CONTENTS

Roland Faley, T.O.R. is a Franciscan priest who holds degrees in Scripture and Theology from The Catholic University of America, Washington, D.C., St. Thomas University, Rome, and the Biblical Institute in Rome. He is the author of several studies in biblical theology and scriptural commentaries, including *The Cup of Grief, To Come and See,* and the commentary on Leviticus in both the early and the revised edition of *The Jerome Biblical Commentary.*

PREFACE

This book was born of the belief that there is nothing more essential to ongoing renewal in the church than quality preaching. Liturgical renewal has had its peaks and valleys, but in the main has had a remarkable measure of success. Serious doubts remain, however, about the overall effectiveness of preaching. And yet if, as the Second Vatican Council exhorted, the treasures of God's word are to enrich continually the lives of the faithful, this will be done principally through the Sunday homily. The homily is a privileged moment. From the preached word, the people are led to apply the teaching of scripture to their daily life and thereby grow in the Lord. But the homily should also be a moment of education in understanding the meaning of God's word, especially in light of the notable gains made in biblical studies in the last fifty years. As much as we may applaud the idea of the ongoing formation and education of the laity, the fact is that the great majority of people will be formed not by classes but by the Sunday homily.

There is a second reason for which this book was written. Today the Sunday lectionary is used by many parishes as the basis for catechetics. By using the scriptures as the principal source, students are brought into direct contact with the word and from there, over the three year cycle, the full body of Catholic teaching is set forth. The catechist then, as well as the homilist, will find here a condensed commentary on each of the Sunday's readings and the psalm. A suggested theme is given for each Sunday or feast day, followed by a brief summary of the content of the three readings, pointing up the weave that unites them. After the commentary on the readings, there is a meditative reflection which is not intended as the "raw material" of the homily or class but simply to open doors and to serve as a stimulus for the reader's own reflection. Finally there is a list of homiletic and catechetical suggestions drawn up to be of

1

help to both preacher and teacher, but with a special eye to the needs of the catechist in relating the Sunday readings to a number of areas of biblical and church teaching.

For the major liturgical seasons, the theme of the Sunday is derived from a consideration of all three readings. For the Sundays of the Year, the first and third readings present the principal theme of the day. The second reading, drawn from the epistolary literature and selected on other premises, does not usually have a clear connection with the major theme. However, the homilist may well decide to construct the homily around the readings of the epistle on particular Sundays.

The commentary is based on the New American Bible translation.

Finally every author has a certain indebtedness, and the length of time required to bring this work to completion has only extended my own list of willing and competent assistants. Special mention must be made of three tireless workers and observers of detail, Theodore Bradower, T.O.R. of Fort Worth, Jose Segovia of New York City, and Gary Dow of Austin whose valuable technical assistance lightened the burden immensely. Finally, but in a sense primarily, for his moral and material support and assistance, due to his personal belief in the value of this undertaking, a deep and lasting sense of gratitude goes to John E. McCarthy, the bishop of Austin, Texas.

FIRST SUNDAY OF ADVENT
Year A

Readings

Is 2:1 - 5
Rom 13:11 - 14
Mt 24:37 - 44

Theme: Watchfulness

The First Sunday of Advent marks the beginning of another liturgical year. Advent affords us the opportunity to reflect on the longing and hope that preceded Christ's birth, just as it beckons us to look forward to Christ's return at history's end. In keeping with the season's note of expectation, today's readings are of one piece in riveting our attention on the inbreaking of God in human history. The Isaian oracle looks to a much desired peace and universal accord for a beleaguered Judah. The gospel reading comes from an era in the early church when Christ's return was strongly anticipated and preparedness was repeatedly counseled. Paul's exhortation to alertness complements the gospel as it highlights the extent to which Christian moral posture actually rests on future hope.

First Reading

This passage from Isaiah is part of a larger collection of oracles which have been inserted here in the editing of the book. This explains the somewhat unusual introduction following so closely on the one given at the beginning of the first chapter (v1). Since the oracle is substantially the same as that found in Micah (4:1 - 3), the introduction may also be identifying Isaiah as the original author.

3

The reference to "days to come" (v2) in itself points to nothing more than an indefinite future. Its appearance, however, in this context gives it a clear eschatological note. At the moment of Yahweh's definitive inbreaking, Jerusalem, made sacred by the presence of the temple and the ark, the place of Yahweh's unique presence from the time of David and Solomon, becomes once again the focal point of Judah's destiny and that of the world. This very positive view of the future should be read against the background of Judah's repeated infidelity and sinfulness which Isaiah himself decries.

This final era will have its distinctive characteristics. In the first place, the temple will be exalted over all other places of worship, with Zion, the mount of the temple's location in Jerusalem, given a very singular status. Yahweh is to have no competing deities; his dominion is absolute. Secondly, not only Israel but the nations as well will recognize Yahweh and seek to be instructed in his law. The scene depicted (v3) is one of pilgrimage to the temple. The Torah (instruction) is here paralleled with God's word and refers here to the Lord's direction and guidance for moral conduct. It may well be a direct reference to the Mosaic law already in the process of codification in Isaiah's time.

The note of universalism struck here is important. Historically there were tensions in Israel between God's concern for all people and the particular status of Israel. The book of Jonah reflects this tension vividly. Here the relationship of Yahweh to the nations is clear in according them a privileged eschatological position, even though there is no indication of any mission outreach to the nations on the part of Israel.

Finally the end time will be an era of universal peace. In the settlement of disputes, Yahweh himself will be the arbiter as the weapons of war are converted into agricultural tools (v4). It is a strikingly idyllic picture of harmony, fertility, and universal accord.

Responsorial Psalm   Ps 122

This song of pilgrimage in proclaiming the centrality of Jerusalem is fitting accompaniment to today's first reading. The pilgrim stands in awe of the holy city because of its impressive fortified structure (v3) and its being a point of prayerful confluence for the entire Israelite population (v4). Since it was also the seat of the royal administration, the joining of just adjudication (v5) with tranquility and good order (v6) echoes today's Isaian oracle (2:4). The psalm closes with a threefold prayer for Jerusalem's peace in favor of the city itself, the temple, the pilgrims and inhabitants (vv 6 - 9).

Second Reading

In his letters, Paul uses a variety of images in enjoining watchfulness upon his readers in the light of the expected parousia. Today's reading utilizes a number of them. The metaphors of awakeness and sleep (cf. 1 Thes 5:6), day and night (1 Thes 5:4 - 8), and armor (Eph 6:13) strongly urge Paul's audience to live in the kairos, the time of salvation, with the moral dispositions proper to a redeemed people. Drowsiness and sleep which accompany the darkness of evil conduct (v13) have no place in the lives of those who live in anticipation of the return of Christ, the bridegroom. It is clear that Paul expected the parousia soon (v12). The military person on watch is armed and prepared. Similarly the Christian's defensive gear is life in Christ. Paul speaks of union with Christ in terms of clothing oneself, clothes being intimately identified with the person in the culture of the times (v14). Those who live in Christ (the spirit) constantly put to death sinful desires (the flesh).

Third Reading

This parable of Jesus on constant vigilance is drawn from the Q source and is found in Luke as well (17:26 - 27, 34 - 35). The account of the flood in Genesis 6 - 7 does not specifically fault those destroyed for their lack of watchfulness. The parable here centers on the unexpected character of their fate. It was sudden and disastrous. Suddeness will also be true of the parousia, with the parable giving repeated emphasis to the Lord's coming (vv37, 39)

The two men in the field replace the less decorous bedfellows of Luke (17:34). The two pair of working men and women, externally indistinguishable, are dramatically consigned to different fates: one is received into the kingdom, the other is consigned to reprobation. Again the emphasis falls on the unpredictable moment and therefore the need for vigilance (v42).

The comparison of the "day of the Lord" with a thief occurs elsewhere in the New Testament (1 Thes 5:2 - 4; 2 Pet 3:10). The work of a thief is by nature secret and surreptitious. That Christ himself is compared to a thief is no more daring than his being likened to a snake (Jn 3:14). Biblical parables stress one main point in comparisons; secondary features are not to be pressed. The point is that the return of the Son of Man will not be pre-announced. Thus alertness undergirds much of the New Testament ethic.

Most of the New Testament authors, like the early church itself, lived with this strong anticipation of the future. Only toward the end of the first century did this expectation begin to recede. Christian belief holds that Christ's return is no less certain for its being delayed. Moreover, it is not identified with one event alone. The inbreaking of God occurs at various moments in history, reminding us that he is the Lord of history and his will be the final word

Nor can we forget that readings such as today's remind us of our personal parousia, our meeting with Christ at the end of life's journey. It too is as certain as it is unknown.

As we look to Christ's return at history's end, we should be aware of the glimpses of that final moment which come in our own lifetime. For centuries people have prayed that swords become plowshares. In view of the increasing realization of war's futility, there are now real possibilities of transforming military might into feeding and clothing the people of the world. Are we drawing closer to Isaiah's vision? Much remains to be seen.

The other return of Christ is personal. We repeatedly say that we know not the day nor the hour. But once said, we tend to put the thought behind us and give as little attention as possible to the final moment.

Advent is a season of anticipation. It recalls Hebrew hopes which we believe were realized in Christ's initial coming. It is also a season of our own future hope. That these hopes are not just wishful thinking but grounded in the reality of faith becomes evident in a posture of moral awareness and wakefulness.

Homiletic and Catechetical Helps

1. Israel's hopes for a Messiah and a messianic age.

2. Jesus as the fulfillment of Israel's hopes.

3. Watchfulness as related to human behavior. The dangers of laxity.

4. The second coming. Its universal and personal significance.

5. Swords into plowshares. Joblessness and world hunger as moral issues.

6. Sinful sleepiness versus gospel awareness: What is my personal challenge?

FIRST SUNDAY OF ADVENT
Year B

Readings

Is 63:16 - 17, 19; 64:2 - 7
1 Cor 1:3 - 9
Mk 13:33 - 37

Theme: Living in Expectation

Isaiah is the prophet of Advent. The reason is obvious when one considers the part that Israel's hope for the definitive intervention of Yahweh plays in the book that bears his name. Today's reading from the third section of Isaiah is a prayer for that inbreaking of God in history to take the form of another Mount Sinai theophany. The gospel points Mark's readers to the second coming with assurance based on the word of Christ himself. They are to be ready. Paul tells the Corinthians that there is no better preparation for Christ's return than to produce the fruits of holiness made possible by the action of God's Spirit within them.

First Reading

Third Isaiah (cc. 56 - 66) is the third division of the book. It is generally agreed today that the greater part of chapters 1 - 39 stems from the prophet himself in the eighth century B.C. Second Isaiah (cc. 40 - 55) is the work of another author actualizing the spirit of the prophet in later and different circumstances: the time of Israel's return from exile in the latter part of the sixth century. Third Isaiah is the book's final addition written after resettlement has taken place, probably in the early fifth century. Like Second Isaiah, it too proceeds from what is frequently called an Isaian school.

The history of Israel's response to its saving God was a checkered one. Infidelity looms as large as do memories of a "golden age." The period of Third Isaiah is a case in point. Once again restored to their homeland, after the edict of repossession of the Persian emperor Cyrus, the Jews have again reverted to the sins of the past while cloaking their infidelity in elaborate ritualism, exclusivism, and religious formality.

The author employs two of Yahweh's most familiar titles: father and redeemer (v19; cf. Ex 4:22; 15:13). The invocation is subtly nuanced with the author basing his appeal for help on Israel's singular relationship with its God. It should be noted that Yahweh is seen as the ultimate cause of all that occurs, even human waywardness (v17). This understanding is common in Hebrew thought although it does not bypass human culpability.

Another Sinai theophany is requested with its attendant cosmic upheaval (v. 19); in this way it is hoped that a senseless people will be brought to a change of heart. The author's "claim" is based on the father-child relationship (v16; 64:7). Moreover, salvation will attest to the nations the greatness and power of the only God (64:1ff). In fact, the present situation has resulted in an impasse. God in his anger is distant and removed, having left his children in their guilt. He cannot forget that as his creatures they are as dependent on him as is the clay on the potter (v7). They live now in hope.

Responsorial Psalm　　Ps 80

This is a lament and a profound plea for help. As in the first reading, Yahweh stands at a royal distance from his sinful people but is persuasively invoked as shepherd and vinedresser (vv2, 15f). Yahweh's enthronement above the ark dates from the pre-temple era when he was "localized" above the two cherubim figures which served as his throne or his footstool (v2b; cf. Ex 25:22; 1 Sam 4:4). Once again Israel is referred to as the vine of Yahweh (Is 5:1 - 7). The first "son of man" reference in 16b is a copyist's erroneous repetition of 18b; it makes no sense in context. Strengthened by the Lord once more, a repentant humankind will pledge fidelity (v19).

Second Reading

In greeting the young Corinthian church, Paul invokes God's charis (grace) and its accompanying harmony in relationships (peace), achieved through the redemptive work of Christ. Paul begins his letter on a positive note while obliquely alluding to more difficult topics to be treated later.

God's grace has not been less evident at Corinth than in any community founded by Paul. They are especially gifted in speech and knowledge (v5), valuable gifts but not the noblest in Paul's eyes (1 Thes 1:3). The "testimony to Christ," difficult to interpret, may well refer to Paul's preaching of the "good news," which, in view of the Corinthians' acceptance in faith, has produced great spiritual benefit (v6; 15:15).

During this interim period prior to the parousia, they are to live in vigilance. It is a faithful God who produces good within them, gifting them with perseverance and uprightness of life, as well as continued unity with the risen Christ (v9). As they remain alert and expectant, their lives will give clear evidence of the Lord's saving action.

Third Reading

The Marcan parable stresses alertness in view of the unknown time of the parousia; note the repeated "You do not know" (vv33, 35). The story is that of the man going on a journey after assigning tasks to his employees, with no indication of a return date. A similar parable in Luke (12:35 - 38) may be a variant, if more elaborate form of the same parable. The parable in Mark has experienced its own development from the time of Jesus. The introductory and conclusive exhortations to watchfulness (vv33, 37) bear the strong imprint of early church concern and are seen as stemming from Mark rather than from Christ himself. What was in the earliest tradition a call by Jesus to live in anticipation of the arrival of the reign of God has become the early church's summons to vigilance in view of Christ's return.

In this opening Sunday of the liturgical year, the spirit of Advent moves us away from lethargy and a business-as-usual attitude to a Christian sense of aliveness. Both our religious and our personal history are linear. We all live in expectation of the end–the end of history with Christ's return and the end of our own earthly sojourn. There are frequent reminders of both. Significant signs of the time point up the relativity and fragility of human existence. History itself undergoes important shifts. Changes in the world picture which we never expected to see still take place. With the eyes of faith, the inbreaking of Christ can be seen well before the end of time. But we do not view the end with terror. We are far from discouraged. As redeemed Christians, we are convinced of Christ's faithfulness. In the eucharistic acclamation we repeatedly proclaim our hope in the returning Christ.

Today's scripture says it well. Do not be fearful but stay awake. And Paul adds: Live faithfully the gifts you have already received. During Advent we look back to the Jesus of history and we look forward to the Christ to come–all of which makes of the present a gifted moment.

Homiletic and Catechetical Helps

1. Advent. Looking to the past and to the future.

2. The gift of perseverance.

3. Being alert and awake in the Christian life.

4. The voice of God in the signs of the times.

5. The Advent wreath: Christian expectation in the home.

6. Advent, the scriptures, and personal prayer.

7. Following Isaiah through Advent.

8. Advent and concern for the poor.

FIRST SUNDAY OF ADVENT
Year C

Readings

> Jer 33:14 - 16
> 1 Thes 3:12 - 4:2
> Lk 21:25 - 28, 34 - 36

Theme: Christ, the Center of Advent Hope

The messianic hope of Israel, launched with Nathan's oracle to David (2 Sam 7:11 - 16), is repeatedly echoed in the prophets. Today's reading from Jeremiah is a clear illustration. Christian belief centers on Christ as the realization of Israel's hope, as it sees the return of Christ at history's end as part of that same faith. Today's gospel, taken from Luke, which will be heard throughout this liturgical year, speaks of this second coming of Christ. Paul's letter to the Thessalonians, the first of his writings, composed in expectation of Christ's proximate return, sees a life rooted in authentic Christian conduct as the best preparation for that eschatological moment.

First Reading

This messianic passage is a late addition to the book of Jeremiah; it is absent from the Greek translation, the

Septuagint. The work of a later editor, the passage is actually a reworking and adaptation of an earlier oracle of the prophet (23:5 - 6). A comparison of the two shows that in the present passage, written in the post-exilic period, the hopes of the prophet center on Jerusalem and Judah, with Israel receiving scant attention (v14).

The hope for a Davidic king, the heir of the covenant promise made to David more than five centuries before, is significant for its constancy in the prophetic tradition. This ideal future king, who stems from the Davidic line, is to be vested with full messianic authority. Unlike so many other descendants of David whose reign had brought little more than disappointment, the future monarch is to be honest and upright for his people (v15).

Messianism centers as much on the nation and the land as it does on the person. Invasion and devastation, so much a part of past history, will be transformed into peace and security in Judah and in Jerusalem, its capital. Jerusalem is designated: "The Lord our justice" (v16). In the oracle's earlier use this was the title given to the king (23:6). Here Yahweh is Jerusalem's justice inasmuch as its restoration and preservation will be convincing evidence of Yahweh's fidelity to his covenant promise. This is his justice (cf. Hos 2:21f).

Of particular interest is the fact that this oracle comes from a period when there was no king and no strong monarchical feeling. It was the levitical priesthood that was in the political ascendancy in post-exilic Judah. That the Davidic hope remains present indicates its deep roots in Israelite faith.

Responsorial Psalm   Ps 25

We find here features of the individual lament and the didactic psalm. In keeping with today's readings, the covenant is emphasized as the broad umbrella touching every aspect of the devout Israelite's life. The sinner who is aware of his wrongdoing is able to cultivate a humble spirit, the fertile soil of Yahweh's saving work (vv8f). It is the Lord's own sense of covenant fidelity that offers instruction (vv4f, 14) and virtue (v9) to those who are receptive.

Second Reading

The first letter to Thessalonica, the earliest of Paul's writings, was composed in 50 A.D. at a time when belief in the imminent return of Christ was intense. Paul shares this sentiment to a considerable extent although he attempts to temper an undue fascination with its proximity. The actual time of Christ's return was not a datum of faith any more then than it is now.

Today's reading is a prayer, expressly directed to Christ the Lord, for the Thessalonians to grow in love both for members of the community and those outside, the example of which has been given by the apostolic missionaries themselves (v12; cf. 1, 5f). This growth in love is equated with holiness and is the guarantee of deliverance and salvation at the Lord's return. The "holy ones" (v13) who are present with Christ at the parousia are those faithful who have died before it occurs (cf. 4:13 - 17).

Paul then enjoins constancy in their Christian comportment (4:1f). He suggests no change of direction, only exhorting them to further growth. Paul has instructed the community with an authority received from Christ himself, which includes directives given by Christ as well as those which Paul interprets as reflecting the thinking of Jesus (cf. 1 Cor 7:10, 12).

The Christ-centeredness of the parousia calls for the elect to be clothed with the virtues of Christ as they look to his return.

Third Reading

Jesus' discourse on the end of time in Luke 21 differs from that in the earlier Mark 13. In the prior tradition, the predictions of the destruction of Jerusalem and the end time were fused. They were two moments of one event. Luke, writing a decade after Jerusalem's destruction, sees that historical event as detached from the still future eschatological moment. This becomes evident from a comparison of the two evangelists.

In today's gospel reading, Luke passes from his earlier treatment of Jerusalem's end to a consideration of the end time still to come, with the cosmic imagery proper to that moment (v26). Many of the images used are drawn from the eschatological descriptions of Isaiah 24 - 25, pointing up the universal, all embracing dimensions of the end time. The convulsion of the earthly and heavenly bodies produces terror in its witnesses but it is offset by the glorious return of Christ as the eschatological Son of Man (Dan 7:13). The title is apt since Christ returns as the firstborn of a new humanity. At that moment the only admissible posture for the believer is the upright and erect position of the free person, not the groveling of the slave (v28). There will be no reason for fear since deliverance is at hand.

Jesus' short exhortation to vigilance (vv34ff) marks the passage's conclusion. Drunkenness, excessive pleasure-seeking, and absorption in worldly concerns are sure ways to lose sight of one's final destiny and to be caught unaware as by a concealed trap. Once again vigilance and prayer are seen as the bedrock of the Christian ethic. They offer assurance of salvation.

The expectation of the early return of Christ is strongly reflected in the New Testament. The fact is that it did not occur as expected. But it would be unfortunate if we were to lose that sense of tension simply for that reason. Israel hoped for its deliverance with the arrival of the messianic king. That hope remained strong even during the periods of a weakened monarchy. It was never lost.

As Christians we believe that Christ is the promised Davidic king, as different as that kingship was. We also believe that Christ is moving toward us from the future, with his advent appearing frequently in signs of the times. History will have an end as will our own personal life story. When this will occur we do not know. When it comes to our individual lives is equally uncertain. Death is something the young seldom think of and the elderly never forget. But none of us knows exactly when that moment will come.

If we live with a certain sense of expectancy, accompanied by a consistent response to God's will, we will be standing tall with heads high at the return of Christ, our brother. He will not disappoint. At his first coming the heavens rejoiced. At his second we shall as well.

Homiletic and Catechetical Helps

1. The Davidic kingship and Israel's hope.

2. Understanding Christ as the Davidic Messiah.

3. The end time discourse in Mark and Luke. Understanding the differences.

4. Salvation as cosmic. The biblical idea of a redeemed world.

5. Postures of prayer. The significance of standing and kneeling.

6. Drugs, sex and alcohol as related to a loss of awareness.

SECOND SUNDAY OF ADVENT
Year A

Readings

> Is 11:1 - 10
> Rom 15:4 - 9
> Mt 3:1 - 12

Theme: The Era of Justice and Peace

The reading from Isaiah is drawn from that section of the book known as the book of Immanuel wherein the future messianic king is depicted as well as the era of peace which he inaugurates. As he concludes his letter to the Romans, Paul stresses the importance of hope, drawn from the teaching of the scriptures, to be lived in a community spirit of harmony and charity. In Matthew's gospel, the beginning of John the Baptist's ministry presents the prophet as an ascetical forerunner whose call for conversion of life sets the stage for the One who is to come.

First Reading

Three characteristics of the messianic age emerge in this Isaian description. First, the era will be presided over by a just and God-fearing descendant of David. Second, it will be marked by the king's execution of justice on behalf of his people. Third, a return to the harmony and peace of Eden will embrace all creation as symbolized by the cohabitation of mutually hostile animal species and their peaceful relations with the human family. Let us look at each of these in turn.

Jesse was David's father and thus the sire of the royal dynasty. The shoot coming from the "stump" and "roots" (v1) represents the state of the dynasty after the branches (unfaithful kings) have been removed (10:33f). The ideal king, then, is rooted in his earliest forebears.

The qualities of the king are highlighted. The "spirit of the Lord" (v2) is an exceptional divine force granted special agents of Yahweh such as Moses, David, and the prophets. It is an enabling spirit which in this case implies keen insight and judgment as well as the ability to execute decisions (counsel, strength, knowledge). "Fear of the Lord" is seen as a fundamental virtue in the wisdom literature (Prv 1:7) and signifies a reverential respect. Its appearance here twice (2b, 3a) is a scribal error. The Greek translation substituted "piety" for the first occurrence, thus giving us what have become known in Christian tradition as the seven gifts of the Holy Spirit.

As an arbiter and judge, the king will be a model of justice (vv3ff) unlike so many of Israel's kings and magistrates (10:1f). Those guilty of malice will be punished while the concerns of the poor and disadvantaged will be addressed. The note of the re-establishment of equity and harmony in the social order is clearly struck.

The scene then moves beyond Israelite society to creation as a whole (vv6ff). The replacement of the predator relationship with one of peaceful ties in the animal world is an allusion to conditions in Eden before the fall. There Adam's dominion over an ordered and peaceful creation is underscored in his naming the animals (Gen 2:19ff). The first note of alienation occurs when the serpent is cursed after the sin (Gen 3:14ff; 9:2). Isaiah's language is symbolic and poetic and not to be pressed literally. But that does not make it unimportant. It highlights the strong biblical theme of the relationships that exist within the whole of the created order. Final justice looks not only to human and social concerns but also to an ordered and peaceful world.

Zion figures prominently as the center of this era of peace

(v9; 2:1 - 4). "Knowledge of the Lord" is primarily experiential not intellectual, referring to the affective internalization of spiritual values which are then reflected in daily life. This knowledge has been sorely lacking in Israel's past (1:3); it will be the touchstone of the future. The passage ends on a note of universalism as the Gentiles acknowledge the king and Jerusalem (v10).

Responsorial Psalm   Ps 72

This is a royal psalm probably composed on the occasion of a king's accession to the throne. Its exalted tone and elaborate description lent themselves to giving it eventually a messianic thrust.

The prayer is for the king and his heir (v1). As in today's first reading, the king is endowed with the suitable qualifications, especially justice to be exercised on behalf of the poor and emarginated. His justice is both eternal (v7) and universal (v8). The parameters of the psalmist's world view are necessarily restricted. The two seas are the Mediterranean and the Persian Gulf; the River is the Euphrates. The final invocation prays for the king in his timeless and world-embracing mission (v17).

Second Reading

Harmony and unity in the Roman community must be rooted in the elimination of all ethnic or religious barriers. Paul had not founded this community nor does he tell us who did. It was evidently made up of Jewish and Gentile Christians, even though the latter were seemingly the majority.

For Paul the scriptures were never so historically conditioned as to lose their relevance. His Christocentrism, coupled with rabbinic praxis, led him to see the scriptures as applicable to any situation (4:23f; 1 Cor 10:11). The word of God with its examples of patience and its words of encouragement can only give hope to a community experiencing trials (vv4f).

Paul is conscious of the need for a unified spirit, unity being the first gift of God's Spirit even in the midst of considerable diversity (1 Cor 12). Unity stands at the heart of true worship, directed as it is to the Father of all (16:25), the source of every blessing (1:7).

A delicately worded plea is made for harmony between Christians of Jewish and Gentile background (vv7ff). Jesus came in service to the Jews as proof of God's fidelity to his promises. But the Gentiles too are part of God's plan. Paul illustrates this from the psalter (Ps 18:50). The Gentile mission is close to Paul's heart; he never hesitates to underscore its origin in God's design. His point is clearly made. A liturgy worthy of God can only be chanted by a mutually accepting and supportive community.

Third Reading

If Isaiah is the prophet of Advent, then John the Baptist is his New Testament counterpart. Ironically, even though much attested to in the gospels, he remains an historically elusive figure. He is known to Josephus, the Jewish historian. While the gospel witness might be said to be abundant, it must be remembered that his person and mission are shaped by the distinct beliefs of the early church, the source of the gospels. The gospels are written with a post-Easter, faith-filled understanding of all that preceded and with a clear apologetic intent. This often makes historical assertions difficult. In Matthew, for example, there is no mention of John's being a relative of Jesus, as in Luke (1:36). In fact the Matthean John, despite his recognition of Jesus at the baptism, has difficulty later in determining his identity (11:2 - 6).

It is certain that John and Jesus were contemporaries. They both preached the dawn of a new era, called to conversion and baptized. John may have once been a member or an associate of the Essene community located at Qumran and known to us from the Dead Sea Scrolls. John and Jesus had parallel ministries and may well have been seen by some as competitors (Acts 18:24ff; 19:1 - 3). The gospels are at pains to present John as subordinate to Jesus for reasons that may well go beyond the prophet's personal humility. Matthew presents John as dressed in the garb of Elijah (v4; 2 Kgs 1:8) and will repeatedly see him as the "Elijah-returned" figure who was to precede and herald the end time (11:14; 17:11 - 13). His diet of locusts and wild honey recalls the exodus desert experience with an accompanying note of penance and vigilance.

Preaching in the region of the Dead Sea, John calls his hearers to repentance in view of the approaching reign of God. Repentance or conversion (metanoia), here colored already by Christian understanding, connotes basically a turn-about on the road (Heb: *shub*), morally a fundamental change of direction from sin to God. Radical and deeply internal, it is externalized in the fruit it produces (v8). Matthew cites Deutero-Isaiah's announcement of the return from exile (v3; Is 40:3) with a free identification of the "voice" with John and the "Lord" with Jesus. Mention is made of the widespread acceptance of John's mission (v5). His baptism was a purification rite with water known to us also from the Essenes at Qumran and other groups at the time. It was accompanied by a change of heart and confession of sin.

John addresses two groups who will be later singled out for their strong opposition to Jesus and the early church (vv7 - 12). The Pharisees were skilled in the law, oral and written; the Sadducees were the priestly class closely linked with the temple cult. They were never comfortable with each other. They found their unity in opposition to Jesus, the possible reason for their being linked here (only) by Matthew.

John opposes their hypocrisy and religious formalism (v9). Blood linkage with Abraham is not sufficient; only conversion and its fruits assure salvation (vv9f). To be noted is the fact that references to John's baptism are somewhat muted; his preaching is to the fore. There is the avoidance of any possible equation between the two baptisms. The superiority of Jesus' baptism lies in its being dominantly the work of God.

The context of John's final words to the two groups (not the crowd) is one of eschatological judgment. The Messiah will separate the wheat from the chaff. The "winnowing fan" (v12) was a tool used at the harvest to toss the wheat in the air to obtain the separation. The Holy Spirit and fire (v11) refer to Christian baptism.

There is an urgency to John's message. Fundamentally it is a call to repentance in view of the arrival of God's judgment.

True conversion will be reflected in life. "By their fruits you will know them."

The reign of God means basically the sovereignty of God's will over all of creation. It is heralded by John and present in Jesus' ministry. In his gospel, Matthew sees it in a more extended fashion. It is present incipiently in Jesus' birth, proclaimed in his ministry, and fully realized in his death-resurrection. The reign will be brought to conclusion with his return.

Justice is part of God's reign, a justice that is linked with peace. The work of God, it is also the work of Christ's disciples and of all people of good will. If our conversion has begun, then we are held to produce the work of conversion. The injustices of today's world are much with us. Poverty, racism, sexism, disregard for life, economic inequality–all plague our society and our planet. True peace can never be expected where such injustice prevails. Working to correct injustice makes us agents of the Lord in re-establishing that biblical ideal of equity and fairness.

The church has a social agenda which is now more than a century old. But how much of it is reflected in Christian attitudes and practice? All too often religion is identified with a personal and private morality. There is a need for all of us to reflect on Isaiah. Justice embraces all categories of people and reaches all nations. Paul today tells us that peace is rooted in a recognition of everyone's place in God's plan. As we hear the Baptist's plea, we are reminded that conversion is continuous and lifelong. It is never too late to start the journey–or to pick it up anew. And for the record it should be noted that the word metanoia means a change of mind as well as a change of heart.

Homiletic and Catechetical Helps

1. Peace: individual, social, worldwide.

2. The cosmic dimensions of sin and redemption.

3. Jesus, Son of David: its meaning.

4. The reign of God: its meaning.

5. To find peace, seek justice.

6. Experiences of ethnic or racial barriers.

7. Ideas on the social teaching of the church.

8. The seven gifts of the Holy Spirit.

SECOND SUNDAY OF ADVENT
Year B

Readings

> Is 40:1 - 5, 9 - 11
> 2 Pet 3:8 - 14
> Mk 1:1 - 8

Theme: New Beginnings

A new dawn breaks for God's people. Isaiah announces that the darkness of exile is over and the Israelites are called to return to their homeland. The gospel of Mark begins with John the Baptist's mission which he sees as an echo of the new beginning proclaimed by Isaiah. The second letter of Peter allays concerns about the delay in Christ's return. When it comes it will bring a new creation not only for humankind but for the entire cosmos.

First Reading

In this reading from the prophet of Advent, Deutero-Isaiah, the author of the second part of the book (Is 40 - 55), announces the end of the Babylonian exile and the return of the Israelites to their homeland (546 B.C.). The poetry is stirring. The scene opens in the heavenly court where, as elsewhere in the Hebrew scriptures, Yahweh converses with his heavenly counsel. He urges them to be agents of consolation to his people (v1). "My people ... your God" is distinct covenant language (Jer 31:33). The reference to Jerusalem here goes beyond the city itself to include all the sufferers in exile (v2). Punishment is complete; servitude to foreign powers is terminated; guilt is doubly expiated.

A member of the heavenly court speaks up (v3). The desert experience of the exodus is to be renewed. Yahweh is once again leading the caravan (Ex 14:2) as the customarily treacherous and uneven road is made level and smooth. The journey is not arduous but refreshing. But "the way of the Lord" has a deeper meaning. It is Israel's new path to salvation, its moral guidance on the journey of life (Is 55:7f).

In a splendid proclamation of redemption, Zion and Jerusalem, which had suffered loss and degradation for decades, are called to herald the new beginning in addressing the other cities of Judah. There is a change in geographical perspective. Jerusalem, the point of the exiles' destination (and destiny), looks out over the plain to watch the approaching procession (vv9ff). From a high vantage point, it sees Yahweh in the lead. With his "strong arm" still indicative of his awesome power (Ex 6:6), the description is tempered with the warmth of the shepherd image (49:9; Ez 34:13). It is a caring and gentle God that carries his people home. The"reward" and "recompense" (v10) may refer to the purified state of the returning exiles.

Responsorial Psalm   Ps 85

The psalm reflects a liturgical setting containing sentiments similar to those found in the first reading. It too reflects a post-exilic optimism for the future. The final part of the psalm which is read today announces peace for God's people, the faithful remnant of Israel (v9). The glory of Yahweh, once identified with his presence in the desert tent (Ex 40:34) and the temple (1 Kgs 8:11), now accompanies the redeemed people to their homeland. A retinue of personified attributes, proper to God and his people, are reunited as they approach each other from heaven and earth (vv11f). All of them are rooted in the covenant. God's forgiveness matches the people's fidelity (kindness, truth); his sense of covenant faithfulness produces well-being and happiness among the people (justice, peace). In this happy wedding of virtues, the Lord's benefits reach both land

and people as his saving attributes accompany him in procession (v12).

Second Reading

The second letter of Peter is a late composition, probably dating from the early second century. It is attributed to "Symeon Peter," linking it with both the apostle Peter and the first letter of Peter. Its date and other factors preclude its being authored by the apostle; its being attributed to him follows a literary custom which links many of the biblical books to prominent personalities. The content of the letter also distances it from the period of Peter's lifetime.

At the time of the letter's composition, the second coming of Christ had still not occurred. Opponents of Christianity continue to make light of this doctrine, one which the author of 2 Peter strongly defends. The time of the Lord's return remains as uncertain as the truth of the return is unquestionable. God is not bound by the confining parameters of humans' limited temporal vision (v8; Ps 90:4). The reason for the "delay" is God's forbearance giving the opportunity for repentance the widest berth (v9). The comparison of the Lord's day with an unexpected thief is a recurring idea (Mt 24:43f; 1 Thes 5:1).

The return of the Lord has a cosmic dimension. Employing apocalyptic imagery, the author describes the old order's demise—the heavens, the celestial bodies, and the earth (v10). Fire has a central role in divine judgment; it has a testing quality as well. Works of value will withstand "the heat"; the worthless will perish. In this way everything will be "found out" (v10b; 1 Cor 3:10 - 14). All of this will be followed by a restoration of creation in a new redeemed state (v13; Rev 21:1). Once more it is to be noted that biblical redemption is more than personal and human; it is cosmic as well.

In the light of this basic belief in the parousia, the author's hearers are encouraged to live a life which will find them blameless when the end comes. Eschatology once more weighs in heavily in conditioning moral behavior. Those who scoff at a second coming are licentious and ill-prepared (2 Pet 3:3f); they will not escape judgment. The believers, on the other hand, by their upright conduct hasten the Lord's coming (v12).

Third Reading

Mark's gospel begins with a brief title and starts at once with the mission of John the Baptist. It is with John, in fact, that the apostolic witness to Jesus in the early church began (Acts 1:21). The title (v1) summarizes the scope of Mark's gospel, i.e. to present the "good news" (Gr: *euangelion*) of God's saving action in Jesus, who in this gospel's dual climax is first recognized as the Christ (8:29) and finally as the Son of God (15:39).

The quotation which introduces the Baptist is attributed to Isaiah but is actually a composite (Is 40:3; Mal 3:1; Ex 23:20). The messenger of Malachi precedes Yahweh's eschatological repossession of the temple and is subsequently identified as Elijah (Mal 3:23). In Exodus, the way is prepared for Israel in the desert. The quotation from Deutero-Isaiah announces the return of the people after the Babylonian exile. The three texts are applied to John (the messenger, forerunner) and to Jesus (the Lord).

The Elijah role of John as the precursor is implied in his dress (2 Kgs 1:8), a role which Mark later makes explicit (9:11 - 13). His diet evokes memories of Israel's desert experience. His baptism (v5) was a purifying lustration practiced rather broadly in this period of Jewish expectation. It is known to us especially from the Essene community at Qumran. The water purification was an external sign of an interior change of heart (metanoia), a radical shift from a worldly path to an engagement in God (v4). The extent of John's popularity is not overstated (v5). His devotees were still present in the time of the early church; he was perhaps even seen as Jesus' competitor (Acts 18:25; 19:3). All the gospels are quick to emphasize his lesser status and subordination to Jesus.

John's words stress this subordinate position (vv7f). To loosen the sandal thongs was the slave's duty in the Jewish household. Hence, John's status is not even that of a slave. An important contrast is made between the two baptisms. With John the water symbolized the internal cleansing and redirection of life; the baptism of Jesus is more clearly the action of God even though the symbolism remains the same. In Mark the clear reference to a Spirit baptism reflects the daily life of the early church. Early references to Jesus' baptism, probably dating from a pre-Easter period, stress more the idea of a purifying fire (Mt 3:11; Lk 3:16). (For other consideration of John the Baptist, see the Second Sunday of Advent, Year A.)

Today's liturgy of the word illustrates the gradual development in revelation. It is much too facile to think that the understanding of God's saving plan and his designs for humanity were firmly understood and fixed at a given moment. The fact is that revelation is still unfolding and neither we nor our posterity will ever grasp it fully. The proximity of the parousia receded gradually in the New Testament literature, as the church's understanding evolved. This means that there is conflicting data in the scriptures themselves. This should remind us, if reminding we need, that the word of God comes to us in the words of human beings, with all the limitations which that implies.

The church wants us to see John the Baptist as a subordinate but important person. He gave himself totally to a prophetic mission but at a given moment he was ready to defer to another whose mission surpassed his own. In our life we often tend to possess our achievements, to preserve our own "turf," to go beyond an understandable satisfaction in our accomplishments. But the Christian call to conversion, to see God as our everything, invests us with a willingness to let go and to move on. For us today, the Baptist is still pointing the way.

Homiletic and Catechetical Helps

1. The meaning of divine punishment.

2. God as redeemer and shepherd.

3. The meaning of development in revelation.

4. Cosmic redemption.

5. Lessons to be learned from the figure of John the Baptist.

6. The difference between the baptism of John and that of Jesus.

7. John the Baptist as an Elijah figure.

8. The time of the second coming.

SECOND SUNDAY OF ADVENT
Year C

Readings

> Bar 5:1 - 9
> Phil 1:4 - 6, 8 - 11
> Luke 3:1 - 6

Theme: The Journey

There are distinct echoes of Deutero-Isaiah in Baruch's account of the returning exiles' journey across the desert. It is the Judean desert that plays a part in the ministry of John the Baptist as Luke applies to him the Isaian call to the Jewish deportees. A new journey in the history of salvation is about to begin. Paul in writing to the Phillipians speaks of the human journey as a continual, on-going growth in faith

First Reading

Baruch is a short book. Although it was originally a Hebrew composition, it has come down to us in its Greek version. It is difficult to date. Attributed pseudonymously to Jeremiah's secretary, the book probably dates from late pre-Christian times, sometime after 200 B.C.

Drawing heavily on the book of Isaiah, Baruch takes up the theme of the exiles' return from Babylon and in the retelling sees its applicability to the Jews of the diaspora. Jerusalem remains always the beckoning homeland. At this point a change of attire for daughter Jerusalem is called for to signify the transition from sorrow to celebration (v1; Is 52:1). The "cloak of justice" (v2) assures Israel of Yahweh's covenant fidelity. Jerusalem enjoys a priestly status, now given the miter of Aaron bearing the sacred diadem with its inscription: "Sacred to the Lord" (Ex 39:30; Is 61:10). In its resplendent glory, Jerusalem becomes to the nations a sign of God's favor.

Jerusalem is called to an elevated position to watch the returning procession (v5). The collection of peoples from "east and west" points to the general diaspora even though the eastern desert route out of Babylon is still retained for literary reasons. The contrast between past and present is striking. A people dispersed for various reasons, frequently deported and deprived of freedom, is depicted as borne home on throne chairs and undoubtedly carried by their oppressors (v6; Is 49:22). The leveling of the terrain to facilitate the journey through the Arabian desert is an image drawn from Isaiah (v7; Is 40:3f). The desert even provides the cool and protection of a forested land as Yahweh leads his people, attended by his personified retinue, the covenant-centered "mercy and justice" (vv8f).

Responsorial Psalm   Ps 126

Written during a time of need, the psalm looks back nostalgically to the time of restoration, once again the time of the journey home. So evident was God's action on behalf of his people that not even the Gentiles could fail to see (v2). There was happiness and revelry.

But times have changed. In the face of the present unnamed distress, the author can only pray to experience that sign of favor once again (vv4 - 6). The agricultural images used may well connect with the concrete needs of a farming population. Praying for an outpouring of blessings like the infrequent downpours which inundated the desert floor, the author pleads for a reversal of the present misfortune. Sowing and reaping image sorrow converted into joy. Restoration would be a rebirth of post-exilic happiness.

Second Reading

The passage from Philippians is full of energy and enthusiasm. Throughout the epistle, Paul's joy comes to the fore despite his imprisonment (v7). Here he speaks of his "partner-ship" with the community (vv5, 7). The Philippians have been Paul's "partners for the gospel." This partnership lies in their joint suffering. Paul currently experiences pain and trials in his imprisonment. The sufferings of the Philippians in witnessing to the gospel (1:29f) not only parallel Paul's but are linked with his in God's Spirit. Suffering for Paul is important for two rea-sons. God's power appears in human weakness (2 Cor 4:7 - 15), and suffering for the gospel becomes one with that of Christ (3:10) in filling up what is lacking in his total offering (Col 1:24).

Finally, Paul addresses the tension between the "now" of Christ's Spirit and the "not yet" of the parousia (vv6, 10). What is important for the moment is a continual growth in grace, a characteristic of the Philippian community (vv6, 9), evident in their maturity of vision and their discernment of values. Their journey is well underway as they move toward the Christ who will eventually return.

Third Reading

The Lucan account of John's baptismal ministry has its own distinctive features. He draws on Mark but paints the narrative with his own theological hues. Following a classical Hellenistic model, Luke places John and Jesus in a precise historical frame-work (vv 1ff). This is not solely a matter of style; he is con-cerned that salvation be clearly placed in a broad historical con-text. He highlights the important political and religious person-alities of the time: the emperor, his Palestinian governor, the Jewish civil authorities, and the religious leadership. But there is an ironic note in this listing. Many of these will come to the fore among those opposed to Jesus as he is sentenced and con-demned: Pilate, Herod, Annas, and Caiaphas.

Luke emphasizes John's prophetic mission. "The word of God came to John" (v2), found only in Luke, places the Baptist clearly in the prophetic tradition (Jer 1:2). His being in the desert near the Jordan would have brought him into proximity with the Qumran community known to us from the Dead Sea Scrolls. Seemingly he shared with them a repentance baptism (v3). The desert and the Jordan have a literary purpose as well, pointing to Jesus' mission as a new exodus.

Repentance (metanoia) connotes an abrupt about-face in moral conduct. This radical redirection signifies a new walking with God, ongoing in nature, in separation from sin. In John's ministry it was accompanied by water purification, signifying the cleansing of mind and heart. Luke clearly distinguishes it from Jesus' baptism (3:16).

The quotation from Isaiah is lengthier than in the other synoptics, concluding with "all flesh shall see the salvation of God" (v6). This enables Luke to highlight one of his major themes, that of universalism. The leveling of hills and the filling of valleys has a strong moral connotation in the third gospel. The Christian life is itself a road or a way (Acts 9:2; 18:25). Jesus' disciples experience their own exodus and make their own journey toward their final engagement in God. The Baptist here echoes the Isaian return from exile, heralds the coming of Jesus, and points to the way of the Christian life. (For further consideration of John's ministry, see the Second Sunday of Advent, Year A.)

It is safe to say that at one point in our earlier Christian life, we saw the church and its message in rather static terms. The church emerged finished and formed from the hands of Christ and remained largely the same for twenty centuries. The answers to questions of faith and morals were clear from the earliest times.

With the Second Vatican Council's biblical image of the church as the people of God, there was a shift, conscious or unconscious, in our earlier thinking. The Christian life is more clearly seen as a journey, and like any journey it has its unknowns, its perils, and its surprises. We are always growing in our understanding of the faith, more willing to admit our ignorance and inadequacies, more accepting of ourselves and others. The basic truth is still there as stemming from Christ but it is constantly unfolding. In journeying toward the heavenly Jerusalem, we listen to the world and ask it to listen to us. We realize better the need to give new expression to old truths, to reconcile long held positions with new insights and developments. As pilgrims, we realize our humanness and that of the church as a whole, convinced as we are that we are guided and directed by God's own Spirit. As Luke is at pains to indicate, our journey is part of history and involves a conversation with the world.

Growth on this journey is essential, as Paul tells the Philippians. It is a growth in love as well as knowledge and discernment.

God's love extends to all people. About that Luke is clear–outreach to other Christians and non-Christians. In different ways, we are joined in a common journey. We cannot be victimized by a religious myopia; our horizons must constantly expand. "The earth is the Lord's and all things in it."

Homiletic and Catechetical Helps

1. The journey as related to the dynamic state of Christian growth.

2. Fellowship in Christ's suffering in Paul.

3. Likenesses and differences in the synoptic accounts of John's mission.

4. The baptism of John.

5. Practical consequences of the Christian life as a journey.

6. The meaning of conversion.

7. Implications of the church as part of world history.

8. The Dead Sea Scrolls and the Qumran community.

9. John the Baptist as a prophet.

THIRD SUNDAY OF ADVENT
Year A

Readings

Is 35:1 - 6, 10
Jas 5:7 - 10
Mt 11:2 - 11

Theme: The Messiah as Healer

Jesus was not the type of messiah that was expected. The puzzled emissaries of the Baptist in today's gospel pose the question of his identity. His affirmative answer hearkens back to Isaiah who spoke of the comfort and healing, not solely the judgment, which was to be part of the final era. In terms of Christ's return at the end of time, James today encourages patience.

First Reading

The 35th chapter of Isaiah serves as a structural link between First and Second Isaiah. Since chapters 36 - 39 are an historical appendix to First Isaiah, chapter 35 originally joined the two parts of the book. In reading it closely, themes common to the earlier prophet are evident, e.g. final deliverance, the "glory of God," imagery drawn from nature. But the chapter also has features of Second Isaiah, e.g. the homeward journey, the verdant desert, the welcoming Zion. The composition comes from the time of the second author who draws on features of the first part of the book.

A redeemed people moves through the desert as if on pilgrimage. Both the theme and its literary expression have much in common with Isaiah 40. What is described throughout is a transformed world, which is the most logical way for a devout Israelite to speak of God's favor. Blessings were anything but abstract. God's kindness found expression in benefits of the world of nature.

As restoration takes place, the desert becomes a verdant garden (vv1f), the handicapped are restored to health (vv5f), and the exiles reach Zion once again (v10). Lebanon, Carmel and Sharon, legendary for their fertility and the green of their landscape, were symbols of disaster in their aridity (33:9) and of blessing in their beauty. This transformation of nature, a manifestation of Yahweh's glory, can only encourage the disheartened and give strength to the weak (vv3f).

The disabled are restored to health (vv5f; 29:18). Quite apart from personal disadvantage, physical handicaps were seen as incompleteness, a lack of wholeness, and any vision of the end time saw them as overcome.

The conclusion (v10) presents the redeemed remnant entering Jerusalem in solemn procession. This same verse appears in Second Isaiah (51:11). While originally looking to the post-exilic repossession of Jerusalem, the image had meaning at an even later date for all the Jews of the diaspora.

Responsorial Psalm   Ps 146

This hymn of an individual believer prolongs the theme of the day in showing Yahweh's concern for the disenfranchised and the unfortunate. To keep faith forever (v6c) is more than trustworthiness. Yahweh's faith (Heb: *mishpat*) is his fidelity to the terms of the covenant, by which he has freely bound himself to his people, especially the neediest. The feeding of the hungry and the freeing of captives are allusions to the exodus, repeatedly highlighted in any litany of God's benefits (v7b). Among the emarginated, strangers, widows, and orphans have a special place (v9a; Ex 22:20f; Deut 10:18): strangers, because as aliens they had no status in Israelite society; widows and orphans, because they lacked a male provider. God's justice is meted out to the wicked as well as to the faithful (v9b). The hymn ends singing the eternity of God's reign (v10).

Second Reading

Patience appears three times in this brief passage from the letter of James (vv7, 8, 10). It is called for in view of the delay in the Lord's return but also because of the trials incurred because of injustices suffered at the hands of the rich (5:1 - 6). Furthermore, there are trials from the interpersonal relations of daily life (v9). In all of this, James' audience is assured that the Lord is at hand, that his coming is imminent. And he comes as a judge who will set the record straight in any matter of injustice.

James' illustrative comparisons appear frequently (1:11f; 1:23f; 3:3f). Here his listeners are to be as patient as the Palestinian farmers for whom the fall and spring rains provide essential and much anticipated moisture (v7). They should look to the biblical prophets for examples of patient endurance (v10); sufferings in the early church are elsewhere compared to those of the prophets (Mt 5:12). Persecuted Christians form part of a long and illustrious tradition. Suffering is transitory; it will fade into insignificance with the full manifestation of the Lord's justice.

Third Reading

Matthew's pointed dialogue between Jesus and John's disciples, shared with Luke (7:18 - 28), comes from the Q tradition. Hence, it is not part of the same tradition which provides the account of John's baptism and the divine recognition of Jesus on that occasion. This episode, quite apart from its historical roots, points up the early church's concern with establishing the true nature of Jesus' messiahship, perhaps arising out of controversy with some of the later disciples of the Baptist. The phrase mentioning the works of the Messiah (v2) is an editorial insert by Matthew within whose circles the question is being discussed. It recognizes Christ as the Messiah and is at some distance from the original event.

In answer to John's disciples (vv3 - 6), Jesus responds from the prophetic literature which pointed to the healing and compassionate character of the final era (Is 29:18f; 35:5f), clearly reflected in the work of the Matthean Jesus in the preceding chapters (cc8 - 9). This is different from the judgment-bent Messiah seen in the Baptist's earlier prediction (3:10f). It should be noted that in the description of his mission, Jesus gives a climactic priority to the poor (v5). Because he is such a different type of Messiah, Jesus finds blessed those who accept him and find him no stumbling block (Gr: *skandalizo*) in view of their own pre-conceptions (v6).

The person and work of John are extolled in Jesus' words to the crowd (vv7 - 11). He poses six questions of a negative character before affirming the Baptist's eschatological role. The questioning implies John's ascetical and determined personality. While certainly part of the prophetic tradition, John is distinctive as the one who is to usher in the final age. The quotation (v10) combines Malachi 3:1 with Exodus 23:20, with Malachi's "before me" (Yahweh) becoming in Matthew "before you" (Jesus).

In this role of immediate forerunner of the Lord, John has no human equal, an unusually strong affirmation (v11). At the same time, the disciples of Jesus, especially with the post-Easter outpouring of the Spirit, are graced and privileged in a way that surpasses anything that John had received. The statement sharply highlights the singular grace of the Christian life.

As Advent reminds us of the end of history, it also deepens our appreciation of the present life. It is not often that, as we bring the child to the baptismal font, we think that this is the greatest gift that God can give, the life in Christ, that not even John the Baptist lived to experience. That idea comes through very clearly in today's liturgy.

But how important it is as well to hear Jesus' identifying description of his own mission. He sees himself not primarily as king, judge, or lawgiver but as a comforting and consoling healer. Not only his contemporaries but we as well are the beneficiaries of that compassion. Moreover, it provides us with the incentive to go and do likewise. It is a blessing to bring healing. Doctors and nurses should see themselves as engaged in much more than a profession. They try to bring God's healing hand to those who suffer. As we hear so much about the problems connected with health care, one wonders if that spiritual perspective is maintained. Jesus brought love and hope to the blind, the deaf, the mute, and the crippled. Every time we see parking reserved for the handicapped, lowered drinking fountains, or the public use of sign language, we become more sensitive and more grateful for our government's greater awareness. Through us Christ today still emerges as a healer.

Homiletic and Catechetical Helps

1. The biblical view of physical and material blessings.

2. The purpose of Jesus' miracles.

3. Healing as overcoming evil in biblical thought.

4. The ministry of healing in today's world.

5. The sacrament of the sick.

6. A corporal work of mercy: visit the sick.

7. The significance of the Spirit in the Christian life.

8. The virtue of patience.

THIRD SUNDAY OF ADVENT
Year B

Readings

> Is 61:1 - 2, 10 - 11
> 1 Thes 5:16 - 24
> Jn 1:6 - 8, 19 - 28

Theme: Christian Joy

This mid-point Sunday of Advent has long been known as "Rejoice" Sunday (Gaudete). Since Advent is not a penitential season but a season of hope and expectation, today's celebration reminds us that we have ample reason to hope in view of our experience of God's goodness. The passage from Third Isaiah speaks of God's anointing the prophet to proclaim a message of liberation and lasting favor. In the midst of rather tense expectations, Paul urges the Thessalonians to rejoice in prayer, thanksgiving, and confidence. In today's gospel, John the Baptist willingly acknowledges his subordinate status as he points to the one who is to come.

First Reading

The prophet of Third Isaiah describes his commission in language evocative of the servant of the Lord. He receives the Lord's spirit (v1a; 42:1) and has a mission to the needy (v1b; 42:7). With post-exilic Israel still in the throes of resettlement, he will proclaim the definitive restoration of Jerusalem. The spirit of the Lord (v1) is a God-given force, beyond the human, supporting and authenticating a determined mission (Jgs 3:10; 1 Sam 10:6). Kings and priests were anointed. The term is used figuratively here in speaking of the prophet's commission; he is sent primarily to the oppressed and the downtrodden, the favored of God. A year of favor (v2) refers to the jubilee year when the land was left fallow, debts were remitted, and property was restored (Lev 25:10ff). The reference here is poetic, pointing to a time of restored justice and equality among the people. God's vindication is his championing those who have no representation.

Zion is the subject of the concluding verses (vv10f), as the Aramaic version makes explicit. The sacred mount is festively adorned and outfitted with the attributes of God's fidelity, a sign to the nations of his lasting concern. It is a moment of eschatological joy.

Responsorial Psalm   Lk 1:46 - 50, 53 - 54

Today's response is taken from Mary's Magnificat. Most commentators see this as a hymn of the early church which Luke applies to Mary in the infancy narrative. Its content is not directly applicable to the context where it appears, except for v48, and it draws heavily on the hymn of Hannah in 1 Samuel 2:1 - 10. The spiritual sentiments which it expresses, however, blend well with those of Mary.

Mary's rejoicing centers on the Lord's greatness and her littleness (the anawim), which have come together in her favored status (vv46ff). While she will be honored in future ages, this is due to no merit of her own but rather to the action of God at work in her life. The reversal of fortunes (v53), a direct echo of Hannah's song, is a strong Lucan theme. In the reign of God, the wealthy are dispossessed and the poor have their fill (12:16 - 21; 16:19 - 31). Although the social categories have an importance in themselves for Luke, it is the greedy rich and the dependent poor that come to the fore. The final reason for joy rests on Yahweh's fidelity to his covenant promises (vv54f).

Second Reading

Paul closes this, his earliest letter, with a series of brief admonitions. Charismatic gifts are operative in Thessalonica; Paul simply counsels caution. It must be recognized that the Spirit is free and cannot be curtailed (vv19f). But discernment is also a gift of the Spirit (1 Cor 12:10) to be used to determine the true and the false (v21).

The apostle prays for his hearers, just as he asks for their prayers (vv23ff). The God of peace (Rom 15:33; 1 Cor 14:33) is the source of all blessings and will safeguard the harmony and spiritual growth of the community. The triad of Spirit, soul, and body is not an anthropological division, rather it looks at the whole person from diverse vantage points—as God-related, living, and corporal. He prays for holiness joined with alertness, in expectation of the Lord's return. The certainty of the parousia is rooted in God's trustworthiness (v24).

Third Reading

The account of John's mission in the fourth gospel differs from that of the three synoptics. It represents a distinct tradition which, while containing features common to all the evangelists, paints the picture of the Baptist in its own distinct hues. These differences should be noted in preaching and teaching.

The first mention of John appears in the gospel's prologue (vv6 - 9) in conjunction with the light-darkness theme. Throughout this gospel, Jesus is presented as the light whose presence some accept while others prefer the darkness. Prominent figures in the gospel, e.g. the Samaritan woman (Jn 4), point to or testify to the light. John the Baptist is one of these. He is "sent" (v6) or missioned, just as Jesus is, in order that he might give testimony. Early in the gospel he directs his own disciples to Jesus (1:35f). The prologue emphasizes the fact that he himself is not the light (v19).

Jerusalem Jews in the person of their delegated authorities (v19) are symbolic of the opposition that appears throughout the gospel. They pass from John to Jesus and consistently prefer the darkness to light. As happens so often in the fourth gospel, particular episodes take on a much deeper meaning. In this case there is a reflection of the antagonism between church and synagogue in the late first century when the gospel was written. In addition, the present narrative may well reflect a later prevailing controversy between disciples of the Baptist and those of Jesus.

John categorically denies that he is the Messiah, the specially anointed descendant of David (Dan 9:25), nor is he Elijah whose return at the end time was expected (Mal 3:1, 23), nor the prophet of Deuteronomy (19:18), another eschatological figure attested to also in the Qumran library (Dead Sea Scrolls) (1QS 9:11) (vv20f). It is interesting to note that John is identified with Elijah in the synoptic tradition (Mk 9:13; Mt 17:12; Lk 1:17); here that relationship is rejected. The Baptist comes simply as a witness without any clear eschatological overtones.

The quotation from Isaiah (v23; Is 40:3) de-emphasizes the notion of forerunner and stresses John as a witness to Jesus which occurs in the following narrative (1:29 - 34), where there is no mention of John's baptizing Jesus. *In the desert* (v23): Here these words refer to the place of John's ministry (the voice); in Isaiah, it accompanies the subsequent part of the verse, the place of the preparatory action.

The questioning continues (vv25ff). If John has no eschatological role, why does he baptize? He replies that his is a water baptism, a Jewish rite of purification, implying a change of heart. There is no immediate or direct comparison with Jesus' baptism; rather the emphasis is on the witness to Jesus as one superior to John. *Whom you do not recognize* (Gr: *know*) (v26): this is one of John's "key" words. The believer is the one who "knows" Jesus in faith; the non-believer remains unknowing. Bethany across the Jordan remains unknown; it is not the Bethany near Jerusalem.

The Johannine narrative centers wholly on the person of Jesus, God's Son, the Word incarnate, light and life.

In a very troubled world, Christian joy is not meaningless. This is not a mercurial joy corresponding to our highs and lows. Rooted in faith, it convinces us that if our lives are properly focused, if they point to Christ, then, like the disciples on the turbulent lake, we can be con-

fident and at peace. Isaiah told a very beleaguered Zion that restoration was near–not because it was merited but because Yahweh is faithful. Paul cuts through the tension in Thessalonica to remind his people that "he who calls us is faithful." As Jesus appears, the role of the Baptist is to make him known and affirm his mission. In Jesus, God's fidelity is unsurpassed. Listening to today's scripture, we have every reason to rejoice. That figure who will meet John in the desert is living proof that we are not and will never be abandoned.

Joy is more than merrymaking, a fleeting laugh, or a bit of euphoria. True joy retains composure, a peaceful smile in fortune or misfortune. It looks at mountains and oceans and sees God's imprint. It looks at teeming metropolises and sees an immense amount of good. Joy looks at Christ and knows he is there.

Homiletic and Catechetical Helps

1. The relationship between faith and joy.

2. Zion as central to Israel's faith.

3. Joy and Advent.

4. Messiah: meaning and history.

5. The meaning of discernment.

6. John the Baptist as he appears in John's gospel.

7. Witnessing to Christ.

THIRD SUNDAY OF ADVENT
Year C

Readings

Zeph 3:14 - 18
Phil 4:4 - 7
Lk 3:10 - 18

Theme: The Judgment of God

Judgment has both its positive and its negative features. Luke's gospel presents John the Baptist as the herald of judgment. The Christ, he says, will separate the wheat from the chaff. The final time means both salvation and rejection. Zephaniah sees the end of Yahweh's punitive judgment of his people with a future marked by his dwelling in their midst. Paul sees the end in terms of rejoicing as long as waiting is marked by a virtuous life, with God's peace dwelling in the human heart.

First Reading

The very short book of the prophet Zephanish (three chapters) dates the prophet in the time of King Josiah (1:1), the latter part of the seventh century B.C. Because the third chapter alludes to the end of the Babylonian domination of Judah in the late sixth century, it is generally considered the work of a later editor.

The prophet himself stands at the end of the Assyrian hegemony and prophesies in the period prior to the rise of Babylon. After a series of oracles proclaiming severe judgment of Judah and Jerusalem (Zeph 1) and the nations (Zeph 2), the book closes with an exultant hymn of deliverance for the remnant of God's people and Jerusalem their capital. This sequence in judgment is something of a prophetic constant. Negative retribution demanded by God's justice is followed by salvation, also required by covenant fidelity.

In today's reading Jerusalem is addressed in personal terms and called to celebration. She is spoken to in family terms as the daughter of Yahweh (v14). The reasons for rejoicing are twofold: retribution is at an end and the Lord is once again taking up his residence in Jerusalem. Historically this refers to the Jews' repossession of the city and the rebuilding of the temple after 546. *In your midst* (vv15, 17): The localization of Yahweh's protective presence ("a mighty savior"), a continuation of his presence with the ark in the desert, is repeatedly seen as cause for rejoicing (Is 12:6; Ps 46:6). Vivid anthropomorphism closes the passage with Yahweh seen as breaking into song in this moment of deliverance (v17).

Responsorial Psalm   Is 12:2 - 6

The note of salvific judgment continues in this thanksgiving hymn from Isaiah. The personal references which pass from singular (vv1f) to plural (vv3f) link the author with the redeemed people. *On that day* (v1): This is the day of the Lord, the time of definitive divine intervention (11:10). Yahweh is twice referred to as "savior" (v2), to be understood in context as both personal and collective. The drawing of water (v3) may reflect a connection between the hymn and the ritual for the feast of Tents, which celebrated Israel's first deliverance from Egyptian bondage. As in the first reading, Jerusalem is called to rejoice as Yahweh again takes up his residence. The hymn seems best situated in a post-exilic setting, added as a conclusion to the first part of the book (Is 1 - 12).

Second Reading

The exhortation to rejoice appears repeatedly in Philippians (1:18; 2:17 - 18; 3:1), even though Paul is writing from prison. It is a joy grounded in the community's solidarity and concern, which Paul feels should be widely known, and the proximity of the Lord's return (v5). The end is near for Paul's suffering as well as those of the Philippian community. Paul again links prayer and thanksgiving (v6; 1 Thes 5:16). Any turning to God in petition should flow from a sense of gratitude for blessings received. *In Christ Jesus* (v7): The unity of the believer with the risen Christ produces a peace of mind and heart even in the midst of seemingly insuperable trials (Eph 3:20).

Third Reading

Luke's account of John the Baptist's ministry contains a number of nuances which are particularly his. For example, the emphasis falls primarily on John's preaching, not his baptism. In today's reading, the chapter begins by highlighting the fact that the word of God has come to him (3:2). In view of the impending judgment (3:9), he calls for repentance and its fruits (3:8).

And what are those fruits? In today's gospel, various categories of the Jewish population pose the question to John. He answers in terms of a very basic ethic, shared, no doubt, by Jew and Greek alike, yet still seen more in the breach than in the observance. The first general norm calls for a sharing of goods with those who are deprived (vv10f). This would come as nothing new to John's Jewish audience (19:8ff; 16:25 - 31) but it is highlighted nonetheless.

Tax collectors (v12) were collaborators with Rome and were commonly viewed as guilty of such unethical conduct as extortion and fraud. Here they are simply advised to "live by the book," asking only that payment which is just. Soldiers (v14), evidently Jewish, were not required to serve with the Roman forces. They served in the employ of the Jewish administrative authorities in Palestine. They are asked to desist from the recognized abuses of the military. These admonitions of John differ considerably from the radical demands of Jesus required for discipleship (5:11, 27; 9:23ff; 9:57 - 62). For Luke this clarifies the difference in role between John and Jesus, with the demands of the latter related to life in the Spirit. John's ethic is one of fairness and equity; that of Jesus, a call to perfection.

The people ... all (v15) goes beyond the context to introduce the important Lucan theme of universalism. As in all the gospels, John excludes any claim to being the Messiah, the promised king of Jewish expectation (v16). The Messiah to come is mightier than John in vanquishing evil. John is not even worthy to perform the slave's task of undoing the sandal strap. Furthermore, he subordinates his baptism to that of Jesus. *The Holy Spirit and fire* combines eschatological judgment (fire) with post-Easter understanding (Holy Spirit). For Luke, fire can also be connected with the Holy Spirit (Acts 2:3f). What is asserted is a clear distinction between John's conversion baptism and the Spirit-filled baptism of Christ.

Separating the virtuous from the evildoer introduces, as in Matthew, the image of the winnowing fan (v17), a tool used in harvesting to toss the wheat into the air to obtain the separation of wheat from chaff. This is John's indication that Jesus' era will be one of judgment calling for exceptional choices (Mt 25:31 - 46). As a forerunner, the Baptist in Luke is seen as closely related to Jesus, e.g. preaching "good news" (Gr: *euangelizo*) to the people (v1), but he is still clearly distinct. Luke concludes the present narrative by introducing John's imprisonment at once (v19), with no specification as to who baptizes Jesus (v21). This careful comparison and subordination in all the gospels would seem to point to an underlying controversy about the two ministries in early Christianity.

The thought of judgment need not be terrifying, the Dies Irae and Michaelangelo notwithstanding. It can be a source of consolation. Rather than being unduly graphic about it, we would do better to consider its theological rationale. To know God and to reject him categorically in an ongoing fashion logically requires some response. Paul asserts strongly that God is not mocked. On the other hand, a life marked by a positive response to God, even with sin and forgiveness along the way, will also not be overlooked. Judgment is a sobering thought but its negative side should never overshadow our realization of God's compassion and love. Remember, it is Luke who gives us in one chapter the lost sheep, the lost coin, and the lost son. Even in the prophets, with Zephaniah among them, judgment repeatedly highlights salvation.

And what is to be said of our readiness to judge? The scriptures remind us that if we refrain from judging, we will not have to worry about our own. It is unfortunate that all too often we serve as prosecutor and judge in examining motives and reaching conclusions. It is far more Christian to interpret motives positively, to refrain from taking sides–in short, to avoid being judgmental. Paul today suggests another source of action–consideration of others, thankful prayer as the door to peace.

With our baptism, inestimably greater than that of John, we already have one foot in heaven. No final judgment need jeopardize that. God's choice for us is already made. Only we can decide otherwise.

Homiletic and Catechetical Helps

1. Understanding the final judgment.

2. Baptism as a fundamental choice.

3. "With death life is changed, not taken away": Preface of Mass of Christian Burial.

4. Advent as a time of personal evaluation.

5. Advent and the sacrament of reconciliation.

6. The indwelling God in our midst: the temple, Jesus Christ, the Christian.

7. John the Baptist and today's marketplace: honesty, fairness, gender respect.

FOURTH SUNDAY OF ADVENT
Year A

Readings

> Is 7:10 - 14
> Rom 1:1 - 7
> Mt 1:18 - 24

Theme: Immanuel–"God With Us"

As Advent draws to a close, the church presents three passages of scripture which bear on Jesus' birth. The Immanuel text from Isaiah has a long history as a messianic text in the Christian tradition. The text from Romans is pertinent as Paul claims to be an apostle who proclaims Christ as Son of David and Son of God. In the infancy narrative, Matthew recounts the conception of Jesus by Mary and sees the Immanuel text of Isaiah as uniquely fulfilled.

First Reading

Eighth century Judah found itself in a difficult position. Two powers to the north—Israel, the northern kingdom, and Syria—had formed a coalition against the major threat, Assyria, and they wanted to force Judah to do the same. Ahaz, Judah's king, was undecided as to whether to submit to Assyria as a vassal and thereby be protected or to form a partnership with the two northern kings. The two kings, then, decide to force Judah's hand (7:1f). Isaiah insists on an independent course of action since Syria and Israel are destined for destruction. He calls for faith in God's word (7:7ff).

In today's reading the wavering Ahaz once gain meets with the prophet. Isaiah indicates Yahweh's willingness to give a sign of his continued support, but Ahaz declines the offer (vv10ff). The prophet responds that a sign will be given regardless of the king's inclination. A young woman of marriageable age (Heb: *almah*) will soon bear a son, who will be called Immanuel (God-with-us). The name will clearly indicate God's continuing presence with his people. The threat from the two northern kingdoms will pass (v16), but chastisement for Judah will not be absent from the Lord's visitation (vv15,17ff). In short, the prophecy is good news and bad news. However, the name itself and subsequent oracles of Isaiah point to the ultimate deliverance of at least a remnant of God's people.

The identity of the child is not specified. Since it was to be a sign to Ahaz, it certainly refers to a proximate birth. As a sign to the "house of David" (v13), the reference may be to the future wife of Ahaz and his son Hezekiah, who at an early age would see the two kingdoms overrun by Assyria.

This text, however, takes on a messianic meaning connected with the Davidic dynasty (2 Sam 7:2 - 16). The offspring is easily connected with the Davidic child who will appear later in Isaiah (9:1 - 6). In the course of later tradition the "young girl" is termed a "virgin" (Septuagint: parthenos), and, as we shall see, earliest Christianity sees the text as uniquely fulfilled in the virginal conception of Jesus.

Responsorial Psalm   Ps 24

This psalm has strong liturgical overtones, probably in celebration of the ark's coming to Jerusalem and Yahweh's enthronement in the temple. With its emphasis on the coming of the Lord, it fits well with today's theme. Yahweh's universal dominion as creator is extolled (v1). Hebrew cosmogony, so clearly reflected in Genesis 1, pictured the earth as a large disc resting upon water. The waters below the earth offer support, just as the waters above the dome of the sky give rain and moisture. The waters below emerge in the form of oceans and rivers (v2).

The theme then turns to cultic worthiness. Only the upright of conscience before God and neighbor can participate in the procession to the temple (vv3f), as God, in turn, extends his blessing (vv5f). *Seeks the face of God* (v6): This is an expression for temple worship; the sanctuary of the temple housed the unique presence of God.

Second Reading

Paul gives expression to his own understanding of "God-with-us" in the opening lines of his letter to the Romans. As a greeting, he uses the classical epistolary form, indicating the sender(s), those addressed, and the greeting. In identifying himself, Paul elaborates with a threefold specification (v1). He is a slave of Christ, not in a servile sense but as one totally given to Christ's service (1 Cor 7:22; Gal 1:10); an apostle, for with his call on the Damascus road, he has been commissioned for the gospel by the risen Christ; and set apart, for even prior to birth he was designated for mission in a way akin to that of the prophets (Gal 1:15). In this letter Paul is the only sender, which is not his ordinary custom.

The gospel which the apostle proclaims is rooted in the Hebrew scriptures which converge on Christ (v2). Paul speaks of Christ as Lord in a twofold way: according to the flesh (v3), he is a human born of the Davidic line, with "flesh" in Paul signifying fragile and weakened human nature, i.e. "like us in all things but sin" (Heb 4:15); according to the spirit of holiness (v4), by reason of his resurrection, Jesus becomes the effective Son of God, the one sanctified and sanctifying, the one who gives the Spirit. Here Paul neither affirms nor denies the pre-existent divinity of Christ. He is not addressing the ontological question. Jesus was known and experienced as God's Son only when he rose and conferred the Spirit (1 Cor 12:3). It is the spirit of holiness present to the risen Christ that is the source of all Christian empowerment.

Among the favors of this same Christ is the grace of apostleship which Paul has received for the benefit of the Gentile
world. Obedience of faith (v5) implies a total submission to the
gospel in a way akin to Paul's being a "slave of Christ." The
"good news" is a call not only to accept Christ but to live in him
(v6; Rom 8:1f).

Paul addresses the Romans as the holy ones of God (v7), the
term used for the sacred, cultic community of Israel (Ex 19:6).
Again, the source of this sanctity is the risen Christ, who, with
the Father, grants them grace (Gr: *charis*) and peace (Gr: *eirene*).
What would be blasphemous to the non-believer Paul unhesitatingly affirms: the Father and Christ together are the cause of
Christian holiness.

Third Reading

The primary scope of the infancy narratives in Matthew and
Luke is a theological statement, not the presentation of the
facts surrounding Jesus' birth. For this reason it is a futile exercise to try to reconcile all the data presented in the two distinct
accounts. Moreover, while serving as an introduction to the
gospels, they are actually a backward projection of many of the
gospels' main features. Like a musical overture, they introduce
many of the themes which the author will later develop.

The theme of Emmanuel (the Greek spelling of the Hebrew
Immanuel) is central to today's narrative. Jesus is both Son of
God and son of Mary. This is effected through the virginal conception by the power of God. Matthew here explicitly carries
the sonship of Jesus back from his resurrection and his baptism
(3:17) to the time of his conception. He does not address the
pre-existence of Jesus prior to his conception as does John 1.

Early on, the reader is advised of the narrative's outcome, i.e.
the virginal conception of Jesus (v18). Formal betrothal had
legal effects. Although not living together, for all practical purposes the couple was considered married. Sexual relations with
a third party were adulterous and, if established, punishable by
death (Deut 22:21ff). Joseph is caught between his concern for
Mary's reputation and the demands of the law. He decides to
divorce her without notoriety. Outside of the author's scope is

any consideration of what Mary's fate would have been when the fact became public.

Joseph plays a central role in Matthew's infancy narrative. Like his Genesis counterpart, he is a "dreamer" (v20), with angels used frequently to express divine communication. Joseph is saluted as a Davidic descendant. The announcement made to him is eschatological, the moment in history for the outpouring of God's Spirit. Mary's conception is the work of God, and the child to be born is Emmanuel, "God-with-us" (vv20 - 23). The account of the conception makes that point alone: Jesus is both God and man. Jesus translates the Hebrew *Joshua* for later Judaism as "Yahweh saves," the name summarizing the child's mission.

The quotation from Isaiah converts the "young woman" of Isaiah 7:14 (Heb: *almah*) into the "virgin" (*parthenos*) of the Septuagint. The text is seen as clearly applying to the virginal conception and is so employed by Matthew.

God-with-us echoes the covenant relationship. In Matthew it appears here and at the gospel's conclusion: "I am with you always " (28:20). That Joseph formally accepts Mary and her child gives Jesus legal paternity and his Davidic lineage (v24).

The Matthean narrative underscores the end time's arrival, Davidic messianism, and the incarnation, the unique presence of God among his people.

One of our earliest faith recollections, originally learned in question and answer form, is that Jesus is both God and man. But it is interesting to note the various ways that the New Testament gives expression to this. Theological pluralism is not a twentieth century invention. Writing for a largely Gentile Christian audience, Paul presents the truth in a different way than Matthew writing for Jewish Christians. Paul's attention centers on the Son of God as the resurrected Christ; Matthew carries it back to conception. Both of them present the truth in very dynamic terms as compared to the rather sterile and static way it has often been later presented. For the early Christian, Jesus was not so much defined as he was experienced. It was not necessary that everything be said or, much less, done in the same way. Every affirmation did not have to be comprehensive and all-embracing. A great deal of adaptation was in the air. It merits our consideration today. In striving for accuracy and uniformity in articulating our faith, we often find that it ends up making little difference in the way we live.

"The Lord be with you" is the liturgical greeting that we hear at every eucharist. It reminds us that the Lord is with us and encourages us to intensify that relationship. During good days, we experience the Emmanuel as did Matthew's end time community, with great joy. At other times it is hard to experience, when difficulties beset us as they did in Ahaz' time when Judah stood on the brink of disaster. But Immanuel was still there. He is no less present today–in sacrament, in scripture, in neighbor, and in the world. Christmas gives us the chance to experience it anew.

Homiletic and Catechetical Helps

1. Understanding Jesus as Son of God.

2. Faith as an experience of God.

3. The unfolding understanding of Jesus' Sonship.

4. Jesus in the flesh and in the Spirit: Paul's understanding.

5. Apostleship in the New Testament.

6. Jesus as two natures in one person: post-New Testament understanding.

7. What are the different ways in which I experience Jesus as God-with-us?

FOURTH SUNDAY OF ADVENT
Year B

Readings

> 2 Sam 7:1 - 5, 8 - 11, 16
> Rom 16:25 - 27
> Lk 1:26 - 38

Theme: Son of David

Mary's conversation with the angel in today's gospel focuses on important truths of our faith. One of these is Jesus' lineage in the line of David. It rests on the promise made to David a thousand years before that his would be a divinely established dynasty to last forever. The first reading from the second book of Samuel contains this oracle of promise. Paul concludes his letter to the Romans with a doxology praising God for the work accomplished through Jesus for the good of all people.

First Reading

This celebrated oracle of Nathan marks the beginning of Israel's messianic hope, which eventually centered on an individual descendant of David. The passage, inserted at this point by the book's Deuteronomic editor, is somewhat more complicated than may appear at a first reading. The word "house" appears repeatedly (five times in the first seven verses); it is a key word which will be nuanced differently as the narrative proceeds.

David's good intention of building a dwelling (temple) for the ark is opposed by the Lord himself, speaking through Nathan (vv1 - 5). This opposition reflects the same tribal tradition that did not agree with having a central monarchy (1 Sam 8). As in the case of the kingship, the temple would present the tribal confederation with a type of political and religious centralization which it did not desire. To appreciate these negative feelings, it is necessary to read the oracle in its entirety (vv1 - 7).

The words of Nathan then take a positive turn, prescinding completely from the proposed temple (vv8 - 11). The picture is one of the simpler past with David leading his people to victory over his foes with divine guidance and protection. Promise for the future centers wholly on the people themselves, to be blessed with a peaceful and prosperous life, free from any military threat. The only reference to "dwelling" at this point turns on the safe dwelling of the people in peace and prosperity (v10).

The concluding section of the oracle (vv11b - 17), read only in part today, is favorable to the idea of the temple and is strongly monarchical. This reflects the "stitching" of traditions that has taken place, so much a part of the Deuteronomic editor's work. Through a play on the word "house," Yahweh promises to build a house for David, i.e. a dynasty. The royal line will continue in perpetuity with unshakeable divine support (v16). This marks the beginning of the monarchical ideal in Israel and the belief that, even in the face of countless setbacks, the line of David would continue. In the course of time, this hope will center on an ideal future king.

Responsorial Psalm   Ps 89

This royal psalm builds on the first reading. It shows the extent to which Davidic messianism continued to play a part in Israel's belief and worship. The psalm is post-exilic, written some five hundred years after Nathan's oracle. It sings of the Lord's covenant faithfulness (Heb: *hesed*) (v2), a kindness that is seen as eternal (v3). Very concretely Yahweh's fidelity appears in the covenant made with David. Written at a time when the monarchy was non-existent and the country laid waste (vv39 - 42), the psalm looks back confidently to the early promise (v4).

The bilateral character of the royal covenant has the king viewing Yahweh as his firm and durable support, his Rock, as well as Father and Savior (v27). Yahweh, for his part, promises to stand by his covenant in lasting fidelity (v29).

Second Reading

Romans concludes with a doxology, glorifying the Father for the plan of salvation, which is at the heart of Paul's ministry. *My gospel* (v25): this is the "good news" which has been committed to the apostle, further defined as the kerygma (proclamation) of Jesus Christ, the mystery revealed in these final times. The kerygma contained the essential truths of faith, focused on the death-resurrection of Jesus (1 Cor 15:1 - 5). This was seen as a secret hidden in God through the ages, partially revealed through the prophets (Heb 1:1), and only in these final days made fully manifest for the benefit of all people (1 Cor 2:6 - 10). *The obedience of faith* (v26): or the obedience which is faith.

This is a central Pauline theme. Faith is an unqualified response to God's action in Jesus which leads to salvation (Rom 1:5).

As the prayer of praise is made to God through Jesus, God is seen as extending a deeper faithfulness to the gospel to those who turn to him in belief (v25).

Third Reading

The account of Jesus' conception in Luke, like that of Matthew, is a central Christological statement. As has been noted elsewhere, the two evangelists, as much as they converge around basic beliefs, show marked differences in their infancy narratives, which preclude any type of historical synthesis. On the other hand, there is no need to force convergence in light of the clear theological and literary perspectives pursued by both.

In Matthew's infancy narrative, Joseph plays a dominant role; in Luke it is Mary. Luke also contrasts, in a parallel fashion, the parentage, conception, and birth of John and Jesus, underscoring the superiority of the latter.

Three fundamental points are made in the passage from Luke read this Sunday. The first is Jesus' descent from David. The narrative begins with mention of Joseph's Davidic lineage (v27), and the initial intervention of the angel concludes on a Dividic note (v32). Since Mary was formally betrothed to Joseph, they were legally joined to each other, although cohabitation had not yet taken place. For Jesus to claim Davidic descent, it was required only that Joseph confer legal paternity. What Luke does here is to connect Jesus with the messianic hope of Israel, which had its beginning in the oracle of Nathan read earlier.

Luke's second major point is to present Jesus as Son of God (vv32, 35). This honorific title was especially used of the king (Ps 2:7) and pointed to a special relationship. As the angel uses it here, especially in view of the context, it clearly has a special transcendent meaning.

The conversation between Gabriel and Mary is a usual way of expressing divine communication in Hebrew thought regardless of what form it might have taken. Akin to his role in the book of Daniel (c. 9), Gabriel is a herald of the messianic age.

Mary is greeted as a highly favored person (v28), a greeting which puzzles her and is explained in the angel's message (vv29ff). In God's plan there is to be the conception and birth of a son whose name Jesus is salvific ("Yahweh saves"). He will be the Messiah and Son of God. Mary's question (v34) simply sets the stage for the climactic response; its purpose is literary. The child will be Son of God through a conception effected in her virginal womb by the exclusive action of God. The child, fathered by God alone, is in that sense God's Son. Furthermore, Elizabeth's pregnancy at an advanced age will substantiate the angel's claim (v36).

The third point of the narrative is to highlight Mary's response. She is recognized as favored (vv28, 30), an appellation which at once points beyond her to the author of salvation. Her own spiritual posture reflects acknowledgement of this in her words of acceptance (v38). In this Mary is the prototype of the Christian. She accepts and activates God's word within her, for which she is and will be blessed (vv45, 48). What becomes increasingly evident in Luke's gospel is that relationship with Jesus is based on word-acceptance, not ties of blood (8:21).

Important to note is that the divine sonship of Jesus, identified by Paul at one point with the resurrection (Rom 1:4), is here carried back to the time of human conception. His pre-existence prior to conception (John 1) will come to the fore as Christian understanding develops.

We speak little today of kings, queens, or royalty in general. Where it still exists, it seems to have lost much of its earlier significance and is but a vestige of a bygone era. As Christians, we are forced to reinterpret Jesus as king as well as the kingdom or reign which he inaugurated. The reign of God means basically the effective sovereignty of God over all creation. For humankind it means universal recognition of that sovereignty. Jesus as king means Jesus at the center of all creation. Everything in the universe is touched by his act of redemption. For us as individual believers, it means that our first allegiance is to Christ and the implementation of his Father's will in our own lives and in society as a whole.

As Son of David, Jesus had an interesting lineage. Some of his forebears were illustrious men of faith, even if flawed, as such David,

*Solomon, and Josiah. However, the greater number of his royal ances-
tors were despicable and are categorically rejected in the scriptures
themselves. They failed Yahweh and his people and as such receive
scant praise. Yet they are part of Jesus' family tree, and he carried that
sinful baggage as he presents himself as Savior. There were skeletons
in his family closet before which he did not blush. We are so often
weighted with guilt. But why should we fear? Christ asks only the "obedience of faith."*

*For Luke, Mary gave her "yes" to God and became the first
Christian! She is honored on many counts. Her privileges are celebrated in feasts throughout the year. Yet she gives all glory to God. Above
and beyond any honors, Mary is blessed because of her humble submission to the Lord's will. She heard the word and kept it.*

Homiletic and Catechetical Helps

1. The virginal conception of Jesus.

2. Jesus as David's Son: its meaning for today.

3. Relation between reign of God and church.

4. Distinguish between the virginal conception and the immaculate conception.

4. The "obedience of faith": faith as commitment.

5. The word of God: hearing and response.

6. The reign of God and environmental issues, social justice,
   and respect for life.

7. Church doctrine: two natures and one person in Christ.

FOURTH SUNDAY OF ADVENT
Year C

Readings

Mic 5:1 - 4

Heb 10:5 - 10
Lk 1:39 - 49

Theme: Humble Origins

Luke's account of Mary's trip to visit Elizabeth offers another opportunity to link Jesus and John, while always stressing John's subordination. In this simple domestic setting, Elizabeth praises Mary for her trust in God's word. Micah anticipated the unborn Savior of the visitation story centuries before. Preaching at a time of considerable sin and corruption, he looked to the Davidic king who, despite his simple origins, would establish an era of universal peace. The letter to the Hebrews touches the core of what brought about that fulfillment of God's plan: the obedience of Jesus.

First Reading

Micah, an eighth century prophet, decries the sins of both Israel and Judah and foretells the downfall of both. Although most of this short book deals with the shadow side of Israelite life, his prediction of the future Son of David presents an interesting and striking contrast.

The prophet singles out the home town of David, Bethlehem or Ephrathah (Ru 4:11), located in Judah, as the place of hope. It was in Bethlehem that Jesse, David's father, lived and David and his brothers were raised (1 Sam 17:12). The town was small and otherwise insignificant (v1). Its importance lay in the fact that as David's home it was the geographical point of origin for the future Messiah. There is no inference in Micah that the Messiah need be born there, although Matthew and Luke will place Jesus' birth in Bethlehem. The emergence of the Messiah is part of God's plan from an early stage. Verse 2 is a parenthesis indicating that the period of exile and separation will last until the Messiah's birth, at which time the dispersed population will once again be restored to its homeland.

Unlike past monarchs who had incurred God's wrath (3:9f), the future king, empowered and fortified by the Lord, will be solicitous for the good of his people (vv3f). His rule will be permanent and universal. With the end of all conflict, he will be identified as peace itself (v4).

Responsorial Psalm   Ps 80

This is the prayer of a beleaguered people for deliverance. The geographical references point to a date of composition in the time of the northern kingdom. While Yahweh's might and power are recognized at once, he is, nonetheless, invoked as shepherd. *Throne upon the cherubim* (v2): At an early date Yahweh is depicted as enthroned above the two cherubim, golden figures placed above the ark of the covenant (Ex 25:18ff). Israel is referred to as God's vine (v15), a frequent metaphor for his people (Is 5:1 - 7; Jer 2:21). The "son of man ... " half verse (16b) is a copyist's error, duplicating v18b. The people are referred to collectively as "man," "son of man." As help is once more requested, there is the promise of covenant fidelity and an authentic spirit of worship (v19).

Second Reading

This passage from Hebrews summarizes Christian soteriology. In contrasting Jewish sacrifices with the offering of Jesus, it sees the latter as both superior and exclusive. The passage begins with a quote from the Septuagint version of Psalm 40:7ff. *But a body you prepared for me* (v5): This is the Greek version; the Hebrew speaks of "ears open to obedience." The body is well suited to the author's intent, referring to Jesus' own corporal and personal offering (v10). The psalm quote refers also to the four types of Jewish sacrifice: peace offerings ("sacrifice"), cereal offerings ("offering"), holocausts, and sin offerings. The semitic use of contrast in the psalm itself would subordinate but not invalidate cultic sacrifice. Its use by the author of Hebrews is obviously different, with Christ's sacrifice replacing the old (v9b). The single sacrifice of the new covenant has unlimited efficacy (v10).

Important to note is the efficacy of Christ's obedience (Heb 5:8). It was God's will that redemption and "consecration" be accomplished through the sacrifice of his Son. Jesus made this "will" his own and through his offering established a new covenant and a new people of God (vv9f).

Third Reading

In this Lucan account of Mary's visit to Elizabeth, the two covenants meet. As in the infancy narrative as a whole, the central figures are the offspring to be born, Jesus and John. Up to this point in the narrative, the accounts of the two have been paired but separate. At this point they are joined.

The story is replete with theological significance. As John leaps in his mother's womb, the inferior recognizes the superior (v44). It is reminiscent of the pre-natal activity of Rebekah's sons, Jacob and Esau, with its own distinct note of inequality (Gen 25:22f). In addition, Elizabeth defers to Mary throughout the narrative. John's role as precursor is underscored as Elizabeth's recognition of the salvific event is due to John's response within her (v44). The one who has conceived at an advanced age is overshadowed by the one who has conceived without a human procreator.

A second point to be noted is the meeting of the two covenants, with Elizabeth, Zechariah, and John representing the old dispensation, Mary, Joseph, and Jesus, the new. The faithful Israel, as seen in the person of Elizabeth, gives a "spirit filled" (v41) recognition of the Messiah and acclaims him Lord (v43), a faith statement to be understood in the light of the church's post-Easter experience. Elizabeth further notes the favored state of both Mary and the child (v42) in words later included in the "Hail Mary." Mary's blessedness rests primarily in her having believed what God had revealed to her (1:25 - 38).

This encomium directed to Mary by Elizabeth will be deflected by the former in her song of praise, the Magnificat (vv46 - 55). Everything has been accomplished by the action of God to whom alone praise is due; Mary expresses the spirit of the anawim, the poor of God. This is well expressed by the visit itself; it is Mary who goes to Elizabeth in a spirit of deference, not vice versa. The concept of the anawim is a major theme in Luke's gospel.

The episode of the visitation in its simplicity and domesticity, so skillfully developed by Luke, also points to the humble origins of the Promised One of the ages.

As Christmas approaches, today's liturgy gives us reason to pause. We are easily impressed by fame and riches; most of us are not averse to notoriety when it comes our way. Jesus followed a very different path. He is born in Bethlehem which, by Micah's admission, apart from being David's home, had little or no claim to fame. The mother of Jesus takes the initiative to visit an elderly cousin presented as living in modest rural circumstances. Mary looks for no acclaim, any more than will her son during his earthly sojourn. There is more than retaining a pious tradition in placing Christ in the manger beneath the Christmas tree. When Francis of Assisi began the tradition, he wept over the poverty of God.

Jesus comes to us as Savior and Messiah. He becomes our Lord through his obedience. We were all badly wounded by Adam's "no" to God, but unlimited possibilities are now open to us through the "yes" of another man. It was not the intensity of Jesus' suffering nor the human hardship that he unquestionably endured that saves us. It was his willingness to respond positively to God whatever the cost. We can do the same in very different circumstances and in largely unnoticed ways. Our every day is replete with opportunities to give God our "yes."

Homiletic and Catechetical Helps

1. Humility in the scriptures: the anawim.

2. The scriptural significance of obedience.

3. The meaning of obedience in our daily life.

4. The sacredness of life in the womb.

5. Jesus and Micah: transcendent fulfillment.

6. Cultic formalism versus true worship.

7. Rank means humility: personal experiences.

CHRISTMAS
Years A B C

Theme: Your Savior Comes

These words from Isaiah, read in the mass for Christmas morning, capture the flavor of all the readings selected for this feast. Selections from the book of Isaiah figure prominently in all the Christmas masses in announcing the dawn of a new era. The second readings today draw on Titus and Hebrews in accenting the arrival of God's salvation in the person of Jesus and anticipating his return at the end of history. Luke's infancy narratives are important interpretative statements on the meaning of the Christ event. In the first two masses of Christmas, Luke does this in story form; in the third mass, the prologue to John's gospel speaks of this saving moment in the highest theological terms: the Word of God has become flesh and has dwelt among us.

MASS AT MIDNIGHT

Readings

Is 9:1 - 6
Tit 2:11 - 14
Lk 2:1 - 14

First Reading

This is one of the Immanuel prophecies, serving as an extended commentary on the promise made to Ahaz, king of Judah, regarding a future king who would liberate his people and rule them with justice and wisdom (Is 7:14f; 11:1 - 9). Evidence points to this assurance being initially centered on Hezekiah, Ahaz's son, but gradually becoming centered on a more distant, ideal figure as messianic hopes grew.

In its immediate historical context, this prophecy looks to the liberation of the Israelite northern tribes from Assyrian rule after their subjugation. They are seen as passing from darkness to light, from sorrow to a joy similar to that of the harvest celebration (vv1f). Assyria, variously described as the yoke, pole, and rod (v3), symbols of oppression, will no longer pose a threat as the signs of its military might, the boot and the cloak, disappear. *Day of Midian* (v3): the occasion of one of early Israel's great victories over its pagan oppressor, when Gideon, with the help of the northern tribes, defeated the Midianites, a major military and political force (Jgs 7:15 - 25).

A child is born to us (v5): The child is Immanuel (7:14; 11:1), with hope centered here on a proximate historical personality, probably Hezekiah. Eventually, however, the prophecy transcends this limited vision and looks to a future descendant of David (2 Sam 7:15 - 25). The child is accorded various descriptive titles which combine heavenly and human qualities (v5). Thus, he will have keen political insight and judgment (counselor), military strength (hero), solicitude for his people (father) and leadership ability (prince). Each of these is enhanced by gifts that transcend human skills (wonder, Godlike, forever, peace). This Davidic king will rule over Israel and the nations in a peaceful sovereignty; it will be a reign marked by fidelity to principles of justice and uprightness (v6).

Responsorial Psalm   Ps 96

This hymn, identified as an enthronement psalm drawn from a cultic celebration of Yahweh's kingship, has a pronounced universalism. The nations are called to extol Yahweh's goodness (v1), as Israel is exhorted to make his glory known (vv2f). In the later verses of the psalm, all of inanimate creation is invited to join in this festive spirit (vv11f). *The Lord will come* (v13a): Ritually this may refer to the solemn entry of the ark into the temple in procession. The motif of Yahweh's arrival to begin his reign reflects the liturgical setting wherein his initial enthronement or "coming to power" is re-enacted. His is a reign marked by covenant fidelity (v13b). This idea of the Lord's arrival finds an appropriate setting in the Christmas liturgy.

Second Reading

While there is no unanimity on the subject, many scholars maintain that Paul's authorship of the letter to Titus is pseudonymous (1:1). This in no way affects its inspired character, however, and clear strains of Pauline thought are present in the letter. In today's passage, the author follows one of Paul's dominant traits in making his appeal for correct moral behavior (2:1-10) on the basis of sound theological principle.

The passage speaks of two "epiphanies" or manifestations of God (vv11, 13): the first in the incarnation, the personalized manifestation of God's grace (v11); the second at the parousia with the return of the Lord in glory (v13). The interim period between these two appearances is one of education (Gr: *paideuousa*) (v12), wherein the Christian is taught or trained to live in accord with his or her new ontological state (v14; 1 Pet 2:9).This embraces a rejection of the ways of the "flesh" (godless ways, worldly desires) to engagement in the life of the "Spirit" (temperance, justice, devotion) (Gal 5:16 - 26).

Future hope is centered on the parousia (v13). *The great God and Savior* (v13): God and Jesus Christ need not be seen as disjunctive here. Christ is "our God and Savior." By the time of the pastoral epistles, the distinction between the Father and Jesus is sufficiently clear, with both of them recognized, in doctrine and worship, as equal as God and Lord (Jn 1:1). At any earlier stage to call Jesus God would not have distinguished him from Yahweh (Acts 2:32, 36), a distinction that was made only with a growth in understanding. The idea of redemption expressed as constituting a people, as a deliverance, and as a cleansing has strong Hebrew and New Testament roots (Ex 19:3 - 6; Ez 37:23; 1Pet 1:18ff).

Third Reading

In this appealing story of Jesus' birth is contained some of Luke's strongest doctrinal statements, something true of the infancy narratives of Luke (cc. 1 - 2) and Matthew (cc.1 - 2) in general. This is to be stressed rather than historical detail, which, if pressed, finds Luke and Matthew at variance in some key areas. This Christmas passage has two major sections, the first describing Jesus' birth (vv1 - 7) and the second, the angelic appearance to the shepherds (vv8 - 14).

Luke's interest in the universal character of salvation sets

Jesus at once on the stage of the Roman international world scene. Mention is made of Augustus and Quirinius (vv1f). Caesar Augustus was the father of the *pax Romana*, an era of universal peace which he inaugurated. He ruled over the empire from 27 B.C. to 14 A.D. There is no extra-biblical record of a universal census during his reign. Quirinius became governor of Syria in 6 A.D., after and not during the reign of the Jewish king Herod (1:5). These are historical difficulties which it is not necessary to reconcile. Luke undoubtedly had some recollection of a census (and there were censuses of a more limited nature), and it serves him well here to account for the journey of Mary and Joseph to Bethlehem (v4). Moreover, the mention of Roman authorities and decrees serves to heighten Jesus' role as Savior of the world and the bearer of a peace that went well beyond that of Augustus.

The birth of Jesus in Bethlehem at the time of a census emphasizes his Davidic lineage. *Firstborn son* (v6): The term establishes Jesus' legal status in the family (Ex 13:2; Num 3:12) and sets the stage for the presentation scene that follows (2:22 - 38). *Swaddling clothes* (v7): The simple, customary vesture of an infant in which even the royal Solomon had been clothed (Wis 7:4ff). A dominant note throughout the narrative is the poverty of the child's birth—the manger, the full inn, the shepherds, the spirit of the anawim or lowliness in both Jesus and his followers being an important Lucan theme (9:3, 24f, 58; 10:21). The Palestinian inn would have housed animals in the inner courtyard and people in the surrounding edifice, usually of two floors with sleeping quarters on the second. In the circumstances of Jesus' birth there is also the preview of his eventual rejection by his own ("no room in the inn").

Shepherds were engaged in the simplest and most basic of occupations. Here they represent the poor of the world as the first recipients of salvation (1:52). The heart of the shepherd story lies in the address of the angel, which affords Luke the opportunity to sketch the person of Jesus along the lines to be further developed in the gospel (v11). He is Savior, the one who delivers his people from the bondage of sin, a title used in the synoptics only by Luke (Acts 5:31; 13:23); Messiah ("in the city of David"), the promised king of the line of David who was to restore Israel (Acts 1:6), literally meaning "the anointed one," with its Greek form "Christos" becoming a surname for Jesus; Lord, a substitute title for the name of Yahweh, pointing to Christ's divine status seen initially as conferred upon him with his resurrection (Acts 2:36). With all of this stated in these titles, this central figure of history is to be found in simple circumstances (v12). *Today* (v11): The note of fulfillment , the divinely appointed kairos, has broken into history now. The notes of joy (v11) and praise of God (v13) will also bring Luke's gospel to a close (24:52f).

The doxology of the angelic choir links heaven and earth. God is praised and humans are favored. *Peace* (v14): not the Roman peace but a restoration of harmony and right order between God and the world, lost by the sin of Adam and restored in Jesus (7:50; 8:48; 24:36; Col 1:20), This peace is then shared within the Spirit-filled community (Phil 4:7; Col 3:13). *Peace to those on whom his favor rests* (v14): the preferred reading of the Greek text, this sees the life of the Spirit as God's gift to humankind, which is thus favored.

In this retrojection of resurrection-faith understanding into the earliest stages of Christ's life, Luke sets the stage for his gospel. The Davidic king Messiah, Savior of the world, lived like the simple people of the earth and is now acclaimed as Lord, giving glory to the Father and the Spirit of peace to the world.

MASS AT DAWN

Readings

Is 62:11 - 12
Tit 3:4 - 7
Lk 2:15 - 20

The shepherds returned home with praise in their hearts after finding the Savior of the world. This Lucan motif of gospel joy is due to the full realization of God's promise found in this morning's reading from Third Isaiah: "Your Savior comes." The letter to Titus comments on the Savior's coming as due wholly to God's kindness and love. It has resulted in our justification and our hope of glory.

First Reading

The passage centers on the rebuilding of the temple and the re-establishment of Jerusalem as the center of Israelite life. Its sense of movement seems to point to a liturgical procession as the poem's original setting (v11; Is 40:10). The Lord brings recompense for his people in terms of total restoration and a rebuilding of the city which is the focal point of faith, the place of engagement with God.

The people are once again called "holy" (v12; Ex 19:6) and "redeemed" (Deut 32:11f). The city too is renamed in accord with its restored character. As stated earlier in the chapter, the city once called "forsaken" and "desolate" is now named "my delight" and "espoused" (v4). Here it is termed "frequented" to underscore the blessing of its repopulation.

Responsorial Psalm   Ps 97

"Yahweh is king" is the liturgical acclamation with which this hymn opens. Despite the stormy elements of Yahweh's appearance (v2; Ps 18:8 - 16), all are called to rejoice because of God's triumph over his enemy, the forces of chaos, false gods, and their adherents (v7). Darkness gives way to dawn; the light brings joy to the just, who are exhorted to give praise to Yahweh (vv11f)

Second Reading

To support his appeal for a spirit of graciousness in community (3:2), the author reminds the people of Crete of their formal sinful state (v3) which lasted until the generosity of God appeared in Jesus. The thought is clearly Pauline.

Redemption proceeds wholly from God's salvific love (v4; 1 Tim 2:3f). It is God who is first presented as Savior (v4) and only later, Christ (v6). The human recipients of this love were favored gratuitously, with no justice of their own (v5; Rom 4:24), a recurring Pauline teaching.

Bath of rebirth (v5): baptism with its accompanying regeneration in the holy Spirit (Rom 6:4). Redemption is accomplished by God in and through Christ, with a corresponding faith which leads to justification, the seed and hope of glory (vv6f; Rom 8:30).

Third Reading

The visit of the shepherds to Bethlehem continues the Lucan motif of God's initial revelation to the poor and humble (1:47f, 52). In finding the child in the manger and proclaiming the message of the angels (v17), the shepherds become forerunners of evangelical preaching. They give expression to the meaning and mission of Christ as Savior, Messiah, and Lord (2:11) but also as the child of humble origins, born just as one of those he came to save.

The circumstances of birth ("When they saw this"), combined with the message of the angel (v17), carry the message of the infancy narrative ahead, beyond the earlier understanding of Christ (1:31ff, 46 - 55). The shepherds' message shared with "all," including Mary and Joseph, leads to amazement (v18). For Mary it means further reflection for her who is the true exemplar of Christian faith (v19; 1:38). The shepherds' praise of God echoes that of the angels (v20; 2:14) and is prelude to the Easter prayer of the disciples (24:53).

MASS DURING THE DAY

Readings

Is 52:7 - 10
Heb 1:1 - 6
Jn 1:1 - 18

Second Isaiah's announcement of salvation in the restoration of Zion and the comforting of God's people was, in the words of today's reading from Hebrews, fragmentary and partial. The way in which human redemption was ultimately realized was truly God's "last word," definitive and non-repeatable. This was salvation in his Son. Hebrews speaks of Christ's pre-existence and his post-resurrection glorification, with emphasis on the latter. Our Christmas gospel from John, on the other hand, carries us back forcefully to that eternal presence of Christ with the Father in clearly identifying the Word with God.

First Reading

This brilliant passage from Second Isaiah combines the images of the messenger running to the ruined city (v7; 2 Sam 18:19 - 33), the watchmen on the city walls, who hear the messenger's words and realize that salvation is at hand (v7bf), and finally the destroyed city breaking into song (v9). The acclamation "Your God is king" has a liturgical ring (v7; Ps 97:1; 99:1) alluding to the arrival of Yahweh in processional form. In the post-exilic setting of a destroyed Jerusalem to be rebuilt at the conclusion of a period of desolation (v8), Yahweh is seen as Savior and reinstated monarch. Thus, the messenger's announcement is one of peace and good news (v7). The restoration will be an epiphany of God's might to all the nations (v10; Is 40:10)

Responsorial Psalm   Ps 98

Commentary on this psalm is to be found on the Twenty-Eighth Sunday of Year C.

Second Reading

These opening verses of Hebrews view Christ from a creative and soteriological perspective. The utterance of God in his Son is compared with the limited insights into God given in past times through the prophetic voices, not only the canonical prophets but the major biblical personalities, such as Abraham, Moses and Elijah. *In these last days* (v2): the equivalent of the "end of days" or the final eschatological period. God's utterance in his Son, termed simply by John God's Word (Jn 1:1), is, by contrast, definitive, comprehensive, and constitutive. This Son is both heir (v4) by reason of his redemptive work and the pre-existent one (vv2bf) through whom, as through Wisdom (Prv 8:30; Wis 7:25), God created all things.

In what may have been a liturgical hymn (vv3f), the author views Christ in his pre-existence and his post-Easter glorification. The pre-existent Christ is seen as God's refulgence (Gr: *apaugasma*), the imprint of God (Gr: *charakter*), and sustainer of creation. Two of these attributes draw on the presentation of

Wisdom (Wis 7:26). As an emanation or reproduction, they mirror God himself. In addition, Christ is the one who is both instrumental in creation and the one who sustains it once creation is accomplished, an idea found also in the Colossians hymn (Col 1:16f).

The redemptive Christ is considered solely in his post-Easter exalted role, seated at God's right hand (Ps 110:1). There is no explicit reference to death or resurrection, even though it is implied in "purification from sins" (v3). He has inherited the name of Son (vv4f), an inheritance that qualitatively enriches his earlier position as the pre-existent Christ. Like the title "Lord" (Phil 2:10f), the inherited sonship of Jesus, following upon his earthly mission, points to an effective and influential sonship with a corresponding recognition of his singular status by angels and humans.

The emphasis on Christ's superiority to the angels (vv4ff) must be seen against the religious and cultural background on the role of the angels in first century Christianity. Angels were seen as mediators of the covenant in some Jewish circles (Acts 7:53; Gal 3:19). There is evidence, as well, that features of an exaggerated angelology had crept into Christian circles, placing angels in competition with the singular work of Christ and thus jeopardizing his exclusive salvific role. Hebrews emphasizes that Christ is as superior to the angels as is the new covenant which he mediates superior to the covenant that preceded,

In freely quoting scriptural texts in support of his argument (vv5f; Ps 2:7; 2 Sam 7:14; Deut 32:43), the author sees the Father-Son relationship as pointing to Christ's superiority, and, in freely adapting the Deuteronomy text, he sees a further indication of angelic inferiority in their injunction to worship him, God's first-born of the dead (Col 1:18), as he enters into his glory, the world to come (2:5).

Third Reading

The structure and content of the prologue to John's gospel, combined with the extraneous prosaic insertions, suggest that this may well have been a liturgical hymn of the early church, which the author of the fourth gospel incorporates.

There are three distinct considerations of the pre-existent and historical Christ in the prologue, each going between the eternal and temporal manifestations. There is the Word's role in creation (vv1ff), the Word's self presentation in the world (vv10f), and the incarnation (v14). Each section is interrupted by the author's comment. In the whole prologue, it is Jesus Christ, not a detached eternal person, who is here presented as God's Word, viewed in both his pre-existent and historical existence. The Word, as applied to Christ, draws on the Hebrew creative word, an expression of God himself (Gen 1) and on the tradition of Wisdom as the expression of God's thought, the designer present with Yahweh in creation (Prv 8:30; Wis 7:25).

The Word in Creation: Opening with the same words as Genesis (v. 1; Gen 1:1), the prologue presents the Word as already present with the God (Gr: *ho theos*) or Yahweh at the dawn of creation. In fact, the Word was God (Gr: *theos*—without the article), i.e. divine, godly, sharing in God's nature. This is one of the clearest and direct affirmations of Christ's divine status in the New Testament. Like Wisdom the Word is both an instrument and an exemplar in creation (v30). Life and light are both the results of creation and here refer to the saving mission of Christ (vv3ff; 8:12; 3:19; 3:15; 3:36). This represents a passage from a pre-redemptive to redemptive thinking, from the pre-existent Christ to the Christ come into the world. The light-darkness dualism, found also in the Dead Sea Scrolls, summarizes the conflict between Jesus and his adversaries in foreshadowing the final triumph of Christ (v5).

A comment is introduced on the person and role of John (vv6f), pressing the fact that he pointed to the light but was clearly subordinate to it (1:26f).

The Word's Self Presentation: The parenthesis concluded, the hymn resumes as it points out the reaction of "the world" to Jesus as the light. "World" has both a positive and negative understanding in John (cf. 3:16f; 15:18f). But Jesus, in presenting himself to the "world," and especially to "his own," the Jewish people, met ignorance and rejection (vv10f).

Commenting once again, the author explains the results of faith acceptance, a new birth from above (vv12f; 3:3ff). This is due to the action of the Spirit and places one in a new family relationship with God. With the normal causes of human birth excluded, this is clearly a birth divinely willed. *Children of God* (v12): The term child used of Christians was seemingly common in the Johannine community (1 Jn 2:12, 18, 28; Jn 21:5).

The Incarnation: At this point the author speaks explicitly of the pre-existent Christ's appearance in human form. *Flesh* (Gr: *sarx*) (v14): complete humanness in all its weakness, an antidocetic note (·1 Jn 4:2). *Made his dwelling* (v14): literally, "pitched his tent," an allusion to the dwelling place of Yahweh during the desert journey (Ex 40:34 - 38). Christ appears with the manifestation of God's majesty, the image of the Father's glory (Gr: *doxa*) (v14; Heb 1:3). *Grace and truth* (v14): two attributes of Yahweh related to his covenant love.

Again the testimony of John is cited, pointing to Christ's anteriority, even though John is his historical predecessor (v15). Christ comes as the communicator of the Spirit ("his fullness"; Col 1:19) received from God, superseding in a new covenant the graced covenant of the past ("grace in place of grace," v16). It is the Spirit over the law. As God's self-revelation, Jesus remains singular and unique as the only avenue to the Father (v18; 14:6).

Christmas may not be the church's greatest feast, but it is surely the one most loved. Perhaps that is because children are so much a part of Christmas. The readings today are filled with joy. One searches in vain for any sense of wrongdoing or guilt. It is a day of great rejoicing, and, if there were not three masses to say it all, we would probably have to create them. The presentation of Jesus' birth presents some interesting questions, but the readings are at one in crying out that salvation is at hand. Sin is vanquished. And God has come among us in human form. The reason? To take us home.

What were the historical circumstances? Where did it occur? What do we actually know about his parents? The answer to all of these questions is "very little." In one way, it is sad that we have overly historicized so much of the infancy narratives. For many of us growing up, that was the historical presentation of the faith. Now, for a variety of reasons, we are not so certain that it all happened that way. It is really taxing to try to bring Matthew and Luke together on many features of the infancy narratives. But does it matter? Not really. They both relate the basic data. The Son of God comes as man, born in simple circumstances, to save us and bring us home. That is Christmas.

All of that having been said, let us not abandon the images, the forms, the things about God that bring children to life. The inn, the shepherds, and the magi portray the Jesus story in the way that Luke wanted to say it. It was not John's lofty theology. It may not have been historical presentation of facts, but it was a warm and engaging presentation in symbolic form of what Jesus meant. Let us not become lost in legend. But let us never forget what legend contributes to faith.

Homiletic and Catechetical Helps

1. The message of the Christmas scriptures.

2. Understanding the infancy narratives.

3. Messianic promise in the readings from Isaiah.

4. David and Jesus.

5. Meaning of symbols: the shepherds, the angels, the manger.

6. Biblical peace on earth.

7. The meaning of gifts at Christmas.

8. Relating John's prologue and Luke's Bethlehem scene.

THE HOLY FAMILY
Years A B C

Readings

> Sir 3:2 - 6, 12 - 14
> Col 3:12 - 21
> Mt 2:13 - 15, 19 - 23 (A)
> Lk 2:22 - 40 (B)
> Lk 2:41 - 52 (C)

Theme: The Family Spirit

The church's intention in this feast is to present Mary, Joseph, and Jesus as a model for Christian families. Sirach, written in the second century B.C., speaks today of reverence for one's parents in words that have a timeless quality. In Colossians, Paul presents practical ways in which the bond of love expresses itself within the Christian community, including family relations. The gospel selections from the Matthean and Lucan infancy narratives, while not written primarily to highlight family values, do, nonetheless, point to the solicitude of Joseph (A), the parents' respect for the law (B), and the obedience of the child (C).

First Reading

The Israelite ethic placed a high priority on respect for parents. The mandate figures prominently in the decalogue, following immediately after the commandments regarding God himself and before consideration of other human relationships (Ex 20:12; Deut 5:16). Sirach insists on obedience to father and mother (vv2, 6). Filial love embraces particularly the declining years when senility frequently sets in (v12df). The rewards for such conduct are blessings in the present life, in keeping with Sirach's traditionalist understanding of temporal sanctions on this side of the grave. Thus, with respectful conduct, one atones for one's sins (v4), is blessed with offspring (v5a), and is assured an answer to prayer (5b) and a long life (v6a).

Responsorial Psalm   Ps 128

Commentary on this sapiential psalm is to be found on the Thirty-Third Sunday of Year A.

Second Reading

Paul lists a number of domestic virtues, common in the Gentile world of his time, and gives them a distinctly Christian significance. Widely recognized virtues such as compassion, kindness, and patience are proper to God's chosen, holy, and beloved ones (v12). These designations, frequently applied to Israel in the Hebrew scriptures, look to the distinctiveness conferred upon the people with divine election. *Put on* (Gr: *endusasthe*): By reason of their baptism, Christians have been clothed in Christ (Gal 3:27). They are now exhorted to be clothed with the virtues which correspond to their new state. In biblical thought, clothing has a very personal stamp, very much an expression of the person and closely identified with the wearer.

These virtues look to inter-personal relationships, forbearance and forgiveness being two of the more important. Here again, forgiveness is related to its divine prototype of which all Christians have already been the beneficiaries (v13; Mt 18:21 - 35; Eph 4:32). Above all other virtues, Christians are to be clothed in love. It is the paramount virtue of Christianity (1 Cor 13:13; Mt 22:37 - 40). Love is the bond of perfection (v14) uniting Christians among themselves under the headship of Christ (2:2, 19) and effecting that holiness of life to which all are called (Mt 5:48).

Another fruit of the Spirit is peace (v15; Gal 5:22). Where charity prevails, peace is present as well. Peace among Christians flows from their unity in the one body of Christ (Rom 12:5; 1 Cor 12:12) and is reflected in their relations with one another. This is the harmony that arises from a restored relationship with God, with one's neighbor, and with the universe as a whole, brought about by the death-resurrection of Christ (1:19f).

The word is to take deep root within them (v16: Mk 4:14 - 19) to be shared within the community in teaching and correcting, always in a spirit of joy as seen in the varied hymnody of the early church. Hymns are not only expressions of gratitude; they are vehicles of formation in the faith, as New Testament examples illustrate (1:15 - 20). Not only is specific moral activity to be offered to God but every action of life (v17; 1 Cor 10:31). United with the risen Christ, Christians are no longer independent actors. There is a saving character to all that they do, and no more fitting thanks can be given to God who has shown his own goodness in Jesus.

Paul next passes to relationships within society (3:18 - 4:6).

He urges a spirit of submission on the part of those who hold an inferior position, according to the cultural outlook of the time, while urging consideration and respect on the part of superiors. Thus he regulates relations between husbands, wives, and children (vv18 - 21).

Third Reading (A)

In the account of Jesus' Egyptian sojourn, Matthew intends to present him as reliving the experience of Israel and thus pointing to him as the representative of the reconstituted people of God. As in the other Matthean infancy accounts, the story is built around the biblical quotation with which it concludes. The quotation here is Hosea 11:1, which speaks of Israel as God's son being called to freedom (v15). "Son" here in its Matthean use is both individual and collective, pointing to Christ as the new Israel (19:28) being called from Egypt. In the story, there are Moses parallels as well. The Jewish historian Josephus relates the tale of the pharaoh's being warned by astrologers of the birth of an Israelite liberator, which leads him to order the death of the Israelite children and results in Moses being miraculously saved.

The second part of the story explains Jesus' origins in Nazareth. The family life of Jesus in Nazareth is a point on which Matthew and Luke agree, even though the basis of these origins is different in each. The angel's directive to return is a direct echo of Moses' injunction to return to Egypt (v20; Ex 4:19). Historical recollection correctly places Archelaus as receiving part of the kingdom of his father, Herod, upon the death of the latter (v22). This would present difficulties for Joseph if he were to return to Judea. What Matthew fails to mention is that Galilee was ruled by another of Herod's sons, Herod Antipas. However, the main purpose of the account is to place Jesus in Nazareth, for the first time in Matthew, while in Luke it is the family's home (Lk 1:26f). *Nazorean* (v23): There is no biblical text that qualifies for this quotation, nor does Nazareth have any messianic associations (Jn 1:46). The main contenders to explain the quote draw on a relationship to "nazirites," consecrated persons (Num 6:1 - 21), or the Messiah as the "bud" (Heb: *neser*), blossoming from the root of Jesse (Is 11:1), and thus pointing to Jesus' Davidic origins. Whatever the background, this forcing of texts shows the importance of Nazareth in the Jesus tradition. The Matthean narrative closes, then, with the new Israel repossessing his homeland.

Third Reading (B)

A collage of biblical texts, by implication and not citation, underlies the arrival of Jesus in the temple, in accord with God's design. The basic text is found in Malachi (3:1) which speaks of the "end time" arrival of the Lord in the temple. The narrative set in the temple unites the two covenants, especially highlighted in the personalities of the story. The dominant note is eschatological fulfillment. The story also bears a distinct resemblance to the presentation by his parents of the young Samuel to the priest Eli for God's service (1 Sam 1:24 - 28).

Fulfillment of the Law: The requirement for the wife only (despite the Lucan "their purification," v22) to be purified after childbirth is found in Leviticus (12:1 - 8). The prescribed offering is also indicated, with Mary and Joseph, unable to afford a lamb, making the offering of the poor (v24). In addition, Jesus, as the firstborn male, was to be offered to the Lord (v23; Ex 13:12). Ordinarily the male was "redeemed" or bought back by an offering of money (Num 8:15f), something Luke would consider theologically inappropriate in the case of Jesus who belongs in God's house. The family of Jesus is here seen as totally observant of the law, as Luke links the two covenants with the temple as a focal point.

Israel Receives the Messiah: The figures of Simeon and Anna, advanced in years and faithful to temple service, represent the remnant of Israel accepting the Messiah. Simeon, steeped in the Hebrew scriptures, awaits the fulfillment of prophetic promise, "the consolation of Israel" (v25; Is 40:1). At the same time, he is led by the Spirit of the new covenant (vv25ff). In his hymn, Simeon recognizes Jesus as Yahweh's salvation for the Jews, and, in keeping with Luke's strong universalism, for the Gentiles as well (vv29ff). This clear mention of the universal mission carries the understanding of Jesus' parents beyond anything theretofore communicated to them (1:35; 2:11f, 17), adding to their amazement (v33).

The words of Simeon to Mary (vv34f) clearly allude to Jesus' "separating" mission. In making a decision for or against him, his Jewish co-religionists will be forced to declare themselves and will rise or fall accordingly (4:28ff). In being an opposed sign of salvation, his will be a contradictory position; in the acceptance or rejection of him, mere formalism will fall, as inner convictions emerge. Mary herself will not escape the hard decisions, since her physical relationship to Christ will not suffice (11:28f; 8:20f).

Anna's name means "grace." Like Simeon, she has spent her life in awaiting the Lord. In their being paired as representative of the faithful Israel, Simeon and Anna share the stage with the elderly, temple-oriented Zechariah and Elizabeth (1:1 - 25)

With their return to Nazareth, whence they will again journey to Jerusalem (2:41 - 52), the city so central to Luke's theology, this narrative of fulfillment, bridging the two covenants in an appropriate temple setting, focuses on the Lord's arrival. Luke has set the stage for much that will follow in his gospel. Eschatological joy does not exclude the thread of foreboding carefully woven into the story. In a Lucan refrain (v40; 2:52), the child's growth in knowledge and grace is reminiscent of John (1:80) and the earlier allusions to Samuel (1 Sam 2:26).

Third Reading (C)

The temple opens and closes the Lucan infancy narrative, as it closes the gospel itself (24:52). Once again the story unfolds in the context of the family's fidelity to the prescriptions of the law (v39; Lev 23:4 - 14). Dominant Lucan themes are easily detected. Jesus is located in the temple as wisdom (v46) imparting knowledge of God in the most sacred setting (v47; 20:47). In journeying to Jerusalem at the time of Passover, he foreshadows the journey that serves as the core of the gospel (9:51 - 19:28; 22:1f) as symbolic of Christ's journey to the Father.

Jesus' separation from his earthly parents in order to be engaged in his Father's "concerns" (v49, the Greek permitting the translation as "house" or "concerns") appears as a distinctive note of Christian discipleship in the gospel. New bonds in obedience to the Father surpass those of human origins (11:28f; 8:20). Jesus, moreover, speaks of a necessity to pursue the Father's work (v49; "I must": Gr: *dei*). This compelling engagement of Jesus in God's plan appears regularly in Luke-Acts (Lk 24:46; Acts 1:16,21)

The anxiety experienced by Jesus' parents (v48) and their failure to comprehend (v50) begin to actualize the pain predicted by Simeon (2:35). Jesus' single-minded devotion to the Father's will is to mark the whole of his ministry. For the time being, it means a humble submission to human parents (v51). It is Christ's obedience that will ultimately bring about redemption (Phil 2:8). Mary continues to ponder the meaning of Jesus, as he himself, in the Lucan refrain, grows in understanding and grace (v52). His mission of surrender to the Father, with separation from earthly ties, has been clearly announced.

As inspiring as they are, the readings for the feast of the Holy Family do not entirely suit our purpose. The three gospels, all taken from the infancy narratives, orchestrate central themes regarding Christ's redemption. They were not written to tell us a great deal about Jesus' family life. The reading from Colossians betrays a certain cultural conditioning in urging the wives' submission to their husbands, followed by a similar exhortation to slaves regarding their masters. The reading from Sirach is, however, in every way suited to today's feast. It envisions situations which are all too prevalent today –senility, even Alzheimer's, the nursing home, children's responsibility to obey. That reading cannot help but remind us that some elderly parents are all but abandoned. One wonders if there can be a greater sin of ingratitude than that of forgetting those who have given us so much. As we look at all of the readings for today, even though other themes may be dominant, we can see an underlying motif of family love and respect. In looking at the family of Jesus, we see a dedication to worship, the anxiety of loss, the joy of finding anew, These are important family values upon which we can reflect. Paul's call to forgiveness, generosity, and gentleness and the exhortation to avoid bickering and badgering have considerable relevance today.

One thing is certain. The scriptures are totally at odds with the decimation and demise of the family, so prevalent today. The solution to many of today's social problems cannot be simply laid at the feet of government. Governments support family values, they don't construct them. Religion has a much greater responsibility for building a solid family life, and religion today must ask some hard questions. Why are family values being discarded? Children will become good Christians and good citizens when they grow up loved, motivated, disciplined, and educated by parents dedicated to religious and social values. We are all aware of today's reality: broken homes, single parent families, latch key children, child abuse, parental addictions. And the list goes on and on. At the other end of the age spectrum, it is true that caring for the elderly is not always easy, and sometimes not even possible. But our parents deserve love in their waning years. And their families have the first responsibility.

When we stop and think, Jesus grew up in a closely knit family in a small Palestinian village. There is no doubt that he absorbed much from his parents, from the way they lived and worked and prayed. He was formed like any other child. At a given moment, they could take pride in their adolescent son. They did their job well. People have to be convinced today that to embark on married life is a great responsibility. When the task is done well, the joys are many. What greater compliment can a child receive than this: "I see a lot of your parents in you."

Homiletic and Catechetical Helps

1. The family: foundation of religion and society.

2. The Bible and responsibility for our parents.

3. Parents' responsibility for formation and education.

4. Parents and church in religious education.

5. Ways to express love within the home.

6. Love as the bond of perfection.

7. The flight into Egypt: its meaning in Matthew.

8. The presentation and Lucan theology.

9. Finding in the temple and the Father's concerns.

10. The home as the first and best school of faith.

MARY, THE MOTHER OF GOD
Years A B C

Readings

> Num 6:22 - 27
> Gal 4:4 - 7
> Lk 2:16 - 21

Theme: Mary in God's Plan

From the infancy narratives, which are written from a post-Easter theological perspective, it is impossible to determine how much Mary understood at the time of Jesus' conception and birth. However Luke's gospel comes back repeatedly to her reflection on what God was revealing in the message of the angel, the words of the shepherds, and the words of Jesus when as a boy he is found in the temple. She is a woman of faith and the church presents her life as an example for us on the first day of the New Year. Numbers, in today's first reading, recounts the priestly blessing conferred upon the Israelites. It invokes an abundance of God's kindness and goodness. Paul then tells us that Yahweh's goodness became incarnate in Jesus who makes us all children of the one Father through the gift of the Spirit. And the humanity of God was made possible through the cooperation of a woman, one of the few references to Mary outside of the gospels. In the gospel the shepherds recount for Mary and Joseph the message they had received: Jesus is Messiah, Savior, and Lord. For Mary the mystery leads to prayer and reflection.

First Reading

The blessing itself probably derives from early pre-exilic times although its reservation to the priest alone (v23) is a later, post-exilic development. Earlier practices portray at least the king as blessing the people (2 Sam 6:18; 1 Kgs 8:14; Hebrew reading: "blessed the whole community"). By the time of the deuteronomic and levitical legislation, it had been restricted (Deut 10:8; 21:5; Lev 9:22).

Of particular note is the the blessing's threefold repetition of Yahweh's name, invoking a richness of blessings upon the people (vv24ff). In two of the verses the image of God's face is used to portray divine solicitude. *Let his face shine* (v25): Seeing the face of God is usually associated with temple worship (Ps 42:3) and thus here may be a liturgical note. In a broader sense, it looks to Yahweh's benevolent gaze conveying well-being and prosperity. At the same time, God's hidden face symbolized misfortune (Ps 44:25; Ps 10:11). *Lift up his face to you* (v26): This too is an anthropomorphism for God's attention, protection ,and providence. It brings with it a peace signifying wholeness, completeness, and a deep sense of God's presence (Ps 4:7ff; 33:18f).

Responsorial Psalm   Ps 67

Commentary on this psalm is found on the Twentieth Sunday of Year A.

Second Reading

Fullness of time (v4): This occurs at the moment fixed by God for his definitive intervention in history (Mk 1:15). The sending forth (Gr: *exapostello*) is more than a simple sending; it connotes a commission or a sending on mission. Here the mission is seen as twofold, expressed in two purpose clauses (v5). First, it was to ransom those who were held captive or "enslaved" under the law, and, second, it was to effect a new status of adoptive sonship for those liberated. To accomplish this God had to become part of the condition of those he wished to save. Thus he immersed himself in the lot of humans and in the lot of the

Jews, coming in human form ("born of a woman) and as a Jew ("born under the law"). He was then in a position to free those who were "enslaved." Even the non-Jew needed to be liberated from the pagan celestial beings, "elemental powers," who were believed to control world events (4:3).

What results from this is a new set of relationships. Through God's conferring the Spirit on his Son, which is in turn shared with the baptized, Christians become adopted members of God's family, enabling them to address God as Father, just as Jesus did (Mk 14:36; Rom 8:15). *Abba, Father* (v6): The Aramaic word for father with the article (Greek translation: *ho pater*) was prominent in early Christian liturgy. This use without a qualifier goes beyond normal Jewish practice in its simple and direct note of intimacy. Such usage was illustrative of the unique status of the Christian.

The Christian is now a son or daughter of God (vv6f); references to childhood in translation do not accurately render the idea, since that stage is now past (3:23ff). As fully mature sons and daughters, they are not to be considered servants in the household either. They are now the true heirs of Abraham, heirs of God's promise (3:29). This means inheriting the reign of God and eventually glory through God's Spirit (Rom 8:16f).

Third Reading

With the exception of the final verse, which speaks of Jesus' circumcision, this gospel is the same as that for Christmas mass at dawn, where commentary on it will be found.

With Jesus' circumcision on the eighth day the family of Jesus is again presented as faithful observers of the law (v21). The teaching of the epistle that Jesus was "born of a woman" and "born under the law" (Gal 4:4) is portrayed once again in this gospel account. Jesus, like John before him (1:59), is fully incorporated into the faith of Israel, the rootedness of Christianity in Israelite belief being another Lucan theme (Acts 22:3; 23:6; 24:14f). It is this faith tradition that has passed into the new Israel, even though rejected by many segments of the Jewish people (Acts 26:5ff, 21ff). The name given the child is Jesus (Yahweh saves) (1:31). What Paul in the second reading speaks of as adoption as sons and daughters, Luke summarizes in the name itself, the one who saves.

Paul has little to say about Mary, the mother of Jesus. He views her solely as the one who made possible God's presence as a human being. Jesus was born of a woman and born under the law. Since the infancy narratives are post-Easter narratives on the meaning of Jesus' person and mission and written as overtures to a gospel already fixed, they have little to tell us about the extent of Mary's understanding of what occurred. But she is repeatedly presented as reflective and meditative. As a woman of faith, Mary remained close to God. She was a woman of prayer.

It is hard for people to realize that their faith life and their relationship with God depends as much on prayer as it does on discernment, study, or counseling. The Lucan Jesus invariably seeks his answers in prayer, as did so many of the biblical personalities. The book of Psalms is nothing more than a prayer book. Luke's gospel opens with the prayer of Zechariah and Mary and closes with that of the apostles. So often we turn to God only after every other resource has been exhausted. Our time spent in prayerful reflection is seldom extended and often shortened. If she who is today celebrated as the mother of God grew in her understanding of what that means through prayer, we who strive to find meaning in our lives can do no better. Prayer is not saying a lot. Prayer is being with, being present to.

The influence of those we love is never far from us in whatever we do. Why should it be less so for God?

Homiletic and Catechetical Helps

1. Understanding the doctrine of Mary as God's mother.

2. The meaning of a blessing.

3. Blessing of a priest, our parents, one another, at meals.

4. The role of Mary in the letter to the Galatians.

5. Pauline transitions: slaves–sons and daughters–heirs.

6. The shepherds: God's concern for the little people.

7. Christian roots in Judaism.

8. Mary: the model of Christian prayer.

SECOND SUNDAY OF CHRISTMAS
Years A B C

Readings

> Sir 24:1 - 4, 8 - 12
> Eph 1:3 - 6, 15 - 18
> Jn 1:1 - 18.

Theme: Jesus, the Wisdom of God

Wisdom comes to the fore in today's readings. Sirach presents a personified Wisdom, sharing God's company from of old and destined to take up her residence in Israel. In John's gospel, wisdom is the Word of God, an agent in creation but also destined to dwell among us. Ephesians speaks of God's decision to bless us in Christ, especially as adopted sons and daughters, and prays that we may have the wisdom to know well the God who has so loved us.

First Reading

Sirach's presentation of Wisdom as personified draws on an earlier tradition (Prv 1:20 - 33; 9:1 - 6). In today's reading she is presented as present to Yahweh at the dawn of creation (vv1 - 4) and dwelling in a special way within Israel (vv8 - 12).

In the presence of the Israelites ("her own people," v1)) and the heavenly council, made up of angelic beings attendant upon Yahweh (v2), Wisdom sings a song of self-description. Even before Yahweh created with a word (Gen 1), Wisdom was spoken (v3). Like a mist she hovered over the earth as did God's spirit over the formless mass of Genesis (Gen 1:2). Her exalted position relates her forcefully to Yahweh himself, as the first-begotten of creation (v4; 1:4). She is to be instrumental in the whole process of creation (Prv 8:22 - 36).

Although active in the universe as a whole (v6), Wisdom is installed in a special way within Israel (v8). Later equated with the law (v22), Wisdom in Israel points to a divine direction for daily life and for worship through covenantal precepts, with a presence in Jerusalem, on Mount Zion, and in the temple (vv10f).

Responsorial Psalm   Ps 147

Like Sirach the psalmist sees God's blessings in creation and its sustenance, and in a special way in his direction of Israel through the law. Commentary may be found on the Feast of Corpus Christi, Year A.

Second Reading

In this liturgical hymn, based on the Hebrew *berakah* or blessing of God, heavenly favor is extended in and through Christ, thus enabling a reconciled and sanctified people to stand before God (vv3f; 5:27; Rom 8:29). It is the pre-existent Christ, present throughout the whole blessing, who is at the center of God's saving plan, even prior to the world's creation. This holy people is made up of God's adopted sons and daughters, united with God's own Son in the bond of the Spirit (v5; Gal 4:4 - 7; Jn 1:12). The visible effectiveness of the grace that comes through Christ redounds to God's glory (v6; Col 1:13).

The author, fully aware of the Ephesians' faith and love, offers a prayer on their behalf. The prayer requests a deeper knowledge of God, enabling the Ephesians to appreciate the ultimate outcome of their election (vv15ff). By reason of their baptism, they are destined to be part of the heavenly community. It is a hope deeply rooted in faith. This is an inheritance among the holy ones, i.e. an aggregation of the elect on earth to the members of the heavenly assembly. A similar union of the two bodies is spoken of in the Qumran literature as well.

Third Reading

Commentary on the gospel is to be found in the Christmas mass celebrated "during the day."

If there never had been sin, would we still have had Christ? Medieval theologians debated the question at length. The Franciscan school, heir to Platonic and Augustinian thought, upheld the primacy of the will over the intellect, thus accenting love as the prime virtue. This school held that Christ was willed by God independently of any foreknowledge of Adam's sin. They found considerable support in texts such as those which appear in today's liturgy. Christ is seen as the incarnate Wisdom of God, present to the Father before creation. Enfleshed among us, he shows us the way to the Father, just as Sirach's Wisdom, encased in the law, led Israel to God.

God's Wisdom was found in a plan to liberate all of us through a great act of self-donation. But more than liberated, we are now sons and daughters and heirs of a future heretofore unimagined. But that same Wisdom embraces more than salvation. It envisions God's continued presence in the world. Dorothy Day saw her call as a Christian as one that was basically counter-cultural. Where Christian values were at stake, she did not hesitate to confront capitalist chiefs or church hierarchs. The Catholic Worker movement became the living wisdom of God in the midst of a society which shows in many ways that it doesn't care, that the poor are dispensable, that the disenfranchised need not obstruct the path to success. The Wisdom of God also continues in thousands of base communities throughout the world which show by their life and action that authentic values are still alive. To speak in human terms, God at some point decided that his love for the world had to be uniquely manifest. It happened in his Son, his Wisdom incarnate. That Wisdom continues today in countless lives which remind us where true wisdom lies.

Homiletic and Catechetical Helps

1. Christian Wisdom in today's world.

2. Christ as God's Wisdom.

3. The Wisdom of God in creation, in Israel, in Jesus.

4. Christ as willed by God from eternity.

5. Wisdom in our daily decisions.

6. God's Wisdom as counter-cultural.

EPIPHANY
Years A B C

Readings

> Is 60:1 - 6
> Eph 3:2 - 3, 5 - 6
> Mt 2:1 - 12

Theme: A Call to the World

Today's feast adds a new and central feature to the Christmas message. Epiphany means manifestation—in this case, manifestation to the nations. Jesus is not solely the Jewish Messiah; he comes for the entire world. In Christ, all barriers will fall. In the reading from Third Isaiah, Jerusalem looks out upon her own people returning from the diaspora, but, on the far distant horizon, appear caravans from all parts of the world. The letter to the Ephesians sees this as the great mystery now revealed in the final times: the total equality of Jew and Gentile in God's plan. The account of the astrologers, taken from Matthew's infancy narrative, summarizes it all in story form. While the Jews, with the scriptural prophecies in hand, remain apart, the foreigners move in faith to Bethlehem.

First Reading

This proclamation of Israel's universal mission is bathed in light, radiance, and splendor, with a poetry strikingly similar to that of Second Isaiah. As the clouds of darkness are dispelled, they are supplanted by God's glory shining upon Jerusalem (vv2f). Early indication is given that Israel is to have an influence on other nations (v3; 49:6). The initial glimpse that Israel receives is that of her own people returning (v4; 43:5f). Yet this is only the prelude to a more impressive spectacle. The image is one of opulence and abundance, with the riches of distant lands being brought to Jerusalem. The gifts offered all look to the reconstruction of Jerusalem; they arrive by land and sea (vv5f). The points of origin of the incoming caravans—Midian, Ephah (Gen 25:4), Sheba and Kedar—are identified with the major trade routes through the Arabian peninsula. They come bringing the wealth of the Orient (1 Kgs 10:1f).

Responsorial Psalm   Ps 72

The major part of this psalm's commentary is to be found on the Second Sunday of Advent, Year A. Of special note for the universalism of the Epiphany is the psalm's geography (vv8ff). The Lord's dominion extends from sea to sea (the Mediterranean to the Persian Gulf), from the River (the Euphrates) to the ends of the earth (the European coastland). Tarshish is identified with traders from the far west, perhaps a port in southern Spain (Ps 48:8; Is 2:16); Arabia and Seba are to the far south.

Second Reading

Paul is presented as speaking to the part he played in the plan (Gr: *oikonomia*) of God's grace (v2). "Mystery" (Gr: *mysterion*) (v3) is an important word in Paul; the reference is to the ultimate salvific plan of God, concealed from ages past and revealed only in the fullness of time (1:9; 2:13 - 17; 1 Cor 2:1). This previously hidden plan is now made known to the holy apostles and prophets. As foundational to the church, their importance as recipients of revelation is of paramount importance (v5; 2:20). The revealed secret is the total equality of Gentiles with the Jews in the saving plan of God (v6). The Greek text emphasizes this equality with the prefix *syn* (with) attached to heirs, body members, and partners. Once made members of the body in the Holy Spirit, the elect becomes heirs of the reign (Gal 4:7). The use of the three compound nouns underscores the note of non-distinction and the elimination of all separating barriers.

Third Reading

The magi story is an important Matthean statement of belief in Christ and his mission, a post-Easter trajectory expressive of that fuller understanding which the church had only after the Spirit was given. Here a number of biblical texts converge to point up the author's intent.

Jesus, the Descendant of David: This comes to the fore in the principal text of the narrative (v6). This combines a text of Micah (5:1, 3) with one from 2 Samuel (5:2). The "clans" of the original Micah become "rulers" in Matthew to highlight the royal associations. Davidic origins are connected with Bethlehem, the home of David's father Jesse (1 Sam 16). The conflated text points also to Christ as a shepherd king. The appearance of the star offers additional Davidic overtones, as related to the Balaam prophecy (Num 24:17) of a royal figure rising out of the line of Jacob. The appearance of a new star in antiquity was popularly identified with the birth of a future leader.

Jewish and Gentile Reaction: Herod ruled from 37 to 4 B.C. The story is well suited to what is known of his character, but beyond that many details of the story need not be pressed. What appears clearly is the enigmatic situation in which the early church found itself. The Jews for whom the Messiah was the promised one refuse to accept him, while the Gentiles come to him in ever greater numbers. Thus, in the story, the Jewish experts, guardians of the tradition, easily identify the child's prophesied birthplace (vv5f). But their response is one of widespread fear ("all Jerusalem with Herod," v3) and duplicity (v8). "Magi" was a term originally applied to Persian priests, and eventually to diviners, here astrologers. They make their way through Judaism (Jerusalem) to the truth of Christ.

The author draws on a number of texts to underscore universalism. Foreigners bring gifts (Ps 72:10), including gold and frankincense (Is 60:6), in reflecting Gentile openness to the gospel. (The mention of "kings" in the psalm text and the three gifts mentioned in the story gave rise to the tradition that the visitors were three kings.) The foreigners' recognition of Christ's position is seen in their act of adoration (Gr: *proskuneo*), the same veneration offered to Jesus by the apostles after the resurrection (28:17).

Jesus, the New Moses: The Matthean infancy narrative in general has Jesus relive the experience of Moses/Israel. This appears in the magi story as well. There is a strong resemblance to the legend found in the historian Josephus about the prediction of Moses' birth given by his sages to Pharaoh and his reaction in the slaughter of innocent children.

The type of literature reflected in this story, often designated "haggadic midrash," draws on biblical and non-biblical texts and narratives to make a strong moral or didactic point. Here it casts light on the meaning of Christ in the light of Hebrew tradition.

Most of us feel that we are devoid of all prejudice. Yet the facts do not always bear us out. People of different racial background create a whole spectrum of reactions from avoidance to fear. As well intentioned as people may be, the fact is that they grow up in different worlds, implicitly segregated neighborhoods and schools. Surprising to say, even after all the consciousness-raising, there is very little interracial contact. We are not really free of racial or ethnic bias because we treat our Hispanic gardener well. Our children are not necessarily free of negative racial attitudes because they play basketball against inner city high school teams. That is something quite different from real acceptance. Within certain neighborhoods, for example, it is rare to see any genuine social inter-action. This writer remembers a Catholic black boy being turned away from the Catholic high school he wished to attend–in pre-civil rights days–and the memory has never left. It seemed as antithetical to the gospel then as it does now.

There are many practical ways in which the Feast of the Epiphany makes its point. It teaches us that in Christ there is no room for religious elitism. It may sound like a time-worn truth, but it still bears repeating: in God's eyes all are equal. And we are not free to build roadblocks of any type. In the early church, this meant not only common worship attended by all but a common table as well. We would do well to ask ourselves how long it has been since people of a different color ate at our table, or visited our house, or swam in our pool. To what extent are our children growing up in both a segregated neighborhood and with segregated attitudes? This is not a textbook issue. It passes quickly from theory to practice. If we are to avoid further volatile civil situations, explosions of violence, or increased polarization, then Christians have to act as such. Today's epistle says we are all co-heirs, co-members, and co-partners. We are called to a classless society in a Christian sense. Each Epiphany reminds us that we still have a way to go.

Homiletic and Catechetical Helps

1. Unity in Christ and equality.

2. The implications of Christ's universal call.

3. Ethnic inclusion: neither Jew nor Greek.

4. Social inclusion: neither slave nor free person.

5. Gender inclusion: neither male nor female.

6. Meaning of epiphany.

7. The magi story as theological statement.

8. Relating today's epistle and gospel.

BAPTISM OF THE LORD
Years A B C

Readings

Is 42:1 - 4, 6 - 7
Acts 10:34 - 38
Mt 3:13 - 17 (A)
Mk 1:7 - 11 (B)
Lk 3:15 - 16, 21 - 22 (C)

Theme: Baptism: Actualizing the Promise

Baptism is called the gate of the sacraments or the entrance way to the church itself. All the promises of salvation, converging from various biblical sources, become real in baptism. The baptism of Jesus is found in three gospels, each with a different shade of meaning. But more than the baptism of Jesus is recounted; the baptismal theophany points to our own baptism as well. The Father acknowledges Jesus as Son and favored one, upon whom God's Spirit rests. In this recognition, there are echoes of the first servant song, our first reading today. In the reading from Acts, there is emphasis on the access to salvation now open to all people.

First Reading

This is the first of the four servant of the Lord songs in Second Isaiah (49:1 - 7; 50:4 - 11; 52:13 - 53:12). Here the servant is introduced by Yahweh as one defended, chosen, and favored. *My spirit* (Heb: *ruah*) (v1b): The word means wind, breath, or spirit. The image is that of a force or power from God enabling a person to act in a manner beyond human capability (Jgs 3:10; 13:25). It was seen as an endowment of the messianic king (Is 11:1). The mission of the servant is to uphold effectively the will of Yahweh in legal decisions ("bring forth justice," vv1, 4, and "law," v4) not on a narrow juridical basis but as the champion of moral uprightness. This instruction in Yahweh's Torah extends to the nations. Both the audience (the nations) and the teacher (a prophet) offer a new dimension to Israelite thought,

The servant's manner is one of calm and reserve (v2) as well as a gentleness of spirit (v3). What is damaged he will not destroy but rebuild. The final verses (vv5ff) envision Israel as the servant. It is a people taken as God's own (Deut 32;10f), fashioned according to the Lord's design (Jer 18:1 - 10), with a universal mission. Just as Yahweh covenanted himself with Israel, so Israel, in its enlightening teaching, becomes a symbolic pact of Yahweh's intent to save the nations (v6). The light

which Israel sheds is to offset the darkness of Gentile ignorance, symbolized by the blind and the imprisoned (v7).

Much debate still centers around the identity of the servant.
That he is at times identified with Israel is certain; in fact at one
point he is called "Israel" (49:3). At the same time the strongly
individualized characteristics of the servant are hard to reconcile with a generic identification. The servant is best seen as an
individual who represents the collective Israel, the saved remnant. This collective individual remains unnamed in the
Hebrew scriptures. The New Testament authors see in Jesus the
fulfillment of the servant prophecies.

Responsorial Psalm   Ps 29

In this hymn a heavy thunderstorm takes on cosmic dimensions in suggesting Yahweh's triumph over the powers of chaos
(Gen 1:1). Mythological overtones connected with a Canaanite
deity's similar victory may point to the original source of the
psalm.

Heavenly beings (sons of El) (v1): originally deities in a pagan
pantheon; in Israelite thought, they are reduced to angelic assistants at the heavenly throne. They are here exhorted to praise
and acknowledge Yahweh's name. *The voice of the Lord* (v3): The
expression appears seven times in the psalm as seven peals of
thunder. In mythology thunder was seen as an expression of
God's might or anger. Yahweh presides above the water which
rests on the firmament (sky). The water is subject to his direction. The hymn goes between the earthly and heavenly liturgy
in calling for acclamation within the temple (v9) as well as in
the heavens (v1; Is 6:1ff).

Second Reading

As part of Peter's discourse in Cornelius' home, this Lucan
passage is primarily directed to the Christian community as a
whole ("you know," v16). The main point being made is the
access of all people to salvation in Christ ("no partiality," v34).
The right of admission of Gentile Christians is emphatically
asserted (v35).

The content of the word (v36) is summarized in what follows. The man Jesus, who announced the era of peace and reconciliation to the Israelites (Lk 2:14; 10:5; 19:38; 24:36), is the one now constituted Lord at his resurrection (2:36) and given a universal sovereignty ("Lord of all").

Luke then traces the historical period on which the apostolic testimony is based. It begins with the Galilean ministry of Jesus, following upon the baptism of John (v37; 1:21ff). It is important to note that the witness begins where Mark's gospel begins, with Jesus' baptism, not with his infancy or early years. *God anointed Jesus* (v38): This refers to the baptism of Jesus in an application of the Isaian text, which speaks jointly of the Spirit's descent and an anointing (Is 61:1), a theme taken up by the Lucan Jesus in referring to the theophany of his baptism (Lk 4:18). Jesus' ministry was then Spirit-empowered, with the work of healing receiving special mention (v38; Lk 4:14).

Third Reading (A)

The three synoptic accounts of Jesus' baptism and accompanying theophany, read at this feast on the three successive years, are at one regarding certain basic data: the baptism itself, the subordination of John, the theophany of divine recognition seeing Jesus as God's Son and favored one. But beyond that each evangelist leaves his own imprint upon the narrative.

In Matthew, Jesus comes from Galilee to Judea expressly for baptism (v13). The problem which this creates for John, as reflected in various ways in the gospels, is actually the problem of the early church in reconciling the sinless Jesus with the reception of a sinner's baptism. This explains John's reluctance to proceed (vv14f). It is further suggested that promoters of the Baptist's cause well into the Christian era (Acts 18:25; 19:2ff) may have found support for their position in this submission of Jesus to John. This may explain the church's apologetic stance (as here) and its repeated emphasis on the subordination of John to Jesus. Whatever the reasons, the fact that there were problems with the baptism is a most convincing argument for its historicity.

To fulfill all righteousness (v15): more than a simple acceptance of God's moral will, the usual meaning; here it is an engagement in that will as salvific. Jesus comes as Savior in sharing the lot of a sinful people and being divinely recognized as God's Son and servant. The baptism itself is marginally treated, reduced to a dependent participial phrase, as Matthew moves the reader's attention to the theophany (v16). *Spirit of God* (v16): This is the power of God directed toward a supernatural mission. The recognition of Jesus as God's Son, a unique form of filiation, is coupled with his being the one "with whom I am well pleased," a reference to Jesus as the servant of the Lord (Is 42:1). He is the one who fulfills the Isaian prophecy in bringing salvation to the nations through a spirit of total submission to God's will. The dove imagery may reflect the hovering Spirit of God in creation (Gen 1:2) or the symbolic agent of peace and reconciliation (Gen 8:8 - 12). It certainly symbolizes the power of mission that Jesus receives (Acts 10:38). In addition to highlighting Jesus' special relationship to God, the term "Son" also points to his Davidic role as the king Messiah (Ps 2:7).

The Matthean Jesus is acknowledged by the Father in the third person ("This is my Son," v17), in contrast to Mark. In Matthew it is clearly for the benefit of others, since the revelation itself has already been made in the infancy narratives. However, Jesus alone sees the theophany (v16).

In the narrative, Jesus is presented as the king servant, identifying with his people, in his salvific mission. The clear trinitarian allusions point to this as a symbol of Christian baptism (Mt 28:19), of which Jesus' own baptism is a prelude and a pledge.

Third Reading (B)

Since the synoptic accounts have a number of common features, the reader is here advised to review the commentary on Matthew (Year A). Here the Marcan differences will be noted. Mark is more primitive, more directly interested in the theophany, and shows no great concern that the innocent Jesus received a sinner's baptism. Before the crowd, John acknowledges his own subordinate status, as well as the difference between the two baptisms (vv7f). The Spirit that empowers Jesus (v10) will also confer effective power upon his baptism (16:16).

The theophany is presented as wholly personal to Jesus; he alone sees the vision and hears the voice (vv10f). This is Mark's first acknowledgement of Jesus' sonship, unlike Matthew and Luke, both of whom address this in their infancy narratives. The intent of this gospel, however, is summarized in its first verse: to present Jesus as both the Christ (Messiah) and the Son of God (1:1). At the gospel's mid-point, Peter will recognize Jesus as the Messiah (8:29), and the Father at the transfiguration (9:7) and the centurion at the cross (15:39) will proclaim his divine sonship. Jesus himself accepts both titles during his trial (14:61f). Here the Marcan theophany concludes, as do the other synoptics, depending on Mark, in presenting Jesus as the Messiah-servant.

Third Reading (C)

Here only the Lucan differences will be noted; for common features, the reader is referred to the Matthean account (Year A). Luke also redimensions the narrative and reduces in importance the baptism itself. He places his main emphasis on the theophany.

The people (v15a), *all* (v15b), and *all the people* (v31) are expressions of Luke's universalism, a central feature of his gospel. As in Mark, in answer to inquiries about his role, the Lucan John subordinates himself and his baptism to the person and ministry of Jesus. *Holy Spirit and fire* (v16): The Spirit conferred upon Jesus (v22) becomes the transforming agent for the apostles (Acts 2:4) and the regenerating force for the baptism which they administer (Acts 2:38). Fire as a symbol of divine power accompanies the Spirit at Pentecost (Acts 2:3).

It should be noted that John is totally removed from the scene prior to Jesus' baptism in the third gospel (3:19f). This not only separates John from the new era of fulfillment in Jesus but also eliminates any indication of his presence at Jesus' baptism. Again as mentioned in the other synoptic accounts, this is evidently due to the early church's difficulty with the baptismal scene as well as any competitive claims from John's advocates. The baptism is treated in a dependent clause (Greek genitive absolute) and attention is drawn to the vision. Jesus is at prayer, a distinctive Lucan note, which characterizes Jesus' posture at every important moment of his ministry (v21; 6:12; 9:18; 9:28f; 23:46).

The eschatology of the scene is seen in the heavens opened (Is 63:19). In Luke, as in Mark, the disclosure is made to Jesus only. There is no doubt, however, that Luke sees an important baptismal catechesis in this account of Jesus, the Messiah-servant, missioned for the world's salvation by the Father.

There are good reasons, of course, why infant baptism has become a part of Catholic life. That is the way that most of us were introduced to Christianity. Yet there is no denying that adult baptism has much to commend it. Anyone who has worked with adults entering the church is aware of that.

The New Testament catechesis on baptism is addressed to people who understand or understood the step to be taken. Baptism brings together the promises of God from the distant past and the redemption brought about by Christ and actualizes them in the life of the person accepting the faith. It is the key and central sacrament, the door to the future, the transition from death to life. Unfortunately, it is all too often little more than a cultural reality, something that every child is born into, a "must" in one's life regardless of what the future holds. In other words, it is simply a given.

Even with the difficulties it presented, the primitive church placed in sharp relief the account of Christ's baptism–and not solely because it linked Jesus and John. It also taught Christians what baptism should mean for them. They were bought at a great price by the Messiah-servant who identified with them in their sinful state. Each evangelist paints the picture with his particular hues. Matthew present a Jesus who is eager to conform to God's saving will. In his brevity, Mark mainly contrasts the two baptisms, pointing to the Spirit as the great vivifier. Luke has Jesus at prayer before this great epiphany of God's love. In all three the triune God is at work.

How fitting it is to finish the Christmas season with the feast that makes the whole season actual in our life. What would the life of Christ mean if it were simply a drama, inaccessible to all of us. Baptism is the most graced moment of our lives. The Easter vigil each year brings new Christians to the living waters. Joy is so evident in their faces. We all rejoice. The same is true when a baptism is celebrated within the

Sunday liturgy. It preaches a homily by itself. We need these moments to stop and reflect. Yes, baptism is where the whole of faith comes together.

Homiletic and Catechetical Helps

1. Jesus as Messiah and servant.

2. The servant as a collective individual.

3. Baptism as a center point of faith.

4. Baptism as the door to sacramental life.

5. Adult baptism and the Easter liturgy.

6. The reasons for infant baptism.

7. Explaining the baptism ritual.

8. The reason for godparents.

9. Baptism as a commitment.

10. The connection between Jesus' baptism and our own.

11. The Trinity and baptism.

SECOND SUNDAY OF THE YEAR
Year A

Readings

> Is 49:3, 5 - 6
> 1 Cor 1:1 - 3
> Jn 1:29 - 34

Theme: Christian Baptism: Election, Forgiveness and Mission

Today's liturgy of the word couples John the Baptist's recognition of Jesus and his mission with Isaiah's second song of the suffering servant. What is said of the mission of Jesus is to be duplicated in the life of every Christian. As Paul indicates in the second reading, the Christian is "consecrated" and "called" just as was Jesus himself.

First Reading

The songs of the suffering servant are four in number, interspersed at various points in the second part of the book of Isaiah (42:1 - 7; 49:1 - 7; 50:4 - 9; 52:13-53:12). Interpretations vary regarding the identity of the servant. He may well represent the faithful Israel and is so called by name in the present song (v3). On the other hand, the gradual progression in the servant's mission and the concrete details of what he endures argue for a specific individual. The servant is best seen as an exceptional, dedicated Israelite who embodies the faithful Israel. This collective individual in New Testament times will be identified with Jesus himself.

In the second song, the servant's mission is becoming clarified. In prophetic fashion, he is chosen prior to his birth (v5; Jer 1:5). His mission is twofold. He shall effect the conversion and restoration of Israel (v5, evidently differentiated from the Israel addressed in v3). His broader commission, however, is universal. He will bring salvation to all peoples (v6; Lk 2:32).

Responsorial Psalm   Ps 40

The psalm touches on the moral dispositions which were at the heart of Jesus' mission (vv8 - 9). They are directly applied to Jesus in the epistle to the Hebrews (10:5 - 7). Prescribed ritual can be formalistic and empty, as was often the case in Israel's history; it is a heart fully attuned to God's will that is the authentic human offering. In reversing the "no" of Adam's dissent, Jesus effects redemption through his unqualified "yes" to the Father's will.

Second Reading

The opening verses of the epistle follow the customary formal salutation. The author of the letter, joined often by others (Sosthenes, possibly the one mentioned in Acts 18:17), salutes the addressees. Paul bases his right to guide and admonish on his own call as an apostle, designated for mission by the risen Christ. He speaks to "the church of God in Corinth." The expression alludes to the local community's election, not unlike that of ancient Israel (Gr. *ekklesia*; Heb: *qahal*), with emphasis on its being a worshiping community. In speaking of Corinth as "the church of God," Paul uses the same appellative applied to the mother churches of Judea, the direct descendants of the Israelite community; when adding the church's particular name ("of Corinth"), he betrays an understanding of church which is beginning to broaden to embrace a wider geographical reality.

To see the Corinthians as consecrated and holy is to see them as set apart or distinct, in accord with the traditional understanding of holiness. This consecration arises from baptism, something shared with all Christians (v2), a point Paul wishes to emphasize in broadening the horizons of his intended readers.

The closing invocation, "grace and peace," expresses the goodness of God showered upon his people and mediated by Jesus. It is God's favor which is the source of whatever holiness is to be found in the church.

Third Reading

In John's gospel, Jesus is identified as the Lamb of God, an echo of the final suffering servant song (Is 53:7, 10), wherein the servant is led to death like a lamb led to slaughter; the gospel reference may also be a reference to the Passover lamb (Ex 12). As distinct from the synoptics the Johannine Jesus is not said to be baptized by John; in fact he is not said to be baptized at all.

Jesus is singled out by John under three headings: (1) He is the one who will effect the world's redemption (v29). (2) He ranks before John and is superior to him, even though the latter had an extensive, and perhaps somewhat competitive, following (v30; Acts 18:25; 19:2 - 5). (3) The spirit rests on Jesus and gives meaning and direction to his mission (v33). The indwelling between Jesus and the Father, and Jesus and the believers, is shared by Jesus and the Spirit as well. Jesus communicates this intimacy of the Spirit to the believers (Jn 20:23). Baptism is the principal channel through which the Spirit is given (v33).

In the Johannine account, the communication between the Father and John the Baptist is silent and internal (vv32f), whereas the synoptics present it in theophany form. John is clear in indicating that the Baptist had no recognition of Jesus prior to God's inspiration and direction, despite the Lucan narrative of a family relationship, and even pre-natal recognition (Lk 1:44).

The theme of Jesus' election reappears in the passage's closing verses, a direct echo of the first servant son, with God's Spirit resting upon Jesus (v33; Is 42:1). Part of the same Isaian verse appears in the synoptic theophany (Mt 3:17; Mk 1:11; Lk 3:22). In John and Matthew, the Father's message is directed to John; in Luke and Mark, to Jesus.

All the gospels point up the likeness between the servant and Jesus; indeed they indicate Jesus as the fulfillment of the Isaian figure. Both are sent with a mission of forgiveness of sins destined for both Israel and the nations. It is a mission in which the Lord's Spirit plays an essential part. As both narratives continue, the mission will require the vicarious death of the two principal agents.

In what is clearly a post-Easter baptismal catechesis, John recognizes Jesus as God's Son (v34). It is with the acceptance of Jesus with such faith that the baptized Christian becomes a sharer in the Spirit conferred upon Jesus (vv32f).

The second reading today ties in closely with the overall theme of election: initiated in the servant, fulfilled in Jesus, and continued in every Christian and the church as a whole. This election results in our forgiveness and is also the source of our mission. The servant theme is also continued in the church's ministry, applied by Paul to his own calling (Acts 13:47; Gal 1:15; Rom 15:2).

We so easily forget that our election carries with it a real sense of responsibility. Our call signifies a consecration or sacredness before the Lord. It also means that we have been forgiven. Yet the Christian life is not restricted to the sanctuary. The servant was missioned as was Jesus. Paul identifies himself as an apostle, one who is sent. The same is true of us, sent to the neighborhood, the workplace, the town or the city. We are called to bring a deep commitment to Christian values to a society of shifting or fading values. The commission is not limited to priests or professed religious. It springs from baptism and is reinforced in confirmation. It is a call that touches all of us.

Homiletic and Catechetical Helps

1. Analysis of the four servant songs.

2. The meaning of baptism: theology, symbol, ritual.

3. Jesus as the Lamb of God: servant theme—Passover theme.

4. Obedience to God, church, state, family, others.

5. The Holy Spirit—in Jesus' life, the church's life, the individual's life.

6. The church, local and universal, eastern and western, worshiping, "other."

7. The baptism of John and the baptism of Jesus—likenesses and differences.

SECOND SUNDAY OF THE YEAR
Year B

Readings

> 1 Sam 3:3 - 10, 19
> 1 Cor 6:13 - 15, 17 - 20
> Jn 1:35 - 42

Theme: Discipleship: Being with the Lord

Discipleship is not something casual. It is a process that requires a growth in understanding, a deeper knowledge of the master, a growth in Christian awareness. To know Jesus is to know the Father (Jn 14:9) but this is possible only when we "stay" or "abide" with Christ. To be truly Christian is to realize that we belong to a new household, living in and with the triune God.

First Reading

The nocturnal call and response of the young Samuel is a vocation narrative, found frequently among the prophets (e.g. Jer 1:4 - 10; Is 6:1 - 10). In this case, it is somewhat different. There is a message conveyed to the young boy which he is to deliver but no indication that he is to have a prophetic mission in life. The message is personal in character and not directed to a broad audience as is customary with the prophets.

But the Samuel narrative, in today's liturgy, has another purpose, which explains its different cast. The portrait of the guileless, innocent Samuel contrasts sharply with the priestly impropriety of Eli's sons, the account of whose unseemly conduct precedes today's passage (1 Sam 2). Their selfishness and greed focused on appropriating for themselves the preferred portions of the sacrificial offerings. In chapter 3, it will be Samuel who is given the task of delivering Yahweh's word of reckoning to Eli's house.

Samuel's innocence is set forth with certain shades of naiveté. The threefold summons tends to highlight the message that is ultimately conveyed. It also points to the unquestioning and transparent submission of Samuel to God's will. Sentiments such as these will characterize the prophet's life.

Two features of discipleship appear in the Samuel story. The boy's extended presence in the Lord's house prepares him for his future task. In addition, his alertness, even when he is called in sleep, shows his willingness not only to remain in the Lord's company but also to be the submissive executor of Yahweh's will.

Responsorial Psalm   Ps 40

The response of the true disciple is an unqualified acceptance of God's will. (The commentary on the psalm may be found on the Second Sunday in Ordinary Time, Year A.)

Second Reading

Sexual license, part of Corinth's port city problematic, is addressed by Paul in his epistle. The language, pastoral and didactic, is not couched in diplomatic nuances. It rests on important Pauline doctrine.

The apostle stresses the sacredness of the human body. Through baptism, the Lord has made it his own and destined it for eventual resurrection (vv13f; Rom 6:3 - 7). This requires seeing the body in a new light and not giving it over to sin (Rom 6:12f).

Paul uses a striking and vivid parallel. The body that belongs to Christ cannot be handed over to a prostitute (v15). In physical sexual union, there is an intimate oneness which is God-designed (Gen 2:24). So, too, in the Spirit, a similar unity takes place between the person of Christ and that of the baptized (v17). The language here is so realistic and concrete as to make any general or esoteric understanding of the body of Christ unacceptable. In its own way, the union with Christ is as personal and real as that which is sexual. Paul argues that since we belong to Christ, any other illicit physical union is excluded. Christian marriage remains intact, however, and in itself actually mirrors the Christ-church union (Eph 5:25f).

In addition, in fornication or sexual license, the body becomes the instrument of sin in a way not common to other forms of sinfulness. The sacredness of the body itself is violated (v18). Paul concludes with the "indwelling" notion: the Christian as body-person is wed to Christ through the work of the Spirit sent by the Father. This makes the body a dwelling place of God (vv19f).

Third Reading

The account of the call of the first disciples in John differs considerably from that of the synoptics. With no mention of boats, fish, or nets, John deals with discipleship on a higher theological level. With his Easter faith perspective, John alters the earlier vocation scenario (Mt 4:18 - 22; Mk 1:16 - 20; Lk 5:1 - 11) and stresses the meaning of being a follower of Jesus.

To emphasize John the Baptist as a transitional figure (Jn 1:23 - 27), the disciples leave him to follow Jesus whom the Baptist has pointed out. Jesus is indicated as being the suffering servant (v37; Is 53:7) and/or the Passover lamb (Ex 12). Only one of the two disciples (Andrew) is identified.

The conversation between the two men and Jesus touches the heart of discipleship. Here the two levels of meaning, common to John's gospel, come to the fore in the use of the verbs "to stay" (v38) and "to see" (v39). This is much more than a cordial invitation. Jesus "stays" with the Father and the Father with him (14:10f), just as true believers "stay" in Jesus and his love (15:5ff, 9). For the two followers to "stay" with Jesus, they must enter into a new communion of life with Son and Father, brought about by the Holy Spirit. This is more than a visit; it is a homecoming.

To do this, one must "come and see." This "seeing" is the recognition of who Jesus truly is. In this first chapter, John masterfully makes the initial encounter of Jesus with all of his new disciples a telescoped picture of their historically gradual growth in insight. He is first recognized as rabbi (v38), then Messiah (v41), Son of God and King of Israel (v49), and finally, as revealed by Jesus himself, the link between heaven and earth (v51). Through all of this, the refrain is "come and see" (vv30, 46).

In this context of a telescoped faith identification, John includes Peter's name change (v42). Simon becomes Cephas or "the rock." It is presented as occurring at Jesus' first meeting with the apostle. Matthew places it later in the public ministry in the locale of Caesarea Philippi. For both, the event occurs in a context of the recognition of Jesus (Mt 16:18). In both cases, catechetical rather than strictly chronological interests are central.

Simon's new name, Rock (Cephas in Aramaic; *Petros* in Greek), indicates his unique role in the community of believers. He will be first among the apostles and serve as a foundation of the church. Catholics believe that this role continues in the bishop of Rome as the visible center and teacher of the faith community. That this office did not end with Peter's demise can be deduced from the fact that both accounts of Peter's designation (Mt, Jn) were remembered and recorded by the faith community well after the apostle's death.

In "seeing" Jesus, one comes to know him as more than a man—a prophet, even a Messiah. He is God's Son and unique emissary. This "seeing" is possible only in faith. Once grasped in faith, this truth leads to a special relationship with the Trinity (the indwelling). The path of discipleship is clear.

It is clear from today's readings that discipleship is far more than an acceptance or adherence to Christ. It means becoming part of God's family. It requires an abandonment of the past and a willingness "to see" and "to stay." Jesus dwells with the Father and we are invited to make our home there as well. Paul speaks of our union with Christ in very bold and vivid terms. This is not simply poetic language. It points to a very compelling reality.

Our home is much more than a place where we eat and sleep. It is an atmosphere of shared values and insights, a focus of love and concern. All things being equal, we should find our home a very warm and inviting place. To be part of the household of God means the same thing. Community has always meant much in our thoughts and worship. We are joined with others at every turn in our Christian life. That is as it should be with God's family. And it is from our union with God that we define our beliefs, our conviction, our way of living each day of our life. It is from this home in God that we are missioned to the world. As Paul reminds us today, this has all been made possible at a great price. We in God and God in us: "Glorify God in your body."

Homiletic and Catechetical Helps

1. The indwelling of the Trinity.

2. Insights derived from the titles of Christ.

3. Being "at home" with Christ.

4. The role of Peter in the church; primacy and collegiality.

5. Chastity; marital union; the proper understanding of sexuality.

6. Sacredness of the body: a positive approach.

SECOND SUNDAY OF THE YEAR
Year C

Readings

Is 62:1 - 5
1 Cor 12:4 - 11
Jn 2:1 - 12

Theme: Marriage as a Scriptural Symbol

In today's liturgy, the close relationship between Yahweh and his people, as well as between Christ and the church, is spoken of in marriage terms. While this says much about God's love for his people, it also underscores the significance and dignity of the married state. Marriage is a secondary theme of the readings, but the use of the imagery, here and elsewhere in the Bible, merits reflection on this way of life to which many are called.

First Reading

The latter part of the book of Isaiah (cc. 56 - 66) is often referred to as Trito-Isaiah to distinguish it from the authorship and history of Isaiah (cc. 1 - 39) and Second Isaiah (cc. 40 - 55). The three parts come from separate authors and represent distinct historical and theological perspectives. Trito-Isaiah is written after the Israelites are once again settled in their homeland after the exile. With a renewed priesthood and spiritual life, prospects for the future are bright. Past sinfulness and punishment are forgotten as the prophet strikes a strongly positive note.

The image of Zion (Jerusalem) as the bride of Yahweh is not new. It appears repeatedly in earlier prophetic literature. Hosea structures a major part of his prophecy around this theme. His tragedy of Israel's infidelity in going after other "husbands" (the baals worshiped in fertility cults) may well be a reaction drawn from the unfortunate circumstances of his own marriage

(Hos 1 - 3). Ezekiel treats infidelity at length, using the same image of the faithless wife (Ez 16).

Here the scenario is totally positive. Re-establishment emerges slowly like the first streak of morning light on the horizon or the light from burning torches that illumined the darkest corners of Jerusalem on festive occasions (v1). The Gentiles witness the emerging wonder although their reaction is muted. Jerusalem is to be renamed (v2). The significance of a name in antiquity is linked to its close identification with the person and his/her fixed destiny (e.g. Gen 17:5). The names given Zion (here representing Israel as a whole) express Yahweh's deep affection and commitment (my delight, espoused); abandoned are the names identified with her former rejection and punishment (v4). She is taken by Yahweh as bride. So complete is forgiveness that Zion is spoken of as one still in a virginal state, untouched and untainted. The picture is one of hope-filled expectations and unlimited prospects for the future, as husband and wife are solemnly united (v5).

Responsorial Psalm   Ps 96

An invitation is extended to all people to recognize Yahweh's sovereignty. The psalm may have originated in a ritualized enthronement of Yahweh in Hebrew liturgy. The central thought of today's liturgy centers on the final manifestation of God's glory which, according to this psalm, has significant ramifications far beyond Israel. Because God's sovereignty and equity know no boundaries, neither should the praise due him. The psalm is remarkable for its strong universalism.

Second Reading

In the early Sundays of each annual cycle, the church draws on Paul's first letter to Corinth. A major portion of the letter deals with the spiritual gifts or charisms which have been given to members of the church for the common good. In Corinth, however, they have become the source of contention and jealousy (1 Cor 12 - 14). This explains Paul's lengthy and theologically important treatment of the one body of Christ with its diversity of gifts.

The gifts listed in today's reading (vv8 - 11) are known in part; what some of them meant we can only surmise. The primary gifts among those listed are those reflective of discernment and good judgment, seemingly lacking in Corinth (v8). Faith is more than the virtue common to all Christians; it was rather an effective belief manifest in exceptional works (v9). Tongues is mentioned last and is considered a lesser gift by Paul (v10). It is to be given extensive treatment in the letter (c. 14). The truth is that we do not have a clear grasp of the distinction among all the gifts of the early church. Paul is very clear, however, about the common features of all the charisms: they are gifts of God (v4); they are meant for the common good (v5); in all of them God is at work (v6). Since they all proceed from the one God and are freely given (v11), they should not be the cause of division.

Third Reading

In this the first of Jesus' "signs" (v11), John begins what is referred to as his book of signs (1:19 - 12:50), which constitutes the first half of his gospel. John's signs differ in literary form and purpose from the synoptic miracle stories. They serve as didactic centerpieces to manifest Jesus' nature and mission.

Similar to the first reading from Isaiah, the Cana wedding feast is replete with themes of fulfillment, joy, and manifestation, connected with the end time. This is done through a number of messianic themes drawn from the Hebrew scriptures, e.g. the marriage of God and his people, the abundance of wine (Am 9:13; Hos 2:24; Is 29:17; Jer 31:5), the replacement of past rituals (vv6f). Jesus' action is seen as an anticipation of the determined time of fulfillment, his "hour" (v4), which in John means the time of death-resurrection (13:1).

Jesus replenishes the failing wine supply by changing water into wine. The "sign" is performed at Mary's request (v3). Her mention of the lack of wine has theological significance connected with the failure of Judaism's deep-rooted hopes. Jesus calls her "woman," a respectful but not familial form of address.

The same term will be used again when, at the crucifixion, the "beloved disciple" is committed to her care (v4; 19:26). To emphasize clearly the true moment of eschatological fulfillment, the author presents Christ here as attempting to withdraw from any anticipation of his fixed "hour" (v4). The abundance of wine produced and its quality (vv6, 10) highlight the theme of messianic fulfillment.

The story should be seen as a sign or manifestation of God's glory made visible in the life and work of Jesus (v11). In his person Christ brings to fulfillment the hopes of the Hebrew people, as illustrated by important biblical images. The role of Mary in this era of fulfillment is significant. There is less emphasis on the miraculous in the story than there is on the eschatological.

The theme of the wedding is important as background to the story. As stated above, it is an important end time theme. As related to Christ and his followers, it appears in the synoptics (Mt 22:25) and in Revelation's account of the final nuptials of the lamb (Rev 21). Ephesians speaks of marriage as mirroring the union between Christ and his church (5:21 - 33).

The liturgy today stresses the finality of all things in Christ and addresses specifically the importance of the final era in which we live. However, the recurring image of marriage allows us to reflect on this calling in life and on its relationship to God's love for his people and the manifestation of that love in Jesus. Church teaching on the unity, indissolubility, and fruitful commitment in marriage has important roots in this scriptural background.

Christianity was never intended to be a grim and dour affair. Joy is essential to Israel's picture of the final outcome. The image used today is that of a wedding. We don't really consider a wedding as "gloom and doom." The end time is to be marked by a clear sign of God's total fidelity as well as the loving response of a converted people. It is often said that many young people are reluctant to commit themselves to a life in the church because they see so few genuinely happy people, or, if they are happy, they have a hard time expressing it. Experience tells us that is an observation not to be casually dismissed. Our actions speak louder than anything. If we are totally involved in a great adventure, the boundless mystery of God's love, then it should show itself.

It is interesting to note how frequently marriage appears in the scriptures as an expression of the God-human relationship. There is no doubt that the Bible sees it in a very positive light. Such was not always the case in the ancient world. There are certainly signs of inequality of the sexes present in the biblical tradition. But there is still a level of appreciation for marriage that surpasses many other cultures. Even if marriage were not a sacrament it would still be highly reverenced in Christianity. So much of everything we are and everything we become flows from marriage. The importance of family values is heard today from many sides. The wisdom of revelation has long presented marriage and family in a positive light. Today more than ever that lesson is to be learned.

Homiletic and Catechetical Helps

1. Marriage as a scriptural symbol of God's love.

2. Marriage as a sacrament; church teaching; its properties.

3. Marriage's twofold purpose: conjugal love and procreation (Vatican II).

4. Mary as cooperator in God's will.

5. Mary as intercessor.

6. The "hour" of Jesus.

7. The use of our gifts in the church.

8. Unity and diversity in the church.

THIRD SUNDAY OF THE YEAR
Year A

Readings

Is 8:23 - 9:3
1 Cor 1:10 - 13, 17
Mt 4:12 - 23

Theme: Radical Conversion–The Heart of Discipleship

In Jesus the messianic age has dawned. Matthew, the gospel to be read during this A cycle, introduces Jesus' public ministry immediately after the account of the baptism by John (3:13 - 17) and Jesus' temptation in the desert (4:1 - 11). As in the other synoptic accounts, the beginning of Jesus' preaching takes place in Galilee. To relate his geography to Israelite messianic hopes, Matthew refers to the Isaian text which is given in its complete form in today's first reading. In writing to Corinth, Paul sees factions as a threat to the singular allegiance due to Christ.

First Reading

During the eighth century invasion of the Israelites by the Assyrians, the two northern tribes of Zebulun and Naphtali proved to be easy prey and were quickly conquered. Since Yahweh is seen as the ultimate cause of everything and the principal agent, he is presented as the "degrader" of the north (8:23). Yet this is but a prelude to a new and better era (9:1ff), one presided over by a faithful Davidic king (9:5f; 7:10 - 15), originally envisioned as a proximate descendant of the eighth century king Ahaz.

The sea road (v23) ran from Damascus to the Mediterranean and was important for trade and commerce. The region had been inhabited by pagans from pre-monarchical times, with part of the territory later carved out by the Assyrians after their conquest in 733.

Upon this land, distant and vulnerable, a new light is about to shine. Light will dispel darkness; brightness, gloom; joy, sorrow. The era of God's reign, seen by Isaiah as proximate, will spell the end of oppression and domination. Victory will come from Yahweh, just as it did in a former time at Midian (Jgs 7:15 - 25).

Responsorial Psalm   Ps 27

Discipleship gives light to the eye, direction to life, and the surety of God's protection. The psalmist yearns for the temple (v4) and that unique presence of Yahweh which lifts up the spirit and assures spiritual and temporal well-being (v13).

Second Reading

Two key areas of Paul's thought are the need for maintaining unity (Gr: *koinonia*) in the Christian community and the power that comes from God's saving word in and of itself. Both concerns figure prominently in the first letter to Corinth (1:24 - 2:10; c. 3; 11:17 - 32; cc. 12 - 14).

The Corinthian community was factionalized. Groups were championing their respective leaders—Apollos, Cephas (Peter), Paul. The chosen favorite may have been the one who had baptized them. The reference to Christ being divided up is ironic in intent. The point is that Christ is one, embracing all: Jew and Gentile (Eph 2:11 - 16), male and female, slave and free (Gal 3:27f). Division of any sort within the community is destructive of that unity, harmony, and peace which is the gift of the Spirit. It is alien to the body of Christ. The problem is exacerbated by the desire to exalt human leadership. It is particularly unfortunate when it centers around rhetorical and philosophical skills ("wisdom of the word," v17). The more that any human ingredient is exalted in the Christian experience, the less apparent is the all-central power of the cross. It is the cross alone, "a stumbling block to Jews" and "foolishness to Gentiles," which is the true power and wisdom of the Christian life (1:23f).

Third Reading

The gospel reading clearly sees the Isaian hope realized in Jesus. In his return to Capernaum in Galilee to begin his ministry, he finds himself, at least in broad geographical terms, in the territory spoken of in the prophetic oracle. The text from Isaiah (vv15f) is compressed and not a literal rendering. Matthew's sea road borders the Sea of Galilee, whereas it is the road to the Mediterranean in Isaiah. Galilee had a relatively large Gentile population by Jesus' time. Matthew's "Galilee of the Gentiles" carries a note of universalism in terms of Jesus' and later the church's mission.

Jesus calls his hearers to conversion (v17). In him the reign of God is present in its initial stage. The reign refers to the universal sovereignty of God's will in every phase of life—religious, political, and social—accompanied by the restoration of Eden's harmony and peace. The reign comes to life in the individual through a change of heart. Conversion (Gr: *metanoia*) is a deeply internal redirecting of one's life from sin-prone humanness to God and his expressed will. It is to be understood as an ongoing, lifelong process, not an instantaneous occurrence. It is conversion, at whatever moment in life, that sets one on the path of discipleship. It is in view of the imminent and final inbreaking of Yahweh in history that Jesus urges his hearers to convert. This sense of urgency colors much of the New Testament writing.

The call of the disciples in Matthew (v22) indicates the decisiveness connected with conversion and the totality of the disciples' adherence to Christ in leaving all behind, even to the point of severing family ties. The leave-taking is done for positive reasons, the desire of a greater good.

The Matthean Jesus restricts his ministry to the confines of Palestine. His present journey continues through Galilee in teaching, healing, and calling to repentance.

If Christianity today has lost some of its "cutting edge," it is due in large measure to our failure to grasp the significance of conversion. The word itself is usually used to express a single act or moment in life when one moves from non-belief to acceptance of the faith. The fact is, however, that it is a lifelong process. In putting one's hand to the plow, there can be no turning back. Discipleship is a call to growth. That is why "being in Christ" has such a dynamic sense in the New Testament. Our life in Christ needs regular assessment, periods of reflection and prayer, retreats, and days of recollection—not in the interests of measuring growth but simply to be certain that we have not settled on a plateau.

It is natural to focus on human leaders or role models, even in the church. It often bespeaks a deep sense of respect and appreciation. But to focus on people or positions can also lead to factions or cliques, with our attention directed away from the sole center of our life, Christ himself. Paul wanted none of it, least of all to have his own band of adherents. In life, it is difficult for us to lose a beloved pastor or to leave an inspiring teacher behind. But in the Christian life, the real measure of their success is the extent to which they have helped us to stand alone with our attention riveted on Christ, whose singular role can never be compromised.

Homiletic and Catechetical Helps

1. The biblical meaning of conversion.

2. Various expressions of discipleship: the single lay person, the married, the religious, the priest.

3. Discipleship in the life of every baptized person; the universal call to mission.

4. Charity expressed in unity: the home, the church, the community.

5. The scandal of a divided Christianity; ecumenism.

6. Position-taking, human heroes, and factions.

THIRD SUNDAY OF THE YEAR
Year B

Readings

> Jon 3:1 - 5, 10
> 1 Cor 7:29 - 31
> Mk 1:14 - 20

Theme: The Call of Discipleship–Universal and Urgent

The account of the call of the first disciples is found in all of the gospels. The Matthean version, strikingly similar to that of Mark (one of Matthew's principal sources) appears on the same Sunday in the A cycle. Today the church couples the account with part of the Jonah story, which contains one of the Bible's strongest universalist themes. Thus the liturgy contains a sense of urgency as well as the note of salvation extended to all people. Mark's gospel will be read during the Year B cycle. Paul's expectation of the parousia finds him appealing to the Corinthians to remain alert and single-minded.

First Reading

The book of Jonah makes good catechesis; it is an engaging story, easily understood, with an important lesson. Attempts to see it as historical have long been abandoned. It is best dated in the early post-exilic period. It combats Jewish exclusiveness (as depicted in Jonah's negative attitude) and shows Yahweh's determination to embrace all people, even the despised Ninevites, in his plan of salvation.

The historical Nineveh, destroyed in 612 B.C., had long lain in ruins before Jonah was penned. But its fame had become the stuff of legend; grandiose, powerful, ornate were terms used to describe it. It had also been a hated foe, the memory of which was deeply rooted in the Israelite psyche. As the story develops, it is to this powerful enemy of the past that Jonah is sent to preach repentance (vv1f).

The reluctant prophet encounters remarkable results. With his preaching mission scarcely begun, the people respond with penance, fasting, and mortification (v5). Yahweh withdraws his threat of destruction and extends forgiveness (v10).

The lesson is clear. No people, regardless how distant, hated, or godless, is to be seen as excluded from Yahweh's concern; the only prerequisite is a change of heart. The spontaneity of the Ninevites' response is, of course, literary, but its theological statement is important. The power of God's grace defies human and practical considerations. It can refashion the heart of a person, a city, a world. Against the background of the narrow and exclusive type of thinking that emerged in post-exilic Judaism (Ezr 9; Neh 13:1ff), the book of Jonah takes a striking prophetic stand. There are no limits to Yahweh's love.

Responsorial Psalm   *Ps 25*

In a prayer for guidance and direction, the psalmist amplifies the Sunday theme. God's call to discipleship and conversion is a gracious act which is really a way of life, a path to walk, light in the darkness. Catechetics is not a task; it is a grace which sets Christians on the path of life. Because Yahweh is upright, faithful, and true, he willingly extends himself in setting forth direction in the light of human weakness.

Second Reading

The reading from 1 Corinthians reflects the sense of urgency found in the first and third readings. Writing in the mid-50s of the first century, Paul expects the imminent return of Christ, the full establishment of God's reign, and the end of history. In the light of the end time, it is foolhardy to treat the transitory as if it were permanent. The passage does not posit an "other world" stance or a "do nothing" attitude. It is not meant to neglect the importance of human endeavor and initiative. Yet one's attention must be riveted on the "higher things" (Col 3:1ff), the true reality, and not become immersed in that which is passing away.

The fact that the parousia did not arrive as expected does not make it less important to Christian faith. At some point Christ's triumph over evil will be definitively evident; the present order of things will cease. Christ will hand the church back to the Father, he himself will be subordinated, and God will be "all in all" (1 Cor 15:23 - 28).

Third Reading

The striking parallel between the first and third reading lies in the immediacy of the response. (For common features of Matthew and Mark, the reader is referred to the commentary for the Third Sunday of Year A.)

In Mark there is an important addition to Jesus' call to conversion. "Believe in the good news" (Gr: *euangelion*). In Mark the call of Jesus emphasizes the end time, the establishment of God's reign, and the need for conversion. The reference to the "good news" is a technical expression in early Christianity which encompasses the death-resurrection-glorification of the life-giving Jesus. Mark incorporates this early church understanding of the meaning of Jesus' mission with the call to conversion. For the early Christian there could be no authentic conversion without this Christological dimension.

That Zebedee was in the boat with the "hired men" (v20) is

one of those vivid Marcan recollections which are characteristic of the second gospel.

The response of the disciples is unqualified, immediate and total. They will continue the mission of Jesus ("fishers of men," v17) in their discipleship role. Central to the liturgy's message is the note of universalism, underscoring the missionary nature of the church. The sharing of the gospel is woven into the texture of what makes the church what it is.

There are some people who want everything to be done yesterday. They may irritate us at times but their sense of commitment is quite clear. They stand in sharp contrast with those who seem never to get around to accomplishing even ordinary things. They procrastinate endlessly. Today's readings teach us that the importance of faith should move us to action. If belief is truly the priority that we claim it is, then it should elicit a certain sense of urgency. Our years may seem to be many, but they pass quickly. Discipleship cannot be relegated to the rank of a commodity. It demands a committed response, which should be accompanied by alacrity and enthusiasm. We cannot say that the Christ-life is something that one day we will address seriously.

The Jonah story is such a strong reminder of God's concern for all people. It highlights the importance of missionary work, not as an imposition of belief or proselytism but as the sharing of a precious gift. It also reminds us that we are gifted by people of other cultures who embrace the faith. They bring values and customs, as well as an outlook on life, which is an enrichment, something to be cherished not abandoned, or, worse still, destroyed. Conversion is a sharing and a mutual strengthening.

Homiletic and Catechetical Helps

1. The church as missionary.

2. The four marks of the church.

3. Reconciling ecumenism and evangelization.

4. Overcoming stereotypes of people of other cultures and color.

5. Detachment in a consumerist society.

6. Christian eschatology: the four last things.

7. Giving faith priority and urgency.

8. Preparing for our personal parousia.

THIRD SUNDAY OF THE YEAR
Year C

Readings

> Neh 8:2 - 4, 5 - 6, 8 - 10
> 1 Cor 12:12 - 30
> Lk 1: 1 - 4; 4:14 - 21

Theme: The Word of God: Call to Commitment

The gospel of Luke will be read on Sunday through most of Year C. For completeness, the gospel should be read with its companion volume, the Acts of the Apostles, both written after 70 A.D. Luke-Acts emphasizes God's saving activity in an historical context and highlights God's outreach to the poor and emarginated.

Today's readings stress the power and truthfulness of God's word. In the first reading, the priestly leader Ezra leads his people in an act of covenant recommitment to God's law. The people express their willingness to center their lives in the saving word. In the gospel reading, Jesus presents himself as the one to whom the Isaian prophecy points. Just as he accepts his designated role, he implicitly asks for his hearers' acceptance. As the chapter in Luke will later indicate, the response of the people did not match the submission of Ezra's hearers (Lk 4:28f).

The second reading today from the first letter to the Corinthians is Paul's call for unity in the undivided body of Christ, endowed with Spirit-given diversity.

The word of God is presented in today's readings as living and compelling. It is God's unfailing disclosure of his will. God has remained faithful; his people are asked to respond in similar terms.

First Reading

The passage is seen by commentators as misplaced in its actual setting in Nehemiah. It fits better the context of Ezra's ministry (after Ezr 8:36). The lay ruler Nehemiah and the priest Ezra were responsible for a major part of Jerusalem's reconstruction, social, physical and moral, after the exile in Babylon (fifth century B.C.).

In the presence of the convened assembly in Jerusalem, Ezra reads from the Torah (probably the final edition of the Pentateuch). At important moments in Israel's history, recommitment to the original covenant with Yahweh (Ex 19 - 24) was ritualized. It occurs at Shechem after the first occupation of Canaan (Jos 24), after the discovery of the "book of the covenant" in the temple during the reign of Josiah (2 Kgs 22 - 23), and again at this moment of restoration after the Jews' return to their homeland. The ritual is a solemn act of the community in which the recognition and formal acceptance of Yahweh's invitation to a covenant relationship is central.

Responsorial Psalm   Ps 19

The second half of Psalm 19, used this Sunday, exalts the Torah. Various substitutes for law are used (commands, decrees, precepts, ordinances) (vv8, 9, 11), all of them illustrating the "grace" of God's law. The psalm echoes the sentiments of the readings; the law itself is an expression of God's fidelity; its observance leads unquestionably to life, for the law, like Yahweh, is trustworthy.

Second Reading

Rivalry was one of the major problems besetting the church at Corinth. It centered around preferred leaders (1 Cor 3:3ff) and, as seen in today's reading, in preferred spiritual gifts. The gifts of the Spirit, intended to build up the church in unity, had become the source of a competitive and jealous spirit.

In dealing with the issue, Paul returns to the image of the body, frequent in his writings (1 Cor 15; Rom. 12:4 - 5; Eph. 1:22 - 23; Col 1:24; 3:15). The risen Christ now lives in the faithful and they with him constitute a new entity, a single body (v12). The Spirit binds and holds together indissolubly this total Christ. This same reality is spoken of in John's gospel as the vine and the branches (Jn 15).

Just as in the human body each member has a determined function which is not dispensable or interchangeable, so it is with Christ. All gifts in the church have their importance; one cannot be played off against another. The elimination of all ethnic and social barriers cannot be supplanted by divisive rivalries (v13; Gal 3:28).

In the human body, no part can dismiss another as unnecessary (vv15 - 18). Nor can one organ preempt another without destroying the balance and harmony of the whole. Organs which might be considered less honorable, or even unmentionable, e.g. the genitals, are covered and cared for in a way not proper to the more visible parts (vv22ff).

Paul then shifts his argument for unity from bonded unity in the one Christ to the mutual need the members have for one another (vv25f).

The one body of Christ—not to be understood as a spiritual or esoteric unity around a leader, but rather a realistic intimate oneness between the risen Christ and the baptized person—expresses itself in various ministries (gifts). Paul lists a number, giving primacy to the apostles, as the foundation of the church (Eph 2:20), the prophets, with inspired insight in preaching, and teachers, as instructors in the faith. The list, which is not exhaustive, underscores the necessity of all gifts for the upbuilding of the body (Eph 4:15f). They are all rooted in the all-embracing and fundamental gift of charity (1 Cor 13).

Third Reading

Today's gospel contains the literary prologue to the third gospel (vv1 - 4). Imitating the Greek writers of his time, Luke summarizes the content of his work and directs it to a distinct person, Theophilus (friend of God); the addressee is usually a patron, in this case perhaps a friend or a literary personification of Luke's intended audience. The prologue is important as an expression of the author's intent. *Narrative* (Gr: *diegesis*): the events of Jesus' ministry, as handed on by eyewitnesses (Acts 1:21f), but from a distinctly kerygmatic or faith perspective. (Lk 8:39; Acts 12:17). These are the events of Jesus' life refracted through the prism of the Easter faith experience and transmitted by ministers of the word (1:3). It is not history or biography which is central; it is a proclaimed catechesis rooted in history.

The transition is made to the beginning of Jesus' ministry in Galilee. The account of Jesus' self-presentation in the synagogue is replete with Lucan motifs. He is led by the Spirit, active from his conception (1:55) and a dominant force in his life and ministry (3:21 - 22; 4:1); it is the Spirit who anoints him for his mission (vv16ff). In another Lucan motif, Jesus is especially missioned to the poor and disenfranchised (vv18f; 6:20, 24; 12:16 - 21; 14:12 - 14; 16:19 - 26; 19:8). He is also a teacher (v15; 5:3, 17; 6:6; 13:10).

The setting of the narrative in the Capernaum synagogue links the two Testaments, or, for Luke the two stages of salvation history. The unrolled scroll would not produce the cited text of Isaiah in a continuous form; it is rather an Isaiah collage (61:1 - 2; 58:6). The message, though, is clear. The first and privileged recipients of the Messiah's mission are the socially and physically deprived, the economically poor, the oppressed, the maimed. Luke's gospel will bear this out in Jesus' personal dealings and his teaching. The year of favor (v19) is an oblique reference to the jubilee year when debts were canceled, property restored to owners, and fields left fallow.

The Isaian text is designedly kept broad in its applicability to people of any background, yet very concrete in its social categories.

Jesus claims that the messianic text is fulfilled in his person and mission (v21). His prophetic "anointing" was to identify him with the lowliest and most forgotten. Written in a post-Easter setting, the temporal reference to "today" is to be read in the light of Christ's death-resurrection (v21). A key idea throughout the narrative is the fidelity of Yahweh to his promises. All New Testament fulfillment carries this connotation of fidelity. It is the message of God's concern.

Unlike Ezra, Jesus will not receive a positive response from his own townspeople. They will react by attempting to stifle his message (vv28f).

There is something very impressive about the seriousness with which God's word is viewed in the Bible itself. In the Nehemiah reading, the post-exilic commitment gives its "Amen" to the book of the law. In the gospel, Jesus reads from the scriptures and then applies its teaching to himself. In a very real sense, we all stand under the judgment of the word. Each Sunday as the scripture is read, it is directed to me, and my responsibility is to examine my own conversion in the light of the word. For this reason, the liturgy of the word requires a dignified presentation, an audible and intelligible reading, and an atmosphere of reflection. The homily is but an arm of the scripture that day, anchored in the meaning of the text and applying it to the congregation's life. God is present to us in his word and in that sense the scriptures are sacramental. Faith comes from hearing. Thus in liturgy both reading and listening are a sacred responsibility.

For example, after hearing today's reading from 1 Corinthians, we ask ourselves if we see that variety of gifts in the Christian community as a blessing or a "threat." Are we jealous of the gifts of others or do we thank God for them? That reading tells us clearly that any form of elitism or separatism is alien to our life in Christ. We should really rejoice in the gifts and successes of others, especially when it means the enrichment of those served. In the light of God's word, then, we ask ourselves where we stand. Are my attitudes towards others' gifts and accomplishments positive? Begrudging? Self-serving? Then, in the light of the answers, personal decision is reached. This is the part of ongoing conversion to which all of us are called. We can't honestly say that we don't know what God wants of us. Every Sunday he tells us.

Homiletic and Catechetical Helps

1. The role of scripture in the church (Vatican II, *Dei Verbum*).

2. The relationship of scripture and tradition (Vatican II, *Dei Verbum*).

3. Private and public reading of scripture (liturgy of the word).

4. The gospels as faith narrative (first catechisms of the church).

5. The word as God's fidelity.

6. The Christian's Jewish patrimony.

7. Ministries in the church.

8. The role of the apostles.

9. The body of Christ.

10. The church and the poor.

11. Unity and diversity in the parish community.

FOURTH SUNDAY OF THE YEAR
Year A

Readings

> Zeph 2:3; 3:12 - 13
> 1 Cor 1:26 - 31
> Mt 5:1 - 12

Theme: Dependence on God

Two important biblical concepts come together in today's readings. These are the remnant of Israel and the anawim or the "poor of God." The prophet Zephaniah speaks of the sacred remnant of God's people and the humble hearts which they are to have. Matthew in the beatitudes moves in the same direction toward a new level of understanding in terms of what it means to be poor. Paul brings this together in the second reading in showing redemption as combining God's loving favor and the recognition of our own poverty.

First Reading

When Zephaniah spoke his prophetic oracles in the late seventh century B.C., Babylon stood as an imposing threat to much of the near eastern world, but especially to Judah. The major crimes of his country were pride and arrogance, and punishment was imminent. Yet the prophet remains convinced of Yahweh's fidelity to the covenant. This means that not all will be destroyed. A remnant will be preserved, the living assurance of Yahweh's faithfulness and saving power. But this will be a remnant characterized by lowliness of heart (the anawim) in sharp contrast to the boastful spirit of the vanquished population.

Originally the remnant was a term applied to survivors after a disaster or military defeat (2 Kgs 19:30; 25:11; 3:12). There was also a constant belief that, in the face of a major threat, some segment of Israel would be saved. This became designated as the remnant and to them the land would ultimately be restored (Is 6:13; 4:2 - 6; Jer 31:7 - 14).

Concurrent with the concept of salvation in the prophetic literature run the moral dispositions that are to accompany it (Hag 1:12). Conversion will take place when attention is directed to the Lord and not the threatening invaders (Is 10:20ff). But it is Zephaniah in the stirring passage read today who succinctly and forcefully summarizes the spirit of the remnant.

The prophets, each in his own time, faced and addressed various evils, e.g. the worship of the baals in fertility cults, the amassing of wealth at the cost of the poor, alliances with powerful nations. Zephaniah deals with a haughty and arrogant spirit in Judah which flaunted its power with a sense of total moral autonomy (1:11 - 13, 16, 18; 3:1 - 5).

With this in mind, Zephaniah sees the spirit of the remnant to be deeply imbued with a sense of lowliness and utter dependence on Yahweh. In the Lord alone is refuge to be found. Moral comportment is to be honest and upright, totally devoid of greed, deceit, and intolerance (vv12 - 13). This emphasis on the moral qualities of the remnant becomes stronger in post-exilic and New Testament literature.

The meaning of the "poor of God" has a similar history. The

anawim in the original Hebrew sense were the poorest of the poor or people "overwhelmed by want." It was a socio-economic category. Since these were the people who had the greatest need of God's benevolence (Ps 35:10; 109:31), they were to be the special concern of the Israelite people. Widows and orphans receive special notice. Having no one to provide for them, they are wholly dependent on the community (Deut 27:19; Sir 4:10).

In the course of time there is a gradual spiritualization of this concept. The ascetical dimensions of poverty came gradually to the fore. Poverty was not seen as a good in itself but valuable in enabling one to understand the meaning of total dependence on God. This is equated with authentic humility, said to be at the heart of God's expectations (Mic 3:8).

Zephaniah combines these deeper theological notions of the remnant and the poor of God. To seek humility is to seek true covenant fidelity (2:3). The remnant finds strength in the Lord alone, as they live an upright life and are blessed with a peaceful existence (3:13). They will be the narrow segment saved from imminent disaster.

Responsorial Psalm   Ps 146

The theme of the day is continued. The remnant of Israel is comprised of those who are the object of Yahweh's special concern: the captives, the blind, the crushed, strangers, widows, and orphans. In championing their cause, God's justice is established and his reign is assured.

Second Reading

The passage from 1 Corinthians fits well with today's major theme. Since salvation is the work of Yahweh and it looks to the lowly and humble, then any form of self-justification or meriting is excluded. In fact, it is through God's choice of the poorest that his salvific action becomes evident.

The Corinthians are to realize that they are not among the city's most intelligent, noble, or affluent (v26). In fact, they were favored by God because they were not (v27). All are sinners, moreover, and fall short of God's glory (Rom 3:23); it is God alone who is their righteousness (2 Cor 5:21). Nothing is their own; all comes from God (vv29f; Rom 10:3).

Since God has chosen them solely because of his love in spite of their unworthiness, there can be no boasting or self-adulation, as the Corinthians were want to do (v31). Their only wisdom is Christ himself. In him God has saved them (redemption), thus making them holy in removing them from sin (sanctification) and placing them before God with covenant uprightness (justice) (v30).

Third Reading

The gospel reading today initiates an ongoing series from the sermon on the mount (Mt 5 - 7). It begins with Matthew's presentation of the beatitudes, which builds on our earlier consideration of the poor of God. Matthew has nine beatitudes where Luke has four (Lk 6:20 - 23). They are not found as such in the other evangelists. Some of the beatitudes derive from a common source used by Matthew and Luke easily linked to Jesus himself in terms of the audience addressed. The rest are either composed by the evangelists themselves or derived from the early church. Some of them clearly reflect early church life (vv10 - 11).

The categories in Luke—the poor, the hungry, and the mourners—are mainly socio-economic in character, the people for whom the messiah was to have a special concern (Is 61:1-4). In Matthew, there is a spiritual adaptation given which deepens the meaning. The three above-mentioned categories, when addressed in Matthew, are all diverse expressions of the anawim. The poor, the mourners, and the meek are bereft of human consolation and support, looking to Yahweh for deliverance.

In Matthew, the poor have become the "poor in spirit" which places emphasis on the spiritual notion of humility and lowliness accompanying poverty (v3). The mourners grieve because they see evil as having the upper hand (v4); the meek experience long-suffering and patience (v5; Ps 37:11).

Luke's hungry have become Matthew's those who "hunger for justice," i.e. those who long for the full establishment of God's reign (v6). The merciful are those who forgive (Mt 6:12 -

14) and are marked by love of neighbor (v7; 5:44 - 47). "Purity of heart" stands close to spiritual transparency, total sincerity in covenant fidelity (v8). Peacemakers, like the merciful, are involved in re-establishing harmonious relations among individuals and communities (v9).

The final beatitudes (vv10f) reflect early church experience where persecution and hatred have been turned on Christ's followers. The distinct Matthean hand is more evident here than is any direct echo of Christ himself.

The people in all of these categories are declared "blessed," favored and extolled by God because the wrongs which attend them are to be corrected with the full arrival of God's reign. Each of the beatitudes' rewards for endurance is to be identified with the time of God's reign.

All of the beatitudes are addressed to the disadvantaged as they attempt to cope with the present world. They are assured a better lot. The first beatitude speaks explicitly of the anawim, but the underlying spirit of an authentic poverty is present in all the Matthean beatitudes. They are based on a confident trust that Yahweh will be their ultimate vindicator.

The readings today carry us from a primitive understanding of those to whom salvation was directed to a deeper perception of what happens to a disciple to whom God's favor is extended. They strongly emphasize the importance of humility and dependence, the avoidance of any spirit of self-sufficiency or arrogance, and the unwavering recognition of God's supremacy.

The reading from Zephaniah takes two important biblical ideas and joins them, that of the anawim and the remnant. The elect of God are to be characterized by a truly humble spirit. The remarkable thing about the Christian ethic is its simplicity; it sounds so easy. It avoids complexity at every turn. But only when it passes from theory to practice is the challenge brought to life. Few people today would place a higher priority on lowliness, humility or meekness. They don't match well with assertiveness, self-reliance, and ambition. Yet the fact is that if God's work is to be truly evident in this world of ours, then we have to get out of the way. The man or woman of God is the one whose transparency lets God appear, like a shaft of light through a window. And that means a spirit of openness and submission, a willingness to let God be good. It appears in every category of the beatitudes–the poor, the mourners, the clean of heart. For all of them, their only boast is in the Lord.

It is not a question of how much we accomplish for God. What matters is what he accomplishes in us. The three vows of religious life take their meaning from the posture of the anawim. They look to self-surrender. That means that we have to let go. In today's world, that is hard to do. But the fact that it is hard does not make it any less true.

Homiletic and Catechetical Helps

1. The poor as the beloved of God.

2. Gospel poverty and human deprivation: the difference.

3. The real meaning of gospel poverty.

4. The danger of riches.

5. Our practical dependence on God.

6. The beatitudes in our daily life.

7. The beatitudes and our competitive, "Horatio Alger" society.

8. Our responsibility for the poor, the unemployed, the homeless, the elderly, those who suffer racial discrimination.

9. Manifestations of pride in our life.

10. Becoming a peacemaker.

FOURTH SUNDAY OF THE YEAR
Year B

Readings

Deut 18:15 - 20
1 Cor 7:32 - 35
Mk 1:21 - 28

Theme: Prophecy

In today's language, prophecy has become almost completely identified with predicting the future. Although this was part of the biblical prophet's function, it was not the major one. The prophet is the mouthpiece of God (Grk: *prophemi*), more concerned about the present than anything. He articulates God's will for his people and usually stands outside the ordinary religious structures. Indeed, it is with the deficiencies of these structures that he often has to deal.

In today's liturgy, Jesus appears as a prophet among his people. The conviction with which he speaks in Yahweh's name is a clear indication of the uniqueness of his mission. Deuteronomy speaks of a prophet like Moses who will guide his people. Paul today speaks of the anxieties connected with various states of life and the necessity of adhering wholly to the Lord.

First Reading

This celebrated passage, which had its own history in Judeo-Christian life, points to a prophetic figure like Moses in words purportedly spoken by the prophet-deliverer himself. Deuteronomy was written centuries after Moses brought his people to the point of occupying the promised land. Its laws and teachings reflect the problems and life of Israel in pre-exilic and exilic times far removed from the era of Moses. The book, finally codified after the exile, finds in Moses a source of some of its law but above all the one who legtimates its authority.

Who is the prophet that is envisaged in this Deuteronomic passage? Seen in its literary context (c. 18) wherein false diviners and soothsayers are to be avoided, the reference is undoubtedly generic. The point is simple and direct. There will always be authentic prophets in Israel as need and circumstances demand (v15).

This is preferred by the people as a form of divine communication in contrast to the frightening aspects of a theophany (v16; Ex 19:16 - 19), the avoidance of which is elsewhere presented as the main reason for prophetic mediation (Deut 5:23 -

28). In its original form, the text makes no reference to a distinct prophet of a later era, messianic or otherwise. It simply assured the continued presence of the prophetic voice.

In the course of time, however, the prophet of Deuteronomy became an eschatological personality in the people's expectations. The messianic era envisioned a prophet. The rule of life of the Qumran community (Dead Sea Scrolls) speaks of three end time figures: the messiahs of Aaron (priestly) and Israel (Davidic), as well as a prophet (1QS 9). This hope will still be alive a century later in Christian times with the hoped-for return of Elijah (Mal 5; 3:23) attached to the figure of John the Baptist (Mk 9:13), and the repeated mention of the expected prophet which appears in the gospels (Jn 6:14; 7:40).

In the Acts of the Apostles, Jesus is identified with the prophet of Deuteronomy who, with his call to conversion, is to usher in the final era (Acts 3:22; 7:37).

In a period of Israel's life beset by fraudulent prophets and priestly leaders (Jer 23:9 - 30) the Deuteronomic passage ends with a note of caution and condemnation (v20).

Responsorial Psalm   Ps 95

The response to the prophetic word must be one of total acceptance. The psalm places this in relief in praying for a heart malleable and open to God's voice. The psalm reflects its original liturgical setting with the emphasis on chant, salutation, and bodily reverence (vv1, 2, 6), accompanied by attentiveness to God's word. With a play on words, the worshipers are exhorted not to repeat the moment of headstrong contestation (Meribah) and testing of Yahweh (Massah) which occurred during the desert sojourn (Ex 17:1 - 7).

Second Reading

Christians are called to be free of distracting anxieties, especially, for Paul, in view of the impending return of the Lord (v32; 7:29 - 31). Human concerns tend to obscure spiritual vision in every state of life. Even those who are single in God's interest tend to become preoccupied with features of their spiritual life. Daily concerns and marital responsibilities place a strain on those who are married. Elsewhere Paul speaks of his preference for the celibate life. Neither state of life is given preference here. The single state may well offer less stress-filled concerns, but it is quite possible that in Corinth it had spawned a form of elitist asceticism.

Paul shows no inclination of being dogmatic in his counsel nor does he indicate a plan of action for his audience (v35). Time is running out. What is paramount is a Christ-centered life. Paul gives the same advice to the married and unmarried and, interestingly enough, to women and men equally.

Third Reading

The gospel passage is taken from a Marcan account of a day in Jesus' ministry. It contains two important characteristics that will serve as a leitmotiv for the public ministry.

The first point centers around Jesus' teaching. He enters the Capernaum synagogue. Like any skilled or learned male Jew of his time, Jesus is afforded the opportunity to teach. The reaction of his audience is to be noted. They are not impressed with his learning but with the authority with which he speaks. His words carry their own weight. Unlike the scribes who gave insight and answers based on biblical and other traditional precedents, Jesus speaks clearly and directly, in what can best be described as a prophetic manner. His authority rests solely on God's claim on his life; he makes appeal to no other sources; he unhesitatingly challenges his hearers (Lk 4:16 - 30). Modern commentators see this authoritative stance of Jesus as an indication of his emerging self-understanding as related to his messianic role. So strong is his teaching that his hearers are left spellbound (v22).

The second significant feature of the account is the miracle account of exorcism. It should be noted that Jesus is presented as combining teaching and miracles. They are mutually supportive (vv27f). The account follows the traditional miracle story form, drawn initially from oral tradition. There is a presentation and brief description of the illness, the action of Jesus, and a statement on the completeness of the cure (vv23 - 27).

Inserted within the miracle story is the dialogue between Jesus and the evil spirit. The case is one of diabolical possession. The story serves as more than an account of Jesus' mercy and compassion. It is an eschatological sign. The end time was to be marked by Yahweh's definitive conquest and defeat of evil. This is seen concretely in the gospels when Jesus confronts evil wherever it is lodged—in sickness, possession, natural upheaval, or death. As Jesus repeatedly cures the afflicted, evil in its various form is vanquished.

In the dialogue, the evil spirit notes the broad chasm that exists between itself and Christ (v24, "What to us and to you?" i.e. "What do we have in common?"). The spirit further reacts by identifying Jesus' singular relationship to God (Holy One of God), which, in Mark especially, is to remain concealed and unknown. The spirit is silenced and expelled (vv25f); the messianic era is advanced as the victory of Jesus over evil announces the reign of God.

The New Testament story builds on the Deuteronomic teaching. In the narrative, Jesus is clearly the prophet; in both his teaching and action, he is the living oracle of God. "In times past, God spoke to our ancestors through the prophets; in these last days, he spoke to us through a Son" (Heb 1:1).

We don't often think of Christ as a prophet. Prophets today are very disconcerting; they challenge the status quo. Not all those who present themselves as prophets are necessarily such. The scriptural prophets are divinely authenticated; modern prophets are not. But prophets raise important questions. They are also counter-cultural. They do not go along with the tide. Many people do not like the prophetic voice. Surely they go against the tide, but on what issues? They oppose destruction, killing the innocent, death, unemployment, poverty and squalor. Their answers may seem simplistic. But Jesus was very simple. It is very important to listen to their voices. The prophetic, unpopular voices come out of a long tradition and we do ourselves no favor to ignore them.

Paul speaks today of anxieties. He does speak to single people. And that is welcome. A large segment of our Christian people are single—unmarried, divorced, widowed—but seldom are they addressed from the pulpit. Single people constitute a large portion of our population. Why do we always speak of families and parents and so seldom of the needs of people who live alone? How often do we preach about the needs of single people?

Homiletic and Catechetical Helps

1. Prophecy in scripture, church, and world.

2. Modern day prophets.

3. Jesus as teacher and healer.

4. Our understanding of the end time.

5. Our understanding of the devil and his works.

6. God-centeredness in the married life.

7. God-centeredness in the single life.

FOURTH SUNDAY OF THE YEAR
Year C

Readings

> Jer 1:4 - 5, 17 - 19
> 1 Cor 12:31 - 13: 13
> Lk 4:21 - 30

Theme: God's Messengers: Discouraged But Confident

The prophet's call inevitably contains difficult, even frightening ramifications. Some of the psychological aspects of the divine call are given in Jeremiah's account, which is read today. The prophet was reluctant to accept the call (Jer 1:6), largely due to the opposition which he knew he must face. Yet the prophetic psychology knows of no way to escape the call to serve.

Jesus' mission was similar to that of Jeremiah. Today's account of the initial negative reaction from his own townspeople is but a prelude to continued antagonism and opposition from his contemporaries that will ultimately culminate in his death. Jesus' repeated attempts to bring hope to his own people were smashed on the rocks of deafness and hostility.

The picture presented is not a bright one. But history has repeated it over and over again. The thirteenth chapter of 1 Corinthians, heard again today, has unfortunately never become a lived reality in many human hearts.

First Reading

Jeremiah's call to be the Lord's prophet in the final decades before Jerusalem's fall is presented as preceding his birth (v5). In fact, it pre-dated his conception. Yahweh models the child (Heb: *yasar*), as does the potter. The child is also set aside (Heb: *qadash*) for the Lord (also translated as "dedicated") and given a mission which is universal, and not destined solely to Israel (v5). This note of universalism is undoubtedly a later reflection on the whole of the prophet's ministry.

But the task is not to be an easy one. The girding of the loins points to a posture of readiness to communicate Yahweh's message (v17; Job 38:3; 40:7). The strongly negative reaction he will eventually evoke is supportable because of the exceptional inner strength he is to receive. The description is of a "fortified city, iron pillar, brass wall" (v18). His opponents are not limited to the masses but include royal and religious officials as well. The prophet is promised ultimate vindication, but it is not difficult to understand his initial reluctance (v6).

The passage is an accurate and later reflection on the prophets's career. It bears a number of distinctive features. Among the prophets, only Jeremiah speaks of a pre-natal destiny. He alone articulates the internal struggle in accepting the task and the inevitable personal disintegration that would have occurred without Yahweh's sustaining hand. Jeremiah will give fuller expression to those sentiments in his confessions (c. 12; 15:10 - 21; 20:7 - 18).

Responsorial Psalm   Ps 71

The words of the psalm could well be those of Jeremiah, Jesus, or any prophet. Its category is that of an individual lament. It is voiced in the face of serious opposition (vv4, 10 - 11), wherein confidence in Yahweh is the only bulwark of support. It is the prophet who proclaims God's justice (v15); there is a Jeremiah-shared reference to a pre-natal calling (v6). Discouragement and confidence are the warp and woof of a prophet's life.

Second Reading

The thirteenth chapter of 1 Corinthians is probably Paul's best known and best loved chapter. It is his ode to charity. It has a literary and lyric quality all its own. The chapter is read today in its entirety.

The section comes in the center of Paul's discussion of the spiritual gifts (cc. 12 - 14). Some commentators argue that it is an independent Pauline composition inserted here because of its bearing on the discussion; others feel that it is well knit, connected with other portions of the letter, and therefore an integral part of the epistle. The latter position seems preferable, but the discussion is of mostly academic interest.

There are three major sections of the chapter, all centering on love as the greatest of the gifts The first major section (vv1 - 3) compares love with the other gifts, elsewhere discussed in the epistle, and comes down strongly on the superiority of love. A gradual gradation is present, proceeding upward and starting with the lesser gifts (tongues and prophecy) through the more insightful (understanding of mysteries, faith) to the special gifts of benevolence or self-sacrifice. All are valueless unless informed by love.

In the second section (vv4 - 7), Paul describes aspects of love's workings in the form of personification. As the positive side is presented there are numerous oblique references to the negative situation in the Corinthian church: the over-bearing and impatient (8:1 - 13), the jealous and competitive (1:10 - 17), the inconsiderate and rude (11:17 - 22), those flouting wrong doing (5:1 - 6). Charity operates in just the opposite fashion; it touches one's neighbor with consideration and gentleness.

The final section (vv8 - 13) looks to the permanent and lasting quality of love as opposed to the transient character of other gifts. Faith, hope, and love remain permanent, while other gifts of seeming importance in the "now" will vanish in the "then" of full maturity (vv9 - 10). There will be no need of prophecy or faulty knowledge when God is known directly. Fuller knowledge, indescribable in itself, will be akin to that of Moses (Ex 33:11; Num 12:8) and will be concurrent with God's singular knowledge of us (v12; 1 Cor 8:3; Gal 4:9). The three theological virtues surpass all others and are inseparable in the present. But they too are prioritized; faith and hope fade in ultimate union with God. Love will perdure even then.

Third Reading

The gospel reading is of a piece with last Sunday's reading (Lk 4:14 - 21). In preaching or teaching, some reference should be made to Jesus' antecedent discourse.

At Christ's claim that the Isaian passage is fulfilled in the eschatological "today," he draws a bewildered and seemingly less than positive response (v21). The best understanding of the difficult v22 is that the favorable comment (22a) is somewhat altered by the fact that he is a local young man (v22b) uttering "words of charity" (Gr: *logoi tes charitos*). The expression may be identified with the salvific word of God (Acts 14:3) that builds up and gives inheritance to the saints (Acts 20:32). Jesus is, then, speaking as a prophet and this is disconcerting to his hearers.

Christ immediately challenges his hearers and builds on their observation that he is of local origin. As he illustrates from the biblical past, such is sufficient ground for non-acceptance of a prophet (v24). The reference to the Capernaum ministry is interesting (v23). Luke is evidently aware of the earlier work of Jesus (Mk 1 - 2) but relocates it in the interests of giving initial prominence to the Nazareth discourse. Jesus alludes implicitly to the people's idle curiosity in the "wonder worker" (v23).

The biblical precedents for non-acceptance are drawn from the Elijah (1 Kgs 17) and Elisha (2 Kgs 5) narratives, in which stories the persons singled out to be the recipients of God's favor are non-Israelites. This notion of universalism and non-exclusion carries forward and applies the prophetic oracle with which Jesus opened his Nazareth discourse (Is 61:1 - 2; Lk 4:18f).

The anger of the people builds on their earlier mixed reaction (v22). It is caused by Christ's prophetic stance in challenging his townspeople, as well as indicating that God's favor is now extended to all people. Their attempts to thwart God's plan by blocking Jesus' "way" (c. 4) are futile as Jesus' escape previews his later victory over death.

This entire narrative is replete with Lucan themes—universalism, the poor of God, the "word of grace," the prophetic stance, the reaction of the listeners, the Easter allusion. It is best read in the light of the whole ministry of Jesus and its outcome. This account of Jesus' beginning is refracted through the prism of a later Easter faith.

Today we are reminded that prophecy produces various reactions, many of them painful. To speak the truth in love is often a difficult task. Jeremiah did it to the point of being exasperated with God. "You have seduced me" (Jer 20:7). Jesus, on an unwavering course, met a continuous wave of opposition even though his word and mission centered on love. He was eventually brought to death.

The truth hurts. But the truth given and received with love and caring, as Paul teaches, is the bedrock foundation of the Christian community.

Homiletic and Catechetical Helps

1. Reaction of today's society to God's word: anger or indifference?

2. The challenge of the word: racism, sexism, minorities.

3. Today's prophets: honored or rejected?

4. The three theological virtues.

5. Charity as the prime virtue.

6. Love as the form of all the virtues.

7. Absence of love—the heart of sin.

FIFTH SUNDAY OF THE YEAR
Year A

Readings

> Is 58:7 - 10
> 1 Cor 2:1 - 5
> Mt 5:13 - 16

Theme: The Christian Life: Light and Salt

Light is the thought that links today's liturgy of the word. Its meaning is developed in the first and third readings. Paul teaches that the light of Christ has its own power when preached and does not depend on human wisdom.

First Reading

The reading is taken from Third Isaiah, the third major section of the book of Isaiah. The author writes after the exile and the people's resettlement in their country. Political and military problems are not his major concern. It is the ever increasing moral malaise and covenant infidelity that pose the greatest threat.

The passage is taken from a chapter dealing with fasting. Empty ritual has replaced the true spirit of religion emphasized so strongly by earlier prophets (Mic 6:8; Hos 6:6). Fasting without an accompanying spirit of outreach to the needy has little meaning. This concern is exemplified in the sharing of food, home, and clothing (v7). When this is done, a new era of light will result; light has both a messianic and a universal significance (Is 8:23 - 9:10; 51:4). It will also be a time of healing with past sinfulness forgotten (Ez 16:59 - 62; Hos 14:2 - 5).

The image of the desert journey again emerges (v8). Like the original ark, Yahweh's covenant fidelity takes the lead, while his glory, present to ancient Israel in the cloud and the pillar of fire, provides protection from behind.

An important ethical note is struck in the passage. Covenant justice includes both the avoidance of proscribed sinful acts (v9), but, even more importantly, a spirit of outreach to the anawim, the hungry and suffering, the favored of Yahweh. This recognition of moral uprightness as including more than legal observance and embracing the positive pursuit of good will reappear in Jesus' ethic, as seen especially in the sermon on the mount (Mt 5 - 7). This active pursuit of justice is integral to Judeo-Christian morality.

Responsorial Psalm   Ps 112

The theme of light as apparent in the just person's life is continued in the psalm. Such a life is characterized by correctness in human dealings (v5), as well as an active outreach to others (vv5, 9), the two aspects of morality discussed above. Trust in the Lord is so total that no human evil is seen as a threat.

Second Reading

Early in his first letter to Corinth, Paul deals with the spiritual elitism present in the church which he had founded. There was an attitude of spiritual elitism present within the community. This was connected with championing early leaders who were adept at rhetorical "wisdom." To call it Christian gnosticism is overstatement, but it bore some of the gnostics' features. Paul develops his corrective teaching regarding this problem which he has already touched on briefly earlier (1:17).

. The apostle came to the Corinthians initially with none of the philosophical or practical skills often identified with human "wisdom" (v1). The verse admits two possible readings. Some manuscripts read God's "testimony"; others, God's "mystery." The latter expression, *mysterion Theou,* refers to the secret of God's salvific plan, withheld throughout the ages until revealed in these final days (1 Cor 2:7 - 10), i.e. the mystery of universal redemption in the death and resurrection of Jesus. It is this mystery alone which Paul has presented at Corinth, with all of his accompanying inadequacies (vv2f). Paul speaks unhesitatingly of his weaknesses (2 Cor 10 - 13); his fear and trembling was that of a human instrument in God's hand bearing a message of such importance and transcendence.

Let the results speak for themselves. Without impressive credentials and forceful rhetoric, proclaiming a crucified Savior (a stumbling block to Jews and foolishness to Gentiles—1:23), there is only the power of God's spirit to explain the results. It is this spirit which is at the heart of their faith and is the strongest proof of his preaching's efficacy. Paradoxically, it is human inadequacy that proves to be a blessing.

Third Reading

The theme of light is continued. The salt and light images are both applied here to Jesus' hearers. Both similes appear in the other synoptic gospels (Mk 9:50; 4:21ff; Lk 8:16; 11:33; 14:34 - 35). Both Matthew and Luke have drawn on Mark but only Matthew has personalized the images in making them explicitly applicable to Jesus' audience.

Salt acts as a preservative and savors food. Light illumines and gives meaning to the surrounding reality. In their lives, Christians are to bring a new vision to a darkened world and are also called to give meaning and enrichment to society. When salt can no longer fulfill its task, it is discarded; the imagery used here is eschatological (v13).

Like salt, the light image is personalized in Matthew. In the scriptures, light is applied to Yahweh and his truth, the virtuous actions of his people (Is 58:7 - 12), to Jesus (Lk 1:79; Mt 4:16) and to Christians (Phil 2:15; Eph 5:8). Just as darkness is equated with sin and the absence of God's presence, so light is God's manifestation in the daily life and work of the faithful. Christ becomes visible in his followers. His spirit is perpetuated; his teaching, upheld; his example, followed.

The sense which Matthew gives to light is different from that of its Marcan source, where it refers to Jesus' teaching and its eventual full manifestation (Mk 4:16 - 25). Matthew clearly applies it to Jesus' followers; the truth in them cannot be concealed or obscured any more than the light from the single oil lamp in the simple one room Palestinian home.

The danger of pride and vanity is envisioned subtly in the

simile. While the Christian life is to be one of clear witness, praise and glory are to be given exclusively to God (v16).

We are often inclined to equate our faith with our knowledge of it, to make study and eloquence a high priority in the Christian life. We can never question our need for an intelligent and skilled deepening of our faith understanding. But in today's liturgy we are reminded that it is not proficiency which saves. Salvation is the work of God whose action within us is to become transparent in our daily life. It is the proclaimed word, alive within us, that makes us "the light of the world" and "the salt of the earth."

Homiletic and Catechetical Helps

1. Christian morality; the decalogue and the sermon on the mount.

2. Penitential rite: "What I have done and what I have failed to do."

3. Social justice as integral to evangelization.

4. Helping the emarginated: individually and structurally.

5. Salt and light–applying the biblical images today.

6. Difference between knowing and living the faith.

7. Wisdom as an obstacle in Paul.

8. Examples of God's power in the powerless.

FIFTH SUNDAY OF THE YEAR
Year B

Readings

Job 7:1 - 4, 6 - 7
1 Cor 9:16 - 19, 22 - 23
Mk 1:29 - 39

Theme: Christian Hope

Chistianity is not simply religion for another world. It is not an "opium of the people" that bases everything on life beyond the grave. Job saw no hope beyond this life and wrestled with present inequities. Christians have a hope that goes beyond; however, just as Jesus responded to illness and discouragement by his healing spirit, we are all called to respond to the needs of people in our world today. Paul speaks of his need to preach the gospel, even to the point of identifying closely with his hearers.

First Reading

Job's spirit was deeply disheartened because he could not understand Yahweh's design. The prologue (1:1 - 2:13) and epilogue (42:7 - 17) to the book tell the original Job story. It is the case of the innocent just man, plagued by unexplained misfortune as a test from God, who at the end of his trials has his fortune restored. The main part of the book (cc. 3 - 42), however, deals with the wrenching problem of the suffering just person and with the various explanations, ultimately unsatisfactory, that Hebrew insight offered as a solution.

In the original story, Yahweh agrees to allow Satan (the "tempter," not yet the devil) to test the faithful Job. Job, unaware of this agreement, soon loses his children and his property, and is subjected to a painful skin disorder. All of this leaves him puzzled, convinced, as he is, of his just life before God. A series of friends visit Job in his grief and become the mouthpiece for Hebrew wisdom on the meaning of suffering. Job rejects all of their explanations as being inapplicable to his situation.

The passage from today's liturgy is from Job's response to his first visitor, Eliphaz. The latter defends the traditional position on retribution. Much like a boomerang, he argues, "evil actions beget suffering and woe." "As I see it, those who plow for mischief and sow trouble bear the same" (4:8). Job protests his innocence to his friend and is stung by Yahweh's silence in the face of this inexplicable duress (c. 6).

There is no sign of optimism in Job's reply to Eliphaz. He

sees human life as little more than futility, like the lot of those engaged in the most despicable jobs: military service (drudgery), hired hands, and slaves (v1). His nights are sleepless, with only the emergence of a dawn of weariness to engage his attention.

When his antagonist assured a bright future if Job would but settle his accounts with Yahweh (5:8 - 27), the sufferer had no reply. His situation is totally enigmatic. The brevity of life is rendered even more tortuous by the futility of its end (v6). Job gives no indication of any afterlife hope wherein present misfortune might be seen in a more understandable light. His life is passing rapidly, filled with misery, and it will end in Sheol, among the shadows of the forgotten dead. He can only question Yahweh: "Why do you not pardon my offense or take away my guilt? For soon I shall lie down in the dust; and should you seek me I shall be gone" (7:21).

Responsorial Psalm   Ps 147

This post-exilic hymn, with its own historical references (v2), lays strong emphasis on the Lord's concern for the downtrodden and disadvantaged (vv3, 6). It is the same Lord who brought his people back from exile, restored their homeland, and presides over the heavenly constellations. Therefore, discouragement can never be such as to conclude that Yahweh cannot reverse the lot of the broken-hearted. The invitation to recognize God's concern (v1) ties together the theme of the day: the need for confidence in the midst of trial.

Second Reading

In the ninth chapter of 1 Corinthians, Paul speaks of his rights as an apostle and the reasons why he has foregone them. It would have been possible for him to marry, to enjoy many things in life (v5), to be sponsored by the community instead of seeking independent income (v6). Paul has personally bypassed his personal interests and well-being because of his vocation to preach. That alone is the priority in his life.

Preaching cannot become a personal boast because he was

not free to accept it or not. He felt compelled (Acts 26:14 - 18). There is simply no choice. If he does it willingly, then his reward is the joy of his work. If unwillingly, it is still a commission he has received and must fulfill (vv16f; 1 Cor 4:1; Gal 2:7).

Paul wryly states that his only remuneration is offering free service and is thus not burdened with any of the by-products connected with payment for service. Paul's allusion to "full use" of his right (v18) may be a nuanced reference to the assistance he received from elsewhere while serving in Corinth (2 Cor 11:9).

In the concluding section of the chapter, Paul presents the paradox of what his freedom has brought him. He is now a slave to all (v14): to the Jew (v20), the Gentile (v21) and the weak (v22). Elsewhere Paul indicates that if, for example, his freedom in the matter of food and drink would cause the weak in conscience to be scandalized or edged toward indifference, because they lacked knowledge of his motives, then he would forego his freedom (1 Cor 8:8 - 13). So in any instance he will not use his liberty at the cost of the weak. Rather, his self-restraint will make him one with the weak in the avoidance of scandal, even though his personal freedom remains intact (1 Cor 10:23 - 33).

Paul's heart, like the gospel he proclaims, is open to all people without exception. If reaching others requires adaptation on his part, even with restricted freedom, he will gladly do so in the interests of the gospel which he preaches.

Third Reading

Jesus' mission begins to expand geographically early in his career; centered in Capernaum originally (1:14 - 39), it will soon extend to all of Galilee (1:39). Whereas Luke begins Jesus' ministry with a teaching episode (4:16 - 30), Mark places emphasis on his healings. This is restricted to illnesses and diabolical possessions (v34) as illustrated in the two miracle stories (vv21 - 31).

The story of Peter's mother-in-law (1 Cor 9:5) is a typical miracle story (vv29ff), with its brief description of the sickness, the action of Jesus, and indication of the totality of the cure ("the fever left her ... she waited on them"—v31). In the mention of Christ "lifting her up" in order for her "to serve," there may be a baptismal catechesis.

In the account of the exorcisms, Jesus silences the demons (v34). This "messianic secret" is an important feature of Mark's gospel. Jesus is frequently recognized by preternatural beings but is only gradually revealed to his followers. Therefore, he consciously avoids public recognition. This developing, slow recognition plays an important part in Mark's theological and literary presentation of his gospel.

It is worth noting the extent to which Jesus is pressed upon, even jostled by the crowd in Mark (v33; 2:2; 3:7 - 9). This almost unnoticeable dimension of Jesus' ministry stresses the extent to which his own comfort and even safety took second place to his concern for the people. Such physical and mental stress form part of his total offering to the Father.

Early on the day after his first full day of ministry (v35), Jesus withdraws to a place of solitude for prayer. This notion of Jesus being alone with the Father is highlighted in the synoptics, and, in Luke, enters Jesus' life before every major event. Jesus is unwilling to return to the place of yesterday's success but desires to move on to territories where the reign of God had not yet been announced (v38). He avoids any form of adulation to be about the Father's work.

Job's soulful plaint asked for relief from his suffering and the vindication of his belief in God's justice. In the course of the book, Yahweh eventually answers Job but leaves the solution to the problem of suffering in the hidden depths of God's knowledge. In Jesus the problem remains, but God is in no way divorced from it. As he moves through the hectic crowd, Jesus brings consolation and hope. Paul goes on to say, years later, that he will suffer anything personally as long as he can bring hope to believer or unbeliever, the strong or the weak.

Homiletic and Catechetical Helps

1. The problem of suffering: why do the good suffer?

1b. A "patient" Job or a "persevering" Job?

2. Biblical development of afterlife belief.

3. Jesus at prayer: its meaning for us.

4. The meaning of Christian hope.

5. Healing: the corporal works of mercy.

6. The mission of Jesus and evangelization today.

FIFTH SUNDAY OF THE YEAR
Year C

Readings:

> Is 6:1 - 2, 3 - 8
> 1 Cor 15:1 - 11
> Lk 5:1 - 11

Theme: God's Power in Human Weakness

The first and third readings today are accounts of a divine call. Heavily accented by the note of human unworthiness, the account of the mission appears clearly as the work of God and not human inventiveness. The second reading contains one of the earliest recorded accounts of the church's kerygmatic proclamation, the good news of salvation.

First Reading

The year of Isaiah's call was 742 B.C., the year of King Uzziah's death. The call is situated in a liturgical setting with the description of the theophany going between the earthly and heavenly sanctuaries. It may well have been that Isaiah's presence at a temple liturgy was the occasion of his call. The imagery, therefore, even when speaking of heavenly realities, relies heavily on the temple setting.

The dominant note is one of Yahweh's transcendence. He is depicted as enthroned with a lengthy royal train (v1). Seraphim (the burning ones) are composite creatures, human and celestial, with six wings, who attend the throne (v2). Their cry extols the holiness of God. Holy (Heb: *qadosh*): The Hebrew word Qadosh stresses otherness and transcendence, with sinlessness necessarily attached to these attributes. This otherness becomes visible in God's glory, a reference to his earthly sovereignty which here extends to all people.

The cultic features of the theophany (praise of Yahweh, smoke, the enthronement) set the prophet's experience in a transcendent atmosphere. His first reaction is one of imminent death because of his unveiled vision of God, something not accessible to humans (v5; Ex 33:20; Jgs 13:22).

The overpowering sense of God's otherness in the theophany only makes the prophet more aware of his human imperfection. Sinfulness is identified with his lips (v5) since his is to be a preaching ministry. His mouth, symbolizing his whole person, is purified, thus enabling him to exercise his prophetic role (v7).

Yahweh's desire to send an emissary "for us" (v8) undoubtedly refers to members of his heavenly council. Once purification takes place, Isaiah's response is one of positive, even enthusiastic acceptance (v8), contrasting sharply with that of the reluctant Jeremiah (Jer 1:6).

Of special note in the narrative is the chasm between God's holiness and human sinfulness. It is Yahweh who bridges this gap and outfits the prophet with the moral integrity needed for his ministry.

Responsorial Psalm   Ps 138

In this hymn of thanks, the psalmist's confidence in Yahweh emerges as a dominant note. Reference is made to the benefit received (v3) but its nature is unrevealed. It is Yahweh's kindness and truth, both terms related to his covenant fidelity, that underlie his gracious response. God's goodness to the psalmist reflects on the creator himself since his existence (name) and covenant engagement (promise) are verified by his beneficent action (v2). Universalism appears in the chorus of voices (vv4 - 5).

The psalm is a response to God's forgiveness, so dominant in today's readings. The sinfulness that separates people from God is overcome by a humble and open spirit (vv3, 7), evidenced in the lives of Isaiah and Peter.

Second Reading

As he begins the section of his epistle dealing with resurrection, Paul cites the kerygma of the earliest stages of the church. It is the gospel of God which he himself had received from others (v3). The importance of this statement of belief lies in its antiquity and its quintessential presentation of the apostolic preaching.

This gospel which Paul proclaims has been both received and owned ("to stand firm") by the Corinthians. It is this accepted keryma—not their own works—which is saving them, but it must be retained in its purity and integrity (vv1f).

The heart of the church's earliest proclamation centered on the death and resurrection of Jesus in the interest of human salvation (vv3 - 5). His death is sealed and assured by his burial (v4), and his resurrection, by eyewitnesses (vv5 - 8). That Christ died "according to the scriptures" (v3) is problematic. A direct allusion may well be to Isaiah 53:5 (cf Acts 8:26 - 35), with the resurrection then pointing to Isaiah 53:11 - 14. Account has to be taken as well of late Judaism's understanding of scriptural data and its adaptability for apologetic purposes in the early church.

The listing of Christ's post-Easter apparitions mentions first Peter; then the twelve; a large number of believers; James, "the Lord's brother" and not one of the twelve (Gal 1:19); other apostles; then Paul himself. A distinction is made between the twelve (v5) and other apostles (v7). For Paul, apostleship hinged on commission from the risen Christ (vv8 - 11; 1 Cor 9:1). The twelve had the added component of having been with Jesus during his public ministry (Acts 1:21f). Thus, while the twelve were all apostles, not all the apostles were among the twelve, as in the case of Paul himself.

The apostle speaks of himself as an abortion (v8), one whose antipathy for the church and whose unusual calling (Acts 9:1 - 9) put him well beyond the pale of normal spiritual gestation (vv9 - 10). But God's favor (as always in Paul) is the only explanation for what he has become, and to God alone is credit due. He is only grateful that God's grace in him has not been dulled by any lack of response (vv8 - 9).

Third Reading

Luke's account of the call of the first disciples differs considerably from its Marcan prototype, on which he draws (Mk 1:16 - 20). The additional source is a post-resurrection appearance of Jesus which appears also in John's gospel (Jn 21:1 - 11). It is a good example of Luke's literary artistry. The two narratives are expertly blended to make a broader theological statement.

Jesus' personal ministry of the word is initially placed in relief (v1). A post-Easter understanding of "the word," much fuller than Jesus' early proclamation of the reign, is intended by Luke. The episode draws on Mark 1:16 - 20.

In Luke, Simon becomes the story's centerpiece; the other disciples, are almost an afterthought. Luke will continue to emphasize Peter's leadership (Lk 23:3ff; 24:34). The account of the disciples' lack of success during the night and the reversal of their fortune at Jesus' direction is found in none of the other vocation narratives (vv4 - 7). Its counterpart is found in the tradition underlying John 21:1 - 11. Although this latter account is fuller and contains other data, the Lucan story is very evidently dependent upon it (cf. vv6, 8, 11). Luke's reference to the future ministry of the disciples as "fishers of men" is paralleled in John by the commission of Peter as shepherd (Jn 21:15 - 19).

Why does Luke combine the two traditions of the call and the catch of fish? His post-Easter telescoping allows him to bring together both the call and the promise of its eventual fruitfulness. From a psychological point of view, the experience of the catch explains the willingness of the three to follow Jesus immediately. In addition, Luke-Acts highlights Peter's leadership roll and is interested in doing so at an early point.

If the account of the miraculous catch had originally a post-resurrection setting, Peter's sinfulness (v8) has by that time become painfully apparent (Lk 22:54 - 62). Like Isaiah, Peter openly recognizes his sinful nature and the breach that distances him from Jesus.

Jesus overcomes this obstacle in his response "Fear not," followed by the mandate to fulfill the apostolic ministry in bringing people to God's reign (v10). The fishing imagery lends itself ideally to the mission. The objective is "to bait" people with God's word and bring them to God's sovereign reign, or, in post-Easter times, to the church. Like the life of a fisherman, the mission will be arduous and painful but made effective by the Lord himself.

The disciples abandon their livelihood and way of life to follow Jesus.

There is considerable commonality in today's liturgy of the word. In the case of Isaiah, Peter, and Paul, the evidence of human inadequacy and sinfulness is clear. This is our human lot and we should no more deny it than flaunt it. But it can be the fertile soil of God's power. God makes great out of nothing. Or "he who is mighty has done great things for me" (Lk 1:49). It is the repeated tale of New Testament personalities and much of Christian history. One thinks of founders and foundresses of religious institutes, missionaries, sainted laity. Rather than be discouraged about our "messed up lives," we would do well to turn them over to the Lord, open our hearts, and ask the Lord to lead.

Homiletic and Catechetical Helps

1. Fishing today—priests, religious, laity.

2. Meaning of "the word": for Jesus and for the early church.

3. Sin as an occasion of grace.

4. The kerygma: the essential message.

5. Power of God–where is it felt in our lives?

6. Explaining kerygma and didache.

7. Defining gospel.

8. Defining an apostle.

SIXTH SUNDAY OF THE YEAR
Year A

Readings

> Sir 15:15 - 20
> 1 Cor 2:6 - 10
> Mt 5:17 - 27

Theme: The Law of Christ

"How I love your law, Lord. It is my meditation all the day. Your command has made me wiser than my enemies for it is ever with me" (Ps 119:97 - 98).

In Hebrew teaching, love and respect for the law is unmatched. It was God's greatest gift to his people. To observe it was to find life and happiness and to be assured blessings from the Lord. The Torah was Yahweh's expressed will for his people; therefore it had a holiness in itself. There were later commentaries and specifications of the law applying it to all features of life.

Jesus came with a new order of things. While respectful of the Torah, he invited his hearers to go beyond it. The new law of Christ was to be observed more in the spirit than in the letter. As the post-Easter church develops, much of the Torah's demands will pass away. Paul will even speak of the former law as being nullified (Gal 3:15f). But tension will continue for years in first century Christianity over the abiding validity of the Torah.

Today's readings reflect both Hebrew love for the law (Sirach) and the way it was superseded with the coming of Christ (Matthew). In 1 Corinthians, Paul speaks of our redemption as the great mystery of God, hidden from the ages and now revealed.

First Reading

As important as the law was in Hebrew life and piety, Ben Sira, writing in the third–second century B.C., reminds his readers that there is always the complete freedom to accept or reject it. God does not constrain or force the will of anyone; he prizes too highly the freedom of the individual. The choice in favor of the law will lead to life (v17) which means peace, harmony, even material blessings; its rejection brings death which, for Sira is total and definitive, with no idea of any afterlife sanctions. Death means Sheol, the pit of the shadows. Retribution for wrong-doing means that death will be preceded by countless misfortunes. God's wisdom and power are seen both in the law itself and in his scrutiny of each person's observance (v18; Ps 33:18).

The reading ends with a strong affirmation of God's justice. Sin never proceeds from God's will (v20); it is a question of human choice. Sin can only be excluded as a possibility with the removal of free will, something which Yahweh refuses to do.

Responsorial Psalm   Ps 119

Only a few verses of this, the lengthiest of the psalms (176 verses) are read in today's liturgy. These verses celebrate the Torah as Yahweh's great gift to his people. With a dominant wisdom theme, the psalmist prays for assistance in observing the law faithfully and assiduously (vv5, 17). It is the only route to fulfillment and true wisdom, as well as life itself (v17).

The psalm points to the deep Hebrew respect and love for the law. Its observance has made a holy people, set apart, a light to the nations. Transposed to another key, the law becomes the law of Christ, in continuity with the past but radically new in its formulation and demand. It too is a gift that leads to life.

Second Reading

In the epistle to Corinth, Paul takes issue with those Christians in the community who see the message of Christ as a type of superior wisdom (c. 1). This gnostic type of elitism is contrary to the egalitarian spirit of the Christian life. Moreover, it does not fit the facts. All people have received the same message and have access to the same truth.

The only wisdom that Paul has to offer is "Christ Jesus ... wisdom from God" (1:30). This he contrasts with the wisdom of political and religious rulers, corrupt and powerless, with a future doomed to futility.

Paul's wisdom is the mystery of God (Gr: *mysterion theou*) (2:1). This is the plan of salvation, effected in and through Christ, which has been hidden in God through the ages and only made known in these final times (vv8 - 10; 1:18 - 25). This is an idea developed at length in Ephesians 1. The plan of God was obviously unknown to Jewish and Roman leaders or they would never have brought Jesus to crucifixion. Ironically, this dreadful act has brought Christ to glory (v8) and them to oblivion (v6). Christians are now being gradually transformed into Christ's glory (2 Cor 3:18).

The quotation (v9) is not scriptural, except in a very broad sense (Is 64:3 with possible Pauline comment). Its purpose is to state clearly that this mystery of God's salvific plan, concealed from the ages, has now been revealed to all believers in the present age (v10). It is the Spirit who makes it known, the Spirit living in the inner recesses of God's life.

Third Reading

In the content of Matthew's sermon on the mount, the Matthean Jesus emphatically states his position on the validity of the law (vv17 - 20). This will be followed by an elaboration of how specific mandates of the law will be fulfilled in the new dispensation: murder (vv21 - 26), adultery (vv27 - 30), divorce (vv31 - 32), and oaths (vv33 - 37).

The Jesus of Matthew's gospel bears a very positive attitude toward the Hebrew Torah. His opening statement (vv17 - 20) reflects this posture, even though in practice he often disregarded Pharisaic interpretations and applications of the law. Matthew writes for a largely Jewish-Christian audience and upholds the abiding validity of the law until the visible universe will be no more, at the end of the age. Both "the passing of heaven and earth" (18a) and "until all things have taken place" (18b) should be understood as having the same eschatological point of reference, identified by early Christianity with the return of Christ.

In this interim period, then, all the precepts of the Torah, even the most insignificant (the yod and the tittle, the smallest features of Hebrew calligraphy), continue to have binding force (v18). Those teaching the contrary, while not excluded from the kingdom, hold only minimal place (the least, v19).

In this teaching, Matthew is obviously at odds with Paul and his segment of the church, with their teaching on freedom from the law (Gal 2:15ff; Rom 3:21 - 31). There is no need to attempt to reconcile the two positions. Suffice it to say that the church had not yet reached a point of total convergence regarding the law. The official gathering in Jerusalem (Acts 15) to discuss the question of the law ends by dispensing the Gentiles from the greater part of the law but left observance intact for Jewish Christians (Acts 15:22 - 29).

It is clear that in the early church, strong currents of thought were at work. One is seen clearly in the Pauline churches; the other was represented more clearly by the Palestinian churches, as reflected in Matthew. In time the question was resolved with the church relaxing the observance of Torah. It should come as no surprise that the weight of time-honored tradition regarding the law was not set aside quickly. It is interesting to note that the New Testament reflects the teaching of both schools. The teaching of Jesus himself on this point is not a factor in this discussion. Although he bore a genuine respect for the Torah in his action and teaching, he seemingly did not set forth any principles on the matter, probably in view of the short future that was envisioned.

Matthew does not enter into polemics on this question and does not give any idea of the breadth of his intended audience. There is no question, however, that he sees Torah observance as the superior approach to the Christian life (v19).

Once his point is made, Matthew goes on to consider the new ethic of the Christian life, an area in which there is genuine New Testament convergence. A new norm of covenant faithfulness has been introduced by Jesus which no longer stops at basic Torah observance (v20). Christians are called to a deeper ethical response going beyond the law and looking at the core causes of evil activity.

Together with this, the way of holiness, with charity as its base (Gal 5:14), will be the basis of all moral activity. Henceforth the emphasis will fall on virtue, not on sin. In going beyond the law, it is clear that the law itself is not being disregarded (Gal 5:22f). Matthew at this point goes on to illustrate this "surpassing righteousness" (v20), in the new law of Christ.

The decalogue forbids murder (Ex 20:13; Deut 5:17). Jesus immediately directs his hearers' attention to the underlying cause of murder and thus internalizes the precept (vv21 - 28). It is anger that is to be avoided, and this applies to all, not solely the plotting killer. There is here both a deeper and an egalitarian dimension of the Christian ethic.

Anger can escalate into abusive language (*Raqa*=imbecile), with accompanying measures of severer sanctions. The local assembly is the court of the first instance; the sanhedrin, the second; and gehenna, the odious, fiery city dump, the third. The imagery underscores the stages through which anger can pass in its rising intensity (v22).

Reconciliation with one's opponent is to precede any cultic offering (vv23 - 24). The existence of temple worship places this logion at some point before 70 A.D., probably stemming from Christ himself. The point has lasting significance. One's sentiments before God cannot be morally upright if relations with one's neighbor are discordant (1 Jn 4:20).

The final statement on anger deals with resolving difficulties "out of court" (vv25 - 26). Again, the complications connected with litigation escalate as the parable proceeds. It is difficult to say what setting it might have had in Jesus' ministry; Luke uses it to urge Christians to avoid pagan judiciaries (Lk 12:57 - 59). The point in Matthew is that forgiveness and a sense of justice should make any form of litigation unnecessary among Christians.

Adultery is forbibben by the law (Ex 20:14; Deut 5:18). Jesus again moves the discourse to another level (vv27 - 30) in surfacing the underlying cause which leads to violating marital rights—human lust. Once again the principle is internalized. It should be noted that it is not sexual issues in general, but specifically adultery that is being addressed. And there is more involved than simply entertaining a lustful thought. It involves an internal decision to act thereon in some way or other. The description of bodily mutilation (v29) is semitic hyperbole underscoring the importance of properly ordering moral imperatives even to the detriment or loss of other less important values.

Divorce was permitted by the law of Moses under certain circumstances (Deut 24:1 - 4). Jesus synthesizes the Deuteronomic exception and then repeals it (vv31 - 33). The indissolubility of marriage is one of the New Testament's strongest and clearest statements (19:1 - 12; Mk 10:1 - 12; Lk 16:18). Only Mark envisions the case of the woman initiating proceedings. In all cases divorce and remarriage are excluded.

Matthew introduces a celebrated "exception" in v32, extensively discussed by commentators. The Jewish-Christian communities, representing a considerable segment of Matthew's audience, were aware of certain degrees of relationship which excluded marriage (Lev 18:6 - 18). It is quite likely that this is the unlawful marriage or "lewd conduct" (Gr: *porneia*) spoken of at the assembly at Jerusalem and forbidden even to Gentile Christians (Acts 15:23 - 29). It is referred to here in the Matthean gospel where divorce is being treated and this type of marriage arrangement is again excluded. Since such relationships were not really marriages at all, severing them is no divorce in the real sense. Hence, Matthew presents no exception to the strongly attested prohibition of divorce found in the synoptics.

This teaching on divorce is not intended to militate against pastoral concern and canonical adjustment, when possible, in dealing with divorce, one of the most painful concerns of our times. At the same time, the Christian concept of marriage as lasting and permanent cannot be muted in Christian teaching and practice, in view of the strong New Testament base on which it rests.

Oaths attest to the truthfulness of what is said and invoke God as a witness. Jesus opposes them categorically in appealing to a transparent spirit of honesty in Christian attestation of the truth (vv33 - 36). The scripture quote is not exact but is rather a synthesis of various sources (Ex 20:7; Deut 5:11; Lev 19:12).

Swearing by other titles, not invoking God's name, still related the action to God in some way and is excluded (vv34 - 36).

A simple and direct answer, wherein falsehood plays no part, is at the heart of Christian truthfulness. The imposition of oaths, whether by church or state, inevitably makes a statement on the extent to which Christian values are seen as lived.

The examples which Jesus cites are not exhaustive but rather illustrative of the new ethic. The Torah teaching of the decalogue is respected. But a new note has been struck with emphasis on interiority and radical response. One cannot lose sight of the authority with which Jesus speaks, juxtaposing his teaching with that of the Torah. If nothing else, this points to a claim that goes beyond being a prophet or rabbi. Jesus is clearly a unique emissary of the original lawgiver.

The lessons of today's liturgy of the word are multiple. There is the continuity between the two laws, that of Moses and that of Christ. It reminds us that ours is not a ten commandments ethic but one which, while encompassing the decalogue, goes much beyond it. It is an ethic that looks to internal motives in all our actions and asks God's grace to heal our illnesses at their root. It is an ethic that calls us not only to avoid sin but to adhere to the positive pursuit of good.

The second reading, not closely related to the main theme, does nonetheless underlie it. We are privileged to be the recipients of the mystery of God's love, not known to the Hebrew scripture's most illustrious personages. Our response to such a gracious God should then be one of gratitude and fulfillment of his will. This is at the heart of compliance with the law of Christ.

Homiletic and Catechetical Helps

1. Law of Moses–law of Christ–continuity and differences.

2. Scriptural inspiration and the presence of different viewpoints, e.g. Paul and Matthew on the law.

3. Anger as the root of hostility.

4. Charity before "coming to the altar."

5. Evil of murder, individual and social: homicide, abortion, euthanasia, death penalty, war.

6. Lust as root of adultery and sexual immorality.

7. Indissolubility of marriage and annulments.

8. Honesty in speech; lying; oaths in the church.

9. Mystery of salvation–hidden and revealed.

SIXTH SUNDAY OF THE YEAR
Year B

Readings

> Lev 13:1 - 2, 44 - 46
> 1 Cor 10:31 - 11: 1
> Mk 1:40 - 45

Theme: Christ and the Emarginated

Leprosy in antiquity put one on the periphery of society. Contact was limited; normal social intercourse was prohibited. But it is precisely to people such as these–the unwanted, the lepers, the poor, the prostitutes, the tax collectors–that Jesus saw his mission principally directed. Today's liturgy gives us a very striking example. In our human conduct, even that which is licit, Paul today exhorts us to avoid giving offense.

First Reading

Within Israel and among its neighbors, leprosy covered a broad spectrum of skin diseases. The reference is not to Hansen's disease but to various dermatological diseases included under the word *sara'at.* The levitic legislation in today's reading envisions the type of curable illness associated with these skin disorders.

The afflicted person comes before the priest, not for prayer or a cure, but for physical examination and diagnosis. The priest determines whether the person is clean or unclean, and whether he or she has been cured or not (Lev 13:24 - 28).

The underlying principle, however, is not medical but religious. Primitively the notion of social exclusion quite possibly sprang from fear of contagion. In Israelite law, however, such illnesses signify a state of cultic unworthiness and consequent exclusion from a cultic community. Israel was designated a "holy people." This refers not solely to moral uprightness; it included physical integrity as well. Holiness and wholeness went together. Anything marred, defective or infected lacked wholeness and the integrity worthy of Yahwistic society and worship. Even corrupting elements like mildew, mold or moss affected this integrity (Lev 14:33 - 57). This means that "the leper" is excluded until his physical health has been restored.

While the illness perdured, the customary signs of religious and social stigma were to be clearly evident: the torn garments, long flowing hair, covered beard (Ez 24:17), and the warning cry "Unclean." The person was to live outside the confines of city, town, or camp.

Responsorial Psalm   Ps 32

The psalm has elements of wisdom and thanksgiving, and is one of the "penitential psalms." Although in the gospel there is no explicit mention of gratitude for the the leper's cure, today's psalm is an individual response of profound thanksgiving for the removal of sin, not illness (although the two are often linked in Hebrew thought).

The sin has been removed and "covered" (v1), parallel expressions for the same idea, i.e. the total forgiveness of transgression. Both sin and accompanying guilt have been lifted—this, from the side of God.

On the sinner's side, there has been a belated confession of wrongdoing with full acknowledgement and sincerity (vv3ff). His reconciliation is accomplished. For all of this God is praised. Both the sinner of the psalm and the sufferer of the gospel have experienced God's favor.

Second Reading

Paul has just completed a section of 1 Corinthians on the question of foods offered in pagan sacrifices (1 Cor 10:23 - 30). He concludes the passage with a strong exhortation, applicable on many levels of the Christian life.

In the choice between right and wrong, whether concerning food or anything else, it is God's glory that must be foremost (v30). Paul has already spoken of his willingness to adapt his own freedom in Christ to the sensitivities of Jews, Gentiles, or the weak (1 Cor 9:19 - 23). He speaks again of his willingness to avoid scandal at any cost (even though his freedom of conscience does not place restrictions) (v31). His only concern is the gospel of salvation (1 Cor 9:23), with anything of personal gain that is conflictive willingly sacrificed (v33). In no way does he wish to be a stumbling block on the path of salvation.

The apostle has personally experienced the risen Christ (Acts 9:1 - 9). As a result, his life mirrors Christ, who is himself the image of God (2 Cor 4:6). Christ has so taken possession of Paul that his own life is now that of Christ (Gal 2:19 - 20). The Christian communities identified with Paul did not have the same experience. His uniqueness as an apostle rested on his direct experience of Jesus (Gal 1:11 - 12). Therefore, he calls on the communities to imitate him as they move toward their sole model, Christ himself (1 Cor 4:16; Gal 4:12; Phil 3:7).

Third Reading

This "leper" is obviously a sufferer of the type described in Leviticus. His skin disease was sufficient to exclude him from the community. The miracle story (vv40 - 42) is typical: description of illness, action of Jesus, completeness of cure. The episode, characteristic of Marcan vividness, is full of emotion. Early catechetical use has not drained it of its pathos.

The man is a true suppliant, insistent but respectful (v40). Divergent manuscript evidence has Jesus as "being angry" or "moved with pity" in v41. The choice will determine whether the unspecified strong emotion in v43 (*embrimesamenos*) points to anger or compassion. The strongest evidence points to pity as being the dominant emotion in both verses. In either case, the scene is fraught with drama.

Jesus' injunction after the cure is twofold (v44). The man is not to publicize the cause of his cure. This is consistent with the note of secrecy regarding Jesus' identity repeatedly found in Mark (1:24 - 25). Gradual revelation, made principally to the apostles, will eventually lead to Jesus' true identity. It will come to its fullness only after the resurrection.

Jesus also has the man submit to the norms of the levitical law (Lev 14). His reinsertion in the community will come as a result of the purification ritual. He is advised to proceed at once to the priest. Both cure and reintegration are part of Jesus' outreach to the suffering man.

The discretion requested by Jesus is disregarded by the cured man (v45). As is usual in Mark, Jesus moves away from adulation and public amazement. Such could easily dull the force of his message of conversion. He retires to a desert place.

Society tends to exclude people and treat them as social lepers today no less than in the time of Jesus. At that time, justification could be found in the law for a certain measure of separation. While Jesus shows a basic respect for the Mosaic law (as distinguished from its many attached rabbinic precepts), he never fails to respect primarily the worth of the human person as transcending every other religious or social consideration.

Our attitudes today are fashioned by social mores, often biased or racist. We have many examples of exclusion of people on the basis of nationality, race, gender, sexual orientation, or social class. It is Jesus' over-riding love for the human person, virtuous or sinful, without qualification, that is his greatest challenge in any age or culture.

Homiletic and Catechetical Helps

1. Christian response to discrimination.

2. The challenge: to seek the good of the emarginated.

3. Respect for just law.

4. Love for the person over legal restrictions.

5. Scandal: definition; attitudes.

6. Relationship between sin and suffering.

7. Using Christian freedom prudently.

8. Seeing God in all that we do.

9. Proper use of food and drink.

10. Gratitude for forgiveness.

SIXTH SUNDAY OF THE YEAR
Year C

Readings

> Jer 17:5 - 8
> 1 Cor 15:12, 16 - 20
> Lk 6:17, 20 - 26

Theme: Rooted in Trust

When things go well, faith is not difficult. Life's necessities are taken care of; we may have more than enough; we live convinced that our life is blessed. It is much more difficult to believe when life seems to be an endless series of adversities. Some of the Bible's major personalities had their faith sorely tested in the fires of adversity. Today's readings remind us, with the use of rich imagery drawn from nature, that God is still present to a troubled world. Our trust must be permanent and deep. Paul speaks of resurrection as a linchpin of the Christian life. If Christ did not rise, we have no hope or forgiveness.

First Reading

The reading from Jeremiah states the importance of trust in Yahweh by drawing on three familiar elements of Hebrew poetry. The first is the use of imagery drawn from nature, used so effectively in Hebrew literature. The person trusting in other humans (v5) is like a withering bush on the desert floor, bereft of water, left to fade into oblivion. The foolishness of trusting in human resources is a frequent biblical theme, repeatedly sounded in the psalms (Ps 118:8f; 146:3f). The image of the person trusting in Yahweh as being a well rooted tree (vv7f), in close proximity to abundant water, is a strong and readily understood simile, also found in the psalms (Ps 1; 52:10).

Secondly, the passage makes use of antithetical parallelism, an important feature of Hebrew poetry. It is readily seen in the short mashal (proverb) wherein the two opposed sections of the verse make a single point. This is done by juxtaposing the positive and negative sides of the issue. Thus Proverbs 10:4 urges industriousness by stating that "the slack hand impoverishes; but the hand of the diligent enriches." The antithesis engages the imagination and elicits the conclusion from the hearer's (reader's) wit rather than by direct statement. The book of Proverbs offers many examples (e.g. Prov 10 - 11).

In Jeremiah 17, there is a simple expansion or development of the same antithetical form in contrasting the lot of the two types of "trusting" persons. Although, the descriptive imagery is more elaborate than in the shorter mashal, the antithesis is the basic genre in the passage (vv5 - 8). The conclusion emerges: deep-rooted confidence in God is the path to peace.

Thirdly, the antithesis makes use of the curses and blessings formula (Deut 11:26 - 31; cc. 27 - 28). It is used to conclude formal legislation. This is more than simple invocation of sanctions; the formula was considered an effective conduit of its sentiments. A blessing or a curse was taken with great seriousness in antiquity (e.g. Gen 27; Num 22 - 23); once uttered, it delivered fortune or misfortune. While eventually the form became more literary and poetic, it still carried a strong indication of future eventualities.

Responsorial Psalm   Ps 1

The psalm today echoes the reading from Jeremiah. There is the contrast between the good and the wicked, the similes of the tree and the wind-blown weeds, the differences between human and divine counsel. The psalm makes specific Jeremiah's trust in the Lord in identifying it with love of Torah (v2), wherein true wisdom lies (Sir 24).

The message remains the same in the reading and the response. It is foolish to give priority to human (or, worse, evil) counsel. What alone matters is God-centeredness in life (v2) which ultimately will not disappoint (v6).

Second Reading

The Christians in Corinth had raised questions about the resurrection. Some saw the idea of a risen body as unsuited to an intelligent faith. The body was material and therefore unrelated to spiritual existence. Either they were deeply influenced by Greek thinking which saw the soul as the only immortal principle, or they had so spiritualized the idea of resurrection that corporeality had been excluded. Paul takes lengthy issue with this viewpoint (1 Cor 15), dealing with both the fact of resurrection (1 - 34) and the manner (35 - 58).

If there is no resurrection, the Corinthians cannot logically uphold Christ's resurrection, which stands at the heart of the Christian kerygma (vv12ff). In excluding Christ's resurrection, everything crumbles. There is no meaning to the faith, even the "enlightened" faith which the Corinthians flaunt. It is Christ's resurrection that brings the forgiveness of sins and justification (Rom 4:24f). If Christ has not risen, then Christians remain in their original sinful state, while those Christians already dead have undergone a death that is total (Rom 5:12 - 14), a death without hope. The situation is dire and renders everything proclaimed and believed totally useless. Verse 19 may be rendered: "If in this life we who are Christians have only hope ...", thus comparing Christians with their Greek counterparts who hold some vague hope of resurrection. The conclusion, however, is clear; without the resurrection, as Paul emotionally states, we are indeed to be pitied.

However, the fact of the matter is quite contrary, Paul has proclaimed it, as have the twelve. It is a keystone of the faith. Christ has indeed risen as the prototype of what will occur in the after-life of his followers (v20).

Third Reading

The Lucan blessings and woes are taken from his sermon on the plain (6:20 - 49), a parallel in abbreviated form to Matthew's sermon on the mount (Mt 5 - 7). Some verses in today's reading are shared with Matthew (Lk 20b - 23), derived from a common source (identified as Q); others are distinctly Lucan (vv24 - 26).

The blessings and woes continue the Hebrew genre of blessings and curses, described in the above comment on the Jeremiah passage. The Lucan and Matthean versions of the beatitudes are quite distinct (for comment on the Matthean version, see the Fourth Sunday in Ordinary Time–Year A). The blessings (vv20 - 23) clearly reflect Luke's over-arching concern with determined segments of society. The people described are people identifiable within the social order. Luke makes no explicit attempt to "spiritualize" the beatitudes as does Matthew.

So it is that, in addressing his disciples, and through them a much larger audience of believers, Jesus speaks of the poor, the hungry, the grieving, and the hated and assures them that their present lot is not permanent. In the reign of God (v23), which is not solely to be identified with heaven, their circumstances will be different. Portions of the Lucan form of the blessings stand closer to the words of Jesus himself, e.g. the view of the poor as being central to Jesus' ministry (Lk 4:18). Others reflect editing adapted to situations in the early church (v22).

The "woes" on the contrary touch disciples who live in distinctly superior circumstances–the rich, the well fed, the care-free, the honored. Their lots, too, will be reversed. They are being challenged implicitly to recognize the authentic demands of the Christian life.

Both categories are strongly suggestive of Luke's parable of the rich man and Lazarus (16:19 - 31). The parable is really an extended commentary on Luke's blessings and woes.

Luke should not be pressed here to give answers to questions that he does not pose, e.g. what should be the moral values of the poor, who are the true poor, etc. His is a clear statement on the "haves" and "have nots" of life and a clear reminder that the ultimate outcome will be measured by Christian standards, not those of the world. God's justice will be manifest in the context of the reign of God. The implicit moral catechesis of the narrative is a reminder of one's Christian responsibility to the needy and the unfortunate. In addition, there must be a willingness to suffer for Christ. The hatred experienced by Christian believers is but a repetition of what was endured by earlier members of God's elect (v23).

The Lucan passage envisions sanctions which are both temporal and eternal. But it loses its strength if given too much "other-worldly" emphasis. Christian men and women, of past and present, have been inspired by this teaching to give their lives for the emarginated and even to institutionalize their concern.

The passage also builds on the main thrust of the first reading. All Christians, even in their most difficult moments, must remain firm in their trust in the Lord's saving work (2 Cor 4:7 - 11).

Two ideas suggest themselves as we reflect on this Sunday's readings. The first is that the way things are is not necessarily the way they should be. In his own way, Jesus was quite radical in speaking of a reversal of the accepted order. Luke's sermon on the plain clearly shows that Jesus felt that his greatest mission was to the poor and downtrodden. When considering the world of our times, that is a message that has important implications for his followers.

Secondly, there are moments when our faith falters and our trust wavers. We too may wonder about the after-life. We may be inclined to doubt at times whether the poor are any closer to a place at the world's table than they ever were. To be human is to doubt. Yet through it all we continue to trust. In faith we take Jesus at his word.

Homiletic and Catechetical Helps

1. The church's option for the poor.

2. Parish responsibility for those who mourn.

3. Sharing our food.

4. Personal and structural sin.

5. The eucharist: sign of solidarity with the needy.

6. Resurrection of the body; life after death.

7. Justification by Christ's resurrection.

8. Praying for the deceased.

9. Explaining the funeral liturgy.

10. Trust in the Lord and times of doubt.

SEVENTH SUNDAY OF THE YEAR
Year A

Readings

> Lev 19:1 - 2, 17 - 18
> 1 Cor 3:16 - 23
> Mt 5:38 - 48

Theme: Forgiveness

The sermon on the mount continues to unfold its teaching for us in the Sunday liturgy. Again we see how the teaching of Jesus goes beyond the Mosaic law. It is no longer the case that our dealings with others call for a measured response. Rather the major concern of a person's dignity and worth evoke unlimited forgiveness and boundless charity in the face of hurt or opposition. Christians are a dwelling place of God—another reason for respect, as Paul speaks of the Christian as belonging to Christ as Christ belongs to God.

First Reading

The reading is taken from the law of holiness in Leviticus 17 − 26, a body of early laws regulating moral conduct and ritual. It is so designated because of its strong call to holiness, which is to reflect that of Yahweh (vv1 - 2).

The fundamental idea of holiness, whether in God or people, was "otherness." While present to his creation, God always stands over and apart from it (Is 6:3 - 5). This distinctiveness is called for in the ritual and ethical conduct of God's people. In this way they approximate God's "otherness." This chapter litanies ways in which this is to be realized. It is not simply a legal or external purity but rather moral rectitude that is called for.

Any spirit of animosity which nurtures hostility toward one's neighbor is excluded. That "fellow man" and "brother" are to be understood as other Israelites only is clear from the "fellow countrymen" parallel (v18).

Fraternal correction is to be observed without incurring sin thereby (v17b). The meaning is rather ambiguous. Sin could be incurred by carrying correction beyond proper limits, e.g. with a spirit of vindictiveness (Ex 21:22 - 25; Lev 24:20). It may, however, refer to the obligation of fraternal correction itself, the neglect of which would be sinful (Ez 3:18 - 19; 33:8 - 9).

The passage ends with the most celebrated verse in Leviticus (v18b). The norm determining the extent of one's love for another Israelite is that of self-love. The roots of self-preservation and self-love are struck deep in human nature. That same concern should be extended to others. In the New Testament, this verse together with Deuteronomy 6: 5 becomes the summation of the entire Christian ethic (Mt 22:37 - 39; Mk 12:30 - 31).

Responsorial Psalm   Ps 103

This is a thanksgiving psalm, expressing an individual's joy at being delivered from sickness (vv3b, 4) and sin (3a, 10, 12 - 13). The psalm, therefore, continues today's forgiveness theme, but entirely from God's part. Sickness and sin are linked in Hebrew thought. The former is often seen as a punishment for the latter (Job; Ps 32:3ff), even though the thesis frequently presented difficulties.

The psalm praises God for lifting the burden of sin and suffering. Verse 8 repeats Exodus 34:6 in underscoring Yahweh's covenant fidelity. It is clear that this is not just a juridical lifting of sin; Yahweh withdraws all its vestiges, removing it from the sinner's sight and his own (v12). His is the posture of a father, not a judge (v13).

Second Reading

Three points are made in today's reading from 1 Corinthians. The first (vv16 - 17) is that the Corinthian community is a temple of God. Its members are the dwelling place of the spirit and by that fact are holy or consecrated (1:2, 30; 6:11). This is not simply a cultic holiness, like that of a church or synagogue. It includes all the moral qualities that properly make Christians a people set apart (Mt 5:48).

Paul had been using the building imagery earlier in the chapter (3:10 - 16) and moves thematically into the temple concept. The imagery should be read together with that of Paul's body of Christ (1 Cor 6:15 - 20; Eph 1:22 - 23; Col 1:18) for a fuller grasp of the community's holiness. Their sanctity derives from their union with Christ in the Holy Spirit. Violence to the Christian community, especially through discord and disunity, is equivalent to vandalizing a holy place. God will deal with it accordingly (v17).

The second point returns to the issue of a Christian's true wisdom (vv18 - 20). What matters is that God's redeemed community be served, not that the community make heroes of its members. Paul returns to the principal idea of this part of the epistle (3:5 - 9). All human standards pale into insignificance in view of God's pre-determined plan of the cross. To accept that plan one has to become a fool in worldly eyes (v19; cf.1:18 - 23). It is "unwise" to exalt human beings. With quotations from Job 5:13 and Psalm 94:11 (with Paul's substitution of "wise" for "men" in the latter), Paul follows the rather loose rabbinic method of freely quoting scripture in support of his thesis that worldly wisdom is passing away.

Finally Paul sets forth the proper ordering of the community's structure (vv21 - 23); there is no room for taking Christian ministers and placing them on pedestals. The reason is that the community's ministers, with their theological concerns, are dedicated to the community and not vice versa. The community, in turn, belongs to Christ alone and Christ, to God. Thus

Christ himself is subjected to the Father (1 Cor 15:27f). This proper ordering of relationships, so easily lost sight of in the course of the Christian life, is vital to any authentic sense of church ministry.

Third Reading

The Christian way of life supersedes any pre-existing norms. It is to be a mirror of God's perfection (v48). In this Matthean passage, which continues our reflection on the sermon on the mount, two issues are addressed: retaliation and attitudes toward enemies.

The first major point to be stressed is that the former teaching on positive relations only with other Jews is broadened to include anyone who is encountered in life. No ethnic or religious distinctions are made in Jesus' teaching. The "neighbor" of Leviticus 19:18 has become that of the good Samaritan (Lk 10:36f), the one who responds to anyone encountered, especially those in need.

The Hebrew law of talion or retribution cited by Jesus (v38) was meant to limit retribution (only an eye for an eye, only a tooth for a tooth). It finds its counterpart in the ancient code of Hammurabi. A sound law in itself, it is repealed by Jesus. One's response to personal injury is to be non-violent and non-aggressive; rather the offender is to be treated with authentic (and surprising) goodness.

A blow to the face was a grave insult (Is 50:6; Jn 18:22f). The only response permitted is acceptance (v40). Lawsuits (v40) are to be assiduously avoided by Christians (Mt 5:25f), especially before non-Christian magistrates (Lk 12: 57f). The idea of being pressed into service (v41) may reflect a relay type of messenger service being rendered, "the extra mile." The final note (v42) moves beyond non-resistance to a positive regard for the needs of anyone who asks, the one with no resources or the borrower. Largess is to be an evident characteristic of Jesus' disciple.

On dealing with enemies, Jesus quotes Leviticus 19:18. There is no explicit Hebrew command to hate one's enemy, although the equivalent is not difficult to find (Ps 137:8f; 139:19 - 22), and it is part of Qumran's teaching (IQS 1:9 - 10). The only

Christian response is love (vv43f). Friends and foes are to receive the same treatment. All of this mirrors God's own way of acting (vv44f). None of it would be thinkable without the Christian's new relationship to God as Father (v44), a state born of God's spirit (Gal 4:6).

The recompense for a love based on mutual compatibility is similarly an increase of the same. But love where there is incompatibility or hostility produces a reward proper to the reign of God (v45; 5:10). Tax collectors were socially demeaned as Roman collaborators and corrupt in their dealings. The rather pejorative reference to Gentiles (v47) is not offensive to the largely Jewish-Christian audience for which Matthew writes.

The inclusion (v48) is a call to be perfect (Gr: *teleios*) rare in the gospels (only here and in 19:21). Luke calls instead for a likeness to God's mercy (Lk 6:36). The meaning of the verse should not be pressed along ontological lines. It is a call to a faithful observance of a God-given ideal; one's dealings with others, moreover, should reflect those of God (vv44 - 45). What it means is illustrated by what has preceded. Christian conduct is not based on customary human standards, nor even those of an earlier revelation. Christians are to be different in the way that God is different. This is how they approximate his own perfection. It is a strong statement and is to be taken at face value.

It is inaccurate to view the teaching of this Sunday's scriptures as an ideal toward which we aspire. Commentators do God's word no favor by allowing human failure to condition their interpretation of the sermon on the mount. The text has no conditional clauses; rather it points to the normative way in which Christians are to live. Every day of our life, in countless ways, we are called to love our enemies, turn the other cheek, and to go beyond the reasonable in seeking reconciliation. We may fall short of what Christians are called to be. But let us say that we do, rather than establish some lesser norm as an acceptable Christian standard. War, for example, is always an evil. The fact that, at times, we feel constrained to wage it does not make it less evil, nor in any way "just."

Another point to be drawn from today's readings is the positive power of non-resistance. It is not simply withdrawal or disengagement.

It is meant to conquer the opposition (Rom 12:19 - 21) and is there-fore a strategy.

In the face of authentic love, even the hardest of hearts will hopeful-ly be affected. Modern history offers some clear examples of the power of non-violence.

Finally, forgiveness of others is but an application of what we ask of God for ourselves in the Lord's prayer. In imitation of God's mercy to us, we extend it to others. Our failure to do so brings a conscious reproach each time we ask for God's pardon. It is in forgiving that we act in a God-like fashion and become perfect like our heavenly Father.

Homiletic and Catechetical Helps

1. The meaning of forgiveness in our lives.

2. Non-violence and non-resistance: ideal or way of life?

3. The meaning of being perfect as God is perfect.

4. Human forgiveness and divine forgiveness as reflected in the communal rite of reconciliation.

5. The penitential rite at mass as related to today's theme.

6. The parish as a temple of God; people over place; practical implications.

7. Hierarchy as service to the community.

8. Christ as belonging to God.

9. The danger of human "heroes" in the church of Christ.

SEVENTH SUNDAY OF THE YEAR
Year B

Readings

Is 43:18 - 19, 21 - 22, 24 - 25
2 Cor 1:18 - 22
Mk 2:1 - 12

Theme: Healing and Pardon

The power of God extends to all areas of life. In today's readings, he is powerful in bringing his people back from Babylon as well as in forgiving their sins. In the gospel, Jesus vindicates his power over sin by restoring the paralytic to health. The remission of sins is not visible; it is not as striking as a healing. But forgiveness comes to us through the same power and mercy of God. 1 Corinthians speaks of Jesus as the definitive "yes" to God.

First Reading

The second part of Isaiah, written in the late sixth century B.C., speaks of the Jews' return from exile in Babylon as a continuation of Yahweh's work in creation (Is 42:5f; 40:28f; 41:4f).

In today's passage he reminds his hearers that the original exodus event (43:16f) need not be reflected on further, for Yahweh is bringing about a new exodus (vv18f). It involves both a journey homeward (v19) and the fashioning of the hearts of a new people (v25).

Past sinfulness and negligence are noted (v24). The prophet sees a continuity in God's power in creation, in exodus deliverance, in post-exilic restoration with the forgiveness of sin as part of this salvific act. Pardon is something which God owes to himself (v25), as the manifestation of his power and glory (Dan 3:43f) and his covenant fidelity (Hos 11:8f).

The passage's importance lies in its showing the connectedness in God's power over human history and human sinfulness. It can be viewed against the broader Isaian theme of his power in creation which continues in later historical events.

Responsorial Psalm   Ps 41

The psalm has the features of a personal lament of one suffering from a debilitating illness (v4); the connection between sin and suffering, seen in today's gospel, is present in the psalm (v5). But the Lord will restore the sufferer to health. His personal integrity will be verified by his restoration to health (vv12f). The psalm ends on a note of trust.

Second Reading

Paul's plans to make another visit to Corinth had to be changed (1:15f). This led to some grumbling and discontent in the community about his alleged vacillation. Paul defends himself in a splendid theological digression on the constancy of God. Paul rejects the idea of his being inconsistent or unpredictable. He is firm and committed, as an apostle of the Lord must be. He begins by speaking of God's fidelity to his word.

There are a number of "yes" responses on which Christian hope is based. The first is that of God himself who has brought to fruition all past promises in the person of Jesus, his Son. The promises made through the prophets (Rom 1:3) and the partial insights given in the past (Heb 1:11) have been completely realized in the salvation brought by Christ (vv19f). Therefore, God's constancy cannot be questioned.

Secondly, Jesus himself was an unqualified "yes" to the will of the Father (Heb 10:9f). As sin came into the world through the "no" of Adam, so grace is even more abundant through the "yes" of Jesus (Rom 5:19). Despite his human fragility and fear, Jesus never wavered in his acceptance of the Father's will (Mt 26:39) and remains an ongoing "yes" to God (v19b).

Finally, Paul and his companions, Silvanus (1 Thes 1:1; Acts 18:5 [Silas]) and Timothy (1 Thes 3:2) share in that same constancy as they give their "amen" to God in apostolic service and worship (vv19f). In this passage only (v19) does Paul explicitly link as one the titles Christ and Son of God (Rom 1:4; Gal 2:20).

At the end of the reading, Paul does an interesting play on words drawn from the language of commerce (vv21 - 22). He points out the security that Christian commitment gives. The "seal" is equivalent to our "signed, sealed and delivered," the "first down payment." The language is used to illustrate a baptismal and trinitarian theme.

In baptism one is united with Christ, anointed by the action of God, and given the pledge of future glory by reason of the Spirit's presence. The conclusion in commercial parlance: God "delivers" on his promises.

Third Reading

In the Marcan narrative of the paralytic, a "stitching" has taken place to link Jesus' authority over sickness and sin. In the gospel, it is situated after a series of miracle stories (c. 1) and before a group of conflict-pronouncement stories (2:13 - 3:6).

Both types of the aforementioned genre are present in the paralytic account. The "stitching" is more noticeable in the Greek text than in translation. Verses 1 - 5a and 11b - 12 relate a miracle story, complete in itself, while vv5b - 10 constitute essentially a pronouncement story.

The miracle story follows the characteristic form. There is the description of the man's illness. He is assisted by four men who ascend the outside steps of the typical Palestinian house and make a hole through the thatched roof (not the Greco-Roman tiles of Luke (5:19). After this description, there is Jesus' recognition of their faith (5a) and his declaration of the cure (11b). In conclusion, the completeness of the cure is noted with the man's departure on his own to the crowd's amazement (12). (With the later addition of the pronouncement story, the amazement of "all" would include his opponents as well, an unlikely hypothesis.)

The pronouncement story (5b - 10) deals with Jesus' power over sin and the accusation of blasphemy. It begins with the questioning of the scribes regarding Jesus' authority to forgive sin. The response of Jesus follows in which he vindicates his power over sin (non-empirical, therefore easier to claim) by curing the man's illness (visible, therefore more difficult). The conclusion of the pronouncement story blends with the conclusion of the miracle story, with a certain amount of overlapping.

It is not likely that Jesus spoke of himself as Son of Man (Dan 7:13) in the third person. There is, however, every reason for the early church to give him this eschatological designation in emphasizing his authority over the evils of sin and sickness. Verse 10, then, would stem from the story's early redactor, who is also responsible for the "stitching."

Worthy of note again is the Marcan emphasis on the crowd's pressing on Jesus (v2), which so often restricts his movements in this gospel (1:34; 3:9).

Instruction easily drawn from today's liturgy centers on an inherent relationship between sin and suffering,. The Hebrew scriptures struggled with the relationship for centuries. It could neither be taken too narrowly nor disregarded.

Physical evil – pain and sickness – often impossible to explain is related to moral evil in the scriptures. To say that a person suffers from any illness because of a sinful life would be inadmissible. But in broad terms there is a relationship between suffering and sin, as even Genesis teaches. Apart from today's gospel, which as we have seen is a redactor's synthesis, Jesus avoids any specific personalizing of suffering and sin. But he himself who takes away the sin of the world does so as the suffering servant. If suffering does no more, it portrays the evil of sin and is often offered for sin's atonement.

The epistle has a lesson that is hard to learn today. It is the lesson of commitment. It is not a word that figures prominently in the modern vocabulary. We know that permanent commitment has become much less frequent today, whether in marriage, priestly and religious life, or other areas.

Paul's words speak volumes of what commitment has meant on God's part. God's reign will never be advanced by a "sometimes" sort of attitude. Commitment means permanence and constancy. Without it, little can be expected; with it, we join Christ in giving our ongoing "yes" to God.

Homiletic and Catechetical Helps

1. Relating sin and suffering.

2. The paralytic story: What did Jesus say? What does the church want to say?

3. Perception of sin in today's world.

4. The paralytic's friends: caring for the sick.

5. Perception of suffering today.

6. Forgiveness of sins–its presence in the church.

7. Permanent commitment in life today.

8. Our amen to God: in liturgy and life.

SEVENTH SUNDAY OF THE YEAR
Year C

Readings

> 1 Sam 26:2, 7 - 9, 12 - 13, 22 - 23
> 1 Cor 15:45 - 49
> Lk 6:27 - 38

Theme: Generosity and Pardon

The story of Saul and David illustrates the gospel's main theme: forgiveness of one's opponent. At the same time we recognize that David's motive for sparing the king is not the same as that which the gospel asks. Taken from Luke's sermon on the plain, the instruction parallels that of Matthew (Seventh Sunday, Year A). Paul speaks of the first and second Adam. The new Adam is a life giving Spirit.

First Reading

The dramatic account of David's penetration of Saul's camp stems from an early tradition found in 1 Samuel 24 in two quite distinct forms. A full appreciation of the story's tension can be grasped only by reading this chapter in its entirety. Today's reading focuses on one feature of the story: the sparing of Saul's life.

With a large detachment of military forces, Saul had gone in pursuit of his rival David. Size and number are an important feature in the deuteronomic history. David's much smaller retinue is victorious, as in the case of fighting Goliath (c. 17), since victory is the Lord's and not the work of human agents (Ps 118:14 - 16).

David's victory over his opponent is achieved by clever strategy and stealth, without compromising principle. With Abisha encouraging David to strike (v8), the tension is heightened, illustrating the ease with which David could have destroyed the king. David refuses to strike Saul since the king is the anointed of the Lord. This is not an act of forgiveness or mercy but the recognition of a sacred responsibility.

The victory still belongs to the young warrior. Escaping with the king's spear and jug, he reminds Saul of how close he was to death at the hands of an insignificant military force (vv22f).

Responsorial Psalm   Ps 103

The psalm is appropriate in today's liturgy with its theme of pardon and forgiveness. The Christian assembly gives its "amen" to the biblical teaching with a psalm that speaks of these qualities in God. Commentary is found on the Seventh Sunday of Year A.

Second Reading

Paul has been dealing with the nature of the resurrected body (15:36 - 44) wherein he argues that, with the natural body being the only point of comparison, one's language is inadequate in speaking of the body yet to come. He then makes a comparison between Adam and Christ (vv45 - 46f; Rom 5; 1 Cor 15:22). Here for the first time he explicitly calls Christ a second Adam. In quoting Genesis 2: 7, both the common noun (*adam*, man) and the proper name (Adam) are used. Popular Jewish belief that Adam would return in the end time allows Paul to draw on the image.

The first Adam was natural, earthly and, of course, living. The new Adam (the prototype of all resurrected Christians) is spiritual, heavenly and a life-giver (Gal 4:6; Rom 8:9 - 10). The Corinthians are to remember that they have experience only of the earthly Adam, whose image they all bear (v49). They have not yet been transformed into the image of the heavenly Adam, even though they already possess the seed.

Third Reading

Much of this gospel is drawn from the Q source and common to Matthew and Luke. The Lucan imprint on the material emphasizes strongly the sharing of possessions. Luke presents the radical teaching, adapts it to his Gentile Christian audience (v27a) and stresses the rewards of the kingdom over any human recompense.

As in the Matthean text, Luke emphasizes forgiveness of opponents (27 - 30). The disciple presents himself or herself for blows and even possible denudement rather than respond to maltreatment with a posture of self-protection. A positive attitude of love for enemies, even social pariahs, is a clear trait of the Lucan Jesus in his dealing with the standard opponents of his time, e.g. Samaritans (9:51 - 56; 17:11 - 19) and tax collectors (19:1 - 10).

In the following verses (vv30 - 37), Luke alters a standard principle of his Gentile Christian audience. This was the ethic of reciprocity. Loans and requests were admissible with the assurance of restoration in the same amount. The Christian, however, is to give expecting nothing in return. Any type of measured negotiations would not be Christian since such was practiced by non-believers as a matter of course. Where Matthew makes a pejorative comparison with pagans (5:47), the Gentile-sensitive Luke refers only to sinners (vv 32 - 33). Instead of the perfection called for in Matthew (5:48), Luke's inclusion calls for mercy (v36).

The non-judgmental, non-condemnatory, pardoning and generous posture of the final verses (vv37 - 38) should be related to the sermon's theme of appropriate sharing without questioning, rather than as general exhortations. The reward will come from God and will be super-abundant, like gifts tightly packed and solid, landing in one's lap. How will the reward be measured? To the extent that the disciple himself is generous (v38). Failure to be generous will limit God's response (16:19 - 31). This theme of generosity and mercy is central to Luke, repeatedly noted in Jesus' comportment and teaching (7:11 - 17; 7:36 - 48; 14:12 - 24).

Once again this year, we have returned to Jesus' challenging teaching on forgiveness and pardon. The dealings of David with Saul were marked by respect, a first step toward, but hardly co-extensive with, Jesus' words on total forgiveness.

The dominant note in Luke is limitless generosity without expecting recompense. This can apply as well to personal hurts as it does to donations and loans. This is the meaning of Christian love. It is the spirit of Jesus himself. It is not correct to call it disinterested since God's recompense will come in its own time and its own way.

This is what Christian holiness or otherness means. God's own nature is reflected in human conduct. "Thus shall all people know that you are my disciples ..." If Christians operate solely on human values, then the salt and light are gone. Christianity, then, has no meaning. We are called to be different.

Jesus teaches with authority. He is breaking new ground and does not hesitate to compare his teaching with the Mosaic law. This throws a strong light on Jesus' understanding of his singular role in the plan of God.

We wonder at times about the resurrected body, no less than did the Corinthians. Paul argues strongly for it as a fact but will not be cornered into describing it. It differs from our present state just as the tree differs from the seed. It is because immortality is so important to Christian belief that Paul does not hesitate to address the question.

Homiletic and Catechetical Helps

1. Giving and lending with no return.

2. The question of interest on a loan; the usury question in the church.

3. Respect for civil authority.

4. Respect for human life; capital punishment.

5. Comparing David's pardon and that of Christ.

6. Attitude toward war in Hebrew scriptures and Christian scriptures.

7. Bodily resurrection and immortality.

8. Concrete ideas on sharing.

EIGHTH SUNDAY OF THE YEAR
Year A

Readings

> Is 49:14 - 15
> 1 Cor 4:1 - 5
> Mt 6:24 - 34

Theme: Trust Versus Anxiety

In the touching image of mother and infant, Second Isaiah gives encouragement to his contemporaries. No more than the mother will God forsake Israel his child. In the same spirit, Jesus in Matthew's sermon on the mount promises his disciples the support and care of a providential God and urges them to put their anxieties aside. Paul today tells the Corinthians that a judgmental spirit is not Christian. God is our only judge.

First Reading

The assurance of a restored Jerusalem at the end of the exile receives one of its most human expressions in this well-known passage from Second Isaiah. Previous words of consolation for the exiles (49:8 - 12) are here matched by encouragement for the desolate city itself. In the context Jerusalem too is seen as a mother who had lost her children in their infancy only to see them return home in their later years, much to her amazement (49:20f).

In today's reading Yahweh reassures the grieving Jerusalem who feels that she has been forgotten (v14). The mother simile is used, not applied to Jerusalem but to Yahweh. In the prophetic literature, Yahweh is father (Jer 31:20; Hos 11:4) and husband (Hos 2; Ez 16); here he is compared to a mother (v15; 46:3).

The bonds between mother and child are of such strength as to preclude the possibility of any fading from memory. As seemingly impossible as that eventuality is, it can be expected to happen before Yahweh would abandon Jerusalem. Once again the motif returns: Yahweh's fidelity to the covenant remains steadfast despite the repeated infidelities of his people.

Responsorial Psalm   Ps 62

The theme of trust continues in today's psalm. Only Yahweh provides assurance of safety and salvation (vv2, 6). This is due to his steadfastness and stability; he is rock (vv3, 7, 8), salvation (vv3, 7), safety (v8) and refuge (vv8, 9), metaphors which invite confidence. The context of the psalm (in verses not read today) speaks of being beset by enemies (vv4f). The psalmist's unwavering trust is to serve as motivation for his compatriots who are encouraged to seek their strength in the Lord (v9)

Second Reading

If Yahweh is worthy of trust, then his ministers should be trustworthy. Paul finishes addressing the issue of criticism and "hero worship" in Corinth (3:21f) by placing apostleship and ministry in perspective. Those called to apostolic service are to be totally subordinate to the message entrusted to them by God. *Mysteries of God* (v1): God's plan of salvation for all people, kept concealed until the appearance of Christ in history (2:1f). Apostles are servants (of a higher Master) and stewards (of a revealed message); as such, they are not to be accorded recognition (3:7) nor judged by human standards (v3).

Paul uses the language of the courts. Since his office has come from God alone (1:1), he has not been commissioned by the Corinthians or much less by himself. They are in no more a position to pass judgment on him than he is himself (v3). He is not aware of any failures on his part (2 Cor 1:12; 2 Thes 3:9); nevertheless he will not be certain of innocence until the Lord's return at the parousia (v5) when judgment will be passed. The Lord who judges not by externals but on the basis of internal motivation will illumine what is hidden in the heart (1 Sam 16:7; Heb 4:13). Where good is present it will be fully recognized (v5).

Third Reading

The Q source has supplied Matthew and Luke with this teaching of Jesus on undivided loyalty (v24) and trust (vv25 - 34; Lk 12:22 - 32)). In Matthew it is part of the sermon on the mount. In linking the two, Matthew nuances the teaching on trust in such a way as to clarify its meaning.

The Christian life does not admit a divided allegiance (v24). To give oneself to the Lord and to someone (or something) else is certain to lead ultimately to the abandonment of one or the other. *Mammon* (v24): the Aramaic word for property, hence material prosperity. Christ does not deny the necessities or the amenities of life. If, however, they take priority and are placed in competition with Christ, then values have been clearly misplaced. Goods of this world are to be used to facilitate dedication to God, not to obstruct it.

Christ in the narrative then passes to the question of trust. There is clear recognition of the need in this life to provide for oneself and others (vv32f). The problem arises when needs take on such importance as to lead to anxiety and preoccupation. Such an occurrence evidences a lack of faith (v30).

The two teachings of Jesus are linked by *therefore* (Gr: *dia touto;* v25). This inter-connectedness is important. If God is first, then other concerns, while admittedly present, have at best a secondary importance. When preoccupation and worry come to the fore, the real sense of God's providence is lost. Christ counsels against worry regarding life, food, and clothing (v25). He allays anxiety in these matters with three arguments. First, life itself is a gift over which the recipient had no control, nor can he add any time to his fixed destiny (vv25, 27). Second, nature is well provided for by a provident God. Birds (v26) and flowers (v28) are prime examples. Men work assiduously in the field, and women in the home (v29), and they have no advantage over the "non-working" flora and fauna. Finally, if God so provides for all the forms of nature, it is logical to conclude that he will direct special concern to his human children (v30; Ps 145:15).

People riddled with anxiety are to be found among non-believers (v32). Christians must be different. Faith is to be active in trust, otherwise it has little meaning. *Kingdom of God and his righteousness* (v33): One is to seek the full establishment of God's reign and his plan of salvation for the world. Righteousness here is related to Yahweh's covenant fidelity, not the human observance of his commands.

Finally, to make the future a cause of anxiety is only to carry a further burden (v34). Future cares will be there when the time comes; for the present, those of today (spoken of as "evil") are quite enough.

These words of the gospel are not meant to discourage the patient and struggling wage earner, nor, on the other hand, to encourage indolence. It is solely a question of priorities. Jesus' figurative language is not to be lifted out of context. It is basically a summons to place our trust in a provident God, and that is to have first place. All other considerations, as justified as they may be, must be secondary.

Reasonable concern about providing for our needs is not excluded by today's scripture. Anxiety is. The basic question is always present: Is God first in our life or not? If he is, then as we make the journey, we are confident that he walks with us. The fact is that trust does work. There are countless cases in our personal experience where people have stepped out in faith and have not been disappointed. They cannot explain how needs were met and bills were paid. Great religious leaders of the past and present have seen a genuine need and with very limited resources have pursued a vision. And yet, it seems that we have reluctance to take such a step, even in God's interest, unless all sorts of safeguards are in place. And even then we are afraid of failure. Today's scripture is speaking to the latter state of mind.

It is so refreshing to read Paul when we tend to lose sight of the forest for the trees. In the church we spend a great deal of time and energy on institutional concerns. This can lead to an absorption in those things which make the body politic function. At times we are all too human in categorizing people and in judging motives. If Corinth had its "camps" and "heroes," we fare no better. And yet the only reason the church has to exist is to be at the service of the word: to proclaim it, to explain it, to promote it. Do we ever reflect on how our conduct as Christians may inhibit the spread of the word? Do we see our divisions as immensely painful? As a counter-witness? We are servants and stew-

ards–all of us, wherever we are in the church. We all stand under the judgment of the word. There is no right to judge. One is our judge. We hope that at his coming we will be found worthy servants.

Homiletic and Catechetical Helps

1. God as Father and Mother.

2. God and mammon: competing forces in our life.

3. The difference between concern and anxiety.

4. Seeking first the reign of God.

5. Servants and stewards: the meaning of ministry.

6. The meaning and role of the diaconate.

7. God's judgment and rash judgment.

8. The meaning of prayer before meals.

EIGHTH SUNDAY OF THE YEAR
Year B

Readings

> Hos 2:16 - 17, 21 - 22
> 2 Cor 3:1 - 6
> Mk 2:18 - 22

Theme: New Wineskins: Living with Change

The early church struggled to determine its relationship with Judaism and its laws and customs. In today's gospel the church found Jesus offering a solution to some of its vexing problems. New times require new measures.

A wedding is not an occasion for fasting. Just as Hosea saw the Yahweh-Israel relationship as a marriage, so Jesus views the new dispensation. In today's second reading Paul employs another one of his metaphors. The Corinthian community, which he founded, is his letter of recommendation, validating his credentials. He, too, speaks of the new covenant of the Spirit which supplants the covenant of the past.

First Reading

Hosea, the eighth century prophet of the northern kingdom, speaks of the covenant bond in marriage terms. It would seem that his own marriage to Gomer (c. 1) had an unhappy ending. The tragedy of his married life colors his prophetic sentiments, giving rise to some of prophetic literature's most touching chapters.

In today's reading Hosea employs the bride-groom figure in speaking of Yahweh's efforts to stem Israel's infidelity. The period of the exodus desert experience remains for Hosea an almost idyllic moment of Israel's fidelity. To experience a true conversion, she must again be led to the desert (v16) where, alone and separated from distraction, she will again hear the voice of her spouse. In being made conscious of her wrong-doing, Israel will turn attentively to Yahweh, in a spirit reminiscent of her forty year desert sojourn (v17; Jer 2:2 - 6).

The renewal of the covenant with the converted Israel continues the marriage imagery (vv21f). The espousal is rich in its use of an important theological vocabulary. The groom brings his dowry ("espouse you in...") in furnishing the qualities which will give the marriage its lasting character. It will be permanent and indissoluble (forever). The bride will be gifted with right (Heb: *sedeq*) and justice (Heb: *mishpat*), qualities which describe upright and correct conduct in human relations; love (Heb: *hesed*) and mercy (Heb: *rahamim*), qualities of covenant faithfulness and compassion; fidelity (Heb: *emunah*), a firmness and stability endowing the covenant with permanence.

Know the Lord (v22): This is an experiential, not cerebral, knowledge—a relationship with God which is deeply personal, the experience of a guiding presence reinforcing the virtues outlined above.

This Hosea passage is significant for the emphasis placed on

Yahweh's initiative. He renews the covenant and brings to it for Israel's benefit the ingredients to make it lasting.

Responsorial Psalm   Ps 103

The idea of Yahweh's compassion and care for his people, expressed clearly in today's first reading, continues in this hymn of praise. Hosea's Yahweh as husband here becomes the Lord as father (v13). The Lord is praised for what is evidently the psalmist's recovery from a serious illness. The connection between sin and sickness (v3) is a frequent biblical theme in both Testaments. With no after-life sanctions, Israel for most of its history saw divine retribution for sin on this side of the grave, mainly in sickness and misfortune (Job; Ps 32:3ff). Thus, the lifting of sin and sickness would signify full forgiveness. *From the pit* (Heb: *sheol*) (v4): Sheol is the shadowy realm of the dead. In being cured, the psalmist is saved from consignment to the underworld in death. Belief in Yahweh's covenant fidelity and mercy, matched by his forbearance, is substantially the same as that expressed in the Moses-Yahweh dialogue in Exodus (34:7). This is illustrated in his clemency (v10), his complete forgiveness (v12), and his fatherly understanding (v13).

Second Reading

In line with today's general theme, Paul sees himself as the minister of a new covenant which supplants the old (v6). The interwoven image of the "letter" is combined in different forms. Letters of recommendation were generally presented by itinerant preachers to legitimate their mission. There are occasional New Testament references to letters of accreditation (Acts 9:2; 18:27). Whether or not Paul had been questioned on this is a matter of speculation. What he does in this passage is exempt himself from any need for letters of this kind, whether to or from the communities he had evangelized (v1).

In the first place, the Corinthians themselves serve as Paul's letter of recommendation (v2). As a Christian community, founded and loved by Paul, they represent the finest commendation that Paul could have, visible for all to see. They are, moreover, a letter from Christ, for whom Paul serves as a "scrib-al" servant, with their lives themselves being the message of Christ's saving action. A certain ambiguity arises at this point (v3), with the "letter" fluctuating between being written on their hearts and they themselves being the letter. At any rate, the message, which the Corinthians now become, is that of the new covenant. It posits a new and deeply internal bond with God (Jer 31:33; Ez 11:19; 36:26f), unlike the former covenant written on stone tablets (Ex 24:12), which proved ineffectual and has passed away. The community, in accepting and living the message of Christ, becomes his letter to the world.

Finally Paul returns to the question of his credentials (vv4ff). His certification comes from God alone. His confidence is root-ed in his call from God through Christ. He is a minister of that new covenant, spoken of previously, which gives life in the Spirit and is not simply codified law, powerless to save and ulti-mately leading to death.

Third Reading

This pronouncement story (vv18f) with the accompanying logia of Jesus (vv20ff) is found together with a number of such stories in Mark's gospel which illustrate the growing conflict between Jesus and the Jewish authorities (c. 2). The question presented to Jesus concerns the disciples of John the Baptist and the practice of the Pharisees. While the Jews were required to fast only on the day of atonement (Lev 16:24), the Pharisees had added their own weekly fast days, as, no doubt, had the dis-ciples of the ascetical Baptist.

Jesus' disciples are exempt from fasting on the basis of the eschatological nuptials (v19). As was seen in today's first read-ing, the use of the marriage metaphor for the bond between God and his people was not uncommon (Is 54:3 - 6; Jer 2:2; Ez 16); here the meaning is clearly directed toward the messianic era. Jesus is identified as the groom (v19), a role formerly held only by Yahweh, hence a recognition of Jesus' singular status. During the time that Jesus is present in his earthly ministry, fasting is inappropriate. The reference to Jesus' eventual depar-ture (v20) is evidently a later addition made by the church, adding a parenthesis to the pronouncement story and dulling the main point of the narrative. It is a clear allusion to Jesus' death and the fasting practices of the early church.

Further parabolic teaching sheds light on the question (vv21f). The laws and practices of the past are not appropriate at the time of a new covenant with its own character and suitable forms. This question of Jewish practice and law was not immediately solved in the primitive church. The teaching here reflects the tensions between the new and the old. The new cloth attached to an old garment will in its shrinking with the first wash tear away, just as the old and worn wineskins will burst under the pressure of new fermenting wine. Mixing the old and the new is destined to fail. A new Spirit-guided covenant will have its own forms of expression. They cannot be pre-determined by practices of a former time.

The account, like most of the conflict pronouncement stories, underscores the radically new nature of Christianity and the accompanying change of outlook which it engendered.

For some people change is admissible in every area of life except religion. Various reasons might explain it. In a sea of change in life, it is felt that religion should be a rock of stability. In addition, people grew up with the idea of the church being as changeless as God. Vatican II altered much of that. But it did not take long for attitudes of retrenchment to come after the first decades of enthusiasm. There was once again a call for stability and order.

Yet Christianity was such a radical departure in its origins. Jesus' life was spent in dealing with opponents of change. While continuity with Judaism may be clearer after two millennia, it was a wrenching institutional rupture when the church began. Christ did not come with a religion of laws. He came with a vital new Spirit. It did not take long to see that the two did not match.

New wine calls for new skins. New times require new methods. Diverse cultures require adaptation. The basic tenets of faith remain but many things do not fall under that mantle. It takes courage to move. Institutions tend to resist change. But it is the promotion of the gospel that Paul keeps reminding us is central. That requires adaptation and creativity. It only comes about when we allow and even encourage change. That means a willingness to let go in order to redis-

cover. In that regard the church of the first century had struggles far greater than ours. And it survived.

Homiletic and Catechetical Helps

1. Marriage as a biblical symbol.

2. The goods of marriage: spiritual, psychological, physical.

3. Fast and abstinence: its application today.

4. Ways to practice mortification.

5. The basic difference between the two covenants.

6. Psychological attitudes toward change.

7. The limits of change in the church.

8. Ministry in the church: mutual enrichment.

EIGHTH SUNDAY OF THE YEAR
Year C

Readings

> Sir 27:4 - 7
> 1 Cor 15:54 - 58
> Lk 6:39 - 45

Theme: Word and Deed: A Window on the Soul

Words and deeds figure prominently in today's readings, with the first reading placing special emphasis on words. Sirach sees speech as the real test of a person's mettle. In the gospel Jesus sees words and actions as reflective of inner dispositions. Both readings point to the fact that our words and actions say a great deal about who we are. In 1 Corinthians, Paul looks forward to the time of resurrection when death, sin, and the law will be definitively vanquished and victory will be obtained.

First Reading

The main point of the four proverbs from Sirach is that speech is a sure key to character. *Sieve is shaken* (v4): Shaking the sieve sort reveals any gross or coarse elements. Speech acts like the sieve in revealing a person's defects. The furnace (v5) serves a similar function. The worth of an object appears when it is fired in the kiln. Flaws in the material become evident at once. The same thing happens in the "kiln" of conversation.

The fruit of a tree evidences the extent to which the tree has been pruned and cultivated. So, too, speech points to the type of formation received (v6). Jesus builds on this image in the gospels (Mt 7:20). In silence nothing is known; the impression is neutral. When conversation begins, strengths and weaknesses emerge (v7).

Responsorial Psalm   Ps 92

The hymn encourages the use of speech to give praise to the Lord. Yahweh is to be acclaimed throughout the day for his love (Heb: *hesed*) and faithfulness (Heb: *emunah*), covenant terminology underscoring Yahweh's attachment, constancy, and fidelity (vv2f). In contrast to the lot of the wicked, described in another part of the psalm (vv8 - 12), the just are destined to flourish like sturdy trees, similar to those planted in the temple area (vv13f; Ps 1:3; 52:10). Well rooted and nurtured in faith, the just grow stronger and more fruitful like the mighty Lebanon cedars to the north. Temple worship will remain an integral part of their rootedness in faith.

Second Reading

This conclusion to the Pauline teaching on resurrection trumpets the victory to be attained by Christ's followers. In combining two texts from the prophets (Is 25:8; Hos 13:14), he carries them beyond their original meaning. Paul sees them as being fully understood only in Christ.

The transformation of "flesh and blood" (15:50) will be complete in the resurrected body, no longer containing any vestige or seeds of corruption. Death will lose its meaning completely (v54). Sin, death, and the law—three important players in the Pauline drama of salvation—will all recede. Death here is both physical and spiritual. Physical death, as a consequence of sin, simply puts the seal of finality on that separation from God, which is spiritual death. It is this total death which has been overcome by Christ. The resurrection is the clear indication of this final triumph, leading to a full life with God.

Death, like a preying viper, has its sting which is sin. It is this venom of sin which destroys life and leads to final death (v56; Rom 7:20f). The law allies itself with sin in making transgressions possible by specifying evil (v56; Rom 7:7f, 13). Christ in his victory turns aside definitively the three opponents: death, sin, and law, all of which are inter-connected. This is the gift of redemption originating in God and brought about through his Son (v57)

Any thought of parousia thinking being identified with Christian passivity is excluded by Paul's conclusion (v58). He exhorts the Corinthians to spend their lives in dedicated service and selfless labor. They stand in the firm conviction that victory is theirs. Paul encourages that steadfastness once again with which he opened his resurrection discourse (15:2).

Third Reading

In the Lucan context, Jesus has been speaking to the disciples and to the crowd about love of enemies (6:27f, 32, 35) and sharing one's goods, especially with the poor (6:29f, 34f, 38). Thus, the parables in today's gospel should be seen as having a particular application against that background rather than expressing generic principles. The parables are four: enlightened leadership (v39), formed discipleship (v40), hypocrisy in correcting others (vv41f), and bringing faith to action (vv43f). The final logion which sees speech as an expression of the heart illustrates the preceding parable on actions flowing from internal values. It is also related thematically to the first reading.

Those who are called to leadership in the community must themselves have a truly enlightened conscience (v39). If they lack understanding of the faith or the conviction to implement it, they will only be an obstacle to others (Mt 15:14; 23:16f, 24).

The disciple always has a subordinate role. Christians must avoid a judgmental attitude which leads from an awareness of others' faults to a desire to correct them, while overlooking one's own, often greater transgressions (vv41f). *Hypocrite* (v42): This harsh expression, usually reserved for the scribes and Pharisees, is here directed to Christians who sanctimoniously find fault with others and neglect their own (Mt 7:1 - 4). Finally actions as well as words reveal a true inner spirit (vv43ff). The use of the tree as a point of comparison appears elsewhere in Jesus' teaching (13:6ff; 21:29 - 32). A living faith finds expression in deeds, such as the forgiveness and charity emphasized in the Lucan context. By the same token, sin is not rootless or inexplicable. It proceeds from a spirit prone to evil. Options in favor of good or evil are not instantaneous; they are the product of a posture or bent in one direction or the other which in time tends to strengthen or weaken the human will when faced with moral choices. Finally, human speech is reflective of an inner faithful or faithless spirit.

Our words and deeds are a true index of character. Agere sequitur esse. *Action flows from what we are. As our lives and thinking are fashioned, we will act. Crime is not overcome by arrest and incarceration but by formation in values. The home, as the most formative element in our lives, will always retain its primary importance. We can expect the disintegration of moral and social values when parents abdicate their responsibility for formation.*

Speech is one of our most powerful tools for good or ill. We hardly realize all that it discloses. To experience the tragic loss of speech through illness, with all its attendant frustrations, makes us aware of how vital this avenue of communication is. God chose to reveal himself through human language. Jesus taught in words, and that teaching was captured by writers in word. The scriptural languages–Hebrew, Aramaic, and Greek–are the language of God. St. Thérèse of Lisieux regretted deeply that she could not read them. Jesus himself, God's Word, is the incarnate language of God. Speech is essentially revelatory. It is a window on the soul. It can reveal courage, honesty, gentleness, and thoughtfulness, or it can reveal cowardice, duplicity, irreverence, lust, and deception. A physically unimpressive person after a ten minute conversation becomes an inspiration. Contrariwise, a very striking and attractive person reveals in the same length of time that looks are everything. Our words and deeds can lead others astray, or they can elevate the human spirit. That is no small responsibility.

Homiletic and Catechetical Helps

1. The proper use of speech: worship, honesty, respect, charity.

2. The improper use of speech: deception, blasphemy, seduction, slander, uncharitableness.

3. Faith expressed in word and deed.

4. The responsibility of the teacher: modeling values.

5. The responsibility of the student: learning to live.

6. The meaning of hypocrisy.

7. Home and family in building character.

6. Resurrection: the end of sin, death, and law.

NINTH SUNDAY OF THE YEAR
Year A

Readings

> Deut 11:18, 26 - 28
> Rom 3:21 - 25, 28
> Mt 7:21 - 27

Theme: Hearing, Speaking, and Doing

Solemn conventions in antiquity were concluded by invoking the deities to bless observance of the agreement and to curse its disregard. Deuteronomy uses this classic formula in invoking sanctions in conjunction with the Sinai covenant. This antithetical mode of teaching appears as well in today's gospel. Those who put Jesus' words into practice and those who do not will suffer the respective consequences. Today's liturgy begins a series of consecutive Sunday readings from Paul's important letter to the Romans. Justification, he tells us today, is a gift of God, made possible through Christ's death and received through faith, not law observance.

First Reading

The curses and blessings which concluded treaties or formal agreements in the ancient near east have become part of modern archeology's contribution to a better understanding of the Bible. They came at the conclusion of the treaty after the terms were agreed upon and recorded and were important as sanctions protecting the accord. Curses and blessings had an irrevocable character with their own inherent force; once spoken, they ran their own course. This is well illustrated in the story of Isaac's blessings for Jacob and Esau (Gen 27).

Today's passage begins with Moses' injunction to take to heart the norms of the covenant, which are recorded in Deuteronomy. The seriousness with which they are to be taken is stressed by the idea of the words being bound to the wrist and forehead (v18). Initially this was probably meant in a figurative sense (Ex 13:9, 16). In the course of time, however, it was taken literally and scripture texts in small boxes or phylacteries were attached to the wrist and forehead at the times of prayer (Mt 23:5). Contained therein were the words of the Shema, Israel's most sacred prayer (Deut 6:8).

The actual content of the curses and blessings (v26) appears later in Deuteronomy (28:2 - 45). The blessings lead to life, i.e. offspring, livestock, productive soil, and peace—all blessings of a very concrete nature. The curses, on the contrary, brought famine, drought, sterility and sickness, war and exile. The blessings come as a result of fidelity to the Lord's commands (v27); curses result from the disregard for those commands, especially in going after other gods (v28).

The dichotomous character of curses and blessings excludes any middle ground between fidelity and infidelity. This polarized form of expression recurs frequently in Hebrew ethics (Ps

1) in presenting two divergent ways of life, the one leading to happiness, the other to despair.

Responsorial Psalm   Ps 31

The "rock" image so prominent in today's liturgy appears also in this lament as applied to Yahweh (vv3, 4). Despite the psalmist's deep distress, he is confident of the Lord's protection and covenant fidelity (vv2, 17). *Face shine* (v17): an expression like "God smiles on us," an anthropomorphic expression for God's favor (Num 6:24ff). In view of God's pledged concern and the psalmist's assurance of his constancy, a final plea is made for courage and perseverance (v25).

Second Reading

Paul here outlines the process of justification in showing the role of God, Christ, and the believer. It has been suggested that the somewhat awkward construction of the passage may be due to the use of a pre-Pauline statement of belief which Paul has edited.

The Action of God: In this moment of the eschatological "now" (v21; 3:26; 5:9, 11), God's righteousness (Gr: *dikaiosyne*) has been made visible. The word refers to God's own fidelity to his promise and himself in acquitting humanity of its sin through a benevolent judgment (1:16f). Even though the Hebrew scriptures (law and prophets) gave ample assurance of this definitive act of God in history (Acts 10:43; Lk 24:44), justification has become a reality apart from the Jewish law (v21). Sanctification has been given freely and without cost (v24) and therefore can never be acquired by works. In this way God's justice (fidelity, uprightness) is established with redemption extended to all people in the removal of all sins of a past era (v24).

The Action of Jesus: God's justice in acquittal is made visible and concrete through the atoning death of his Son (v24f). Justification or correctness before God occurs through redemption (Gr: *apolytrosis*), the act of buying back a slave or captive from bondage. Redemption in Paul refers to Christ's "buying back" an alienated sinful people. Christ is, moreover, our expiation (v25), literally, our mercy seat (Gr: *hilasterion*). The mercy seat was located in the temple's holy of holies before which expiation was made for sin on the day of atonement (Lev 16:2, 11 - 17). As the instrument of definitive atonement, Jesus becomes the new "mercy seat." This is done through his death on the cross ("by his blood," v25), here clearly presented as an atoning death.

The Action of the Believer: All people were in a state of separation from God because of sin (v23). There was nothing they could do to overcome their alienated condition. Here the Christian life is described as a sharing in God's glory through life in the Spirit (2 Cor 3:18; 4:6); without redemption it remained unattainable. In the "now," however, humanity may appropriate God's action in Jesus through faith in the Son of God who has accomplished this on their behalf (v22). It is this faith in Christ as Savior, and it alone, which results in uprightness before God in the Spirit life. The works of the law have no role to play at all (v28; Gal 2:16).

Third Reading

Two teachings of Jesus treat of those who speak the words of faith but fail to act upon them (vv21ff) and those who hear God's words but fail to do anything about it (vv24ff). They conclude the sermon on the mount, with the same type of antithetical sanctions found in the covenant's curses and blessings.

Charismatic enthusiasts were a part of the early church's life. Paul endorses the charisms while fully aware of their dangers, with his emphasis on love as the greatest gift (1 Cor 12 - 14). The Matthean Jesus addresses members of the Christian community who share diverse charisms—prophecy, ecstatic prayer, exorcism, miracles—but whose lives are not in conformity with their belief (vv21f; Lk 6:46). The teaching is important for the distinction it makes between spiritual gifts and the life in the Spirit. The former can be present without the latter. In fact, the conduct of some charismatics was undoubtedly corrupt to merit these harsh words of condemnation (v23)

The final parable is a classic example of antithetical parallelism. *Words of mine* (v24): a reference to the teaching of the preceding sermon on the mount (cc. 5 - 7). Jesus addresses two distinct categories: those who hear the word and act upon it (literally: "does them"; Gr: *poieo*) (vv24f) and those who listen but fail to act (vv26f). The former course of action leads to salvation; the latter, to destruction. In the Lucan account of the same parable, faith is likened to a house built with a solid foundation which withstands flood waters when they arise (Lk 6:47ff). Matthew compares the faith to an edifice built upon rock, much like the church (16:18), which remains firm in the face of rain, flood and storm. Both teachings are geared toward the expected parousia with its accompanying reward and punishment.

What the house built on solid rock looks like in fact is illustrated in other parables of Jesus, e.g. the sower and the seed (13:18 - 23). The story is illustrative of the fact that the church of the present world is made up of the good and the bad (13:24 - 30); it is not an invisible church of the elect alone. Faith is seen as vibrant and growing, expressing itself in the ethic which Jesus has proposed in his extended discourse to the disciples (cc. 5 - 7).

Paul's justification through faith has not avoided the pitfalls of history. The distinction between faith and works was one of the major points of contention at the time of the reformation. That hurdle seems to be safely behind us. The official conversations between Lutherans and Roman Catholics since the Second Vatican Council have found essential agreement on this issue. Redemption can never be merited. We can never attain it through works of our own. It is totally gift. Once justification takes place, however, there is nothing in Paul that would suggest that it is not brought to life in good works. That now seems clear to everyone. But it took four hundred years to put that "chestnut" to rest. Paul is undoubtedly pleased to know that he is no longer an obstacle to church unity.

In fact, Jesus' teaching on faith without works emerges clearly in today's liturgy. It is not enough to say "I believe" or "I pray" or "I am involved in ministry." Faith goes a lot deeper. There is a real inconsistency in belonging to a prayer group and exempting oneself from social concerns. Faith does the worthwhile things mentioned above. But it also loves enemies, seeks forgiveness, cares for disabled persons, is concerned with the homeless. True believers examine their conscience with the sermon on the mount as the basis. Today's scripture reminds us that it is not meant to be an easy life. The comfortable pew is not the answer. It is a question of bringing Christ to the struggles of humanity. That is the cost of discipleship.

Homiletic and Catechetical Helps

1. Understanding justification through faith.

2. Results of the Lutheran-Roman Catholic dialogue.

3. The difference between God's justice and our justice.

4. Faith: personal examples of saying but not doing.

5. Faith: personal examples of hearing but not doing.

6. Practical ways to bring faith to life and action.

NINTH SUNDAY OF THE YEAR
Year B

Readings

> Deut 5:12 - 15
> 2 Cor 4:6 - 11
> Mk 2:23 - 3:6

Theme: The Spirit and the Letter

Jewish law tended not only to become more detailed; it became absolutized as well. The sabbath law, for example, in today's reading from Deuteronomy, called for the recognition of Yahweh as Israel's true provider. But it became much more in the course of time, and Jesus, in today's gospel, noted that observance of the letter was killing the sabbath's true spirit. Paul today speaks of our dying to self in order that the life of God may emerge more clearly in our lives.

First Reading

The decalogue (ten commandments) is found in Deuteronomy and Exodus (20:7 - 17), where in the latter it forms part of the covenant law code. The sabbath has no exact parallel outside the Bible; it seems to be a distinctly Israelite practice. One day each week was given over to rest and the ordinary work of the other days was foregone (vv12ff). Both presentations of the decalogue relate the sabbath observance to some point of the scriptural tradition. In Deuteronomy this is the experience of slavery which was part of Israel's past (v15). The sabbath is here given humanitarian motivation, looking especially to the well-being of the land owner's slaves (v13). In Exodus (20:11) the motivation is inspired by Yahweh's rest after the six days of creation in the Priestly narrative (Gen 1).

Attention is directed to the beneficiaries of the observance: members of the family, slaves, livestock, and the resident non-Israelite (in that order). Resident aliens were treated with respect (Ex 23:9) but were never accorded the rights of the Israelite population. Rest is suitable for humans and animals alike (Ex 23:12). A period of "rest" was also to be accorded the land, vineyards, and groves every seventh year (Ex 23:10f), during which time the poor and the livestock could roam freely and avail themselves of what grew from unplowed and uncultivated land.

Responsorial Psalm   Ps 81

A pilgrimage hymn, probably connected with the fall harvest at the time of the feast of Booths, with its emphasis on observance of the Lord's precepts (vv5, 9f), ties in with today's theme. The feast is inaugurated on the new moon (v4; Num 29:6) with trumpet accompaniment (Lev 23:24). The precept of observance is connected with the exodus (vv5f).

A temple official speaks an oracle (vv7 - 11) which recalls events from the exodus. The basket (v7): a reference to the containers used to carry the clay for bricks during the time of Egyptian slavery. It was during the time of oppression that Yahweh's deliverance was experienced. Again referring to the time of the covenant, the oracle recalls the precept on the exclusive recognition and worship of Yahweh as their God (vv10f); Ex 20:2f).

Second Reading

This impressive passage highlights the activity of the risen Christ in the sufferings and trials of Paul. In citing the Genesis creation of light (1:3), Paul returns to the idea of the light that shone in the face of Moses (3:7 - 18) as being inferior to the light of God's glory now shining in the face of Christ (v6). In thus contrasting the two covenants, Paul points to the presence of Christ in the Christian heart as an experience (knowledge) of the glory of God. In other words, through the Spirit God imparts knowledge of himself by the revelatory presence of his Son in the human heart.

Union with Christ in Paul's thought is a twofold experience. Christ is known in the power of his resurrection and in the sharing of his sufferings (Phil 3:9f). The two are complementary. It is in the weakness of human suffering in union with the dying Christ that the emergence of the resurrected Christ, the power of God, is made possible. God's power becomes visible in the powerless human form. It is this idea that Paul develops here.

Earthen vessels (v7): the human person, fragile and disposable, in whom any accomplishment becomes revelatory of God's power. Results are clearly not due to the human agent (3:5; 13:4). Paul illustrates his point in a series of antitheses (vv8f). Repeatedly forced to the edge, the apostles do not succumb. Their survival and hope are the "bright side" of Christ's presence in them, his power at work. The dying of Christ is present in their tribulations. Hence, Paul's entire apostolic experience is rooted in the dying and rising Christ; his sufferings unite him with the death, his survival (salvation) with the resurrection. All of this is endured for Christ and with him to be part of his victory (v11).

Third Reading

By the time of Jesus, the sabbath observance was so detailed as to exclude almost any form of human exertion. The two narratives of today's gospel, which form part of the conflict-pronouncement series in Mark (2:1 - 3:16), deal with the sabbath question.

In the first account (vv23 - 28), Jesus' disciples are stripping grain on the sabbath to satisfy their hunger. Since this was seen as a form of harvesting, it was prohibited on the day of rest (Ex 34:21). Whether, in addition, the disciples had exceeded the prescribed limits of walking is not mentioned. Jesus justifies his disciples' action on the basis of a biblical precedent, the high priest's sharing the sanctuary's sacred bread with David's hungry soldiers (vv25f; 1 Sam 21:2 - 7). The priest is identified in the Samuel story as Ahimelech, the father of Abiathar; Mark identifies him as Abiathar. The parallel lies in exemption from a religious law on the basis of human need. The argumentation is rabbinic, sparring with one's opponent through appeal to the scriptures for support.

Jesus' final statement is strong in seeing the original law with its humanitarian purpose inverted by the imposition of burdens on people by Pharisaic legalism (v27). The statement is omitted by Matthew (12:1 - 8) and Luke (6:1 - 5), probably because it was too controversial. The concluding logion, with its third person reference, is an early church addition; it clearly recognizes Christ's divine authority in according him authority over the sabbath law (v28).

In the account of the cure (3:1 - 5), the pronouncement of Jesus is situated within the context of a miracle story. The same occurs in the first story of the series, the healing of the paralytic (2:1 - 12). The miracle story form is present: description of the illness (v1), the action of Jesus (vv3, 5a), and the account of results (vv5b, 7). The pronouncement is inserted into the narrative (v4).

The Pharisees want to see if Jesus will cure on the sabbath, something forbidden by their law except in danger of death. Jesus raises the discussion to a different level in presenting his opponents with a broader dilemma (v4). In a choice between good and evil on the sabbath, the response would have to be in favor of good. The argument as stated allows for no tertium quid, i.e. to do nothing. Jesus affirms that the performance of an act of mercy is wholly consistent with the sabbath precept, transcending the limits imposed by any law. The spirit takes precedence over the letter. The account also points to Jesus' authority over any law. As a logical climax to this unit of pre-Marcan conflict stories, although too early in the gospel itself, Jesus' opponents make plans to kill him (v6).

Jesus met a great deal of legalism in his day and dealt with it directly. Many would argue that our problem today is not so much legalism as laxism. It is not a question of observing Sunday too exactly but of observing it at all. The word "obligation" seems to have become anathema in some quarters. There is something to the argument, and to the extent that it is true, it is regrettable. But Jesus here is not turning his back on reasonable precepts. His problem is with that type of religion which becomes so taken up with law that the real meaning of faith is lost. All too often people will define their relationship to God in terms of observance. The means becomes an end. For example, people with perfectly valid excusing cause, even involving a work of charity, still believe that they sin in not attending mass. And they are people who never neglect worship. Examples could be multiplied. It is so important to understand the reason behind the law—and for lawmakers to keep law to a minimum.

The real meaning of religious experience calls us repeatedly to those great Pauline images. No precept will ever substitute for looking on God's glory in the face of Jesus. Christ is our window on God. To live in that light is at the heart of what we are. And when we do, the law is always fulfilled—spontaneously, willingly. Can we see our sufferings in the service of God as part of Christ's dying? Can we see our weakness as a gain? What is our experience of God during prayer? These are reflections that require time.

Prayer time is quality time. Without reflection we never know that Christ whom Paul knew. And so we end up observing rules. Good, but too little.

Homiletic and Catechetical Helps

1. The Sunday observance: its meaning in our life.

2. The difference between the Jewish sabbath and the Christian Sunday.

3. Sunday and a sense of community.

4. The meaning of Sunday rest.

5. Examples of a legalistic spirit in religion.

7. The spirit over the letter: examples.

8. Charity as the first law.

9. Understanding life in Christ: dying and rising.

10. Our understanding of weakness.

NINTH SUNDAY OF THE YEAR
Year C

Readings

1 Kgs 8:41 - 43
Gal 1:1 - 2, 6 - 10
Lk 7:1 - 10

Theme: Stranger in God's House

In the reading from 1 Kings, Solomon envisions a day when foreigners will visit the newly constructed temple. The pagan centurion in Luke approaches Jesus, the new temple of God, with a faith superior to any Jesus had encountered among his own people. Paul tells the Galatians that there is only one authentic gospel, the one which he had received from God and preached to them; any other, as the one being promoted among them, is simply counterfeit.

First Reading

The deuteronomic editors who are responsible for the books of Samuel and Kings have shaded this prayer of Solomon in their own exilic and post-exilic hues. This chapter in 1 Kings describes the solemn dedication of the Solomonic temple (8:1 - 21) and presents the prayer of the king which followed (8:22 - 66). Among the intentions for which the king prays is the spiritual well-being of the foreigner. The day will come when

Yahweh's deliverance of his people at the time of the exodus will become known among peoples who do not share Israel's faith (vv41f). With an incipient belief, the foreigner will come as a worshiper. Solomon requests the granting of the foreigner's petition for reasons which are both apologetic and astute (v43). It will lead to the honoring of Yahweh's name and the politically agreeable recognition of the impressive temple.

The universalism of the passage is relative. It does not speak of the nations but of certain Gentile proselytes. There is no notion of Israel actively sharing its faith; the initiative comes wholly from the foreigners. This seems to reflect the early post-exilic period when this phenomenon was occurring in Israel.

Responsorial Psalm   Ps 117

Universalism is the dominant note of this hymn, the psalter's shortest psalm. All the people of the earth are called upon to acclaim the Lord. In the typical style of the hymn, the motive is given immediately after the exhortation. This is the recognition of Yahweh's fidelity to his covenant with Israel in manifesting his two major attributes: his love (Heb: *hesed*) and steadfast faithfulness (Heb: *emeth*). The psalm is a succinct summary of Hebrew historical theology.

Second Reading

In this passage taken from the opening of Paul's letter to the Galatians, Paul vindicates his apostleship (v1), the singular and unique character of his gospel (vv6 - 9) and his personal integrity (v10).

Apostle (v1): The word is related to the Hebrew word for a fully delegated messenger or agent. In the New Testament it becomes a technical term for one divinely commissioned to preach the gospel. Paul's right to the title of apostle had been questioned since he was not one of the twelve who had been with Jesus during his earthly ministry (Acts 1:21f). His claim to the office rests solely on his being commissioned by Christ and the Father (v1). It is interesting that Paul identifies the source of his calling as God the Father, the one who put a seal on Jesus' mission by raising him from the dead. The call which he received from Christ dates from his conversion on the Damascus road (Acts 9). Here Jesus and God are spoken of in co-equal terms. He is clear that his was not the type of commission received by lesser emissaries in the church (Phil 2:25). Paul is joined by all of his companion Christians (brothers) in sending this letter to Galatia, located in what is now central Turkey.

The blessing which he invokes from Jesus and the Father (again) is for grace and peace (v3). It is the grace of the life-giving Spirit which results in a state of restored harmony or peace between God and humankind.

Paul bypasses the customary note of thanksgiving to manifest his irritation at the conduct of the Galatians. Judaizing Christians in Galatia were urging the integration of parts of the Mosaic law into the Christian message and therefore nullifying the all-sufficient work of Christ (c. 3). Paul finds it incredible that Christians among whom he had preached are so quickly abandoning the authentic gospel which they had earlier received. Their vocation was from God himself, made possible through the saving work of Christ (v6). Deeply incensed, Paul excludes from consideration any other form of "gospel," even if mediated by an angel, a role which Judaism had assigned to angels in God's original giving of the law. There is no other authentic gospel other than the one he had preached in their midst (v7). In verbalizing his decree of condemnation, once repeated (vv8f), Paul sternly upholds his apostolic claim and message.

Finally, Paul recognizes that his reaction and his anger are hardly geared to win him friends (v10). If he wanted to draw human favor in his direction, he would have remained a Jew and continued to persecute the church instead of becoming a slave of Christ. As a slave, he has substituted the yoke of the Mosaic law (5:1) for the sweet yoke of the gospel (Rom 6:22). Paul is emphatic in keeping the lines of his mission and message clean and unequivocal.

Third Reading

The idea of the Gentiles' coming to the truth, found in Solomon's prayer, is well illustrated in Luke's account of the cure of the centurion's servant. The narrative was particularly helpful in legitimating the Gentile mission of the early church. In fact, the story bears a striking resemblance to the account of the conversion of Cornelius, the centurion (Acts 10), with its principal point of showing that God makes no distinction among peoples in his plan of salvation (Acts 10:34f). Today's account of the centurion is found in a more condensed form in Matthew (8:5 - 13).

The centurion (so designated because he was responsible for one hundred soldiers) approaches Jesus through intermediaries. The positive qualities of the man's character emerge in the story's telling. He has been a benefactor of the Jews (v5) and now shows a marked concern for one of his sick domestics (v2). Two delegations approach Jesus; the first, from the Jewish elders (v3), the second, from the man's friends (v4). As Jesus directs his steps toward the centurion's house, the latter, recognizing the legal impurity incurred by a Jew in entering a Gentile home (Acts 10:28), expresses his unworthiness (v7). The Jews had earlier spoken of him as worthy of the favor (v4). The soldier makes an act of faith in Jesus' power: Just as a word suffices for his own orders to be executed, the same must be true of Jesus (v8).

This clear recognition of Jesus' power over death is seen as a full faith affirmation, surpassing anything Jesus had encountered among the Jews (v9). The man's servant is at once restored to health (v10).

The basic miracle story form has here given way to a didactic piece on the Gentile mission, which comes to the fore much more strongly than the healing. The mission of the early church to all people without distinction is seen as fully justified in the words and deeds of Jesus.

There is really nothing about our faith which is esoteric or restricted. There is an incredible openness and all-inclusiveness about the gospel. It was proclaimed so openly and publicly that manipulators in Galatia had no trouble distorting it. There were questions connected with the gospel that had to be settled. But this was done in an open forum. None was more thorny than the relation of the church with the Mosaic law. Convinced that the law could never be imposed on

Gentile converts, Paul struggled for freedom. Nothing could be allowed to compete with the singular work of Christ.

The Gentiles had a worthy and credible spokesperson in Paul. But the impetus to find a place in the church for all people came from Jesus himself. Christianity could not remain an exclusive Jewish sect and remain faithful to the memory of the One who reached out to everyone, even though he never left the confines of Palestine.

Discrimination today is much more subtle, but forms of elitism and separatism are still with us. Perhaps it's part of nature to want to feel somewhat superior. As American Catholics, we have been quite slow in reaching black Americans or the indigenous people of our continent. We grew up thinking that we were the bearers of civilization to a backward people. And then we brought slaves from Africa to make our installation complete. There is a lot of history to be rewritten and reread.

A total equality, even in the church, has been slow in coming. Prejudice today is much more subtle and therefore more difficult to uproot. Listen to today's scripture. A multi-colored, multi-ethnic, multi-national church is not an option, or a matter of largess. It is a gospel mandate. And it means total equality–in theory and in fact. We can't wait for the centurion to come to us. We have to find him–to share life and faith. We may be surprised to find more faith there than "elsewhere in Israel."

Homiletic and Catechetical Helps

1. Vatican II and the world religions.

2. Discriminatory attitudes in our experience.

3. Recognizing the positive in other faiths and cultures.

4. Belief in God's power over death.

5. Maintaining the gospel's integrity.

6. Deepening our faith: importance of theology.

7. Definition of an apostle.

8. Meaning of the church as apostolic.

9. Responsibility of the catechist and teacher.

10. Pleasing humans instead of God.

FIRST SUNDAY OF LENT
Year A

Readings

> Gen 2:7 - 9; 3:1 - 7
> Rom 5:12 - 19
> Mt 4:1 - 11

Theme: Overcoming Evil

Lent reminds us of many things. It recalls our baptism, the beginning of God's life in us. We think of this especially as we follow the journey of our catechumens toward their baptism at Easter. Lent also reminds us of sin and our own weaknesses. It leads us to a greater dependence on Christ as we move toward holy week. And finally we are reminded of the need for penance in our life, to die more to self and to live more for God. All of these ideas are present in today's readings. The Genesis story introduces sin on the world stage; it is the beginning of our undoing. Paul then reminds us that what Adam "undid," Christ has "redone"—and more so. The gospel tells us that the same Christ in his human weakness was tempted as we are. He was drawn to follow Adam, but he did not. In his classical triptych of Christ and the devil, Matthew teaches us all how to overcome evil.

First Reading

In the "twilight zone" of human origins, as distant and misty to the eyes of the Yahwist editor as it is to modern anthropologists, there is situated the account of the beginnings of sin. There is no pretense at historical accuracy here. Such is well beyond the author's intent and hardly necessary for the main point he wishes to make. However it began, sin is a tragedy. In no way part of God's plan; it was humanity's undoing.

In the Yahwist tradition of Genesis cc.2 - 3, God is presented in very human terms. He walks, talks, is pleased, and becomes upset. Today's reading presents him as an artisan. Like a potter, he fashions man (Heb: *adam*) out of earth clay (Heb: *adamah*) and then breathes into his nostrils (v7). The play on words—*adam-adamah:* man-earth—presents this new creature as being directly related to the earth (3:19). He is animated, however, by a breath from God which in turn initiates his own breathing process. Hence a *living being* (v7) is an animated or breathing creature. This life force is not an immortal principle, a soul; if it is withdrawn, humans perish like any other creature (Job 34:14). Immortality in this account will come from other quarters, not the human composite. Adam is a special creature in Genesis not because of an immortal life force but because he is formed directly by God in a way distinct from any other creature.

Yahweh then surrounds man with a garden of beauty. *Eden* (v8): Geographically located in Mesopotamia (vv10 - 14), it is intended to be a mythical land of pleasure. In fact, the probable etymology of the word means a "plain" or "steppe," a place of fertility in a parched desert. There are two trees of note in the garden: one is of primary importance in the narrative; the other takes on significance only when the man and woman are excluded from the garden (3:22f). *The tree of the knowledge of good and evil* (2:9): the two extremes (good and evil) are used to point up the entire spectrum spanning the two. Thus, it is the tree of all knowledge with a strong emphasis on experiential, not solely mental cognition.

As the narrative develops, the serpent (a tempter but not identified as Satan) plays a psychological game in moving the protagonists toward the forbidden fruit. The vast span of forbidden knowledge is made very appealing. The couple are told that they need not fear death regardless of God's prohibition (3:4ff). Death here would mean not only physical death but total separation from God. *Like gods* (v5): in other religions, the pantheon of deities; in Israel, heavenly beings, attendant on Yahweh's court. The two eat of the fruit and immediately experience the shame of nakedness. The sexual motifs in the narrative—the interplay between the couple; the experiential, even sexual implications of knowing "good and evil"; the shame about nakedness—suggest that the narrative may contain a subtle polemic against the sexual fertility worship practiced commonly by the resident Canaanites in early Israelite life.

The fact is, however, that regardless of the influences that produced the story, the author is not informing us about the exact nature of the first sin. He is depicting it in an understandable way for his contemporaries. This in no way detracts from the force of his principal argument: sin was introduced by humans and from it has come a flawed humanity alienated from God.

Responsorial Psalm   Ps 51

As is fitting for the opening of Lent, the celebrated *Miserere* strikes a note of sinfulness and the need for repentance. Its Hebrew title (vv1f) relates it to David's contrition after his sin with Bathsheba. Much of the psalm is, however, much later than David, referring even to the time of Jerusalem's destruction in the sixth century.

The psalmist begins with an ardent plea for forgiveness in four verses of synonymous parallelism, in which he expresses his sinfulness and the need for God's purifying action (vv3 - 6). The cleansing requested is deeply internal; it is a pure heart and a forceful spirit that are needed (v12; Ez 11:19). Once purified, the psalmist will give acknowledging praise to God (v17). The psalm touches on the radical nature of conversion, with the gravity of sin overcome only by the power of God.

Second Reading

The Genesis reading serves as a springboard for Paul's refection on the sin of Adam. In this passage from Romans, he considers the widespread consequences of the initial revolt against God. Death and sin are the patrimony which humanity has inherited and from which there is no escape. Yet, as dire as these negative results have been, they are more than offset by the salvific work of Christ. In fact, we have gained much more than we lost. Paul draws a striking parallel between Adam and Christ.

In this reading, sin, which is personified and spoken of in the singular, represents all sinful activity which has occurred since the beginning. Sin's companion on its earthly journey is death, also personified (vv12 - 14). Sin entered the world through one person but it has been ratified and appropriated by everyone thereafter. It has had a cumulative, "snowball" effect in its head-long descent through history. In this context sin has its own existence as it passes to each generation. Paul does not seem to speak of this as a personally transmitted sin; it looks rather to a sinful ambience coupled with the proclivity of a weakened will. The church has long rooted in these verses its teaching on origi-nal sin.

Inasmuch as all sinned (v12): This is a much discussed and controverted clause. It is best understood as the personal ratifi-cation of that sin introduced with Adam's revolt. People of every age have made it their own through personal sinfulness, as the subsequent verses illustrate. From a theological perspec-tive, there might have been one era which was exempt from the universality of sin's reign (v13). There was no law between Adam and Moses. In the absence of law sin cannot be imputed since no one transgressed a given precept as did Adam (Gen 2:17) or the Jews of the Mosaic and post-Mosaic era. The fact is, however, that sin did exist, even if not labeled, and was accom-panied by death, during the pre-Mosaic period (v14). This pres-ence of death during that early period is incontrovertible proof for Paul of sin's all-prevailing presence.

Paul concludes with the Adam-Christ parallel (vv15 - 19) The gift that comes through Christ far surpasses in its effects the sin of Adam. This is his argument. *Sin* brings judgment and con-demnation, universal in scope; Christ brings the cancellation of the entire debt through the gift of *grace* for the "many" (=all, v18). This means atonement for Adam's sin in addition to the whole body of human sin (v16). *Death* is the second part of Adam's patrimony. For Paul death is both physical, i.e. the nat-ural termination of human life, and spiritual, i.e. a definitive separation from God. Both aspects must be kept in mind to appreciate the restored *life* in Christ (5:21). This life is still future in the text; its present seed is grace and justification.

Finally the root of both chaos and beneficence is the human will. Through the *disobedience* of Adam, all were made sinners, just as through Christ's obedience to the Father's will, redemption is assured and will be shared with "the many" at the time of Christ's return (v19; Heb 5:8f).

Sin, then, for all its dire consequences, is for Paul a *felix culpa*, a happy fault. It provided God with the opening for redemption in his Son, which in its beneficent effects far surpasses the evil for which it is an antidote. It should be noted that Paul's understanding of Adam as an individual would be wholly consonant with the thought of his time and, moreover, lends itself well to his parallelism. It does not mean to address later theological questions on the singular or collective origins of sin.

Third Reading

Matthew and Luke share this threefold temptation narrative taken from the Q source. Mark simply states that Jesus was tempted. The nature of this narrative betrays its intent; it is a type of midrash or theological illustration, presenting in cameo form the type of temptation Jesus experienced repeatedly during his earthly ministry. For Matthew this is viewed against the background of Israel's desert experience at the time of the exodus. Unlike the majority of the events from Jesus' public life, the account here is made up of illustrative examples rather than factual events. One does not think of Jesus as being drawn from desert to temple top and mountain top by the devil nor being placed on a summit from which could be seen "all the kingdoms of the world." The fact is, however, that Jesus was less dramatically tempted during his ministry to provide bread, to perform wonders, and have himself proclaimed king. Usually the disciples or his followers, not the devil, were the provocateurs. The present narrative brings the temptations of Jesus together and expresses them in a condensed triptych form; in Matthew this is placed against the background of Israel's desert experience.

The location in the desert (v1) relates the narrative at once to Israel. *Forty days and forty nights* (v2): this recalls Moses' fast on Sinai (Deut 9:9) and that of Elijah in journeying to Horeb (1 Kgs 19:8). The tempter's reference to Jesus as *Son of God* (v6) goes back to the baptism (3:17) as well as Israel as a type of Jesus (2:15).

The first temptation (vv3ff) appeals to Jesus' hunger. To make stones bread would be to resort to the miraculous rather than await God's will. As in the other temptations, Jesus' response is from Deuteronomy (Deut 8:3), the great testament to Israel's desert experience. It is far more important to hear God's word in submission and patience than to provide pre-emptory solutions. Israel had argued about food (Ex 16:3); Jesus awaits the Lord's word.

In the second temptation (vv5ff), the devil matches Jesus' scriptural bent. Quoting Psalm 91:11, he urges Jesus to presume on God's staying power. Jesus refuses to force God's hand as the Israelites in their anger had done at Massah, the "testing place" (Ex 17:7). Jesus' quote appropriately refers to the biblical event (Deut 6:16).

The final temptation (vv8ff) is reminiscent of Moses on Mount Nebo in its geographical setting. It is an appeal to a sense of power—riches and dominion in exchange for recognition of the evil one. Was not all of this assured to the Messiah anyway (Ps 2:7f)? Idolatry is the allusion here, the sin to which Israel had fallen prey more than once in its history. It was categorically excluded by the law, as Jesus makes clear in his deuteronomic response (Deut 6:13).

Jesus defeats the devil in three key areas of human weakness: the sensual appetite, self-aggrandizement, and the will for power. The new Israel succeeds where the old had failed. And this he does repeatedly, if less notably, in the course of his public ministry.

No one likes to dwell on sin, especially in light of the havoc it has created in our lives. Nonetheless it is salutary to reflect, especially as Lent begins. The Genesis narrative, symbolic as it surely is, still hits a raw nerve. "Being like God" or "playing God" is what so much of life is about today. Modern society holds moral precepts in very low regard. The temptations of Jesus are matched today. Many burn incense at the altar of drugs, sex, and alcohol. Sheer egotism is the motive behind so much that is labeled ambition or initiative. And in the desire for power and wealth, ethical principles vanish. All of this is idolatry in one form or another. Few of us escape its wiles. The lesson of today's gospel is to deal with temptation quickly and effectively. Living in the risen Christ, we are empowered to do so.

That sin of Romans continues to seek its prey. There is no reason for us to become morose or guilt-ridden about sin. But reflection on the havoc it creates is helpful. It holds a mirror up to our own lives and causes us to assess our relationship to God. And, above all, as Paul makes clear, it makes us aware of the abundance of God's love. In the Adam-Christ parallel, we see that all the evil in the world cannot overshadow God's goodness. In Christ we can deal with sin. And that alone should give us courage.

Homiletic and Catechetical Helps

1. Sin in paradise: what Genesis is and is not teaching.

2. Original sin: its biblical and theological meaning.

3. Adam and Christ: the meaning of both for Lent.

4. Relating the temptations of Christ to our experience.

5. Human appetites: control and moderation.

6. Acting like God: its meaning for today.

7. The riches of this world: greed or generosity.

FIRST SUNDAY OF LENT
Year B

Readings

> Gen 9:8 - 15
> 1 Pet 3:18 - 22
> Mk 1:12 - 15

Theme: A Covenant People

If there is one thread that runs through the entire fabric of the Bible, it is that of covenant. Genesis today speaks of

Yahweh's covenant-making with Noah for the benefit of all of creation. The first letter of Peter draws on the Noah theme in pointing to baptismal water as the saving element of God's new covenant. Mark's brief account of Jesus' temptation concludes with Christ's proclamation of the new covenant's arrival. "The reign of God is at hand." The beginning of Lent is a good moment to consider what it means to be a people bonded with God.

First Reading

The major moments in Israel's history were marked by covenants. There is the central covenant of Sinai made with the people as a whole (Ex 19 - 24), preceded by that with Abraham (Gen 17:1 - 14), and the pre-history covenant with Noah, recounted in today's first reading. In addition, there is covenant language in the God-Adam story (Gen 2), although the relationship is not specified in those terms. The covenant with Noah is singular inasmuch as it is unilateral. There are no binding conditions placed on Noah or his descendants. Yahweh alone binds himself in solemn promise.

This narrative is part of the Priestly tradition (P) of the Pentateuch. Some editorial "stitching" has taken place as seen in the frequent repetitions (vv11, 15; 12:17). Biblical covenants are constructed along the lines of political treaties, common in the ancient near east. Noah's covenant, however, is of a particular type. Where ordinarily the two contracting parties bind themselves to the terms, here it is Yahweh alone who is bound. He allies himself with Noah, all of humanity, and all living creatures (vv9f). The terms assure a certain tranquillity in nature which precludes any future destruction of all forms of life such as Noah had experienced (v11). The subordinates in the covenant, here Noah and his sons, have no terms imposed upon them unless it be the prohibition against homicide and blood meats in the preceding section (9:4f), an unlikely possibility.

Another feature of the ancient treaty was the external sign, a permanent and lasting record that agreement had been reached. Today this is expressed in similar terms: "I want that in writing." Here the visible pledge of Yahweh's lasting intent is

the rainbow (vv13 - 16). Its over-arching character as it spans
the sky is seen as joining heaven and earth. It appears at the
conclusion of the rain, serving well as a reminder that Yahweh
has established pluvial limits.

The significance of this pre-history covenant, part of Genesis'
theological retrojection to beginnings, lies in the stress it places
on Yahweh's relationship, not solely with Israel as in subsequent
covenants, but with the whole of creation, or more precisely
with all forms of life. Israel saw it as divine protection for all
peoples of the earth.

Responsorial Psalm   Ps 25

This psalm, constructed on the Hebrew alphabet (each verse
beginning with a subsequent letter of the alphabet), reiterates
many of the key concepts of Israel's faith. The *ways* of the Lord
or his guidance are the terms of the covenant, the path of
upright living, for which light is requested (v5). It is God's kindness (*hesed*, vv6, 7, 10) or covenant love that binds him to his
people as well as to individuals, bringing him to the remembrance of promise and a total forgetfulness of sin. The dispositions of the petitioner are those of the humble (*anawim*) (v9).
One can follow the Lord's way and invoke his kindness to the
extent that a lowly spirit is present. In treating of Yahweh or the
suppliant, the psalm is covenant-centered.

Second Reading

The first letter of Peter draws heavily on the baptismal catechesis of the early church. Here the experience of Noah's "salvation through water" becomes a figure of Christian baptism
(vv20f).

Christ's sufferings result in Christian deliverance (v18). His
offering was made to God in his weak and sufferable humanity
(*in the flesh*); this with his resurrection led to his becoming a vivifier, the one who communicates new life (*in the spirit*) (Rom
1:3f). *The spirits in prison* (v19): The reference is to an activity of
Christ after his resurrection, when he was "in the spirit." Who
the spirits were to whom Christ preached remains unclear.

Ordinarily, unspecified "spirits" refer to celestial beings, in this case fallen angels. In context (v19) this would point to the angels who had sinful intercourse with humans prior to the flood and were at least partially responsible for the punishing deluge that followed (Gen 6:1 - 4). They appear also in the early Christian apocrypha. Or the reference may be to those humans who died in the flood itself because of their wrong-doing. Elsewhere both the fallen angels and sinful humans of Noah's time are treated jointly (2 Pet 2:4f). In any case the text relates Jesus salvific work to the pre-Christian era.

Mention of God's patience during the time of the ark's construction (v20) is followed by the comparison of the two "saving waters." Baptism is not an act of "the flesh," a mere physical cleansing but rather a *pledge* (Grk: *eperotema*) to God of an unstained life made possible by the power of the Lord's resurrection, the life in the Spirit (v21). This same Christ now presides as Lord (Phil 2:9ff) over all the heavenly beings (Eph 1:20f).

Third Reading

In the synoptic tradition, the more primitive Mark presents only the essentials of Jesus' temptation (vv12f) in contrast to the more extended depiction of Matthew (4:1 - 10) and Luke (4:1 - 13). The same Spirit present to Jesus in his baptism (1:10) now leads him into combat with the evil one. The topical reference is to the Judean desert, the place of John's ministry. The *forty days* (v13) echo the desert sojourns of Moses (Ex 34:28) and Elijah (1 Kgs 19:8) with a possible allusion to Israel's forty years in the desert. *Satan* (v13): Originally the prosecutor or the heavenly adversary (Job 1), he eventually became the leader of Yahweh's opposition. It is in this latter role that he is present to Jesus. The mention of the ministering angels and protection from the desert beasts suggests the psalmist's assurance of Yahweh's assistance to his faithful one (Ps 91:11ff).

Victorious in the newly given Spirit, Jesus begins his ministry. It is important to note that his announcement of salvation takes place only after his forerunner is removed from the scene (v14). Their ministries belong to different eras and do not overlap.

Jesus leaves Judea and returns to his native Galilee. *The gospel of God* (v14) includes announcement of the time of fulfillment, i.e. the end of the era of Israel and the time of eschatological realization; the proximity of the reign of God, i.e. the time of God's total sovereignty over the whole of creation; and finally the need to repent, i.e. to experience a radical change of heart in light of this final moment. *Believe in the gospel* (v15): This is to be read in its full Christian sense, implying more than the gospel preached by Jesus. For Mark in a post-Easter setting it includes the work of redemption accomplished in Christ's death-resurrection.

Since we no longer make covenants, it is at times suggested that we should find better terminology to describe this all-important relationship. But it is hard to do so. Contracts in modern parlance are legalistic and fall short in expressing divine largess. Agreement is too weak a word, and testament has become almost as obsolete as covenant. So we keep the word and try to give it meaning.

Covenant, properly understood, speaks volumes about God's concern. In the covenant with Noah, coming so close on the heels of the flood, Yahweh comes as close to saying "I am sorry about all of this" as he could. Yes, sanctions were called for, but he foreswears forever this type of punishment.

The ark symbolizes salvation. It is a figure of the church and is related to baptism. We are all protected by God's love as was Noah and his family. In addition, baptism confers the Spirit enabling us to cope with evil. Baptism is the seal of the new covenant made by the living God with each one of us and all of us together in his Son's blood. "If God is for us, who can be against?" Only one question underlies it all: Do we really believe?

Homiletic and Catechetical Helps

1. The meaning of covenant.

2. The relationship between baptism and covenant.

3. The relationship between eucharist and covenant.

4. Universal salvation: God's concern for all people.

5. Environmental salvation: God's concern for the world.

6. Noah as a type of the Christian; the ark as a type of the church.

7. Understanding the angels.

8. The gospel: its meaning for Jesus and for the early church.

9. Conversion and coping with temptation in life.

10. Understanding the reign of God.

FIRST SUNDAY OF LENT
Year C

Readings

Deut 26:4 - 11
Rom 10:8 - 13
Lk 4:1 - 13

Theme: Salvation

In the ritual for the giving of thanks after the harvest, the Israelite offerer prayed a brief summary of salvation history. This actualizing of past experience is contained in today's first reading. It stresses the collective dimension of salvation. Paul reminds us that salvation in Christ is personal, deeply internal, a question of heart and lips. The Lucan account of Jesus' temptations exemplifies what the Christian response to evil should be. In view of its many similarities with that of Matthew, the reader is advised to refer to the commentary for the First Sunday of Lent, Year A.

First Reading

The Hebrew believer presented a part of the annual harvest to the Lord as an expression of gratitude. The credo which the offerer recites (vv5 - 10) blends appreciation for personal benefits with those received by Israel as a whole. The identification of the individual with the larger community is central to covenant faith.

The time of offering may well have been during the feast of Weeks (Deut 16:9f) or may have been made at any time depending on the farmer's harvest. When the priest accepts the offering and places it on the altar (v4), the offerer makes his profession of faith.

Thanksgiving is at once connected with the exodus experience. *A wandering Aramean* (v5): Aram Naharaim in northern Mesopotamia is Abraham's land of origin where he lived a pastoral or nomadic life. The reference is not to any specific person but rather to the patriarchs as a whole. When oppressed in Egypt, the plight of the people is recognized and prompts Yahweh's deliverance (vv6 - 9). It is interesting to note that the credo passes from Egypt to the land of promise with no mention of the Sinai covenant. This is not a singular occurrence in Israel's liturgical life (Ex 15:1 - 17). This may be due to the existence of two distinct traditions: one, the Sinai covenant; the other, the Egypt-Canaan deliverance. They were merged only in the course of time. Or the omission may be due to a type of narrative which wanted to portray solely Yahweh's beneficence to his people. Since the covenant was a bilateral agreement, it would not be included.

In appreciation of God's gifts to his people as well as to the offerer, the farmer presents the produce of his land and, joined by the priests in service at the sanctuary and the foreigners in his employ or in his surroundings, celebrates Yahweh's goodness (vv10ff). *In his presence* (v10): Originally this would have referred to local sanctuaries. Under the deuteronomic reform of King Josiah in the seventh century, Jerusalem became the only legitimate place of cult. At that point the expression would have referred to the temple.

Responsorial Psalm   *Ps 91*

The psalmist stresses confidence in Yahweh who at the psalm's end pledges salvation (v16). The psalm is centered on the temple, the place where God's protective hand is assured (v1). The two speakers are a cultic authority, probably a priest, and Yahweh, who at the end addresses the believer. The worshiper is urged to give expression to his confidence (v2), with the protection of the Lord described as angelic guidance and deliverance from all harm (vv11f). Belief in the angels as protectors and guardians is a recurring theme in the Hebrew scriptures (Gen 24:7; Ex 23:20; Ps 34:8).

Yahweh speaks a word of assurance as the psalm ends (vv14ff) Clear indications of Yahweh's saving hand were deliverance from any evil and the conferring of a long life. Where there is authentic dependence on Yahweh, salvation is guaranteed.

Second Reading

If Deuteronomy sets forth the collective dimension of salvation, Paul here touches on its personal and internal aspect. In this tenth chapter of Romans, Paul regrets the failure of the Jews to recognize true salvation (10:1f). They continue to strive for their own "law" righteousness instead of that which comes as a total gift from God. This is not something distant or remote; that word of faith, the proclaimed salvation in Christ the Lord, is close and within reach. Or, more accurately, it is deep within (v8).

Salvation for Paul consists in a personal appropriation of what Christ has done for us. It entails a recognition in faith that the man Jesus of Nazareth now enjoys with Yahweh the title "Lord." And this is a faith that requires public expression. The pairing in vv9 and 10 should be seen as appositional, not sequential. Thus, *confessing with the mouth* and *believing in the heart* are two aspects of the single act of faith. Also, to say *Jesus is Lord* and to believe that *God raised him from the dead* are inseparable (Acts 2:33 - 36; Phil 2:9). *Justified* and *saved* express the same basic reality (Rom 8:30).

What Paul means by faith is a deep adherence and commitment to the Lord Jesus, who alone justifies and saves. This is a salvation open to all people, not the Jews exclusively (v12). To invoke Jesus as Lord is not "cheap grace." The New Testament itself attests that many of those who did so in early Christianity paid a dear price (Mt 10:18; 1 Thes 2:2; Phil 1:29). Faith reflects itself in one's values and whole way of life. Paul here emphasizes its simplicity, its interiority, and its gratuity.

Third Reading

As part of salvation, the Christian is called to deal forcefully with temptation. In this, Jesus is the model. The account of Jesus' temptation in Luke parallels closely that of Matthew (see First Sunday of Lent, Year A). But there are significant differences which will be touched upon here.

The Holy Spirit is a principal actor in Luke-Acts, as influencing both Jesus and the early church. Jesus has received that Spirit in baptism (3:22) and it now leads him to the contest with the devil (not designated as Satan). Unlike Matthew, Luke does not develop the concept of Jesus as a new Moses or a new Israel. While there are elements of that typology already present in his source (Q), which are highlighted and developed by Matthew, Luke does not choose to follow that line of thought, as he writes for a Christian audience with little background in Jewish tradition.

The reference to *forty days* (v2) does not have the Mosaic-exodus connotation. It simply refers to an extended period of time (Jon 3:4). The Spirit-filled Jesus survives because of another food, God's will (v4). Although he does not eat, it is not referred to as a fast as in Matthew (4:2). *This stone* (v3) is more plausible and realistic than the "stones" of Matthew. The same is true of the manifestation of the *kingdoms of the world* (v5). Luke avoids the Matthean mountain top, from which a world view would be impossible anyway, and presents it as an instantaneous vision (v5). There Luke has the devil offer Jesus power (*exousia*) as well as glory. Power in Luke is something to be studiously avoided (9:48; 18:17).

Luke also reorders the temptations. The final temptation takes place in Jerusalem (vv9ff), always the point of climactic destination in Luke. It is to Jerusalem that Jesus' journey or exodus takes him (9:51); from there he proceeds from the cross to the glory of the Father.

As in Matthew, the temptations present a literary triptych of the types of temptation to which Jesus was subjected during his ministry in a less dramatic fashion. The fact is that he resolutely put them down. The account is a paradigm for the Christian in responding to attractions that are not dissimilar in his or her life.

All of us tend to think of salvation in rather personal terms. If we saw it as collective, as Israel certainly did, we would undoubtedly have greater concern about other members of Christ's body, their struggles, their strengths and weaknesses. The homeless, the addicted, the unemployed would have to become more real. Those who have left the church for one reason or another would be more than a statistic. The church poster displayed in subway cars simply says "Come home for Christmas." It makes believers and non-believers stop and think.

Looking at ourselves, we know that Paul's short formula for salvation is simple but not simplistic. To say "Jesus is Lord" is to put him at the center of our life. We are called to see Christ as the great gift of our existence. If we accept him–and him alone–as our Savior, then our lives will be changed and salvation is assured. This is far more than repeating a few words and far more than Sunday morning religion. It means altering many things in life. It affects commitment, marriage, family, work, and play. Evil of the sort confronted by Jesus is with us at every turn. But victory–and salvation–are within our grasp.

Homiletic and Catechetical Helps

1. Salvation: personal and collective.

2. First fruits for God: church support, tithing, charities.

3. Theology of the offertory collection.

4. The meaning of salvation by faith alone; the place of works.

5. The unity of heart and words.

6. Lutheran-Roman Catholic dialogue on justification.

7. Interpreting Jesus' three temptations in contemporary life.

SECOND SUNDAY OF LENT
Year A

Readings

> Gen 12:1 - 4
> 2 Tim 1:8 - 10
> Mt 17:1 - 9

Theme: The Favored of God

God's engagement in the life of his people has meant blessings and favor. The scriptures today make that abundantly clear.
In Abraham's call to venture forth to an unknown country,
there is the assurance of blessings for the aging patriarch, his
descendants, and, finally, all peoples of the earth. In the transfiguration narrative from Matthew's gospel, Jesus is designated
by the Father as being the favored emissary of redemption.
That redemption touches all of us, as the second letter to
Timothy states, and results in our being favored in Christ who
brings us from death to life.

First Reading

The epic of sin found in the Genesis pre-history (cc. 1 - 11) is
immediately followed by the beginning of a new era of blessing.
This begins with the call of Abraham. The darkness of widespread evil is followed by the glimmer of a new dawn, the emergence of a saving light.

Abram, whose name has not yet been changed (Gen 17:15),
is called by Yahweh to leave Haran where his family had settled
after leaving Ur of the Chaldees in southern Mesopotamia
(11:31). He was to set forth for an as yet unspecified land (v1).
Being of nomadic origin, Abram was not unaccustomed to a
migrant life. In Genesis, however, this sense of movement
assumes religious value with this first of a number of patriarchal journeys undertaken at the Lord's command. Abram
becomes the archetype of the willing spirit open to God's direction. Thus, the cascading deluge of sin in Genesis 1 - 11,

incurred by disobedience, is offset by submission. The saga of repeated curses will be reversed by one of blessings.

Abram receives a sevenfold blessing (vv2f). The first is the assurance of progeny, resulting in a new people, a new nation. His name itself will become sacred, even used in blessing. Then this blessing for Israel is extended. *Communities .... shall find blessing in you* (v3b): literally, communities will bless themselves in you. Abram's name will be invoked as people extend greetings and salutation: "May you be blessed as Abraham was" (Gen 48:20). This verse contains a clear note of universalism. Yahweh's protection will follow the patriarch. His friends and foes will be reckoned such by God himself (v3).

It should be noted that blessings and curses had an inner force of their own. Much more than a passing word, a blessing unleashed an independent power which followed the one blessed through good times and bad.

This classic blessing is derived in its final form from the Yahwist tradition in about 1000 B.C. Thus it is refracted through the prism of Israel's experience while still attaching itself to the patriarchal figure.

His age notwithstanding, Abram with his nephew Lot sets out for his unknown destination (v4).

Responsorial Psalm   Ps 33

This hymn lauds the fidelity of Yahweh. His favor is not transient but worthy of trust (v4). The integrity of his word can be seen in the creation which it produced (v6). The covenant partner's justice and right meet their match in Yahweh's covenant kindness and fidelity (v5). The psalmist speaks of the Lord's watchfulness over all humankind but notes that he is especially attentive to those who reverence him and turn to him in the face of peril (vv18f). The psalm ends with the petitioner's expression of confidence (vv20, 22).

Second Reading

After admonishing Timothy to be willing to suffer for the gospel (v8), the author sets forth a condensed summary of soteriology of the type which appears frequently in the epistolary literature (Rom 6:3f; 1 Pet 2:9f). The favor of God reaches all believers through the actualization of God's salvific will. This was the eternal plan of God, realized with the appearance of his pre-ordained Son (v9; Tit 1:1ff).

Salvation is a transition from alienation to holiness (v9), from death to life and immortality (v10). It is attained *through the gospel*, i.e. the proclaimed death and resurrection of Christ. He destroyed death in its fullest sense, which is a total separation from God (Rom 6:5 - 11), in bestowing grace upon his followers. All of this is God's favor; in no way do works or merit make it attainable (v9).

Third Reading

The transfiguration in the synoptic tradition is best described as a theophany. Like the experience of Moses on Sinai or of Jesus at his baptism, it comes to us with a heavy theological overlay which makes sorting out the actual historical kernel very difficult. And it is unwise to try to do so. The evangelists present the account in its present form for very clear reasons, and it is our task to determine that message.

The event centers on the Father's recognition of Jesus as his Son (Ps 2:7), as the favored servant of the Lord (Is 42:1), and as the end-time prophet like Moses (Deut 18:15). The three references are contained in the heavenly voice's statement (v5) and point to Christ as the unique fulfillment of these major biblical themes. Furthermore, the Son of God designation is a link with the voice at Jesus' baptism (3:17) and confirms Peter's earlier confession (16:16).

The narration is accompanied by apocalyptic imagery, giving the event a strong end-time significance. Jesus experiences a metamorphosis, enveloped in a strong and blinding light (v2). There is considerable dependence on the apocalyptic language of Daniel—the shining face and clothes (v2; Dan 10:6, 7, 9), the prostration of the disciples with the consoling touch and word of Jesus (vv6f; Dan 10:9f, 18f). The three tents (booths) would seem to be a reference to the end-time celebration of Tabernacles, which Peter wishes to inaugurate at once (v4).

There is, in addition, an emphasis on fulfillment in the account, an important feature of Matthew's gospel. This is seen in the aforementioned voice of recognition. Also, Moses and Elijah represent the law and the prophets as they converge on the person of Jesus; both are important end-time figures (v3). Jesus appears as the new Moses on the "high mountain," Sinai-like setting (Ex 24:12 - 18), with the enveloping cloud (v5; Ex 24:15). As at Sinai, the revelation occurs after six days (v1; Ex 24:16).

The final remark of Jesus points to another meaning of the theophany (v9). It is a preview of the resurrected Christ, of the glory that will be his after his servant role as the Son of Man is brought to completion.

In two short verses, the letter to Timothy summarizes what it means to be favored by God: from slavery to freedom, from death to life, from sin to grace—and favor means pure gift. We did and could do nothing to deserve it. In faith we know that everything is ours because Christ obtained it for us. It is hard to see how our belief can become a burden or a threat. It may well be that gifts and favors have become so commonplace that we have lost sight of the goodness that underlies them. So often it seems that we try to live a Christian life in order to attain something. Actually we should do it gratefully because we already have something.

Another interesting note appears in today's readings. Both Abraham and Christ were favored in order to serve others. Abraham was singled out and chosen so that he might become the father of a nation. Jesus is identified as the favored Son of God, destined to be the suffering servant who would die for others. Favor does not eliminate suffering. So often pain is woven inextricably into the fabric of love. If God's favor led Jesus to the cross, the trying of our faith in the crucible of hardship in no way diminishes God's love for us.

Lent is a good time of year to reflect on what salvation means. A glance at the cross reminds us that we have much for which to be thankful. We are favored sons and daughters. But that does not spell elitism. If biblical examples mean anything, then it is a call to serve.

Homiletic and Catechetical Helps

1. Is faith seen more as a gift or a duty?

2. The Abraham story: faith as commitment.

3. Abraham a blessing to Jew and Gentile.

4. Distinction between faith and merit.

5. Christ: Son of God, servant of the Lord, and prophet.

6. Jesus as the new Moses.

7. Salvation and future glory.

SECOND SUNDAY OF LENT
Year B

Readings

> Gen 22:1 - 2, 9, 10 - 13, 15 - 18
> Rom 8:31 - 34
> Mk 9:2 - 10

Theme: A Father's Sacrifice

Christian tradition has long seen in the moving Genesis story of Abraham's willingness to sacrifice his son Isaac a type of the relationship between God and his Son Jesus. This is alluded to in today's gospel, Mark's account of the transfiguration, with the Father's enunciation of the mission of his Son. Paul sees God's willingness to give up his Son as a source of great strength and comfort for the Christian.

First Reading

This masterfully composed story from the Elohist (E) tradition intends to illustrate Abraham's total and unquestioning acceptance of God's will. In his son Isaac, the promise of God was incarnate, a promise that was to involve the destiny of many people. His son's death would not only mean the death of his "beloved" son but would also nullify Yahweh's pledge (Gen

18:10, 18; 21:12). Our tendency to raise questions about the legitimacy of God's request is not pertinent. The author focuses the drama on one major point only—Abraham's submission—and does it as forcefully as possible. Moreover, the reader is early advised through dramatic irony that this is to be a test of Abraham (v1), something of which he himself remains ignorant.

The frightening nature of the command is heightened by stressing the tenderness of the relationship—"your only one," "your only beloved son" (vv2, 12)—which in turn highlights Abraham's obedience. *Ready* (v1): literally "Here I am," the model response of the obedient believer (1 Sam 3:4; Is 6:8). *Moriah* (v2) is later identified with the mount of the Jerusalem temple (2 Chr 3:1), perhaps for theological reasons; there is no certainty as to its location.

The drama of the narrative builds continually: the altar, the wood, the tying of Isaac, placing him on the wood, the poised knife. All of this is prelude to the last-minute intervention of the angel, a surrogate for God (vv9 - 12). With his spirit of total acceptance, Abraham passes the test and is blessed once again.

The substitution of the ram for the boy (v13) is a subtle polemic against human sacrifice, common among Israel's neighbors and at various moments introduced in Israel itself (2 Kgs 16:3; 21:6: Mic 6:7). The Hebrews recognized God's right to the first-born with their law of reacquisition or "redeeming" the child (Ex 34:19f). But any type of human sacrifice was excluded. In this literary retrojection, Abraham is presented as complying with the law of substitution.

The solemn blessing repeats those of earlier chapters (12:2f; 13:14ff), and comes to rest on Israel and the nations. Here it rewards Abraham's fidelity to God's will. *Shall find blessing* (v1): literally "shall bless themselves," i.e. "May you be blessed as were Abraham's descendants."

Responsorial Psalm   Ps 116

This thanksgiving psalm dates from the post-exilic period; its sentiments express the posture of both Abraham and Jesus in the face of adversity. It was recited on the occasion of presenting a votive offering of thanks after deliverance from a misfortune—in this case, it would seem, a serious illness. Even in the midst of great trial, the offerer's faith was not diminished (v10). *Death of his faithful ones* (v15): The meaning is controverted since death in itself had no positive significance for God. It could well point to a life span, without emphasizing its natural termination. Hence, a life spent in fidelity even to the end is sacred to the Lord. In gratitude for his cure, the offerer proceeds with the temple sacrifice in liturgical solemnity (vv17ff).

Second Reading

Christian confidence is rooted in what God has accomplished, i.e. the death-resurrection of Jesus. If God has gone this far, he will hardly abandon his own now. The passage contains a series of rhetorical questions. Invested with God's power, which comes through Christ's victory, the Christian can have no matching foe (v31). The reference to God's not sparing his own Son (v32) is a clear echo of the Abraham-Isaac story, today's first reading. *Handed him over* (Gr: *paredoken*) (v32): a theological expression for the voluntary surrender of precious life (Jn 3:16; 19:30). God has already acted as the exonerating judge; in the face of acquittal, there is no case for the prosecution (v33).

The reason for trust is Christ's salvific act, both death and resurrection, with the accent here falling on the resurrection (v34). It is the risen Christ who gives the Spirit, the pledge of glory, the reason for future hope. No distinction is made between the risen and glorified Christ; they are simply two aspects of the same mystery. Christ is also our intercessor, a role that the letter to the Hebrews connects with his priesthood (Heb 7:25; 9:24).

Third Reading

Both Matthew and Luke have drawn on the more primitive Mark in recounting the transfiguration. Since many features are shared in common, the reader is referred to the more extensive commentary on Matthew (see Second Sunday of Lent, Year A).

Here particular attention will be directed to the distinctly Marcan features.

In the theophany the three disciples are given a glimpse of Christ's future glory. The mountain is unspecified, but, like the time reference ("after six days"), echoes Israel's Sinai experience (Ex 24:12 - 16). Since the scene is revelatory of who Jesus is, the time reference may also be a conscious effort to link this narrative with the preceding profession of Peter (8:27 - 30). As a glimpse of the glory of the kingdom, the account is also closely connected with the kingdom promise at the end of the last discourse (9:1). The three apostles are the same who later share his human sufferings (14:33). In Mark, Elijah is center stage in the conversation with Jesus, Moses being subordinate (v4). This is an unusual order if the idea is the fulfillment of the law and the prophets. Elijah is a major end-time figure and for this reason is dominant in Mark; discussion about his return will follow the narrative immediately (9:9 - 13).

After the appearance of the enveloping cloud (the shekinah or symbol of the divine presence), the heavenly voice identifies Jesus as divine Son and prophet (v7). In a post-Easter composition, much more is implied here than a royal or adoptive filiation. It goes much farther than Peter's earlier recognition of the Messiah (8:29) and fits with the Father's identification at the baptism (1:11). It is this full expression of Jesus' nature that will be understood only at the termination of Jesus' earthly ministry and thus is appropriately placed on the lips of the centurion at the crucifixion (15:39). The heavenly voice also makes reference to the deuteronomic prophet (Deut 18:15), who is to be heard in the final days. Mark does not allude here to the servant of the Lord theme.

In the descent from the mountain, Jesus again refers to his approaching death, with which the preceding revelation must be reconciled (v9). With Jesus excluding any disclosure of the insight they have received on the mountain, there is a return to Mark's messianic secret. Repeatedly in this gospel, the full manifestation of Jesus' nature is reserved for a determined moment. Their quandary about the resurrection (v10), deleted in Matthew and Luke, centered both on its meaning for Jesus and the necessity for Elijah to return before any end-time rising from the dead (vv11f).

Straight as an arrow–that is the message which comes home very clearly on this Second Sunday of Lent. We are more prone to the curves and the detours as we look at Abraham's dilemma. How could God even ask such a thing? How could Abraham acquiesce in willingness to take his son's life? But the story is not addressing these questions. Abraham does not pose any questions. He gave himself to God completely.

In a different but similar way, the Father of Jesus also has to surrender his Son. The transfiguration speaks of two things: future glory and the pain of the cross. Speaking in human terms (and we have no other), we witness the pain of God and the meaning of love.

And all of this is done for us. The cards are stacked in our favor. We have far more to be glad about than to fear. That is Paul's message today. With such incredible signs of God's concern for us, how can we help but hold our heads high? Our faith should speak to us strongly of a salvation already achieved, not simply striving for one to be attained. Even though the Father loved his Son, he was willing to surrender him for our sake. That says a lot about God, and a lot about us.

Homiletic and Catechetical Helps

1. The meaning of obedience.

2. The meaning of salvation: present and future.

3. The inseparable causes of salvation: death and resurrection.

4. The meaning of theophany.

5. Relating the transfiguration to our Lenten experience.

6. Relating the transfiguration to our future life.

7. Christ as our intercessor.

8. The prayer of petition.

SECOND SUNDAY OF LENT
Year C

Readings

> Gen 15:5 - 12, 17 - 18
> Phil 3:17 - 4:1
> Lk 9:28 - 36

Theme: Citizens of Heaven

In ancient times the making of a covenant or treaty was done in the interests of a just and peaceful future. In today's reading from Genesis, an unusual form of covenant-making between God and Abram speaks to the future of people and land. In the Lucan transfiguration scene Jesus manifests his future glory as he speaks with Moses and Elijah about his journey home. And in the midst of too much world-centered thinking, Paul reminds the Philippians of where their real citizenship lies.

First Reading

This covenant account comes largely from the Yahwist (J) tradition. Childless and advanced in years, Abram (the name not yet changed to Abraham) receives the promise of descendants numerous enough to constitute a nation, an incredible assurance (vv5, 13). Abram's faith receives Yahweh's acknowledgement. *Act of righteousness* (v6): Abram's trust is recognized positively by Yahweh or "is credited to his account." This trust is rooted in belief in God's power to realize the promise. Paul will later use this verse to support his position that it is Abram's faith, not his works, that wins justification (Rom 4:2f).

In addition to progeny, the patriarch is promised land. He asks for a sign (v7f). Yahweh responds in the form of a covenant, binding himself to the agreement. The only obligation on Abram's side is the trust which he has already expressed. Covenants in the ancient world took various forms; the one cited here is foreign to the western contemporary mind (vv9f).

Treaties were made between individuals, tribes, or nations. The present treaty was usually made between individuals.

Before the ritual begins, Abram falls into a deep sleep, a state suitable for divine communication (v12). The severing of the animals into two parts allowed the covenant partners to walk between the separated members. This underscored the closeness of the bond and the seriousness of the obligation, with the two parties invoking a similar loss of life on themselves for failure to comply with the covenant (Jer 34:18ff).

There is mention only of Yahweh's involvement in the ritual, with his presence symbolized by the oven and torch (v17). Either Abram's commitment is implied by his earlier acceptance or the author may wish to underscore the divine initiative and favor underlying the promise of people and land. Either way the rite is clearly designated a covenant (Heb: "cut a covenant," v18) bilateral and binding on both sides, even though not made by parties of equal status.

The promise of land extending from Egypt to the Euphrates in Mesopotamia represents ideal rather than real boundaries; the closest historical approximation occurred in the Davidic era (tenth century B.C.) (v18).

Responsorial Psalm   *Ps 27*

The psalm in today's liturgical context builds on Abraham's trust. The Lord's assurance removes all reason for fear (v1), with the petitioner turning in confidence and praying for consolation and guidance. *Your presence* (v8): Worship in the temple is desired where Yahweh was singularly experienced. Even in the face of adversity and disappointment, the psalmist advises constancy and a stalwart spirit (vv13f). *The land of the living* (v13b): Cultic or temple overtones do not seem to be implied. It is better seen as a reference to a life spared to be lived in the land given by God.

Second Reading

Paul's ethical demands continue to be strongly eschatological; it is the Christ coming toward the Christian that calls for an appropriate moral posture. The present passage has considerable "body" talk, a reaction against Judaizers with their "flesh" interests. Christians are assured of a heavenly body in a new country in which they have already obtained citizenship. Their conduct should reflect their status.

Pauls' encouragement to see him as a model is not self-serving (v17; 4:9; 1 Thes 1:6; 1 Cor 11:1). Example was as integral a part of apostleship as was preaching or teaching. *Enemies of the cross* (v18): In the context they appear to be Judaizers (3:2 - 5), former Jews still promoting circumcision and some Jewish practices as necessary in the Christian life. For Paul their position nullifies the all sufficient work of Christ's redemption and thus sets up an adversarial position. *God is their stomach* (v19a): This probably points to Jewish dietary laws, now also nullified. *Their "shame"* (v19b): a reference to the circumcised male genital organ, usually discreetly concealed (1 Cor 12:23), now figuratively flaunted by the promoters of circumcision. With circumcision and other Jewish practices now relegated to worldly or "flesh" concerns, their proponents cannot rise above a material or terrestrial plain.

The Christian, however, has other goals and another homeland. The return of the Lord will see the Savior bypass present "bodily" concerns as he effects a total transformation of the corporal nature (v21). This he will accomplish by the vivifying Spirit in transforming the Christian into the image of himself, the prototype of resurrection (Col 1:18; 1 Cor 15:45 - 49) and in bringing all creation into final subjection (1 Cor 15:25). All of this is prelude to Christian possession of "the land," the heavenly reign of God where true citizenship lies. In view of this future reality, Paul's readers are exhorted to remain steadfast (4:1).

Third Reading

Because of the strong likenesses that exist in the three synoptic accounts of the transfiguration, the reader is advised to review the commentary on the Matthean narrative (Second Sunday of Lent, Year A). Here the commentary will address mainly the Lucan differences.

In Luke Jesus has just predicted his passion and its victorious outcome. He also stresses the part that suffering is to play in discipleship (9:22 - 27). In the transfiguration narrative, the Father confirms this teaching of his Son (v35).

After eight days (v28): The time reference simply links the narrative with the preceding prediction of the passion. Thus the vision of glory, the outcome of the cross, is closely tied to Jesus' suffering. Unlike the other synoptics, Luke makes no concerted effort to relate events in Jesus' life to their biblical precedents. For example, the mountain here is neutralized, becoming for Luke simply a place of prayer (vv28f). In this gospel, it is in the posture of prayer that Jesus is found before the major events of his life (6:12; 9:18).

In the end-time setting (changed countenance, brilliant garments), the two prophetic figures, Moses and Elijah, representing the law and the prophets or the body of scriptural tradition, appear engaged in conversation with Jesus (vv30f). Both of them are also end-time personalities, believed to be destined for a role in the ushering in of God's reign. Only Luke mentions the subject of their conversation: Jesus' *exodus* or journey. This refers to his steady movement toward Jerusalem and from there to the cross and glory. The Hebrew exodus from Egypt is background to this as well, but the theme is central to Luke's gospel which is largely constructed around Jesus' journey to Jerusalem (9:51; 19:28) where his definitive leave taking will occur (24:50 - 52).

Only Luke has the three apostles in a semi-sleeping state (v32). As in Abram's case, seen previously, sleep is a state which lends itself to supernatural communication. It should be noted that the same apostles will struggle with sleep in the garden as Jesus' passion begins (22:45). Luke also stresses the *glory* (Gr: *doxa*) (vv31f) surrounding the three heavenly figures, an end-time note, proper to Yahweh and indicative of the Christian's future. Peter wants to hold fast to this final moment, relating it to the end-time feast of Tabernacles (tents) (v33), as the three are enveloped by the cloud, symbol of the divine presence (v34).

The Lucan Christ is identified by the Father as the fulfillment of scriptural promise (v35): Son (royal filiation, Ps 2:7), servant of the Lord ("chosen one," Is 42:1) and the prophet like Moses ("listen to him," Deut 18:15). In addition, there are distinctly Christian notes: sonship is divine and singular (3:22). "Listen to him" would point to Jesus' own teaching, especially that on his salvific destiny (9:22), as surpassing that of the two other prophetic figures in the apparition.

The apostles are not held to silence in Luke but are respectfully circumspect (v36).

In Luke's writings salvation history moves forward. In the gospel he moves us with Jesus toward Jerusalem and then onward to death and glory. This is the call of the Christian as well. Today's Scripture reminds us not to become so involved in temporal concerns, even legitimate ones, that we forget our ultimate destiny, our own transfiguration into the image of Christ. Since we are citizens of another realm, our baptismal passport must condition our way of life.

Abram was promised descendants and land. His blessings were very concrete. It reminds us that as we journey toward our homeland we are not to neglect our responsibilities here. Heaven is not just a question of the hereafter. It begins here, and all peoples have a human right to a foretaste of what heaven means—justice, equality, a fair standard of living, mercy. Christians lend their hands to this task.

But the ultimate truth remains. Life does not end here. We know what citizenship means in daily life: the broad smile on the faces of immigrants as they take the oath of allegiance for the first time; the security that a passport gives; stepping off a plane to realize that one is home again. Why should our feeling about the ultimate reign of God be any different? Ours is to be a homecoming worthy of the name. Lent gives us the chance to pause and reflect.

Homiletic and Catechetical Helps

1. Faith transmitted from Abraham: How we receive the faith.

2. The land: material blessings to be shared with others.

3. What is our understanding of heaven? of resurrection?

4. How does our future life influence the present?

5. Relate Luke's journey theme to the Christian life.

6. Prayer in the life of Jesus and our own.

7. The law and the prophets as related to Jesus.

8. Jesus as Son, servant, and prophet.

9. Lent and our future destiny.

THIRD SUNDAY OF LENT
Year A

Readings

> Ex 17:3 - 7
> Rom 5:1 - 2, 5 - 8
> Jn 4:5 - 42

Theme: Baptism and Commitment

Baptism is very much in the foreground during Lent. There are good reasons for this. As we examine our lives during this penitential season, we do it in the light of our baptism and the commitment that accompanies it. In addition, we are making our Lenten journey with those people in our parish and diocese who are preparing for baptism. The Easter vigil will bring all of this together when we renew our own baptismal commitment and welcome newly baptized Christians into our community.

Today's scripture appropriately highlights baptism. It is prefigured by Moses' providing water for the exodus journey. In the gospel, Jesus refers to himself, the Spirit-giver, as the source of living water in his conversation with the Samaritan woman. Baptism is the symbol of this living water. Paul's letter to the Romans reminds us that this water of the Spirit has been poured forth in great abundance.

First Reading

The story of God's supplying water for the people during their desert journey comes to us in two forms. This is the first; the second is found in Numbers 20:1 - 13. At an earlier point in the journey the people were displeased with the bitter water which Moses had provided (Ex 15:22 - 25); here there is no water at all, a fact which triggers considerable dissension. This narrative is part of the Yahwist (J) tradition. The stress on "quarreling" and "testing" (vv1f) will subsequently be explained in terms of the name of the location. Although the crowd argues with Moses, it is clear that their argument swirls around Yahweh himself. Their sin lies in their failure to appreciate what the Lord had already accomplished for them. They regret having begun their journey, a sin to be aggravated later by a desire to reverse God's plan by returning to Egypt (Num 14:3f).

To assuage their discontent, Yahweh commands Moses to strike the rock for water, accompanied by the elders as witnesses (vv5f). Water immediately appears.

The location bears a twofold name, Massah and Meribah, and involves a play on words. Massah means "testing place" and Meribah, "place of quarrel"; in this way the events are made to tie in with the place names and are thus fixed in the memory. The tradition found in Numbers from the priestly (P) school links the event with a Meribah at Kadesh in the Negeb and places it at the end of the journey. In this latter tradition, Moses and Aaron are also guilty of sin. It is evident that these are two accounts of a single event which has been differently located and nuanced in the course of time. The closing question in the Exodus narrative (v7) summarizes well the ambivalent, even hostile sentiments of the people.

Responsorial Psalm   Ps 95

The psalm is often identified with a feast of Yahweh's enthronement. Whatever the occasion, the chant has strong liturgical features. The reference made to Meribah and Massah (v8) makes it appropriate for today's liturgy. Yahweh is recognized as Savior by the approaching procession as it raises its voice in song (vv1f). Upon entering the sanctuary, prostration is the suitable posture as Yahweh is further acknowledged as Creator and Shepherd (vv6f). A temple oracle is enunciated exhorting fidelity. The worshiping Israelites are to refrain from the sins of their forebears who ungratefully spurned their God at Meribah and Massah; again there is the play on words: the "testing" of Yahweh (vv8f).

Second Reading

The passage's main thesis is that God's grace has been poured forth superabundantly after the death of Jesus in the giving of the Spirit. This was in no way merited by an unjustified human race.

One of the results of the enmity between sinful humanity and God was an alienation beset by anxiety and hardship. This has now been reversed (vv1f). Through faith-justification, which Paul has been treating in chapters 3 - 4, access to God through Christ's redemptive act has been achieved. The life of the Spirit (grace) places the believer in a state of peace with God; former hostilities have passed. This same gift of grace is a pledge of the future. This is the basis of hope for Paul (v2). In this sense hope is an unrealized certainty not wishful thinking or mere aspiration. *We boast*...(v2b): This is ironic. The human boast here is about something not humanly achievable. God's grace, wholly gratuitous, gives assurance of an eventual share in the glory or radiance proper to God alone, attained with the resurrection (8:17; 1 Cor 15:42).

The Holy Spirit, a present reality, gives certainty of future glory. *Has been poured out* (v5): God's gifts are communicated effusively (Sir 1:8; 18:9; Ps 45:3). This lavish goodness serves Paul well in his Adam-Christ comparison, with the gift from Christ far outweighing the evil inherited from Adam (5:15).

Paul anchors hope in another consideration (vv6ff). Christ took the first step when humanity was non-justified and "guilty before God." In the context of society, it might happen that one would die for a good (just) person but hardly for a malefactor. But Christ did precisely that, and this gives added credence to the certain hope of future glory. The major impasse has been overcome; the next step is virtually assured (8:28ff).

Third Reading

A baptismal leitmotiv emerges in the fourth chapter of John, which is read almost in its entirety today. The treatment here will be made with broad strokes, pointing up the major themes: living water, faith in Jesus, true worship, and mission.

The Samaritans were located between Judea and Galilee. They were heterodox in Jewish eyes, having departed from a number of traditional beliefs. In John's gospel they are seen as "half-Jews." On his journey to Galilee, Jesus passes through Samaria and there, at the well traditionally identified with Jacob's family, he engages a woman in conversation.

It is important to recall that, for John, occurrences in Jesus' life serve as a backdrop for full-blown, post-resurrection faith discourses. This is strikingly evident in the Samaritan woman story. In addition, it is to be noted that the conversation proceeds on two levels. The non-believer or incipient believer speaks on a lower or natural level while Jesus responds on a higher or spiritual level. This bifurcation will often center around a single word or phrase capable of being used equivocally or in two senses, e.g. water, bread, light, sight.

Living water: The well at which Jesus stops to rest is initially presented as something akin to a fresh water fountain (Gr: *pege*) (v6); only later will it become a cistern (Gr: *phrear*) of contained ("non-living") water (v11). After Jesus' request for water meets a reluctant response, he introduces his own claim to have another water, which is not contained or stagnant but "living" (v10). For John this is the life of the Spirit, given by the risen Christ, as the pledge and source of eternal life.

It is at this point that the two levels of understanding enter, the woman continuing to speak of common water and Jesus, of the spiritual water. The woman does not understand Jesus' meaning (vv11f) but in her questioning gives him the opportunity to speak of a "water" that surpasses anything which Judaism offers (vv12ff). Both the Torah and Wisdom were referred to as water in biblical and rabbinic sources (Sir 24:22 - 25; 24:20). Hence Jesus' water is superior to natural water as well as Jewish and Samaritan beliefs. While the woman's request for water (v15) remains on the natural level, it marks her first opening in faith to Jesus' teaching.

In this Johannine context the first meaning of "living water" is life in the Spirit, attainable through faith in Jesus. But, as elsewhere in John, the image immediately suggests baptism; this is further confirmed by the observations on baptism with which the chapter begins (4:1ff). There is, moreover, a continuity between the concepts of the Spirit and baptism.

Growth in faith: This is woven into Jesus' conversation with the woman. She begins far from Christ as an "outcast" Samaritan and much married (vv16ff). But her growth in faith and mission is constant. She recognizes him as a prophet (v19) and the Messiah (vv25, 29—a Johannine interjection since the Samaritans had no Davidic messianic expectations). The people, whom the woman draws to Jesus, acclaim him as Savior of the world (v42). In the conversation the woman repeatedly refers to Jesus as Sir or Lord (Gr: *Kyrios*) (vv11, 15), a word with a double significance not to be lost on John's audience.

As the discourse continues, Jesus too is engaged in self-disclosure. He acknowledges messiahship in words which, on the spiritual level, say much more (v26). "I am he" is the "I am" of Yahweh's self-identification to Moses (Ex 3:14).

The point is clearly made. The effectiveness of Christ's "living water" depends on a corresponding growth in faith on the part of the believer.

True worship: On the natural level this meant a choice between Jerusalem (Jews) or Mount Gerizim (Samaritans) (v20). Jesus moves the discussion to another plane. Future worship will not be anchored to any location; it will spring wholly from the interior action of the Spirit imparting the truth of God to every believer (vv23f). The new era will be marked by new relationships, not external forms. Just as Father and Son are joined in the Spirit, so too will the Christian be united (14:20) and the Spirit will convey its own enlightenment (truth) (14:26). This worship means internal "family" conversation; discussion about place has no significance. True worship will mean an understanding of Jesus in precisely the terms which the woman's faith elicits in the narrative.

Mission: The woman's growth in faith, similar to that of the apostles (1:35 - 50), results in her move toward mission. She is the bearer of "the word" (vv39,42), as she enters the town and brings others to Christ (vv39 - 42). In the meantime, his disciples speak to Jesus of food (on the natural level), while Jesus' food is identified with his Father's will (vv31 - 34). In speaking of mission, Jesus speaks in harvest terms, as do the synoptics (vv35 - 38). His reference to the proximate harvest could look to the coming-to-belief Samaritans. However, the mention of harvesters who did not do the sowing (v37) seems to reflect the mission of the early church which, by the time of the composition of John, could have missioners reaping the results of earlier preaching.

Baptism says so much more than church membership, as today's scriptures so clearly illustrate. The water that Moses provided slakes the Israelites' thirst for a period of time. The living water of Jesus is not provisional or temporary. It is not cistern water but a living fountain that springs up and leads to a life beyond. It makes possible our growth in faith in the person and mission of Jesus. And faith is the important word. This is not just the acceptance of certain truths, as significant as that may be. It is our commitment to a person—the Christ, Messiah, Savior, Son of God. It is a commitment that is destined to color the whole of our life. New doors are opened. Baptism gives a vision that is meant to grow and expand. And it means service of the word.

The Samaritan woman, once confirmed in faith, moved unhesitatingly. She even left her water jar behind (symbol of a former faith?). The word of Jesus is destined for the world. The woman received her faith in the marketplace and she took it to the marketplace. Missionaries are not a select group in the church. Every Christian is called to bring the perspectives of faith to everyday situations as diverse as they are numerous. The woman was accepted by Jesus in her sinful state. She was gifted with an understanding of who it was who spoke to her. The only thing that remained was for her to bring that word to others.

Paul reminds us that our hopes are high. And they will be realized. But those hopes are meant for others as well. Every time we bring the touch of Christ to a bruised or wounded person, to one beset by tragic circumstances, to the family struggling for a livelihood, to someone in prison, we are messengers of hope. The Samaritans first believed because of the woman. Faith is not something private or closeted. It calls for conviction and courage. Baptism is no small thing.

Homiletic and Catechetical Helps

1. The symbolism of water in baptism.

2. The role of godparents in baptism.

3. Infant baptism and adult profession of faith.

4. "Testing the Lord": ways in which we fail.

5. The role of women in the mission of the church.

6. Missionaries to developing churches

7. Being a "local" missionary.

8. Baptism, commitment, and mission.

9. Explanation of the rite of baptism.

10. Growth in faith.

11. The virtue of hope.

THIRD SUNDAY OF LENT
Year B

Readings

> Ex 20:1 - 17
> 1 Cor 1:22 - 25
> Jn 2:13 - 25

Theme: A New Temple and New Law

The new covenant was more than a fulfillment; in its own way it was a revolution. One of the basic expressions of the former covenant was the decalogue, commonly referred to as the ten commandments. They are found in the book of the covenant (Ex 19 - 24) and serve as the first reading of today's liturgy. As important as the decalogue is to the formation of our lives, we realize that Jesus went far beyond it in the ethic which he proposed, particularly as seen in the sermon on the mount. Jesus as the new temple is more than a substitution; he represents a whole new way of living, a new set of values. As Paul states today, this was all brought about by a crucifixion, a dreadful form of execution. By human standards this seems incomprehensible. By God's standards, the new was born in power and wisdom.

First Reading

The commandments (in Hebrew, "the words") are central to the book of the covenant and are seen as fundamental ethical norms by both Jews and Christians. As will be noted, their original meaning was often more restricted than the sense which later tradition has given them.

Initially there is a short prelude or introduction (v2) in which Yahweh identifies himself as Israel's deliverer. This is geared to inspire allegiance and a willingness to comply.

The first precept (vv3 - 6) is an expression of practical monotheism. It excludes the worship of other deities, without theoretical considerations about their existence or non-existence, and forbids as well the making of any images whether of Yahweh or other gods. *Besides me* (v3): i.e. within the temple sanctuary, the exclusive domain of Yahweh. Israel remains throughout its history a non-iconic faith. Images of Yahweh militated against divine "otherness" and could easily convey the idea of a form of control to be exercised over the deity. The consequences of sin could be felt by future generations, with a force being unleashed that was almost physical. Depending on its gravity, sin continued to wreak its havoc. Without discounting human culpability or the force inherent in the act, Yahweh, as the primary cause of everything, is presented as inflicting punishment. *Jealous God* (v5): demanding unqualified and undivided allegiance. God's mercy far surpasses his justice where fidelity is maintained.

The Lord's name is sacred and unutterable (v7). "Yahweh" was not pronounced; the surrogate "Adonai" (Lord) was used. This precept looks rather to the invocation of the deity rather than the direct use of the name. This could not be done in unbecoming ways, especially in false oaths, the probable reference here.

The sabbath occurrence each week assured rest for all—land owner, family, employees, and livestock (vv8 - 11; Ex 23:12). Like the sabbatical and jubilee years, it led to reflection on God as the provider, with human industry given a secondary role. Yahweh is seen as the model of the precept (Gen 1), but it remains a question of the "chicken or the egg" since the evidence points to the Genesis narrative as drawing on the sabbath observance already in place. Honor to parents (v12) looked to their age and maturity, as well as being the preservers of a transmitted wisdom. The prohibition against killing (v13) looked to planned homicide only, not other forms of killing. Adultery (v14) respected the rights of the man only with reference to his wife or intended spouse. The verb used in speaking of theft (Heb: *ganab*) (v15) looks to stealing a person, i.e. kidnapping. Lying publicly about another or perjury is destructive of honor and a good name (v16). Coveting another's home or property (v17) involved more than desire. The verb (Heb: *hamad*) implies a plot or an effort to attain the desired end.

These "words" of Yahweh looked to specific and determined violations. Nonetheless, they are a remarkable ethical summary, a fact which lent itself to their fuller development in Christian teaching.

Responsorial Psalm   *Ps 19*

The law is the centerpiece of this latter part of the psalm. The earlier part sees the wisdom of God in creation (vv2 - 7), followed here by a hymn to his wisdom as seen in the law. Spoken of in a variety of synonyms, the law is uplifting (v8a), instructive (8b, 9b), rooted in Yahweh's truthful nature. Rather than being a burden, the observed law adds a savor to life and provides a sound set of values. (vv10f)

Second Reading

Today Paul speaks of the great paradox. The cross of Christ, which appears to human eyes as weak and foolish, is from God's part strength and wisdom. Neither Jew nor Gentile would find in the cross a convincing apologetic.

The Jews looked for signs and wonders, prodigies like those experienced in the exodus. The Gentiles, on the other hand, built their religious belief on a rational construct, a logic that pointed to a higher wisdom worthy of acceptance (v22). And what does Christian preaching offer? A crucified God.

The death itself offers no convincing sign that Christ's claims should be accepted by the Jews. A death of disgrace and ignominy offers to the Gentiles no logic or understandable rationale. It would seem that Christ's death was self-defeating (v23). But to the believer, the elect of God, just the opposite is true (v24).The cross effects deliverance from sin through an act of love and results in the giving of the Spirit. The Spirit of the dead and risen Christ is invested with power to vanquish sin and bring about redemption (Phil 3:10; Jn 20:22f). Moreover, Christ, preordained before creation, the one who gives meaning to and reconciles the whole of the created order, is the perfect wisdom of God (Col 1:15 - 20; Eph 1:7 - 10). The paradox remains. God's "foolishness" surpasses all human insight and his "weakness" effects more than any demonstration of human strength (v25).

Third Reading

The account of the temple's purification appears in all four gospels. In the synoptics, it precedes Jesus' arrest at the end of his public life, coinciding with his only visit to Jerusalem during his ministry. John places it at the beginning of the ministry as part of the "book of signs" (1:19 - 12:50). In addition, distinctive features of the Johannine account argue for its coming from a source distinct from that of the synoptics. However, all four gospels converge around the essential features of the event. In John, the event becomes a "sign" which Jesus offers for belief. In this case it is a sign of substitution. Jesus, the new temple, replaces the old.

In the fourth gospel, Jesus makes several trips to Jerusalem. The occasion at this time is Passover (v13). Animals were sold for use in sacrifice (v14). The money changers collected the sale price and also served to collect the "redemption" tax required of every male Jew at nineteen years of age (Ex 30:11 - 16). Jesus'action takes on a highly symbolic value (vv15f). Scripture had spoken of the temple's purification at the time of the messianic era (Mal 3:1 - 4; Zech 14:21). Hence, Jesus' action is seen as eschatological, precipitating the Jews' request for his messianic credentials (v18).

Zeal for your house will consume me (v17) is a quotation from the psalms (Ps 69:10). The disciples' recall, or, more amply, the early church's recall, is oracular. The original psalmist, using the present not the future tense, is speaking of his strong attachment to the temple; here the quote presages the hostilities between Jesus and the Jewish religious authorities which will ultimately "consume" or destroy him.

Jesus' response to the "sign" request is another example of John's "two level" approach. The word "temple" takes on two meanings (vv19f). Jesus responds on the higher, spiritual level, speaking of his body as the temple; his adversaries remain on the natural level, speaking of the material edifice (v20). In other words, through Jesus' death-resurrection, the temple will be superseded by the new reality of a "Spirit-filled" Christ. As the passage makes clear (v22), it is only in the post-Easter reality that the full significance of the words and event will be understood. At that time Jesus' words will have equal weight with all of God's revelation ("scripture" and" the word of Jesus").

The substitution of Jesus for the temple points to him as the locus of the divine presence in the new era (1:51), a fact which will call for an entirely new approach to worship, centered in a new relationship between God and the believers, not tied to physical location (4:22ff).

The "signs" which the Johannine Jesus performs were intended to be the key to a deeper faith understanding (2:11). However, reaction ran the gamut, extending even to total non-acceptance. Jesus is therefore wary of the people's response (vv23ff). His profound understanding of human nature (v25; 1:47) is elsewhere cited as a divine attribute (1 Chr 28:9).

People are usually reluctant to change a given mindset, especially in religious matters. Changes in liturgy, church law and practice, and theological perspective often produce negative reaction. If change is to be accepted, we are told, it must come slowly. One can only marvel, therefore, at the flexibility and openness of the first Christians, especially those of Jewish background. The acceptance of Christ represented an incredible upheaval in traditional faith and practice. There were those who would not accept him at all. Many of those who did paid a dear price, even life itself. The Spirit, of course, did the convincing. But it was no small feat.

Christ is the new temple. Christian faith is not anchored in any particular place, regardless of where nostalgia may want to carry us. Our relationship to God depends essentially on the indwelling Father, Son, and Spirit; it is God who makes temples of us all. Liturgy is a vitally important expression of the Christian community as the continuing temple of God. And yet worship continues in all that we do and say. Our life becomes an uninterrupted prayer.

Christ is also the new lawgiver, the new Moses. Most of us spend a good deal of time on the ten commandments. Although their meaning expanded in the Christian era, they are basically the ethic of a former covenant. For us they are important as the outer parameters of Christian conduct. They remain an essential base. But from there we have mighty steps to take. The ethic of the new lawgiver is found in the sermon on the mount. We should examine our conscience on the teaching of Matthew 5 - 7. That is the litmus test of what it means to be a Christian.

Homiletic and Catechetical Helps

1. Explanation of the ten commandments, the decalogue.

2. Relation of the decalogue to the sermon on the mount.

3. The temple theme: Jerusalem, Christ, the Christian.

4. Christian worship: communal and private.

5. Explanation of the indwelling of the Trinity

6. Lent, the examination of conscience, reconciliation.

7. Confession: "What I have done and what I have failed to do."

8. Wisdom and power in the cross.

THIRD SUNDAY OF LENT
Year C

Readings

> Ex 3:1 - 8, 13 - 15
> 1 Cor 10:1 - 6, 10 - 12
> Lk 13:1 - 9

Theme: The Call and Complacency

On the occasion of Moses' call to liberate his people from bondage, God also chose to reveal his name. This is one of the great moments of the Hebrew scriptures. But election is not synonymous with salvation, as Paul today reminds the Corinthians. Election calls for a continuing response, an ongoing conversion. In Luke's gospel, Jesus reminds us that there is a day of reckoning for all. We should learn from misfortunes that occur rather than feel that we are immune. Now is the time to bear fruit. Every day is a gift and a moment of growth.

First Reading

Moses has fled Egypt and has settled and married among the Midianites (2:15 - 22). It is while pasturing his sheep that he receives the call to free his people. *Angel of the Lord* (v2a): a designation used interchangeably with an appearance of the Lord himself. Since Yahweh here is the partner to the conversation, the expression is best understood as an appearance of the deity. Fire is the sign of God's presence; the bush is *seneh* in Hebrew, a probable play on the word Sinai.

The passage is largely derived from the Elohist (E) tradition. Horeb is the customary name for Sinai in the E tradition. The geographical identification here links two major events: the Sinai covenant and the mission of Moses. Moses approaches and removes his shoes, a customary sign of respect for sacred space.

Yahweh first identifies himself with the God of the patriarchs, establishing an important continuity between past and present. The Egyptian interlude notwithstanding, the God of the patriarchs is still present (v6). Moses' initial fear is understandable; to see God and live is not possible (Ex 33:20; Gen 32:31). Yahweh further identifies himself as the God who directly intervenes ("I have come down") on behalf of his people (v8). He intends to take them from oppression to a land of plenty ("milk and honey," a proverbial expression for agricultural abundance—13:5; Num 13:27).

The protest of Moses' inability for the task is met by the assurance of Yahweh's accompanying presence (vv11f). Moses then requests to know the name of the deity (vv13f). It should be noted that in antiquity knowledge of the name implied some control over the person; the giving of a name often fixed the person's destiny (Gen 17:5). God's response is his third and final identification in the narrative. *I am who am* (v14): or "I am who I am" or "I am who I shall be." This is intended as a proper name, as is clearly indicated at the end of the verse: "*I am* sent me to you." The name is enigmatic and there is no clear consensus on its meaning. It is intended as an explanation of Yahweh's name, already known much earlier in the Yahwist tradition (Gen 4:26). Here the name is receiving a descriptive definition. It is related to the verb "to be," perhaps in the sense of an effective and dynamic presence of God, a God who actually is and will be, one whose existence has been and will be experienced.

In the closing verse of Moses' commission (v15), Yahweh is linked again with the patriarchal tradition. The sacredness of the revealed name is underscored. In fact, "Yahweh" was not pronounced by the Hebrews, even in cult, *Adonai* (Lord) being substituted.

Responsorial Psalm   Ps 103

This thanksgiving psalm recounts God's goodness to Moses and the Israelites (v7). The psalmist has been delivered from grave misfortune, perhaps an illness (v4). Sickness is closely linked with personal wrongdoing in Hebrew thought (v3). God's "benefits" (v2) are not only personal; they extend to the nation as well, especially evident in the events of the exodus.

His covenant-centered attributes have been experienced: mercy, forbearance, and forgiveness (v8), but above all his covenant love (Heb: *hesed*) (v11).

Second Reading

To make his point on the danger of over-confidence, Paul sets forth a typology between events of the exodus and the Christian experience. The presence of the cloud and the sea (Ex 13:21; 14:19 - 22) foreshadow baptism (v1). *Baptized into Moses* (v2): a free theological adaptation suggested by baptism into Christ. The "spiritual" nourishment, manna (Ex 16) and the water from the rock (Ex 17:1 - 7), is related to the eucharist. *The rock was Christ* (v4): The typology is made explicit, even if somewhat forced. As baptism was projected back to Moses in v2, so the desert rock is directly related to Christ. Yahweh was the rock of his people (Deut 32:4). Rabbinic literature has the water from the rock follow the Israelites through the desert. All of this is seen as symbolic of Christ's continued presence with his elect.

Yahweh's displeasure with his rebellious people and their subsequent demise (Num 14:26 - 38) is to be a warning to the Christians (vv10ff). The Israelites were favored no less than the Christian elect, yet they were not spared God's punishment. The Corinthians are not to see themselves so assured of salvation as to have nothing to fear. *The destroyer* (v10): the reference is to an angel of death (Ex 12:23; Wis 18:25), with Yahweh thus spared direct intervention in human catastrophe.

All of these biblical events happened for the benefit of the Christian community, which is now living in the final age (v11). This is the moment toward which all former generations pointed. No one should presume on his or her ability to withstand the present danger. The examples of the past amply illustrate how even the most favored succumbed to the forces of evil.

Third Reading

Luke deals with a not uncommon problem in the early Christian community: a sense of complacency in view of the delay in the Lord's return. It is not unlike the situation in Corinth which Paul addresses in the second reading. In the preceding chapter (Lk 12), Jesus has emphasized the need for alertness and repentance.

One way to escape self examination is to stand apart from the plight of others with an attitude of "This couldn't happen to me." There is no extra-biblical testimony to Pilate's barbaric act (v1) or to the tower's collapse at Siloam (v4). The traditional Hebrew understanding of the direct relationship between one's sin and subsequent disaster, although much questioned, was still in possession in many quarters in Jesus' time. Jesus bypasses any consideration of this just retribution theory and reminds his hearers that there is a lesson in tragedy for everyone (vv3, 5). Before God there is no exception of persons. The only lesson to be learned is one of alertness and repentance.

The story of the fig tree (vv6 - 9) could have been used to point out God's patience and forbearance in dealing with human failure. In its present context, however, it is a warning. At a given moment, if conversion does not take place, time will run out. This is a recurring Lucan theme (12:16 - 21; 17:20 - 31).

Beginnings are wonderful moments, filled with enthusiasm, the excitement of novelty, new horizons. But there is nothing in life that does not lose its initial glow. The new soon becomes a customary part of life; it can even become dismally normal. We then look forward to the next moment of exhilaration. With faith, however, it should be different. In fact, prayer and meditation are geared to make of faith an ongoing challenge.

The call of Moses was a high point in his life as well as in that of his people. He was sent by God and assured of continued guidance. But in time even he had to bear the bitter burden of ingratitude and rebellion. He had his own moments of doubt and anger and was not permitted to enter the land of promise.

All of us can settle into that sense of security which prevailed at Corinth. Today we hear much of God's love and mercy. And for that we can be grateful. But there is another side of the coin. God is not as tolerant as we sometimes think of him. Or, as Paul says, God is not mocked. Complacency can easily lead to a loss of control, indifference, and back-sliding. *When we learn that someone has a dreaded illness or that some disaster has occurred, after our initial shock we tend to distance ourselves from the reality. But today's scripture teaches us to internalize whatever occurs. Let it become an occasion for deeper repentance and conversion. Each day we pray for perseverance. The greatest saint can look at a condemned criminal and say: "There but for the grace of God go I."*

Homiletic and Catechetical Helps

1. The meaning of vocation.

2. The name of God: its meaning.

3. Reverence for God's name.

4. The grace of perseverance.

5. Understanding ongoing conversion.

6. The danger of complacency.

7. Cite contemporary events which have taught a moral lesson.

8. In what areas of my life is reform most needed?

FOURTH SUNDAY OF LENT
Year A

Readings

> 1 Sam 16:1, 6 - 7, 10 - 13
> Eph 5:8 - 14
> Jn 9:1 - 41

Theme: Light and Darkness

Lent moves us steadily through the mist of our humanness to the light of Easter. Today once again the Johannine Jesus is the focal point of faith, the source of light, the giver of sight.

Appropriately for Lent, the gospel also has a distinct baptismal motif. Paul encourages the Ephesians to live in the light and avoid the darkness of sin. From relative obscurity and total unpreparedness, the young David, in today's first reading, is brought into God's light to be anointed king. Unequipped by human standards, he is singled out by the God who places little stock in appearances but sees the depths of the heart.

First Reading

The story of David's selection and anointing serves several purposes. Following imediately upon notice of God's rejection of Saul (15:35), the account points up Yahweh's intention to see the monarchy continue without a debilitating hiatus. In addition, having David anointed at the moment he is introduced fixes his destiny as the narrative of his youthful life unfolds, especially with the continued antagonism between himself and the rejected Saul.

Only much later will David be formally recognized and acclaimed as king (2 Sam 5:1 - 5). Because of the similarity in the two anointing narratives, it may well be that they represent two separate and independent traditions dealing with David's selection. In fact, David's initial anointing is unknown even to his own brothers in the next chapter (1 Sam 17). Whatever merit such a position has, the fact is that in the final composition of 1 and 2 Samuel the two accounts serve different functions. David's secluded and relatively private selection here paves the way for his ascendency and the public recognition of his position at a later date.

The selection of David is clearly the work of the Lord. Samuel's role is quite secondary. *Bethlehem* (v1): The town of Jesse and his family is some five miles south of Jerusalem. The choice of the youngest son is characteristic of Yahweh's wont to choose the lowly to confound the mighty (1 Sam 2:4 - 8). Samuel's conclusion that the oldest sibling Eliab would be selected is misguided (v6). However, the dictum that the choice of God focuses on internal qualities, not external appearances (v7) is partially offset by the description of David's handsome features (v12). David's qualities of character will emerge as his story continues. The spirit of the Lord takes hold of David forcefully after his anointing (v13), a clear indication that his effectiveness will now be due largely to God's action.

There are shades of today's light and darkness theme in this first reading. In the call of David, the darkness of human standards give way to the penetrating light of Yahweh's insight and decision. It is he who determines the qualities of the future king.

Responsorial Psalm   Ps 23

This poetic masterpiece is cherished in the Judeo-Christian tradition. The Lord is described as both shepherd (vv1 - 4) and host (v5). The shepherd image for near eastern kings is not uncommon and is repeatedly applied to Yahweh (Gen 49:24; Is 40:11; Ez 34:11 - 33); it is an image with rich significance for a largely pastoral society. Here the shepherd pastures and waters the sheep (v2), guides and directs (v3) and brings them through dangerous terrain (v4). This pastoral description is applied to the life of the psalmist, the recipient of Yahweh's favor. The rod and the staff were for guiding and protecting the sheep.

In the second part of the psalm, Yahweh is the psalmist's host. The meal is served as adversaries look on, in strong poetic contrast (v5). Anointing need not be seen as royal here, but rather as a poetic description of God's goodness. The psalmist has no fear of the future, pursued only by Yahweh's covenant love. His greatest joy will be to continue always in temple worship (v6).

The sentiments of the psalm can be applied both to David and the man cured in today's gospel.

Second Reading

Light and darkness as applied to the moral life was common in the Jewish literature of Paul's time and an earlier period. It appears in the Qumran literature in much the same way that it is used here. The Ephesians lived once without faith but through baptism have been enlightened (v8). Their works must now correspond to their new life in the light.

Light in the moral life is important for two reasons. It is the arena where good is produced (v9). What is done in daylight is patent for all to see; it is darkness or night that offers the opportunity for hidden and unseemly activity. Secondly, light is important for unmasking sinful activity (vv11f). Works of darkness can be seen as they really are in their unmentionable depravity. Once exposed to light, they lose their force.

The appeal to live as "light" people closes with a section of a hymn, probably used in conjunction with baptism (v14). The theme, however, is distinctly Pauline (2:5f; Rom 3:5f). Sleep like death was a figure of sin; it too belongs to the night. The transition from sin to grace appears in the New Testament in various images: sleep to being awake, blindness to sight, dark to light, night to day.

Third Reading

The story of the cure of the man born blind, with its running theological commentary, is another of Jesus' "signs" in John's book of signs. The miracle is a springboard for a presentation of Jesus to the believer through the eyes of one community in the late first century church. This chapter of the gospel is read in its entirety in today's liturgy. Its treatment here will deal mainly with the chapter's principal theme.

At the chapter's end Jesus presents himself as judge (v39). Yet he is not a judge who reviews a case and pronounces sentence but rather the occasion which results in self-sentencing by reason of acceptance or rejection (3:17f). The meaning of the story of the blind man focuses on the single affirmation that Jesus is the light of the world (v5). To come to him in faith is to accept the light; to reject him is to embrace the darkness (1:3 - 11).

The blind man symbolizes the alienated person without faith to whom Christ comes as Savior. The entire chapter will develop the blind man's coming to sight, from non-belief to belief, while the "seeing" Jews plunge into ever greater darkness. The story also contains a baptismal motif, consistent with John's sacramental concern in the gospel.

The chapter begins with an indication that the man's blindness is to be the occasion for the manifestation of God's work as Jesus immediately introduces the light-darkness theme (vv2 - 5). *This man or his parents* (v2): The traditional Jewish position on divine retribution extended beyond the sinner to embrace his/her progeny as well. As the narrative unfolds, the blind man, who earlier received his physical sight (vv6f), grows in his spiritual vision through his recognition of Jesus. To his inquirers, he responds that his healer was *the man called Jesus* (v11), then *a prophet* (v17), *a man from God* (v33), *Son of Man* (vv35 - 38). Finally, Christ is recognized and worshiped as *Lord* (v38). Thus the man's cure takes on symbolic value in terms of coming to Christ in faith.

The Pharisees, on the other hand, claim to have "sight" (vv40f). They have knowledge of the scriptures and theological skill, and they are the teachers of Israel. Yet as the story unfolds, their "sight" leads them into ever deeper darkness. Their identification of Jesus is in strong contrast with that of the cured man. Jesus is *sinful* (vv16, 24) because he violated the sabbath in making clay and healing. Their *disbelief* leads them to discredit Jesus (v22). They claim to be *disciples of Moses* as they disavow knowledge of Jesus' origins (v29). They uphold the traditional position on retribution as they abuse the witness (v34). This counter-witness of the Jews is framed in an almost frantic movement: to the man, then to his parents, back to the man, and then to Jesus.

This drama of parallel cross-passage from blindness to sight and from "sight" to blindness receives the definitive sentence of Jesus at the chapter's end (v41). Those truly blind, without faith but open to Jesus, are far better off than the "seeing" Pharisees who are actually deep in darkness and sin but fail to recognize it in their certainty that they have the truth. The blind man's gradual growth in faith is similar to that of the apostles (1:35 - 51) and the Samaritan woman (c. 4).

Baptism is a secondary theme in the narrative. The man's cure is effected through his washing in the pool of *Siloam* (v7), related by John to the Hebrew verb "to send" (*shalah*). The waters of baptism are made effective by the One who is sent, Jesus. The man speaks of the anointing (v11) which was part of his cure; it was also part of the baptismal ritual. It is interesting to note that this incident was repeatedly given baptismal significance in the art of the early catacombs. Faith and baptism, then, are joined in the narrative.

The account also reflects the growing conflict between the early Christians and Jewish authorities toward the end of the first century. In a sense the "departure" of Jesus had brought on considerable darkness (v4). At the time Christians were formally excommunicated from the synagogue (v22). These hostilities are reflected in the widening gap between Jesus and his adversaries in the narrative.

One of the memorable quotations from scripture appears in today's reading from 1 Samuel. Humans see appearances but God looks at the heart. Externals entrap us so often. We are carried aloft by our heroes in life and so often are dashed to the ground when we discover that they, alas, have feet of clay. We are taken up, even within the church, with titles and honors as barometers of worth. But is it not the "little people" that inspire us the most? The elderly person who, whatever the weather, attends mass each day. The person for whom menial work is a sacred trust. The bedridden invalid whose acceptance reveals an incredible faith. There are the people who have little to give but do so and in receiving have a grateful smile that speaks volumes. God sees more in the simple unsung people of our daily life than human criteria would ever admit. But then God's ways are not ours.

How ready the blind man was to come to Jesus! His gratitude was boundless as he unhesitatingly responded to his formidable opponents. He simply spoke the truth as they avoided the truth at all costs. There was too much at stake to accept Christ–hence, the chosen course to make him unworthy of faith by twisting the evidence. Do we not often act in a similar way? Candor and transparency get lost in vested interests. We defend positions not out of conviction but because we have too much to lose. We do not assess our motives as we should. Rather than admit our faults we make others culpable. Rather than address sensitive or controversial issues with honesty, we equivocate rather than displease. As Christians we are called to light, to sight, to alertness. In human affairs that means transparency, candor, and charity. In baptism we were cleansed with clear water. Perhaps we should reflect on the symbol more than we do.

Homiletic and Catechetical Helps

1. The dangers of judging by appearance.

2. The biblical significance of David's humble origins.

3. The Lord as shepherd.

4. Sleep as spiritual lethargy.

5. What it means to grow in faith.

6. Our spiritual blind spots.

7. Faith and inflexibility.

8. Baptism, clear water, and transparency.

9. The "muddied" water of disbelief and duplicity.

10. The sacraments in John's gospel.

FOURTH SUNDAY OF LENT
Year B

Readings

> 2 Chr 36:14 - 17, 19 - 23
> Eph 2:4 - 10
> Jn 3:14 - 21

Theme: Deliverance Through the Cross

Only the exodus from Egypt was more strongly emblazoned on the Israelite psyche than the return to Jerusalem after the exile. The chronicler retells this latter story of deliverance today. Christ in John's gospel speaks of another deliverance, the one made possible through his own being "lifted up" on the cross. The passage from Ephesians is a forceful reminder that deliverance is due entirely to God's love. We are favored and did nothing to merit it.

First Reading

The two books of Chronicles were written about 400 B.C. They betray strong cultic and priestly interests with the monarchy viewed against that background. Chronicles' moral teaching is clear: If Israel is to have any future, it must learn from the mistakes of the past. It is in this light that history is recounted.

The tragedy of the exile was due to the sins of the collective Israel—royalty, clergy, and people—with special mention made of cultic violations. Yahweh's admonitions were not wanting, conveyed through the prophets and other agents (Jer 7:25f), but they were spurned. Divine retribution was brought to bear in Nebuchadnezzar's invasion of Jerusalem in the early sixth century, with the slaughter and deportation of much of the population (vv17, 19f). With a distinctly theological reading of history, the chronicler sees the anger of Yahweh as the immediate cause of the nation's tragedy (v16). *Lost sabbaths* (v21): The period of exile would result in the non-cultivation and over-growth of the land to compensate for unobserved sabbaths and sabbatical years (Lev 25:4). In fulfillment of Jeremiah's word, this is to last seventy years (Jer 25:12), until the rise of the Persian emperor Cyrus.

When the books of Ezra and Nehemiah were detached from their original unity with Chronicles, the beginning of Ezra (1:1 - 3) became also the conclusion of Chronicles (vv22f), lending a positive note to the end of the book. Cyrus, having conquered Babyon, orders the restoration of Judah, the return of its citizens, and the rebuilding of the temple. His presentation as a believing Yahwist (v23) is an over-statement but theologically in tune with the expanding post-exilic vision which viewed Yahweh's relationship to other people and nations more broadly than in the past. Cyrus is consistently viewed in a very positive light (Is 44:28; 45:1).

Responsorial Psalm   Ps 137

Stressing the sorrowful lot of an Israelite deportee during the exile, this lament was probably composed shortly after the exile's end. The *streams of Babylon* (v1) were irrigation canals stemming from the Tigris and Euphrates. The psalm reflects more than nostalgia for temple and homeland. It finds its roots in the very concrete juncture of land, worship, and God. Yahweh had gifted the people with the land, and only there was legitimate worship possible. The taunting of their Babylonian captors is then sacrilegious (v3). To compromise authentic worship by transferring it to a foreign country would be to neglect the importance of Jerusalem (vv4f). The psalmist goes so far as to invoke punishment on himself if he should ever be unmindful.

A broader outlook will arise in the post-exilic period, already seen in Jeremiah and Ezekiel, wherein Yahweh's presence and guidance in a foreign culture will be admitted. The present psalm remains a strong expression of the traditional mindset.

Second Reading

The salvific plan of deliverance as pre-designed by God is here set forth in Pauline and some post-Pauline terms. Salvation is wholly due to God's mercy and unconditional love (v4). It involves three steps, presented here as already realized: transition from the death of sin to new life, resurrection, and exaltation (vv5f). The Christian relives the phases that Christ himself experienced and is ultimately joined with him (1:20). This form of a totally realized eschatology, including exaltation, is not customary in Paul's thought; even here it is modified by the subsequent reference to what remains to take place in the age to come (v7).

This action of God's grace is completely gratuitous and in no way due to personal achievement. The *works* (v9) are not explicitly the works of the law but remain unqualified. One does not come to justice through works, but works after justice are not excluded, in fact are pre-ordained (v10). This distinction of the two types of "works" may be intended to clarify earlier Pauline thought. What is certainly Pauline in the passage is the unity of the Christian with Christ in the process of salvation, as well as the gift that salvation is.

Third Reading

This passage from John stresses the centrality of the cross in God's plan of deliverance. The bronze serpent "lifted up" by

Moses on a pole in the desert brought deliverance from the plague of snakes to those who looked on it (Num 21:6 - 9). In Jesus' conversation with Nicodemus, this becomes a type of the crucifixion. Jesus on the cross is revealed as the divine "I AM" (8:28); acceptance of his claim means salvation. In the Johannine presentation, the various moments of the salvific act are joined together. Christ on the cross is already revealed as Lord and is the source of life.

Jesus here looks at salvation from its two sides, that of God (vv16f) and that of humans (vv18f). It was love alone that launched this divine initiative. The measure of that love is gleaned from the form it took. *He gave his only son* (v16): The "handing over" (Gr: *edoken*) and the "only son" echo Abraham's willingness to sacrifice Isaac. God is willing to offer his Son to bring the world to salvation. The idea of God's sending his Son with a sentence of condemnation is excluded (v17). The only motive for God's acting is universal salvation. Notice that John's eschatology is realized. Belief and eternal life are contemporaneous (v15) as are non-acceptance and condemnation (v18). The various stages are not considered.

Jesus then takes up the human aspect of salvation. If Jesus is not the judge, how then does sentencing take place? Jesus is the occasion, not the cause. Faced with the options of acceptance or rejection of Christ, the world encounters the dualistic light and darkness (vv18f). In accepting light, good works emerge and are totally visible (v21). A positive verdict is already passed. In preferring to stay in darkness where evil works remain invisible, self-condemnation takes place (vv19f; 1:10ff). So it is individuals who pass sentence on themselves, not Christ whose work remains solely salvific.

To accept the light is to embrace the truth; it is to appropriate the crucified and risen Christ with the commitment that faith entails. Eternal life has begun.

There is a strong sense of movement in today's readings. The edict of Cyrus moved the Jews out of Babylon through the desert to their homeland. In John's gospel, Jesus moves from his life to glory via the cross. In fact the cross in John captures both moments, suffering and victory. When the Second Vatican Council spoke of the church as the people of God, that same sense of motion was conveyed. Our life in God is not fixed or static; it moves us through hills and valleys over a terrain that holds many unknowns. The journey is one of growth, grappling with faith, seeking answers to unresolved questions. Life today is not what it was in our parents' time. This is true of our life in the church as well. There are constants, of course. It is the same Christ yesterday, today and forever. However, there has been enough change to prove disquieting to some and exhilarating to others. But we are all a little less secure and a little more a pilgrim people. Yet that is what faith is all about–holding on tenaciously when the path gets difficult to find.

The cross is central in today's liturgy. It is the great sign of God's love. But it is still a cross. Today society wants as little of the cross as possible. Suffering is meaningless. Sacrifice is a word seldom heard. When it comes to illicit sexual activity, it is safety that is counseled, with scarcely a passing nod to self-denial. Christianity without the cross is a half truth at best. As we share the joy of an eternal life already begun, we have to integrate our crosses into our life of faith. This is the only way to follow the One who has gone before us.

Homiletic and Catechetical Helps

1. Deliverance: Israel, Christ, the Christian.

2. The cross and resurrection as the cause of salvation.

3. The cross and self denial.

4. Deliverance: gratuitous and God-initiated.

5. Cyrus: the hand of God in world events.

6. The meaning of realized eschatology.

7. John's understanding of Christ as judge.

8. Sacrifice and Lent.

9. The crucifix: the principal Christian symbol.

FOURTH SUNDAY OF LENT
Year C

Readings

Jos 5:9, 10 - 12
2 Cor 5:17 - 21
Lk 15:1 - 3, 11 - 32

Theme: A Ministry of Reconciliation

The Christian life is basically one of reconciliation. All of us move from sin to grace, from alienation to friendship. Every ministry in the church is in some sense a reconciling one. For the Hebrews, the possession of the land was a symbol of reconciliation, just as the time spent in Egypt stood for their life of alienation. The first reading from Joshua speaks of their arrival in Canaan. As in today's gospel story, it too was a homecoming. The parable of the forgiving father, found only in Luke, speaks as eloquently about God's desire for reconciliation as does any page in scripture. Against this background of the exodus and Christ's act of redemption, Paul speaks of his own ministry of reconciliation.

First Reading

Egypt was the symbol of separation from Yahweh. The exodus and covenant restored relations, and with entrance into Canaan reconciliation was complete. Soon after Joshua brings the people to the promised land, the passover is celebrated there for the first time. The shame or reproach of Egyptian bondage has been completely removed (v9). *Gilgal* (v9): there is a play on words here, a popular way of linking place and event. "I have removed" or "driven away" (Heb: *galothi*) sounds similar to Gilgal.

Passover and the feast of Unleavened Bread (vv10ff) were originally distinct and unconnected celebrations. Both of them antedate Israel. Passover was a pastoral feast marked by the killing of a spring lamb; Unleavened Bread was an agrarian feast celebrating the spring harvest. Israelite cult joined and "baptized" the two feasts in the spring of the year in celebration of the exodus. It may be that the Joshua account conceals the fact that this was originally a celebration of Unleavened Bread only. There is no mention of the lamb, and the Septuagint does not have the twofold references to "the day after Passover" (vv11f). The Hebrew text would then represent a textual adaptation to insert Passover. On the Hebrew calendar, the feast was celebrated on fourteenth Nisan, with Unleavened Bread observed on the following seven days (Lev 23:5f).

Whatever is to be said of the original historical circumstances, the Joshua narrative wants to relate the first celebration of Passover to the occupation of the land after crossing the Jordan (cc. 3 - 4). The latter event paralleled the crossing of the Reed Sea after the first Passover. This linkage is important in establishing continuity in the deliverance from bondage to freedom.

Now that the blessing of the land has been conferred, the providential manna, which has provided for the people in their need, ceases (v12).

Responsorial Psalm   Ps 34

Trust in a providential God is the central theme of this thanksgiving psalm. When the psalmist turned to God, he was heard and saved from his affliction (v5). Conversion to the Lord does not disappoint but rather brings its own joy and peace (v6). The refrain *Taste and see* (v9) underscores the importance of a knowledge of God that is experiential, not simply cerebral.

Second Reading

This selection beings with an affirmation of the basic reality. As in the exodus passage from bondage to freedom, the Christian too has passed to an entirely new creation (v15; Gal 6:15), the new life in Christ, which is not only personal but has touched the whole of he universe (Col 1:10). This is effected by the initiative of God who in and through his Son restores humanity to its earlier relationship of friendship with him (vv18f). Culpability for earlier sins is now cancelled and of no account. *Made him to be sin* (v21): Christ, sinless himself (Heb 4:15; 1 Pet 2:22; 1 Jn 3:5), became sin in the sense that he was born in weakened "flesh," took upon himself all human sinfulness, and paid the price of sin (Rom 5:8). Here Paul uses two figures of speech, with the mutual appropriation of qualities. Christ becomes sin; the Christian becomes God's righteousness.

Paul's eschatological tension between the "now" and the "not yet" appears as he speaks of the continuing application of Christ's reconciliation. In one sense it has already taken place (vv18f); in another, it is still ongoing (v20). The fruits of reconciliation must be appropriated by each person in turn and then continually re-enkindled through a spirit of conversion. Paul works to accomplish this through his proclamation of what God has achieved, in his role as an "ambassador of Christ" (v20). As an emissary or delegate, he continues in his apostolic calling; this is a vital ministry in the church. He makes his strong appeal for reconciliation in the imperative (v20).

Third Reading

No more striking account of God's understanding and love for the sinner is to be found in the scriptures than in Luke's story of the forgiving father. To call it the story of the prodigal son is an unfortunate and misleading misnomer, even though it is joined with the "lost sheep" and the "lost coin" (c. 15). The father is the centerpiece of the story, flanked by the differing postures of the two sons. Found only in Luke, the story is told with the literary artistry of the Lucan pen.

The opening verse situates the story and gives a key to its interpretation (vv1f). The "righteous" religious leadership takes issue with Jesus' association with recognized sinners. This offense is aggravated by table fellowship, food sharing being a sacred act among those of accepted religious standards.

In the story which Jesus tells, the two sons are reminiscent of the younger Jacob's ascendency over his brother Esau (Gen 25:27 - 34). The younger son's conduct is unwarranted in a variety of ways. He requests his inheritance in anticipation of his brother to whom deference would ordinarily be shown (v12). He then squanders his share in disreputable ways (v13) and ends up living the life of a Gentile, caring for pigs (v15). His decision to return home is not based on remorse but on need (vv17f). It can scarcely be called a genuine conversion.

The father, on the other hand, is considerate (v12b) and compassionate (v20), and he breaks with propriety in running to meet his errant son (v20b). The forgiveness is unhesitating and total, the son not even permitted to conclude his prepared speech (vv18ff, 21). He is completely restored to his family position: sandaled, robed, and given the authoritative signet ring (v22). But the return calls for even more. A festive banquet is prepared (v23). The reason: life has been restored to a dead son (v24).

The older son rounds out the interesting triangle. The words loyal, obedient, and subservient best describe his filial posture. But his very sense of duty has clouded his vision. He finds his father's forgiveness and generosity incomprehensible (v29). He can no longer bring himself to identify the younger son as brother ("your son," v30), eliciting a subtle reproof from his father ("your brother," v32). The story ends without the older son's participation in the feast.

The parable brings to the fore the important Lucan theme of the inversion of human values. It is the last who shall be first (13:30). Also there is the implicit recognition of Gentiles entering the church while the Jews remain without. But, above all, it is God's limitless love for sinners that brings Jesus unhesitatingly into close association with them. He brings them the message of reconciliation. They listen but his opponents remain aloof.

There is great consolation in reading Luke 15. When moments of discouragement come and our spiritual failure tends to overwhelm, there is no better antidote than a prayerful reading of the story of the forgiving father. It tells us that no one escapes God's love or ever gets too far away. This is no ordinary love; it defies all human standards. When it comes to us poor mortals, God is a striking non-conformist.

The more we experience the peace of reconciliation, the better prepared we are to be its ministers. If we feel forgiveness, we want to bring it to others. *Today there are so many welcome ministries of outreach to the divorced, children of broken homes, gay and lesbian people, the imprisoned, and others who may feel lost or alienated. Many of these are conducted by lay people. Theirs is a true ministry of reconciliation, as is the priest's who administers the sacrament. It is truly a joy to be present to people who often see religion in aloof and distant terms. It is a gift to accompany a wounded person on the journey.*

Homiletic and Catechetical Helps

1. Understanding the boundless mercy of God.

2. The sin of discrimination: who, what, how.

3. Reconciliation with God and neighbor.

4. Lent, reconciliation, and the sacrament of penance.

5. The personal and communal dimensions of the sacrament.

6. Reflecting on our personal experience of father and mother.

7. Passover and eucharist; the seder service.

8. Self-righteous pride and the poverty of alienation.

9. General discussion of lessons learned from today's gospel.

FIFTH SUNDAY OF LENT
Year A

Readings

> Ez 37:12 - 14
> Rom 8:8 - 11
> Jn 11:1 - 45

Theme: From Death to Life

The climactic "sign" of Jesus in John's book of signs (1:19 - 12:50) is the raising of Lazarus, which serves as the occasion for

Jesus' enemies to make plans for his death. This account is the gospel for today's liturgy. The first reading is Ezekiel's oracle predicting the "resurrection" of his people with their return to their homeland at the end of the exile. All of the readings point to our own rising to new life, not only in the future, but in our introduction to the Christian life, about which Paul speaks in today's reading from Romans.

First Reading

Ezekiel speaks of the exiles' restoration in the symbolic language of resurrection. This is an image added to that of the enlivened "dry bones" on the desert plain (vv1 - 11), both dealing with a death-to-life theme. Just as Yahweh brought the breath of life to clay in forming the first man (Gen 2:7), so his spirit (Heb: *ruah*) will lift up an inanimate and defunct Israel and give it new life (v14).

In giving this breath of life in the form of a restored homeland, Yahweh will be recognized as Israel's only Lord in a work effected by his power alone (v13). The reference to resurrection here is symbolic and has no reference to a personal or bodily resurrection.

Responsorial Psalm   Ps 130

This is one of the six penitential psalms used by the church in its liturgy for the deceased. It is an individual lament in which the psalmist prays for forgiveness (vv1 - 4) and concludes with a deep expression of trust (vv5 - 8). The community of Israel is addressed at the psalm's end, presumably after the psalmist has experienced God's pardon (vv7ff). *Out of the depths* (v1): Submersion in deep water is symbolic of great psychological distress (Ps 69). The question as to "who can stand" (v3) probably reverts back to this submersion image. *That you may be revered* (v4): divine forgiveness produces a reverential gratitude for the favor received (1 Kgs 8:39f). There is a confident waiting for the Lord to utter his "word" of forgiveness and deliverance.

Israel as a whole is encouraged to sense this same assurance of salvation (vv7f). God's redemptive power is vast and able to embrace all of his people, rooted, as it is, in his covenant love and fidelity (Heb: *hesed*).

Second Reading

Paul speaks of what death and life mean in a Christian context. He utilizes the dichotomy of "flesh" (Gr: *sarx*), the human person weakened and debilitated by the effects of sin in a non-redeemed state, and "spirit" (Gr: *pneuma*),the vivifying presence of God's power which justifies and makes holy. To live "in the flesh" is to live solely for personal and egotistical concerns (v9).

Christian existence, however, is wholly centered in the indwelling spirit. Paul goes between "spirit" and "Spirit" (v9), the former accenting God's action in the individual, and the latter indicating the agent responsible for this activity. The indwelling of the Spirit is the first fruit of Christ's resurrection, and it is Christ who communicates this Spirit to the world. What results in the human person is a wholly new ontological mode of existence, establishing a frame of reference for a new vision.

The passage has trinitarian insights, if only incipient. God (Father) is the author of this new mode of being, known as life in the Spirit (v9a). There is also reference to the Spirit of Christ (v9b) because it is through Christ that the Spirit has access to the world. Finally there is mention simply of Christ dwelling "in you" (v10). It is, then, the indwelling Spirit who binds the Christian, Christ, and God in intimate unity.

The dichotomy is clear. Without the spirit, there is a total absence of life (v9b). If one does have spirit life, the bodily death, which sin has brought (5:12ff), is transformed by a new life, the result of justification (v10; 5:17). Here (v10) Paul uses "spirit" in another twofold sense. The term was commonly used for the vivifying principle of the human body, much as "soul" would be used today. Here it refers both to this principle and the vivifying divine Spirit.

Just as the Spirit brought Christ to life, that same Spirit is the pledge of human immortality (v11). For Paul resurrection is the logical end of justification (8:30). In short, spirit life is a share in God's own life and therefore cannot be extinguished by physical death. The most important life-giving moment is baptism (6:3f) from which everything else flows.

Third Reading

Bethany was a town near Jerusalem where Jesus was evidently a frequent visitor (Mk 11:11; 14:3: Lk 10:38); Mary and Martha are presumably well known to John's readers, Mary being identified as the woman who anointed Jesus' feet (v2;12:1 - 7; Mk 14:3 - 9). It can be presumed that, in view of this close friendship, this was the family with whom Jesus stayed.

The story of the raising of Lazarus is found only in John; this seems unusual in view of its importance as a miracle and the role that it plays in John in bringing about Jesus' death (11:45 - 53). The incident is given a strong theological interpretation in the fourth gospel. It will be treated here in three main features of the narrative: the principal symbolism, the two levels of understanding, and the faith response.

The Symbolism: Lazarus represents the faithful Christian, the true believer. He is the one whom Jesus loves (vv3, 36), the one for whom he weeps (v35). As in the other instance of this expression of love in John (13:23; 21:20), the person takes on symbolic significance. The raising of Lazarus, then, symbolizes the resurrection of the Christian. The story will go back and forth between the circumstances of Lazarus' death and raising and the event's broader meaning for the Christian life.

There is a twofold dimension to the raising of the Christian: the initial acceptance of Jesus in faith and the future final resurrection. Both are present in the narrative (vv24ff). In Johannine eschatology, the two moments are blended and are not seen as disjunctive (5:24 - 30). Whoever comes to Jesus in faith will never experience spiritual or total death. The believer has already passed from death to life, and final resurrection will simply confirm what has already taken place.

In the case of Lazarus, the evangelist wishes to emphasize the true state of death; he is not simply in a comatose state. Thus Jesus delays his departure for two days (v6); Lazarus is already four days dead when Jesus arrives (vv17, 39). The stone is set and in place (v38). This is a longer period than had transpired in any of the gospel accounts of a recall from death. It clearly shows Jesus' power over physical death; on another level it points to his life-giving power over spiritual death.

Two Levels of Understanding: This is one of the main characteristics of John's gospel. In his conversations, the respondent(s) speak on one plane and Jesus on another; the transition is made possible by the use of a word or a phrase capable of being understood in two ways.

Jesus' first response on hearing of Lazarus' illness is that he will not die but rather will be an instrument of God's glory (v4). The meaning is that, as in the case of the man born blind (9:3), his impaired state is to be a visible "sign" by which God's power will be made manifest. The apostles' failure to press the issue indicates that they understand Jesus' exclusion of death literally whereas he is speaking on a distinctly different level. This is borne out by the disciples' confusion when Jesus later speaks of Lazarus being asleep (vv11 - 14). The disciples take "sleep" literally and see no cause for alarm. Jesus is speaking of the physical death of the believer, which amounts to no more than a sleep.

The two levels continue. Jesus speaks of going to Judea (v7) where the death has occurred and where he will later die himself. Remaining on the natural or human level, the disciples attempt to dissuade him in the interests of caution (v8), with Jesus seeing the need for the light's continued presence before the "nightfall" of his death arrives (vv9f; 9:4 - 5). The disciples' decision to accompany him is also capable of a twofold meaning (v16): the actual journey to Jerusalem and their eventual martyrdom.

The lack of comprehension continues in Martha's first response (vv23ff). She believes in a final resurrection. Jesus replies that for the believer new life is already present and resurrection in that sense already realized. Upon Mary's arrival, she expresses the same regret already spoken by her sister (v32). In this whole preliminary discourse prior to the "sign" itself, Jesus continually lifts his hearers understanding to a higher faith level. The sign value of the event is to present to the believer God's power at work in Christ, a power that overcomes death at all levels. This is the "glory of God" (vv40, 42). Even Jesus' anger (Gr: *embrimaomai*) (v33) is directed at the evil one who rules in death. Above and beyond the circumstances of the event itself, it is the Johannine faith community that is being addressed in the entire narrative.

Faith Response: No one comes to eternal life and resurrection without faith. In the narrative, there is an expression of faith in Jesus akin to that of the apostles (1:35 - 51), the Samaritan woman (c. 4), and the man born blind (c. 9). At the beginning Jesus indicates to his apostles that the experience ahead will intensify faith (v 15), a note repeated when Jesus is at the tomb (v42). When Jesus states that he is the life-giver and the cause of resurrection, he asks for Martha's acceptance of that truth (vv24ff). Her faith response reflects a high Christology (v27). Jesus is the Messiah, i.e. the promised and anointed of God, the longed-for Davidic descendant. Moreover, he is God's Son, the pre-existent Word who became flesh in time (1:1 - 14). This is an affirmation of a divine filiation which is unique and singular. Finally he is the one sent into the world to disclose the life of the Father (3:31 - 36) and to be the agent of salvation (3:16f).

In summary, the raising of Lazarus is a sign of Christian resurrection, both realized and future. This is made possible by the life-giving power of the risen Jesus whose claims are to be accepted in faith.

In the mass of Christian burial, the preface reminds us that, for the Christian, in death "life is changed, not taken away." Death is a transition, not a terminal experience. The major death-life moment for the Christian occurs in baptism. From that point on, there is a growth in life which ultimately blossoms into full engagement in God. In every death, of course, there is the wrenching pain of separation. But there is also cause for rejoicing—that is, if we truly accept the word of God, if we do believe in the Lazarus story. It is not the "grim reaper" who greets us but the loving Lord who has gone before us. To paraphrase Paul: Why are we afraid? If God loved us enough to give his Son for us, will he abandon us now? If someone close to us in life tells us that he or she will see us in a week, we believe unhesitatingly. God promises us that he will see us. Christ will come to us as surely as he came to Lazarus. Do we truly take him at his word?

Living in faith is a different way of living. If we have passed from death to life, it means that we have also passed from flesh to spirit. We cannot have it both ways. Faith and life have to correspond. Belief in the spirit life points to a great present and an even greater future. But by choice it excludes a life that is improper, tawdry, and "flesh" centered. The message is simple. Be what you are. Live what you profess. With Lazarus we have come to life. We have only to leave behind the burial bands and cloths of past death and walk in a resurrection spirit.

Homiletic and Catechetical Helps

1. Faith as a passage from death to life.

2. Resurrection as present and future.

3. The Christian burial liturgy: white vestments, paschal candle.

4. Paul's use of flesh and spirit.

5. The Hebrew scriptures and the after-life.

6. Lazarus: symbol of the believer.

7. Martha and Mary: symbols of the believer.

8. Lazarus and Christ: the meaning of friendship.

FIFTH SUNDAY OF LENT
Year B

Readings

> Jer 31:31 - 34
> Heb 5:7 - 9
> Jn 12:20 - 33

Theme: The Path to Glory

The successful outcome of God's salvific plan appears in all three readings today. In the midst of exile and dispersion, Jeremiah sows the seeds of hope with God's promise of a new and more effective covenant. The authors of the letter to the

Hebrews and the fourth gospel see the outcome of Jesus' work in his deliverance or glorification. But both of them state forcefully that this is realized only by Christ's following the path of suffering and endurance. The outcome is certain but it comes at a great price.

First Reading

This has long been recognized as one of the most important passages in all of the biblical literature. The mission of Jesus centering on a new covenant (Lk 22:20) and the division of the scriptures into two "testaments" or covenants find their *raison d'être* here. This teaching plays a part in prophetic eschatology (Ez 36:24 - 28), but it is Jeremiah who gives it the most succinct but comprehensive treatment.

The context is important. In chapter 31, the present passage follows that which deals with individual responsibility for sin in a move away from the idea of collective guilt (vv27 - 30). This new emphasis on personalism blends well with the new covenant oracle.

The future relationship will find a responsive Hebrew people unlike their forebears who repeatedly violated the Sinai covenant (v32). It will be a covenant with the nation as a whole, with explicit mention made of both kingdoms (v31).

The covenant to come will be internal (v33), not written on stone tablets but on the heart (Heb: *leb*), the seat of intelligence and volition, not affection. In other words, it will be an observance of the law marked by conviction and personal appropriation. The stress on the Yahweh-people relationship (v33b), a recurring Jeremian theme (7:23; 24:7), underscores the continuity between the two covenants.

This future pact will also be characterized by a direct experiential knowledge of God (v34). It will emerge particularly in the realization of forgiveness. Communication through mediators or secondary agents will be unnecessary. The heart will learn from and respond to God directly, with the idea of personalism again coming to the fore. Conformity will not depend on external sanctions but will spring from a conviction surrounding the truth.

It should be noted that the new covenant does not mean a new set of laws. The content of the first covenant remains intact. Rather the change is in the human partners to the covenant. The new covenant becomes in fact what the former was in theory. Christians have long seen in the Jeremian oracle an unusually clear insight into the covenant of Jesus.

Responsorial Psalm   Ps 51

The "clean heart" for which the psalmist prays in the *Miserere* (v12) gives the psalm a logical place in today's liturgy. The basic plea for forgiveness rests on Yahweh's covenant love and deep sense of mercy (v3). But the petitioner asks for more than forgiveness. The removal of sin is to be total, with the offense blotted from memory, as if it had never occurred (vv3f). Furthermore, he prays for a completely renewed spirit. There are allusions to this new heart in the oracle from Jeremiah (first reading); it is mentioned explicitly by Ezekiel (11:19). What is requested is a "fleshy" responsive heart. *Your presence* (v13) refers to attendance at temple worship. There is a plea for the joy that comes from experienced forgiveness and the strength of conviction in observance (v14). In gratitude the psalmist will share his experience and promote the conversions of others (v14).

Second Reading

The epistle to the Hebrews here addresses Jesus' passage to glory. The general context of chapter 5 speaks of Christ in his role as high priest who has now entered the heavenly sanctuary but who as man was able to empathize with a broken humanity.

Jesus is the prototype of glory through suffering. In the days of his mortality (flesh), he prayed to be delivered from suffering, especially from his pre-destined death (v7). The reference could well include Gethsemane but is broader in scope (Jn 12:27). It deals with the general posture of Jesus in facing a future with so many shadows. The description of Jesus' anguish (prayers, loud cries, and tears) is exceptional in its emphasis on the depth of his human suffering.

He was heard (v7b): not in the sense that he was saved from death but rather that he was brought through death to resurrection-exaltation. This is parallel with v9. *Son though he was* (v8): This could be a reference to the sonship conferred with his exaltation (Rom 1:4) or the eternal, pre-existent filiation. The latter is a rather late development; the former is more primitive. Either is possible in the letter although emphasis in this passage falls on exaltation.

The hardships of Jesus taught him obedience (v8), which is the key to Christian soteriology and central to the thought of this epistle (10:8ff). The submission to the Father's will is what brought Jesus to the heavenly priesthood (v9, "he was made perfect"), a sacerdotal role now exercised perpetually and uninterruptedly on behalf of those who will now, in turn, obey him.

Third Reading

Jesus' discourse on his path to glory through crucifixion is triggered by the arrival of Gentiles who seek an interview with him (vv20f). These may well have been proselytes converting to Judaism who had come to Jerusalem for Passover. Here, however, they become part of John's symbolism, with the words quickly taking on a deeper meaning.

The Gentile mission of the church is about to be launched as the request of the inquiring "Greeks" is meant to indicate. It should be noted that this incident follows the unwitting prophecy of a universal mission (v19). The request is brought to Jesus by his disciples and is met with his response of a forthcoming death-glorification (vv22ff). The whole incident has passed to a higher faith level: the Gentiles wish to *see* Jesus (v21), i.e. to come to him in faith, which is only possible with the giving of the Spirit in death-exaltation. The *hour* of Jesus (v23) is a consistent Johannine reference to his passion and death (2:4; 17:1), with death and glorification being two moments of a single event. The Father glorifies the Son as the result of his obedient submission. Jesus then reigns from the cross. Jesus is deeply disturbed in facing his "hour" and requests of the Father, *Glorify your name* (v28). There is an exchange of glory on the cross. Jesus glorifies the Father through his death (v28) as he has through the "signs" performed during his ministry. At the same time, in accepting his Son's act of self donation and gifting him with the Spirit, the Father also glorifies Jesus (v23).

The "hour" of Jesus is here described in three ways. First, it is a death that gives abundant life (v24). The "grain of wheat" may have been a popular proverb (1 Cor 15:36), here adapted to apply to Jesus' death. The grain that is planted ("dies") is productive; otherwise it produces nothing. In Jesus' case a death is called for if the Spirit is to be given and the Gentile mission opened. Thereupon John's audience is addressed in the ensuing paradox (vv25f). Love of life results in loss; the surrender of life produces gain. The lesson is clear to first century Christians enduring persecution. This antithetical proverb is found in all the gospels (Mt 10:39; Mk 8:35; Lk 9:24).

Second, the "hour" is a moment of crisis. The "now" occurrences (vv27, 31) refer back to the "hour." Jesus' dismay in facing his passion is reminiscent of Gethsemane (Mt 26:39) but need not be so limited in John's understanding. What is foreseen is a moment of great suffering which will ultimately issue in glory given to the Father (vv27ff).

Finally it is an "hour" of judgment (v31). Through Jesus' exaltation on the cross, access to eternal life is afforded to all (v32; 3:14ff). Judgment is passed on Satan whose rule is abolished (v31). In this verse, "world" is used in a negative sense as the arena where evil presides; in other instances in John it is seen positively as the locus of God's concern (3:16). Those who live for this "world" will bring judgment on themselves (3:18).

In ancient times crucifixion was a dread form of execution and the death of Christ was not readily depicted. In the history of Christian art there have been moments when it came to be depicted in rather grotesque ways. What captures any student of Johannine thought are those artistic expressions of the crucifixion, ranging from El Greco to Dali, which capture a certain serenity and radiance. The glory of God emerges through all the ugliness of this event. The cross is the throne from which Christ rules, or, as Hebrews expresses it, it is the door to the heavenly sanctuary where Christ the priest has entered once and for all. The new covenant of Jeremiah has become a fact.

As Jesus reminds us in today's gospel, discipleship means walking our own distinct path to glory. It involves a loss of life if life is to be gained. No two people walk the same path. For some people the loss of life is literal; they are called to martyrdom for the gospel. We have our modern examples. There have been inspiring Christians who have faced totalitarian, sometimes "Christian" regimes in defense of the rights of others. There are others whose entire lives are spent for the poor. Think of the people who accept a terminal disease with serenity, even joy. Then there are those who are always available, never inconvenienced, who never count the cost: those who give love to the children of broken marriages, those who nurse their elderly parents in their final years. Yes, there are many paths to glory. There is a great destiny before us. But on that path the seed must die, for only death brings life.

Homiletic and Catechetical Helps

1. The covenant: Sinai, Jeremiah, Jesus, the eucharist.

2. The experience of God: What does it mean in my life?

3. The law written in the heart: its meaning today.

4. Christ as priest.

5. The Catholic priesthood: its meaning.

6. The single sacrifice of Christ and the mass.

7. Understanding the human suffering of Christ.

8. Modern examples of the "seed dying."

FIFTH SUNDAY OF LENT
Year C

Readings

> Is 43:16 - 21
> Phil 3:8 - 14
> Jn 8:1 - 11

Theme: The Power of the Resurrection

Second Isaiah sees the impressive events of the original exodus as but a prelude to the Jews' repatriation after the exile. It is God's creative power that is at work in both events. Paul summarizes the meaning of his life in being identified with the dead and risen Christ. The power of God which effected the resurrection is now brought to bear in the life of every Christian through the work of the Spirit. Nowhere is God's saving power more evident than in the forgiveness of sins. In today's gospel Jesus forgives the sinful woman and restores her friendship with God

First Reading

The return from Babylon is seen as a singular act of God's saving power. This passage from Isaiah is introduced by Yahweh's self presentation: "I am the Lord, your Holy One, the Creator of Israel, your King" (v15). What follows is an illustration of that power. What was seen first in the creation of the universe continues in the triumph of the Hebrews over the Egyptians and is to be manifested again in the return from the Babylonian exile.

The passage through the Reed Sea is recalled as Yahweh triumphs over the sea and the Egyptian army (vv16f; Ex 15:19ff). As great an event as that was, it can be overlooked in light of what is to come (vv19ff). The on-going creation will produce irrigation in desert regions and a new highway to be traversed. Even the wild animals will see the "hand of God" in all of this (v20). Finally a new people will be formed that will see and honor Yahweh as their benefactor (v21). Yahweh who is identified as Creator in the opening verse of the chapter continues to manifest his power in acts of redemption.

Responsorial Psalm   Ps 126

This is a prayer for assistance in time of need. It can be divided into two parts: a recalling of past favors (vv1ff) and a plea for present assistance (vv4ff). The psalm is best situated in the post-exilic period, probably in a time of hunger and drought. As in the first reading, the return from exile as a moment of divine favor is strongly underscored (vv1ff); it had apologetic value as well, with the Gentiles recognizing God's deliverance.

As the floor of the Negeb in the south of Palestine is inundated by the winter rains, may Yahweh's favor be experienced by his people (v4). The contrast between the sorrowful sower and the joyful reaper may be proverbial (v9). The imagery is vivid of fertility and abundance following quickly in the wake of agricultural hardship.

Second Reading

The passage is one of the richest in the entire Pauline corpus and can be divided into two parts: Paul's present life in Christ (vv8 - 11) and that which it augurs for the future (vv12ff).

The great gain for Paul is *the knowledge of Christ Jesus* (v8), i.e. an experience of Christ arising from the intimate unity which binds Christ and the Christian. For Paul it is termed "living in Christ" (v9a; Gal 2:20). This "knowledge" makes all former accomplishments or titles, like those mentioned earlier in the chapter (vv3:5f), fade into insignificance as something disposable, simply rubbish (v8). The "knowledge" of Christ for Paul has two dimensions: a fusion into Christ' suffering and death and into his resurrection with its life-giving power (v10). The Christian in his or her death to self becomes conformed to the death side of Christ (Gal 2:19f) by which, through the cross, the Christian dies to the world and the world to the Christian (Gal 6:14). But there is more than that. The Christian's suffering, especially that on behalf of the church, becomes an extension of what Christ endured; it is appropriated by him and bcomes part of his total offering to the Father. This offering of both the head and the body makes up for what is lacking in Christ's personal offering (Col 1:24).

The second dimension of this "knowledge" of Christ is to experience the power of the resurrection. Christ rose from the dead constituted Son of God in the "spirit of holiness" (Rom 1:4). This is the Spirit which has brought about his resurrection and is destined to be shared with those who come to him in faith. Paul "knows" Christ because of the Spirit, received at the time of his conversion (Acts 9:17). It is this same Spirit that makes possible death to the flesh (Gal 5:16 - 25) and empowers Paul in his apostolic mission (Acts 13:2f). To live in Christ, then, means conformity to him in his death and resurrection.

In this passage Paul also presents a succinct summary of his teaching on justification (v9), given at length in Romans and Galatians. If one is "found in Christ," it is because he or she has first been found by Christ. Righteousness justifies. It has its source in God's righteousness or covenant fidelity which is extended and conferred on the believer (Rom 3:21f). This justification is not due to any human achievement or law observance. It is pure gift and comes solely through faith in the saving work of Christ.

Finally Paul speaks of the future aspect of justification (vv12ff). There is a "not yet" connected with the "now" of personal righteousness. That is the final summing up or terminal point, a destiny arrived at through fidelity and growth. *Perfect maturity* (v12): a possible allusion to the stages of development found in the mystery religions of Paul's time. In speaking of the future eschatological moment, Paul uses the athletic imagery of the race. He presses on toward the prize with the hope of having the race's judge call him to the raised platform to confer the honor (v14), "upward calling" (literally "call from above"). As the athlete focuses on his goal and sacrifices all to reach it, so too Paul concentrates on the finish line. It remains only for him to persevere.

Third Reading

This is one of the most poignant and touching accounts of Jesus' ministry. Quite apart from its inspiring lesson, the narrative has long been beset by difficulties of acceptance. The main problems center around its canonicity, i.e. recognition as an authentic part of the scriptures, and its authorship, i.e. whether or not it was originally a part of John's gospel. As regards the canonical question, the story is absent from the major Greek manuscripts of the gospels. This absence from important ancient sources militates against canonicity, although the passage does appear in later Latin manuscripts. Since it appears in the Vulgate of St. Jerome, its authenticity as inspired scripture has never been contested in Catholic circles. The story itself has an authentic ring in terms of Jesus' ministry. There are reasons why it may not have appeared at an early date, e.g. its seeming incompatability with the strict penitential discipline of the early church.

A stronger case can be made for its not being Johannine. It reflects neither the language nor the style of John. In some manuscripts it is placed after Luke 21:38, which makes reference to Jesus' stay on the Mount of Olives (v1). Its present location in John may be due to the context of Jesus' claim to being non-judgmental (8:15). At any rate, this question should not detract from its important teaching on sin and forgiveness.

The woman has been taken in the act of adultery, punishable by death according to Jewish law (Deut 22:23f). At this time the carrying out of the punishment would have been academic, since Rome had withdrawn Jewish authorization for capital punishment (Jn 18:31). It does, however, place Jesus in a serious dilemma. In stating his position, he would have to uphold either Moses or Rome (vv5f). Jesus' writing on the ground remains enigmatic; there is only room for conjecture. A plausible case can be made for an allusion to Jeremiah 17:13; the Hebrew reads: "Those turning aside (from you) shall be written on the earth," a reference to the woman's accusers.

Jesus proposes a counter-dilemma (v7). Ordinarily the witnesses to the crime are the ones to execute judgment (Deut 17:7). Since Rome had withheld the right to execute, Jesus' proposal is didactic in character. Clearly the sinless person is not be found. As the accusers depart and the two remain alone, Jesus removes any hint of condemnation. Her acquittal means forgiveness, with the single injunction to sin no more (v11). The action of Jesus is certainly one of compassion. But it is also an exercise of the power proper to God alone. Elsewhere Jesus implies that a spiritual healing demands more than one which is physical (Mk 2:7 - 11). God's creative power continues as salvific in the ministry of Jesus.

There was nothing that evoked stronger reaction in Jesus' opponents than his claim to forgive sin. It was seen as blasphemous, an appropriation of power proper to God alone. What is true on both sides is that sin was considered a serious and weighty matter. One wonders if the same can be said today. Jesus' compassion for the sinner is real. His treatment of the woman in today's gospel is sensitive and non-threatening. But his final words tell her to desist.

Sin is something only God can eradicate. Other miracles are only a shadow of what it means to overcome sin. Jesus does it, and willingly, but he is anything but casual about it. The mindset of today is often just the opposite. Modern society dismisses sin; it is explained away in terms of culturally conditioned attitudes or guilt-producing anxieties. If ours is a biblical faith, then we have to say that the Judeo-Christian tradition sees it differently.

Paul's treatment of the sorrow and joy (death and resurrection) dimensions of faith has much more than academic value. Our union with Christ makes our suffering his and his resurrection ours. Those two great moments in salvation are woven into the fabric of every Christian's life. Our final victory, the attainment of the prize, will not be ours alone. It will be his as well. And our suffering, especially in the interests of faith, is not borne alone. In a very real sense Christ bears it with us. We are an extension of his offering on the cross. This is not merely consoling language. Paul's body of Christ may be hard to grasp but it is very real. The battle and the victory are shared. Our lives become part of Christ's gift to the father.

Homiletic and Catechetical Helps

1. Creation: Genesis, the exodus, post-exilic return, Christian redemption.

2. The power of God: creation, redemption, forgiveness.

3. Power: its Christian and its worldly meaning.

4. To know Christ in his death and resurrection.

5. Examples of experiential knowledge.

6. Athletic imagery and the moral life: examples today.

7. Lessons to be learned from Jesus and the sinful woman.

8. The power of God in relation to sin.

9. Personal attitudes toward sin.

10. Personal attitudes toward forgiveness.

EASTER
Years A B C

Readings

> Acts 10:34, 37 - 43
> Col 3:1 - 4
> 1 Cor 5: 6 - 8
> Jn 20:1 - 9

Theme: Living a New Life

In his first contact with the Gentile world, Peter presents the Christian kerygma, the "good news" of Jesus. He highlights the resurrection to which he personally attests. The gospel gives us the Johannine account of Peter and the beloved disciple reaching the empty tomb, with the latter being the first to come to faith recognition of what had transpired. In both of the alternative second readings, Paul stresses the moral dimension of resurrection faith. In whatever we do, our attention is riveted on the heavenly values which Easter makes manifest to all humanity.

First Reading

Acts is the companion piece to Luke's gospel. They are really two volumes of a single work, beginning with Jesus' earthly ministry, moving through his death-resurrection, and finally bringing the "good news" to "Judea, Samaria, and the ends of the earth" (Acts 1:8).

Peter's speech is but one of numerous kerygmatic discourses in Acts, some to Jewish hearers (2:14 - 39; 3:12 - 26; 4:9 - 12), others to Gentiles (14:15 - 17; 17:22 - 31). All of them betray their origins in the catechesis of the early church, which Luke has adapted to his own purposes. This speech to the members of Cornelius' Gentile household is especially tailored for a Gentile audience. These discourses in their primitive form centered on the key features of Jesus' redemptive act: his death in accord with the divine plan, his resurrection as foretold in scripture, and his post-resurrection appearances (1Cor 15:3 - 7). Eventually the kerygma also included a brief summary of Jesus' earthly ministry, to which the apostles were recognized witnesses (1:21f). This latter inclusion eventually developed into the whole body of teaching which constitutes the full gospel (Mk 1:1). All of these aforementioned features are found in this Petrine discourse: earthly ministry (vv37ff), death (v39), resurrection and manifestation (vv40f).

Jesus brought God's "word" (the "good news" of salvation) first to the Jews in fulfillment of prophetic promise (10:36; Is 52:7). According to Luke's gospel schema, Jesus' ministry begins in Galilee and terminates in Jerusalem, with the greater part of his teaching or didache given to the people as he makes his journey south. The two geographical focal points of Galilee and Jerusalem come to the fore in the speech. The ministry of healing receives emphasis with Jesus *led by the holy Spirit,* a key Lucan motif (LK 3:22; 4:1,14). *God anointed Jesus* (v38): In the sense of consecrate for mission, at the time of Jesus' baptism by John (Lk 3:21f).

The testimony of the apostles, beginning with the baptism and continuing to the resurrection, is an essential witness for Luke (vv39, 41; 2:21f). Jesus' appearances after the resurrection were reflective of his new transcendent form of existence. He was not seen by everyone but only by those so designated (v41a). *Eating and drinking* with Christ, on the other hand, maintains a continuity with the earthly Jesus. Even with a corporeality now totally transformed, he is not a mere phantasm or internal vision (v41b; Lk 24:36 - 43). The witness of the apostles is intended to link the proclaimed risen Christ with the terrestrial Jesus (v42; 1:8).

The concept of Christ as universal judge is prominent in the Gentile discourses (v42; 17:31). This is not so in the Jewish speeches where scriptural attestation and Jewish culpability in Jesus' death are more to the fore. The discourse ends on a note of universalism. Everyone without exception has access to God's forgiveness in Jesus' name (Lord), a forgiveness made possible through faith recognition and repentance (vv43, 36; 2:38; 3:19).

Responsorial Psalm   Ps 118

This thanksgiving psalm echoes the sentiments of an individual, perhaps the king, who here represents the experience of the collective Israel. The psalm expresses gratitude to Yahweh for deliverance in liturgical terms connected with temple worship.

The exhortation to collective praise of Yahweh for his covenant fidelity is extended to the nation (v2), then to the priests (v3) and Jewish converts (v4). *The right hand* is the warrior's source of strength and protection, here used figuratively for Yahweh's power to deliver his people (v16). He has brought Israel ("I") back from the edge of defeat and destruction to live again in his presence (v17). This insignificant country, demeaned by the great powers of the time, has become a centerpiece of the international scene solely because of Yahweh's evident favor (v22).

This psalm finds its place in the Easter liturgy in being applied to Christ brought back from death to life (v17) and in his rejection by his own people leading to his becoming the cornerstone of a new people of God (v22). This latter verse is repeatedly applied to Jesus' ironic position in the new dispensation (Mt 21:42; Acts 4:11; 1 Pet 2:7). The refrain acclaiming the day of the Lord, fitting for Easter, expresses the psalmist's sense of joy (v24).

Second Reading

The Colossians passage illustrates the consequences of union with the risen Christ. A commentary on the passage is found on the Eighteenth Sunday of Year C.

Alternate Second Reading

In the context of Paul's insistence that a man living in incest within the Corinthian community should be ejected, he uses today's image to point to the infectious nature of misconduct. His exhortation views the Christian experience against the background of the Jewish liturgical calendar.

The Jewish feast of Passover, with its paschal lamb, commemorated solemnly the Israelites' deliverance from Egypt (Ex 12:1 - 13). It was followed immediately by the week-long celebration of Unleavened Bread, during which time fresh bread with no yeast was eaten as part of the exodus remembrance (Ex 12:14 - 20). Paul views Christ's death as the death of the new paschal lamb, a new Passover (v7b). The Christian identifies with this death in baptism. Now purified, the Christian must continue in a post-Passover spirit of unleavened bread (v7a). Yeast was seen as a corruptive force which quickly permeated the whole mass of dough (v6). In order to retain personal and collective integrity, no element of sin (yeast) can be introduced. The past leaven of misconduct is to be set aside and the fresh bread of correctness of life must characterize the Christian community (v8).

Third Reading

It is difficult to harmonize the different accounts of the empty tomb and appearances of the risen Christ in the four gospels. They represent different traditions, some emphasizing the role of the women, others, that of the disciples. They all converge, however, around the basic fact: the tomb was empty and the Lord was risen.

Only John has Mary Magdalene as the sole visitor to come to the tomb in the early hours of the first day of the week. In the synoptics she is in the company of other women (Mt 28:1; Mk 16:1; Lk 24:10); even the Johannine account evidences an earlier plurality ("we," v2). The present narrative may well come from a joining of the Matthean and Lucan accounts. Mary does not enter the tomb nor is there any angelic apparition. She simply concludes that the body has been removed on the basis of the rolled-back stone (v1). She comes to Easter faith only later with Jesus' appearance (vv11 - 18).

Peter and another disciple, upon receiving the news, hurry to the tomb. *The disciple whom Jesus loved* (v2): He is never identified in terms other than "the beloved." Closely linked to Christ at the supper (13:23 - 26), he is present at Calvary (19:26f). His role is more theological than historical, representing the believing and loving Christian who never wavers in his constancy and fidelity. It is the beloved disciple who arrives first at the tomb (v4). His deference to Peter may be explained in terms of Peter's position in the early church as a witness to the resurrection. In the narrative, however, his secondary position gives him a particular prominence, when, after Peter's bewilderment, he becomes the first to believe (v8). This flows from his unwavering love of the Lord.

The burial cloths lying in order and even folded pave the way for faith; they indicate that the body was not stolen in haste (vv6f). The disciples' failure to believe (apart from "the beloved") is attributed to a faulty scriptural understanding (v9: Lk 24:26). It is not clear, however, wherein the clarity of the scriptures regarding a dead and risen Messiah lies. There was evidently a Christian rereading of the scriptures in the light of the resurrection. Thus, this may refer to the servant of the Lord (Is 53:1 - 12) and other allusions now read in a new light (Ps 16;10; Hos 6:2).

Newness of life–that is the message of Easter, the Church's principal feast. It comes in the spring of the year when nature begins to burst forth anew. The new clothes and the Easter eggs are symbols that point to new life. It is the resurrection itself that is the major statement about life.

Christ's emergence from the tomb has importance for three major reasons. First of all, it is God's endorsement of everything Jesus claimed and taught. His life ends in victory not defeat. He was not destroyed by cynical machinations, political manipulation, or military power. In Jesus' resurrection, God has the final word. Secondly, this faith event is a cause of our salvation. Paul tells us that if Christ did not rise, then we are still deep in sin. It is the risen Christ that gives the Spirit, our sanctifier. The "firstborn of the dead" gives assurance to all of us that we are called to a similar destiny. Finally, it is the risen Christ that represents the starting point of Christian faith. It is the prism through which everything in his earthly ministry is now viewed. The risen Christ is read into the events that preceded his death. Jesus of Nazareth, the Jewish rabbi instructing his disciples, is truly God's Son and Lord. Easter stands at the heart of faith.

Paul always looks at the practical dimension. We now have a heavenly homeland, a new vision, and eternal truths to shape our thinking. This does not mean that we live only for a world to come. To bring the Easter spirit to life in a suffering world is very much our task in the here and now. There are the disheartened and the discouraged, the terminally ill, youth in need of credible role models, the poor who people the world's barrios and favellas. The point is, however, that it is our spiritual vision of the new reality which directs all that we do. Easter opens the door to a future heavenly banquet. It is the ultimate Easter dinner to which all are invited by the Lord who rose and was first accepted in faith by one who loved.

Homiletic and Catechetical Helps

1. Easter symbols: the candle, the Alleluia, water, the clothing, the egg, the lily.

2. Easter and baptism.

3. The resurrection: the triumph of God.

4. The meaning of Jesus as Lord.

5. Easter: the beginning of the gospels.

6. Easter background: Passover and unleavened bread.

7. Easter and the Gentile world.

8. Explaining the resurrection.

9. The beloved disciple: connecting love and faith.

10. The impact of the life above on our moral conduct.

SECOND SUNDAY OF EASTER
Years A B C

Readings

Acts 2:42 - 47 (A)
Acts 4:32 - 35 (B)
Acts 5:12 - 16 (C)
1 Pet 1:3 - 9 (A)

1 Jn 5:1 - 6 (B)
Rev 1:9 - 11, 12 - 13, 17 - 19 (C)
Jn 20:19 - 31 (A B C)

Theme: Growth in Faith

The Sunday readings during the Easter cycle take a different tack. They are not woven together in the way to which we are accustomed. All three readings deal with the effects of the resurrection both on the individual believer and on the community as a whole. The first reading from the Acts of the Apostles directs our attention to the growth of the early church under the Spirit's lead. The gospel, generally taken from John, speaks of the Spirit's action in guiding the human soul to its destiny. The second reading, generally taken from Peter or John, reinforces this gospel direction.

There are three brief summaries of early church life found in Acts. They appear as today's first reading in the A B C cycles. Faith grows as a new community begins to evolve, just as it grows in the soul of an incredulous Thomas.

First Reading (A)

The reading describes the daily life of the first faith community in the early church. There are three such summary presentations which Luke has incorporated into Acts (4:32 - 37; 5:12 - 16). Although they betray a certain idealization, they are to be regarded as an authentic portrayal of the central values at work in primitive Christianity.

The teaching of the apostles (Gr: *didache ton apostolon*) (v42): The apostles were official witnesses to Jesus' resurrection and his public ministry (1:1f, 21f). Once baptized, Christians were instructed further on the deeds and teaching of Jesus. This material eventually became the content of the canonical gospels. *Communal life* (Gr: *koinonia*): Now constituted a new family in the Lord (Lk 8:19ff), the faithful recognized a common responsibility for each other. It probably included a certain amount of living in common, although such was not a general practice. The general sharing of goods (vv44f) was an ideal rather than an actual practice; in another summary it is seen principally as a responsibility of the wealthy for the needy (4:34f). *Breaking of the bread and prayer:* The former was a technical expression for the eucharist, the earliest distinctive form of Christian worship. It was conducted in private homes, while the temple continued to serve as the gathering place for ordinary worship (v46: 3:1). There was as yet no rupture between the church and the temple, or Judaism in general, the belief prevailing that the Jews would soon recognize Jesus as the Messiah. Only later in the first century was there a separation of church from synagogue.

The early church enjoyed the favor of the people because of the quality of their life, and the number of converts was notable (vv47f). This popularity was short-lived and soon gave way to violent persecution against the faith community (8:1ff).

First Reading (B)

The effects of the Spirit's work in unity and concern for others again comes to the fore in this second of the summaries on the early Christian community (2:42 - 47; 5:12 - 16). That they were of *one heart and one mind* (v32) is reflective of the Hellenistic ideal of friendship, and having *no needy person among them* (v34) is a reference to the Deuteronomic ideal in Israel (Deut 15:4). Luke places them both in a Christian context as flowing from the teaching and example of Jesus (Lk 8:3; 12:32f; 16:9, 11, 13).

Holding everything in common is related to Jesus' teaching on renunciation. It remains a Lucan ideal even though the evidence of retention of private property (5:4), with emphasis falling on the wealthy's responsibility toward the poor (vv34f), is present. The apostles' witness to the resurrection in power looks principally to the convincing signs and wonders that accompanied their preaching (v33; 5:12; 3:15f). In attesting to the resurrection of Christ, the apostles witness to God's power, which is also at work in their Spirit-filled ministry.

First Reading (C)

In this third of the summaries on early Christian life (2:42 - 47; 4:32 - 37), the notion of the apostles as the adhesive force of the community is much to the fore. Their gathering regularly in the general temple area (v12; 2:46; 3:11) links the apostles with Jewish worship and would have occasioned no surprise at a time before the split between Judaism and the church. The respect of the people for them reached the point of awe (vv13, 11), as the number of converts continued to increase (v14). The gathering of the sick and resulting cures finds the apostles continuing the ministry of Jesus (vv15f; Mk 6:55f). The church continues to grow with evident signs of accompanying power and a numerical increase in members.

Responsorial Psalm (A B C)   *Ps 118*

The commentary on this psalm is to be found on Easter Sunday.

Second Reading (A)

This letter addresses Christians in the Gentile world, recently born in the faith but already enduring persecution. Beginning with the Christian form of a traditional Jewish blessing (v1; Gen 9:26; 1 Kgs 1:48), Peter speaks of the gift of baptism which contains the seeds of hope in a life beyond, a conviction rooted in the Spirit of the resurrected Christ (v3).Thus, rebirth is directed ultimately to a future life which is described as "an imperishable inheritance, kept in heaven for you" (v4), "a salvation to be revealed" (vv5, 9). It is God's spirit (power), expressing itself in trust, that keeps the faithful in readiness for that future day, the proximate arrival of which is part of the epistle's eschatological data.

The trials of the present time cannot still the spirit of joy (v6). The troubled lot of the Christians, which ran from social exclusion to persecution, is a major concern of the letter (1:11; 5:9; 2:19f), to be seen as a test or form of purification in preparation for the life to come (vv7f). Trials also join the believer with the suffering of Christ (5:1; 2:21ff).

Faith is described in terms of a love and a trust without sight (v8). Joy in the midst of trial springs from the realization that the road to salvation has been secured (v9).

Second Reading (B)

The first epistle of John is as much a treatise as a letter. It deals with problems within the Johannine community at the end of the first century about which we can only conjecture. There were dissidents in the church whose arguments are being refuted in this positive presentation of doctrine. The strong emphasis on the pre-existence of Jesus and the importance of the life of charity in the letter give some insight into the problematic.

Faith and love are interwoven in this passage and are inseparable in the living of the Christian life. Only the baptized ("the begotten by God") can profess the messiahship of Jesus (v1) and his divine sonship (v5). It is this faith that is capable of overcoming the world and its allurements (v5), just as Jesus himself did (Jn 16:33). The world is viewed in two ways in John, as the arena of evil (17:14f) and as the object of God's salvific love (17:18; 3:16f). The evil of the world is vanquished by a living faith.

To believe in God is to love him as well. Moreover, the love of the Father is inextricably connected with the love of other Christians ("the one begotten by him") (v1; 3:17; 4:7f). Love of neighbor reflects the extent to which love of God and observance of his commandments play a part in life (vv2f). By the same token, the love of other Christians is the clearest indicator of an authentic love of God (4:12, 20). The two loves are inseparable, as are faith and love.

Christ communicates the Spirit through the waters of baptism made effective by his sacrificial death. The reference to water and blood points to both baptism and crucifixion (v6). It is the Spirit that witnesses to the truth of Jesus. At his death, the Johannine Jesus hands over the "spirit" as his pierced side produces water and blood (19:30, 34). It is the Spirit that links the atoning death and baptism and makes possible the Christian profession of faith.

Second Reading (C)

An unknown Christian named John is exiled to the Roman penal colony of Patmos in the Aegean Sea, not far from Ephesus, because of his Christian beliefs (v9). This is not the author of the fourth gospel, nor is there any historical evidence for his being John the apostle. That he may be a pseudonymous John the apostle, thus adding to the stature of his work, is conjecture at best. Establishing authorship, however, is not essential to the inspired character of the book.

The vision of John is of the victorious, post-Easter Christ in glory. *The Lord's day* (v10): the day of the resurrection, Sunday. *Loud as a trumpet* (v10): the accompaniment of biblical theophanies (Ex 19:16, 19). The seer is enjoined to write on papyrus the content of the vision of Christ in its apocalyptic (veiled and symbolic) setting.

Christ as the fulfillment of Israelite hopes appears against the backdrop of the temple lampstand (Ex 25:31 - 38), which in Zechariah's prophecy has seven lamps (Zech 4:2). *Son of man* (v13): Christ as the fulfillment of Daniel's prophecy regarding the restored remnant, the faithful Israel (Dan 7:13f), a title frequently used in the gospels. The Lord is clothed in the apparel of a celestial figure (Dan 10:5).

Echoes of the apocalyptic Daniel reappear, as the visionary, unable to look upon God and live (Ex 19:21; 33:20), falls prostrate only to be lifted up by the son of man (Dan 8:18). Christ describes himself as pre-existent and immortal (first and last) (v17), the one who has returned from death to life (v18a), with full authority over creation, extending even to its outer limits, Sheol, the abode of the dead (v18b; 20:13f).

That which the seer writes is to be sent to the seven churches (v11) and will include descriptions of present ills (cc. 2 - 3) and God's plan for the future, the apocalyptic content of much of the book.

Third Reading A B C

The Johannine Jesus' first appearance to his disciples occurs on the evening of the resurrection. He has already gone to the

Father (20:17); his now glorified state is indicated by his appearance behind locked doors (vv19, 26) and his conferral of the Spirit and its accompanying peace (v19, 21, 22, 26). John, unlike Luke, does not adhere to an extended temporal sequence of post-Easter events: appearances, ascension, and Pentecost. For John these are but different aspects of a single transcendent event, the resurrection-exaltation of Jesus.

The Johannine narrative is in basic accord with earlier tradition on Jesus' appearance, although the author has shaped the material to fit his own design. The Lucan account of the post-Easter appearance has interesting parallels: peace is extended (Lk 24:36), hands and feet are proffered as signs (v39), forgiveness of sins is to be preached (v47) a promise of apostolic commission is given (v49).

The conferral of the Spirit is central to the first part of the narrative. Clearly a gift of the resurrection, the Spirit conveys peace and the power to forgive sins.

Peace (vv19, 21): The restoration of harmony between God and creation and within the created order itself is effected by the Spirit life of the resurrection (Col 1:20). It is a fulfillment of Jesus' promise at the supper (14:27). *I send you* (v21): This is the mandate given to the apostles as witnesses to the risen Jesus. It is conferred in all the gospels (Mt 28:19; Lk 24:47; Mk 16:15). *Whose sins you forgive* (v23): The power to bind and loose within the church (Mt 16:19; 18:18) is here further elaborated in the power to forgive or retain sins. It connotes an authorized act of judgment, here given to the apostles. As the first gift of the Spirit (v22), it looks to baptism or first forgiveness but also includes subsequent pardon for sin in the Christian life. The Catholic Council of Trent saw in this text the basis for the church's authority to forgive post-baptismal sins. The act of breathing the Spirit evokes the image of God's breathing the spirit of life into Adam (Gen 2:7). Here it is the new life from God that is bestowed (v22).

The narrative also establishes a continuity between the crucified Jesus and the risen Christ. This is seen in the presentation of hands and side (v20). The exchange with Thomas serves several purposes. It too reasserts a continuity between the mortal and transformed Christ (vv25ff). In Thomas' words, it also gives the fullest faith affirmation of Jesus as both Lord and God, offering an important inclusion with the gospel's prologue (1:1). Finally the narrative speaks to the early Christians who had never seen or known the risen Christ. Their faith is applauded as not derived from contact but from the action of God's Spirit (v29).

The narrative closes with what may well have been the conclusion to an earlier edition of the gospel (vv30f). It points out that the evangelist was selective in choosing events from Jesus' life (and thus was in no sense a biographer). Moreover, what was written was fashioned with a determined perspective: to promote faith in Jesus as Messiah and Son of God, a goal imprinted upon the fourth gospel from the start (1:41, 49). *You may believe* (v31): Manuscript differences permit either a coming to faith or a continuing in faith. In view of the gospel's being destined for a faith community, the latter seems preferable, even if not incontestable.

Those first several years in Jerusalem were undoubtedly exciting times. Even with Jesus' death by execution in that city, a fact which on the human level could very well dampen expectations, the apostles soon saw the energizing efforts of the Spirit at work. As prayerful and dedicated people, striving to live and grow in the teaching of their Master, the first believers were an example to all. And their numbers were increasing constantly. There is something captivating and promising about beginnings. Fervor and enthusiasm run high. These were mainly people who had not known Jesus of Nazareth, even more so as the faith began to spread. They were convinced by the preached word and openness to God's Spirit. But in the course of time, and in the wake of opposition, the faith of many began to wane, as the New Testament itself indicates. That may have been a singular case but it is reflected in so many human experiences. Enthusiastic beginnings end up with a "laissez-faire" mentality. Within the church, we have experienced, even in our lifetime, any number of new beginnings. Much of it has left some good in its wake. But novelty of itself does not hold adherents. Those early believers who persevered in the faith were those who had built their house on solid ground.

Today's gospel is for all of us who have not seen and have believed. Thomas doesn't get "the best press." He turns out to be another rather disappointing apostle. For him seeing was believing. And the Lord's words are so clear. How important it is to believe because God is truthful. And in honesty we can say that is where we are. Struggle with belief, yes. Moments of strength and weakness, yes. We do not live in a state of vision, so we struggle with doubt. And there is very little novelty in the lives of most of us. But day after day, in season and out, we profess with our lips and our lives that Jesus is our Lord and God. We believe that our sins are forgiven—not "confessed to a man" but brought humbly and sacramentally before a forgiving God. We believe that Jesus gave authority to the church to forgive sin. We are convinced that we are reconciled and completely restored to his love. No small comfort that.

Sight is a great gift. We love to see new places, new faces, and make new friends. And yet the central feature of our lives is not seen. It is believed. But we are no less certain. And there is nothing novel about a faith two thousand years old. But that is fine, because the Jesus who was seen by Thomas is the same—yesterday, today, and forever.

Homiletic and Catechetical Helps

1. The gospels as the teaching of the apostles.

2. Common life: responsibility for other Christians.

3. Breaking of the bread: eucharist as central to faith.

4. Growth of the community: seeking out the unchurched.

5. Growth in the faith: the RCIA program.

6. Forgiveness of sins: baptism and reconciliation.

7. Forgiveness of sins: sacrament of the sick.

8. The role of the apostles in transmission of belief.

7. Relationship of faith and love.

8. The meaning of apocalyptic.

9. The use of symbols in faith.

10. The testing of faith.

THIRD SUNDAY OF EASTER
Year A

Readings

> Acts 2:14, 22 - 28
> 1 Pet 1:17 - 21
> Lk 24:13 - 35

Theme: Stay With Us

In rising from the dead, Christ inaugurates a new life on our behalf. He accompanies us on our journey of life as we prevail upon him to remain with us. Today's first reading is taken from one of Peter's major discourses to the Jews, the substratum of which is the fact that Christ is alive. In the Lucan account of the two disciples' journey to Emmaus, there is a strong catechesis on Jesus' continued presence, especially in the scriptures and the eucharist. The reading from 1 Peter speaks of the great price that was paid for our freedom and our responsibility to act accordingly.

First Reading

This is the first of six major kerygmatic discourses in Acts in which the "good news" of Jesus is proclaimed. In this first speech to his Jewish co-religionists, Peter points up Jesus as the Messiah, Israel's expected one. These discourses may well have been independent units which found their original setting in the preaching of the early church. All of them have common features. Luke, however, has given them his own distinctive stamp. In both style and content they are an integral part of Luke-Acts.

With the eleven (v14): Peter speaks for the twelve, who represent the twelve tribes of Israel. Thus it is not outsiders who address the Jews about their Messiah but rather the symbolic faithful Israel speaking to the opponents of God's salvific plan.

The following are the main features of the Petrine discourse:

The Kerygmatic Proclamation. The early kerygma centered on the basic elements of Christ's salvific work (1 Cor 15:3ff) including a brief summary of his ministry, with the proclamation of his death and resurrection (vv22ff).

The Design of God. Emphasis on the plan of God as realized in Jesus moves the discussion away from the human machinations that brought about his death. This was not a triumph of Jesus' enemies but rather the realization of God's eternal "foreknowledge." Thus, the Jews are told that Jesus was "commended to you by God" and that "God worked through him" (v22). In his death he "was delivered up by the set plan" (v23), and in his resurrection "God raised him up" (God regularly seen as the cause of the resurrection).

The scriptures are drawn on extensively to support the argument of divine design. Here Psalm 16 is given a very literal interpretation as applied to Jesus' resurrection. His soul was not abandoned to Sheol nor his body to corruption; rather God led him back to life (Ps 16:8 - 11). In this way the events of Jesus "passage" are seen as foretold in scripture.

The centrality of the death-resurrection has a strongly apologetic value here; there is no redemptive perspective or mention of the salvific effects of the passage of Jesus.

The Culpability of the Jews. From the Lucan point of view, primary responsibility for Jesus' death on the human level falls on the Jewish leaders and not on the Romans (3:13ff; 4:10f; 5:30). This corresponds with Luke's passion narrative where the Jewish leaders are the major provocateurs of the death (Lk 23). Specific, almost redundant mention is made of Israelites "staying in Jerusalem" (v14), the capital of Israel, the city that kills the prophets (Lk 13:34f). It was this man sent by God whom "you killed, using lawless men to crucify him" (v23).

Their guilt notwithstanding, the plan was ultimately God's, and the conversion of Christ's opponents is already initiated in the gospel (Lk 23:48) and serves as the climactic plea of the Petrine discourse (2:38f).

Responsorial Psalm   Ps 16

The psalm, already cited in the first reading, continues the Easter theme. Commentary is found on the Thirty-Third Sunday of Year B.

Second Reading

The exhortation to Christian conduct in the midst of a pagan milieu (a place of sojourning or temporary exile, v17) rests upon respect for the God whom the faithful call Father but who is also the one who judges (v17). The action of Jesus is seen as a ransom or "buying back" from the moral alienation of paganism to a life with God. Although it was no financial transaction, the price was very high (v8; Is 52:3; 1 Cor 6:20); it was accomplished through the atoning death of Christ. *The blood ... as of a lamb* (v19): For the Hebrews life was in the blood (Lev 17:14). The reference here is to the Passover lamb (Ex 12:5), a type of Christ (Jn 1:29; 1 Cor 5:7).

Christ is the "mystery of God" (1 Cor 2:1). This is the secret hidden in God from eternity, sometimes made known to the heavenly court, but only revealed in these final times (v20). Praise is directed through Christ to the Father who is consistently seen as the principal agent in the resurrection (v21a; Acts 2:24; 3:15). Faith and hope are coupled, indeed inseparable (v21b). The hope of future glory is rooted in the seeds of faith (Heb 11:1).

The Petrine moral catechesis, like that of Paul, calls for upright conduct on the basis of a redemptive theology. More than an ethical precept, correct living is a grateful response.

Third Reading

The engaging story of the two disciples on the road to Emmaus is a major theological statement. It is replete with reflections of early church belief, something of a ready-made homily on Easter faith. Here we shall deal with its major theological themes.

The Risen Christ. Emphasis falls on the transformation which has taken place in the pre-Easter Jesus. He is not immediately recognized (v16); in fact, recognition only comes with faith and charity (v31). He vanishes as quickly as he appears. All of this highlights the transcendent, wholly new dimension of Christ's risen life. The two disciples. moreover, have wavered from discipleship. Instead of remaining in Jerusalem (24:47, 52), they are moving away. The journey, so central to Luke's literary-theological schema (Lk 9:51 - 19:27), has taken for them a deviant turn, until they are redirected by their meeting with Christ (v33). They recount the kerygma (vv19 - 24) but without belief, providing a sharp contrast with the women who were prompt to believe (24:4 - 12). It is the risen Christ who overcomes the disciples' disbelief.

The Kerygma. The disciples, still lacking in faith, give expression to the fundamental belief of the early church (1 Cor 15:3 - 7). It includes the ministry of Jesus (v19), his death (v20) and resurrection (vv22f). The customary inclusion of the resurrection is lacking only because it appears in the story itself.

The Scriptures. The early church found in the scriptures ample attestation to Jesus' salvific role. This was often done with an "after the event" rereading, a common procedure in Jewish exegesis. Thus it is said that there is a general convergence of the scriptures on the death and resurrection of Christ (vv27, 44). Yet there are no texts cited, as elsewhere in Luke (Acts 2:17 - 21, 25 - 28, 34f), to support that view. And the disciples later indicate that it was in the sharing of the scriptures that their resurrection faith began (v32). Without entering into scriptural detail, Luke here indicates that it was vital to the life of the early church to place Jesus within the framework of God's design, as the point of convergence of the law and the prophets (9:30).

Generosity. As in the case of the journey theme, Luke regularly underscores the value of charity as manifest in generosity (Lk 10:38 - 42; 10:7; 1:39f; 10:29 - 37). The coming to faith of the two disciples is facilitated by their hospitality in inviting Jesus to dinner. *Stay with us* (v29): This is more than a simple invitation for the evangelist. It is a desire for Jesus' abiding presence.

The Meal. There are various theological overtones. An eschatological meal was part of the end-time imagery. At the final supper, Jesus indicated that he would no longer share the Passover meal with the disciples until the kingdom was realized.

Thus, the resumption of table fellowship. a Lucan sign of unity and love (7:36; 11:37), points to eschatological fulfillment.

There is also a clear eucharistic imprint on the meal, with its evident allusion to the last supper liturgical formula (v30; 22,19). In hearing this story, the early Christians were reminded of the eucharist, known as the "breaking of bread" (Acts 2:42), wherein they shared the life of the Lord and grew in their faith knowledge of him.

Witnesses to the Resurrection. Restored by the presence of the risen Christ in scripture, breaking bread, and generosity, the two disciples retrace their steps in a return journey to Jerusalem where they, with the apostles, become witnesses to the resurrection (vv34f). They will preach a real Christ but one recognized only in faith and for future generations to be encountered in scripture, eucharist, and a living charity.

"Stay with us." These words marked a turning point in the disciples' faith journey. They began their walk dejected and disappointed. They finished with enthusiastic faith. The transition began when they showed concern for a stranger on the road. Everything in the Emmaus story is directly applicable to our life as Christians today. As the Second Vatican Council teaches, we meet Christ in the scriptures. The word of God is sacramental, an external sign that brings us to Christ. And yet are we attentive to the word? Do our lectors understand the importance of what they do? With all the developments in scripture, how updated are we in our understanding? Every eucharist brings us both scripture and the breaking of the bread. Full participation should deepen faith. That is the message of Emmaus. Yet how routine it can become, a very customary matter. Perhaps deprivation would help intensify our love. With no possibility of celebrating mass in the distant Orient, Teilhard de Chardin once wrote poetically about offering Christ on the altar of the world. If Emmaus is correct, then Christ surrounds us. Yes, he stays with us through the entire journey of life.

And he is present in generosity and concern. The first letter of Peter today spoke of life as a grateful response for our ransom. And that means showing generosity to others. A dinner invitation in biblical thought was a genuine expression of goodness. We should try to recapture some of that sentiment in our matter-of-fact world. When our home becomes a point of welcome for others, especially the less fortu-

*nate, then the spirit of "stay with us" comes to life. Generosity takes
many forms: availability to the elderly; time given to hospital ministry;
parenting the parentless; standing with another in bereavement; assisting the wayfarer in need.*

Stay with us, Lord. Stay with us.

Homiletic and Catechetical Helps

1. Faith proclamation (kerygma) and teaching (didache).

2. The Christian life as a journey.

3. The scriptures as a sacrament of God.

4. Understanding the scriptures.

5. Meal sharing and Christian generosity.

6. The eucharist as a meal.

7. Witnessing to Christ.

8. Moral uprightness as an act of gratitude.

9. Christ as the Passover lamb.

THIRD SUNDAY OF EASTER
Year B

Readings

> Acts 3:13 - 15, 17 - 19
> 1 Jn 2:1 - 5
> Lk 24:35 - 48

Theme: Resurrection and Repentance

The resurrection has much more than apologetic value.
Inasmuch as it effects the forgiveness of sins, it is redemptive.
Today all three readings emphasize repentance. At the conclu-
sion of his strongly worded address to the Jews, the Peter of Acts

urges them to repent of their sins. The letter of John views Christ as a sin offering for the world and reminds us that if we sin, we have in him our personal intercessor before the Father. In his summary of the risen Christ's first appearance to his disciples, Luke concludes with the apostles' post-Easter mandate. They are to preach repentance, for now access to God has been definitively achieved.

First Reading

This discourse of Peter, given in conjunction with the healing of the crippled man, has a strongly polemic tone when it turns to Jewish culpability for Jesus' death. It is equally forceful, however, in its call to conversion and the desired participation of the Jews in the reign of God. Lucan themes are readily detected, and, therefore, regardless of its source, the speech is an integral part of Acts. In looking at Jesus' death and the accompanying responsibility, it is a speech of contrasts.

The God of Abraham, Isaac, and Jacob (v13): The mention of the patriarchs places Jesus in the line of the authentic Israel, with the same God who acted on behalf of Israel's ancestors now vindicating Jesus (Ex 3:6). *Glorified* (v13): God has given glory to Christ in raising him from the dead and seating him at his right hand (Jn 12:23). The "servant" designation alludes to the servant of the Lord who was also vindicated by Yahweh (Is 52:13). The contrast here is between God who champions the cause of Jesus and the Jews' public denial of him before Pilate, who sought to release him (Lk 23:15, 20, 22).

The Holy and Righteous One (v14): The title places Jesus' personal sanctity and integrity in bold relief. He is so identified by the angel at his conception and the centurion at his death (Lk 1:35; 23:47). The contrast here is seen in the Jews' rejection of one who was sinless in favor of Barabbas, a criminal (Lk 23:18f).

Life and death (v15): The final contrast is between life and death. The Jews chose death for one who pointed the way to authentic life and who was vindicated by the Father with the conferral of new life. The note of apostolic witness to the resurrection is again underscored.

The ignorance that excused in the past is now excluded in the

face of divine and human testimony (vv17f). There is an underlying note of irony in the Jews' being ignorant of something to
which the scriptures amply attested. There is a distinction made
between the crowd and the Jewish leaders (v17). In Luke's gospel,
the crowd is joined to and allied with the priests and leaders at
the trial (Lk 23:4f, 13 - 23) but is detached from them in showing
repentance at the crucifixion (Lk 23:48). *Through all the prophets*
(v18): This generalization is again unspecified (Lk 24:27, 45ff).
There was a Christian rereading of the Hebrew scriptures in light
of the death-resurrection, with allusions found to this salvific
event not intended by the original author. Examples of this are
found in Peter's first discourse (2:17 - 21, 25 - 28, 34).

The injunction to conversion is equated with the forgiveness
of sins through the gift of the Spirit. This is accomplished by
the acceptance of Jesus as Lord and Messiah (v19; 2:36, 38).

Responsorial Psalm   Ps 4

This individual lament expresses confidence in Yahweh's
favor in the face of trial (vv2, 4). The Lord's doing "wonders for
his faithful one" (v4) by adaptation is today read in the light of
the Easter event. The psalmist prays for the continued support
of Yahweh's blessings, which give him a deep sense of peace
and security (vv7ff).

Second Reading

These verses may have been originally drawn from an initiation rite within the Johannine community which emphasized the
separation from sin incumbent upon the believer. For those who
have sinned, forgiveness is attainable in and through Christ's
atoning death. *Advocate* (v1): In legal parlance, Jesus is the
defense attorney. He is the first intercessor; the Spirit is the second, also termed Advocate (Jn 14:16). *Expiation for our sins* (v2):
Jesus' death is compared to an atoning sacrifice (4:10; Heb
7:26ff); it touches not only the Christian community but the
entire world.

With forgiveness established, the Christian is called to resolute moral rectitude. *Knowing the Lord* and *keeping the com-*

mandments are co-extensive concepts (vv3ff). Knowledge connotes the experience of God's presence, not mere conceptualization, and is to be found in fidelity to his teaching and mandates. Contradiction inevitably arises in claiming the experience of God and yet disregarding his commandments. In such a case, as in that of aversion for one's neighbor (4:20), there is no authentic love of God.

Love of God (v5): A subjective genitive, this is God's love for the human person. The observance of God's word results in the internal upbuilding of God's redemptive love with the indwelling of Father and Son (Jn 14:23f).

Third Reading

The conclusion to Luke's gospel centers on the singularly important meeting of Christ and his disciples after the resurrection. Today's reading begins where the story of the two disciples journeying to Emmaus terminates (v35). An outline of the central features of this post-Easter appearance follows.

Peace (v36). The Lucan note sounded in the angelic hymn at Jesus' birth returns here (2:14). With Christ's resurrection the harmony and accord between God and the world, lost by sin, is restored (Col 1:20). More than a mere greeting, the expression is pregnant with meaning as part of the Easter message (Jn 20:19, 21, 26).

Reality of Christ's Presence (vv37 - 42). The fact that Jesus ate with his disciples appears elsewhere in the resurrection narratives (24:30; Jn 21:12). While the themes of the messianic banquet and the eucharist explain part of this, continuity between the pre-Easter and post-Easter Jesus plays a key role. This apologetic feature was part of the later apostolic preaching (Acts 10:41).Here it is complemented by emphasizing the actuality of his crucified body. This note, repeatedly struck, opposes any suggestion of a purely internal experience or a discontinuity between the terrestrial and risen Jesus. A careful balance is maintained between a transformed and transcendent Christ and that same Christ's relationship to the experienced Jesus of the earthly ministry.

Scriptural Fulfillment (vv44 - 47). This recurring Lucan theme sees much of the Hebrew scriptures converging on the Messiah's death and resurrection (v26; Acts 3:18; 17:3; 26:23). As has been noted elsewhere, much of this implies a Christian reinterpretation of scriptural texts in understanding them in a Christological sense. The Acts of the Apostles amply illustrates the procedure (Acts 2:25 - 28, 34; 3:22f; 4:25).

Apostolic Mandate (vv48ff). While there is some evidence that others may have been with the apostles on this occasion (24:9, 33), the emphasis falls on the witness of the twelve, who assume an official role in attesting to the earthly ministry and resurrection of Jesus (Acts 1:21 - 26). Their witness is to be accompanied by the forgiveness of sins, effected by the atoning death and the Spirit, and attainable through the acceptance of the proclaimed Lordship of Jesus (v47). Their preaching is to start in Jerusalem, the focal point of Lucan geography, and then expand to the ends of the earth (Acts 1:8).

It is difficult to describe the resurrection. The holy card image of Christ emerging from the tomb clothed in white with banner in hand probably serves as well as any other visual representation. The fact is, however, that no one saw Christ rise. It is really a question of a theological statement more than a captured historical moment. His resurrection was known from his appearances and from the empty tomb, not from eyewitnesses to the event. The gospels struggle with expressing the risen reality. It was not just another phase in the history of Jesus of Nazareth. In a real sense he was totally "other," living now the indescribable life of God. And yet he was the same person and in some ways objectively identifiable. However, the resurrection was known principally by its fruits, the faith proclamation of unlettered fishermen. It changed people's lives and continues to do so. To watch people move from a state of alienation to conversion and a new direction in life is the clearest proof of the risen Christ. To see a faith-filled person galvanize the forces of other people to pursue an ideal, to see hatred and animosity become love and forgiveness, to see an ecumenical council change the face of a church: these things tell us that "Christ has truly risen and appeared to Simon."

There is simple and unvarnished truth in John's letter today. Most of us register our experience of God in terms of our conduct. We are not given to ecstasy, apparitions, or levitating experiences. But if we earnestly strive to live his teaching, even with failure, we do experience peace. We draw life and courage, as well as solace, from being faithful. And when God's word becomes less significant or relativized or just disregarded, God becomes distant. Frequently people feel "short-changed." Their prayer is dry. They don't "feel" close to God. There are few spiritual "highs." But they are faithful. And they strive to live as Christians. They should take courage. God is close. He is present every step of the journey. And his message is that of Easter: "Peace."

Homiletic and Catechetical Helps

1. The meaning of conversion.

2. The relationship between the resurrection and conversion.

3. Forgiveness of sins and amendment of life.

4. Knowing God and keeping his commandments.

5. Explaining the resurrection.

6. The Christian meaning of peace.

7. Apostolic witness to the earthly and risen Christ.

8. Christian mission to the world today.

THIRD SUNDAY OF EASTER
Year C

Readings

> Acts 5:27 - 32, 40 - 41
> Rev 5:11 - 14
> Jn 21:1 - 19

Theme: Fishing and Shepherding

The liturgy today moves between earth and heaven. The gospel finds the apostles engaged in their now highly symbolic occupation as fishermen and Peter is given his mandate to provide for Christ's flock. The first reading from Acts has the apostles arraigned for fulfilling their mission of "catching" people for God. Revelation carries us to a higher realm where the risen Christ, carrying the marks of his passion, is praised by heavenly and earthly voices. Their joy prolongs that of the apostles in Acts, who rejoice in their lot of suffering for the Lord.

First Reading

This is the second arraignment of the apostles before the Sanhedrin. In the first instance (4:5 - 18), only Peter and John were accused; here it is all the apostles. The two accounts are similar, with the dramatic build-up between the disciples and the Jewish leaders at this point more intense. Major features of the narrative are the following:

The Kerygmatic Proclamation. At the heart of the narrative stands the announcement of the "good news" in the presence of the Jews (vv30ff). It centers on the death and resurrection/exaltation, the witness of the apostles, and the call to repentance. *The God of our ancestors* (v30a): This is an apologetic of continuity. The validation of Jesus' mission in the resurrection is accomplished by the God of Jewish history, the God of the patriarchs (3:13). *Hanging him on a tree* (v30b): This reference to the Deuteronomic impaling of a dead criminal (Deut 21:22f) adds a further negative note to the accusations against the Jewish leadership in treating Jesus as a common criminal. Christ is leader as the "firstborn of the dead" (Col 1:18) and, for the first time here, *Savior,* the one who forgives sin and confers the Spirit (v31). The witness of the apostles is subordinate and instrumental; it is the Spirit who ultimately testifies to the truth of the kerygma (v32).

The Apostolic Mission. The apostles fulfill the mandate given by Christ quite literally (Lk 24:47f), beginning in Jerusalem, indeed before the highest Jewish authorities (v27), whence the mission will proceed to Samaria and the far reaches of the earth (Acts 1:8). Again, in fulfillment of Jesus' prediction, the reply of the apostles is not derived from human skill but is rather a spontaneous utterance as the need arises (vv29 - 32; Lk 21:14f);

they rejoice in persecution, realizing that they are being treated as were the prophets (v41; Lk 11:50f).

The Posture of the Sanhedrin. The hostility of the Jews toward the apostles intensifies. The latter had disregarded the earlier order of the Sanhedrin (v28; 4:18). The apostles answer in the same vein as previously: obedience to God, not humans, is the higher priority (v29; 4:19. *Blood upon us* (v28): The saying is prophetic irony in view of the Matthean acclamation during Jesus' trial (Mt 27:25).

Responsorial Psalm   Ps 30

Resurrection allusions in this psalm (v4) account for its use in the Easter season. The commentary is found on the Eleventh Sunday of Year C.

Second Reading

The picture is one of Christ in glory with the Father, receiving the adoration of all creation, as seen by John, the seer of Patmos (1:9), In the first vision, the chorus is celestial, made up of angels, the four living creatures, and the twenty-four elders. The *living creatures* are animal and human composites, the imagery drawn from Ezekiel and Isaiah (4:6ff; Ez 1; Is 6:2). The *elders* are representative of the twelve tribes of Israel and the twelve apostles (21:12ff).

Lamb that was slain (v12): The redeeming Christ is seen as the now glorified slain lamb. This echoes the Baptist's identification of Jesus (Jn 1:29) and may refer to the Passover lamb (Ex 12:1 - 10), the servant of the Lord depicted as a lamb in his suffering (Is 53:6f; Acts 8:32), or both. The hymn of praise resembles that accorded the Roman emperor, here replaced by Christ the redeemer.

The second vision (vv13f) has praise extended by the whole of creation, with cultic equality accorded the Father ("one who sits on the throne," 4:1 - 9) and the Son (the lamb). This recognition of total parity emerged gradually in the early church, with cult playing a major part in understanding the full meaning of divine filiation.

Third Reading

This chapter in John complements chapter 20 with its account of other appearances of Jesus. The chapter may derive from an independent non-Johannine source, in the light of differences in both style and content, and been incorporated and adapted by the gospel's author. We shall treat in rather broad strokes the main themes of the reading.

The Fishing Scene (vv1 - 10). This is seemingly a variant of Luke's fishing scene (Lk 5:1 - 11), with which it shares notable likenesses and differences. There are seven disciples in the account (unless "Zebedee's sons" is a scribal gloss identifying the two unnamed disciples). The "fishing" is identified with the apostolic mission (v3; Mt 4:19; Mk 1:17); the fruitfulness of the mission is attributed to the presence of Christ (v6; Lk 5:4). The number "one hundred and fifty three" (v11) remains enigmatic. If it is symbolic, the symbolism has been lost. If it is an actual memory, it probably took on the significance of a very large number, representative of the growth of the church.

Children (Gr: *paideia*) (v5): The term was one of endearment used within the Johannine community (v5; 1 Jn 2:14, 18).

Recognition. As is characteristic of resurrection appearances, Jesus is not recognized at once (v4); recognition comes with growth in faith (vv7, 12; 20:15f; Lk 24:30f). *The disciple whom Jesus loved* (v7): This unnamed disciple, representative of the authentic and faithful believer, remained close to Jesus at the supper (13:23), stood faithfully at the cross (19:26), and was the first to believe in the resurrection (20:8). Here his faith and love enable him to recognize the shore figure as the Lord. Upon reaching shore with the large catch, the other disciples too express faith-recognition (v12). Peter's attempt to come to Jesus on the water resembles a similar narrative in Matthew (Mt 14:28 - 31).

The Meal (v12). Jesus' eating after the resurrection has apologetic value in overcoming suggestions that he was a mere phantom or ghost (Lk 24:30, 42). It also reminded the early Christians of the eucharist. Jesus' action here (v13) has distinct likenesses to the loaves story (6:11) and the synoptics' last supper formula (Mk 14:22). Moreover, even though fish have been predominant in the narrative, they clearly become subordinate to the bread in the moment of sharing (v13). Hence, three strong catechetical notes are present in the narrative: apostolic mission, faith recognition, and eucharistic presence.

Peter. The apostle's threefold denial is overcome by the threefold attestation of love (vv15ff; 18:17, 25, 27). With each question, the responsibility of feeding and tending the flock comes to the fore. Peter's singular role in the church appears in different forms in the gospels (Mt 16:18f; Lk 22:32). They all point to an authority within the faith community, with the emphasis here falling on the pastoral dimension. In Catholic belief, the Petrine authority continues to be exercised through the bishop of Rome.

Reference is made to Peter's future martyrdom at the hands of his persecutors by adapting a proverb dealing with the problems of aging and applying it to Peter's eventual loss of freedom (v18). In this he will be quite literally "following" Jesus.

Evangelization and pastoral care–these two ideas are clearly linked in today's liturgy. The fishing of the apostles is symbolic of the church's effort in evangelization, a process which begins with the apostles' preaching the Lordship of Christ before the Jewish leadership and general population in Jerusalem. The early preaching was as dauntless as it was dangerous. Yet the church has no other choice but to proclaim and to evangelize. This should not be seen or conducted as a preemptive strike or a form of proselytizing. It is the sharing of a gift. Undoubtedly there have been sad chapters in the history of the church's mission with forms of moral coercion and the destruction of important human and cultural values. This is best admitted and repented. But there are many stirring chapters as well–missionaries who gave their lives with unlimited generosity and dedication; men and women who truly bettered the lot of others; yes, and people who learned and received as well as gave.

In this age of new evangelization, however, the planting of the seed of faith and its nurturing overlap. Evangelization and pastoral care often become one. There are many people baptized, and there it stops. In a number of countries, Christians never enter a church from their baptism to their burial. This is a nominal faith and hardly that of the scriptures. Many Catholics have reached a plateau where growth in faith has stopped—mass on Sunday, rare reconciliation, some financial support. Pastoral care today means deepening the faith; in many cases it means re-evangelizing. It moves us beyond the comfortable pew. It brings people to a willingness to stand with faith conviction, to find a place in programs of outreach, to be part of the church's mission. For a parish it means much more than being a center of sacramental service. It means being a vibrant center of formation and education, the center of a cluster of neighborhood base communities. It is a call, in short, to revitalize the faith. And for this Peter does not serve alone. It is a community responsibility—to fish and to shepherd. Today they often overlap. The unchurched are often the baptized. Distinctions are not the important thing. The task is. We are all part of the apostolic mission—in the boat or on the shore.

Homiletic and Catechetical Helps

1. The meaning of evangelization today.

2. Evangelizing and re-evangelizing.

3. Examples of "obeying God rather than humans."

4. Faith as the courage of conviction.

5. The equality of Jesus and God in worship.

6. Recognizing the risen Christ in the scriptures.

7. Shepherding—promoting growth in the faith.

8. The authority of Peter in the New Testament.

9. The pastoral role of the pope.

10. The meaning of martyrdom today.

FOURTH SUNDAY OF EASTER
Year A

Readings

> Acts 2:14, 36 - 41
> 1 Pet 2:20 - 25
> Jn 10:1 - 10

Theme: The Sheepgate

The Johannine Jesus speaks of himself as the way to God. Today on Good Shepherd Sunday, Jesus elaborates on that idea in describing himself as the sheepgate. In his first discourse on Pentecost, Peter calls upon his contemporaries to recognize that singular role of Christ by accepting him in faith. In his redemptive mission, Jesus is seen as both the lamb and the shepherd in Peter's first letter.

First Reading

Peter is joined by the eleven in making his initial appeal. The twelve are the faithful Israel, representatives of the twelve tribes (v14; Lk 22:30). This establishes a continuity with the past as Peter (the new Israel) addresses his Jewish co-religionists and through them the whole of Israel. The discourse is entirely geared to a Jewish audience.

The expected response to the Petrine-expanded kerygma (2:14 - 35) is the acceptance of Jesus as *Lord* (Gr: *Kyrios*) and *Messiah* (Gr: *Christos*) (v36). Both titles play a part in Peter's discourse in the quotation from Joel (vv20f) and Psalm 6 (v25), as well as Peter's own commentary (v31). To call Jesus Lord is to accord him the title given traditionally to Yahweh. This recognition of divine status comes with Jesus' resurrection/exaltation (Phil 2:9ff) and is the key to salvation (Rom 10:9). The Messiah is the promised one of Israel, a descendant of David (2 Sam 7:12ff), who is to preside over the restored Israel in the final era. Both titles coalesce in the person of Jesus.

The response of "the house of Israel" is positive (v37). In his gospel, Luke spoke of the people's initial contrition at the crucifixion (Lk 23:48); hence, an affirmative reaction at this point is not unexpected. The crowd, moreover, is distinguished from the antagonistic Jewish leadership (4:1 - 18). In response to their question, Peter outlines the steps of incorporation: repentance, baptism, and Holy Spirit (v38).

Repentance (Gr: *metanoia*) represents a basic change of life from a sinful past to a life of engagement in God. Rooted philologically in the Hebrew word for a change of direction in walking or on a journey, it is a moral "turnabout" in one's goals and objectives, not simply a marginal change of perspective. Baptism accompanies repentance as a visible expression of internal change. It is received "in the name of Jesus Christ," i.e. the name "Lord." This profession of faith, centered on the recognition of Christ as Lord and Savior, is necessary for baptism's effectiveness and may reflect an early baptismal formula ("Jesus is Lord"), which antedated the trinitarian formula (Mt 28:19). It is baptism with its accompanying faith expression which results in the forgiveness of sins. *The Holy Spirit* distinguishes Jesus' baptism from John's (Lk 3:16). It is the empowering divine gift conferred by the risen Christ, the outpouring of which is the sign of the final era.

These three aspects of conversion, although distinguishable, are joined together in a single reality and are inseparable (10:43 - 48). Where there is an extended period of time between one and the other, it is done to link the apostles in Spirit conferral on new believers (8:15f; 19:2, 6).

The gift of faith is destined for Jews and non-Jews ("those far off"); election comes from the freedom of God's choice, as Acts will later attest (v39; 10:44f; 11:15ff). The response of the Jews to Peter's message is immediate and numerically impressive, although the number cited is primarily symbolic of the success of the apostolic mission (v41).

Responsorial Psalm   Ps 23

The theme of the Lord as shepherd continues in the psalm, the commentary for which is found on the Fourth Sunday of Lent, Year A.

Second Reading

In counseling a spirit of long-suffering for those who are slaves (2:18), the author presents Christ as the example. In so doing, he draws on what may have been an early confession of faith, which sees Christ as the servant of the Lord (vv21 - 24) and as the shepherd of souls (v25).

Endurance and patience under duress are part of the Christian calling in living a life conformable to that of Christ himself, who has set the example (vv20ff). The description of Christ as the suffering servant is taken from Isaiah 53:4 - 12, the last of the servant songs. Thus "he committed no sin" (v22; Is 53:9); he was not vindictive, suffering in humble submission (v23a; Is 53:7); he places himself confidently in the hands of the just judge (v23b; Is 53:10ff). His atonement was vicarious, effected for the spiritual liberation of the many (v24a; Is 53:5, 11); his wounds are productive of healing in others (v24b; Is 53:5).

The servant as a lamb is implicit in the profession of faith; it is explicit in the Isaian hymn (Is 53:7). The pastoral image continues here, however, with Christ becoming the shepherd (Gr: *poimen*) and overseer (Gr: *episkopos*) of the flock. Both terms are related to ecclesiastical officeholders in the early church. The linking of the two points to the essentially pastoral dimension of church authority. The shepherd image is a frequent identification of Yahweh (Ps 23; Is 40:11; Ez 34:1 - 16) and of Jesus as the provider for the people of the new covenant (Lk 15:4 - 7; Mt 18:10 - 14).

In this passage, then, Jesus is depicted as the sheep who gives his life for the redemption of others and the shepherd who guides and protects the forgiven flock.

Third Reading

In speaking of himself as the gate for the sheep (vv7, 9), the Johannine Jesus uses two different images. The first is that of legitimate access to the sheep for those responsible for pastoral leadership in the church (vv1 - 3a); the second deals with the sense of security that proper access affords both shepherd and sheep. Jesus as the sheepgate is the divinely constituted and sole avenue to the Father (14:6). Jesus is here speaking to the Pharisees. In the preceding chapter, they had opposed Jesus and excommunicated the man he had cured (9:34f). They are the "thieves and robbers" who not only reject Jesus' claims but mislead others who would attempt to follow him. But because of their inauthenticity, their efforts are doomed to failure (v8).

The opponents of Christ resemble the evil shepherds of Ezekiel who ignore the sheep and pursue their own interests (Ez 34:4 - 8) only to be replaced by Yahweh himself (Ez 34:11f). Evildoers enter the sheepfold deviously and surreptitiously. But the fact is that it is Jesus who offers the only authentic insight into God and his designs. It is he who presents the plan of salvation. Faithful shepherds who adhere to Christ's teaching will elicit a positive response from the faithful (vv3b, 4f). This is undoubtedly a polemic against people within the Johannine ecclesial community whose heterodoxy had become problematic (1 Jn 2:18f; 4:1),

Strangers, i.e the Pharisees and false teachers in the early church, will not succeed in diverting the true disciples. It is adherence to Jesus' teaching that removes all equivocation and makes the voice of the shepherd recognizable (vv4f). Elsewhere Jesus states that it is the Advocate, the Holy Spirit, who assures the preservation of truth in the hearts of believers (14:26). This custody of the word is an important Johannine theme. The Spirit effects a closeness and recognition between leaders and the faithful. The contrast between the two approaches is underscored. False teachers seek only death and destruction, whereas the message of Jesus leads to abundant life (v10).

Failure to accept Jesus as the single way to God explains the inability of Jesus' listeners to understand his figurative language (Gr: *paroimia*, proverb, parable) (v6). This lack of comprehension is appropriate for those who, because they think they see well, in fact remain blind (9:41).

The message of Jesus has not been saved from misrepresentation and distortion. History bears that out. Moreover thieves and robbers have entered in more ways than through heretical teaching to wreak havoc

within the fold. Examples of people using religion to amass personal fortunes evoke very painful memories in the minds of many sincere people. In terms of adherence to truth, there is wisdom in a teaching church, a living custodian of God's revelation. As early as the time of the Johannine writings, orthodoxy was undergoing strain. Not many centuries later councils would be called to establish authentic teaching. To allow distortion to prevail would have caused havoc within the body Christian. The sheepgate had its parameters; it was not broad enough to embrace every shade of thought. When it comes to an area as sensitive as religious belief, error is not helpful.

On the other hand, today's gospel cannot be used as a weapon to champion a type of narrow orthodoxy which fails to see the organic character of revelation or the need for reformulation. The sheepgate is not overly wide nor is it extremely narrow. Attempts to understand revelation more clearly, to express it in a more acceptable way, or to address problems not heretofore encountered require respect and patience, not a negative "knee-jerk" reaction. To solve any mystery involves a fair amount of unraveling. To shed light on God's mysteries is the task of theology, and it often requires breaking new ground. Theology today is an encounter between faith and modernity, faith and science, faith and culture. There are challenges to the theologians today that the New Testament did not envision. The fact that the basic truths are there does not exempt us from the task of working for answers that respond to the needs of today. Our belief in the Spirit's guidance remains secure. That must be accompanied by respect for those who faithfully seek the answers. They are not "thieves and robbers" but servants of the church who, in facing new realities, want to lend us assistance in entering and exiting through the sheepgate.

Homiletic and Catechetical Helps

1. The relationship between faith, the Spirit, and baptism.

2. Jesus as the model of innocent suffering.

3. Pain and suffering in the Christian life.

4. Jesus as the biblical lamb and the shepherd.

5. Jesus as the gate of the sheepfold.

6. The sheepgate and the teaching office of the church.

7. The role of theology in the life of the church.

8. The Holy Spirit: teacher in the church.

9. Examples of new questions facing the church.

10. Remaining open to the Spirit.

FOURTH SUNDAY OF EASTER
Year B

Readings

Acts 4:8 - 12
1 Jn 3:1 - 2
Jn 10:11 - 18

Theme: The Model Shepherd

The reading today from John's gospel presents Jesus as the model shepherd in his spirit of dedication and willingness to surrender his life for his sheep. The letter of John speaks of the graced outcome of the shepherd's death: our becoming children of God. This Jesus, moreover, is the only way to the Father as Peter tells his hearers in Acts. In him alone is salvation, which is now extended to all humanity.

First Reading

This short kerygmatic discourse of Peter before the Jewish religious authorities is couched in the apologetic language which these speeches assume when directed to such an audience. It centers on the proclamation of death-resurrection with the strong Lucan antithesis: "you crucified," "God raised" (v10). It is in the name of Jesus as Lord (v10; 2:36; Phil 2:11) that the cripple was healed (v9) and that salvation is offered to the world (v12).

Contrast appears again in the quotation from Ps 118 (v11). This familiar text, which in its original sense saw Israel as the rejected stone, is applied to Christ, the one rejected by his own people and now become the foundation stone of the new covenant. It was evidently a commonly cited text in the early church (Lk 20:17; Mk 12:10; 1 Pet 2:7). The note of contrast is carried forward: rejection by his own, acceptance by God. Both the effectiveness and the exclusiveness of the professed Lordship of Jesus is strongly affirmed (v12; 1 Cor 3:11).

Responsorial Psalm   Ps 118

A commentary on this psalm may be found on Easter Sunday. Verses added here point to the superiority of the Lord's protection over that of any human agent. V. 26 is an invocation of the priests upon the temple pilgrims. The sense is: "Blessed in the name of the Lord be he who comes (enters)...."

Second Reading

Children (v1): A term of affection in the Johannine community (2:1; 2:18; 2:28; Jn 21:5), it arises, like the Pauline "sons of God" out of the new relationship in Christ that constitutes believers as members of God's family. *We may be called ... we are:* with the latter given particular emphasis in the Greek text, it moves the designation beyond a mere figurative appellation.

This passage makes three affirmations. First, the failure of the world to acknowledge their new relationship to God should come as no surprise to the Christian community, since it failed to recognize Christ as well (v1; Jn 15:18f; 17:14ff). "World" is used here not as the object of God's love (Jn 3:16) but as the arena of evil. Second, the love of God, which is the Spirit life, is also a pledge of the glory yet to come (v2). This notion of the new life initiated here as issuing forth in the life to come is a strong Johannine theme (Jn 4:14; 6:40). Since Christ is the "firstborn of the dead" (Col 1:18), believers are destined to be transformed as he was; this is a transformation already begun in the recognition of God in the face of Jesus (2 Cor 3:18).

Third, by reason of their hope and their conformity to Christ, Christians are held to duplicate in their lives the virtues of Jesus (v3; 2:29).

Third Reading

The Johannine Jesus is the model (rather than "good") shepherd. The shepherd theme, not infrequent in the Hebrew scriptures, appears early in the gospel tradition (Mk 6:34; 14:27) and here receives a later and more explicit elaboration. This is a late first century reflection on Christ's pastoral mission. Under two headings, Jesus is presented as the dedicated shepherd. First, he gives his life for his flock, something alien to the thinking of a hired hand. The latter's mercenary interests are in no way comparable to the unqualified dedication of the true shepherd (vv11f). Second, the true shepherd is personally familiar with his own. There is a mutual experiential knowledge between Christ and the Christian which is a reflection of the knowledge of the Father and Son. This motif of the mutual relationship between Jesus and the Father being extended to include the believer (the indwelling) figures prominently in Jesus' later priestly discourse (Jn 17).

I have other sheep (v16): A probable reference to the Gentile mission of the early church (11:52; 12:20 - 23; 17:20). The verse stresses the church's universal mission.

The Father's love for Jesus is linked to his redemptive offering (v17). The verse is important for early Christian soteriology. Christ's offering is the new Adam's positive response to God which cancels the first Adam's disobedience (Rom 5:15 - 19; Heb 10:5 - 10). It is through this generous offering of Christ that the love of God for humanity is manifest (Rom 5:8). Moreover, John is also at pains to show that Christ's death was part of the divine plan (v18). It was not due to human machinations or the manipulating efforts of his opponents. This is verified by his resurrection, an act impossible to anyone held captive by human mortality. This is a more developed soteriology wherein Christ is the principal agent in the resurrection and not the Father as in earlier sources (Acts 2:24; 4:10; Rom 1:4; 4:24).

Words say a great deal. There are, for example, interesting differences between shepherding and herding. A flock is shepherded or pastured; cattle are herded. Both terms pass figuratively into our everyday speech. Herding, generally applied to a group or a crowd, conjures up images of coercion and restriction. Sheep, however, require a different type of treatment than cattle. They are fragile and mostly defenseless in the face of a threat. They are handled with care and their domestic bent results in a bonding between shepherd and sheep. The Bible is strongly attached to the shepherd image because it is so rich in expressing love and concern. The term "pastoral" has long been a part of church language and is often contrasted with more detached and objective sounding expressions as "legal" and "structural." Pope John XXIII called Vatican II a pastoral council, one that was to point up the care for people and a concern for humanity. And to a very considerable extent, it succeeded in doing just that. But to "herd" people evokes images of frightened masses jammed into boxcars headed for Auschwitz or of people led out to die in mass graves.

Shepherding and pasturing have a warmth that tell us so much about what is expected. We call our local religious leader our pastor. It is applied, of course, to pope, bishop, or parish priest, but most frequently it is used of the person on the local scene. And the truth of the matter is that the title says so much that it readily becomes a measuring stick for performance. Today, the many lay people who collaborate with the pastor in ministry are called the pastoral team. The mandate is simply to be what we are called. Jesus remains our model shepherd. He gave his all for each of us and now calls us each by name. To mirror Christ is to manifest availability and a true sense of service–as the scripture says, when it's convenient or inconvenient. And, in addition, we know our people–their needs, their concerns, their joys and sorrows. To reach the twilight of life with that accomplished confers a joy all its own. Shepherding, pastor, pastoral. What's in a word? Sometimes, very much indeed.

Homiletic and Catechetical Helps

1. Understanding "shepherd" in an urban society.

2. Seeing Jesus as the model shepherd.

3. Lord: the name of Jesus.

4. The cornerstone and the stone rejected.

5. Salvation in Jesus' name and the salvation of non-Christians.

6. What it means to be God's children.

7. The meaning of resurrection of the dead.

8. Other sheep: explaining our faith to others.

9. The significance of the baptismal name.

FOURTH SUNDAY OF EASTER
Year C

Readings

> Acts 13:14, 43 - 52
> Rev 7:9, 14 - 17
> Jn 10:27 - 30

Theme: Following the Shepherd

Good Shepherd Sunday in the three year cycle follows the shepherd discourse in John's gospel in presenting three different themes: Christ as the sheep gate (A), Christ as the model shepherd (B), and the care of the flock (C). Today's gospel speaks of the Christian response to Christ as a willingness to hear his voice and follow his lead. Paul and Barnabas in the reading from Acts follow the Spirit's lead in proclaiming the message of the Shepherd before Jew and Gentile alike. In the passage from Revelation, Christ is both the enthroned lamb and the shepherd. It is those who have followed the lamb through trial and persecution who now stand in the heavenly sanctuary.

First Reading

Paul's first missionary journey to Asia Minor brings Barnabas and him to Pisidian Antioch in the province of Galatia (v14).

The highly stylized presentation of their first encounter with the local population is a typically Lucan presentation of the Spirit-guided movement of the church outward (v52). The message is first preached to the Jews, and, with their rejection of it, the thrust goes toward the Gentiles, as Paul himself states in his summary (v46). Paul consistently visits the synagogue upon entering a town (9:20; 14:1; 17:1f) and only then moves to the broader population. In this way, with the Spirit guiding the church's growth, the mandate of Jesus himself is fulfilled (Acts 1:8) as well as the pre-ordained mission of Paul (9:15).

According to pattern, there is an initial positive response from the Jews (v43). This is followed by a negative reaction to the apostles' success on the part of some of the Jews, which takes different forms in varying circumstances (v45; 13:8; 14:5, 19). Paul then explains this course of events in the light of scriptural prophecy (Is 49:6; Acts 9:15). As in the case of Jesus' betrayal and death, Luke emphasizes the divinely ordained plan at work; it is not simply a question of human obstruction.

At this point the lines of demarcation are clearly drawn: the Gentiles' acceptance becomes widespread, while Jewish opposition hardens (vv48ff). *They shook the dust* (v51): A symbolic gesture of complete separation from the attitudes of an opposed or discourteous population (Lk 9:5; Mt 10:14). The motif that runs through Acts, set forth also by Paul, sees the rapid growth of the Gentile mission as due to the Jews' rejection (Rom 11:11f).

Responsorial Psalm   Ps 100

A commentary on the psalm, with its accent on the Lord's flock (v3), is to be found on the Eleventh Sunday of Year A.

Second Reading

This is the second vision of those who have attained salvation given to John the seer of Patmos. The first (7:1 - 8) was of the elect of Israel, precisely determined as twelve thousand from each of the twelve tribes. The present vision is of universal election, people gathered from all the nations of the earth and too numerous to count (v9). They stand before Christ, the enthroned lamb, with the signs of victory and celebration: white robes (3:5) and palm branches (2 Mac 10:6f).

Revelation was written during the period of Roman persecution of the church. The adorers are identified as those who have endured this trial and remained faithful by one of the twenty-four elders in attendance at the throne (vv13f). The jarring image of washing white vestments in blood is characteristic of apocalyptic (v14). Clothing, closely identified with the wearer, reflects a state of soul, soiled or clean (3:4; Gal 3:27). Here it points to the effects of baptism, an interior purification which is the result of Christ's redemptive action.

In this tableau, the lamb is seated at the center of God's throne. Through a juxtaposition of images, God is seated on the throne (v10), and the lamb shares enthronement as well (v17). Both receive the worship of the throng. In terms of cultic recognition, there is no distinction between the two.

The lamb is both redeemer and provider (shepherd) (vv14, 17). As the Passover lamb he brings about the liberation of his people (Ex 12:1 - 11); as shepherd he nurtures his flock (Ps 23:1f).

Life-giving water (v17): More than the psalmist's restful water, this is the Spirit-life, the living water of John's gospel (Jn 4:4 - 15). The suffering of the elect is past (v16), as God comforts them (vv15, 17b) and the lamb guides and provides for them (v17a).

Third Reading

The church of John's time was beset by persecution from without, especially with its definitive break with the synagogue (9:34f) and the opposition of Rome, and with difficulties from within on the part of false teachers (1 Jn 2:18; 4:1). The end of the shepherd discourse encourages the believer in the presence of these hardships. The mutual recognition of Christ and his followers bespeaks a close adherence and assures the Spirit-life which begins here but continues into eternity (vv27f; Jn 6:40).

There is, moreover, no need to fear the marauders who attempt to invade the sheepfold (10:1). That overarching protective power of the Father will protect the faithful. The Father has entrusted them to Christ and thus they will never be wrested from his grasp (the hand of the Father and the Son here become one) (vv28f). The Father and Jesus work in perfect concert. They constitute an inseparable unity (v30; 1:1; 12:45; 17:21).

Nothing is clearer in Acts than the fact that good comes out of misfortune. God indeed writes straight with crooked lines. Rebuffed by his own people, even persecuted by them, Paul moved unhesitatingly toward the Gentiles. The Spirit was always at work. And the missionary efforts, although beset by countless difficulties, were crowned with success. So often in life, misfortune or tragedy becomes a moment of grace. However, that is not easy to see at the time of trial. It takes that perseverance about which Revelation speaks in today's liturgy. Faith has to be tested—belief in an explanation in the face of the inexplicable. Anyone ministering in the church is repeatedly amazed at how faith-filled souls hold on when there is nothing left but God—loss of work, loss of health, loss of a child, the suffering of addictions. To see faith alive in the midst of tragedy is the real sermon that is preached in life.

Most impressive about the model Shepherd whom we recall in today's liturgy is that strong note of encouragement. The church has lived two thousand years of a very turbulent history—persecuted from without, betrayed from within. But it is still here, and very much alive. The Father remains the one who is most powerful. He has entrusted us to his Son. That is the dimension of church life that can never be lost, regardless of how much time we spend trying to improve the human face of the church. What keeps us all going is the realization that we are Christ's and Christ is God's. No path is too treacherous, no mountain too steep, no burden too heavy to bear. As the moving spiritual has it: "He's got the whole world in his hand." And, Jesus adds, no one will snatch us away.

Homiletic and Catechetical Helps

1. The growth of the church in adversity.

2. The message of Acts: first to the Jew, then the Gentile.

3. Sacrament of confirmation: courage and perseverance.

4. Revelation: relationship of the One enthroned and the lamb.

5. Eucharist: this is the lamb of God—its meaning.

6. Biblical background of Jesus as shepherd.

7. The shepherd and Christian trust and confidence.

FIFTH SUNDAY OF EASTER
Year A

Readings

> Acts 6:1 - 7
> 1 Pet 2:4 - 9
> Jn 14:1 - 12

Theme: Living Stones

Our reading from 1 Peter today describes the church as a spiritual building constructed of living stones with Christ himself as the cornerstone. Christ is the church's sole foundation because he alone is God's full revelation remaining forever, in the gospel's words, our way, truth, and life. In that spiritual edifice wherein we are all the living stones, there are a variety of ministries, all contributing to the community's welfare. Our reading from Acts today recounts the beginning of diverse forms of service in the church.

First Reading

This account of the designation of seven men to "serve at table" leaves a number of questions unanswered, yet its main purpose remains clear enough. It serves as a link between the Jerusalem-centered activity of the infant church (Acts 1 - 5) and its gradual outreach to the broader world, beginning in Samaria (Acts 8) and from there to the "ends of the earth" in the later chapters of Acts. The men chosen, all bearing Greek names, were evidently prominent members of the Hellenistic (i.e. diaspora background) Christian community. The narrative introduces Stephen and Philip, both of whom will assume important roles in the ensuing narratives (Acts 6 - 8). As important as the Hellenists were to the ongoing growth of the church, the rite of commissioning (v6) clearly subordinates and binds them to the apostles.

That Luke's overall picture of the early church's serenity and accord was rather idealized (2:42 - 47; 4:32 - 35) surfaces in accounts of conflict such as this. *The Hebrews ... the Hellenists* (v1): two segments of the early church, the Aramaic-speaking (Hebrews), being of local origin, and the Greek-speaking (Hellenists), identified with the diaspora. It was more than a question of linguistic difference; there was a sharp cultural breach as well.

The reason given for the dissension between the two groups was the insufficient attention given to the daily needs of the poorer Hellenist widows in the program of works of charity. Whether or not there were deeper issues that separated them remains uncertain. That Hellenists were designated to provide this ministry while at the same time holding a subordinate role reflected good administrative thinking. The twelve consulted the community about the problem (v2), and it was the community which selected the candidates (v3).

At least in theory, the distinction of roles is important. The twelve are to be given entirely to the *ministry of the word*, i.e. the preaching and teaching concerns of the church (v4). The seven are to *serve at table*, i.e. supervise the charitable undertakings of the community, a function of lesser importance than that of the apostles (vv2f). Although deacons were accredited ministers in the early church (Phil 1:2; 1 Tim 3:6 - 12), it is not certain that the ministry cited here was their proper role, nor can this passage be cited as the time of the diaconate's institution. The seven are not called deacons; there is no record of their performing the role for which they are chosen. In fact, two of them, Stephen and Philip, are later engaged in the ministry of the word. The narrative evidently serves more in uniting

Hebrews and Hellenists than in institutionalizing a new ministry.

The commissioning of the seven exhibits features of similar nominations in the Hebrew scriptures (Ex 18:13 - 26) and of rituals which signify power sharing and official designation (Num 27:18 - 23; 1 Tim 4:14; 5:22) (v6). Luke again highlights the growth of the Jerusalem church, with converts including members of the Jewish priestly rank (v7)

This account serves to propel the church beyond Judea toward the Hellenistic world through the prominence given this ministry "of the Greeks." While it leaves much unsaid about the exercise of the ministry, it serves the Lucan purpose of showing the broadening of ministries within the church.

Responsorial Psalm   Ps 33

Commentary on this hymn, which invites the upright to an expression of gratitude, is found on the Second Sunday of Lent, Year A.

Second Reading

In one of the most expressive passages of the New Testament, Christians are described as living stones in that spiritual edifice which is the church, having Christ himself as its foundation stone. The church as a building appears in different forms, with Christ as the foundation (1 Cor 3:11f) or as the head of the household (Heb 3:6). Using a rich scriptural background, this passage moves around two focal points: Christ and the faithful.

Christ is the primary "living stone" (v4), the source of the Spirit which enlivens the members, the other "living stones" of the building. By a free adaptation of Isaiah (28:16), Christ is depicted as the cornerstone, a position recognized only in faith (vv6, 7a). For those without belief, he is simply the one rejected by his own and now the recipient of another allegiance (Ps 118:22). He has become a stumbling block to his own people (Is 8:14; Rom 11:11; 1 Cor 1:23). The "rejected stone" appears elsewhere to highlight Christ's victory (Acts 4:11); here it is simply an obstacle to the unbeliever (v8).

The believers are described with a variety of expressions, originally applied to Israel and here given a Christian sense. Besides being *living stones* (v5), they are a *holy (royal) priesthood* (vv5, 9; Ex 19:6), offering their lives to God as a spiritual sacrifice and prolonging in time the sentiments underlying the priestly ministry of Christ (Rom 12:1; Phil 4:18; Heb 10:9f). Like the former Israel, Christians are now the *chosen race* (v9), the people of God's election. By reason of this election, they are a people set apart, separated from a sinful paganism and now consecrated to God as a *holy nation* (Ex 19:6). Continuing the exodus theme, the author sees the Christians as being a singular acquisition of the Lord, *a people of his own* (Ex 19:5). Their priestly mediation of God to the world includes the proclamation of their "exodus," a call from the darkness of paganism to the light of God's truth (v9; 1:18; 4:3; Is 43:21).

Third Reading

In a strong appeal for faith, centered as much in him as in God (vv1, 11), Jesus speaks of his leave-taking in death-resurrection, and of his eventual return (vv2f). This is not the traditional parousia which is envisioned. By the time of John's gospel, the imminence of the return of Christ had receded; here the emphasis falls on Christ's meeting with the disciples at the time of their death.

The questions of both Thomas (v5) and Philip (v8) remain on the natural or "flesh" level of misunderstanding or misconception. As happens frequently in John, their questions serve as a catapult for Jesus' "faith"-level response. Thus, the "way" which Jesus affirms (v4) and Thomas misconstrues (v5) moves the discourse forward toward Jesus' climactic statement. *I am the way and the truth and the life* (v6). The "way" is not a spiritual road map or book of instructions. It is Jesus himself as God's revelation. To know Jesus is to know God, the goal of human existence. Jesus verbalizes in his person the mind of God (1:1). It is interesting to note that the earliest designation for the Christian life in Acts was simply "the way" (Acts 9:2; 18:25, 23).

The "truth" and the "life" are not separate categories; rather, they explain the meaning of the "way." God is truth itself and Jesus is the only one to have captured that truth and the only one to have revealed it (1:17f; 18:37). Faith acceptance, then, is directed toward God's self-disclosure, the authentic truth of the Godhead, Jesus himself. In being the "way," Jesus is also the Spirit-life of God. It is the Spirit that makes the acceptance of Jesus possible and is the wellspring of eternal life (5:26; 11:25f). Jesus thus is the exclusive "way" to God, as well as the source of "grace and truth" (1:17).

Jesus then dwells on his relationship to the Father. The Johannine Jesus never speaks of God in a detached or separated fashion. It is not some far-off God of whom he gives his followers a glimpse, as Philip's question implies (v8). Rather it is the mutual indwelling of Father and Son that is underscored. They not only "live together," they are one, with the result that to see Jesus is to see the Father. This high Christology of John is present from the beginning of his gospel with his designation of the Word as God (1:1). Jesus does not simply point to God but is identified with him and as such can claim to be the way, truth, and life.

If faith acceptance cannot be based on Jesus' authentic teaching, at the minimum it should be based on the works that he performs, those "signs" of God's power that he manifests (v11). In fact, following his resurrection- exaltation and the conferring of the Spirit, similar manifestations of God's power will accompany the church's preaching (v12).

Thematically today's liturgy can be approached from a number of angles. "Living stones" is one of them inasmuch as it links the strongly vertical thrust of the gospel and the horizontal direction of the reading from Acts. As living stones, Christians are engaged in both worlds. We live in the risen Christ, the self-disclosure of God. If he lives in the Father and we through baptism live in him, then we are constituted members of the same family. Questions such as "What is God like?" and "How can I know him?" really have no meaning. God is close and as real as death on a cross. God's mind is as clear as the sermon on the mount. God's forgiveness is as close as the prodigal son. God is, moreover, the empowerment of every sacrament. We are living stones because we are united with the one irreplaceable foundation, Christ the Lord. We "live" because the life that binds him and the Father reaches us as well.

But there is also a horizontal dimension. The living stones are involved in ministry. Acts today speaks of shared responsibility, of a move away from a top-heavy structure of authority. And ministry is a diakonia, a form of Christian service. With the great variety of out-reach ministries in the church today, it would be wrong to see this pre-ponderantly in terms of religious life. Yet it is undeniable that histori-cally religious life has given a very striking and vivid expression to the ministry of service: accompanying immigrants, assisting the dying, nursing during epidemics, instructing the unlettered, health care for the poor. Today religious life is at something of a crossroads, with the vision of the road ahead somewhat unclear. Whatever the future, that sense of undivided service cannot be lost. It has an incredible history. The Christian life is not limited to contemplation. Those who see the Father in Christ meet that same Christ in the faces of the poor and needy. Living stones are then transformed into precious jewels.

Homiletic and Catechetical Helps

1. Ministry of the word and ministry of service.

2. Modern expressions of Christian service.

3. The role of the deacon in the church.

4. The imposition of hands at ordination.

5. Explaining Christ the cornerstone and Peter the rock.

6. Hebrews and Hellenists: conflict resolution in the church.

7. Jesus as the revelation of God.

8. Jesus as way, truth, and life.

9. The priesthood of all believers.

10. Christians as a chosen people.

11. Christian passage from darkness to light.

FIFTH SUNDAY OF EASTER
Year B

Readings

> Acts 9:26 - 31
> 1 Jn 3:18 - 24
> Jn 15:1 - 8

Theme: Vine and Branches

The Easter message of life in the risen Christ continues in today's gospel of the vine and the branches. Apart from Jesus the vine, there can be no Spirit-life for his disciples. The letter of John reminds us that it is this same Spirit that enables us to recognize Jesus as God's Son and to keep his commandments. The Spirit at work in Acts moves the recently converted Paul to present his message in Jerusalem regardless of the personal danger involved. Thus the vine and branches constitute a living reality within the human soul and within a growing church.

First Reading

Paul's first visit to Jerusalem after his conversion differs in its Lucan form from the account given by the apostle himself (Gal 1:18f). Although the length of time between conversion and the visit is not specified in Acts, Galatians speaks of a three year interval. The two are difficult to reconcile if it is to be thought that there was still fear of the converted apostle after such a long period of time (v26). In Galatians, the trip is not attributed to a hurried escape (vv24f) but to a planned meeting with Cephas. Paul indicates that of the apostles he saw only Cephas, while Acts speaks of his meeting all the apostles (v27). His movements in Jerusalem were free and evidently extensive (vv28f), although Paul states that he remained largely unknown to the churches of Judea (Gal 1:22).

This passage undoubtedly represents one of Luke's schematic and condensed presentations of the data. Regardless of the actual time sequence, Luke wants to legitimate Paul's mission in the eyes of the twelve prior to the start of the apostle's Gentile mission. Therefore, he presents himself and his case to the apostles (v27) and joins them in their Jerusalem preaching (v28). Paul's engagement in the preaching ministry not only links his message with that of the twelve but also provides a foretaste of the opposition he will repeatedly receive from his former co-religionists (v29). The Hellenists were Greek-speaking Jews in Jerusalem characterized by strongly traditionalist views.

After Paul's departure, Luke presents an idyllic picture of peace and serenity, together with a steady increase in numbers. The Holy Spirit, the principal actor in Acts, is here the comforter, just as elsewhere he is the guide (v31). *Galilee* (v31): Again Luke is schematic. Thus far there has been no mention of preaching in that part of the country.

Responsorial Psalm   Ps 22

These concluding verses of the individual lament, celebrating the sufferer's deliverance, have a strong universalist bent (v28). The *poor* (anawim) (v27) were initially the needy in society for whom Yahweh was the provider, with the category receiving the later internal or spiritual emphasis of lowliness and dependence. The acclaim of the Lord and his reign comes from all the people of the earth (v28) and embraces the present, the past ("all who sleep in the earth," v30) and the future ("descendants, generations to come" (v31).

Second Reading

Voicing belief is not sufficient; faith must come to life in action (v18; Jas 1:22). The self-accusation of a disturbed conscience ("a condemning heart") can be allayed by the realization that ultimately it is God who forgives and justifies (vv19f). Moreover, there is an objective criterion that determines the heart's stance before God, namely, the observance of his commandments (v22).

In summarizing the command of God in terms of faith and

love of neighbor, John may be giving his version of the great gospel mandate (v23; Mk 12:28 - 31) since in Johannine thinking faith in God and love of him coalesce (Jn 16:27). This would be in line with the Johannine dictum on the inseparable character of love of God and neighbor (4:20f; Jn 13:34f). The belief spoken of here is an adherence to Jesus as Lord and Son of God (v23).

The indwelling of Father and Son (Jn 14:10ff) is extended to the believer through the action of the Spirit who binds the three together (v24). To observe the aforementioned commandments of faith and love is to be assured that the indwelling is a reality, verified by the Spirit itself.

Third Reading

This extended metaphor has four allegorical components: the vine grower (the Father), the vine (Jesus), the branch (the disciple), and the fruit (commandment observance). In speaking of himself as the *true* vine (v1), the Johannine Jesus uses the adjective in contrast with something of the past (4:23; 6:32). Israel was the biblical vine (Is 5:1 - 7; Jer 2:21; Hos 10:1), now supplanted by Christ. In the vine and the branches, the relationship between Christ and the believer is expressed in terms more intimate and personal than in the preceding image of the shepherd (c. 10). It is the language of the indwelling, the "remaining together" in friendship, that here comes to the fore in characterizing the bond between Jesus and his followers. Because of the mutual love and unity of Father and Son, Christ can give assurance of the Father's response to prayer (v7; 14:13).

It is this "abiding" of the believer in Jesus that is productive of good (vv4f). Failure to produce fruit results in a severance of the branch, i.e. an end time separation from Christ by the intervention of the Father (vv2a, 6) through pruning; on the other hand, the true believers are strengthened (v2b). The disciples are consoled in being told that their fidelity has been established (v3). Just as the Father is glorified by the obedient death of his Son (12:27f), so also does the virtuous life of the disciple give glory to God (v8). Finally the fruit-bearing is specified in terms of the commandments (v10), made explicit in 1 John as faith in God's Son and love of neighbor (1 Jn 3:23).

The Easter shepherd theme presents Christ as our leader and guide. The image of the vine carries us to an even deeper level. Christ is as intimately one with us as he is with the Father. And it is this unity that produces the good that we do. Even if we are not always as aware as we should be, Christ lives in us as long as we do not sin. If we are striving to live as uprightly as possible, then we are assured of his presence. Serious sin, then, is the betrayal of our closest companion on life's journey. And what is the betrayal? What is God's commandment? To believe in God's Son and to love one another. Belief is far more than a simple assent; it is to be open to transformation, to become like the One in whom we believe. And to love our neighbor is to respect his or her person in every sense of the word. In the words of Paul, that means patience, kindness, generosity, fidelity, gentleness and self-control. It also means a "no" to hatred, rivalry, jealousy, anger, envy, lust, and debauchery. John's commandment, then, says much in a few words.

The church places a great deal of stock in continuity and linkage. We are symbolically linked with the church in different ways when we are missioned. Just as the apostles authenticated Paul, bishops commission priests in ordination, missionaries are "sent" by their superiors, and theologians receive a mandate to teach. Religious profession links the person with a very distinctive historical corporate personality. Catechumens preparing for baptism are acknowledged and incorporated by the parish community. We share a common understanding of the faith. We worship in a corporate way. Religion has its private and personal dimension about which today's liturgy speaks. But it also makes us part of a larger whole, to which and for which we have a shared responsibility.

Homiletic and Catechetical Helps

1. Vine and branches: related to the sacramental life.

2. Living in Christ: its meaning.

3. Living in Christ: motivation of Christian conduct.

4. Christian summary: faith in God and love of neighbor.

5. The three theological virtues.

6. The twelve and Paul: unity in belief.

7. Christian mission at home and abroad.

8. The place of unity and diversity in the church.

FIFTH SUNDAY OF EASTER
Year C

Readings

> Acts 14:21 - 27
> Rev 21:1 - 5
> Jn 13:31 - 33, 34 - 35

Theme: Welcoming the New

There is newness in all three readings today. At the end of their first missionary journey, Paul and Barnabas enthusiastically report on the admission of Gentiles to the church. In the Easter season, the growth and spread of the church is much to the fore. The seer of Patmos in Revelation witnesses the end time marriage of Christ and his church in the midst of a creation made completely new. And before his leave-taking, Jesus in today's gospel presents his disciples with his new commandment of love. These are readings well suited to the freshness of the Easter season.

First Reading

The first missionary journey of Paul and Barnabas (46 - 49 A.D.) carried them from Antioch in Syria to cities in Asia Minor, in the territory of Galatia, Pisidia, and Pamphylia. The return to Lystra, Iconium, and Pisidian Antioch brings them once again to cities from which they had been forcefully ejected (v21, cc. 13 - 14). Their encouragement of the new disciples (v22) offers the opportunity for a Lucan reflection on the role of suffering in Jesus' life (Lk 24:26) and that of his disciples (Lk 9:23f). *Presbyters* (Gr: *presbytreroi*) (v23): Never mentioned in the Pauline writings, they played a significant role in local church administration in later times (1Tim 5:17 - 23; Tit 1:5). Luke, here and elsewhere (11:30; 15:2, 5), may well be reflecting later church structures.

After reaching coastal Pamphylia and visiting two cities there, the apostles sail for Antioch in Syria where there was a large Christian community and where they had been originally missioned (13:2f). In announcing the Gentile mission, according to the consistent Lucan motif, it is the action of God that directs the church (v27; 15:4, 12; 21:8). The church's move toward the "ends of the earth" has begun (1:8).

Responsorial Psalm   Ps 145

This alphabetic hymn praises Yahweh's covenant "virtues" of fidelity and forbearance in a direct echo of Exodus (Ex 34:6). God's reign is extolled (vv11f). Believers as well as the works of creation make known to all people God's majesty (v12) and eternity (v13). For further commentary, see the Thirty-First Sunday of Year C.

Second Reading

In this final climactic scene of Revelation, the vision is one of a totally new beginning. The heaven and earth of past experience pass away and are substituted by a new universe (v1). The reign of God, embracing the entire created order, is definitively established. *The sea was no more* (v1): Often identified with evil as the home of mythological sea monsters and the realm of the dead (20:13), the sea is vanquished and eliminated as part of the old order. The church, seen as the "new Jerusalem," the "holy city," and as a bride, is at the center of this end time picture, which highlights the definitive marriage between Christ and the elect (v2; 19:7ff). This brings to its final phase a union begun with Christ's death-resurrection (Eph 5:25ff).

A celestial voice heralds this espousal in a collage of scriptural references (vv3f): God's dwelling (Ez 37:27), God and people (Jer 31:33), elimination of tears and sorrow (Is 25:8; 65:19). It is to be an era of uninterrupted peace, with God's reign firmly established and his elect as the recipients of final salvation. God is the Creator of a new order.

Third Reading

The passage introduces the final discourse of Jesus at the supper with his disciples (cc. 14 - 17). This introduction centers on two main ideas which will later reappear: the leave-taking of Jesus (vv31ff) and the new commandment (vv34f).

Jesus' Leave-Taking. The death-resurrection is the moment of glorification, which Jesus solemnly announces. It was pre-announced with the request of certain Greeks (Gentiles) to "see" him (12:20 - 33), a request to be granted with the Spirit-directed universalism of the post-resurrection period. Now glorification is proximate with Judas' departure from the supper to betray him (v30). Jesus is glorified through the Father's recognition of his self-donation in liberating him from death and bringing him to resurrection. Christ is further glorified in being the source of eternal life for all who believe (17:1ff). At the same time, Jesus gives glory to the Father in his total obedience and by manifesting to the world God's love for a lost humanity (17:4f).

The added glorification of Jesus "at once" is difficult to interpret (v32). Its temporal allusions, so closely connected with his approaching leave-taking (v33), probably refer to his departure from this world to be with the Father, the period in the early church's life when the apostles proceeded without Christ's experienced presence. Only later would he return and take them to the Father (v33; 16:16 - 22).

The New Commandment. This mandate of love appears again in the last discourse (15:12, 17). Love of neighbor is not in itself a new commandment (Lev 19:18). In Leviticus it refers to other Israelites only; here it refers to other Christians, in a similarly restricted sense (vv34f). Its novelty lies primarily in its being the major precept of a new covenant, a covenant that establishes a new heart-centered relationship between God and his people

(Jer 31:31 - 34). It is new as the expression of the Spirit which makes its observance possible. This precept is also new in its exemplarity. It is based on the love that Christ has shown for his disciples in handing himself over to death for his followers, a greater love than which cannot be envisioned. This type of love within the community, which will inevitably become manifest to others, is to serve as the true apologetic of Christianity (v35). Not by word or teaching or even martyrdom will the followers of Christ be recognized but by the intensity of their mutual charity.

There is something exhilarating about novelty. Looking forward to an event often outdoes the joy of the occasion itself. And how quickly the new becomes routine. Commercialism is built on keeping our sense of novelty at a high pitch. New things quickly become old, like the child's Christmas toys strewn throughout the house a week after Christmas. We thrill at new thresholds but the thrill doesn't last. Today, however, we are reminded that certain things are part of God's gifted newness and should never become "old hat."

The wonder of new converts—Paul spoke joyfully about it at Antioch and repeatedly in his letters. Each Easter we welcome new converts to the faith. But how many of us make that faith journey with them in sponsoring, teaching, extending welcome through the rite of Christian initiation of adults. Those new disciples are so much a part of Easter, expressing the perennial newness of the church. Its message springs eternal!

And what of Jesus' new commandment? Is our love for one another, even within the church, a true sign to an unbelieving world? We might have to say that it could be if we started to live it. Instead we settle for negativism and pettiness. We have no shortage of ethnic slurs, racial dislike, and ill feelings toward minorities. We believe that we are free of sexism, but that can be sorely contested. The newness of that commandment lies partially in the motivation for observing it. Christ's love is to be mirrored in our own. But is it? God continues to make things new. A new heaven and a new earth. Think of a cleaner environment. A world free of destructive weapons. We can help construct a better world even in the here and now. But do we take personal and social newness seriously? Or is it mostly business as usual.

Homiletic and Catechetical Helps

1. Conversion to the faith.

2. The rite of Christian initiation of adults.

3. The missionary dimension of the faith.

4. Suffering as related to the reign of God.

5. Christ and church: the husband and wife image.

6. Explaining a new heaven and a new earth.

8. The glorification of Jesus.

7. The love of neighbor: the motivation in John.

8. Examples of lack of charity in the faith community.

SIXTH SUNDAY OF EASTER
Year A

Readings
Acts 8:5 - 8, 14 - 17
1 Pet 3:15 - 18
Jn 14:15 - 21

Theme: Another Advocate

The first Advocate in the Johannine writings is Jesus himself, who represents the interests of his disciples before the Father. The Spirit is the second Advocate, sent after Jesus' departure. The Advocate serves as the defense attorney but also as prosecutor in the case against the world and a witness to the truth of Jesus. It is this same Spirit, who in today's reading from Acts, leads the infant church from Judea to Samaria with the preaching of Philip. In the first letter of Peter, Christians are advised to heed the Spirit of truth in speaking clearly and honestly under persecution so that their opponents may find in them no semblance of deception but only the work of God.

First Reading

The importance of the arrival of the faith in Samaria is best appreciated when read against the background of centuries of hostilities between the heterodox Samaritans and the Jews of greater Palestine. In Luke's gospel, Jesus has contacts with Samaritans but does not venture into their territory. That step is reserved for Acts in the execution of Jesus' mandate to the apostles before his leave-taking (1:8). Today's reading, with its emphasis on God's power at work, is often termed the Samaritan Pentecost.

Philip's preaching in Samaria is attributed to the dispersion created by Saul's persecution of the church (8:3f); it is a mission undertaken by the Hellenist segment of the church, represented by Philip. His mission is accompanied by healings and the vanquishing of demons (v7). The positive response of the people is surprising considering the isolation and hostility of the Jews that was long a part of their history. The city where this mission occurs is unnamed; the mention of Samaria after the Judean mission suffices for Luke. The joy accompanying the proclamation of the Messiah sounds a familiar Lucan note, first heard with the Savior's birth (v8; Lk 2:10).

It was to the apostles that the mandate to bring the faith to Samaria had been given, and the ratification of this new endeavor in the conferral of the Spirit is reserved to them (vv15ff). This is evidently more than an internal activity of the Spirit since it attracts the attention of Simon the magician (vv18ff). In the interests of authenticating this new mission and subordinating it to the authority of the apostles, Luke separates the giving of the Spirit from baptism, reserving its conferral to the apostles. The coming of the Spirit will at times follow baptism as here (vv16f; 19:5f), or precede it (10:47f). It is a Lucan literary device to highlight the Spirit's initiative and to maintain important links with the apostles. In other circumstances, the customary unity of baptism and the Spirit is maintained (Acts 2:38).

Responsorial Psalm   Ps 66

The theme of universalism is dominant in this psalm, the commentary for which is to be found on the Fourteenth Sunday of Year C.

Second Reading

This is part of an exhortation to Christians suffering persecution. In the face of opposition, the Christ who abides with them through baptism is their surest bulwark and source of confidence (v15a; Gal 2:20). *Your hope* (v15b): Christ present in the believer is the pledge of future glory (Col 1:27). It is the innocence of the accused that is ultimately their vindication, as well as the "shame" of their accusers (v16). Their upright conduct keeps their suffering from being tainted by any insinuation of moral deformity (v17). Ironically they suffer only for doing good.

In this they are one with Christ who, as innocent, suffered for the guilty (v18). Once again Christian morality is rooted in the example of Christ. Put to death in his truly human and mortal state ("in the flesh"), he was vindicated in being exalted with the total transformation of a life-giving Spirit (v18; Rom 6:9f).

Third Reading

The passage deals with the indwelling of Father, Son, and Advocate in the Christian, the verification of which is to be found in the observance of Christ's commandments.

The Advocate (Gr: *parakletos*). This is the second Advocate, Jesus being the first (1 Jn 2:1). The Advocate or Holy Spirit, here sent by the Father (v16) and not Jesus (16:7), performs a number of functions. He dwells within the Christian (v17) and also continues Jesus' teaching ministry (14:26). As the *Spirit of truth* (v17; 15:26), the Advocate ratifies the teaching of Jesus, who is himself the truth, the authentic revelation of God (14:6). The world, immersed in untruth and perversity, does not recognize the Advocate, who comes as the prosecutor to convict the world (16:8 - 11). The Dead Sea Scrolls use the expression "Spirit of truth" as a positive moral force opposed to the angel of darkness or iniquity.

The Indwelling. The return of Jesus (v18) refers to the indwelling and not the parousia. The passage speaks of the mutual cohabitation of Father, Son, and Spirit within the believer. The Spirit of truth dwells "in you" (v17). Since Christ lives in the Father, from whom he is inseparable, then Christ's presence in the believer unites Father, Son, and believer (v20). This is the life of the triune God in the believer. Since Jesus is the exclusive way to know the Father, his presence in the Christian is revelatory as well. The use of the future tense throughout refers to Christ's coming to dwell with the Christian, as the context makes clear.

This presence of God in the believer is made manifest through the observance of Christ's commandments (vv15, 21; 1 Jn 2:5), specified principally as the commandment of mutual love (15:12; 1 Jn 3:23f). The "love of Jesus" (vv15, 21) is not that common in John; it is usually faith that is stressed. In Johannine terms, however, the two are mutually inclusive. The love of Jesus, then, is to be found in the observance of his teaching. This love, centered in God's Son, evokes a similar response from the indwelling Father, in an all-embracing circle of knowledge and charity (v21).

It is amazing to think of all that is implied in the rather static traditional expression, "the state of grace." Life in the Spirit has a very dynamic dimension, as is so evident in the missionary thrust of the church as seen in our Easter season readings from Acts. But it is John who is at his best in describing the inner workings of the Advocate. Today's gospel is the source of ongoing meditation. Father, Son, and Spirit make their home in the faithful Christian. That belief is a summary of our life and our destiny. It carries us from baptism to the final vision of God. We are accompanied on life's journey by the family of God; in fact we, too, are admitted as members. In truth, if not in sentiment, we are as close to that family as we are to any. That is what makes sin such a tragedy. It ruptures such a close bond. It means turning our back on family so that we can go it alone.

To call the Spirit our Advocate says a lot more to most of us than Paraclete. An advocate is one who represents our interests, our defense, the one who goes to bat for us. The scriptures say so much about God's concern for us. It is expressed in so many ways. Loved by God, redeemed by his Son, made holy by his Spirit. And then, as Advocates, the Son and Spirit are pulling for us at every turn. Hope stands between presumption and despair. We cannot simply presume that we will get where we're headed. But we certainly do have the scales weighted in our favor. To paraphrase Paul: If God has gone this far for us, will he let us down now?

When judgment is pictured like a courtroom scene, it can be a little frightening–until you remember who your lawyer is.

Homiletic and Catechetical Helps

1. Baptism and the Holy Spirit.

2. Acts: The separation of baptism and the Holy Spirit.

3. Christian ecumenism: overcoming historical barriers.

4. Christ in our heart: the source of hope.

5. Suffering injustice.

6. Explaining the Trinity.

7. Understanding the indwelling.

8. The Spirit as Advocate.

9. Love of Christ and observance of commandments.

8. Beliefs expressed in the sign of the cross.

SIXTH SUNDAY OF EASTER
Year B

Readings

Acts 10:25 - 26, 34 - 35, 44 - 48
1 Jn 4:7 - 10
Jn 15:9 - 17

Theme: Chosen as Friends

All three readings today highlight God's initiative in the world. In the first reading, it is God who launches the Gentile mission in conferring the Spirit upon Cornelius' household. In the familiar Johannine refrain on the primacy of love, today's second reading reminds us that it is God who first loves us, and the gospel says the same in referring to our election as disciples. We did not have to search God out. He found us.

First Reading

This account of the first apostolic contact with the Gentile world emphasizes the role of the Spirit as the mission's inaugurator. Cornelius' reception of Peter is actually an act of adoration (vv25f). On other occasions, the wonders which accompanied the apostles' ministry led to the conclusions among Gentiles that they were deities (14:11 - 18; 28:6). Although a visit to a Gentile home would not have been favorably viewed in Jewish circles (v28), Peter sees it as legitimate on the basis of his earlier vision abolishing the distinction between the clean and unclean (vv9 - 15). Moreover, his miraculous summons to the house of Cornelius (vv30 - 33) convinces him of the boundary-breaking character of the gospel. Suitability for baptism is determined only by moral posture (v35). *Partiality* (Gr: *prosolemptes*) (v34): from the Greek, meaning literally "lift up the face" or to show favor to one over another (Rom 2:11). At the heart of Christian universalism is the elimination of any sort of elevating distinction.

The definitive authentication of the Gentile mission comes from the Holy Spirit, who even before baptism descends upon those in Cornelius' house. To the surprise of the Jewish Christians present, the effusion of the Spirit, rooted in Joel's prophecy (3:1), parallels that of the Jerusalem Pentecost, with the same accompanying charismatic phenomena (vv44ff; 2:4). That the Spirit precedes baptism is part of the Lucan schema, underscoring two ideas: the Spirit legitimates the subsequent baptism and the Gentile mission, and the descent of the Spirit is linked with the apostles and the Jerusalem church in the person of Peter.

The baptism, then, is divinely mandated (v47).

Responsorial Psalm   Ps 98

Universalism emerges strongly as today's psalm. Commentary is found on the Twenty-Eighth Sunday of Year C.

Second Reading

The knowledge and love of God are inseparable. Without love one is truly ignorant of God (vv7f). Elsewhere the author states that to bear hatred for another disciple, who can be seen, is antithetical to the love of God, who is unseen (4:20). Moreover, since the very nature of God is love (v8), one who is lacking in love knows nothing of God (v16). *Begotten by God* (v7): In John, the conferral of the Spirit life is spoken of as a conception and birth (Jn 1:13; 3:5). Fathered by God, the disciple henceforth belongs to the triune family (Jn 14:15 - 20).

Relations among Christians reflect the love of God manifest in Christ. Christ alone mirrors the Father (Jn 1:18). Christians love for two reasons: they are inspired by the love portrayed in the atoning death of God's Son, and they realize that all love begins in God who seeks out the elect independent of any action on their part (vv9f).

Third Reading

Just as Jesus shares his knowledge of the Father with his disciples (14:20), he shares his love as well (v9). Once again it is the observance of Christ's commandments that is the clearest assurance that one abides in Christ's love (v10; 14:21). Just as Christ's obedience was the measure of his love of the Father, the same can be said of the disciples in relation to Christ. It is interesting to note how knowledge, love, and obedience are three-tiered and inter-related in John: Father, Son, disciple.

Jesus' love is shown in three ways. First, he surrenders his *life* for the sake of the beloved, the highest form of love (v13;

10:15). Second, the beloved are no longer called slaves but *friends*. Slavery in John is connected with sin, from which the disciples have been freed (8:33 - 38). But friendship goes beyond freedom in being a relationship of mutual trust and communication (v15). The friends of Jesus are those who have the closest relations with him (13:23ff; 19:26f; 11:3). As such they are privy to the revelation of the Father and united by the same bonds which exist within the "household" of God (14:20). Third, it is Christ who *chooses* the beloved, not vice versa. This was seen in the case of the twelve, the first disciples (6:70). The Christians' election as friends makes them one with Christ in a fruitful life and in access to the Father in prayer (v16; 15:5; 14:13). Again, love within the Christian community remains the master plan of growth in discipleship (v17).

The Easter message continues to unfold as the church's growth appears in Acts and the depth of the Spirit life is presented in John. The evangelist has given us the picture of Christ as shepherd and vine, images which are rich in meaning. Today Christ is the one who chooses us as friends. In life there are many things for which we apply–acceptance at a university, a scholarship, employment. And usually we are one of many. If we are accepted, we have the feeling that we earned it in one way or another. But it is something else to be chosen. This may mean notoriety–a Nobel or Pulitzer prize or the baseball Hall of Fame–or something closer to home–diocesan or parish honors, employee of the month, mother of the year. But whatever it may be, it makes us two inches taller. We have been singled out of the masses and given recognition.

It is wonderful to be chosen as a friend. Friendship is one of life's greatest gifts. There are many givens in life over which we have no control, but our friends are ours by choice. To speak of our being Christ's friends says something different than brother, sister, or other family designations. Why? Because friends are chosen. Our acquaintances in life are many; our friends are relatively few. A friend is always there, always trustworthy, always a support. The friend is the one to whom we can confide anything and be assured of understanding. As a famous writer once put it: a friend is one in whose presence we don't have to say anything. That is what Christ is to us. The other titles of Christ appear with such frequency. Churches are named Holy Redeemer, Christ the King, Christ Our Savior, but seldom Christ Our

Friend. After all, it is the friend who stands by us in every trial. The friend understands. Think of David and Jonathan, Ruth and Naomi, Jesus and the beloved disciple. We are chosen as friends–another reason for Easter joy.

Homiletic and Catechetical Helps

1. Bringing faith to the world.

2. Knowing and loving God in John.

3. The household of God: the Trinity and the believer.

4. The equality of all peoples before God.

5. Christ, the revelation of God's love.

6. The difference between freedom and friendship.

7. Ways to "choose" others in daily life.

8. Friends and acquaintances.

9. The meaning of being a friend of Christ.

10. Sin as a loss of friendship.

SIXTH SUNDAY OF EASTER
Year C

Readings

    Acts 15:1 - 2, 22 - 29
    Rev 21:10 - 14, 22 - 23
    Jn 14:23 - 29

Theme: The Gift of Peace

In today's gospel, the Johannine Jesus promises his disciples the Spirit as well as his farewell gift of peace. The latter signified the restoration of harmonious relations between God and humankind but also a bond of accord among believers themselves. The danger of rupture within the early church is overcome by peaceful agreement between Jew and Gentile Christians in today's reading from Acts. In Revelation, John of Patmos sees the new Jerusalem, the church, as a city without a temple, signifying that the believers themselves are the new temple of God.

First Reading

This account of the conference held in Jerusalem to take up the question of Gentile observance of the Mosaic law differs in a number of ways from that given by Paul (Gal 2:1 - 10). Today's reading dwells mainly on the final decision taken by the church leaders. Paul's visit to Jerusalem is occasioned by the insistence of some Jewish Christians that the provisions of the Israelite law be observed by Gentile converts, who were far removed from any knowledge of Jewish observance. Since such observance was being set forth as essential to salvation (v1), the leaders of the Gentile sector of the church, Paul and Barnabas, with other representatives, carry their concerns to the authorities of the mother church in Jerusalem (v2). Luke presents the Jerusalem conference as a major gathering (vv4f), whereas Paul speaks of it as a private discussion (Gal 2:2).

After considerable debate, not included in today's reading, accord is reached on the question. James, "a brother of the Lord," not the apostle, was head of the Jerusalem church and the spokesman for the conference's majority view (vv13, 21). There are three major points in the final decree. First, those proponents of the law who had disturbed the Gentile community were unauthorized. In now sending two representatives of the Jerusalem church, Judas (Barsabbas) and Silas, the present decision is authenticated and formally linked with the Jerusalem community (vv24ff). Judas remains an unknown figure; Silas accompanied Paul on the second missionary journey (15:40 - 18:5). Second, the Gentile church is henceforth free of any responsibility to observe the law of circumcision and the Mosaic law in general (v28). Finally, there are a few legal provisions of sufficient weight within the Jewish Christian community to warrant observance in the church as a whole (v29). They are four in number, largely based on the holiness code of Leviticus (Lev 17 - 18): abstention from meat offered in pagan sacrifices, meat with blood in it, meat of an animal which had not been slaughtered according to ritual, and the prohibition of marriage with close relatives. The food prohibitions had special importance in view of the increased meal-sharing among Jew and Gentile converts. *The holy Spirit and us* (v28): an important Lucan note. It is the Spirit who takes the lead in Acts in guiding and directing the church. Human agents are secondary.

The difficulty with the decree lies in the fact that Paul makes no mention of these legal stipulations in his account of the Jerusalem visit (Gal 2:7 - 11) and later in Acts seems to learn of it for the first time (21:25). What we may have here is another example of Luke's telescoping different events: the first, exempting the Gentiles from all Mosaic law observance, and the second, the later issuance of a decree prescribing certain laws. Luke gives the whole process sanction by linking it all to a Jerusalem gathering of church leaders.

Responsorial Psalm   Ps 67

Universalism remains an important theme in this psalm; the commentary is found on the Twentieth Sunday of Year A.

Second Reading

The eschatological description of the church as the heavenly city of God draws on Ezekiel's vision of the end time Jerusalem. Thus, Revelation's seer, like the prophet, is taken to a high mountain from where the city becomes visible (v10; Ez 40:2); the twelve gates of the city are representative of the twelve tribes (v12; Ez 48:30 - 35); and there is the all-pervading presence of God within the city (v23; Ez 48:35). The new and old Israel merge with the symbolism of the twelve tribes (the gates) and the twelve apostles (the twelve stones on the foundations). The radiance of precious stones draws on Isaiah's depiction of the restored Zion (v11; Is 54:11f).

Since God and the lamb are all pervasive in the end time

city, there is no temple (v22). Localized cult, so much a part of
Israelite tradition, is superseded in Christianity by a new, deeply
internal form of worship not dependent on place (Jn 4:23f).
Jesus' risen presence is assured even in the smallest gathering
(Mt 18:20) as well as in the church as a whole (Mt 28:20; Col
1:18). As Isaiah had foretold, the all-enveloping presence of
God's glory overrides any other form of light (v23a; Is 60:1f,
19f). This is an illumination channeled through Christ, who himself reflects the brilliance of God's glory (v23b; 2 Cor 4:4ff).

Third Reading

In his leave-taking discourse, the Johannine Jesus enunciates
a recurring principle: the indwelling is concomitant with the
observance of his word or commandments (vv23f; 14:21; 1 Jn
3:24). There is a basic incompatibility between living in God
and disregarding his will, which, though articulated by Jesus,
finds its ultimate source in the Father. *Our dwelling* (v23): The
earlier notion of a heavenly dwelling for the elect (v2) is actually
superseded by their earthly dwelling in God, which begins here
but continues into eternity.

The *Advocate* (intercessor, mediator) is identified with the
Holy Spirit (v26), and one of his major roles is highlighted: continuing the teaching mission of Jesus and shedding light on the
salvific meaning of the death-resurrection ("remind you of all
that I told you").

Peace is clearly related to the Spirit's mission (v27). It is
promised here but is not imparted by Jesus until the Spirit is
given on the night of the resurrection, the time of Jesus' return
(v28; 20:19 - 23). Not the elusive peace of earthly powers, this
peace arises from the restoration of harmony and accord
between God and the believer, lost in the rebellion of Genesis
and regained through the saving death of Jesus (Col 1:20). The
giving of the Spirit and the gift of peace will be possible only
after Jesus' passage to the Father. This departure should be
marked by joy, not sorrow, in view of its ensuing benefits. *Father
is greater than I* (v28b): Jesus' equality with the Father does not
supplant the diversity of roles. Jesus' inferiority lies in his filial
obedience and submission to the Father in the fulfillment of his

mission (v31). Jesus' foretelling of the Father's plan will be supportive of the disciples' belief when the hour of his passage arrives (v29).

The argument over the role of the law in the early church was more than heated discussion. It had the potential to cause a major split in the fledgling body or, if the interests of the Judaizers had prevailed, could have resulted in Christianity's being no more than a splintered segment of Judaism. People are children of their own hour. We often think today of the difficulties in keeping the church together. Yet Vatican II introduced major and sweeping changes with comparatively little fall-out in terms of division. Diversity in outlook and concern abounds, to be sure, but in the main we are still together. For Luke it was the Spirit that held the early church together, just as it was the Spirit that prompted change. "The Holy Spirit and we have decided." The Spirit of God is unifying and not divisive. In any major decision, if we truly and sincerely try to discern God's will and not impose our own or predetermine the outcome, then solutions will be found. James and the Jerusalem leaders could well have insisted on the sacred character of a revealed law and ended discussion. Paul, with his theology of freedom, could have resisted any form of imposed Jewish legalism. In fact, most of the provisions of the Jerusalem decree were rather short-lived anyway. But the fact is that both sides showed their ability to listen, and the Spirit carried the day.

The Spirit also teaches and is the agent of peace. The teaching of Jesus continues in and through the Spirit. That teaching role has a primary importance today. There are so many areas where scripture may establish broad principles but few specifics. The Spirit continues to work in a special way through the teaching office of the church but also through theological research and the Christian body as a whole. While it is not easy to bring all of that together in a posture of openness and learning, there is really no other way to hear the Spirit's voice. The Spirit also brings peace–a restored and renewed relationship with God, begun in baptism, reinforced in the sacramental life, and sealed with our passing to God in death. It is a peace that no one can take from us. Peace for many people is defined in terms of an absence of war. But Christian peace is a positive force that convinces us that there is more right with the world than wrong. And the reason for that is simple. Christ alone is our peace.

Homiletic and Catechetical Helps

1. The significance of the Jerusalem decision.

2. The major councils of the church.

3. The councils and the church's teaching office.

4. Peace and compromise.

5. The Holy Spirit: Advocate, Teacher, Agent of peace.

6. The Christian: the dwelling place of God.

7. Reasons for the non-observance of the Jewish law.

8. Relating the indwelling to observance of Jesus' commandments.

9. Father and Son: equality and distinction of roles.

SEVENTH SUNDAY OF EASTER
Year A

Readings

> Acts 1:12 - 14
> 1 Pet 4:13 - 16
> Jn 17:1 - 11

Theme: Constant Prayer

Constancy in prayer does not mean continuous prayer. Rather it is a prayer that is unfailing, a posture of dependence on and openness to God that makes an ongoing relationship a normal part of life. This type of prayer appears in all three readings today. Gathered in the upper room in anticipation of the coming of the Spirit, the apostles and the women followers of Jesus lived in a climate of prayer. Jesus in John's gospel in his inseparable oneness with the Father typifies the spirit of prayer as he prays today in a special way for his followers. The first let-

ter of Peter encourages us to thank God for the sufferings we
have to endure as Christians.

First Reading

Important Lucan themes emerge in this brief account of the
disciples' post-ascension life. Jerusalem remains the focal point
of this transitional period (v12). It was toward Jerusalem that
Jesus was directed in fulfillment of his earthly destiny (Lk 9:51),
and it was from there that the witness of the apostles was to go
forth (Acts 1:8). It is Jerusalem's theological importance that
accounts for its repeated references (Lk 24:9, 33, 52). Olivet was
in close proximity to the Lucan ascension site at Bethany (Lk
24:50), and also close to Jerusalem, the distance permitted for a
sabbath walk about a half mile. Olivet is mentioned because of
its eschatological significance, befitting the present context
(v11; Zech 14:4).

The list of the apostles does not differ from that given in the
gospel (v13; Lk 6:14ff). John and James are "upgraded" because
of the mention they later receive (3:1 - 11; 4:13; 12:2). Judas, of
course, is not listed. Since the twelve play such a key role as witnesses to Jesus' ministry and the subsequent gospel proclamation, Luke sees it as essential that they be at full complement
before the coming of the Spirit (vv15 - 26). Present with them in
prayer are Mary, Jesus' mother, the living personification of
faith (Lk 1:26 - 38; 11:27f), and the "brothers" of Jesus, who
probably included James, the later head of the Jerusalem
church (v14; Gal 2:9). The women present were undoubtedly
those present at the crucifixion (Lk 23:49) and later at the burial (Lk 23:55f). Prayer is prelude to the important events of
Luke-Acts (Lk 3:21; 6:12: Acts 2:46f), and Jesus sees it as an
accompanying feature of the Spirit's conferral (Lk 11:13).

Responsorial Psalm   Ps 27

Trust and lament are joined in this psalm which stresses the
role of prayer in the believer's life (vv4, 7f). The Lord's assured
presence is the psalmist's great consolation in the face of adversity (v11). The psalmist's one great desire is union with the

Lord in temple worship, expressed in terms as living in God's presence and gazing upon him (v4). There he will be safe from his foes. It is for this temple worship that he ardently prays (vv7f).

Second Reading

Admonitions here directed to Christians undergoing persecution reflect features of the Pauline theology on suffering and glory. Baptism unites the Christian to Christ in his death and rising (Rom 6:3f). To live in Christ is to experience and even prolong his suffering (Col 1:24) as well as to be empowered by his risen life (Phil 3:10). Therefore, suffering is reason for joy (v13), in terms of both companionship in Christ's suffering and the assurance of glory which accompanies the Spirit's presence. It is the Spirit's presence with its future promise that makes the bearing of insults tolerable (v14; Is 11:2).

There is a pronounced difference between suffering as a wrongdoer and suffering as a Christian (vv15f). In the former case it may well be deserved; in the latter case it is conformity with Christ, the innocent sufferer (2:19ff; 3:16f).

Third Reading

The final section of Jesus' supper discourse is a lengthy prayer to the Father (Jn 17). In today's gospel, the first section prays that Jesus' work be brought to its salvific conclusion (vv1 - 5) and the second is a prayer for the disciples (vv6 - 11). The formative influence of the author on the whole of Jesus' discourse appears clearly at various points, as, for example, v3, a parenthetical explanation which even includes a third person reference to Jesus. *Hour* (v1): a characteristic Johannine reference to the eschatological time, i.e. Jesus' death-resurrection (2:4; 12:23). It is through his life-giving death, climaxing a life of total submission, that Jesus glorifies the Father (v4). Jesus, in turn, is glorified by the Father in assuming his rightful position as Son and Lord, a position held by the Word before creation itself (v5; 1:1f). Jesus further glorifies the Father by extending to others the life he enjoys with the Father (v2; 3:35f), a life obtainable through an unqualified acceptance of the God revealed in Jesus (v3; 1:18).

The cross in John serves basically as the avenue to Jesus' glory. As Jesus concludes the supper, then, he prays earnestly that the human machinations leading to his death be set in motion in order that the path to glory be opened.

Jesus then prays for his disciples. They have been the recipients of the revelation which Jesus has received from the Father and are presented as having been totally receptive to the Word (vv6, 8). *Your name* (v6): Probably the name "I AM," drawn from Yahweh's self-identification in Exodus (3:14) and conferred upon Jesus with his resurrection. This is, of course, anticipated in John who reads the resurrection-glorification into Jesus' earthly life. Thus the repeated I AM statements of Jesus (8:24, 28, 58). This points to Jesus' identity in nature with the Father.

Jesus prays for the apostles prior to mission (vv9ff). Because of their acceptance of the truth, they are no longer part of the world (v9). Although the world in John is the object of God's love (3:16; 17:18), it is also the arena of evil, inimical to God's interests (15:18f). The disciples have been taken from the world to be sanctified that they may be missioned to the world (17:17f). Jesus' life-sharing with his disciples extends his glory received from the Father to them. This prolongation of glory allows for the continuation of the Father's work, even though Jesus takes his leave (vv10f). This mutual sharing of glory is but another expression of the indwelling God in the life of the Christian.

Prayer is an attitude or state of mind, not simply something done at stated moments. All of us have to give ourselves regular fixed points to turn to God formally. But God is met in countless ways in the course of every day—in human dealings, in nature, in solitude. Our prayer is constant when we view reality from the vantage point of faith. Realizing the presence of God places prayer at the center of our lives, whether in the middle of a forest or in a crowded airport. Today's readings offer us something of a litmus test. In Acts the disciples are at prayer in expectation of an important event, the coming of the Spirit. In 1 Peter, Christians are encouraged to pray in the face of suffering.

Important moments come in all our lives. And they often consume our interest. Some of them are joyful; some are sorrowful. All of them full of anticipation. Yet often, as far as God is concerned, our thoughts are centrifugal rather than centripetal. For counsel we may turn in various directions before we turn to God. In a flurry of excitement, it is the human solution that is sought, not the mind of God. A prayer that is constant does the contrary. God is such a part of life, as was the Father in the life of Jesus, that turning to him is spontaneous. A closeness is there that finds many words unnecessary.

The same is true in the face of hardship. Fear in the face of the stark reality of suffering is normal. Yet God can and will save us in the way he deems best. The psalms are full of confidence in the midst of distress. Misfortune can and often does make us people of deeper faith. The examples are many: the imprisoned hostage with his Bible; the priest without bread and wine praying daily the eucharistic prayer; the terminally ill patient simply repeating the name of Jesus. Suffering is itself a form of prayer. We have no simple answer to its meaning. But we worship a God who has experienced it, a God who is never far from us. For prayer to be constant, it need not follow a neat inflexible schedule. It is the consciousness of an indwelling God, the realization that in God we are really at home.

Homiletic and Catechetical Helps

1. The meaning of prayer.

2. The "why" of prayer.

3. Forms of prayer.

4. Prayer in Luke-Acts.

5. Suffering in the Christian life.

6. Endurance without retaliation.

7. The death of Jesus and the glory of God.

8. Eternal life as faith in Jesus.

7. Discipleship: a continuation of Christ in the world.

8. Constancy in prayer.

SEVENTH SUNDAY OF EASTER
Year B

Readings

> Acts 1:15 - 17, 20 - 26
> 1 Jn 4:11 - 16
> Jn 17:11 - 19

Theme: Disciples: Elected and Missioned

It is hard to separate vocation and mission. In the Acts of the Apostles, the Holy Spirit chooses Judas' successor with the help of the Christian community. In today's gospel, the twelve are missioned to the world from which they were chosen. The message which they carry is captured in today's epistle.It is one of faith and love, to be lived as much as to be preached.

First Reading

The first discourse of Peter, clearly a Lucan composition, is indicative of his prominence as a spokesman for the apostles. It reflects Peter's position within early church life and for Luke is a fulfillment of Jesus' prayer for him prior to his death (Lk 22:32). *One hundred and twenty persons* (v15): The multiple of twelve by ten looks to the full complement of the new Israel. The twelve tribes are represented by the apostles, who are in turn responsible for "groups of ten" (1 Mac 3:55). Peter calls for a replacement for Judas whose betrayal of Jesus is not attributed to his own wiles but, in Lucan terms, was part of God's plan, even foreseen in the Davidic psalms (vv16f, 20). The substitution for Judas is seen as called for by a free adaptation of Psalm 109:8.

The incorporation of a new *apostle* (v26) is more specifically a reconstitution of the twelve, who represent the continuity between the old and new Israel. While Luke is generally inclined to limit apostleship to the twelve, though not always successfully (14:4, 14), there were other broader views in play

(Gal 1:1; 1 Cor 15:2 - 9). Luke's criteria for apostleship among the twelve are two: part of the company of Jesus during his public ministry and the experience of the risen Christ (v22). The latter related to the former as providing linkage between the two phases of Christ's existence. In addition, the early church viewed the earthly ministry in the light of the resurrection with the fuller understanding of the person and mission of Jesus which it provided. At the same time, it anchored the proclamation of the risen Lord in his earthly preaching and teaching.

Of the two candidates chosen by the community, nothing more is known from New Testament sources (v23). The prayer highlights the selection as the Lord's, to match the choice of Jesus in the case of the original apostles (vv24f). In the prayer, the play on the word "place" is ironic. Judas leaves his apostolic post to finish in a Field of Blood, remembered for reasons of infamy (v19). The drawing of lots rather than election lifts the choice from human calculation to the realm of divine determination (v26). *Apostolic ministry* (literally, ministry and apostleship) (v25): This is an appositive or epexegetical use of two substantives. Apostleship is clearly identified with service and not simply office (1 Cor 12:5, 28; Eph 4:11f). Matthias is designated to accede to the position.

Responsorial Psalm　　Ps 103

The Easter acclamation of the Lordship of Jesus finds echoes in this hymn. It begins with a personal recognition of God's goodness (vv1f). His forgiveness is seen as limitless and truly paternal (vv12f). With the Lord enthroned above the heavens, the whole of the heavenly court is invited to acclaim him (vv19f) in addition to the order of creation (v22).

Second Reading

The reading gives three assurances of the divine presence within the Christian: the testimony of the Spirit, of love, and of faith. The idiomatic "No one has ever seen God" is repeatedly used by John to uphold the singular character of Jesus' revelation of God (v12; Jn 1:18; 5:37). Here the absence of sight is compensated for by the experience of God dwelling within. That experience is born of the Spirit (v13) and manifests itself in mutual love (v12) and faith (v15).

Love is a Christian requisite because God has shown it first in his Son's sacrifice (vv11, 16; 4:9f). That experience of the love of the Father in Jesus' self-donation leads to its being brought to life anew in the love of Christians for one another (v14). God's love grows or is perfected with the increase of mutual love (v12). Here faith and love become one and inseparable. To believe in Jesus as God's Son is to know him in terms of the Father's love (vv15f). This then calls for a similar love within the Christian community.

Finally, God can be defined in terms of love (v14). The person who lives in a Christian spirit of mutual charity and centers his or her life thereon is assured of the indwelling presence of God (v16).

Third Reading

This gospel passage treats of Jesus' presence with the disciples (vv11f), his imminent departure and their state in his absence (vv13 - 17), and their mission to the world (vv18f).

Holy Father (v11): This is exceptional in John and may well reflect a liturgical formula. *Your name* (v12): The name is shared by the Father and Jesus. In the fourth gospel it is the name Yahweh (I AM) (8:24, 28, 58). The name, like Godhead itself, is now seen to embrace more than one person. This is the new revelation of God in Jesus. The disciples' faith in Jesus as God's Son was equivalently faith in God's name. This faith confirmed the disciples in the truth and preserved them safe and untouched by the world (v12). Judas was the only exception. Both the preservation of the elect and the loss of the one are elsewhere explained by the scriptures (18:9; 13:18). In Johannine terms this points to the divinely ordained character of the events surrounding Jesus' death-resurrection.

The passing of Jesus to the Father will lead to the Spirit-filled joy of his disciples (v13). In accepting his teaching and his commandments, the disciples clearly set themselves apart from the world, which is guided by antithetical principles. The disciples incurred the world's hatred as did Jesus himself (v14; 15:18 - 25). However, unlike Jesus now in transition to the Father, the disciples can still be seduced by the world and Satan, its overlord (v15; Mt 6:13). *Consecrate them in the truth* (v17): Consecration is here sanctification in the Spirit. Specifically it is a consecration in God's word and commandments, the "truth" that Jesus has imparted (14:6). This ultimately means a consecration in Jesus himself, who is the way, truth, and life. Consecration and mission are inseparable (v18). Just as Jesus was missioned to the world, so too are the disciples (20:21).

Jesus passes to glory through his death-resurrection. In cultic terms this is seen as a consecration, somewhat akin to Hebrews' understanding of Jesus' sacrifice as an act of priesthood (v19; Heb 9:11ff). His heavenly consecration will then result in that of his disciples through the conferral of the sanctifying (consecrating) Spirit. In this way the mission of Jesus to the world will continue in his disciples (v18).

There is no divinely prescribed way for leadership to be named in the church. No system has been formally canonized. While the final decision on the new apostle in Acts was left to God, the proposal of candidates went beyond the twelve to the believers in attendance. There is a certain wisdom there. Collaborative processes of decision making in the church have become broader since Vatican II. However, this has left largely untouched the method of selecting church authorities. It seems logical to involve the faithful in some way in the selection of bishops and pastors. Most religious communities have long operated on a broad-based process of election, something which they would surrender only with great reluctance. The faithful in Acts presented the names of the candidates in the Lucan account. The church would have much to gain in allowing broader participation in making selections. It would manifest confidence in the Holy Spirit and show greater sensitivity to our belief in God's presence within his people.

Are consecration and mission to be viewed in some sort of a detached fashion? Not according to John. Biblical consecration, even in the Israelite priesthood, looked to a determined role. Kings, priests, and prophets were made holy in order to do something. Today we speak of men and women religious as consecrated, not to stand apart in holy iso-

lation, but to be missioned for the salvation of the world, from cloistered nuns to foreign missionaries. Every baptized person is bathed and anointed. The symbolism is clear. Anointing looks to consecration and that means a mission to the world. It is a consecration carried to the halls of government, to executive offices, to TV studios, and to plant assembly lines. The comportment of salespersons in a department store can say much about Christian values. Christ prays that when we are sent to the world, we do not lose ourselves in it. The danger is always there. But consecration for mission means that there is no escaping the danger.

Homiletic and Catechetical Helps

1. Possible methods of designating church authorities.

2. Differences in the understanding of apostleship in the New Testament.

3. Mutual love: sign of the Spirit's presence.

4. Relation of faith and love in John.

5. Consecration in religious life.

6. Consecration in the Christian life.

7. Understanding "the world" in John.

6. The anointing in the sacraments of baptism, confirmation, holy orders, and the sacrament of the sick.

SEVENTH SUNDAY OF EASTER
Year C

Readings

> Acts 7: 55 - 60
> Rev 22:12 - 14, 16 - 17, 20
> Jn 17:20 - 26

Theme: Come, Lord Jesus

In today's first reading, Stephen, shortly before his death, sees Jesus as the eschatological Son of Man who is to return on the clouds of heaven. The sense of expectation of that return runs high in the reading from Revelation today. The heavenly Christ, who is the beginning and the end, speaks to his bride the church about his approaching return. In John's gospel, the idea of the returning Lord is muted with the coming of Jesus identified with the indwelling which draws together the triune God and the believer.

First Reading

Stephen's death comes at the termination of his trial and his lengthy apologia which is a resume of salvation history (7:1 - 53). The Stephen narrative links his death with the beginning of the Gentile mission (c. 8) and introduces Saul (eventually Paul), the apostle of the Gentiles, in joining him with the Stephen event which launches the Gentile movement (8:4).

The martyrdom of Stephen serves two of Luke's literary-theological aims. The first patterns the death of the proto-martyr on the death of Jesus himself. The second integrates Paul into Acts before the beginning of the persecution of the church, which subsequently becomes considerably intense.

Stephen's vision brings to fulfillment Jesus' prophetic words at his own trial (v55; Lk 22:69), the only variation being Jesus' standing rather than sitting at God's right hand. In both instances, the strong reaction of the sanhedrin is caused by what is considered a blasphemous assertion (vv56f; 22:70f). The death of the church's first martyr is modeled on that of Jesus in the expression of identical sentiments. He commends his spirit to the Lord, here the Lord being Christ, not the Father (v59; Lk 23:46), and he asks forgiveness for his enemies (v60; Lk 23:34).

Paul is inserted as something of an adjunct figure in the narrative (v58). His presence, however, prefaces his role as a persecutor (8:3), links him with the beginning of the Gentile church, and makes him one of the first beneficiaries of Stephen's prayer for pardon.

Responsorial Psalm   Ps 97

In this hymn identified with the celebration of Yahweh's enthronement, the Lord approaches in an awesome theophany (vv1f), recognized jointly by the celestial and earthly spheres (v6). Yahweh's power contrasts sharply with the nothingness and impotence of foreign deities and their adherents (v7). Poetic acknowledgement is accorded the existence of other gods only to accent their total subordination to Yahweh (vv7, 9). Hymns exalting the kingship of Yahweh appear regularly in the Easter season, with Christ now sharing in Yahweh's glory.

Second Reading

Christ is the speaker in these oracles which bring the book of Revelation to a conclusion. The expectation of the Lord's imminent return gives the words a sense of urgency. He will return as the judge rewarding and punishing according to conduct (v12; Mt 25:31 - 46). He is the eternal One, here applying to himself the words earlier used by God himself (v13; 1:8). Alpha and Omega, the first and last letters of the Greek alphabet, express his eternal nature.

Those who *wash their robes* have done so in the Lamb's blood. Not only baptized, they have also endured the suffering of hardship and persecution, but not necessarily martyrdom (v14; 7:14f). Eden's tree of life (22:2; Gen 2:9) and the city with gates (21:12) symbolize eternal redemption. Jesus is *root and offspring of David*; in bearing these messianic titles, he is the heir to the Davidic promises (v16; 5:5; Is 11:1). As the *morning star*, he is victorious over darkness and death (v16; 2:26ff).

The Spirit with *the bride* receives the elect. The bride is both the church (21:2) and biblical wisdom inviting her listeners to salvation (Prov 8; 9:5). The *life-giving water* offered is both end time abundance and, in Johannine terms, the Spirit issuing into eternal life (Jn 4). The book concludes on a note of expectation and a liturgical response requesting the parousia (v20b; 1 Cor 16:22).

Third Reading

In concluding his prayer at the supper, Jesus directs his attention beyond the apostles to those who will respond in faith to their mission (v20). He prays for their unity in faith and love (vv21 - 23) and for their eventual union with him in heaven (v24). There is to be a deepening in their knowledge and love in the future (vv25f).

The unity on the vertical level which already binds Father, Son, and believer now takes on a horizontal dimension as Jesus prays for those who will come to him through the apostles' mission. In addition to being united with Father and Son, he prays that they will be characterized by a mutual love among themselves (v21). This will make manifest to the unbeliever the same type of love the Father had in sending his Son. Thus, love has an apologetic value as well (v.23).

The glory you gave me (v22): This is the glory of Christ's exaltation in the Holy Spirit, here viewed by the author as already accomplished. This is glory shared in the conferral of the same Spirit upon the disciples after Jesus' death-resurrection. It is the Spirit which is the source of unity. God's working in Jesus and Jesus in his followers is a dynamic, on-going presence by which love is perfected in becoming an evident sign of God's presence in the world (v23).

It is Jesus' desire that his followers join him in heaven. The glory which they now see is only partial (1 Cor 13:12; 1 Jn 3:2); in the future they will see the fullness of his glory, which he had eternally with the Father (v24; 17:5; 1:1). The world does not know Jesus (15:18 - 25), and thus does not know the Father whom Jesus reveals (1:18). However, this knowledge, not merely intellectual but identified with the experience of God, is shared by the believers (v25). *Your name* (v26): The name is Yahweh, used also of Jesus (I AM), in view of their common nature. To know the name was to know the person. Through Jesus, the Father is known and loved. *I will make it known* (v26): through the activity of the Advocate after Jesus' departure (16:12f). With this on-going communication of love and knowledge, the indwelling is intensified and perfection realized (v23).

The return of Christ at the end of the age is much to the fore in today's liturgy, clearly in Revelation and at least implicitly in Acts. It was a belief important to the church in its early years. The Christ who had departed would soon return for the full inauguration of his reign. John's gospel is quite different. Written late in the first century, it places its emphasis on the continuing presence of Christ in the believer and the church. To live in God in anticipation of history's end makes the now of our salvation an inestimable value. Easter's importance does not lie mainly in its apologetic value, as important as that may be. Of far greater moment is the beginning of a whole new life. We are no longer strangers in God's household. We are now members of the family. All of this is made possible by the risen Christ's gift of the Spirit.

Today's gospel speaks of unity and continuing revelation. Charity is the benchmark of our Christian life, and it expresses itself in a spirit of unity. Division within Christianity is the very antithesis of Jesus' teaching. If division doesn't bother us, it should. We have to be convinced–all of us–that historical division can be overcome with a true openness to God. Yes, fidelity to truth is important but so is a healthy measure of flexibility. Further division can be avoided if we do not allow differences to become barriers. Legitimate differences are a healthy sign and can lead to growth. Unfortunately they often escalate into a state of polarization. Then charity is lost. It is important to remember that the scriptures say more about love than any other virtue. And yet we so often treat its violations casually.

God continues to reveal himself. Jesus is followed by the Spirit, the teacher. As much as some people might oppose change, the fact is that we are changing constantly. Even in our belief and understanding of God, most of us are not where we were a decade ago. To live is to grow. To live in God's triune family is to know the family better. Come, Lord Jesus–at the end of history, yes, but in so many other ways that lead us to growth in faith and love. Our God is not solely coming on the clouds of heaven. Ours is a God who is never far from us. In fact, the Lord walks every step of the way with us.

Homiletic and Catechetical Helps

1. The meaning of martyrdom.

2. Examples of contemporary martyrdom.

3. Stephen's configuration to Christ.

5. Christ as the beginning and the end.

6. The Christ of the future and the Christ of the now.

7. The sign value of Christian unity.

8. Attitudes toward a divided Christianity.

9. Understanding on-going revelation.

10. Explaining the Trinity.

PENTECOST
Years A B C

VIGIL

Readings

> Gen 11:1 - 9
> Rom 8:22 - 27
> Jn 7:37 - 39

Theme: Birth from Above

There are a number of options for the vigil's first reading. The Genesis Babel narrative is selected here because of its connection with the Pentecost account in Acts. The reading from Romans looks at our future destiny in the light of our present struggle and strongly accents the virtue of hope. The Spirit groans within us in its tireless desire to realize our final redemption. The Johannine Jesus speaks of the Spirit as a fountain of fresh water, a precious resource in the land of Jesus; the Spirit quenches the believer's thirst in time and eternity. The readings for both the vigil and the feast itself speak exultantly of new life, a birthday for the believer and the church.

First Reading

The story of Babel, which is part of the Genesis epic of sin (Gen 1 - 11), is a graphic illustration of human disobedience and pride. Disobedience appears in the unwillingness of Noah's descendants to migrate to those parts of the world which God had designated. They preferred to settle in a place of their choice and become city dwellers. The sin of pride is present in their desire to build to the heavens, to construct an edifice as tall as the legendary Babylonian steppe temples, which towered over the flat level plains.

While migration is taking place, a decision is made to stop and settle in the valley of Shinar, ancient Sumer in Mesopotamia, the land where Babylon was located (v2; 10:10). In their pursuit of work in brick and mortar (v3), the people abandon a pastoral nomadic life in favor of urban living, with the story thus shaped to reflect the existing hostilities between these two segments of near eastern society. The construction of an edifice patterned on a pagan temple, the tallest building on the Mesopotamian horizon, subtly portrays an opting for false religious values (v4).

Yahweh is portrayed anthropomorphically as an observer of these events (v5). In conversation with his heavenly attendants (v7), he decides on a punishment in the form of confusing speech, with diversity of languages viewed as a major barrier to communication. This is a popular or folkloric explanation for a "disorder in nature" in terms of human sinfulness, in much the same way as other human trials are explained in the early chapters of Genesis. *Babel* (Babylon) (v9): The name is given a pejorative explanation in view of its resemblance in sound to the Hebrew verb "to confuse" (balel). The people's destination for other lands, part of Yahweh's original plan, comes about now by their being scattered (vv8f) and also impaired by an inability to communicate.

Responsorial Psalm   Ps 104

This hymn praises Yahweh for the works of creation while describing the inter-dependence of all creatures, provided for by a beneficent God. Yahweh is enshrined in effulgent light, as near eastern deities were often presented (v2). Not only is he the origin of all creatures (v24), he sustains everything in a well-ordered dependence. Planting leads to harvest, harvest to food and nourishment. When he withdraws life or its supports, creatures cannot survive (vv28f). *Breath* (vv29f) (Heb: *ruah*): This is the cause of life emanating from God, which when "breathed" into Adam initiated his existence as a man (Gen 2:7). It is the cause of animation but not to be equated with the "soul." It may here also be identified with a "wind" that brings the perennial change of seasons, the rainfall and the harvest. The rather broad spectrum of meanings given the word *ruah* (breath, wind, spirit) accounts for the adaptation of v30 to the Pentecost liturgy.

Second Reading

Here Romans speaks of the role of the Spirit in the life of the baptized. Creation itself is in a state of spiritual parturition in expectation of its birth in God or final salvation (v22). To speak of nature's annual re-emergence as a giving birth was a common metaphor in antiquity. The Christian shares in this period of anxious anticipation. This is so because the Spirit, already present, is a pledge of future destiny. *Firstfruits* (v23): The initial produce of the harvest was given to God, symbolic of the whole harvest (Lev 23:15 - 21). Here the Spirit anticipates the final fullness. The resurrection of the body is assured by the Spirit's presence, even though the Spirit is housed in the weakness of flesh from which the believer yearns to be released (v23). *Adoption* (v23): The word is not fully attested in manuscript evidence. Moreover, adoption takes place with baptism, not resurrection (8:15). If the reading is retained, it would refer to a fullness of adoption with final redemption.

Assurance is rooted in hope. Because hope is centered on the as yet unattained, it is accompanied by a spirit of endurance which patiently awaits the final outcome (v24). This interim period of travail finds the Christian assisted by the Spirit. Weakness or the "flesh" side of human existence includes ignorance. The human inability to know what is best before God is compensated for by the Spirit's prayer (vv26f). The Spirit prays within the elect (in groanings), and the God who "searches hearts" (1 Sam 16:7; 1 Kgs 8:39) finds mutuality in encountering the Spirit. It is the Spirit who understands God's will and directs human prayer accordingly. In addition, it is the Spirit who makes prayer intimate and familiar (8:15; Gal 4:6f).

Third Reading

The feast of Tabernacles (v37a), at which Jesus is in attendance, had a distinctive ritual with water brought by the priest to the temple from the area of the Siloam pool. This was done in conjunction with prayers for the fall rains. The rite serves as an appropriate background for Jesus' presentation of himself as the source of living water.

Jesus' invitation to come to him as the source of water alludes to biblical texts wherein wisdom is the source of food and drink (v37b; Prov 9:5; Sir 24:19ff), without being a specific citation. *Whoever believes in me* (v38) is awkwardly placed and disturbs the flow of thought which points to Jesus (not the believer) as the source of water. It may be the author's didactic insertion to point up the necessity of faith in order to come to Christ. The major quotation (v38) is also of dubious origin, although the thought is characteristically Johannine (4:10, 13f). The text may be related to a number of scriptural "water" texts referring to Yahweh's life-giving power (Ez 47:1; Is 12:3).

The reader is left with no doubt as to the meaning of Jesus' statement. The Spirit is the living water proceeding from its source, the risen Christ (v29). Although the gospel is written in the full light of Easter faith and the Spirit's presence, the author does not hesitate to avert to the historical fact that the Spirit was not given prior to the resurrection (20:22).

PENTECOST

Readings

Acts 2:1 - 11
1 Cor 12:3 - 7, 12 - 13
Jn 20:19 - 23

First Reading

It is important to note that only Acts has a distinct episode for the Spirit's descent with the phenomena that surround it. Much is compressed in this dramatic presentation which should be read as an important theological statement rather than as an actual presentation of historical data. There are a number of features which bear emphasis.

Pentecost (v1). This major feast occurred fifty days after Passover-Unleavened Bread, sufficient reason in itself to explain the Lucan choice. However, there is evidence that by New Testament times the feast included the celebration of the giving of the law on Mount Sinai. In fact, the narrative contains some phenomena connected with the Sinai experience. If this correlation is correct, the narrative would highlight the new law of the Spirit as supplanting the Mosaic legislation. As scriptural background to the event, in terms of both the elements of theophany and the universal mission, the strongest claimant is a passage in Third Isaiah (Is 66:15 - 20). In addition, the loud noise and fire are connected with the Sinai theophany (Ex 19:16, 18).

Tongues. The first result of the Spirit's presence is the gift of "tongues" (v4). Originally this may well have been a reference to a type of unintelligible ecstatic speech, one of the well-established gifts of the Spirit (10:46; 1 Cor 14). Here, however. "tongues" is clearly understood as languages (vv4, 6, 11) and functions as part of the narrative's message of universalism. This may have resulted from a reworking of a previous "tongues" text. At any rate, here it is intended to reverse the confusion of Babel where, as a result of sin, language was an obstacle to communication (Gen 11:1 - 9). The Spirit now supplants sin, bringing reconciliation and mutual understanding.

Universalism. The rapid transition from the upper room to a public forum in Jerusalem is a literary device. The Spirit moves the apostles at once to preview the program of Acts' outreach to the nations. The audience is composed of Jews and Jewish proselytes, mostly people of foreign origin (vv9ff). The list of countries, probably not Lucan, is unusual; few of the places have any significance in Acts' missionary accounts. However, although the purview at this point remains restricted to a proclamation to a Jewish audience, the broad geographical sweep clearly points to the universal character of the church. To the astonishment of the hearers, the apostles are understood as they proclaim "the mighty acts of God," centering on the salvific death and resurrection of Jesus (v11: 2:36)

Responsorial Psalm   Ps 104

Commentary on the main lines of the psalm are to be found on the Pentecost vigil,

Second Reading

Paul here underscores the diversity connected with the Spirit's presence in outlining its work among the faithful. He first cautions his readers to be wary of pseudo-spirits which can easily delude. There are criteria for determining the authentic Spirit within the church. The Spirit will never label the true as false or vice versa. In citing the customary baptismal formula as an example (v3b; Acts 2:38), he argues that any profession of the Lordship of Jesus is certified as being prompted by the Spirit of truth.

The diverse manifestations of the Spirit are identified as gifts (v4), forms of service (v5) and workings of God (v6), all of which are interchangeable. Whatever proceeds from the Spirit is the action of God, totally gratuitous, and ordained for the good of the whole. Each is attributed to a different expression of God: the Spirit (v4), Christ the Lord (v5) and God himself (v6), which will eventually find full articulation in the doctrine of the Trinity. Emphasis is given to the gifts of the Spirit, not as directed to individuals, but given for the common good (v7).

Paul then introduces the image of the body as the living organism in which all members adhere. So too is it with Christ. This concept of the living union between Christ and the believer expressed in body imagery is a central feature of Pauline theology (vv12f; 10:17; Rom 12:4f). Diversity is not destructive of unity any more than the parts detract from the one body. It is the Spirit which unifies, and that Spirit is shared by people of diverse ethnic or social backgrounds (v13; Gal 3:28). In the one baptism, all have "been given to drink of one Spirit."

Third Reading

Comment on the appropriate verses of today's gospel are to be found in the commentary for the Second Sunday of Easter.

The readings of Pentecost are full of new life. This is truly a birthday. Ministers of baptism today often remind parents to make the remembrance of the baptismal day something special in the child's life. In some countries, celebration of the Christian name day takes precedence over the birthday. Baptism marks the day when all of us began a new life in Christ, the day when Pentecost became a lived reality. It is that day which sets the direction for our life. Without Pentecost Christ's work would have been incomplete, His death may have proved his love for us, but it would not of itself improve our lot. We would be able to admire him at a distance. But there would be no effective following of him, nor the right to call Christ "brother," or God "Abba." It is the Spirit of Pentecost that makes all of that possible. But today's celebration is not just personal; it is communal as well. Today the church was launched on its mission. It celebrates two millennia of life. And the church is the mother who accompanies us from the cradle to the grave.

Unity and diversity–both are so pronounced in today's readings. In Acts there is a clear foretelling that an open door policy will be followed. The church is open to all people. There are to be no distinctions of race, gender, nationality or social status. We find our unity in one Lord, one faith, and one baptism. But unity does not mean a measured marching to the same tune. There are many ways in which life is lived and service is rendered in the church. It took us a while to learn that cultural differences are to be respected, but now we see what an enrichment they represent. We have diverse liturgical expressions in the church, different approaches to theology, different forms of government. Religious communities have quite divergent forms of ministry and ways of living community life. All of this goes hand in hand with a unity in faith. All too often differences are seen as a threat. It is labeled non-conformist. But conformity is not necessarily a virtue. The Spirit breathes where and as it wills. Pentecost reminds us of that as unlettered Palestine Jews go forth as empowered Christians.

Homiletic and Catechetical Helps

1. Explaining the Holy Spirit.

2. The gifts of the Spirit.

3. Unity and diversity in the church.

4. Relating the Babel and Pentecost stories.

5. Redeemed creation and environmental concerns.

6. The Spirit praying within us.

7. Jesus, giver of the Spirit.

8. The importance of the Gentile church.

9. Remembering our day of baptism.

10. The significance of the Christian name.

11. The Spirit and the sacraments.

TRINITY SUNDAY
Years A B C

Theme: Love in Three Persons

YEAR A

Readings

Ex 34:4 - 9
2 Cor 13:11 - 13
Jn 3:16 - 18

The understanding of a God in three persons was alien to the Israelites. It is unique to Christian faith. At best, a Christian reading of the Hebrew scriptures sees a background to later belief in earlier texts. Thus, it can be said that the attributes of mercy and fidelity in the Exodus reading today foreshadow qualities that will be later seen as personal in God. Paul's prayerful invocation in today's second reading relates three distinct divine activities to God, Jesus Christ, and the Spirit. The work of the triune God is implied in the Johannine Jesus' conversation with Nicodemus. Love prompted the Father to send the Son who was the bearer of the Spirit, the source of eternal life.

First Reading

The "calf of gold" incident in Exodus is something of a watershed in the account of Israel's desert journey (Ex 32). Because of this sin, Yahweh indicates to Moses that he will no longer accompany the people (Ex 33:3). On the basis of his friendship with Moses, he later retracts his decision (33:15ff), at which point Moses requests to see Yahweh's glory, a request that cannot be granted because of the spiritual chasm that separates God and mortals (v20). Nonetheless, Moses is promised a "glimpse of God," a view of his back and no more (vv19 - 23).

Today's reading can be seen as a commentary on that "glimpse of God." In compliance with the divine injunction, Moses takes to the mountain the two tablets which are to replace the former set of "broken" commandments (v4; 34:1). Moses ascends Sinai as he did in preparing to enter into covenant-making the first time (19:3). The anthropomorphic view of God is interpreted in Yahweh's revelatory words to his friend. He initially identifies himself with the God of the burning bush (vv5f; Ex 3:14). In addition, as the God of the covenant, *kindness* (*hesed*) and *fidelity* (*emeth*) are expressive of central covenant attributes (v6). They point to Yahweh's concern and constancy seen in his willingness to initiate a covenant and his unfailing faithfulness to the commitment (Ps 117:2). These two qualities are rich in their expression of covenant love.

But insight into God goes further. He is a God of justice (slow to anger), who will not leave transgressions unpunished. In the narrative, his qualities of goodness and compassion outweigh the punitive dimension (v6), but, as his words go on to say, evil has to be dealt with (v7). Yet he is also a forgiving God where repentance is present (v7a). This notion of pardon goes a step beyond Yahweh's earlier self-description where mention of his justice in rewarding and punishing is not matched with that of forgiveness (Ex 20:5f).

Moses' view of God, then, is basically a deeper insight into Yahweh, a faithful covenant God, a God of sanctions who is also willing to forgive.

Responsorial Psalm   *Dan 3:52 - 56*

This doxology is part of the hymn of the three youths in the fiery furnace in Daniel. Here Yahweh is addressed directly. Reflecting its original liturgical setting, the hymn repeats the people's response at every half verse, with soloists or choir singing God's various attributes in the first part of the verse. To bless God's name (v52) is but another way to bless his person. Yahweh's presence among his people in the temple receives special recognition, with the temple and cherubim throne references (vv53ff). This movement between Yahweh's heavenly and earthly throne brings the two realms together in worship (Is 6:1f). It is God's majesty that is strongly underscored in exalting him over all creation.

Second Reading

The troubled Corinthian community, to which Paul contributes the lion's share of his epistolary correspondence, is given advice and encouragement in these final verses of the second letter. Joy and peace are central, both the result of the Lord's presence among them (v11; 1 Thes 5:16; Lk 2:10, 14; 24:52; Jn 20:19, 21). God himself is the author and model of peace and love, which will become manifest in the divided Corinthian community in a spirit of harmony and encouragement. *Holy kiss* (v12): a possible allusion to liturgical practice, the early "kiss of peace" (Rom 16:16; 1 Cor 16:20). *The holy ones* (Gr: *hagioi*): the Christian community where Paul is residing in Macedonia (Phil 4:21f; 1 Thes 5:26).

It is difficult to conclude from the final blessing how developed Paul's belief in the three persons of God is (v13). It stands in striking proximity to Trinitarian belief. Christ stands at the center as the immediate source of grace (Rom 16:20; 1 Cor 16:23). It was the love of God that brought about the mission of Christ and is the ultimate source of all spiritual gifts, including the Spirit. Finally, the Spirit binds the community together in *fellowship* (Gr: *koinonia*), creating the type of unity which Corinth sorely needs.

Third Reading

The Johannine conversation of Jesus with Nicodemus, with its Trinitarian implications, receives commentary on the Fourth Sunday of Lent, Year B.

The understanding of God as one in three came only by degrees. As today's Exodus reading indicates, the most that the Israelites perceived was that God was multi-faceted. The New Testament itself evidences a gradual growth. But the interesting feature of New Testament thought on the question is that of relationship. These diverse insights into God's nature are never treated abstractly or in a detached doctrinal way. They are seen in relation to the human situation, to the life of the baptized. The invocation from 2 Corinthians, with which the celebrant regularly greets us at liturgy, points to God's love as the cause of our salvation. That love has become personalized in Jesus Christ, whose offering to God has been "graced" by the gift of the Spirit. And there is nothing abstract about the Spirit who builds up the community in support, forgiveness, and understanding. Again, in John's gospel, the Trinitarian motif is situated in an account of what God did for the world in his Son.

There are times when the sign of the cross is a true profession of faith in a God who is our Creator, Redeemer, and Sanctifier. At other times it is an unrecognizable, distracted gesture with no semblance of reverence. It might help to remember that this distinguishing sign of our faith really identifies us as members of a very specific family. Today's readings make it very clear that it is a question of Father, Son, Spirit, and you. We are enveloped in the love of three persons and challenged to bring that love to our community. Just as Matthew's gospel ends with the Trinity, so our life begins with it. We are baptized in the name of the triune God.

A personal memory recalls a Dublin bus driver, carrying a full complement at a very busy hour of the day. Noticeable was the fact that he

*blessed himself at every church he passed. And then when the elderly
had trouble ascending the bus steps, he stopped the bus, rose, and gave
them personal assistance. And when this writer found to his chagrin
that he was far from his destination due to misdirection, the driver took
great pains to make certain that he would take the right route. A trifle?
Perhaps. But trifles make perfection, and perfection is no trifle. For
that person the Trinity was much more than a theological definition.*

Homiletic and Catechetical Helps

1. Explaining the mystery of the Trinity.

2. The Trinity in relation to salvation.

3. Symbols of the Trinity in the Christian life.

4. Revelation as a gradual process.

5. Christian love: a mirror of the Trinity's love.

6. The Trinity and the liturgical greeting.

7. God's love for the world and the Trinity.

YEAR B

Readings

> Deut 4:32 - 34, 39 - 40
> Rom 8:14 - 17
> Mt 28:16 - 20

The majesty of a God who wants to take a people and make
them his own is the teaching in today's first reading. This is a
God of unsurpassed greatness who comes close to a people
whom he chooses. The Trinity speaks to us of the "otherness"
and the closeness of God, transcendence and personal love.
That note of relationship is well expressed by Paul who in
Romans speaks of the Spirit of God's Son now enabling us to
address the Father with the same intimacy as Jesus himself. The
gospel of Matthew gives us one of the New Testament's clearest
Trinitarian expressions. Baptism plunges us into the life of the
Trinity and enables us to call God "Abba."

First Reading

This passage is one of the high points in Deuteronomy. It makes its appeal for covenant observance (vv39ff) on the basis of Yahweh's over-arching and singular might and power, which were used to the advantage of the Israelite people (vv32 - 35).

The rhetorical questioning by Moses centers on the Sinai event (v33) and the Egyptian liberation (v34). On Sinai God spoke to his people in awesome theophany (5:22ff; Ex 20:18f). In Egypt he used many signs of his power to effect the people's liberation, especially the plagues (testings) which beset Pharaoh and the Egyptians (7:19; 26:8; Ex 15:3 - 10). None of this had ever been witnessed before either in Israel or by any other people.

All of this must lead Israel to moral commitment. First, the recognition solely of the One who saved his people, in the observance of a strict monotheism, a faith that is to be deeply internalized (vv39f; 6:4ff). This points to the first commandment of the decalogue (5:6f). Moreover, there is to be an adherence to all the Lord's commandments, preeminently the decalogue (to follow in the next chapter, 5:11 - 21). A positive response will lead to blessings in the form of prosperity and longevity (v43)

Responsorial Psalm   Ps 33

Commentary on this hymn praising the Lord's fidelity and justice is to be found on the Second Sunday of Lent, Year A.

Second Reading

The Spirit does more than place the believer in a state of uprightness or justice before God. There is a new relationship established as well. Just as Jesus was constituted Son of God with the conferral of the Spirit of holiness at his resurrection (1:4), the sharing of that same Spirit enables the believer to enter into a state of sonship of God (v4). This posits a new relationship, moving one beyond a form of servility to the state of a family member (Gal 4:5f).

Paul plays on the word "spirit" (Gr: *pneuma*). A *spirit* of slavery refers to a mentality or outlook whereas spirit of adoption combines the same meaning with a reference to the Holy Spirit (v15). The point is that the position of the Christian is not like the slave in a household but rather that of a member of the family, with all the recognition attached thereto. This happens by way of *adoption*, a social procedure better known to the Greek world than that of the Jews. There is the understanding that this is not a question of entitlement but the result of a free choice on God's part. *Abba* (v15): the Aramaic word for father (with the definite article), taken over with the Greek translation (*ho pater*) in the earliest liturgies. With its strong note of familiarity, it was not a common form of addressing God in Jewish circles. It was, however, used by Jesus in a deeply personal way (Mk 14:36). All of this is the work of God's Spirit within the believer.

Sonship, then, bears certain consequences. The son is an heir, in this case a co-heir with Christ, the firstborn of the dead (Col 1:18). The Christians' inheritance is shared jointly with Christ (v17). Theirs is the pledge of glory provided that they, configured to Christ, participate in his sufferings in anticipation of a share in his glory (6:3f; Phil 3:10)

Third Reading

The Matthean account of the apostles' mandate to teach and baptize is treated on the feast of the Ascension, Year A.

The approach of Deuteronomy has much to commend it. Before we can appreciate the closeness of God in our life, we have to appreciate his greatness and otherness. That closeness comes home strongly in the reading from Romans, where the Trinity is deeply personalized. Paul's conclusions are quite startling, or would be, if we were not anesthetized to that powerful dimension of our faith. Adoption in our society, which used to be something of a quiet, private affair, has been ennobled in recent times. It really requires a great deal of courage to bring a child into the world at a time when other options are available. It shows a deep respect for human life. To offer that child to people who want to provide a home is a choice that says a great deal about the birth mother and the adopting parents. In every sense, that child is wanted. So it is between God and us. To speak in a single breath of our being co-heirs with God's Son, after realizing the price he paid for all of us, is truly "mind-boggling." That is the meaning of the Trinity.

Some people have scarred and hurtful memories of their father. There was no warmth or concern, no time spent in play and recreation. Sometimes there was cruelty and abuse. For these people it is hard to relate to God as father in the biblical sense. Other people, for one reason or another, never knew their father. But it has a meaning which is important to capture, even if through a transfer of memories. Think of parents whose love for their child is real and warm. In our transferral we don't have to stay with the father image. The scripture uses it and with certain nuances that cannot be disregarded. In this regard we cannot rewrite the scripture but we can translate it personally into terms that have significance. What is important is to grasp the meaning. We go beyond concepts to reach affectivity. We are speaking of the bonds of love, And that, too, is what the Trinity means.

Homiletic and Catechetical Helps

1. Work of the Spirit: sons and daughters of God.

2, Work of the Spirit: brothers and sisters of Christ.

3. The meaning of being a co-heir.

4. Baptism in the name of the Trinity.

5. The teaching mission of the church.

6. Christ's presence with the church.

YEAR C

Readings

> Prov 8:22 - 31
> Rom 5:1 - 5
> Jn 16:12 - 15

A major theme of these readings for Trinity Sunday is that of the Spirit as God's wisdom. Proverbs' personification of wisdom finds her present with God in the entire process of creation. In John's gospel today, Jesus speaks of the Advocate whom he will send as a guiding light on the path of truth. In the passage from Romans, Paul tells us that, now justified by faith, we are reconciled with God through Jesus and are fortified by an unwavering hope through the Spirit's presence within us, the incontrovertible sign of God's love.

First Reading

The feminine personification of Wisdom as God's prime attribute here finds her present in creation providing the Lord with the blueprint or plan (v30). The notion of "the Lord begetting me" (v22a) is not that clear in the Hebrew text. The verb *qanah* means basically "to acquire" or "to possess." The subsequent phrase is best translated "the beginning of his ways" (not "firstborn"). The sense is that of Yahweh's taking hold of Wisdom to utilize her in the process of creation. This possession of Wisdom precedes any of God's creative work (v22b). *Poured forth* (v23): The ethereal quality of mysterious forces was often expressed in terms of a fluid motion (Wis 7:25).

Hebrew cosmogony comes into play in the description of the universe (vv24 - 29). The *depths* (v24) were the waters below the earth, pictured like a large disc or platter over the abyss (Gen 1:2, 9; 7:11). At various points on the earth, the water emerged (lakes, rivers) in *fountain*-like eruptions. The mountains, hills, land, and fields are all placed in order after the watery abyss is contained and the earth set in place (vv25f). The waters above the earth are prevented from inundating the earth by a large *dome*, which made of the sky or *heavens* a permanent fixture, containing and withholding the waters above. It served the same purpose as the earth vault over the waters below (vv27ff; Gen 1:6 - 10). With land and sea created, limits were established for the sea to prevent its covering the earth (v29).

Before this whole process begins, Wisdom is present to Yahweh and serves as his *craftsperson* in drawing up the plan of the ordered universe (v30; Wis 7:17 - 22). She is youthful and personable, enjoying human company (v31).

Responsorial Psalm   *Ps 8*

This hymn contrasts God's majesty with human lowliness and marvels at God's treatment of humankind. In looking at the works of creation in their grandeur and permanence, as well as the skill with which they were fashioned, the psalmist can only wonder at God's concern for inferior mortals (vv4f; Gen 1:14 - 19). Humans are placed at the summit of creation and then associated with Yahweh in its direction (vv6ff). *Less than a god* (Heb: *elohim*) (v6): The term often applied to pagan deities is also used in Israelite thought of attendants or "angels" present in the heavenly court (Job 1:6; Gen 1:26)

Second Reading

The Pauline presentation of justification through faith finds God, Christ, and the Spirit actively engaged (vv1, 5). In concluding his treatise on faith, and not works, that effects reconciliation with God (3:21 - 4:25), Paul sees this new-found justice as eliminating hostility and restoring harmony with God, thus making Christ, through his reconciling death, "our peace" (v1; Eph 2:14; Col 1:20). This has provided entree to God's realm through the life of grace. *We stand* (v2): This is not a transient or passing justice but a constitutive and permanent reality, placing the Christian in a gospel way of life (1 Cor 15:1).

Faith is the root of a *hope* which assures the believer of the ultimate transition from a graced state to one of final glory. This hope is not wishful thinking or illusory; it is the certainty of a future not yet attained. Ironically it is a "boast" not of something merited but of a destiny wholly unmerited.

Even trials (Gr: *thlipsis*) which might be thought of as obstacles to union with God (8:35) contribute to the hope of glory (vv3ff). It is hardship that produces patient endurance (Gr: *hypomone*), and endurance produces strength which reinforces hope. It is a hope solidly rooted (Ps 22:6) and not simply human aspiration. It will not disappoint because the first fruits have already been given in the presence of the holy Spirit, the gift of God's love. *Love of God.* (v5): a subjective genitive, i.e God's love for us, as evidenced in the gift of the Spirit.

Paul moves from justice to glory through God's love manifest in Jesus and given lasting expression in the Spirit.

Third Reading

The Advocate to come will serve two important functions. First, the Spirit enlightens the disciples in the fuller understanding of Jesus and his teaching (v13). Then, in so doing, he will give glory to the person of Christ because the Spirit's sole function is to present Christ as the sole mediator, the "truth" of God (vv14f).

In this passage the Johannine Jesus explains the disciples' pre-Easter lack of comprehension and the faith-understanding only possible when the Spirit is given after the resurrection (vv12f; 14:26; 20:22). *All truth* (v13): Jesus is the truth of God in the sense that he is the sole mediator between God and humankind. All other claimants are deceivers, guilty of the untruth. In being the truth, Jesus then is the way to God as well (14:6). The Spirit is not an independent agent. He is dependent upon the Son for all that he teaches, drawing on that fullness which Christ has received from the Father (v13). *The things that are coming* (v13): Jesus here speaks from a pre-Easter vantage point. The discourse precedes his death. The Spirit will interpret the death-resurrection in the light of God's saving plan. His declaration will not exceed the parameters established by the Son (v13). In so enlightening the disciples in the true meaning of Christ, his mission, and his relation to the Father, and drawing exclusively on the Son's fullness from God (1:16), the Spirit will give added glory to the person of Jesus (vv14f).

We often speak of the Spirit as empowering and life-giving. Today's readings take a slightly different tack in seeing the Spirit as wisdom, a wisdom that sheds light on the meaning of reality. It is somewhat akin to social analysis. Analysis evaluates a given situation, looks at the factors that have shaped it, and raises questions about systemic rather than surface causes. Proposed solutions flow from this whole process. The Spirit leads the individual and the church to an examination of fundamental issues. The Johannine Advocate shed light on the entire Christ event in the light of world history. The same Spirit in an ecu-

menical council led the church through a process of deep self-evaluation wherein it could see itself as part of the world, not above or apart from it. It is the Spirit that has led us to seek the presence of God in the plight of the poor and persecuted, in other world religions, in other Christian churches. There is a wisdom that is timeless in all of this, a wisdom which enriches faith.

Wisdom brings out the feminine dimension in God. God is, of course, genderless, but speech about God is not. And that speech, enshrined in biblical books we consider inspired, cannot be denuded without eliminating important dimensions of the human insight into God. As partial and figurative as speech about God may be, it is still part of our understanding. God's plan for the universe with all the intelligence which that presumes is expressed in feminine terms. This is not an image of softness or passivity. It is creative and aggressive. Stereotypes are always dangerous. As soon as we say that this is masculine and that is feminine, our thesis meets countless roadblocks. Both men and women are endowed with the same gifts and make an equally valid contribution to church and society. The gender differences in character and manner are complementary and an enrichment. Rather than being competitors, they are better seen as partners or associates. Women have had a longer struggle. But they have made us much more aware.

Homiletic and Catechetical Helps

1. The Spirit as the wisdom of God.

2. Wisdom as a female personification.

3. The Hebrew view of the universe.

4. Justification by faith.

5. Relation between faith and hope.

6. The role of the Trinity in justification.

7. The meaning of Christian endurance.

8. The Advocate as teacher.

9. The ongoing character of revelation.

10. The Spirit as a guide of the church.

CORPUS CHRISTI
Years A B C

Theme: Covenant Making: Sacrifice and Banquet

YEAR A

Readings

Deut 8:2 - 3, 14 - 16
1 Cor 10:16 - 17
Jn 6:51 - 58

Today's readings point to the eucharist as the bread for our journey of life. The experience of hunger coupled with God's providence was to remind the Israelites that material needs do not exhaust life's meaning.As the reading from Deuteronomy explains, God's word is food in itself. That same word of God gives us the assurance in today's gospel that Christ's body and blood will bring our earthly journey to its divinely determined end. Today's reading from 1 Corinthians highlights the social dimensions of the eucharist. The one loaf which we share intensifies our unity in the one body of Christ. The eucharist bonds Christians throughout life. Therefore, the motif of the body and blood of Christ as our food or our meal is to the fore in today's liturgy.

First Reading

Deuteronomy's reflections on the events of the exodus look to the lessons which they provide. The trials that the people endured during their forty year journey were to test them and to see how resolute their commitment to Yahweh was (v2). At times their resolve left much to be desired in their willingness to put Yahweh to the test (6:16f). They had been allowed to experience hunger and then witness God's providential care for them in the gift of manna (Ex 16; Num 11:16 - 23). This was done that they might realize that true life lies in conformity with the will of Yahweh, the provider, and not merely in satisfying material needs (v3). It is this quotation that is used by Jesus in rejecting Satan's attempt to have him change stones into bread in order to satisfy his hunger (Mt 4:4).

In fact, all the major events of the desert experience—deliverance from bondage, from poisonous serpents (Num 21:6 - 9), from hunger and thirst (Ex 17)—were intended to be instructive. When well-being and prosperity arrive, with the taking of the land, the temptation will be great to forget. It is then that they must remember (vv14f).

Responsorial Psalm   Ps 147

The hymn praises God for a restored post-exilic Jerusalem (v2). In attributing to Yahweh the blessings of security and offspring (v13), peace and plenty (v14), the psalmist, like the Deuteronomist, finds instruction in these experiences and reason to glorify God. Yahweh's commands are simply another aspect of his blessings, a part of his direction of the whole created order (vv18ff). Israel's providential status alone is sufficient motivation for praise.

Second Reading

In speaking against the dangers of idolatry (v14), Paul cites three types of sacrifice as an example: Christian (vv16f), Jewish (v18) and pagan (vv19f). All sacrifices promote union with the deity. Not only should Christians avoid the other forms of sacrifice in creating bonds that are inappropriate, but they must be ever conscious of the preeminence of the Christian offering.

Paul distinguishes two distinct elements of the Christian offering: the cup (blood) and the loaf (body). Participation in both creates two effects. The first of these is a unity with the deity—in this case, with Christ of whose body and blood all partake. It is this sharing in the one loaf which led to the common expression for eucharist as the "breaking of bread" (Acts 2:42). The Greek word for "participation" (*koinonia*) is the New Testament word for community or fellowship (v16). Therefore, communion or participation with Christ implies as well a relationship with the community of believers (v17).

The symbolism is strongly accented here. The unity of believers is seen in the single loaf in which all share. In eating of the single loaf or body of Christ, the believers constitute another single body of Christ, i.e. the body brought together in the risen Christ by the Holy Spirit. Thus the two "bodies" coalesce in the symbolism of the one loaf. The loaf, in turn, when shared, reinforces the bond of unity among believers.

Third Reading

Commentary on the Johannine teaching of Jesus as the eucharistic source of life is to be found on the Twentieth Sunday of Year B.

The feast of Corpus Christi reminds us in a very concrete way of the extent to which the journey is aided by the Lord's eucharistic presence. What begins in first communion continues until viaticum with many sustaining pauses along the way wherein the eucharist is repeatedly seen in faith as the road to eternal life. At each mass we are dinner guests of the Lord. "Blessed are those who are called to his supper." In a prayer, "O Sacred Banquet," which is not heard as much today as it once was, we are reminded of the three moments of eucharist: the memory of Christ's passion, the present experience of grace, and the promise of future glory–every step of the journey.

Paul brings out today the social dimension of the eucharist. The one loaf is shared in Africa, Asia, and North and South America. It is the one loaf in which the lowly and the exalted, the chief executive officer and the person on welfare, the powerful and the powerless partake together. And it makes brothers and sisters of us all. Where there are the downtrodden and forgotten, I too am present. We all eat of the same loaf. Within Christianity there are no first and second class dining rooms. This writer has a very powerful memory of a migrant community of people in a large U.S. city whose closest church happened to be one of the most affluent. Efforts to have mass celebrated for the Hispanic community were received half-heartedly by the Anglos. Celebrated once a month, it was a well attended mass. But soon the migrants were looking for another place of worship. They simply did not feel wanted. It was a sad commentary on the common table and the single loaf. We all have growing to do.

Homiletic and Catechetical Helps

1. The place of communion in the mass.

2. The sign value of separated bread and wine.

3. Christian unity and the eucharist.

4. Eucharistic ministers: serving at the local table.

5. The eucharist and division in church and society.

7. The eucharist: pledge of eternal life.

YEAR B

Readings

> Ex 24:3 - 8
> Heb 9:11 - 15
> Mk 14:12 - 16, 22 - 26

The mass is both sacrifice and banquet. The celebration of Corpus Christi this year views the eucharist in terms of covenant, with special emphasis on its sacrificial character. In the reading from Exodus, the covenant between Yahweh and his people is formally concluded with sacrifice and a bonding blood ritual. Mark's gospel today finds Jesus in the upper room celebrating his final Passover with the disciples. In memorializing the new covenant in ritual, his words over the cup are a distinct echo of those of Moses in finalizing the Sinai covenant. In the reading from Hebrews, Christ is high priest and mediator of the new covenant. In his own blood, he has cleansed our conscience and given us access to God.

First Reading

The solemn ritual of covenant making is recorded in this final chapter of the book of the covenant (Ex 19 - 24). Moses first seeks the consent of the people to the covenant terms, spoken of as "words" (Heb: *debarim*), referring to the decalogue, and the "ordinances" (Heb: *mishpatim*), the remaining covenant laws (v8). With consent given, Moses gives the law permanence in consigning it to writing. On the following day, he erects both the altar and memorial pillars (v4). The latter (Heb: *massebah*) were large erect stones which memorialized important religious events or which were used for cultic purposes (Gen 28:18). Because of their origins in pagan circles, they were later excluded by Israelite law (Lev 26:1).

The essential sacrificial act resided in the use of the blood as carried out by Moses in the narrative. The actual slaughter, an act of death, was necessary as the means of obtaining the blood but was not seen as a priestly act. The priest's function lay in the blood rites (vv5f; Lev 1:3ff; 13:1ff). The blood ritual follows the reading of the covenant norms and the consent of the people. The covenant bond is established with part of the blood, the sign of life, sprinkled on the altar, which symbolized Yahweh, and part on the people. Rite and words are combined in Moses' solemn pronouncement, which will be modified and carried forward into New Testament covenant texts (v8; Mt 26:28; Mk 14:24; Lk 22:20).

Responsorial Psalm   Ps 116

In thanksgiving for his being saved from mortal danger and loss of life (vv3f), the psalmist gives cultic expression to his gratitude. *The cup of salvation* (v13): perhaps the container used for libations that were poured out rather than consumed as an act of gratitude to God (Num 15:5, 7, 10). The death of the good is "costly" in God's eyes, and therefore not desired (v15). The temple exerts a magnetic pull over the grateful psalmist (v19); there he will offer sacrifice and invoke God's name (v17), as well as fulfill his promises before the assembly (v18). For the Christian reader, the reference in the psalm to the "cup of salvation" has eucharistic implications.

Second Reading

Like the high priest on the day of Atonement, Jesus, the harbinger of good things to come, has now entered the heavenly sanctuary to perform the rite of purification (v11). *Perfect tabernacle* (v11): This is the heavenly sanctuary which Christ enters with his resurrection-exaltation (4:14; 9:24). As belonging to another realm, this heavenly tent is not a human artifact, i.e. not of the created order. Unlike the earthly priest, who made repeated atonement, Christ enters once and for all in a definitive act of reconciliation (10:11f). Moreover, his offering was in sharp contrast to the preceding; the blood of animals is replaced by the blood of the high priest himself (v12). *Heifer's ashes* (v13): Ashes mixed with water were used as a lustration to purify those who had become defiled (Num 19:9, 14 - 21).

If it is possible for that which was *defiled* to be cleansed by animals' blood and ashes, how much more will the One, himself *undefiled* or unblemished, by the offering of his blood, in the eternal spirit life of his resurrection (7:16), bring about an internal cleansing from lifeless works (flesh) to the worship of God (spirit) (vv13f). It should be noted that the author does not juxtapose the earthly death of Jesus and his heavenly atonement, as if they were two distinct events. Rather he views the death-resurrection through the prism of the Israelite liturgy of the day of Atonement.

Third Reading

Commentary on the Marcan narrative of the last supper and eucharist are to be found on Palm Sunday, Year B, under the sub-headings, *Passion Preparation* and *The Eucharist*.

The sacrificial imprint on the death of Jesus is unmistakable. His blood is carried into the heavenly sanctuary in atonement and is also offered to his disciples as the living symbol of the sealing of a new covenant. Both Moses and Jesus speak of the blood of the covenant. Jesus has brought it all together in realizing Jeremiah's promise of a new covenant.

We learned from an early age that sacrifice is deeply woven into the texture of the mass. With separated bread and wine, the symbolism itself proclaims the death of the Lord until he comes. There is pain in eucharist as well as joy. Each mass reminds us that we were bought at a very great price. It is important to dwell on the sacrifice involved in redemption. It reminds us that a measure of it is needed in our own life as well. At some point we will all have to suffer and accept it in a

Christian spirit. It may mean sharing the lot of the unloved. It may mean a grinding poverty, children who no longer practice the faith, the pain of a divorce, the haunting memory of an abortion, an illness that draws us slowly away from our dear ones, the sudden realization of our own mortality. But fear not. In the Christian life pain and joy go hand in hand. Pain is not the end. Our high priest has entered the heavenly sanctuary. Every mass says it all: union in his sufferings and the power of his resurrection.

Homiletic and Catechetical Helps

1. The meaning of a covenant bond.

2. Explaining the Exodus covenant ritual.

3. "The blood of the covenant": old and new.

4. The Passover setting for the new covenant.

5. Eucharist as sacrifice and meal.

6. The meaning of the real presence.

7. Reservation of the eucharistic species.

8. Jesus as the high priest in Hebrews.

9. The mass as covenant renewal.

YEAR C

Readings

Gen 14:18 - 20
1 Cor 11:23 - 26
Lk 9:11 - 17

The symbolism of bread comes to the fore in these Corpus Christi readings. Melchizedek, a king and priest, makes his fleeting appearance in Genesis as the one who blessed Abram. Although the scriptures make no further comment about his bringing bread and wine, church tradition has long seen inferences in the gesture. The New Testament does, however, see other Melchizedek-Christ likenesses, as, for example, his being a priest outside of the levitical line. In today's second reading, Paul draws on the liturgy of his own day in recounting how Jesus gave bread and wine new meaning as the memorial of his death. In the Lucan gospel narrative, Jesus' act of providing bread for the crowd is seen as symbolic of the eucharist.

First Reading

After Abram's impressive victory over the Canaanite kings in effecting the release of his nephew Lot (vv13 - 17), he is honored by other Canaanite monarchs upon his return. It is here that the figure of Melchizedek is briefly introduced. He is both a king and a priest. *King of Salem* (v18): Salem was an ancient name for Jerusalem (Ps 76:3), a fact that probably accounts for this episode's preservation.

God Most High (Heb: *El Elyon*) (v19): Both El and Elyon were the names of Canaanite deities.Their combination points to the chief Cannanite god. The title was eventually given to Yahweh in Israelite tradition and is so intended here, as the description of his activity makes clear. The bread and wine were intended as a gift to celebrate Abram's victory.

In the epistle to the Hebrews, Melchizedek is seen as prefiguring Christ by reason of his unknown ("eternal") origins (7:3), and by a free interpretation of his name as meaning "king of justice" and his being "king of peace (Salem)" (7:2). Most importantly, his priesthood, like Christ's, was outside of the line of Levi (7:4 - 11). Hebrews sees no symbolism in the bread and wine reference.

Responsorial Psalm   Ps 110

The psalm is addressed to the king ("my lord"), perhaps on the day of his coronation or its anniversary (v1), by a court singer. It is one of the major messianic psalms, applied to Christ repeatedly in the New Testament. The king is presented as enthroned and at Yahweh's invitation is seated at his right hand. *Enemies your footstool* (v1): an ancient image of submission of enemies to the power of a victorious king. The verse has repeated New Testament appearances (Mt 22:44; Acts

2:34). The scepter was the symbol of royal authority (v2). The original sense of v3 has been almost completely lost in textual transmission. The sense adopted here sees the king's power as predating creation, i.e. before the sun, or "daystar," was created. The king was begotten in mystery like the nebulous evanescent dew. He is acknowledged as a priest (v4), with his priestly credentials derived from his assimilation to the priesthood of Melchizedek (Gen 14:18), who was both a non-levitical priest and a king. The king of the Davidic line was unrelated to the line of Levi-Aaron.

Second Reading

With 1 Corinthians written in the mid-50s A.D., this is the earliest written version of the eucharistic formula in the New Testament. As predating the epistle, it was already fixed in the tradition of the church, here quite probably the church of Antioch. Although it bears a strong resemblance to the Lucan formula (Lk 22:19ff), it nonetheless betrays its independent existence. Paul has taken over the formula, including its "remembrance" rubric (vv24ff). The passage's importance lies in several areas. It shows, first of all, that the eucharist was part of a fixed tradition, which Paul has *received* and *handed on* (v23; 10:16f). The celebration of the rite, then, by the mid-50s was fixed in the life of early Christianity. Second, the realism of the formula (in all its appearances) cannot be neutralized or diminished. It is because of this recognition of the true presence of Christ that the eucharist is to be accorded the greatest reverence (vv27ff). Third, the presentation of the inseparable life components of body and blood in a separated form clearly "remembers" Jesus in a state of death. It is Christ in his free offering of self-donation ("body that is for you," v24) who is recalled.

In addition, in being one with the offering of Calvary, this action effects a new covenant (v25). The repeated emphasis on this in the synoptics (Mk 14:24; Lk 22:20) echoes Moses in the first covenant ritual (Ex 24:8). This is the blood of a new covenant, which brings about a binding and lasting, as well as deeply internal, union between God and his people, as foretold by Jeremiah (31:31 - 34).

Finally this is a rite to be done as a remembrance (Gr: *anamnesis*) of Jesus, in a repeated rubrical indication (vv24f). Much discussion centers around the meaning of this "memorial," some seeing it as an act by which God will "remember" the offering made by his Son in saving love. Here the interpretation is given in the text itself (v26). The liturgical action is a symbolic proclamation, a making present in reality of the death of the Lord. It is a living remembrance of his act of love (Rom 8:39) which is both a recall and a salvific actualization of his death. Through participation (eating and drinking), it integrates one into that death. The action is to continue until the parousia.

Third Reading

In all of the synoptics, and perhaps most notably in Luke, this is much more than an account of one of Jesus' miracles. It is a catechesis on eucharist and ministry. In adapting the narrative to Hellenistic city dwellers, Luke situates the action of Jesus in the vicinity of Bethsaida (v10) and has the crowd "recline" as if at table gatherings (v14). Jesus has been involved in preaching and healing (v11); the feeding is an extension of his ministry, as is the distribution role of the disciples (v16).

The eucharistic motif is strongly imprinted on the narrative. Although there is mention of both loaves and fish, it is the bread that is predominant, even to the collection of the *fragments* (Gr: *klasmata*), the technical term for the eucharistic bread. The action of Jesus in *taking, blessing, breaking,* and *giving* the bread (v16) reproduces almost exactly the last supper formula (22:19) and the Emmaus meal (24:30). Whatever the original setting of the story, Luke clearly intends to present a eucharistic catechesis. In the church, Jesus continues to feed and nourish his followers through the ministry of the apostles and others in the sacramental celebration of his saving death.

The notion of abundance (v17) points to the lasting and durable character of the eucharist in the life of the church. As the bread which issues in eternal life (Jn 6:58), it is completely satisfying (v17). The twelve baskets may well symbolize the twelve apostles, who represent the reconstituted tribes of Israel.

The eucharistic tradition in the church is one of our oldest and most well-documented beliefs. By the year 50, it was fixed in the life of the church, and the death of Jesus of Nazareth was being memorialized. Multiple New Testament witnesses, as diverse as they may be, all converge around this central belief. In celebrating the feast of Corpus Christi, the church bring us into contact with a tradition that is as old as the belief in Christ as Son of God. It links us with Christians of all ages and all cultures.

Paul reminds us that we are proclaiming the death of Christ, announcing God's love for the world, in a sacrament which will perdure until the Lord's return. It is no wonder that this sacred action is surrounded by reverence the world over. It has inspired some of the finest music in the history of the arts. It centers around a simple, short formula which is pronounced with the same effect in a cathedral church or in a humble village chapel. It is a powerful moment–the risen Christ in a state of death for the salvation of the world.

"Do this in my memory." "He gave them to the disciples." In the absence of the eucharist, the church is impoverished. The use of paraliturgies, scripture or communion services is not living out the memory. Only the mass fulfills the mandate. The church is essentially a eucharistic community. While there are many features of belief and practice that can be altered or reduced in importance, the eucharist is not one of them. Nothing so epitomizes the total belief of the church. We are disturbed–and we should be–when people show indifference about their Sunday responsibility. We don't like to see the eucharist's significance diminished in our own life or in that of another. Even more so, we as a church cannot become complacent about the absence of Sunday liturgy due to a shortage of priests. Certainly we must make provision for exceptional cases. But we pray against the day when the exceptional becomes the accepted.

Homiletic and Catechetical Helps

1. Melchizedek and Christ: likenesses.

2. The death of the Lord in the eucharist.

3. The real presence of Christ in the eucharist.

4. The eucharist and charity.

5. The antiquity of the eucharistic tradition.

6. The eucharist and priesthood.

7. The story of the loaves as catechesis.

TENTH SUNDAY OF THE YEAR
Year A

Readings

> Hos 6:3 - 6
> Rom 4:18 - 25
> Mt 9:9 - 13

Theme: Mercy, Not Sacrifice

Hosea exhorts his hearers to know the Lord in experiencing his love. Their lives are too fickle, their faith is too identified with external observance. The Matthean Jesus in today's gospel expands on the "sacrifice" quote from Hosea in pointing up the true nature of the religious response. In continuing the Sunday series from Romans, today's reading presents Abraham as a prime example of that faith which makes one upright before God.

First Reading

The eighth century Hosea warns his contemporaries that their instability will inevitably incur God's judgment. Early in the reading, the afflicted population is presented as turning to Yahweh. The call to internalize God's presence ("know the Lord") is urgent in view of his forthcoming intervention (v3). The coming of the Lord in terms of either deliverance or punishment is as inexorable as the return of the cycles of nature (v3).

Yahweh's response is directed to both the north (Ephraim) and the south (Judah) (v4). *Piety* (v4; Heb: *hesed*): This important covenant term is better translated "love," as elsewhere (v6; 2:21). It expresses a heartfelt loyalty to the terms of the covenant. This quality is so lacking in Israel's comportment that it is likened to transient phenomena of nature (v4). The people's unpredictable conduct contrasts sharply with the constancy and stability of Yahweh (v3).

Cultic observance is meaningless without an authentic internal religious spirit. *Love* and *knowledge of God* refer to the experience of God which finds expression in conviction and fidelity. *Sacrifice* and *holocausts* are symbolic of all cultic worship (v6). Semitic emphasis often expresses itself in antitheses, highlighting the superiority of one thing over another. Here it is not meant to nullify sacrifice in any of its forms despite the absolute form of expression. It is simply meant to say that love is better than sacrifice. However, in a later period, when the temple was destroyed, the text was used in Jewish circles to support religious expression without its sacrificial dimension.

Responsorial Psalm   Ps 50

Possibly connected with a covenant renewal ritual, the psalm builds on today's theme of a spirit marked by a desire to fulfill Yahweh's will as having more importance than cultic observance. Yahweh summons witnesses to a type of trial of his people. Those called are the heavenly court, the nations, and the people themselves (vv1 - 5). *Rising of the sun to its setting* (v1): from east to west. The Lord indicates that sacrificial offerings are incomplete forms of covenant response (vv8, 12f). In the anthropomorphic suggestion of Yahweh's hunger being abated by animal sacrifice, incongruity points up the emptiness of their offerings. Sacrifice is relegated to a second place. It is the praise of a correct life and the fulfillment of covenant responsibilities in ethical uprightness that have value (v14). Examples of their wrongdoing are litanied later in the same psalm (vv16 - 21). Once lives are converted and lived in accord with Yahweh's will, invocations will be heard and needs addressed (v15).

Second Reading

Abraham is the man who prefigures Christian faith. The parallel lies in his belief that despite his old age and deteriorating body, he could still become a father, solely on the basis of

Yahweh's promise. Paul's teaching centers wholly around Genesis 17:1 - 17, with no reference to the tradition that, even later than this, Abraham had other children (Gen 25:1f). The faith of Abraham goes beyond the promise of a son to that of becoming "the father of nations" (v18; Heb 11:8 - 12). His "hope against hope" lay in maintaining this conviction in spite of the fact that both he and Sarah were so old. Christian parallels begin to appear in Sarah's "dead womb" being vivified by the God "who gives life to the dead" (v17).

Because Abraham's faith did not waver but found expression in gratitude to God, he was reckoned as just (vv20f). In the Genesis narrative, because he believes the promise of a progeny as numerous as the stars in the heavens, Abraham is considered upright before God (Gen 15:5). Paul takes the Genesis text, quotes it twice (vv22f), and applies it to a wholly new situation in the form of a midrash. This was a type of literary adaptation common in Judaism and used by Paul on different occasions (1 Cor 9:9f). Paul sees Abraham's justification through faith as extending into the Christian era. Christians are the true descendants of Abraham (Gal 3:29) and their faith is basically the same (v24). The likeness lies in faith in a God who has power over death: for Abraham, power over a dead womb; for Christians, power over the dead Christ. In both cases life is brought out of death. Here again it should be noted that it is God who brings Jesus to life (v24; Acts 2:24).

Paul concludes with what is possibly an early credal formula (v25). It parallels death-resurrection in an allusion to the vicarious atonement of the servant of the Lord (Is 53:4f, 11f). The verse is not be understood disjunctively as if the death were for sin and the resurrection for justification. It is the twofold cause that produces the double effect. Death-resurrection results in the eradication of sin through the life-giving justice of God's Spirit.

Third Reading

The Matthean account of the tax collector's call to discipleship centers on Jesus' summons to one who was a sinner (vv9, 13), as well as the question of table fellowship with recognized

sinners (vv10 - 12). Both features converge in the three concluding pronouncements of Jesus (vv12f).

The tax collector is identified as "Matthew" (v1) only in the
first gospel; both Mark (2:13 - 17) and Luke (5:27 - 32) call him
Levi. Double first names were not the custom. In his list of the
apostles, Matthew mentions "Matthew, the tax collector"
(10:13). He evidently makes this change of name from his
sources for particular reasons. Perhaps it was to make the
known apostle, "Matthew, the tax collector," the recipient of
this very singular call. This same Matthew may have made a distinct contribution to the material in the gospel which bears his
name, even though he did not author the final work.

The immediacy of Matthew's response is theologically stylized
(v9), the point being that this is the only response worthy of a disciple (10:16 - 23). The setting for the discussion with the
Pharisees moves quickly to a dinner table, presumably in
Matthew's house. Tax collectors were social and religious pariahs
who consorted with pagan conquerors and were notorious extor-
tionists. Since Matthew was such, the gathering of "likes" finds
both tax collectors and other unseemly company gathered at the
table with Jesus (v10). Table companionship, or even a social
visit, with such people was excluded by law (Acts 10:28). For Jesus
it is an anticipation of the eschatological banquet. The sacred
character of food sharing, moreover, lay in its symbolic sense of
well-wishing, an expression of genuine concern (Ps 41:10).

The vocation account becomes a pronouncement story as the
Matthean Jesus is questioned (indirectly) about his conduct,
which is in violation of the law (v11). His response is threefold.
The first speaks of God's outreach to those most in need, as religious outcasts and sinners, much the same as the physician's *raison d'être* lies with the sick (v12). Then follows the Hosea quotation, found also in today's first reading, via its Greek translation
(the Septuagint). It is mercy or compassion which is called for,
not the concerns of law (v13a). Here the Matthean Jesus is using
"sacrifice" in a more extended sense than in Hosea, since it covers ritual impurity as well. In the Lucan and Marcan accounts of
this same incident, the Hosea quote does not appear. Finally
Jesus' mission is specifically for those alienated from God (v13b).
Literally this would mean everyone since all are in a state of sin

(Rom 5:12), and there are no "righteous." Here, however, the contrast appears once again in the antithesis. The quote highlights the importance of that disregarded segment of people, with no particular concern about who the righteous might or might not be.

The three final logia point clearly to the religiously and socially disenfranchised as the special concern of Jesus. In fact, he does not hesitate to call an apostle from their midst.

In an era of the centrifugal family and fast food service, meal sharing has lost much of its meaning at the center of life. For a variety of reasons, many families no longer share the main meal of the day, and it is a great loss. Many cultures, even modern ones, retained the custom until comparatively recent times. Undoubtedly some still do. But modern life has made it more difficult. Sharing food is a sacred act, accompanied by a sharing of experiences and insights. For Jesus it was both reality and symbol. In sharing food, he shared himself and he did it with people who were not considered acceptable. His final testament was given at a meal where the common elements of bread and wine spoke and continue to speak of God's love for the world. The tragedy is that the eucharist, the great sign of oneness and sharing, is now the sign of a divided Christianity. We agonize over our disunity as we pray that these walls will one day tumble and bring us together as Christ desires. Divisions within the church which focus on the eucharist are addedly painful. The table of the Lord is one place where we have to be united and where we grow in unity.

Mercy and love have to be greater than laws and regulations, as legitimate as the latter may be. If we believe strongly and avoid hostility and further wall-building, then the God who gave a child to Abraham and new life to his own Son will bring us together as well–Christians at a common table, Catholics themselves united in a common purpose. Christ wants the table enlarged to seat us all. And he wants people there who are still out on the street. A few verses of scripture give us much food for thought.

Homiletic and Catechetical Helps

1. The religious and social significance of meal sharing.

2. The meaning of Jesus' eating with sinners.

3. Examples of mercy taking precedence over law.

4. Meal sharing and the eucharist.

5. Religious division and the eucharist.

6. Faith: active or passive?

7. The Jews as descendants of Abraham.

8. Christians as descendants of Abraham.

9. Meal sharing and our family life.

TENTH SUNDAY OF THE YEAR
Year B

Readings

> Gen 3:9 - 15
> 2 Cor 4:13 - 5:1
> Mk 3:20 - 35

Theme: Overcoming Evil with Good

The Genesis reading today recounts the results of sin's arrival on the human scene. It brought alienation and division; there is at most a slight glimmer of good's eventual triumph in the narrative. In the gospel Jesus stands as the irreconcilable foe of Satan. Those who stand with him, the hearers of God's word, will join him in the ultimate triumph over evil. Paul also heralds the ultimate victory. While his physical forces diminish, he grows stronger in the Spirit, convinced that he is destined to live with God forever.

First Reading

The sin of Adam and Eve has already taken place before Yahweh begins his late afternoon walk in the garden (Gen 3:8). As is characteristic of the Yahwist tradition, God is presented in very human terms, walking and conversing with his human creatures. The first result of sin is the recognition of nakedness, here directly related to the eating of the forbidden fruit (vv10f). The blame passes from the man to the woman to the snake. Punishment will be meted out in the order of culpability, the first being the snake, the most responsible (vv14 - 19).

Just as the man and woman are individuals representative of all humanity, so too the snake represents the overall forces of evil. In all three cases, the punishment for the sin is drawn from the author's lived experience. The disorders in nature which were part of everyday life are presented as the consequences of sin. In short, the author begins with the experience and works back to the proposed cause. Today's reading presents only the retribution directed to the snake, and it is drawn from the natural appearance it makes. Its slithering form and alienation from other creatures suggest its wrongdoing (v14). It is cursed by God in its flat and groveling condition.

Between the serpent and humans, antipathy is to be perpetual (v15). The "offspring" of both refers to all future generations. The descendants of Eve (he: singular in Hebrew; they: sometimes plural in English) will be locked in unending conflict with the forces of evil. The struggle is depicted in the strike and counter-strike of the two opponents. That is as far as the Genesis text goes. Later tradition, including the biblical, saw the devil in the snake (Wis 2:24; Jn 8:44). The human's superior physical position in stepping on the snake's head has also been seen as the earliest indication of humanity's eventual triumph over evil in Christ. There is a lengthy Christian tradition which sees in this text the first announcement of the gospel.

Responsorial Psalm   Ps 130

One of the penitential psalms, this is an individual lament of one who is suffering great distress. *Depths* (v1): The watery formlessness suggestive of the chaos of Genesis is figurative for severe trouble and discouragement (Ps 69:3, 15; Is 51:10). The psalmist's woes are related to his sins, a common connection in Hebrew thought. Yet deliverance should not be forestalled on this basis since before God all are guilty (v3). Pardon, moreover, will lead to a reverential respect for God's goodness (v4).

The psalmist waits for an oracle (vv5f) with the anticipation of a night watchman awaiting the first glimmer of morning (v6). The oracle is an announcement of deliverance (vv7f). The psalm passes from the individual to the collective Israel, a transition customary in a culture where the individual and community are intimately linked (Ps 22). Both Israel and the individual are beneficiaries of the Lord's covenant love.

Second Reading

Paul will not speak from the discouragement of his earthly trials but rather from faith, as he indicates in his free adaptation of the psalm (116:10). His faith directs his attention to the end time; he is convinced that the same God who raised Jesus will also raise him and the Corinthian community and present them before Christ (v14; Rom 8:11). Paul's apostolic energy has been spent in the service of the community so that the acceptance of God's truth by ever greater numbers will ultimately redound to God's glory through the life and praise of his children (v15; 1:11).

Therefore, Paul is not disheartened. *Outer self* (v16a): the person as perceived visibly by externals and appearance. *Inner self* (v16b): the person with reference to intangible and imperceptible qualities. The outer self is being spent in afflictions, persecutions, and abandonment (4:7ff), while the inner self continues to grow stronger (4:11). This inner force will ultimately arrive at God's glory, the invisible eternal verity, totally distinct from those earthly elements which are passing away (v17). He remains convinced that the earthly body person (here described as a house or tent) will be transformed in resurrected form in the future (5:1; 1 Cor 15:42ff). The dwelling image has echoes of Jesus' prediction of his death-resurrection in the language of a destroyed and restored temple (Jn 2:19 - 22).

Third Reading

Today's gospel is a clear illustration of the ongoing conflict between the Son of Man, the new humanity, and the forces of evil. The episodes and pronouncements, which may well have had an earlier, independent existence, have been carefully stitched together to make a coherent whole. This includes the concern and lack of understanding of Jesus' family (vv20f), further incomprehension from his opponents in a double accusation (v22), Jesus' response to the accusations of the Jews (vv23 - 29), and finally a return to Jesus' family and a response to their charge (vv31 - 35). Opening and closing with the family question offers a parenthesis or inclusion for the narrative.

The Marcan crowd pressing upon Jesus and giving him little respite or space is a recurring theme in the second gospel (v20; 2:2; 3:9; 4:1). Jesus' own family did not understand his mission and thought that he was mentally disturbed, the equivalent of diabolical possession in the thinking of the time (v21; Jn 7:20; 8:48). This controversial statement of Jesus' relatives has no parallel in Matthew and Luke, both of whom knew of its existence. It would not fit well with the narratives of Jesus' childhood found in both gospels.

The expression of disbelief from Jesus' family is prelude to the stronger accusations of his opponents (v22). It is a two-pronged charge: he is possessed by an evil spirit and is an agent of Satan. Jesus responds to both in parables (v23). Answering first to the second accusation (vv23 - 26), Jesus states that internal division leads ultimately to the downfall of a kingdom (v24), a house (v25) or Satan (v26). If Jesus is an agent of Satan, then in his working to cast Satan out, they are at cross-purposes. Satan is doomed to fail.

A single parable, not wholly consonant with the preceding train of thought, is introduced here (v27). Jesus' action against evil is a form of binding the evil one prior to the final conquest, achieved definitively in Christ's death-resurrection.

To the accusation that he is himself possessed, Jesus responds in particularly strong terms (vv28ff). *Beelzebul* (v22): Origins and etymology are difficult and confusing. By this point it is the name of a recognized unclean spirit. To refer to Jesus as possessed is the "unforgivable sin." The sin is clarified by the context. What is unforgivable is to call the work of God evil or to call an emissary of God an agent of Satan. It is to call light darkness. To do so is to reject the reign of God and thus by one's own decision to move oneself to an unforgivable position. Yet all sins can be forgiven, even the one here cited, with repentance. What Jesus does here is underscore its extreme seriousness and the unlikely chance of reconciliation.

Jesus' relatives are here identified as being his mother and brothers (Gr: *adelphoi*) (v31). The logical and normal understanding of "brothers" would be as blood brothers. The term carried that customary connotation, and Mark gives no indication from anything in his gospel that he meant otherwise. The semitic use of the term, however, includes relatives in a broader sense (Gen 14:16), and such may be the meaning intended here. The church's long held belief in the perpetual virginity of Mary has led commentators to interpret "brothers" in this broader sense.

Jesus concludes in responding to the earlier incredulity of his relatives (vv31 - 35). In so doing he enunciates a principle which goes beyond the actual scenario. There are bonds among his disciples which are stronger than those of blood. Those who accept and actualize God's will as Christ has expressed it constitute his real family (vv34f; Mt 12:46 - 50; Lk 8:19ff). There is a new order which goes beyond that of the flesh (Lk 11:27ff). In the post-resurrection era, the bonds of the Spirit between Christ and his followers will add a further dimension to the understanding of the new family of God (Rom 8:14 - 17).

One of the major differences between the Bible and modern society is that the Bible takes evil seriously. Biblical faith sees evil as an independent force in conflict with the interests of God. It makes its appearance in Genesis and continues through to the book of Revelation. A low point in Jesus' ministry came when his opponents accused him of being an instrument of Satan. Their reason probably rested on his willingness to bypass Jewish law on many occasions in the interests of his mission. It is clear from Jesus' speech, as well as that of his enemies, that evil was so real that one stood on one side or the other, with Christ or with the evil one. There is room for discussion about the nature of evil. But to say that it is simply a human construct flies in the face of biblical teaching.

Evil is yet to be finally vanquished. What Christ accomplished is still to be actualized in our lives. Evil is overcome by those who are brothers and sisters of Jesus, those who take his word to heart and live it. Evil exists. Its emergence in modern times in the form of the holocaust speaks for itself. But it comes in many lesser forms. To do battle with evil is to live the Christian message each day. Conversions are just as real as is evil. Christ is still binding the strong man. A good beginning is to acknowledge evil, then take issue with it. The battle lines are clearly drawn, but the resources are there as well. It is the force of good that overcomes evil.

Homiletic and Catechetical Helps

1. The sources of evil: external and internal.

2. Understanding Satan.

3. Interpreting Genesis 3.

4. The central truth of Genesis 1 - 3: creation and sin.

5. Explaining the sin against the Holy Spirit.

6. Being mothers and brothers of Christ.

7. Mary and doing the will of God.

8. Ministry to others as the praise of God.

9. The dying and rising of Christ in my life.

10. The meaning of personal resurrection.

TENTH SUNDAY OF THE YEAR
Year C

Readings

1 Kgs 17:17 - 24
Gal 1:11 - 19
Lk 7:11 - 17

Theme: Lifegivers

In today's scripture, both Elijah and Jesus restore life. Both incidents are restorations to earthly life and not resurrections, although Christians will undoubtedly read them in the light of eternal life. Paul, in the face of continued opposition in Galatia, speaks of the authenticity of the gospel which he preached. It had been directly revealed to him and was not given to him "second hand," not even from the hands of the apostles.

First Reading

The story forms part of the Elijah cycle of stories which recount major events from the prophet's life (1 Kgs 17 - 19). This incident takes place among Gentile people in Phoenician territory. The widow in the story is the same who, in the preceding narrative, provided food for the prophet in time of drought. The death of the woman's son leads to her reproach of the prophet (v18). The presence of the prophet as a divine emissary cast a shadow on the woman's life, bringing her sense of guilt to the fore. Thus she interprets the death of her son as punishment for her sins.

The intervention of Elijah involves intercession on the family's behalf and then physical contact to effect resuscitation (vv19ff). The prayer of the prophet is more a reproach than a plea, underscoring the hospitality which he had received (v18). The act of restoration to life may have been a form of respiration or simply a life to non-life proximity. It clearly reflects a Hebrew anthropology. The life breath (*nephesh*) has left the boy, and its return is the object of the prophet's prayer (v21). This is the same life principle that makes Adam a living being (Gen 2:7); it is a principle of animation not identical with the human soul as understood today.

The restoration of the living son to his Gentile mother results in her recognition both of Yahweh and of Elijah as his prophet. In view of what the Lord has accomplished, his word in Elijah's mouth is henceforth completely validated (v24; 17:1).

Responsorial Psalm   Ps 30

Restored life continues as a theme in today's hymn of thanksgiving. The psalmist's praise goes to God for his being raised up (v2), a restoration to health from what was evidently a mortal illness. This involved being snatched from Sheol, the shadowy realm of death where real life and even God were absent (v4). Punishment for sin is seen as momentary at best, with the time of God's anger being minimal in comparison with his enduring largesse (v6). The psalmist then describes his feelings during his sufferings, only the last verse of which is read in today's liturgy (v11). Finally, the joyful transition from death to life is described in the language of a festive dance and a change of clothes from somber garb to the bright attire of celebration.

Second Reading

At pains to uphold the authenticity of his credentials, Paul claims that he is an apostle by reason of his call from the Lord and that the gospel which he preaches was received from the Lord and not from others nor adapted by him afterward to suit the Gentile world (vv11f). *Gospel* (v11): Jesus as the God-Man now constituted Lord and Savior of the world (Rom 1:1 - 4). It does not mean the extended form of the gospel, the Christian *didache*, which Paul would certainly have received from others. Paul insists that he received the gospel by a direct revelation from Christ and not from any human agent (v12; Acts 9:1 - 22). A brief autobiographical sketch is given to substantiate the point (vv13 - 19).

His first argument is based on what might be termed the humanly inconceivable. In the past he had been a person deeply steeped in Jewish tradition as a Pharisee (v14; Acts 26:4 - 6), as well as a persecutor of the primitive church (v13; Acts 8:1 - 3). The complete reversal of his religious posture cannot be explained apart from his call, a pre-determined destiny which, in prophetic fashion, antedated his birth (v15; Jer 1:4; Is 49:1). Called in grace, his was a vocation and revelation centered wholly on Christ (v16). *Flesh and blood* (v16): the human dimension of church life (Mt 16:17). Paul's message like his call was wholly from God.

After his conversion, Paul's mission took him to the Gentile world in Syria, the location of both Damascus and Roman Arabia (v17). Only three years after his return to Damascus did he make his first journey to Jerusalem. *Cephas* (v18): the Aramaic form of Peter's (Rock) name, underscoring Peter's foundational role (Mt 16:18). Paul spent two weeks in consultation with Peter. *The apostles* (vv17, 19): This refers to the twelve, the first chosen, who were commissioned by the risen Christ and shared in his earthly ministry (Acts 1:21 - 25). *James, the brother of the Lord* (v19): This is not a James from among the twelve. He was a relative of Jesus (Mk 6:3), a leader in the Jerusalem church (Acts 12:17) with a position of notable authority in the church as a whole (2:9; Acts 15:13 - 21).

Third Reading

The life-giving motif continues in this New Testament parallel to the Elijah story, the restoration to life of the widow's son at Nain. The account is found only in Luke and is one of the few resuscitation narratives found in the gospels. It fits well in the Lucan context where shortly Jesus' words will include restoration to life as one of the messianic signs (7:22).

The narrative follows the lines of the typical miracle story: a description of the circumstances (v12), the action of Jesus (v14), and the validating consequences in restoration to the former condition (v15). The woman is described as a widow who has lost her only son and is therefore without any means of support (1 Tim 5:3ff). With Jesus early designated as Lord (v13), the stage is set for a clear manifestation of God's power over death itself. The compassion of Christ (v13) explains his spontaneous outreach to the woman, with no request from any side. The act of restoring the son to his mother repeats almost exactly the action of Elijah (v15; 1 Kgs 17:23).

The reaction of the crowd is one of fear and praise (v16). They recognize in Christ the prophet of the end time, the moment of God's definitive visitation of his people (1:68). His fame now spreads beyond Judea to the Gentile regions (v17). As one of the more important Lucan miracle stories, the account presents Jesus in direct combat with evil in one of its main staging areas, the arena of death. Death will be ultimately vanquished in the death-resurrection of Jesus. Thus, the account serves as a pointer to the resurrection of Jesus, as well as those who will follow after him.

The church can do no less than be a strong promoter of life. The scriptures speak only of life and have little sympathy for death. The psalms ask repeatedly for deliverance from death and restoration to life. Admittedly, death was a rather grim subject in Hebrew terms. Life meant a great deal in comparison with Sheol. But the biblical God is always the God of the living. Jesus came with a message of life. In fact he restored it. The accounts of Lazarus, the widow's son, and Jairus' daughter all point to final resurrection. But they also present a feeling Jesus in the face of the grim reality of death.

Controversy or partisanship should not dim our view today. To deny unborn life the chance to experience what full life means is a position that cannot go unchallenged. It is more than a Catholic position or even a biblical position. It is a human stance. Life is too sacred a value. War is hideous because, even if the term "just" could ever be used, it leaves in its wake the strewn bodies of the young, the old, and the defenseless. To extinguish life lethally, whether in an abortion clinic or a hospital, is to appropriate authority that belongs to the God of life. Jesus did not see a funeral cortege in Nain and then walk away disinterestedly. Nor can we when it comes to the gift of life.

Homiletic and Catechetical Helps

1. The breath of life in Hebrew thought.

2. The distinction between resurrection and resuscitation.

3. The miracle at Nain: symbol of resurrection.

4. The morality of taking human life.

5. Abortion, euthanasia, war, capital punishment.

6. Consequences of the gospel being exclusively God-given.

7. Distinguish between the twelve, Paul, and James.

8. Paul and Cephas: the importance of consultation in the church.

ELEVENTH SUNDAY OF THE YEAR
Year A

Readings

 Ex 19:2 - 6
 Rom 5:6 - 11
 Mt 9:36 - 10:8

Theme: Mission to Israel

God's appearance in history occurred at a determined time and among a specific people. It was to the people of Israel that God spoke. Today's reading from Exodus speaks of his intention to form a covenant with the Israelites, the bond that was to give them a unique identity among the peoples of the world. In the gospel, Jesus selects and missions his apostles, directing them to the Jewish people. In the reading from Romans, Paul considers deliverance from a sinful past the best assurance of our ultimate salvation.

First Reading

This chapter of Exodus serves as a prelude to the covenant with Israel which follows immediately. At this initial encounter Yahweh formally proposes to bond with the people. This occurs shortly after the people's arrival at Sinai following the exodus from Egypt (vv1f). The location of Mount Sinai cannot be determined with certainty; it is most frequently identified with one of the desert's highest mountains, Jebel Musa, on the Sinai peninsula. The dwelling of the gods on lofty cloud-shrouded mountains was common in Oriental antiquity. Thus, it is not surprising that Yahweh at an early stage was considered a "mountain God." Moses ventures forth to meet Yahweh on the mountain (v3).

Yahweh's invitation is a carefully constructed poetic unit, evidently drawn from a later liturgical source (vv4ff). In its attempt to convince the people to accept the Lord's proposal, it recalls his initial act of deliverance on their behalf (v4). The vivid "eagle's wings" imagery appears again in one of Israel's great lyric poems, the song of Moses (Deut 32:11). *Covenant* (Heb: *berith*) (v5): This was an agreement among individuals, tribes, and eventually nations to observe certain norms in order to protect mutual rights. It might look to property or land rights, boundaries, or treaty terms between warring countries. There were standard forms for major conventions of this type; with some alterations, the agreement between Israel and Yahweh is expressed along the lines of these conventions. In his proposal, Yahweh states that if there is agreement around the covenant terms (cc. 20 - 23), Israel will enjoy a special status among all the nations (v5). *Special possession* (Heb: *segullah*) (v5): a term expressing a singular closeness between the object and owner, found especially in royal documents. It is used here to highlight Israel's value in God's sight in spite of its political insignificance when compared with other countries of the world (Deut 7:6; 14:2; 26:18).

Kingdom of priests ... a holy nation (v6). The two descriptive phrases may be synonymous or complementary. Most commentators opt for the former in seeing the country which has a consecrated and sacred character in the midst of the nations as also called to the worship of God. Thus, the people enjoy a mediating or priestly role, although distinct from that of the official priest. Other authors see the text as reflecting the post-exilic political structure wherein the high priests ruled the country wielding full religious and political power, a kingdom ruled by priests.

In this passage the broad terms of the covenant are set forth: divine providence and protection hinging on fidelity to the covenant law.

Responsorial Psalm   Ps 100

Related to a thanksgiving liturgy, this hymn speaks of Yahweh as the benevolent provider of Israel. All the earth is invited to join in the joyful liturgy (v2) in giving thanks for the kindness shown to God's chosen people (v3). Thus the nations praise God for Israel's blessings. These include God's election of his people as well as his steadfast love and fidelity as a result of the covenant (vv3, 5).

Second Reading

This passage is full of hope. Christian hope is not wishful thinking but confidence in a future which rises from a past and present experience. Paul's argument runs thus: All people were at one time alienated from God as sinners and enemies, burdened with weakness (v10). Then, at a given moment, Christ overcame alienation through his death, with justification here attributed solely to Christ's death (v9; 4:25). Reluctantly Paul admits that death on behalf of a just person might occur (v7). What is unthinkable is that one would die for a sinner. This is precisely what Christ has done (v8). In this case it is not simply wrongdoers who are made just but those in direct opposition to the lifegiver himself.

At this point Paul separates justification from salvation (v9), two ideas which at times coalesce. Those made just by the death of Jesus and the conferral of the Spirit will be ultimately brought to salvation and glory (vv8f; Rom 8:30). *The wrath* (v9): God's final intervention which in Jewish apocalyptic often highlights God's punishment. For the unrepentant it was to bring condemnation (1 Thes 1:10).

Thus, if God has gone as far as he did to accomplish the first stage (justification), he will not disappoint at the end (salvation). The present state of reconciliation is the basis of confidence for the future.

Third Reading

At this point in Matthew's gospel there is a transition between Jesus' self-presentation in word and deed (cc. 5 - 9) to his commissioning and instructing his apostles (c. 10). The bridge shows Jesus' compassion for his leaderless people (9:36ff) and his missioning the twelve (10:1 - 8).

Jesus shows deep pity for his people, who lack spiritual leadership (v36; Mk 6:34; Jer 50:6). The verb used to express his emotion (Gr: *splanchnizo*) is related to the term for "entrails" and is the closest Greek can come to the modern "gut" reaction. Lack of guidance will be met only by missionaries sent from God. Therefore, prayer is urged (vv37f).

"Disciples" in Matthew is generally used more broadly than it is here where it is restricted to the twelve (v1) They are called both "disciples" and "apostles" (v2), the single occurrence of the latter term in Matthew's gospel. With its basic meaning of "one sent," its use here is appropriate. The listing of the twelve differs little from the other lists in the New Testament (vv2ff; Mk 3:16 - 19; Lk 6:12 - 16; Acts 1:13). They represent the eschatological twelve tribes of Israel. Most of them have not been heretofore mentioned; the earlier selection of four of them is recounted (4:18 - 22). The listing without comment evidences the early church's knowledge of them, with Peter, once again, accorded first place.

The mission of the twelve is patterned on that of Jesus, with power over demons, disease and death (vv1, 8a). With the final battle directed against Satan, disease and death are attacked as a major arena of his presence. The apostles are to announce the kingdom's arrival (with no explicit mention of conversion) (v7; 4:17). At this point they receive no teaching mission, since their instruction is not yet complete. After the resurrection they will be formally assigned to teach (Mt 28:20). Their mission has clear eschatological tones.

The recipients of the message are exclusively the members of the Jewish community (vv5f). They are the lost sheep spoken of previously, here identified with the entire Jewish population. The apostles are not to venture into either Samaritan or Gentile territory. In this way they adhere to the boundaries established by Jesus for himself (15:24). Only after the resurrection will the Gentile mission be formally inaugurated (28:19). This emphasis on the Jewish mission would read well in the strongly Jewish Christian community for which Matthew wrote. Giving of their services without cost, a sentiment also voiced by Paul (2 Thes 3:8; 2 Cor 11:7), sees faith as a pure gift to be dispensed accordingly.

The claim that we are all spiritual semites goes back at least to Pope Pius XI. Vatican II made a strong statement on our spiritual affinity with the Jewish people. The truth is that the Jews have had a long history of persecution and disdain at Christian hands. Hatred reached its most dreadful expression in the holocaust. As Christians we must mend our fences by setting the groundwork for a more positive future. Admittedly the picture becomes complex when political considerations enter over which there may be legitimate differences. But on the basic truths there is only one Christian viewpoint. This is a people with a unique spiritual history. Jesus during his earthly life saw them as the people for whom he had a very distinct mission. He himself and his immediate followers came from the Israelite population. Paul regretted the Jews' failure to accept the Messiah but spoke of a day when they would, a day of great rejoicing. We have a common heritage. Unkind or contemptuous stereotypes have no place.

At any time when we feel low or burdened with guilt, we should read today's passage from Romans. It contains so much hope. Paul gives us a slap on the back and a strong voiced "Coraggio!" Do we see how much God has done for us? Intellectually, probably yes; emotionally, no. Our faith touches many areas of our life; one of them is to give us courage. The hand of God has appeared so often in our life. We may be unfaithful. God is not. That guiding hand has been with us thus far. We have every reason to believe that it will continue to be.

Homiletic and Catechetical Helps

1. Israel as God's elect in the Bible.

2. Vatican II and the Jewish people.

3. The sin of anti-semitism.

4. The message of Jesus: first to the Jews, then to the nations.

5. The apostles and their mission in Matthew.

6. Understanding mission today.

7. The virtue of hope.

8. Confidence from justification to salvation.

ELEVENTH SUNDAY OF THE YEAR
Year B

Readings

>   Ez 17:22 - 24
>   2 Cor 5:6 - 10
>   Mk 4:26 - 34

Theme: Steady Sustained Growth

The first reading is part of an allegory from Ezekiel; the gospel has two of Jesus' parables. Both use plant life to image the work of God on the human scene. So much of the good that is accomplished in life is due to the action of the Lord. In the second reading, recognizing the condition of human weakness, Paul longs to be with God.

First Reading

The Ezekiel reading today is of a single piece with the allegory of political power that is found earlier in the same chapter. The latter speaks of the competing powers of Babylon and Egypt as two great eagles (17:3, 7). The Davidic dynasty, a mighty cedar, is in turn dominated by and attracted to the two great powers (17:3 - 8).

Here the cedar, representing the line of David, appears again in a quite positive context. Yahweh takes a descendant of the Davidic line and installs him in Jerusalem, the lofty mountain (v22). This is a clear messianic note, sounded repeatedly in the pre-exilic and exilic prophets. The planted tree offers umbrage to all species of bird, pointing to the future king's international if not universal sway (v23). The kings of other nations, represented by the trees of the field, acknowledge the Davidic king's sovereignty (v23a).

All of this is done at Yahweh's bidding. It is not to be explained by diplomacy, treaties, or military conquest. This is done at the word of a God repeatedly seen as the Lord of inverted values—the lowly rise and the mighty fall (v23; 1 Sam 2:7f; Lk 1:52f).

Responsorial Psalm   Ps 92

The image of the tree firmly planted and flourishing continues in this psalm. For the commentary, see the Eighth Sunday of Year C.

Second Reading

In today's reading Paul compares his present "bodily" existence with that which is to come and for which he longs. In this chapter of his letter to Corinth, he uses a variety of images, at times somewhat confusedly. At one point the body is a dwelling (5:1f), then a suit of clothes (5:2ff). At this point he moves to the idea of a homeland from which he is presently exiled.

Paul is forced to walk gingerly as he realizes that there is a certain segment of the Corinthian community which sees the human body in very negative terms. The present body impedes the desired union with Christ, who is understood here as the final point of Christian destiny. In the present mortal existence, the vision of God is lacking; therefore, human assurance rests on faith (vv6f; 1 Cor 13:12f). In view of this imperfect situation, Paul's strong desire is to leave the body and go to Christ (v8; Phil 1:21ff). This passage and similar ideas in the chapter have led to speculation as to whether Paul envisions an interim state with Christ after death but prior to the parousia. The possibility is there, but the very ambiguity of verses such as this makes the hypothesis inconclusive.

Whether in this world or that to come, Paul wishes only to live in accord with Christ's will (v9). This is his mainstay. In fact, the present body, which at times wears him down, remains the arena of his human activity upon which he will be judged at the parousia (v10; Mt 25:31 - 46; Rom 2:16f).

Third Reading

The first of these two parables is found only in Mark. In the face of the struggles and difficulties being experienced by early Christians, both parables urge patience and reassurance. The first presents the growth of the reign as determined and brought about by God, quite independent of human resources (4:26 - 29). The second contrasts the inauspicious beginnings of the reign with its ultimate impressive success (4:30 - 34).

The first seed story has the farmer seeding the land; this is then followed by a period of steady unassisted growth (Gr: *automate*), while the farmer goes about other pursuits (vv27f). The plant matures at every step: blade, ear, grain, and harvest. The harvest theme points to the eschatological character of the reign of God (Jl 4:13). While not intended to diminish apostolic fervor and labor, it does point clearly to the Author of the church's growth and development upon whom all ultimately depends. Paul uses the same argument in reminding the Corinthians not to have their ecclesiastical "heroes" (1 Cor 3:6 - 7).

Small beginnings produce great things. This is the point of the mustard seed parable (vv30 - 33). This tiny seed produces a plant eight to ten feet in height. Full-grown, it is here seen as offering protection for the birds, which, like the Ezekiel allegory on which it is based, may be pointing to the church's universal character. It certainly emphasizes the impressive character of God's reign as it grows and expands within the world.

The passage ends on a distinctly Marcan note (vv33f). The parables were ordinarily seen as teaching tools, imaginative ways of clarifying abstract truth. However, since they communicated the truth obliquely, parables also had an illusive side, a restricted presentation of the truth, a sort of riddle (4:10ff). In Mark this second aspect comes to the fore as he indicates that the parable (Gr: *parabole*, Heb: *mashal*) communicated only a certain measure of truth about God's reign, adapted to the people's ability to understand. However, as was his wont, Christ gave fuller explanations to his disciples privately (4:13 - 14); it is they who will later have the responsibility of instructing the faithful.

Pope John XXIII, it is said, was having a restless night shortly after being elected pope. The concerns of the church and decisions to be made were pressing upon him. And so he turned fitfully from side to side. Finally he verbalized his sentiments. "Listen, Lord, this church is yours, not mine. I'm going to sleep." And, as he said, he fell quickly asleep. We all have moments when we wonder if it is all worth it. In a single lifetime we have all met people who were deeply upset because the church veered too far to the left and then those who were equally disturbed when it went to the right. The church is ultimately Christ's, as today's liturgy teaches clearly, and he will see it through the storm. The early Christians also had trying times. They saw some of their earliest enthusiasts fall away in the course of time. Others started well but soon got detoured. It is enough to read the parable of the sower and the seed that fell along the path. Things were not all encouraging but Christianity survived. The church is stronger than all the people who try to make it or unmake it, because it's in God's hands, and God is at the helm. Yes, the church has its share of humanness. But with all its warts, it is still a beacon and a great source of strength. And how often things turn out better than we thought. Just when we felt that walls were crashing down around us, the lay people in the church emerged with a vitality and sense of ownership not previously imagined. Even while we sleep, God's reign is growing–blade, ear, ripe wheat.

Paul so often speaks of his desire to be on his way. How often do we think about "going home"? We are very much this-world centered. Much of our ministry is geared to a better world. It certainly would not be appropriate to live only for the next world. But it is our home. And the older we get, more of our dear ones head in that direction. After we have done our level best, let's leave it to God and think about home. Paul never shows the slightest fear of death. He knew that God would never work against him. He longed for that great moment and so should we.

Homiletic and Catechetical Helps

1. Christian mission as primarily the work of God.

2. In what way has the church grown in your experience?

3. The parable as a way of presenting the church.

4. Events in our life that convince us that God is at work.

5. Reconciling world mission with authentic values in other religions.

6. Death as a homecoming.

7. Ministry: helping others prepare for death.

ELEVENTH SUNDAY OF THE YEAR
Year C

Readings

2 Sam 12:7 - 10, 13
Gal 2:16, 19 - 21
Lk 7:36 - 8:3

Theme: *Expression of Repentance*

God's pardon is extended to two people in today's scripture. One is the illustrious David whose adulterous conduct led him as far as murder. The other is an unidentified sinful woman who evidently enjoyed a certain notoriety. Upon their recognition of wrongdoing, both are forgiven, with the woman's repentance given a very public expression. In leaving the law behind for a life in Christ, Paul experienced his own forms of crucifixion. He speaks about this in the second reading.

First Reading

There is little in David's character to lead one to believe that lust could carry him to the lengths recorded in the second book of Samuel. In the present chapter, the prophet Nathan confronts the king for his sinful conduct in the parable of the ewe lamb (12:1 - 5). This leads to a further reproach and finally an admission of guilt, as presented in today's reading.

Nathan first recounts David's blessings (vv7f): his consecration as king of Israel (5:1 - 3), his deliverance from Saul (1 Sam 19 - 20), a permanent dynasty (7:11ff) and sufficient wives (5:13f). This only adds to the gravity of David's sin the added note of ingratitude. His action is clearly enunciated as a turning his back on the Lord (vv9f). Specifically he is guilty of an adulterous union with Bathsheba, Uriah's wife (11:1 - 5) and his direct intervention in arranging for her husband's death (11:14 - 17). Retribution is clearly called for with the prediction that death and humiliation will hover over David's house (vv11ff, 15 - 18).

David's recognition of his sinfulness is seen as repentance (v13). Although retribution will not be bypassed, as the remainder of the chapter makes clear, David's life will be spared and his sin blotted out. The part that the recognition of sin plays in its being forgiven should not be overlooked.

Responsorial Psalm   Ps 32

Although the psalm is one of thanks for forgiveness, it is cast in a didactic mold with its emphasis on the sinner's experience of pardon. Total remission of sins brings joy in its wake (vv1f; Is 1:18). Having endured a period of physical suffering (vv3f), the psalmist acknowledged his sin and repented, the two basic elements which lead to forgiveness (v5). Seeing Yahweh as his safeguard, he calls the just to rejoice in God's deliverance (vv7, 11).

Second Reading

Of particular importance for Christian anthropology, this reading describes the new existence in Christ realized in baptism. It also contrasts the deadening effect of life under the law with the vivifying power of the Spirit.

The Pauline axiom, expressed in juridical (courtroom) terms, states that no justification or uprightness before God comes from law observance but only through faith in Christ (v16; Ps 143:2; Rom 3:20, 28). Paul, Peter, and other observant Jews in their company (vv11 - 15) have reached this conclusion on the basis of their own experience as well as their new-found faith in the total sufficiency of Jesus' work.

Paul explains that it was through dying to the law, and only in that way, that life in Christ was open to him. *Through the law I died to the law* (v19): The law brought nothing but sin in its wake. Unable to confer holiness, it led only to further transgression and spiritual death (3:10f; Rom 5:12ff). Christ himself was cursed by the law and brought to his death (3:13); ironically this was the death that made liberation from the law possible. This human state of helplessness under the law led to its abandonment and a belief in Christ. *I have been crucified with Christ* (v19): In baptism the Christian brings his sinful body to be united with the death of Christ (Rom 6:5 - 11). Just as Christ passed through crucifixion to new life, the Christian must enter into that death as well. This is the symbolism of baptism, a burial and a rising with the Lord (Rom 6:4).

On the psychological - spiritual level, this ontological incorporation has its own consequences. Union with the dead-risen Christ means that a new life now pulsates within the Christian, the life in the Spirit (v20; Rom 8:10f). Although the human body in its weakness still remains, in fact there is a real symbiosis of flesh and spirit. The whole thrust of life now rests on faith in Christ who died and rose for his followers and on the presence of the vivifying Spirit. Therefore, even now in mortal flesh, "Christ lives in me."

Hence, unlike the Judaizing disturbers in Galatia with their concern for law observance, Paul refuses to reactivate the law to which he is already dead and nullify the all-sufficient work of Christ (v21).

Third Reading

The Lucan sinful woman is not identified; the story with some variations appears in all the gospels (Mk 14:3 - 9; Mt 26:6 - 13; Jn 12:1 - 8). She is termed a sinner but there is no indication of what her sin might have been. A strong element of contrast marks the story: the self-righteousness of the Pharisee host (v39) and the authentic openness and sorrow of the woman (vv37ff). The Pharisee sees Jesus as a (possible) prophet; the sinful woman by her actions recognizes him as Lord.

The question of table company and food sharing emerges once again, sinners being excluded from the circle of the righteous. Hence the Pharisee's indignation at the woman's action (v39). The story contains some authentic Palestinian customs: the reclining at table (v36), the welcoming kiss (v45), the washing of feet (v44), and the anointing of the head (v46).

Jesus explains his acceptance of the woman, even in defiance of religious custom, on the basis of the outpouring of her love seen in the footwashing, the reverent kiss, and the anointing (vv37ff), none of which had been extended by the host (vv44ff). At this point the question of forgiveness is introduced. The woman had experienced it and the Pharisee had not, with the result that the moral posture of each is quite different.

The parable used by Jesus (vv41ff) points to greater love being the result of a more extensive forgiveness. The sense of the text sees the forgiveness as preceding the gestures of love. She is forgiven much, with the result that she loves much, not vice versa. The translation is justified on grammatical grounds (the final clause being one of result—introduced by the Greek *hoti*—not cause). In addition, the sense of the parable requires the forgiveness before the love. In his final statement (v48), Jesus simply affirms what has transpired in her life. At the root of everything was the woman's faith in Jesus' power to forgive, the component which she added to the act of deliverance. Her reconciliation is complete (v50).

The short inclusion on Jesus' journey actually opens the next section of the gospel. It is Luke who brings to the fore the role of women in Jesus' ministry. Jesus continues his preaching mission, announcing the reign of God (v1). The apostles accompany him as well as a group of women (v3), only three of whom are mentioned. *Mary Magdalene*, inflicted with "seven devils," need not have been a sinner. She may well have suffered from a serious illness from which Christ cured her. Even if she were a sinner, there is no scriptural evidence that Mary Magdalene's sins were of a sexual nature. Joanna was a woman whose husband held an important post in Herod's household. *Susanna* is not further identified. It was quite unusual that Palestinian women would travel in a religious teacher's entourage. Perhaps Luke cites it for more than information. It is women who are the first witnesses to the resurrection (24:9ff, 22ff) and are in the company of the apostles in the upper room after the ascension (Acts 1:14).

It is impossible to be sorry for sin when it is not even acknowledged. What stands out clearly in today's scripture is the need to call sin by name. David clearly admitted his fault, as did the sinful woman. Jesus recognized the presence of sin. Today there is a reluctance to label the wrong that we do. Sin is very relative. The social mores of the time fashion our thinking more than does biblical teaching. Reception of the sacrament of reconciliation ranges from "highly infrequent" to "practically never." We surely do not want guilt-ridden Christians, but we have to acknowledge our wrongdoing. Once that is done, there is nothing to fear, certainly not from an all-forgiving God. "Sins red as scarlet become white as snow." There is no doubt about how far God is willing to go to meet us, just as there is no doubt about the joy of the person whose burden is lifted. But we can't run from the reality. We begin by facing it.

Paul lets nothing obscure the work of Christ. He fought valiantly to uphold the all-inclusiveness of faith. It was the same Jesus who forgave sinners that saved Paul and all of us—and he alone. We have to be wary of competition. We can never come before God with "bargaining chips." We were lost and now are found—totally gratis. Every day we come back to the same truth. No self-righteous Phariseeism. Just a weeping woman—weeping for joy.

Homiletic and Catechetical Helps

1. The Lord's Prayer: Forgive us our sins.

2. The penitential rite in the liturgy: its meaning.

3. Naming sin.

4. Understanding the sacrament of reconciliation.

5. Women in the New Testament.

6. Women in today's church.

7. Women in religious life.

8. Explain Paul's "being crucified with Christ."

9. David and the sinful woman: likenesses and differences.

TWELFTH SUNDAY OF THE YEAR
Year A

Readings

> Jer 20:10 - 13
> Rom 5:12 - 15
> Mt 10:26 - 33

Theme: The Courage of Conviction

Stand tall! Jeremiah, faced with a serious threat to his life, remains confident of God's power and will to save him. Jesus encourages his disciples to have similar courage in the face of persecution, which, as Matthew writes his gospel, is already occurring. A celebrated and controverted passage from Romans on our inheritance from Adam is our second reading today.

First Reading

Jeremiah's "confessions," found at various points in his writing, represent as personal and intimate a self-portrait as is contained in the Bible. The passage read today is part of one of the "confessions" which contains particularly strong language and reflects an anguished spirit. To appreciate Jeremiah's experience, one has to know him as a cultured and refined person of considerable sensitivity. He neither sought nor wanted the prophetic career to which he was called (1:6f), even claiming in the present chapter that Yahweh had "seduced" or "duped" him (20:7). Through it all, however, his confidence in the God who had called him did not waver.

Terror on every side (v10): Originally these were the words of the prophet himself, foretelling the destruction of Jerusalem and its people (vv3ff). The words were evidently seen as traitorous and are used by his accusers to remove him from the scene. Even former friends wait to catch him in his words to have him killed (v10; Job 19:19).

A sudden change of temperament moves Jeremiah from discouragement to trust. His enemies will be brought to shame and the nature of their works brought to light. Yahweh who has selected him is certain to vindicate him (v11; 1:8; 15:20). Assurance is based on faith in Yahweh's word. Moreover, the Israelite concept of justice required a tangible and unmistakable retribution in the absence of any after-life sanctions. Hence, the prophet asks that his vindication be clearly evidenced; before Yahweh as his judge, he has presented his case (v12; 12:20)

Yahweh, seen as the provider of the poor in Israelite society (v13; Ps 109:30f; 35:10), evokes concern for them on the part of the people as well (Ex 22:24ff; Lev 19:10). By the time of Jeremiah, the poor represent more than a social category; they are those who have the accompanying internal dispositions of dependence and trust.

Responsorial Psalm   Ps 69

A sense of confidence in the midst of adversity is a key feature of this personal lament. In those verses appearing in today's liturgy, the psalmist speaks of scorn and rejection suffered at the hands of his own relatives (vv8f). *Zeal for your house consumes me* (v10): Quoted in the gospel in reference to Jesus' cleansing of the temple (Jn 2:17), the verse here speaks of a profound commitment to Yahweh's concerns, which meets only destructive opposition. The psalmist confidently requests God's intervention, recalling his covenant fidelity and compassion (v17). In conclusion, envisioning his deliverance, he urges the anawim, the poor of God, to turn to the Lord (vv33f). The lowliest are the closest to God, and therefore the first to experience his love (Ps 22:25ff). The universe itself is invited to participate in the joyful hymn (v35).

Second Reading

At this point in Romans, Paul parallels Adam, the cause of sin, and Christ, the source of grace. In today's passage, he points up the universality of the sin that springs from Adam and contrasts it with the superabundance of grace that stems from Christ (vv15 - 21).

The actors in this drama, all personified, are Adam. death, and sin. As the result of Adam's transgression, sin is the first to appear (Gen 3:11 - 13; 1 Cor 15:21). Once sin is unleashed, death follows immediately in its wake (v12; Wis 2:24). Death is understood here as total, both physical and spiritual. The human demise simply put a seal on the deeper death, i.e. a definitive separation from God. Both sin and death, then, pass to all humanity. *Inasmuch as all sinned* (v12): This much discussed clause is best understood as the personal appropriation of Adam's sin. It looks to a solidarity in Adam's sin by personal transgression, without disregarding the ambience of sin which Adam initiated. All have been guilty of sin just as all have died.

Objection: How could there be sin in the world when there was no law? Adam sinned against a determined precept. But before Moses and the giving of the law, there were no precepts. There can be no culpability where there is only ignorance (v13; 4:15). Paul's response to the objection lies in the universality of death. Sin was present from Adam to Moses, even though it was not the direct violation of a precept, because death was never absent. Sin and death are inseparable (v14). The conclusion: sin and death reigned over all human beings from Adam to Christ.

The Catholic Council of Trent solemnly affirmed that the church's traditional teaching on original sin is found in Romans 5:12. The responsibility of the exegete and theologian is to determine how it is found there. The text reflects both a collective (original) and personal sin. A climate of sin, which is both external and internal, has passed from the original transgression to all people in all ages. They in turn ratify it. In Romans there is room for both original causality and descendants' culpability.

Third Reading

After completing his assurance that future opposition and persecution would come (10:17 - 25), the Matthean Jesus now encourages his disciples to stand firm. Three times they are told to have no fear (vv26, 28, 31). They are to proclaim the gospel publicly (vv26f), to be certain of God's protection (vv28 - 31) and to be assured of final recognition (vv32f).

The instruction of the apostles, still not complete at this point in Matthew's gospel, will remain private until they are commissioned as teachers after the resurrection (vv26f; 28:19ff). The Matthean text is much clearer than Luke (12:2 - 9) in stating that the private and exclusive instruction is to be proclaimed openly in the apostles' future ministry. This distinguished first century Christianity from the concealed teachings of the Gnostics and other Hellenistic mystery cults.

In advising them not to fear death, Matthew, in contrast to Luke, uses the Hellenistic body-soul distinction (v28), failing to indicate, however, how the soul is to be destroyed in an after-life existence. Persecutors may bring the disciples to death for their belief, but they can do no more; they cannot deprive them of eternal life. It is more important to fear the evil one who is capable of destroying the person completely in the after-life. The inestimable value of the human person is illustrated in the comparison with the sparrow, the cheapest edible bird in the public market (v29). God's care for the elect far surpasses any concern of his for other forms of nature (vv30f; 6:25 - 34).

Especially cited are those who profess Christ publicly (vv32f). The setting is juridical. Jesus' apologist will find in him an advocate before the eternal judge. The parallel probably envisions a defense of the faith before a civil court of law (vv17f). Earthly profession merits heavenly commendation; earthly denial will result in heavenly condemnation. The main point made throughout is courage in the face of the human threat.

We all pray that if ever brought before a human tribunal for our beliefs, we will remain strong. The present age has seen some compelling examples. This may happen simply because of one's belief. Or it may happen because a human law has been transgressed as being unjust in the light of a higher divine law. The latter cases are more difficult and complex. Discernment and prayer are certainly necessary before action is taken. But it all proves that faith can be costly. Conviction can often result in intolerance and hostility–on either side. Yet charity must be the over-arching consideration. Opposition is overcome with charity and understanding, as hard as that may sound. But conviction is still necessary, otherwise faith becomes a weak and comforting construct. Position-taking is not easy. But we are increasingly asked to do so.

Years ago we learned that sin is both original and actual. Original sin is differently explained today than yesterday. But it is a truth of faith and a reality. We have a bent toward selfishness that begins early and stays late. Some would say that it is just an expression of self-preservation, but experience indicates that it is a bit more than that. There are many things that we have never done and yet feel drawn to do. Sin has a hold on us even before it is committed. Today's scripture has two important lessons. Take courage! And be on your guard!

Homiletic and Catechetical Helps

1. Contemporary examples of faith lived with courage.

2. Faith and courage in our own lives.

3. Seeing God as father and provider.

4. How does my faith waver?

5. Defining original sin.

6. The meaning of death in the scriptures.

7. Understanding Adam and Eve.

8. The distinction between original and actual sin.

9. Martyrs and martyrdom.

TWELFTH SUNDAY OF THE YEAR
Year B

Readings

> Job 38: 1, 8 - 11
> 2 Cor 5:14 - 17
> Mk 4: 35 - 41

Theme: Troubled Waters

Modern developments in oceanography continue to reveal the great wonders of the sea. If much still remains hidden from us, we can understand the awe with which the mysteries of the sea were held in antiquity. The ocean was at once serene and terrifying. It was believed to house mythological sea monsters. In Job today, Yahweh recounts how he first harnessed the burgeoning power of the sea. Jesus, in the gospel, tames its terrorizing force with a word. The second reading recalls that Christ's death meant death to an old order and that the life he brings opens new doors and brings a new set of values. Paul states that it is this new order which must fashion our thought.

First Reading

At this critical moment in the book of Job, Yahweh breaks his long silence. In preceding chapters Job has protested innocence in the face of the intense suffering he has endured. He has even questioned Yahweh's justice and rashly called for a response (31:37). In his answer, the Lord prescinds from the question of Job's lot and simply stresses his wisdom and power in creation, in what is some of the Hebrew scriptures' finest lyric poetry. The creation of the earth (vv1 - 7), sea (vv8 - 11) and light (vv12 - 15) are depicted.

The sea from its "birth" was expansive and encroaching in its outreach. It was the Lord who set its limits in establishing the shorelines of separation between land and water (vv8, 10). The sea often takes on the personification of its inhabiting sea monsters, such as Leviathan (3:8) and Rahab (9:13; 26:12). These became the symbols of evil, the primeval chaos which Yahweh subdues in creation (Gen 1:1f). In placing shorelines and establishing the depths and the height of the water, God places limits on the sea (v8; Gen 1:7). The white clouds as well as the gathering darkness on the horizon tended to hug the ocean in the view of the eye looking outward. Here they become the infant clothing of the vivacious newborn (v9).

Limits are set by a large gate, securely locked, beyond which the sea cannot pass (v10). The ocean depths are also connected with Sheol, the realm of the dead, the gates of which are also secured by Yahweh (38:16f). The rolling waves striking the shore as they complete their journey are also observant of the Lord's directives on boundaries (v11).

In this vivid poetry, Yahweh's dominion and sovereignty are seen as extending to those realms where the mythological forces of evil had long dwelt. The natural forces are powerless against him (Ps 74:13f; 104:26; Is 27:1).

Responsorial Psalm   Ps 107

Stormy waters continue in today's psalm. Courage and trust in Yahweh in the face of insurmountable odds is at the heart of this thanksgiving psalm, envisioning a series of circumstances from which Yahweh saves his elect. These include desert wandering (vv4 - 9), imprisonment (vv10 - 16), serious illness (vv17 - 22), and a stormy sea (vv23 - 32). Only the last set of circumstances is read in today's liturgy.

As has been noted, the sea, as the realm of the mysterious, could be one moment a placid friend and the next a raging enemy. It housed hostile forces which God had the power to vanquish. Therefore, prayer in the face of shipwreck takes on these cosmic dimensions (Jon 2:3 - 10).

The mariners are involved in international trade (v23). The ultimate cause of the storm is Yahweh, who, while not discounting secondary causes, is always finally responsible for what occurs (vv24f). The storm is nothing short of a tempest described in terrifying terms (vv26, 28). Upon turning to the Lord, the mariners, like the sea itself, experience calm and serenity (vv28f). Confidence is rewarded as full of thanks they head for port (vv30f).

Second Reading

Paul here speaks of a new way of thinking which flows from the Christian way of being. Both the ontological and the psychological components of the "new creation" come to the fore.

What constrains Paul to conform his way of thinking and acting is the love which Christ has shown for his people. *The love of Christ* (v14): The context here calls for a subjective genitive, i.e. Christ's love for us. With Christ's death, a new era has begun. Through their own baptism, Christians are assimilated to Christ in his act of dying. In being configured to Christ's death, the Christian puts off the old person with its sinfulness and weakness and lives with that life which characterized Christ himself in his self-giving (v15; 4:10f).

The result of this is a whole new mindset by which the Christian judges no longer by human "fleshy" criteria, seeing only the weak, the sinful, and the perishable. This was the actual state of the Corinthians at one time—weak, foolish, lowly, and despised (1 Cor 1:26ff). Indeed, before his conversion, Paul saw Christ in this way. The message of the cross was "foolishness" to the unredeemed (1 Cor 1:18 - 21).

Now a "new order" has changed all of that (v16;Gal 5:24f). *New creation* (v17): Judaism used the term of a radical change of life or a conversion with forgiveness of sins. Paul sees it as the new covenant (3:6), the putting on of Christ (Gal 3:27), a transformation which will ultimately transform all of creation (Rev 21:1). To live in this new order, then, is to view human conduct in terms of the works of the Spirit (Gal 5:22f) not those of the flesh (Gal 5:19).

Third Reading

This is the first of a series of four miracles in Mark (4:35 - 5:43). It reflects some of the mythological cosmogony of the time but basically asserts the Job position, i.e. the control of God (here Jesus) over all the forces of nature, notably those considered to be most distant from the divine realm. Here the miracle story form is complete: a description of the disorder (vv37f), the action of Jesus (v39a), and the complete restoration of order (v39b).

Jesus sets out for the east side of the Lake of Galilee with his disciples at the onset of evening (v35). Sudden storms with the wind sweeping down from the steep surrounding cliffs are not unusual on the lake. Marcan "close to the event" features appear in his vivid description of the listing boat filling with water, with Jesus himself asleep on a cushion (vv37f). The sleep of Jesus symbolizes his spirit of total trust in the Father (Ps 4:9), with the apostles, weak in faith, frightened and rash in their request for help. This is all softened considerably in Matthew and Luke in what becomes basically a reverential prayer for deliverance (Mt 8:26; Lk 8:24).

Jesus addresses the elements in personal terms (v39). The sea is "rebuked" and told to "be muzzled" (Gr: *pephimoso*). This is again the notion of evil spirits dwelling in the sea, with Jesus using the same language as in exorcisms (1:25). He then rebukes his disciples for their lack of faith (v40). The identity question so important in Mark is raised again (v41), a question to be gradually answered as the gospel progresses (8:29f; 15:39).

There is a strong catechetical imprint on this narrative, going beyond the miracle story. The disciples' cry becomes that of the early church beset by persecution (Mt 10:16ff), rejection (Mt 10:21f) and desertions (Mk 4:13 - 19). In the midst of the stormy sea, Christ's presence is not to be doubted (Mt 28:20); confidence and trust will bring believers safely to shore (Jn 14:1;16:33)

The sleep of the just–Christ on the storm-tossed lake was perfectly relaxed in his confidence and trust. His disciples were in a frenzy. How human, how true to form. We professedly claim that Christ is first in our life And yet in the face of a crisis or severe problem, we spontaneously turn in many directions for support before turning to God. Great steps have been taken in history with no assurance of the outcome. Founders of religious institutes were sometimes rejected by their own members. Others lived long enough to see their stated ideals profoundly altered. But their projects did not make them saints. The Spirit did. What they all had was an unwavering trust. Many people are deeply upset about the church today–and for a vast variety of reasons. What will it look like tomorrow? Will it be better or worse? It is hard to say. But one thing is certain. It will *be here. And the one who knows best will still be at the helm of this embattled vessel as it traverses the sea of life.*

Paul sees a whole new set of criteria for Christian judgment, and they have nothing to do with civil courts. The church should be viewed from the vantage point of joy, peace, patience, and a whole raft of virtues. The fact that such sounds so utopian only reminds us of how short we fall. What a difference if we Christians spent as much time on the good in people as we do on their shortcomings. History sees a lot of the church's shortcomings–wars fought in Christ's name, the overrunning of indigenous cultures, the crown and the cross. But in all of it there was some good. Church history has some inspiring passages. We are flesh and spirit. Today it helps to hear more about the spirit.

Homiletic and Catechetical Helps

1. Mythology in the Bible.

2. The continuing presence of Christ in the church.

3. Explaining the church as divine and human.

4. The role of the teaching office in guiding the church.

5. Personal example of our trust in God or lack of it.

6. Judging by the spirit and not by the flesh.

7. Understanding infallibility in guiding the church.

TWELFTH SUNDAY OF THE YEAR
Year C

Readings

    Zech 12:10 - 11

Gal 3:26 - 29
Lk 9:18 - 24

Theme: Cross-Bearing

In the Zechariah text, as difficult to translate as it is to interpret, the Davidic house and Jerusalem look upon an unknown sufferer as they grieve over the one they have pierced. Suffering is a central motif of the gospel as well, as Jesus turns his disciples away from an exalted notion of Messiah to one of suffering. Moreover, it is a pain which they themselves will one day endure as well. Paul tells the Galatians that life in Christ breaks down all barriers that stand between people. As Christians all are equal.

First Reading

The obscurity of the text has long made of this an "interpreter's cross." To call it a messianic text would seem to exceed the evidence. The wounded figure bears a resemblance to the equally mysterious servant of the Lord in Deutero-Isaiah.

The prophet Zechariah appears in the early post-exilic period, closely connected with the priestly class in Judea. The context of the present passage deals with Yahweh's vindication of Jerusalem and Judah in the messianic era. At that time, Yahweh's favor is poured out on the Davidic house and the people of the city; their conduct reflects their new status as a purified and prayerful remnant (v10a). Then, in a disturbed and still unclear Hebrew text, the citizens are looking upon someone whom they have killed, with a grief as profound as that for an only child (v10b). There is no indication that the one pierced is of the Davidic household or of the priestly line. The language bears a striking resemblance to that which speaks of the onlookers gazing upon the dead servant of the Lord (Is 52:13ff). In John's gospel, the text is applied to the dead Christ, as prophecy fulfilled (Jn 19:37).

This sense of loss is compared with that which took place at Megiddo at another time. *Hadadrimmon* (v11): Megiddo was the place of the illustrious King Josiah's death (2 Chr 35:22 - 25), although the present text does not seem to allude to him. The name may be a compound for two known pagan deities, Hadad and Rimmon, for whom mourning rites of death and resurrection, symbolizing fertility, were held.

The text yields only the sense of the Jews and their rulers mourning over a sainted martyr. That the chapter in which the passage is found is messianic cannot be denied. However, the specific messianic character of these verses appears only in its New Testament application. The Davidic Messiah does not enter here. That there is here an eschatology connected with the servant of the Lord is hypothesis only.

Responsorial Psalm   Ps 63

The pain of discipleship does not overwhelm the psalmist's sense of trust and confidence. For a commentary on the psalm, see the Twenty-Second Sunday of Year A.

Second Reading

In this passage from Galatians, Paul underscores the closeness of the Christian's union with Christ, which, in turn, creates a unity among the disciples themselves so strong as to make other differences inconsequential.

Sons and daughters of God (Gr: *uioi,* sons) (v26): The translation "children" fails to put in relief one of the chapter's major points, viz. that childhood under a disciplinarian (tutor) was the case under the law. Through baptism the Christian comes into his or her majority as a son or daughter, no longer in the state of a child (vv23ff; 4:6f).

Through faith and its accompanying baptism, the Christian has been fused into Christ through water immersion (v27). The baptism "into" is important in conveying a sense of movement. With baptism the Christian is *clothed* in Christ. The imagery may be based on the white baptismal robe worn in the liturgical rite. Clothing, closely identified with the person, is often applied to the virtues of one's life (Job 29:14; Is 59:17). Being clothed with Christ is another way, like being a member of the body, to speak of the symbiotic unity that takes place in baptism.

The bond between Christ and Christians also binds the elect among themselves (v28). It is of such overriding importance as to make other distinctions of ethnicity, social class, or gender become relegated to an inconsequential status when viewed from the order of faith. Another result is that the descendants of Abraham do not proceed from an ethnic strain. They arise now out of union with Christ in whom one becomes a true heir of the promise (v29; 4:21 - 31).

Third Reading

Peter's faith recognition of Jesus (vv18 - 21), the prediction of the passion (v22) and the cross in discipleship (vv23ff) are joined in all the synoptics, with each one introducing particular nuances. In Luke, Jesus' being at prayer signals, as always, the approach of an important moment in his ministry (v18; 3:21; 6:12; 9:28). The response to the question about his identity is basically the same as what Herod had heard (v19; 9:7f): a resurrected John the Baptist, the eschatological figures of Elijah (Mal 3:23) and the prophet. *Messiah of God* (v20): This says more than Mark (8:29) and less than Matthew (16:16). Christ is the Messiah, i.e. the promised one of Israel, the Davidic descendant of the final age. As the Messiah of God, Luke situates Christ in his eschatological mission, the emissary of God for the spiritual salvation of the people. This becomes clear in the prophecy of the passion that follows. His messiahship is identified with the salvation of others through the cross (23:35). As the Messiah of God's plan, Luke goes beyond any religio-political considerations to a salvific plateau.

The reason for Jesus' command of silence is clear from the description of his future suffering (v22) where he passes to the Son of Man title. While Jesus' foreknowledge of impending death is reasonable enough, the Lucan particularization with detail comes from a post-Easter reflection after the event (24:26). That Jesus must execute the Father's plan lifts his passion out of the realm of simple human machination (v22).

This important gospel apogee of a suffering Messiah then

incorporates disciples in its scope. What is true of Jesus will be true of his disciples as well. Cross-bearing is woven into the fabric of discipleship (v23). This leads to the Christian paradox. Attempts to preserve the present life will lead to its loss, while the surrender of life in cross-bearing will lead to its being saved (v24; 14:27). *Daily* (v23): This is a Lucan addition which moves the statement of Jesus away from considerations of a single moment of crucifixion, or any type of literalism, to an ascetical way of life which embraces all types of Christian endurance. The saying is directed to all of Christ's followers without distinction.

Christ bore his cross in obedience to the Father for the love of the world. It is interesting to note that the lot of Jesus' followers is joined to that of the master in the earliest passion prediction. Cross-bearing for Jesus involved many things, among them the hardships of his earthly ministry; his desire for rest, so often denied; his need for space, so often curtailed. Mark's gospel portrays vividly the extent to which Jesus was confined, jostled, prevailed upon. Yet he gave his all "for the sheep without a shepherd."

In our lives we don't have to seek the cross. It will find us. Our response is so important. Can we accept it in faith? As "fellowship in his suffering"? Illness, poverty, financial loss, rejection, giving of ourselves for others, generous presence to one in need–the cross is certain to come in one form or another. We pray for the grace to bear it with love.

Our unity as Christians makes other differences become secondary. Nationality or ethnic differences, differences of social status, gender differences–they are still present. But within the context of the faith they assume no importance. If they ever become dominant or areas of conflict, then difference becomes division and the Christian life loses its meaning. Human biases or prejudices really have no place. There is a truth in today's short reading from Galatians that we are still trying to actualize. Differences can enrich; division destroys. Unity in Christ respects differences and overcomes division.

Homiletic and Catechetical Helps

1. Discipleship and cross-bearing.

2. Peter's profession of Christ: differences in the three synoptics.

3. Luke's Messiah of God: its meaning.

4. Daily cross-bearing in my life.

5. Baptism as being clothed with Christ.

6. Christian unity and ethnic, social, and gender barriers.

7. Racial or ethnic prejudices in our neighborhood.

8. Christians as descendants of Abraham.

THIRTEENTH SUNDAY OF THE YEAR
Year A

Readings

> 2 Kgs 4:8 - 11, 14 - 16
> Rom 6:3 - 4, 8 - 11
> Mt 10:37 - 42

Theme: Hospitality

It is not the Lord's emissaries who are praised in today's first and third reading but rather those who show kindness to them. The hospitality shown to the prophet guest by the Shunammite woman is rewarded with the birth of a much desired child. Matthew's gospel in speaking of church leaders congratulates those who offer them even the ordinary kindnesses. Continuing our readings from Romans, we are today reminded that our baptism into the dead and risen Christ should reflect itself in our lives through death to sin and life for God.

First Reading

This story is part of the engaging account of Elisha's friendship with a very forthright and aggressive woman from northern Israel. She is left unnamed but hardly undefined. A resourceful person, she takes initiative with an undaunted spirit. In the complete story, Elisha assures her of a son (vv8 - 17), is later summoned by the woman when her son dies (vv18 - 30), and finally restores him to life (vv31 - 37). Today's reading covers only the first part of the story. Shunem was a town located in the Galilee region of Israel, not a great distance from Mount Carmel on the coast where the woman later goes to meet with the prophet (v25).

The woman is conspicuous for her thoughtfulness in providing food (v8) and lodging (vv9f) for Elisha. As the narrative proceeds, the strength of her personality makes her, rather than the prophet, the focal point of the chapter. In response to her kindness, Elisha asks his servant Gehazi what he can do for her. The prophet's attempts to deal with the woman via Gehazi, a third party, will be thwarted by the woman as the narrative proceeds (vv25ff). The prophetic promise of a child is something of a biblical constant (v16; Gen 18:10; Jgs 13:3; 1 Sam 1:9 - 19; Lk 1:5 - 13, 26 - 38). In this case it is divinely affirmed recognition of a woman's thoughtful hospitality.

Responsorial Psalm   Ps 89

The psalm is a royal lament recalling Yahweh's promise to the Davidic line (vv2 - 5, 20 - 38) in the face of a disheartening military defeat (vv39 - 53). The verses read today recall the covenant made with David (2 Sam 7), an expression of Yahweh's love and fidelity, with the emphasis on its perpetual character (vv2f). There is a transition to the covenanted people (vv16 - 19). They experience God's presence in worship (vv16f); he is their protector and guard. *Our horn* (v18): the animal's horn was a symbol of strength. With Yahweh's assistance his people accomplish remarkable feats.

Second Reading

Just as Christ had to experience death before he could live a new life as the risen Lord, so too must the Christian. Baptism, then, is an incorporation into the death of Christ through

which one must pass in coming to new life (vv3f). *Into Christ...
into his death* (v3): The use of the preposition with the
accusative here conveys a sense of motion, of an authentic lived
incorporation. Death and sin are inseparable. Christ passes
through the realm of death to vanquish sin definitively. That
done, he passes to a new life where neither sin nor death has
any sway. So too the Christian. In baptism, the person dies to a
sinful existence through incorporation into the death of Christ
and is then empowered to live a new life (v4; Col 2:12). *Glory of
the Father* (Gr: *doxa*; Heb: *kabod*) (v4): The external and awesome experience of God's power in wonders (Ex 15:7, 11), the
greatest of which is Christ's resurrection, here is attributed to
the action of God. The immersion baptism of the early church
with its descent into water and subsequent ascent symbolized
the concept of dying and rising.

Christ's resurrection is the certain pledge of the Christian's
as well (v8). The triumph of Christ over death is definitive, a
once-for-all event never to be repeated; his life now is wholly for
God (vv9f; 2 Tim 1:10). As for the Christian, everything is done
"with" Christ by incorporation. But that which is done in fact
must become real in conscious reflection. The Christian must
"think" the reality of a death to sin and a new life and then
must act accordingly (v11; 2 Cor 5:15; 1 Pet 2:24). Here again
Paul's ethic builds on his ontology.

Third Reading

These verses bring the Matthean Jesus' missionary discourse
to a close (10:1 - 42). They address the requirements of discipleship (vv37ff) and the posture expected of those who receive disciples (vv40ff).

Christian discipleship sets up a completely new set of relationships in the Spirit, which take priority over those of blood
(12:46 - 50). Christ's relatives are to be found in his disciples,
and the same is true of the disciples in reference to him. To
attempt to reverse this order once one has accepted the call is
to reject the voice of the master and thus be unworthy of him
(v37). Matthew softens Luke's (ultimately Q's) "hatred" (Lk
14:26), a semitism used for emphasis, to the less abrasive "love

more"; both, however, say the same thing. In the Matthean expression,the legitimate love of family is explicitly upheld (15:4ff), although it is clearly subordinate to the love binding the disciple to Christ.

Cross-bearing is a fundamental feature of the Christian life (v38; Lk 14:27). This is Matthew's first mention of the cross, and in a context of discipleship. The cross was an infamous form of Roman torture; its application to the life of the disciple is figurative. But Jesus' literal cross-bearing and that of his followers are linked by the common spirit of dedication to God's will. To seek one's own good (life) in escaping the cross leads to doom (life lost). To set aside one's interests (life) for the cause of Christ is gain (life found) (v39; Lk 17:33; Jn 12:25).

Discipleship also merits respect and charity. The second section deals with reward for those who are attentive to the disciples' needs. Four categories of disciple are indicated: the apostle ("you"), the prophet, the righteous person, and the little one. The *apostles* (v40) are those "sent" by Christ, the specially delegated twelve. As special emissaries, their position is unparalleled; their reception implies reception of Christ and the Father. It was proverbial in Judaism that to receive the messenger was to receive the sender. Failure to receive the apostles is highly reprehensible (10:14f).

The *prophet* (v41a) is the Lord's mouthpiece. A recognized charism of the early church, prophecy built up the church through instruction (23:34; 1 Cor 14:1 - 12). As in the time of the former covenant, prophets could be authentic or fraudulent (7:15f). The *righteous person* (v41b) is ideally any Christian but here probably looks to a respected and saintly member of the Christian community (1:19). To accept the prophet or the righteous person in a spirit of faith entitles one to the reward given to the person being received.

Finally *the little one* (v42) refers to the humanly insignificant members of the community—the poor, the unprotected, the more vulnerable (18:6; 25:40). Even a cup of cold water, in a land where extreme heat and thirst were common, is a sign of hospitality and respect that will not go unrewarded. In all of these examples, very simple acts of acceptance become significant acts of faith.

The human person, unlike many other lower forms of life, cannot live long without food and shelter. Biblical hospitality is rooted in these basic needs. To wish another well in the most fundamental fashion is to offer food and lodging. Neither is a superfluity; without either the guest would not long survive. We certainly practice these acts of hospitality, but one often wonders if we capture the significance. To invite someone to spend the night or to come to dinner carries a sense of the sacred, a very basic wishing well of which the inviter and the invited should be conscious. Awareness enriches what we do. Moreover, to extend this spirit to an emissary of Christ is to facilitate the spread of the gospel, to be consciously missionary, to be a partner in the guest's work. We might well meditate a bit on the next invitation we receive–and on the next one we extend.

Paul is an expert at backing up his demands with solid reasons. After outlining our death experience and our new life, he says, "Now act that way." There is something contradictory and incomprehensible about slipping back into death by turning to sin. We have to live what we are. The Christian life doesn't begin with precepts. It begins with what happens to each of us at the baptismal font. The best starting point–in preaching, in teaching, above all in living–is to realize what God has done for us.

Homiletic and Catechetical Helps

1. Hospitality as a religious act.

2. Christian love in offering food and lodging.

3. The love of Christ and the love of family.

4. Christian values fashioning human love.

5. The cross in our daily life.

6. The lay missionary.

7. Assisting the missionary.

8. Baptism: symbol of death resurrection.

9. Dying to sin and walking in new life.

THIRTEENTH SUNDAY OF THE YEAR
Year B

Readings

> Wis 1:13 - 15; 2:23 - 24
> 2 Cor 8:7, 9, 13 - 15
> Mk 5:21 - 43

Theme: God of the Living

When death means the end of everything, it is abhorred. It has always been so. Wisdom in today's first reading tells us that God is the author of life and has given us a destiny that is immortal. In today's gospel, Jesus brings life to a woman after many years of suffering and to a young girl who had a premature death. Life is at the heart of Christ's mission. In the reading from 2 Corinthians, we are reminded that our generosity is but a faint image of that of Christ who impoverished himself for us.

First Reading

The book of Wisdom comes from the Alexandrian Jewish community of the first century before Christ. Hellenistic philosophy flourished there, and the author of Wisdom has a certain indebtedness to it. In today's reading he speaks of human imperishability, a concept for which Greek philosophy, it would seem, served at least as a catalyst.

As the author of life, it is only with life that God is concerned (v13). Death here is understood as spiritual death, i.e. a total and final separation from God. Physical death does not figure prominently in the author's thought. God is not responsible for nor does he desire the death of any person. All things came from the hand of God as good (Gen 1), with God endowing much of the world with life (v14). *Destructive drug* (v14): a lethal power in nature capable of causing spiritual death. Sheol or the nether world, the realm of the dead, here personified, had no hegemony or sovereignty in the created order. The reason for this is because God conferred justice on the first human beings, and it is justice, a share in one of God's attributes, that is immortal (v15; 1:1 - 6; 15:3).

The author of Wisdom never argues from the natural immortality of the human soul although it may well have helped to fashion his thinking. Immortality comes from a life of justice and the unjust will not experience it (v24). As Spirit life in the New Testament, it is justice that confers eternal life. In referring to the Genesis creation account (v23; Gen 1:26), the author speaks of the sharing in God's nature as conferring immortality. Again, this is not a natural immortality but creation in God's justice. Uprightness of life constitutes the likeness of God in humanity (6:18f). Death which is the loss of justice makes its entry through the devil. Those who espouse evil are destined for death. For them there is no immortality (v24; Gen 3:1 - 24; Rom 5:12f). This is the first time that the scriptures have explicitly identified the Genesis serpent with the devil, as well as speaking of the devil's motive as envy, probably of Adam's pivotal role in the created order.

Responsorial Psalm   Ps 30

The gift of life over death continues in today's psalm. For a commentary, the reader is referred to the Tenth Sunday of Year C.

Second Reading

The needs of the church in Jerusalem form the basis of an appeal Paul makes to the Christians of Corinth (cc. 8 - 9). A pastoral call for help rests on a solid and inspiring Christological principle.

In setting the tone, Paul cites the charisms or gifts which the Corinthians have received, to which he adds the gift of his own love (v7; 1 Cor 1:5; 2 Cor 6:11ff). Just as they have received, they should be willing to give. They have been especially enriched by the Christ who impoverished himself on their behalf (v9). This sense of Jesus' identifying himself with the disenfranchised in order to bring them to a state equivalent to his own appears in various forms as part of the Pauline dialectic (5:15f; 5:21). In surrendering the expressions of divinity to become totally human, even more a sufferer, Christ brought to the poverty of the human the riches of divinity in sharing the life in the Spirit (Phil 2:6 - 11).

At this point Paul passes to an argument based on equality (vv13ff). Sharing between Corinth and Jerusalem will eventually be mutual, with the result that neither will experience excess or shortage. Sharing will have an equalizing effect. Allusion is made to the providential manna at the time of the exodus (v15). At that time God as the equalizer provided in such fashion that what seemed to some gatherers an abundance and to others a shortage actually proved simply sufficient for both (Ex 16:18).

Third Reading

Two miracle stories are woven together in this lively Marcan narrative. They are recorded in the same way, although in abbreviated form, in Matthew (9:18 - 26) and Luke (8:40 - 56), both of which depend on Mark. The story of Jairus' daughter (vv21 - 24, 35 - 43) is interrupted by the healing of the sick woman (vv25 - 34).

The stories retain many of the Marcan vivid features, often illustrating the human tensions surrounding Jesus' ministry. After Jesus reaches the western side of the lake, a large crowd surrounds (v21) and follows him (v24). It is the pressing crowd that makes the woman's access (vv27f) and her later identification (v31) difficult. The rude, almost caustic question of the disciples (v31), omitted in Matthew and softened in Luke (8:45), is illustrative of the short tempers that the crowd occasioned. Jesus' concern for the one who touched him (v30) persists in spite of the apostles' negative response (v32). As they approach Jairus' house, there is the loud weeping (perhaps professional mourners) (v39) and the ridicule (v40). Only Mark has Jesus usher the people out (v40), and he retains the Aramaic expression used to resuscitate the girl (v41). It is the Marcan Jesus who sees that the girl receives something to eat (v43). This entire scenario draws the reader closer to the event and underscores the human and often trying dimensions of Jesus' ministry.

The account of both miracles, which follows closely the traditional miracle story form, constitutes an important catechetical piece from the early church's life. The healing and the revivification are symbols of salvation and the work which Christ effects in the life of each believer. All of this carries the reader beyond the historical event itself. Thus, Jairus, a Jewish official, adopts the posture of a suppliant and asks that his daughter *be saved* (Gr: *sozo*) and *live* (Gr: *zao*). The physical contact in both accounts is a link with the miracle worker's curative power. The woman's abnormal flow of blood had cost her pain and money for years (v25). Moreover, she was legally unclean (Lev 15:25), and therefore fearful of having direct contact with Jesus.

But in the woman's story, the Easter faith overlay again comes to the fore. She had heard the *reports of Jesus* (Gr: *ta peri tou Iesou*) (v27) which at a later date will refer to the kerygma centering on death-resurrection (Lk 24:19, 27; Acts 18:25). By touching his garment she *will be saved* (Gr: *sozo*) (v28). Finally Jesus assures that her faith is the cause of her *salvation*, with the healing almost an appendage at this point (v34).

As Jairus' story continues, the notice of his daughter's death requires of him an added measure of *faith* (v36). The inclusion of Peter, James, and John at this critical moment signals an important manifestation of God at work in Jesus (v37; 9:2; 13:3; 14:33). *The child is not dead but asleep* (v39): In fact the child was dead. However, in the faith perspective, the period between physical death and resurrection was known as one of sleep (Gr: *koimasthai*) (Mt 27:52; Jn 11:11f; 1 Cor 11:30; 15:18). The verb to *arise* (Gr: *egeire*) is used of Jesus' resurrection (14:28; 16:6). The injunction to silence (v43), difficult to understand if historical, is actually part of Mark's messianic secret, the restricted unfolding of Jesus' identity in determined steps.

This gospel is important on both the historical and the transcendent levels. It reflects the ascetical response of Jesus to human need under the often pressing circumstances of his daily ministry. It is also a catechesis on Jesus as the cause of resurrection and life, as he meets every Christian in healing and eternal life-giving.

The old must die and the young can die. We don't know whether the woman who suffered from the hemorrhage was old or not. But twelve years of pain, plus any number of doctors, must have given her at least a drawn and wizened look. Jairus' daughter is reported to have been twelve. A pressed and harried Jesus came to both of them. And, at the heart of the narrative, is the teaching that he comes to us as well. The message is clear. Do not fear! Life is eternal! The gates of death do not separate us from those we love. To know that a dear child or a beloved grandmother lives on is immensely consoling. And it is not wishful thinking. There are natural reasons to believe in immortality when one looks at the accomplishments of the human spirit in the arts and sciences. Even the controversial Norman Mailer has stated that he would be very surprised if there were no afterlife. But we are convinced with the certainty of faith. We share God's justice, and justice is immortal.

In this day and age with many demands made upon Christians for financial support, it is not surprising that pastors and congregations pray to be delivered from any more special collections. Yet it is an inspiring expression of bonding with people throughout the world. In offering of our abundance, their lack can be overcome. We may not be able to give endlessly, but Paul would urge us to keep trying. Christ gave completely and did not hold back. And we are richer for it. Every time we give, Christ is better served.

Homiletic and Catechetical Helps

1. Immortality as a share in God's life.

2. Immortality known from reason.

3. Spiritual death.

4. Assisting the young to live a Christian life.

5. Ways of being present to the suffering and the elderly.

6. The difference between resurrection and resuscitation.

7. Christ's poverty as our enrichment.

8. Ways to share our abundance.

9. The meaning of the collection during liturgy.

10. The injustices of wealth and poverty in the world.

THIRTEENTH SUNDAY OF THE YEAR
Year C

Readings

> 1 Kgs 19: 16 - 21
> Gal 5:1, 13 - 18
> Lk 9:51 - 62

Theme: Journey of Commitment

The word conversion is derived from a Hebrew word meaning a basic change of direction. Commitment follows conversion. There is no turning back. Elisha's discipleship meant a last farewell at home and then an unwavering allegiance to Elijah. Today's gospel builds on that first reading theme. Christ wants no ambivalence. As he makes his own journey to Jerusalem, he asks of his disciples a journey of commitment. Paul's thought today points to the same kind of journey, one from flesh to spirit. Once freedom in the Spirit is ours, there can be no "backtracking" to the slavery of the flesh.

First Reading

Yahweh gave Elijah a threefold commission: the anointing of two kings and the designation of a successor (vv15f). He actually performs only one of these, the choice of Elisha to continue his work. Elisha was evidently a farmer of means, hard at work in the fields (v19). The conferring of succession and authority is symbolized by the giving of the mantle, a symbol which returns at the time of Elijah's final leave-taking (2 Kgs 2:13ff). With this act, Elisha's calling is confirmed.

The enthusiasm of Elisha's response and his readiness to follow the prophet miltate against the idea of a rebuff in Elijah's answer to the request which is made (v20). The slaughtering of the oxen does not appear to have any sacrificial significance (v21). With their being dispatched and the burning of the farm equipment, the completeness of the prophet's commitment is underscored, as well as his generosity in distributing the meat. Elisha sets out on the path of discipleship.

Responsorial Psalm Ps 16

The exclusive character of the psalmist's love for Yahweh fits well with today's scriptural theme. For a commentary on the psalm, see the Thirty-Third Sunday of Year B.

Second Reading

The Judaizers in Galatia want to place the Christians there under the law from which Christ has freed them (2:4). Paul emphatically states that to advocate a new legalism is to run the risk of being enslaved anew and to abandon their new-gained freedom (v1; 4:9)

The Spirit-flesh dichotomy is the guiding principle of Paul's ethical challenge. Christian freedom is a freedom for the Spirit who places one at the service of love. Freedom is not unbridled license. To follow that path would lead back to the flesh, the worst form of slavery (v13; Rom 6:18; 1 Cor 8:9). Paul's teaching on love of neighbor (without citing love of God) as the summary of the law probably draws directly on the teaching of Christ (Mt 22:39) rather than being an independent application of the Leviticus text (Lev 19:18). It is Paul's thesis that the Spirit does not neglect the fundamental demands of the law. On the contrary, the single dictate on love of neighbor fulfills the precepts of the decalogue (v14; Rom 13:8ff). Personal attacks within the Galatian community militate against this spirit (v15).

In the ontological order one dies to the flesh in baptism; in the experiential and psychological order its effects are still felt. The flesh tries to draw the person away from the Spirit, its arch-enemy. Caught between these two warring factions, Christians must ally themselves with the Spirit (vv16f; Rom 8:7ff). Furthermore, since law is allied with sin and death (Rom 6:14), it has no place in the Spirit-allied life of the Christian (v18). In summary, the Spirit, life, and resurrection stand on one side; on the other stand flesh, sin, law, and death. There is no middle ground. One must walk (Gr: *peripateo*) by the Spirit (v16).

Third Reading

This opens a new section in Luke's gospel which will reach its completion only at the gospel's end. Jesus begins his journey to Jerusalem, a dominant motif of the Lucan gospel (9:51 - 24:53). The commentary here will look at the narrative from the perspective of Christ himself and from that of his followers.

Jesus' Journey to Jerusalem. Although the literary setting is a geographical journey from Galilee to Jerusalem, its import is theological. The reference is to Jesus' journey to the Father in death-resurrection, which finds its geographical locus in the city where he is sentenced and killed. Luke's vocabulary discloses his intent. *The days were fulfilled* (v51) looks to the time set by the Father for his salvific mission to be accomplished. *His being taken up* (Gr: *analempsis*) (v51): The same word is used of Christ's ascension (Acts 1:2, 11, 22). *He resolutely determined* (v51): literally "he set his face." It points to Jesus' complete dedication to his mission. This notion of the *journey* recurs in today's reading (vv53, 57) and appears repeatedly in carrying forward the theme in this second part of the gospel.

At an early stage in Jesus' journey, there is opposition from foreigners (vv52 - 55), not unlike that received from his own people at the beginning of his ministry (4:16 - 29). The Samaritans, located between Judea and Galilee, were considered heretical, "half Jews" at best, who differed from standard Judaism in some important aspects of belief. Ordinarily their country was bypassed in travel (Jn4). They did not worship in Jerusalem but on their own Mount Gerizim—hence their hostility regarding Jersualem (v53). Jesus rejects any form of retaliation against them (v55) as contrary to his teaching (6:27ff). He will later cite Samaritans as examples of a genuine religious spirit (10:30, 37; 17:11 - 19), and the church will make early inroads among them (Acts 8:4 - 7, 14, 25).

The Disciples' Journey to Jerusalem. As Jesus imparts his *didache* or teaching on the journey, Luke's intention is to incorporate Christ's followers as well. This is not only in reference to his immediate disciples but all who would come after him in making their own journey to the Father. Here Jesus imparts an important teaching on renunciation and commitment (vv57 - 62).

Followers must be prepared to leave possessions (vv57f), human responsibilities (vv59f) and personal ties (vv61f). In the examples cited, Jesus emphasizes the primacy of commitment to the reign of God; all else is secondary. The imagery used is typically semitic and strongly worded to drive the idea home. Details should not be pressed, e.g. in asking who are the dead left to attend to the burying or in explaining an injunction against saying goodbye to family. To break the sayings down into fractions is to lose their impact. The main point is clear: human considerations are insignificant and negligible in comparison to God's reign. Family ties have elsewhere been indicated as secondary (14:26), even conflictual (12:53). The Palestinian one-hand plow cannot be easily guided without full attention given to the furrows. So, too, the reign of God calls for undivided commitment. Where one's treasure is, there also is one's heart (Mt 6:21).

Every journey has a measure of the unknown. This was true of Christ as he moved toward Jerusalem. It is true of every Christian who accepts the radical call and who, as Paul states, makes his journey as the "Spirit walk." Every day of our life presents new challenges, new problems of faith, new moral choices. There is great force in Luke's statement about Jesus. "He set his face" for Jerusalem. One thinks of a finely chiseled face of stone, with head erect, and steely eyes looking directly forward. It all speaks one word: commitment. In the face of the unknown, Christ never wavered. Our age has many difficulties with commitment. Great hesitation surrounds any life commitment. Those which are made are regularly broken. Judging the situation of others is not ours to do. But it is a regrettable fact of our times. True love does not shrink from commitment. To opt for God in our life is a very important choice. How reassuring it is when we know people who remain strong and firm in that Christian decision throughout life. If there is one thing we need today, it is a witness of stability. And when we find it, it is a great inspiration.

Once we begin our "Spirit walk," there is no reverting to the "flesh" life. Paul really does not envision a form of passing back and forth from grace to sin and vice versa. Certainly, in life there are struggles and "fall-out" as well. But to opt for the Spirit is to strive continually to walk God's path, to move toward the Lord's goals, and, insofar as possible, to make our choices based on his directives. We will not always succeed. But that doesn't end the game or even retire the side. With the willingness to build on what has been started, the journey continues.

Homiletic and Catechetical Helps

1. The meaning of Christian commitment.

2. The journey theme in Luke's gospel: its meaning.

3. The journey theme in the Christian life.

4. Renunciation on the journey.

5. Family relations and our relation to Christ.

6. The meaning of flesh and Spirit.

7. The irreconcilable character of living in flesh and Spirit.

8. Love of neighbor fulfills the law.

9. Understanding mortal sin.

FOURTEENTH SUNDAY OF THE YEAR
Year A

Readings

> Zech 9:9 - 10
> Rom 8:9, 11 - 13
> Mt 11:25 - 30

Theme: A Gentle and Humble Spirit

Zechariah paints a picture of the messianic king in very peaceful hues. A king of a different cut, he is neither militant nor political but rather lowly and humble. The Jesus of Matthew's gospel reinforces that image of lowliness. He invites his followers to see in him an example of humility and points out that it is the little ones of this world who receive God's message. In encouraging Christians to live the Christ-life, Paul points to the resurrection to glory as the certain outcome for those who do.

First Reading

The ninth chapter of Zechariah depicts the destruction of Israel's traditional enemies (vv1 - 7), as well as the deliverance of God's people (v8). The next oracle, read in today's liturgy, centers on the emergence of the messianic king, the Davidic descendant (vv9ff).

With the arrival of the king, Jerusalem is exhorted to give full expression to its joy. The first notable characteristic of the new king is that he is a man of peace (v10; Mic 5:3); the weapons and instruments of war shall exist no more in the north (Ephraim) or the south (Jerusalem) (Hos 1:7; Is 2:4). His rule is seen as universal, although obviously circumscribed by the world boundaries known at the time, extending from the Mediterranean to the Persian Gulf (sea to sea), and from the Euphrates (the River) to southwestern Europe (v10; Ps 72:8)

The profile of the king is sharply defined. *Just savior* (v9): literally, "just and saved"—a king who is upright before God, not the savior but the one saved, delivered and protected by God for his important destiny (Ps 33:16). He is meek (Heb: *hani*), with the spirit of the poor of God, clearly dependent on Yahweh. He is the opposite of the bellicose warrior (Jer 17:25). He is mounted on the *foal of an ass*, a beast of burden, not an example of equestrian warfare; he resembles the pastoral leader of an earlier Israel (Gen 49:11; Jgs 5:10). Zechariah envisions the deliverance of Israel not through military might but through justice, gentleness, and a lowly spirit of openness to Yahweh.

For the evangelists this text finds its fulfillment in the entrance of Jesus' into Jerusalem (Mt 21:4ff; Jn 12:14f).

Responsorial Psalm   Ps 145

This psalm extols Yahweh's kindness and compassion as well as his outreach to the lowly and forgotten. The commentary is to be found in the Thirty-First Sunday of Year C.

Second Reading

Paul is here engaged in his dialectic of flesh and Spirit in the Christian life (8:1 - 17). By reason of baptism, the Christian incorporation into Christ through the action of the Spirit connotes a dying to the flesh in all its demands. "Flesh" here differs from the contemporary understanding of "carnal." Rather it is that dimension of the human person which is unredeemed, weakened by sin and prone to follow its promptings. *Spirit of God...Spirit of Christ* (v9): The Spirit stands in opposition to the flesh. Conferred on the risen Christ by the Father (1:4), the Spirit is communicated by Christ to the believer (1 Cor 3:16). Thus, the Spirit can be termed as being of God or Christ. So diametrically opposed are flesh and Spirit that co-existence is excluded. This is not to deny the existential persistence of the flesh in the person's daily life (Gal 5:17), but the Christian is ontologically rooted in the Spirit which wholly fashions his or her goals.

It is the Spirit-life which is the pledge of resurrection (v11). God alone is the cause of resurrection in the case of both Christ and the Christian. But again Christ is always the channel of the Spirit that will bring the elect to a new life, and he remains the exemplar of the risen life (1 Thes 4:14; Phil 3:21).

With his ontological base established, Paul now makes his moral appeal (v12). To live according to the flesh ultimately leads to destruction. To produce the works of the flesh is to live a life of serious immorality (Gal 5:19f), terminating in spiritual death. To live the Spirit-life is to produce its fruits (Gal 5:22f), which ultimately issues in eternal life (vv12f).

Third Reading

Words of reproach and dismay on the disbelief encountered precede this encomium of the believer and its accompanying invitation spoken by the Matthean Jesus (11:16 - 24). In his pronouncement, Jesus speaks the language of the Wisdom literature, indeed presents himself as the true Wisdom. The passage is a praise of God for his revelation (vv25f), a description of revelation itself (v27), and an invitation to come to Jesus as God's revelation.

Jesus' praise of the Father is drawn from Q and shared with Luke (10:21f). The revelation of God is given to those with a spirit of lowliness and openness—sinners, publicans, tax collectors, the outcasts—just as it is concealed from the self-righteous—lawyers, Pharisees, scribes. This is God's will (v26) according to the Hebrew sense of divine causality, which bypasses secondary causes without, however, excluding human responsibility.

What is this revelation? It is the mystery of God revealed in Jesus who is both the agent (v27a) and the content (v27b) of the revelation. As the Word of the Father (Jn 1:14; Heb 1:2), Jesus is the personal expression of God, manifest in his deeds, his teaching, and his salvific death-resurrection. There is an intimacy and exclusivity about the relationship between Father and Son, long retained as a mystery within the Godhead, which has now been revealed in Jesus. It is those who are open to God (the little ones) who receive this message. This high Christology, which sounds very Johannine, is not, however, foreign to Matthew who elsewhere emphasizes the presence of God in Jesus (1:23; 28:18).

The invitation to come to Christ as the divine revealer is a distinct echo of Sirach's call to approach Wisdom (51:23 - 27), which is also preceded by the praise of God (51:1). Those who come to Wisdom will find her yoke pleasing (v26). Those who come to Jesus will be freed of the burden of the law (v28; 23:4) and receive the yoke of a leader who, in the spirit of Zechariah, comes in the spirit of the anawim as lowly and gentle (v29). Jesus offers the teaching of the upright way and offers the spiritual force to observe it. While requiring a righteousness that surpasses that of the Jewish leaders (5:20), Jesus' yoke offers both the end and the means, which makes the commitment both simpler and profoundly engaging.

Power tends to corrupt. The saying of Lord Acton has been verified countless times. So much of our modern society is geared to power. It can be wielded ruthlessly with little regard for other humans. It can also be used more subtly in forms of control and manipulation. At times the use of power is blatant; at other times it is concealed. Jesus stood for totally contrary values and was considered a total paradox. He avoided messianic titles because of their implications. He controlled no one and wanted to avoid any sense of earthly power. Acceptance of Jesus was personal, free, and liberating. The assistance of others is never more rewarding than when it results in maturity, a sense of self-worth and personal empowerment. Christ's magnetism lay in the example of his life and his teaching–nothing more. That lesson has proved difficult for his followers and has often been forgotten.

Life is a paradox. The flesh is always attractive in its various expressions, and yet it is the Spirit that really impresses. So often it seems that the forces of evil are galvanized to destroy the human spirit–injustice, dishonesty, role models with feet of clay, the debasing of sex, character assassination. On the other hand, we are so uplifted by lives oriented by authentic values–generous self donation–sainted sufferers, champions of the poor and the forgotten, courageous conviction. Such examples can offset so much of the negative. There are people–many people–who are not debtors of the flesh. The Spirit truly guides their lives. We all need to be inspired, and the "inspiring" Spirit has not left us wanting.

Homiletic and Catechetical Helps

1. The meaning of the gentle and humble king.

2. Power and powerlessness.

3. Lowliness: the power to accept God's word.

4. The Trinity: relationship between Father and Son.

5. The lightness of Jesus' yoke.

6. The meaning of life in the flesh.

7. The meaning of life in the Spirit.

8. Fruits of the flesh.

9. Fruits of the Spirit.

FOURTEENTH SUNDAY OF THE YEAR
Year B

Readings

> Ez 2:2 - 5
> 2 Cor 12:7 - 10
> Mk 6:1 - 6

Theme: The Rejected Prophet

No prophet has ever faced a simple challenge. The prophets' message inevitably flies in the face of accepted standards. Ezekiel's message of retribution will find a very difficult audience. But at least God's word will be delivered. The Marcan Jesus is a classic example of the prophet facing the hometown congregation. His local origins are as good a reason as any to ignore him. Paul sees strength emerging from weakness. In his own powerlessness lies the reinforcing power of God.

First Reading

A note of human failure and rejection is often sounded early, appearing even in the prophet's call, as in today's reading from Ezekiel (Is 6:9f; Jer 1:17f). Even though they are part of the vocation form, such shadows may well have been composed as a later reflection on the prophet's career. *Spirit* (Heb: *ruah*) (v2): literally, a breath or wind. This is the divine force, invisible but effective, that brings order out of chaos (Gen 1:2), makes humans capable of extraordinary feats (Jgs 11:29; 14;6), raises to ecstasy (1 Sam 10:10) and empowers the prophet to grasp and convey God's message (8:3; 9:24). *Son of Man* (v3): Equivalent for "man," it here highlights the gap between the human agent and the divine source of prophecy. Its frequent use in Ezekiel makes it almost the equivalent of a name.

The prophet was to face an obstinate Israel, already paying the price for its sins with the destruction of Jerusalem and the deportation of the people in 586 B.C. *Thus says the Lord God* (v4): Ezekiel's oracles are presented as direct and detailed communications from Yahweh, with no elaboration. He is in the strict sense of the word a mouthpiece of the Lord (2:1 - 4; 3:27). He will be met with acceptance or rejection, a sign of salvation or condemnation. Before Yahweh's word, the people will either obey or resist. The Lord's support of the prophet is to be, at least, a sign that they have not been abandoned (v5). In addition to the call for conversion, the prophetic role also indicates God's constancy and fidelity.

Responsorial Psalm   Ps 123

Like the prophets, the psalmist has met rejection (vv3f), in the midst of which he expresses his unshakable trust in the Lord. The enthronement of Yahweh in heaven (v1) may be figurative only or reflect its earthly localization in the temple (Is 6:1). Both the male and the female servants have their gaze riveted on the distributing hand of their employer; so too the psalmist never loses trust in Yahweh's favor (v2). Increased hostility has only deepened the petitioner's confidence (vv3f).

Second Reading

Special revelation accorded Paul is no occasion for self-aggrandizement. To avoid any sense of pride, he was given a particularly strong affliction to help in keeping his feet firmly planted on the ground (v7). *Thorn in the flesh* (v7): The reference is probably to personal opponents (Num 33:55). The "angel of Satan" is best understood as personal in Pauline usage (11:13ff). Thus the leveling factor in the apostle's exalted experience came from personal opposition, whether individual or collective, regarding his person and his ministry. The threefold request for relief signifies persistence in prayer (v8; Mt 26:39 - 44); the response assures the apostle of continued and sufficient support (v9).

It is in the ground of human weakness that the seed of God's strength takes root (v9; 6:4 - 7). This again is the Pauline dialectic: dying, we live; weak, we are strong. The apostle can take comfort in his weakness and opposition, because, in the face of his evident inability and inadequacy, positive results will not be attributed to him. They will be seen as the work of God, and therein lies his strength (v10; 4:7 - 11).

Third Reading

The Marcan Jesus meets repeated alienation early in his ministry, coming from the Jewish leaders (3:6), his relatives (3:21) and at this point from his townspeople. He returns to Nazareth, his native place (v1; 1:9) and there enters the synagogue for the sabbath service. Like any Jewish man, he enjoyed the right to read and discourse on the scriptures. In the questioning mode, characteristic of Mark's gradual identification of Jesus, the citizens first marvel at his exceptional deeds and teaching and in their attempt to find a human explanation fail to see the hand of God (vv2f).

The people then move toward discounting Jesus on the basis of his simple and unimpressive origins. Only in Mark is Jesus called a carpenter (v3; Mt 13:55). *Son of Mary* (v3): This would be an exceptional, even unsettling way for a person to be identified, with no mention of the father. Yet Mark has already identified God as Jesus' Father (1:1, 11) and will again (9:7; 13:32). He makes no mention of the virgin birth, but this expression may be an indication of his awareness of Jesus' singular origins. *The brother of James and Joses* (v3): As in the case of the virgin birth, Mark does not expressly indicate knowledge of Mary's perpetual virginity. The ordinary understanding of the Greek *adelphos* is "brother" in the sense used today. Yet in both Greek and Hebrew it can be used of relatives in a broader sense (Mt 13:55f), and elsewhere Mark names another mother for two of the men cited, if it is to be presumed they are the same (15:40).

The attitude of the crowd passes from wonderment to hostility (v3). At this point Jesus' ability to communicate further with his audience is impeded by lack of faith (v6). The proverb (v4) appears in Jewish literature applied to various functionaries, not usually prophets. Here it explains Jesus' rejection by his own people. Since faith is a necessary concomitant of Jesus' miracles, he is rendered powerless in Nazareth because of the negative and incredulous attitude (v5).

Disappointment and failure seem to come to the fore this Sunday. In view of the role that lack of success plays in the human endeavor, such is not too surprising. It is encouraging to know that it was endured painfully before us. Rejection is a very difficult thing to handle. It strikes at our sense of self-esteem, which is only a mite less forceful than that of self-preservation. Then, when it comes to competition, someone else is chosen, not I. In selection, I am bypassed and someone else is singled out. In friendships someone else is preferred to me. In all of this there is often a deep sense of hurt. This came to Jesus from various quarters. As far as his townspeople were concerned, he was just too local to be important. As a modern wit puts it, an expert is somebody who tells us everything we know already but he comes from out of town. But even Jesus' relatives thought that he was "out of it." The Jewish leaders rejected him. Barabbas, a common criminal, was preferred to him. We may never be hounded to death as Jesus was, but we will certainly suffer a sense of rejection. So did he. And that gives us great consolation.

With all the "thorns in the side" that we experience, it is gratifying to know that Paul had one in his flesh. Like rejection, opposition comes in many forms. It is quite different from disagreement. Lack of accord can be very fruitful in clarifying thought and ironing out wrinkles. One should presume good will in disagreement. But hostility breeds endless "roadblocks." It often springs from personal dislike, and in its negativism, even cynicism, it is clearly unproductive. In the throes of human existence, we can only do our best—and, Paul would add, let Christ do the rest. We know our weakness. But God writes straight with crooked lines. We do not always succeed. But with right motives and a believing heart, we never really fail.

Homiletic and Catechetical Helps

1. The prophet and opposition.

2. The prophets of our times.

3. The teachings of faith as prophetic.

4. The experience of rejection in our life.

5. The brothers and sisters of Jesus.

6. Mary's virginal conception and perpetual virginity.

7. Jesus the carpenter: the value of work.

8. The eighth commandment.

9. The sinful use of speech.

FOURTEENTH SUNDAY OF THE YEAR
Year C

Readings

>   Is 66:10 - 14
>   Gal 6:14 - 18
>   Lk 10:1 - 12, 17 - 20

Theme: The Joy of Fulfillment

Happiness carries the day in the scriptures this Sunday. Religion was never meant to be gloomy or solely duty-oriented. In Christianity there is every reason for joy. Isaiah sees joy in the fulfillment of God's promises to mother Jerusalem as she contentedly nurses her offspring. The apostles find their happiness in the success of their mission, in banishing demons and inaugurating God's reign. In the Lucan gospel, Jesus tells them that even greater things are in store for them as the elect of God. Paul's joy centers on the cross of Christ, the source of his new re-created life.

First Reading

The note of rejoicing, so pronounced in Second Isaiah, is much to the fore in the concluding verses of Third Isaiah (cc. 55 - 66). The announcement of the end of Jerusalem's trials and the launching of a new era are expressed is some of Isaiah's most vivid imagery. Feminine images of God play a part in Second Isaiah (42:14; 45:10; 49:15); here the picture of a woman in the advanced stages of pregnancy giving birth to a child (vv7ff) whom she suckles with joy and contentment is particularly apt (v11). Eschatological joy compared with the happiness that follows the pain of parturition appears again in Jesus' teaching (Jn 16:21f).

The citizens of Jerusalem live the experience of salvation as the contented children of a devoted mother, nourished and caressed (vv12f). The centrality of Jerusalem to the faith of Israel is poignantly underscored. The riches of the earth converge on her like a river and cascading waterfalls (v12). After years of pain, destruction and evil, the final days have burst open, bringing boundless joy in the realization that God has favored his people (v14).

Responsorial Psalm   Ps 66

A sense of joy permeates this hymn which begins on a collective (vv1 - 12) and ends on an individual note (vv13 - 20). An invitation extended to the earth's ends calls for acknowledgement of Yahweh's strength in dealing with his opponents (vv1ff). All are called to see the *works of God*, the great acts of the exodus, litanied in Israel's cultic poetry (vv5f; Ps 114; Ex 15:1 - 17). Finally, the psalmist, perhaps the king, speaks of the benefits he himself has received for which he asks that God be praised (vv16, 20).

Second Reading

The Judaizers at work in Galatia have been the object of much of Paul's anger in this letter. They remain so to the conclusion. Among their objectives in restoring the force of the Jewish law was the reintroduction of circumcision. Here Paul speaks of the only mark which he will ever bear as a new creature in Christ. The Judaizers wanted to pride themselves on their distinctive Jewish heritage of which circumcision was the seal. Paul sees the cross as his only (figurative) boast, i.e. all credit must be given to the saving work of Christ of which the cross is the visible expression.

The world (v14): the created order in opposition to God, with its attractions and enticements, everything that appeals to the unredeemed (flesh) in human nature. To all of the world Paul has died, and it has lost its control over him (v14). This death occurs through incorporation into the death-resurrection of Christ in baptism (2:19; 5:24; Rom 6:1 - 4).

Consequently, any discussion of circumcision is useless. The only thing that matters is a personal transformation into Christ, which is the gift of God's spirit at work. This is the *new creation* (v15; 2 Cor 5:17; 1 Cor 15:45). Paul extends his final prayerful salutation to all who accept this basic teaching (this rule: vv14f) and all the church. *Israel of God* (v16): This is the church itself, the new Israel, the true descendants of Abraham (3:29; 4:21 - 31).

The marks of Jesus (Gr: *stigmata*) (v17): the brand of ownership borne by a slave in his body to mark him as his master's property. The visible signs of apostolic suffering and physical hardship (2 Cor 11:22 - 31) are the marks of Christ which Paul bears to the exclusion of the physical sign of circumcision upheld by his opponents.

Third Reading

A similar note of joy and urgency characterizes the Lucan account of the sending of the seventy-two disciples. In the manuscript evidence, there is a discrepancy over the number: seventy or seventy-two. If the figure is based on the number of people Moses chose to assist him in administration (Num 11:16 - 25), then it is seventy. A later scribal addition of two in some manuscripts may refer to the two people added to Moses' lot at a later moment (Num 11:26 - 30). The sending of the seventy follows closely upon Luke's similar account of the sending of the twelve (9:1 - 6).

The missionaries travel in pairs (v1; 7:18; 24:13; Mk 6:7), evidently as a matter of custom. The mandate they receive deals with the *how* of their mission rather than the content. They are to speak by example as well as by word. The presentation of the mandate is colored as much by the procedures of the Lucan post-Easter church as it is by the actual ministry of Jesus.

The readiness of the people for conversion sets the tone for the commission (v2; Mt 9:37f; Jn 4:35ff). The danger lies in opposition to the gospel (v3; Mt 10:16ff). The disciples are to move with urgency and a strong emphasis on the end-time character of their message (v9; Mt 10:7 -14). Their deprivation is practical (travel light!); money is not necessary since their needs will be met. The order to avoid even salutations simply stresses the urgency of their task (v4). *Peace to this household* (v5): Peace arises from a restored relationship with God. Destroyed by sin, peace and harmony between God and humankind are restored in Christ. A blessing, like a curse, has a force of its own once uttered. Like a trajectory, it will inevitably come to rest at some point, even if that means returning to the well-wisher.

The host community was to provide for the needs of the missionaries, during the time they performed their ministry (vv7ff; Mt 10:10f; 1 Cor 9:6 - 14). The disciples are to expect the type of opposition that Jesus himself experienced (vv10ff, 13 - 16; Mk 4:16 - 30). Once rejected, they are to leave all traces of contact behind (shake the dust) and depart. The final lot of their opponents will be worse than that of the sinful cities of the scriptures (vv12ff; Mt 10:15; 11:24).

Joyful enthusiasm marks the disciples' return from mission, as they witness the overthrow of the powers of evil (v17). Jesus describes their success as a striking downfall of Satan (vv18f; Mk 16:18). But even more important than their missionary success is the assurance of their place in the reign of God (v20; Mt 7:22f; Phil 4:3; Heb 12:23).

Everything we believe gives us reason for happiness. "To suffer or to die" may have made a saintly motto for some, but it is hardly an appealing way to live for God. There should be a great deal of happiness connected with our pursuit of often difficult objectives. There is a really Hebrew earthiness in Israel's description as a full-breasted mother. Yet what brings out the idea of contentment better than a cuddled child being nursed? There is something electrifying about Luke's account of the disciples' first mission. Jesus tempers their enthusiasm but does not extinguish it. He tells them that there are even better days ahead! The church always needs people who lift the spirit. Some great enthusiasts became dour and negative in the post-conciliar church. Others are so bogged down in administrative detail that the sight of the big picture—the great adventure—is lost. The basic message is clear: God wants us so badly that he sent his own Son to say so. No wonder the first missionaries moved too fast to carry luggage. We could use a little of that enthusiasm today.

It is small wonder that Paul is impatient with "circumcision or no circumcision." With so many major issues to die for, why become involved in dead issues? The marks of Christ; a new creation–such phrases came tripping off his tongue and flowing from his pen. Yes, his pain at times was great. But his joy was limitless. And he worked for others so that their joy could be complete.

Homiletic and Catechetical Helps

1. Hebrew poetry and the feminine in God.

2. Christian joy distinguished from passing pleasures.

3. Liturgy and joy.

4. Christian simplicity as a missionary imperative.

5. Mission in my life.

6. Explanation of Paul's crucifixion to the world.

7. Our crucifixion to the world.

8. The new Israel of God and the Jewish people today.

FIFTEENTH SUNDAY OF THE YEAR
Year A

Readings

> Is 55 - 10 - 11
> Rom 8:18 - 23
> Mt 13:1 - 23

Theme: Preparing for the Harvest

Using agricultural language, today's scriptures speak of the effectiveness of God's word. Isaiah tells us that just as the rain brings about desired results in fertile soil, so too God's word moves inexorably toward its fixed finality. However, in Jesus' parable of the sower, we are also reminded that not even God can effect in the human heart more than good will permits. The letter to the Romans teaches that not only are we destined for glory, but all of creation is joined with us in that hope.

First Reading

In antiquity the spoken word was an avenue of self-disclosure as well as an extension of the person, even invested with the characteristics of the speaker. God can create with a word because it bears within it the power and might of divinity. Words were not readily lost; they had a permanent and lasting quality, seen especially in blessings and curses. The word of God, then, spoken in both events and in teaching had a sacredness proper to God himself.

Second Isaiah today speaks of the effectiveness of God's word in bringing about determined results. This looked especially to Israel's return from exile (55:12f). The event will take place, indeed is on the horizon, because of Yahweh's veracity and ability to accomplish. Comparison is made with the rain and snow sent from the heavens (v10). Its mission does not occur haphazardly, nor is it a question of possibility only. The waters from above accomplish their mission and are viewed as returning ultimately to their heavenly source. So too will God's word achieve its end. In this case it looks principally to the return from exile.

Responsorial Psalm   Ps 65

The use of agricultural imagery continues in today's psalm in illustrating God's providence. Thanks to Yahweh for the blessings of creation characterize this hymn which begins by extolling Yahweh's goodness (vv2 - 5), then his power and might visible in creation (vv6 - 9), and finally his providential care (vv10 - 14).

The interchange between heaven and earth is vividly depicted. Yahweh produces the earth's fertility by providing the rain (v10; Is 30:23, 25). *God's stream* (v10): the waters stored above the sky or heavenly firmament (Gen 1:7; 7:11). This provides moisture at the time of planting and early growth (v11). *Your paths* (v12): perhaps tracks made by Yahweh's "cloud" chariot (Ps 104:3), which provide an opening for the rain to fall. The natural irrigation results in a verdant landscape of grain and flocks (vv13f).

Second Reading

In this reading Paul sees all of creation sharing in humanity's hope of final redemption. He contrasts present anxiety with the personal manifestation of God's Spirit (glory) to be part of final redemption (v18; 2 Cor 4:17). This revelation of God's "children" (better: "sons and daughters"; Gr: *uioi*) is anticipated by all of creation, destined to be part of that final moment (v19). Creation has been linked with humanity from the time of the fall. The sub-human order was cursed with Adam (Gen 3:15 - 19) and was made part of Noah's covenant of restoration (Gen 9:9ff). Thus it *was made subject* to the chaos and disorder of sin by God at the time of the fall but with the same *hope* of liberation that belongs to humanity (v20; 2 Pet 3:12f).

In the meantime, the human cries of frustration, looking to a full redemption yet to be achieved, are matched by that of creation as a whole, as if in labor (v22). *First fruits of the Spirit* (v23): the pledge of the "full harvest" to be realized with resurrection and final redemption. *Adoption* (v23): Accomplished in baptism (Gal 4:4f), it will reach its final stage with resurrection.

This concept of cosmic redemption, realized by the saving work of Christ (Col 1:20), unites humanity and the sub-human world in the spirit of the graced creation before the fall (Gen 1) and in anticipation of a new creation to be part of the end time (Rev 21:1 - 4).

Third Reading

The parable of the sower opens Matthew's book of parables (13:1 - 52), which contains seven illustrative stories, drawing on Palestinian life and culture. Today's reading presents the first parable (vv1 - 9), a digression on the purpose of parables (vv10 - 17), and finally an allegorical explanation of the sower parable (vv18 - 23). Jesus is presented as teaching from a boat because of the large crowd that lined the shore (v2).

The Story of the Sower. The Palestinian farmer scattered the seed before plowing, with the result that a fair amount was lost even though there was a sufficient yield where the soil was fertile. The point of Jesus' parable, grasped by the ears of faith (v9), is that the message which he delivers, despite its apparent ineffectiveness, will ultimately meet with great success. Just as the seed was lost if sown on a well-worn path, or on a thin layer of soil, or among thorns, so too with God's word. Many people will not be receptive. But just as there is always good soil to receive the seed in spite of the fall-out, so too the authentic hearers of Jesus' message will be many and strong in faith. As initially enunciated by Jesus, the parable makes the single point of steady and fruitful growth despite initial disappointments.

The Purpose of Parables. This is an insert into the narrative, introduced by Mark (4:10ff) and followed by Matthew and Luke (8:9f). It deals with parables in general and is otherwise unrelated to the sower story. *Parables* (Heb: *mashal*) (v10): The essence of the parable is the use of comparison. An intangible truth is clothed in the language of daily life so that the analogy illustrates the truth being presented. The *mashal*, then, may be brief, as in proverbs, maxims, or riddles, or more extended, as in many of the gospel parables and allegories. What the parable does in any form it takes is to present the truth in an oblique fashion. *Mysteries of the kingdom of heaven* (v11): truths concealed in God through the ages made manifest in the mission and teaching of Jesus.

Matthew gives his explanation on the use of parables from the perspective of the early church seeing an Israel which had not accepted Jesus. Therefore, contrary to the customary enlightening purpose of parables, this metaphorical presentation of the truth is seen as a hindrance to understanding, a punishment for the Jews' obduracy in opposing the truth. The teaching of the first part of the gospel (cc. 5 - 12) had fallen on deaf ears; only Jesus' disciples had remained open to the truth. Therefore his followers will continue to grow in their understanding of his mission and his parables (vv18 - 23) but to the unbelievers the parables will remain puzzles (v12). The words of Isaiah are seen as applicable (vv14ff; Is 6:9f). The parables, then, basically an avenue of communication, become in the actual circumstances a way of concealing the truth in punishment for lack of faith.

The disciples are singularly blessed for their openness to and receptivity of the truth (vv16f). What the great figures and upright personalities of the long Israelite tradition had longed to see was now the privilege of the disciples to experience with the dawn of the messianic era,

The Explanation of the Parable. At this point the experience of the early church is much to the fore as the initial parable becomes an allegory, with an interpretation given to each of the secondary features. While some allegorization of the parables by Jesus himself is not excluded, the detailed presentation of the categories of believers, as well as a certain awkwardness in the author's adaptation, points to this as an early church teaching.

In the original parable, the seed was the message sown among potential believers. Here the seed becomes the hearers (vv19, 20, 22, 23). These are respectively those who do not respond (the "path" seed), those who after initial enthusiasm fall away in adversity ("rocky ground" seed), those overcome by material concerns or worldly allurements ("thorny" seed), and those who embrace the truth and deepen their commitment ("good soil" seed). The allegory finds its natural setting in a church experiencing apostasy and persecution, as well as encouraging growth.

Many people do not realize the rich scriptural sources that undergird our environmental concerns. Humanity and the world are intimately linked from the first pages of Genesis to the last chapter of Revelation. The imprint of God is present in the nature that surrounds us. While nature itself "groans" through the calamities of earthquake, hurricane, and flood, that same creation can give us the beauty which some people, free of concrete pavements, see each day and others pack the van to move out and enjoy each vacation season. Each time we take a stand on industrial waste or volunteer for highway beautification, or even take seriously the recycling of disposables, we are showing reverence for a world that has a blessed destiny. For many environmental questions, there is no easy answer. But we are all more aware of the problem. And that in itself is a plus.

That fruitful harvest stands on the horizon. The picture is not all bright. Some seed never takes root. Faith never had a chance. In other cases faith is lost. How all of that works out cannot be answered in human terms. What is gratifying in reading the sower parable is to realize that in the end the positive results will far outweigh the negative. Salvation will be more to the fore than condemnation. In the meantime, the call is clear: nourishing and cultivating the faith; a life of prayer; ongoing formation and education in the faith; living our belief in service of others. It's the best way to prepare for the "new creation."

Homiletic and Catechetical Helps

1. The effect of God's word in our life.

2. The providence of God in the seasons of nature.

3. The parable as a tool of instruction.

4. Faith without roots.

5. Faith in adversity.

6. Faith and serious temptation.

7. Ways to deepen our belief.

8. The Bible and the environment.

9. The link between humanity and the world.

FIFTEENTH SUNDAY OF THE YEAR
Year B

Readings

Am 7:12 - 15

Eph 1:3 - 14
Mk 6:7 - 13

Theme: Mission

Amos was not a prophet by his own choice, nor would he cease to be one by another's decision. Yahweh had missioned him. The Marcan account of the missioning of the twelve is marked by a sense of urgency. In the first chapter of Ephesians, we are reminded of our calling as sons and daughters of God, its cost, and our concomitant responsibility.

First Reading

Amos arrives with the dawn of classical prophecy. Although a native of Judah, his prophetic career carried him to Israel, the northern kingdom. There he preached in the first half of the eighth century when Jeroboam was king of the north. Amaziah, a priest of the Bethel sanctuary, issues his peremptory dismissal of Amos only after the latter had predicted the demise of the king and the conquest of Israel (7:11). In derogatory terms, the priest refers to the prophet as a seer or visionary and orders him to leave the country (v12). Undoubtedly Amos' prediction was viewed as traitorous. He was excluded from Bethel, the main sanctuary and place of pilgrimage in the north, erected by the king to sever the people's religious ties with Jerusalem (1 Kgs 12:26 - 32)

I am not a prophet (v13): Although the verb is not expressed in Hebrew, the use of the present is normal. Prophets were a recognized group or guild in Israel and Judah. Distinct from the Bible's classical prophets, they were a mix of authentic and false claimants, traveled in groups, and were characterized by ecstatic behavior (1 Sam 10:10, 13; 1 Kgs 20:35; 2 Kgs 2:3, 5, 7). Amos makes a disclaimer of having any ties with these cult prophets. His work had been that of a shepherd and horticulturist. Since he is not a prophet by trade, he is not free to opt in or out. The Lord had called and commissioned him to Israel. His word will be the same wherever he is located. His predictions against

Israel (7:16f) will be effective independently of any action taken against him (v15).

Responsorial Psalm   Ps 85

The missionary proclamation of "peace" appears again in today's psalm. For a commentary, see the Second Sunday of Advent, Year B.

Second Reading

If today's first and third readings give insight into the nature of mission, the second deals with its content. Based on the Hebrew blessing of God or *berakah*, this passage betrays its liturgical origins, similar in both style and content to the early Christian hymn of Colossians 1. A trinitarian motif gives unity to the blessing in highlighting the work of the Father (vv3 - 6, 11f) acting through his Son (vv7 - 10) to bind humanity and all of creation to himself in the Holy Spirit (vv13f).

God extends heavenly blessings in and through Christ in order that a reconciled and sanctified people might stand before him (vv3f; 5:27; Rom 8:29). It is the pre-existent Christ, present throughout the blessing, who is at the center of God's saving plan prior to the world's creation. This holy people becomes adopted sons and daughters, united with God's own Son in the bond of the Spirit (v5; Gal 4:4 - 7; Jn 1:12). The process of sanctification redounds to God's glory through the visible effectivness of the grace that comes through Christ (v6; Col 1:13).

All of this is made possible by the death of Christ. Here *redemption* and *forgiveness* are equated (v7). Redemption signifies God's acquisition or "buying back" of his people from the domain of sin, and it effects at the same time the pardon of transgressions (v7; Col 1:14). *The mystery of his will* (v9): The "mystery" is common in inter-testamental Judaism, pointing to the concealed plan of God withheld from past ages and now revealed. Here that plan is universal redemption through the death-resurrection of God's Son.

The concept of all creation sharing in redemption is an important Pauline theme (Rom 8:20 - 23; Col 1:20). Christ at the epicenter is encompassed by two concentric circles—the first, the redeemed people of God, and the outermost, the entire sub-human creation.

Predestined by God's choice as part of the mystery, the elect give praise to God (vv11f; Rom 8:29f). *His glory* (v12): This is the external and perceptible manifestation of God's wisdom and power, seen in the mighty deeds of the exodus and now seen preeminently in his plan of salvation. The Christians, for their part, must respond in faith after receiving the preached kerygma, committing themselves to Christ (v13; Rom 10:12f, 17). The believer is stamped and *sealed* in the Spirit, clearly delineated as a member of God's household, and the same Spirit is the pledge (first installment) of a glory yet to come (v14; 2 Cor 1:22; 5:5)

Third Reading

Mark's account of the sending of the twelve, two by two according to custom, comes immediately after Jesus' rejection at Nazareth. Their mission to performs exorcisms and healing of the sick (vv7, 13) is basically an extension of that of Jesus himself. An anointing with oil (v13) had medicinal value in itself (Lk 10:34); by a logical extension it plays a part in healings as well. The practice continued to play a part in the ritual of the early church (Jas 5:14f). The apostles' preaching mission is a call to repentance in light of the kingdom's arrival. It is strikingly similar to the preaching of the Baptist (1:4) and different from that of Jesus (1:15). There would seem to be an effort here to distinguish this from their "full gospel" preaching after the resurrection (16:15f).

The austerity in travel is largely practical, not a distinctive asceticism (vv8f). It enabled them to move unhindered, underscoring the urgency of their task. Contrary to Matthew (10:10) and Luke (9:3; 10:4), the Marcan Jesus permits a walking stick (v8) and sandals (v9), best explained as accommodation to differing locales and customs. The local host community was to provide for their needs (Mt 10:10; 1 Cor 9:6 - 14); this, coupled with their sense of trust, excluded the carrying of money (v8). In not leaving the house of lodging, there was no temptation to seek better quarters (v10). The *shaking of dust from the feet* (v11) was a symbol of rejection and hopefully a thought-provoking gesture. In refusing hospitality to the twelve, the people were refusing the gospel. The apostles then set forth on their mission (v12), with their return reported later in the same chapter (6:30 - 33).

When action flows from deep conviction, it cannot be halted by simple decree. How much more is this the case when mission proceeds from God's personal directive. Amos may have been rebuffed but he couldn't be silenced. The twelve were so driven by their commission that human comforts and other considerations had no place. When faith becomes a passion, things change. Unfortunately too often religion becomes quite matter of fact. People are well served but seldom challenged. We have to remember that enthusiasm is infectious. There was a time when people, mostly in religious congregations, went willingly to bring the gospel to foreign lands with no likelihood of their ever returning. And they never lacked a sense of fulfillment. Our lives today become too circumscribed. It's always: "Yes, but. . ." We are hemmed in by caution, programs, administrative detail–and the list goes on. It may be very prudent, but somehow it lacks apostolic fire.

Ephesians summarizes the whole message: from sin to family status, universal redemption, all accomplished through the blood of God's Son, a first installment on an even better future. That is what got missionaries excited! And today the church has made it very clear that all of us are missioned. More than what we say or teach is the message of our lives. Doctor, lawyer, priest, civil servant, construction worker–all are called to place their skills at the disposal of God's reign. Some give medical service; others provide legal assistance for the poor. Some people donate their time to help the uninformed prepare their taxes. Others work collectively to repair houses and make them livable. In this way the good news of Ephesians receives multi-faceted expression.

Homiletic and Catechetical Helps

1. The lay mission in the church.

2. The sacrament of the sick.

3. The value of a simple lifestyle.

4. Providing for the needs of missionaries.

5. Predestination and free will.

6. Cosmic redemption.

7. The Holy Spirit as a first installment.

8. Chosen for the praise of God: importance of liturgy.

9. Redemption and forgiveness.

FIFTEENTH SUNDAY OF THE YEAR
Year C

Readings

> Deut 30:10 - 14
> Col 1:15 - 20
> Lk 10:25 - 37

Theme: The Concreteness of Faith

The call of faith is anything but esoteric or abstract. The will of God, says Deuteronomy, is within hearing distance. The decrees and commands of the Mosaic law now resided within the human heart. They were as near as the voice of conscience. In Luke's timeless tale of the good Samaritan, we are told that our neighbor is anyone in need and thus as close as the person next door. The hymn of Colossians places in relief the centrality of Christ in the church and in the universe.

First Reading

Unlike Saul who had to journey to the witch of Endor (1 Sam 28:8 - 19) or David's consultation with the ephod (1 Sam 30:7ff), the Israelite believer in daily life had no doubt of Yahweh's will in his or her regard. *This command* (v11): This is the observance of the book of the law, spoken of previously

(30:10). In communicating his will in the covenant ethic, Yahweh removed any element of the esoteric or remote. His will is to be found neither above (v12) nor beyond (v13) the grasp of his people. Not only is it heard in cult and teaching, but it is implanted within the heart. *In your mouths...in your hearts* (v14): The law is frequently taught (6:7; 11:19) as well as being the object of reflection (6:6; 11:12).

Responsorial Psalm   *Ps 69*

God's concern for the needy is much to the fore in this psalm. Commentary may be found in the Twelfth Sunday of Year A. The psalmist's confidence continues in spite of suffering and bitter rejection; his assurance rests on God's justice in vindicating the cause of the poor. The psalm's conclusion (vv36f) is a key to its exilic date in speaking of the rebuilding of Jerusalem and Judah. That God's concern for the needy is often channeled through other human beings gives the psalm linkage with today's liturgy of the word.

Second Reading

A commentary on the Colossians hymn is found in the Feast of Christ the King, Year C.

Third Reading

Jesus is tested by a lawyer, an expert in the Jewish law, probably a scribe (v25). In the ensuing process of question and counter-question, it is the lawyer himself (v27) and not Jesus (Mk 12:28f) who gives the summary of the law in quoting the combined Pentateuchal texts (Deut 6:5; Lev 19:18). It is this synthesis of the law and the prophets which is upheld by Jesus and eventually embedded in the life of the early church (v28; Mt 22:37ff; Rom 13:9; Gal 5:14; Jas 2:18). The joined love of God and neighbor lies at the heart of the Christian ethic.

The lawyer then poses the question as to who one's neighbor is (v29). In the subsequent parable (vv30 - 35), found only in Luke, Jesus makes the central figure a *Samaritan,* a religious and social outcast, ritually unclean in Jewish eyes (Jn 4:9). It is he who befriends and provides for a dying Jew. The latter is bypassed by cultic personnel, a priest and Levite, who avoid the apparently dead man to avoid becoming ritually unclean (Lev 21:11). On the other hand, the Samaritan goes beyond the demands of basic charity in providing for the man's needs (v35).

At this point Jesus reverses the lawyer's original question. The lawyer would have interpreted "neighbor" in Jewish terms as another Israelite. But the true answer emerges clearly in the story. The "neighbor" is anyone in need. But the final question of Jesus centers around the one who *acted* as neighbor (v36). The answer, of course, is the Samaritan. Though not a Jew, he is the true observer of the law, placing love above any other consideration. The fact that the lawyer cannot bring himself to speak the word "Samaritan" but only "the one" (v37) shows how difficult it is for him to accept the teaching. The lesson of the parable is that love of neighbor embraces a Jew, a Samaritan or anyone else.

For the Christian, the parable's importance lies in its upholding the priority of the spirit over the law and its note of openness to all people.

Many great minds have dedicated themselves to understanding the truths of faith through the centuries. Libraries are full of attempts to plummet the depths of revelation. But, when all is said and done, the heart of the Christian faith is open to everyone, even the illiterate. Its beauty lies in its accessibility. The truth of Christianity has become incarnate in every culture, in ways adapted to the understanding of all. Its basic ethic is not hard to grasp or difficult to interpret. It has no gnostic secrets understandable only to the enlightened. Christian moral teaching meets us in a constant variety of choices at every turn in life. The results of our moral choices come home to roost at the end of every day. This is the concreteness of faith.

The Christ that Colossians enthrones is the image of God, firstborn from the dead, the head of the church. But he is also the Christ who meets us in the person in need, like the man beaten and robbed lying along the road. How often a homeless person asleep on a park bench seems just as lifeless. This is also the Christ who calls us to see our neighbor in people of any color or race, religion or social category.

That is the teaching of today's parable. And isn't it interesting that a Samaritan, a member of a despised sect of untouchables, has been known for centuries as the man who is "good."

Homiletic and Catechetical Helps

1. Relationship between love of God and neighbor.

2. Applying the Samaritan parable to life today.

3. The spirit over the law.

4. The evil of discrimination: racial, ethnic, social.

5. The body and Christ the head.

6. Christ as the center and redeemer of the universe..

7. Christ, the firstborn of the dead.

8. Faith and environmental concerns.

SIXTEENTH SUNDAY OF THE YEAR
Year A

Readings

> Wis 12:13, 16 - 19
> Rom 8:26 - 27
> Mt 13:24 - 43

Theme: The Patient Judge

Wisdom today speaks of a God who judges justly, and, if the scales are tipped in any direction, it is on the side of leniency. In a series of parables, the Matthean Jesus draws again on the world of nature in pointing up the quite imperfect state of God's reign in its present existence. With considerable patience, God offers more than ample opportunity for conversion. In the reading from Romans, we are told not to worry about the perfect prayer. The Spirit, praying with us, compensates for our deficiencies.

First Reading

The justice of God in Wisdom contrasts sharply with the injustice of the wicked (1:10 - 2:24). In the events of the exodus (cc. 11 - 12), Yahweh's might and power were much in evidence, even though tempered by his patience (12:2). It is these two qualities of justice and mercy that appear in today's reading. When God is accused of acting unjustly, what is the measure against which he is judged, since there are no other gods with whom to compare him (v13; 6:7; Is 44:6, 8)?

The wicked in their evildoing became their own norm of justice, letting their strength bend any objective norms to their own will (2:11). It was a rule of power. But Yahweh has authentic power, as witnessed in the saving events of the exodus, which is used in the cause of right and finds expression in moderation toward the weak (v16; 12:2) His is a rule of understanding.

In the face of disbelief in his power, Yahweh does not hesitate to perform convincing deeds, as in the case of the Egyptians (12:27). It is in recognition of Yahweh as God that conversion can be attained and immortality can be reached (v17:15:3). The wicked use their limited might as an instrument of cruelty, whereas Yahweh with boundless might is restrained by the concerns of leniency and forgiveness (v18). The action of God against Israel's enemies was not geared to be death-dealing justice but an opportunity for repentance (v20). This was a lesson for the Israelites to administer justice with mercy and to strengthen the hope of repentance. In short, the experience of God's power pointed up his justice as well as his compassion.

Responsorial Psalm Ps 86

This lament places emphasis on God's patience and forbearance, in line with today's theme. The psalmist, perhaps the king, appeals to Yahweh because of his willingness to forgive (v5). The implicit recognition of sin as the cause of suffering is consonant with the traditional Hebrew linkage between wrongdoing and pain. Soulfully he recognizes Yahweh's singularity and universal sovereignty (vv9f). Again, in traditional thinking, he reconciles Yahweh's justice and mercy, with the latter much more in evidence, and the former elicited only after endurance has been spent (vv15f; Ex 34:6f; Ps 103:8). He asks for deliverance from his ordeal in an outpouring of mercy and strength (v16).

Second Reading

In the Christian's present condition, Spirit and flesh are still at war within the person. Even though one is rooted in the Spirit, the danger of reverting to the flesh remains present (8:12f). The Spirit gives access to God in prayer and enables the Christian to address God as "Abba," an otherwise unutterable expression (8:14f). This familiar form of intimate address was proper to Jesus, who now shares his Spirit of sonship with the believer (Gal 4:6).

Left to their own human resources, Christians would find their prayer ineffective and inadequate. But the Spirit overcomes human weakness and adds its own God-given effectiveness (v26). It is a question of God addressing God, with the Spirit here clearly distinguished from the Father. *One who searches the heart* (v27): As a reference to God in various biblical passages, it points up the interiority of his knowledge of the person (1 Sam 16;7; Ps 17:3). There is perfect coordination between the Spirit-filled heart and the Father because the Spirit has been missioned by the latter, with the Spirit's intent ultimately proceeding from the Father himself. The efficacy of Christian prayer, then, springs from its being Spirit-assisted.

Third Reading

Three parables drawing on images common to the Palestinian culture speak of the reign of God in its various manifestations. The *reign of heaven* in each parable is likened to the story as a whole, not the person or object first mentioned. The parable of the wheat underscores the coexistence of good and evil in the reign's present state (vv24 - 30); the mustard seed and yeast illustrate the remarkable growth of the believing community (vv31 - 34). A short digression deals with the use of parables (vv34f); finally the parable of the wheat is explained in a Matthean allegorization (vv36 - 43).

The weeds or darnel (Gr: *zizania*) (v25) resembled wheat in the early stages of growth and, entwined with the wheat, made an initial sort very difficult. At the time of the harvest separation was more easily made. The biblical image of the end time as a harvest is fairly common (Jer 51:33; Jl 4:13; Hos 6:11).

The point of the parable acknowledges that good and evil are present together in the reign of God. Unlike some Jewish eschatological thinking, this was not to be a company of the elect alone. The presence of both categories of people tempers any false hopes or rash action on the part of the disciples or later zealous church leaders. The parable as it stands is found only in Matthew, with some possible dependence on Mark's parable of the seed growing secretly (4:26 - 29).

The mustard seed (vv31f; Mk 4:30ff; Lk 13:18 - 21) is common to the three synoptics; the parable of the yeast is taken from Q by Matthew and Luke. In both, the main point centers on the remarkable growth of the reign after insignificant beginnings. The seed produces the large plant, with the reference to the birds of the air adding a note of universalism, a reign open to all people (v32; Dan 4:7ff; Ez 17:23; 31:6). Yeast is usually seen as a corruptive element (16:6, 11 - 12; 1 Cor 5:6 - 8); here it is viewed positively as bringing about an unusually large mass of dough (v33).

Unlike the enigmatic purpose of parables expressed earlier in Matthew (13:13ff), this text sees the parable as a vehicle for conveying the truth, even if in a clothed fashion. *The prophet* (v35): Actually the quotation is from the psalms (Ps 78:2) but for Matthew it is seen as a prophetic utterance pointing to Jesus' ministry. The parable, moreover, discloses the *mystery of God*, i.e. the plan of salvation, withheld from the ages past and revealed only in this final time (v35). The fact that the parable does not express everything unequivocally enables Jesus to give further instruction to his disciples (vv36f). As he does this, he dismisses the crowd (the unbelieving Jews) and will henceforth concentrate on instructing the disciples.

The allegorization of the parable (vv36 - 43), like that of the sower (13:18 - 23), reflects the conditions of the later church and should be seen as a Matthean interpretation. There are no less than seven allegorical elements (vv37ff), and the tilt of the parable is less on the aforementioned presence of good and evil as on the serious, even frightening character of final retribution (vv40ff). Christ coming as Son of Man and eschatological judge fits well his later post-Easter role (v41).This reign belongs to Christ until the "end of the age" (vv39, 49; 28:20) when it will pass to the Father (v43; 1 Cor 15:24).

The allegory runs thus. Christ sows the seed in the world (v37) with mixed results (v38). At the parousia retribution is definitive, particularly severe for the evildoers (vv40ff), and triumphant for the elect in resurrection glory (v43; Dan 12:3). *Wailing and grinding of teeth* (v42): a typically Matthean expression for misery and travail (8:12; 13:50; 25:30).

There probably was a time when, rather naively, we thought that the church was already the spotless bride of Christ. The fact is that the church is beset by humanness no less than its individual members. The good is there, and it is widespread. But there is no doubt that the weeds are there also and give every indication of remaining until the harvest. Neither the good nor the bad is restricted to single segments of the church. Both are found on all levels. We really shouldn't be scandalized although we are often hurt. After all, the prophets called Israel, the elect of God, a prostitute–strong language. However, it shows us the extent to which the sacred is capable of profaning itself. But remember the patient judge. As long as evil is present, there is a chance of conversion. All of this says that the church has an indispensable role to play as an instrument of God's love. But it still points beyond itself to God. There alone is perfection. It is on God that our gaze must be centered.

Even when we pray, we fall short. So much of our weakness emerges–distractions, weariness, carelessness. In a spirit of quiet prayer, or centering prayer, we are simply conscious of God's presence; we don't have to verbalize or keep ourselves "busy." The Trinity is at work within us. We don't have to get high marks. There is no scoring record. It is enough to be aware and to grow in that awareness.

Homiletic and Catechetical Helps

1. The church as the body of Christ.

2. The church as human and sinful.

3. The meaning of divine judgment.

4. The meaning of the reign of God.

5 The reign of God and the church.

6. Prayer in the Holy Spirit.

7. The different forms of prayer.

8. My experience of prayer.

9. The steady growth of God's reign.

SIXTEENTH SUNDAY OF THE YEAR
Year B

Readings

> Jer 23:1 - 6
> Eph 2:13 - 18
> Mk 6:30 - 34

Theme: The Tireless Shepherd

A careful reading of Mark's gospel makes the reader sensitive to the pressures that surrounded Jesus' ministry. It is a picture of rushing, pushing, and shoving crowds of people. In today's gospel, Jesus stands before them full of compassion. Jeremiah foresees a day when the neglectful shepherds of his time would be replaced by a king whose reign would be marked by solicitude. Ephesians celebrates the unity of Jew and Gentile achieved by the one reconciling act of Christ.

First Reading

The chronicles of the kings of Judah present a disappointing picture of the Davidic kingship, the line which was the channel of prophetic hope (2 Sam 7) and cultic promise (Ps 2; 45). Jeremiah is an exponent of the corruption and neglect which these leaders had visited on their people (ch. 22). Today's passage breaks from the litany of faithless kings as it looks to the future. After issuing his "Woe" to these past kings (vv1f), the prophet speaks of an era of restoration (vv3f) to be presided over by a messianic king, who will represent everything that his predecessors failed to be (vv5f).

The first duty of the king in a theocratic state was to uphold the interests of the deity, in this case, fidelity to the covenant and instruction in Torah. However, Judah's kings had been guilty of social injustice, luxurious living, and a variety of corrupt practices (22:13f, 17). Their people had been deprived of guidance and been sorely mistreated (v2; Ez 34:4 - 10).

Therefore, Yahweh himself will act as shepherd, first in restoring the people to their homeland by bringing the exile to an end (v3; 29:14; 32:37), and then by raising up kings faithful to the Davidic ideal (3:15; Ez 34:11 - 16).

An oracle is introduced at this point with a change from the prosaic to the poetic style and from consideration of future leaders to that of a single future king. This will be an era preceded by anticipation ("the days are coming"), still situated in an historical context, in which the messianic king will preside on the throne of David with total covenant fidelity (v5). *Righteous shoot* (Heb: *semah sadiq*) (v5): The descendant stemming from the line of David is referred to as a branch or shoot (Is 11;1; Zech 3:8; 6:12). As righteous, he will be a concrete manifestation of Yahweh's own justice (v6). The word "justice" (*sedeq*) appears in various forms three times in these two verses. At the same time, the king's reign will be marked by uprightness and wisdom.

This will be a time of joy for both kingdoms, with both north and south consistently present to Jeremiah's prophetic consciousness (cc. 30 - 31). *The Lord our justice* (v6): The ideal king is so designated because in his person God's saving justice in fidelity to his promises becomes evident (16:14f; Is 9:5f; 45:25; Ps 103:6). There is also a play on the name of the actual king of Judah, Zedekiah, in the repeated use of the word *sedeq*, implying, not too subtly, that the future king will be everything that the present one is not.

Responsorial Psalm   Ps 23

Today's theme of the Lord as shepherd makes this celebrated psalm appropriate. For commentary, see the Twenty-Eighth Sunday of Year A.

Second Reading.

The word "peace" appears four times in these verses, in one instance defining Christ simply as "our peace" (v14). Harmony between God and humanity was destroyed through Adam's sin; this resulted as well in an alienation among people themselves, as is highlighted in the Cain-Abel narrative (Gen 4).

Christ has restored the primeval relationship on the vertical (Rom 6:10) and horizontal (Gal 3:27f) plane. With that right order re-established, peace now exists between Jew and Gentile with the elimination of the barrier that stood between them (v14), brought about by the death-resurrection of Christ (v13). What results is a new creation and a new order centered in the formation of a new person, the body of Christ, wherein all find their unity (vv15f; Col 1:20ff). Christ is so much the cause and focal point of this whole process that he can simply be defined as "our peace" (v14).

A major obstacle to regaining this unity between Jew and Gentile was the role of the law in Jewish life. Central to Jewish faith, it was foreign and unknown to the non-Jews. In Christ the law has been abolished (v15), thus leveling the plateau between the two groups to effect the desired unity. The enmity that distanced God and humanity dies with Christ on the cross (v16). The Jews ("those who were near") and the Gentiles ("those who were far off") now become a single people (v17; Is 57:19). It is the action of the Spirit that not only binds the two groups but also gives both a direct avenue of communication with the Father (v18; Rom 8:14f).

Third Reading

This passage is transitional in Mark. It brings to a close the first mission of the twelve (6:7 - 13) and is a prelude to the story of the feeding of the five thousand (6:34 - 44). The term "apostles" (v30) is used of the twelve in this instance only, probably to distinguish them from John's disciples mentioned in the preceding verse. They will be apostles in the full sense only with their post-Easter commissioning. After they report their success (vv30, 12f), Jesus calls them to a desert place by themselves (v31). This note of isolation sets the scene for the hungry crowd without food in the following narrative. It also echoes the desert experience of Israel where Yahweh had provided food (Ex. 16). That Jesus calls them "by yourselves" is a Marcan lead phrase pointing to imminent revelation (4:34; 7:33; 9:2).

The pressure of the crowd is a Marcan motif. The large number precluded any respite for the disciples (v31). Moving with alacrity and determination, they arrive at the destination on foot ahead of the disciples by boat (v33). There is no shade of annoyance in Jesus' attitude despite the crowd's thwarting his desire to rest. He begins to teach at once, bringing to life the prophetic word of Jeremiah and others that Yahweh's people would be shepherded (v34; Num 27:17, Ez 34:5f).

Today's gospel bears many of those vivid Marcan features. It is one of those rare instances where Jesus' stated intent is thwarted by the needs of the crowd. His desire to be alone with the disciples after the excitement and enthusiasm of their first mission could not be realized. What a striking lesson as Jesus puts personal concerns aside because of his pastoral concern for others. Most of us are generally willing to help or to be present to others, but very often it is on our terms. We have an agenda which we like to have respected without undue disturbance. We don't like to be taken off-guard. The unforeseen easily becomes an irritant. But shepherding in the church, which today embraces many people in diverse ministries, calls for a Christ-like openness and responsiveness. How we do things is as important as what we do. That is the asceticism of Christianity. Jesus himself admitted that he had not a great deal to say on fast and abstinence. But when it came to being inconvenienced and put upon for the good of others, he gave us all a sterling example of self-sacrifice.

Peace is a word that is often on our lips. But today's epistle reminds us that peace is within our grasp; it has already been attained. We only have to actuate it. We have been reconciled with God, our neigh-

When was a time that you were "inconvenienced" for the good of others.

bor, and the universe. If that peace is disrupted, the fault is not God's. Violations of peace extend from the hostile remark to international conflict. Its absence has been keenly felt–families at odds, relationships destroyed, racial and ethnic divisions. It is all so contrary–not to what we are called to be, but to what we actually are. To be a Christian is to live in peace. It is much more than just the cessation of hostilities between wars. Peace is a state of being, uniting heaven and earth, and bought at a dear price, the death of God's Son.

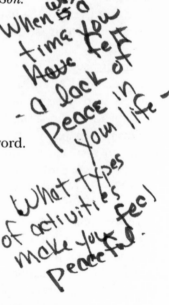

Homiletic and Catechetical Helps

1. Christ, the shepherd of his people.

2. The parish priest as pastor.

3. Serving others when inconvenient.

4. Teaching by example as well as by word.

5. The scriptural meaning of peace.

6. The walls of hostility in my life.

7. The single body of Christ.

8. Discrimination in our society.

SIXTEENTH SUNDAY OF THE YEAR
Year C

Readings

> Gen 18:1 - 10
> Col 1:24 - 28
> Lk 10:38 - 42

Theme: Ministry and God's Word

In the readings from Genesis and Luke today, a spirit of service comes to the fore in the offering of hospitality. In Greek the same word means both service and ministry, a twofold meaning that emerges in the gospel. In both readings, as service is being extended, God's word reaches the hosts. Abraham and Sarah are promised a child; Mary ponders the words of Jesus. In Colossians, Paul tells us that his sufferings for the church supplement those of Christ, as he proclaims the mystery now revealed, "Christ in you."

First Reading

With its strong emphasis on hospitality, this narrative from the Yahwist tradition is a classic example of semitic story-telling. To wish another person well by sharing a meal was an act of good will which concretely enhanced the existence of the person through the nourishment offered. It had such an aura of benevolence about it that it was unthinkable for it to be contradicted by an internal spirit of hostility or deception.

Abraham's visitor(s) fluctuate between being Yahweh himself (vv1, 3, 10) and three visitors (vv2, 4f, 8f). The narrative is oracular and intends to be an apparition of Yahweh, made visible in the form of the three men. It would have been impossible to look upon God (Ex 33:20), hence this visible expression. Abraham's immediate response to the three men is one of prodigious hospitality. An allusion to the true nature of the guests is present in Abraham's profound act of reverence (v2) and his addressing the leader as Adonai (Lord) (v3).

The host initially offers water for tired and dusty feet, an appreciated sign of cordiality in near eastern cultures. He then offers the chance to rest. The meal that is later offered with its abundance was reserved for special guests. *Three seahs* (v76): about half a bushel. *Curds* (v8; Is 7:15, 22): This was a cream or milk product in a semi-solid form like yogurt. The guests say very little in the narrative, placing in relief the aura of mystery or otherness (v5). Before their leave-taking, God's word is communicated in an atmosphere of cordiality and respect. Within a year, Sarah, already beyond the age of childbearing, will have a child (v10).

Responsorial Psalm   Ps 15

The upright person is the one who lives by the covenant norms and who readily distinguishes good from evil conduct. Abraham and the two women of today's gospel more than qualify as examples of the just person. For a commentary on the psalm, see the Twenty-Second Sunday of Year B.

Second Reading

Paul speaks of the joy that is his in being able to suffer for the church (v24), serving in the ministry of making known the mystery of God in Jesus (vv25 - 28).

The apostle suffers for the sake of the Colossians and for the church as a whole. In complementing "what is lacking in the afflictions of Christ," Paul adds nothing to Christ's all-sufficient act of atonement (Heb 9:26ff). But the total offering of Christ at the parousia will include the sufferings of those who endure apostolic hardship and tribulation. It is this which is still lacking. As a member of Christ's body, Paul is joined to the Lord in his sufferings, just as he has a share in the power of his resurrection (Phil 3:10). With his initial saving act completed, Christ continues to vanquish evil in and through the members of his body. Only when evil is completely subjected to Christ will he turn his reign back to the Father (1 Cor 15:24 - 28). In the meantime apostolic suffering on behalf of the church prolongs Christ's sufferings in bringing evil into subjection.

Paul serves as a minister of the gospel in bringing to fullness the effects of the word of God among them. *The mystery* (v27): As found in inter-testamental Judaism, as well as in the Hellenistic mystery cults, this was often concealed by the heavenly powers and made known only to the spiritual elite. For Paul, it is the saving work of Christ, the mystery concealed from past ages but now revealed for the benefit of all (v27). Destined for the Gentiles as well as the Jews, the mystery is summed up as "Christ in you" (v27), i.e. by his death-resurrection Christ now communicates his Spirit, through whom he lives in the Christian (Gal 3:20). This same Christ living in the believer is the "hope of glory," i.e. the concrete pledge of final salvation at the resurrection (1 Cor 15:22). Paul works to bring the believing community to a deeper understanding and growth in the truth that they may pass from the imperfect to the perfect (v28), from the immaturity of childhood in the faith (1 Cor 3:1ff) to the full stature of maturity in Christ (Eph 4:12f).

Third Reading

Early in the church's life, a problem arose centering on the primacy of the word of God over other forms of ministry (Acts 6:2). The solution in favor of the word is reflected in this engaging story of domesticity, found only in Luke. The context is important. It is part of the Jerusalem journey during which time Jesus imparts his teaching on discipleship (v38). Therefore, the story has a clear catechetical import. In addition, it follows immediately after the story of the good Samaritan (vv29 - 37), where the "active" dimension of the Christian life was to the fore in the Samaritan's act of charity. The present narrative will highlight the "contemplative" nature of faith.

Often noted is the singular role of women in the narrative. Jesus accepts the invitation to a woman's home (v38); her sister adopts the posture of a disciple before the master in sitting at Jesus' feet (v39; 8:35; Acts 22:3), and Martha becomes a type of Christian ministry or *diakonia* in *serving* (Gr: *diakonein*) the Lord (v40).

The Lord's response to Martha evolves around her anxiety and upset, not the value of her work. Her problem arises out of the plethora of concerns which face her (v41). However, the singular concern of the disciple must be the contemplation of God's word ("hearing the word," v39). Everything else is of secondary importance. It is the word of God that feeds ministry; without reflection on the word, ministry loses its meaning. This is the better part (v42). It is for this same reason that the apostles in Acts will dedicate themselves to God's word and leave the table ministry to others.

These two aspects of the disciple's life are not to be seen as contrasting. They are complementary but subordinate. In fact, it is within the context of charitable service (Martha) that the word of God is heard (Mary).

Women play a prominent part in Luke's gospel. In today's scriptures, two women express the heart of discipleship: contemplation and service. God's word and ministry are coupled, even though it is sometimes difficult to keep the balance. A life immersed in the active ministry without the contemplative dimension tends to become arid. A life lived wholly in contemplation with no sense of outreach resembles more an esoteric cult than the faith of the New Testament. The two are not dichotomized. Our faith perspective and awareness of God's presence flow into ministry, just as ministry becomes contemplative when God is seen in human need. Today's gospel, however, gives priority to contemplation—and justly so. It is only in an every deepening perception of "Christ in us" that our sense of mission remains strong. It was in the desert that Christ strengthened his disciples for mission.

And what is it that we contemplate? I no longer live my own life but Christ lives in me. So close is that unity that our sufferings in the faith become his. We are actually a part of his saving work just as we shall share in his resurrection. We are never alone. Our joys and sorrows are shared. Our work for God's reign may often seem so unproductive, so isolated, so little appreciated. But in faith we know it is not so. Christ in you, your hope of glory.

Homiletic and Catechetical Helps

1. Food sharing: the significance of the family meal.

2. The sacredness of hospitality.

3. Action and contemplation in the Christian life.

4. The complementarity of men and women in ministry.

5. The meaning of sharing in Christ's suffering.

6. How does my faith mature?

7. The meaning of the mystery: Christ in you.

8. A universal or catholic faith.

SEVENTEENTH SUNDAY OF THE YEAR
Year A

Readings

> 1 Kgs 3:5, 7 - 12.
> Rom 8:28 - 30
> Mt 13:44 - 52

Theme: The Gift of Wisdom

Wisdom is not the same as intelligence, nor is a smart person necessarily a wise one. Wisdom directs knowledge properly in life. It understands what is best for oneself and for others and then works to attain it. Solomon, in today's reading from 1 Kings, asks for this gift to arrive at correct and just decisions in directing his people. Wisdom in today's gospel lies in appreciating the value of God's reign and then sacrificing everything to be part of it. In the passage from Romans, Paul outlines the stages of God's election from foreknowledge to the final moment of glorification. True wisdom is also found in living fully every stage of that call.

First Reading

Sanctuaries were sacred places of divine communication. Revelatory dreams were associated with places of worship where Yahweh was in a certain sense localized. For Jacob it was Bethel (Gen 28:11 - 19); for Samuel it was Shiloh (1 Sam 3:2 - 18). For Solomon the dream comes at Gibeon, a sanctuary northwest of Jerusalem, one of the country's important cultic sites prior to the construction of the temple (v4).

To Yahweh's offer to grant a request (v5), Solomon's response has its own measure of wisdom. He is reassured in asking in view of God's promise to David regarding his son and successor (v7; 2 Sam 7:13ff). His request is based on two factors: his own inexperience (v7) and the growing size of the population (v8). These are formidable obstacles for the young king. *Understanding heart:* (Heb: *leb shomea:* "a listening heart") (v9): Since the heart is the seat of the intellect more than of the emotions, the request is for a sensitive and discerning mind. This would give the king the ability to distinguish the just cause from the unjust and to arrive at the best decisions in the people's regard.

The Lord commends Solomon's sense of priorities in not seeking personal gain or revenge against enemies (vv10f), and he accedes generously. Solomon's gift comes into play in the subsequent narrative of the two harlots (vv16 - 27).

Responsorial Psalm   Ps 119

The psalm is didactic as it sings the praises of the law. It is the longest in the psalter and is alphabetical, with each stanza beginning with the successive letter of the alphabet and each verse within the stanza beginning with the same letter. The wisdom of the law is upheld throughout, and the pursuit of that wisdom is the psalmist's all-consuming good. Torah has a value far beyond the most precious material goods (v127), and the desire to live is related to a continued and joyful observance of the law (vv76f). The great value of the law is the guidance and direction it gives to life. It is a clearly marked path, present even to the unlettered, which brings fulfillment and joy (v130). Strongly accented is the note that it is the law itself which attracts the conscience of the faithful Yahwist (vv127ff). The psalmist needs no exhortation to observance nor does he register any temptation to desist.

Second Reading

This celebrated "predestination" text has been variously used and misused. It should be read in its entirety as the divine plan for "those who love God" (v28), i.e. those who have responded to the call of Christian discipleship. The passage highlights God's providential care for the believer at every stage. It is this purpose and plan which has set election in motion, a plan which terminates in the glory of resurrection (v30; 2 Thes 2:14). God's free election preceded human existence (v29; 1 Pet 1:2) and was guided toward a life in Christ. Image of his Son (v29):

The Christian is called to reproduce within himself or herself a likeness of Christ, perfected through an ongoing transformation in grace (2 Cor 3:18; 4:4ff). Christ then becomes the first-born of many followers, who are born anew in the Spirit and destined for glory (v39). Therefore, at every step—foreknowledge and election, call, justification, and eventual glorification—the plan of God's love is being realized (v30).

Third Reading

Three short parables, all exclusively Matthean, concludes the evangelist's "book of parables" (c. 13). Two of these, the hidden treasure and the pearl (vv44 - 46), point to the great value of the reign of God; the third speaks of the coexistence of the just and unjust within the kingdom prior to the parousia (vv47ff). Finally there is a rather typical Matthean version of the role of the teacher in the church (vv52f).

Wisdom presented as the much desired prize, worthy of every effort to attain, is an oft repeated motif of the wisdom literature (Prov 2:4; 4:7). In comparing the possession of God's reign or Christian discipleship with a hidden treasure (v44) or a pearl (v45), the value is set at a very high price. Pearls were as precious as gold or silver. A treasure would be hidden in a field by a harried landowner in a country beset by invasion and turmoil. That efforts to live discipleship are expended joyfully underscores the true nature of Christian asceticism. It is not a question of denial and hardship in search of a good. Rather, it is the good in hand, of an inestimable worth, that prompts whatever sacrifice is needed. True wisdom, then, sees God's reign and the following of Christ as the greatest good beside which all other things fade in comparison.

The parable of the fishnet (vv47f) hearkens back to the parable of the wheat and the weeds (13:24 - 30, 36 - 43). The picture is one of the large net drawn by several fishermen in different boats. In its large sweep it picks up all types of fish, the fresh and the rotten, the clean and the unclean (Lev 11:9 - 12). The sort is made only when the shore is reached (v48). So too the final separation of the just and unjust will be made with the return of the Son of Man at the parousia. As in the case of the parable of the wheat and weeds, emphasis here falls on the severity of punishment (vv49f; 13:41f); no mention is made of the future lot of the just. It is the church's concern with "backsliding" that comes to the fore (13:18 - 23).

In concluding his section on parables, Matthew ends on a characteristic note, an appreciation for the old as well as the new. The disciples continue to grow in their understanding of Jesus' mission (v51). *The scribe ... instructed* (v52): The Jewish scribes were those skilled in the knowledge and interpretation of the law. Christian scribes (23:34) were evidently teachers of the new law within the faith community. The scribe was able to draw on the old (the law and the prophets) as well as the new (Jesus' teaching). Matthew shows marked respect for the Jewish Torah and upholds its validity, while calling the Christian community to go beyond it (5:17 - 20). Hence, both play a part in Christian teaching at this period in the church's development. In placing this logion where he does, Matthew evidently sees the parables as part of the "new" in the scribe's storeroom.

It was at great personal cost that many people became Christians in the early days of the church. Yet they saw it as the pearl of great price, the treasure hidden in the field. Many died for the faith long before it had stood the test of time. Many of us were born into the community of faith. But how many of us see the faith as the precious gift about which the gospel speaks. That sense of excitement about the faith may well have faded. It is all so much taken for granted. Not too many years ago, a trip to Europe in one's lifetime was little more than a dream. Today it is often considered another part of the high school experience. What is left to anticipate or enthuse over? Self-denial today is unpopular because people do not see the reason for it. If one denies oneself to get something, then it is presumed that the goal is worthwhile. If there is no real goal, then there is no need for exertion. If there were no Olympics, would we expect years of rigorous and exacting preparation? If Christian discipleship really filled our being, if that gift were really appreciated, then self-denial would fall into place. If we were full of Christ, everything else would be of lesser value.

Paul tells us that we have been called, elected by God, supported by grace, and destined for eternal life. Again, how conscious of that are we? A call from anyone important has to generate enthusiasm. But religion is seen by so many as a chore, a duty, rules to be observed. It is all rather lackluster. True wisdom looks to the proper ordering of our life. The Christian message is unparalleled as a way of life, demanding certainly, but full of peace and hope. It tells us that God will not abandon us. The gift of Jesus is the greatest wisdom, the pearl to be cherished. Indifference or passivity just does not fit the bill. If other things count more than our faith, then it's time to ask the central question: Is it God's fault or ours?

Homiletic and Catechetical Helps

1. The difference between wisdom and intelligence.

2. Wherein lay Solomon's wisdom?

3. Faith as the dominant value in our life.

4. The lesson of the fishnet parable.

5. Examples of combining the new and the old in our faith.

7. Predestination and free will.

8. The meaning of Christian vocation.

9. Growing in appreciation of the faith.

SEVENTEENTH SUNDAY OF THE YEAR
Year B

Readings

> 2 Kgs 4:42 - 44
> Eph 4:1 - 6
> Jn 6:1 - 15

Theme: The Bread of Life

Today's scriptures inevitably bring the eucharist to mind. In 2 Kings, Elisha provides for the needs of a multitude with twenty loaves of bread. In John's gospel, Jesus feeds five thousand with five loaves and two fish, in an account which bears a strong eucharistic imprint. The unity which marks the church should be reflected in Christian conduct. This is the lesson from today's reading from Ephesians.

First Reading

The providential nourishment of God's people begins with the manna and quail of the exodus (Ex 16). In the Elijah-Elisha cycle of miracle stories, connected with the prophets' career, the miraculous feeding of a hungry widow and her son by Elijah is done with prodigality (1 Kgs 17:7 - 16). Since events in the life of the two prophets are frequently paralleled, it is not surprising to find a feeding in the Elisha cycle as well. This story has also had an influence on the loaves and fish account in Jesus' ministry, as the pairing in today's liturgy suggests.

The offering of first fruits of the soil to the Lord at the sanctuary was customary; here the same is offered to the prophet as well, suggesting the esteem in which Elisha was held (v42). The donor comes from Baal-shalishah, a town southwest of Samaria. The calm directive of the prophet to the incredulous questioner throws into strong relief the subsequent miraculous action, an exchange closely paralleled in the New Testament account of the loaves (v42; Mk 6:37ff). As is typical of the feeding miracles, there is not only enough to eat but food left over (v44).

Responsorial Psalm   Ps 145

This psalm appears at different times in the liturgical year in celebration of Yahweh's kindness. (See the Twenty-Fifth Sunday of Year A.) The verses read today emphasize Yahweh's providential care as recognized by humans and the works themselves in creation and salvation (vv10f). The natural order is so regulated in its dependence on providence that no creature goes lacking (vv15f). The Lord is never far from those who depend on him.

Second Reading

The picture of Paul as a prisoner is evoked in an epistle which on critical grounds is generally regarded as being of non-Pauline authorship. The author here argues for a spirit of unity on the basis of the objective unity which the church possesses. These virtues center around mutual respect and a humble spirit, as befits those who are called as the elect of God (vv1f). The Spirit received in baptism unites Christians among themselves and re-establishes that harmony and peace which had been lost through sin. Thus love, unity, and peace become inseparable (vv2f; Col 3:14ff).

There are seven objective "unities" which undergird the moral imperative. In the *one body* of Christ, all have been baptized. This insertion into the body of Christ is effected by the *one Spirit* (v4a; Rom 12:5; 1 Cor 10:17). It is the Spirit who is the pledge of future glory, *the one hope,* which is the common destiny of all (v4b; 1:13f). Converts from a Gentile background are reminded that their *Lord is one* (1 Cor 8:6). Within the framework of an evolving church there is emphasis on the *common faith* professed by all and the common rite of *baptism* (v5). The *one God* (v6; Rom 3:30), who is also Father, remains transcendent but all-pervasive (Acts 17:28); the fourfold use of *all* (Gr: *panta*) underscores God's intimate presence to the whole of creation and not just the human population.

Third Reading

The miracle of the loaves in John is part of his "book of signs," portraying events in Jesus' life all of which point to a deeper reality in the life of the faith community. In the Johannine miracles, there are two levels of understanding, one centering on the event itself, the second on its meaning in the life of the church.

The Event Itself. The miracle of the loaves is the only miracle of Jesus to be found in all four gospels (Mk 6:34 - 44; Mt 14:13 - 21; Lk 9:10 - 17). *Sea of Galilee of Tiberias* (v1): Tiberias was a later name given to the Sea of Galilee, with the completion of the Roman city of Tiberias. Here it is an appended gloss. More so than in the synoptics, here the initiative of Jesus comes to the fore. He wants to satisfy their hunger (v5), and, after performing the blessing, distributes the loaves himself (v11). Cast so prominently, Jesus is something of a Moses figure, recalling God's provision of bread in the desert. Again, the abundance is characteristic of God's generosity (v13).

The Second Level of Understanding. It should be noted that this narrative precedes the bread of life discourse in the same chapter. Hence, the bread is already seen as symbolic of Jesus himself as well as of the eucharist. The providing of food symbolizes the nourishment to be found in the person and words of Jesus as well as in the sacrament. The question posed to Philip on the natural level (v5) is answered on the same plane (v7). For Jesus, however, it is transitional, moving toward a fuller faith level, i.e. his willingness to provide miraculously, and, secondly, the people's need for more than material bread (v6). The Passover is near (v4), the feast that figures prominently in the death of Jesus and, in the synoptic gospels, in the institution of the eucharist. Jesus "took" the loaves, "gave thanks" (Gr: *eucharistesas*), and "distributed": all three verbs appear in the synoptics' liturgical account of Jesus' action at the last supper (Mk 14:22; Mt 26:26; Lk 22:19). The order to "gather the fragments" (Gr: *klasmata*) uses the same term employed in the early church to refer to the eucharistic elements.

There can be no doubt that John carries the narrative to a level of eucharistic catechesis. The Christians hearing or reading the account were called to realize that Christ provides for them no less than for the people of his ministry. He feeds now in his word and especially in the eucharistic offering.

The people recognize Jesus as the prophet, the figure of Elijah returned, the herald of the messianic era (v14: Mal 3:1, 23). The reference to kingship is a recurring Johannine motif. Jesus wants to avoid at all cost any confusion over current notions of kingship as related to his own mission (v15; 18:36).

In John's account of the loaves and fish, Jesus takes the initiative. He observes the people's need, responds, and himself distributes the bread: Jesus at the total service of his people, the humility of God.

The eucharist stands not only for God's willingness to accompany us on the journey but also for his keen awareness of our needs in our weakness. In fact, it is God who takes the first step toward us, not once but repeatedly. In John there are no distinctions made between disciples and the crowd in Jesus' outreach. It is simply Jesus and people. In the eucharist there is total equality; we are all one. This is the real image of what the Christian community is to be. Before God's altar stand rich and poor, the learned and illiterate, Asiatics, whites, blacks, and native Americans. Other than for being disciples, they are indistinguishable. There is no precedence in approaching the table of the Lord. And that same spirit should carry into life.

The seven basic "unities" of Ephesians would cause no discord at an ecumenical gathering. They are central, and around them we would all concur. These are areas in which many Christians already find their unity. The next section of that same chapter of Ephesians then goes on to speak of the church's diversity. We need both. Unity with diversity is the hallmark of Christianity. Unity is not uniformity. Healthy diversity, arising from culture and custom, enriches the church. It is not always easy to keep the balance between unity and diversity. But try we must. It is part of a two thousand year heritage.

Homiletic and Catechetical Helps

1. The eucharist as an expression of God's providence.

2. The eucharist as a meal.

3. The eucharist as a sacrifice.

4. The connection between the miracle of the loaves and the eucharist.

5. John's gospel and the sacraments.

6. The eucharist as an act of thanksgiving.

7. Unity in Christian essentials.

8. Diversity within the church.

SEVENTEENTH SUNDAY OF THE YEAR
Year C

Readings

> Gen 18:20 - 32
> Col 2:12 - 14
> Lk 11:1 - 13

Theme: Importuning God

Like a shrewd customer at an Oriental bazaar, Abraham presses Yahweh to bargaining limits in today's first reading. To determine how far the Lord's will to save will go, he works skillfully to save as many citizens of Sodom as possible. The Lucan Jesus reminds us that God is to be pursued aggressively. Annoyance reflects well on the petitioner and eventually elicits a positive response. The Christian passage from death to life and from flesh to Spirit is succinctly presented in today's reading from Colossians.

First Reading

The three men of the story represent collectively an appearance of Yahweh, who earlier in the chapter has promised Abraham and Sarah a child within the year (18:9 - 12). The three of them set out for Sodom, a city clearly destined for divine punishment because of its wickedness. *Their sin* (v20): There are differing shades of interpretation on the nature of the sin, even within the Bible. In the Genesis narrative, if the subsequent lot of the men is to be understood as the sin characteristic of Sodom (19:1 - 11), then it is homosexual conduct, addedly serious when directed against visitors in violation of hospitality—thus the origin of the word "sodomy." In Ezekiel, while this is not excluded, the sin is viewed generically as high living with a lack of social concern (Ez 16:49f). Jeremiah evidently sees it as a general moral decay (Jer 23:14).

The two men, later referred to as "angels" (19:1), continue

their journey together, leaving the stage occupied only by Yahweh and Abraham (v22). Abraham's dominant interest is not with saving Sodom but with determining Yahweh's sense of justice. Since evil was viewed as a corruptive force infecting the whole of a social body, the destruction of the innocent with the sinners would not have been looked at askance. Total war was an accepted reality, with the elimination of all inhabitants of an enemy town or village (1 Sam 15:1 - 3). This narrative, however, will show Yahweh as selective in the execution of justice.

The patriarch bargains with Yahweh for the lives of the just, speaking respectfully, even obsequiously in pressing his case (vv23ff, 30ff). As an astute bargainer, he drops the figure first by fives (vv28f) then by tens (vv30ff), as the Lord proves himself increasingly flexible. He stops at ten because below that number Yahweh can easily provide for individuals (v32:19:12ff).

The story is anthropomorphism at its best in the Yahwist tradition from which it comes. The scene of Yahweh and Abraham engaged in spirited conversation highlights the closeness of the patriarch's relationship with the Lord.

Responsorial Psalm   Ps 138

The psalm is a song of gratitude for Yahweh's response to prayer. A commentary is found on the Fifth Sunday of Year C.

Second Reading

The effects of baptism are here outlined in what appears to be part of an early Christian hymn. It is strikingly similar to the description of baptism given in Romans (6:3f). Building on the baptismal ritual of submersion and emersion, the prior step is seen as incorporation into Christ's death, which is prolonged in the Christian's ongoing death to the life of the flesh (12a; 3:5). The second step of the process, connected with emerging from the waters, is a joining to Christ's resurrection. On the part of the baptized, this requires faith for its effectiveness, a faith in the power of the God who brought Jesus himself to life (v12; Rom 1:4). This twofold dimension of union with Christ in his death and resurrection is central to Paul's Christian anthropology.

The death-life passage is also a move from sinfulness to Spirit-life (v13). Formerly the Colossian community had lived a life of sin, a spiritual uncircumcision of carnal concerns (v11). The transition through baptism to new life is here explicitly identified with the pardon of all sin. Legal language is used to describe the effects of redemption. *The bond* (Gr: *cheirographon*, "handwritten note") (v14): Used in the transactions of creditors and debtors, it would here refer to human indebtedness before God (Eph 2:14ff). This bond with all its demands was affixed by God to Christ's cross, nailed thereto, and thus made extinct.

Third Reading

Jesus' teaching on prayer includes his own prayer given to the disciples (vv1 - 4), joined to two parables emphasizing the importance of perseverance (vv5 - 13). It can be safely presumed that there was some concern about unanswered prayer within the Lucan community.

As before every major teaching moment (6:12; 9:18; 9:28), the Lucan Jesus is at prayer. As was common for disciples with their own rabbi, the apostles ask for a prayer that would be as distinctive as that given by John the Baptist (v1). The Lord's Prayer in Luke is briefer than in Matthew. Although the two coincide in the major petitions, there are different nuances growing out of the experience of distinct churches.

Luke places strong emphasis on the eschatological features of the prayer, while considering the daily life of the Christian community. *Father* (v2): This direct and unqualified address of the Father was initially proper to Jesus and is now shared by all Christians in light of their baptism (Gal 4:6). Their incorporation into the inner life of the Godhead assures them an access in communication which is familial and unmediated. God's name shares in his own holiness as an extension of his person. The petitioner prays that this holiness may be augmented by the sanctity of the believers, who reflect God's glory (v2a). Then may the reign of God, already inaugurated in Jesus, be brought to its conclusion with the final return of the Son of

Man (v2b; 21:27). *Daily bread* (Gr: *arton epiousion*) (v3): The meaning of the adjective is much controverted. It is frequently translated, with reason, as "our *future* bread." The bread of the heavenly meal was often identified with the end time yet to come. This would then be a request, accompanying the desire for the kingdom's coming, for the ushering in of the final heavenly meal. Its anticipation in the present ("each day") would be a reference to the eucharist, the foretaste and pledge of the final banquet. Other commentators, translating the adjective as "daily," see it as a prayer for the material needs of daily life (v5).

In view of the tribulation to precede the end time, there is a petition for the forgiveness of sins, based on the petitioner's willingness to forgive offenses in the commerce of daily life (v4a). In fact, the petition in Luke flatly states that this spirit of forgiveness is already normative in the petitioner's life (17:3f). Finally returning again to eschatological language with its cosmic and human upheaval (21:25 - 28), the prayer asks for deliverance from the "test" (Gr: *peirasmon*), that moment of trial with its dread and terror before final salvation (v4b). In its eschatology and its brevity, the Lucan prayer may be closer to the words of Jesus than its Matthean counterpart.

While retaining the heart of its original meaning and intent, the Lord's Prayer as canonized through centuries of tradition has been adapted to later needs and circumstances in the course of time.

The parable of the importunate friend (vv5 - 8) seeking assistance late at night stresses perseverance in prayer, a virtue evidently in need of strengthening in Luke's time (18:1 - 8). Moreover, the father-son parable makes the point of a favorable response to persistent prayer (vv11ff). The examples used of a good friend (v5) and a human father (v11) point up the close bond existing between God and his sons and daughters. If in human affairs, wherein there is a proneness toward evil, good is extended in need, *a fortiori* God will do the same.

The Holy Spirit (v13): Luke's substitution here is important. The heavenly Father's response does differ from that of humans. He does not necessarily bestow the "good things" of life, as desired (Mt 7:11). But what is never lacking is the gift of the Spirit for guidance in dealing with human necessities and directing the person's will. What is all-important is to avoid discouragement and to remain constant in prayer. Even if it does not always elicit the response desired, it is never disregarded (vv9f).

There is something very human about today's scriptures. God is certainly not accorded an aura of otherness or aloofness. His exchange with Abraham is lively and engaging. Jesus' parables on perseverance are very down to earth, even humorous. That dimension of our faith should not be overlooked. Paul has God hammering away at Christ's cross as he does away with the charges against us. The transcendence of God is important for faith, for liturgy, and for forming a Christian conscience. But there is also a charm about inspired human speech regarding God. That too is part of the message. Jesus' homespun Palestinian parables really don't lend themselves to being sanitized. We don't serve religion well in identifying it solely with spotless sanctuaries and shining marble, with floral arrangements and flowing vestments. A crying baby, a hearty laugh, a good round of applause—even in church—are an integral part of the mix of faith.

Are not all those ways in which liturgical art and practice try to incarnate the Christian message attempts to do exactly what Jesus did? Faith is not just about a world beyond. Much of it is about living in the here and now. And we do that as people, as men or women, as citizens of a nation, as part of a city or region. God did not hesitate to plunge into the human scene. In so doing he accepted limits. He spoke to us in books, written not in universal tongues but in three languages—Hebrew, Aramaic, and Greek. And in becoming flesh, he laughed, cried, told interesting stories, and mixed with both men and women quite freely. In today's scriptures, God lets Abraham strike a good bargain. Jesus tells us that his Father can be pestered and importuned into answering—fascinating insights into God, but also interesting dimensions of faith.

Homiletic and Catechetical Helps

1. Personal impressions of Abraham's bargaining.

2. The Lord's Prayer in our Christian life.

3. The prayer of petition.

4. How God answers prayer.

5. Sodom and understanding human homosexuality.

6. Baptism: our union with Christ.

7. Death-resurrection as related to our moral choices.

EIGHTEENTH SUNDAY OF THE YEAR
Year A

Readings

> Is 55:1 - 3
> Rom 8:35, 37 - 39
> Mt 14:13 - 21

Theme: Food in a Desert Place

Today Second Isaiah tells the returning exiles that if Yahweh is truly the center of their lives, their aspirations will be fulfilled and their needs met. The Matthean account of the loaves finds Jesus in a desert place with a hungry crowd. His response to the physical hunger of the crowd in a more than ample fashion suggests the eucharist where the Lord continues to feed his people. Paul finishes the eighth chapter of Romans with a burst of song in praise of Christ who has loved us with such force that it eliminates any obstacle between the lover and the beloved.

First Reading

The exiles' return to Jerusalem was marked by emphasis on a new theocratic state. Rather than highlighting the traditional institutions of kingship and the Sinaitic covenant, Second Isaiah prefers to look at God's engagement with the people in actualizing a new covenant (Jer 31:31 - 34).

Drawing on a wisdom motif, an invitation is extended to the restored people to turn wholeheartedly to Yahweh (v1). The call is like that of Lady Wisdom, attracting the person who is willing to enter her halls in search of understanding and in abandonment of folly (Prov 9:4ff; Sir 24:18ff). Yahweh is the speaker here who addresses those who are without material resources. They need only an open spirit to be fully satisfied. Much of that which ordinarily attracts the human spirit is deceptive and unfulfilling. It is foolish to become ensnared in the inauthentic (v2).

The Everlasting Covenant (v3): This goes beyond the covenant of Sinai. Second Isaiah elsewhere speaks of the ancient covenant with Noah (55:9 - 10) and Abraham (51:2); he sees the new relationship with the people as actualizing anew God's earliest covenants (24:5). The new covenant will bring to life in a lasting fashion God's primitive contact with his people. No great emphasis is placed on the covenant of Sinai nor on that with David (2 Sam 7:8 - 16), with the latter treated in a summary fashion (v3). The promise made to David is seen as benefiting the people as a whole. In this scenario for the future it is a personal and direct relationship with Yahweh, with no emphasis on mediating structures, that is envisioned.

Responsorial Psalm   Ps 145

This psalm highlights God's goodness, covenant love, and forgiveness, especially as seen in his providential care. For further commentary, see the Seventeenth Sunday of Year B and the Twenty-Fifth Sunday of Year A.

Second Reading

These verses conclude a section of Romans wherein Paul has discussed the role of the law, the freedom acquired in Christ, and the meaning of life in the Spirit (cc. 6 - 8). In light of all that has been said, the apostle sees nothing in the whole of the created order that is able to separate the believer from the love of God that reaches him or her in the saving death-resurrection of Christ. No human or spiritual accuser (vv33f), no human distress (v35), nor preternatual power (vv38f) can sever the Christian from that overwhelming love communicated in God's Spirit.

Paul speaks of the difficulties and hardships arising from the Christian mission, many of which he had himself experienced (v35; 2 Cor 4:8f; 11:23 - 28). Christians not only bear patiently their lot of suffering, they actually triumph over adversity through the power of Christ (v37). So convincing is this power of love that Christians are not intimidated by the most powerful forces of the universe. *Angels or principalities* (v38): celestial beings who exercised control over the universe; whether for good or ill is not specified (1 Cor 15:24; Eph 1:21). *Present things...future things* (v38): Probably astrological predictions, pointing to the influence of the stars on human behavior. *Height...depth* (v39): A reference to the planetary system in which stars were so positioned as to effect conditions on earth. In gradually ascending stages of natural and preternatural forces, Paul, after setting forth the extent of God's love in bringing the elect from death to life, hymns that love as invincible.

Third Reading

There are striking similarities in the loaves and fish story which appears in all four gospels. The reader is, therefore, referred to the commentary on the Johannine account (Seventeenth Sunday of Year B). The comment here will be largely restricted to the differences from John in the Matthean narrative.

The withdrawal of Jesus in the first gospel is occasioned by news of the Baptist's death (14:3 - 11), pointing up the sorrow that Jesus experiences with his forerunner's demise (v13). Jesus' motive for responding to the people's need is compassion, a point made also in Mark (6:34) but an emotional note rare in Matthew. Here it leads to a healing of the sick (v14), whereas Mark speaks only of teaching (v14).

As in the other accounts, the episode is to be read against the background of the feeding in the desert at the time of the exodus (Ex 16) and Elisha's feeding of the crowd (2 Kgs 4:42ff). Its eucharistic language (*blessing...breaking...giving*) places the account with the other gospels in the category of a sacramental catechesis (v19; 26:26). This is further accentuated when the action of Jesus centers wholly on the bread; the fish have lost their significance and are no longer mentioned.

Matthew differs from John in emphasizing the ministerial role of the disciples. They are the ones who bring the people's situation to Jesus' attention (v15), bring the loaves and the fish to Christ (v17), and distribute the bread to the crowd (v19). This throws into relief the ministerial dimension of the eucharist as an important form of apostolic service.

Divine goodness is stressed in the great abundance of bread provided (v20). Only Matthew explicitly enlarges the crowd by mentioning the women and children (v21). This adds to the sense of divine largesse.

Matthew emphasizes the ministerial role of the apostles in the eucharist. This is not a feature in John, where Christ is the sole and central figure around whom the entire initiative rotates. Matthew always shows considerable concern for church structure and the role of the apostles in the direction of the church. In the mass today there is a variety of ministerial roles. We have the priest, lectors, eucharistic ministers, gift bearers, and servers. The sanctuary which was once the sole domain of the priest celebrant is now the locus where various functions surrounding the eucharist come into play. This all came about over a few years' time, and now we are hardly conscious of the difference. But there is an important difference. The mass now conveys a much more communal sense. It is the one Lord, the one Spirit, and many gifts. It is so important that these ministries be exercised well, all of them in convergence around the altar. They point to the one Christ who ultimately "blesses, breaks, and distributes." This all carries into life where education and new structures illustrate everyone's participation in the life of the church, blending together as the one voice of Christ. People of every ethnic or national strain, female and male, priest and lay person, work together in building up the one body of Christ. Although we get discouraged at times, when things don't always work that way, it is still a great time to be alive.

The message of Paul this Sunday sings its own song. It is so encouraging. There is nothing in the world that can rob us of God's love. Has anyone else ever told us that we were loved that much? It almost defies description. And that is the message of every crucifix. God just can't give up on us. Some people are so inhibited that they can't even use the word "love." In God's language it is used boldly and unequivocally and with all the meaning possible. Paul simply says that nothing is going to take us away from God—unless we opt out. And how could that happen in the light of all this Sunday has taught us.

Homiletic and Catechetical Helps

1. The eucharist and ministry.

2. The eucharist and the priest.

3. The eucharist and Christ's compassion.

4. The scriptural symbolism of food and drink.

5. The invincible love of God in Romans 8.

6. Relating Paul's love of Christ with the story of the loaves.

7. Human suffering in the light of Christ's love.

8. Explaining the loaves story as a eucharistic catechesis.

EIGHTEENTH SUNDAY OF THE YEAR
Year B

Readings

> Ex 16:2 - 4, 12 - 15
> Eph 4:17, 20 - 24
> Jn 6:24 - 35

Theme: Jesus, the Bread from Heaven

This Sunday the liturgy continues to draw on the bread of life chapter in John. In the Exodus narrative, the grumbling of the Jews in the desert results in the wondrous provision of manna and quail. Jesus builds on this theme in the gospel by presenting himself as the true bread from heaven. Ephesians reminds us that our new life in Christ calls for a new way of thinking, proper to a people created anew in God's image.

First Reading

It was not long after the exodus had begun that the grumbling of the people against Yahweh began (Ex 16). The gravity of the complaint lies in its pitting life under the Pharaoh against life in the desert with Yahweh (v3). The pre-Sinai response of Yahweh is one of unquestioning acquiescence (v4); after the Sinai covenant, punishment for such misconduct comes more to the fore (Num 11:1 - 6, 31 - 34). *Bread from heaven* (v4): The basic idea was that of heavenly bread, a divine gift, poetically described as a rainfall of bread. The instructions on collecting the manna (v4) are given in considerable detail (vv16 - 30), with the limitation to the quota of a single day established to avoid greed and accent providence.

The provision of food comes in two forms. The small quail migrate to Sinai and Palestine in the spring in large numbers. Manna, the bedouin *mann*, is a sweet-tasting substance found on the tamarisk tree, probably the excretion of plant lice. Both phenomena, natural in themselves, are miraculously provided for the Israelites on their journey.

What is this? (*Man hu'*) (v15): an Aramaic rather than Hebrew expression; the question is a play on the word *manna*, giving the word a popular etymology.

Responsorial Psalm   Ps 78

This didactic psalm written to promote fidelity, in explaining Yahweh's rejection of the northern kingdom, recounts many of the events of Israel's history. There is emphasis on the oral tradition by which sacred history is passed on (vv3f). The gift of the manna is cited (vv23ff) but here it becomes an expression of God's wrath (vv21ff) due to the people's lack of trust (v20; Num 11:16 - 34). Rather than a sign of favor, in this psalm the feeding is a form of punishment.

Second Reading

This passage places in relief the moral imperatives that accompany the new life in Christ. The people's former life in Gentile idolatry was a life of darkness, ignorance, and sinfulness (v17), an oft repeated Christian evaluation regarding pagan life and practice (Rom 1:21ff). The Pauline description of Christian transformation in baptism as a vesting or clothing in the person and thinking of Christ (v24; Gal 3:27) calls for an ongoing assimilation into the image of the Creator (v24; Col 3:10f). Like a tattered suit of clothes, the old self is put aside completely (v22).

Third Reading

The pivotal verses in this passage, which leads into Jesus' bread of life discourse, are found in the comparison between the bread of the old and new dispensations (vv31ff). They also link today's first and third readings. It is the *bread from heaven* that brings the manna and Jesus together.

The crowd, made up of those who had witnessed the miracle of the loaves (vv1 - 15), follows Jesus to Capernaum. Each of their questions has a Johannine importance, pointing beyond their surface significance to a deeper faith meaning. The questions enable Jesus to respond on a deeper level of faith.

"Rabbi, when did you come here?" (v25) can be understood as simply relating to Jesus' movements. It can also be understood as a question on Jesus' origins, which are ultimately with the Father (1:38f; 14:3). The crowd's search for Jesus is due to the fact that their hunger had been satisfied not because of *the signs*, here not referring to the miracle but to its deeper significance, Jesus himself as the bread of life. They should *work* (a word to be further developed) not for material bread, even miraculously provided, but for the teaching of God, which like the spring water earlier presented (4:14) is the true nourishment that remains for eternity and need never be replenished (v27).

"What can we do to accomplish the works of God?" (v28): The works of God are those that God accomplishes in and through humans. Jesus performs *the works of God* in restoring the blind man's sight (9:3f). The crowd asks how such acts may be performed. Preparing for the bread of life discourse, Jesus specifies only one work of God, i.e. faith in the person of his Son (v29). Faith is not a human accomplishment but is effected by God himself.

"What sign can you do?" (v30): The crowd remains on the natural (flesh) level. Even though they had seen the sign of the loaves, they ask for another in order to believe in Jesus, one akin to that of Moses. The exodus bread "rainfall" reference is a combination of a number of texts (v31;Ex 16:14; Ps 78:24). Jesus moves the "sign" request to a deeper level. At the miracle of the loaves, they had not seen the real "sign" (v26), only the wonder itself. Moses was not the author of the bread in the desert; it was God himself, who now gives a new bread leading to eternal life. They must look beyond material bread and wonder-working to grasp the meaning of the true bread, attainable only in faith (vv32f).

The crowd's final request remains on a non-faith level: "Give us this bread" (v34). This request for an uninterrupted supply of bread is full of Johannine faith possibilities Those who accept the truth of his revelation will never again suffer spiritual hunger or thirst (v35). The bread here is not eucharistic but refers to Jesus himself and his divine teaching.

Hardness of heart. Failure to understand. Israel begins complaining as soon as its deliverance takes place. It is hard to believe that the people's life in Egypt had been that rewarding, but that is where they would rather be. In John's gospel, the Jews are repeatedly missing the point. They flock after Jesus for many wrong reasons. As long as he remains a "bread god," they will stay with him. And yet is it that unusual for people to want God on their terms? Many people today pick and choose the areas of religion that appeal to them. We are probably more partial to the preacher who encourages us rather than the one who challenges. Jesus presents himself as the bread of life. But that means accepting him and his message integrally. We, too, like our "signs and wonders"; that is the appealing side. But the cross-bearing and the dying and rising are also pieces of that bread of life–difficult, challenging, totally engaging. But to eat of that bread is to hunger no more.

Clothes were part of a person in ancient times. A change of clothes affected what you were. When Paul speaks of putting on Christ, he thinks in those terms. To be clothed with Christ is to become Christ. You become what you assume. And there is no turning back. One does not vest and unvest at will. So much of our change is artificial. We go through the motions but nothing really happens. That is because we don't think differently. Christians do have a very distinct view of reali-

ty. *That mindset impacts much of what we do. If it doesn't, then we simply fade into the woodwork. We are still wearing the same old clothes. If we really began to think like Christ, every day would make a difference. All that means is being what we say we are.*

Homiletic and Catechetical Helps

1. Explaining the miracle of the manna and quail.

2. Verbalizing our dissatisfactions in life.

3. Greed in today's society.

4. Jesus as the bread of life and the eucharist.

5, Moral life as related to Christian transformation.

6. Examples of a new way of thinking.

EIGHTEENTH SUNDAY OF THE YEAR
Year C

Readings

> Eccl 1:2; 2:21 - 23
> Col 3:1 - 5, 9 - 11
> Lk 12:13 - 21

Theme: Vanishing Wealth

In his rather sardonic way, Qoheleth (Ecclesiastes' Hebrew name) looks at experience and sees nothing but irony in the fact that those who work hard to achieve a certain position in life end up leaving everything to someone who has made little or no contribution. This is part of life's folly. Luke's largely self explanatory parable of the wealthy farmer points up the foolishness of investing energy singlemindedly in the passing things of this life. Paul rounds out today's theme by telling the Colossians to set their gaze on the things of God where our true destiny lies. Where our treasure is, there will our heart be.

First Reading

The author of this very unusual book, Qoheleth (the preacher or presider of the assembly) believes in a divine plan, although he feels that it remains largely concealed from the human mind. Attempts to understand the grand picture are simply futile. The best one can do is to live each day as a God-fearing believer, confident that the Lord will ultimately make sense out of the nonsense of daily experience. The case cited in today's reading is for Qoheleth a classic example.

Vanity of vanities (Heb: *hebel*) (v2): The Hebrew repetition renders the superlative, i.e. the greatest vanity. The word means a "vapor" or a "whisp of smoke." It is figurative for futility or emptiness. On this negative note, the author sees any decoding of the human experience as an impossible pursuit. He ends his treatise on the same note (12:8).

A case in point is the person who has labored assiduously throughout life (v21). His toil produces a great deal of worry and concern (v22). The accumulation of wealth is accompanied by a generous measure of hardship and grief. Then, with the person's passing, everything is left to someone else who has invested neither time nor energy. Attempts to give all of this a rational explanation fail. It is simply "vapor."

Responsorial Psalm   Ps 95

Greed also produced the "hardened hearts" of the Israelites who tested Yahweh at Meribah. It is a joyful openness to God that characterizes the disciple's life. For a commentary on the psalm, see the Fourth Sunday of Year B.

Second Reading

As is his custom, Paul establishes the theological basis (vv1 - 4) for the moral imperatives which he lists (vv5 - 11). Baptism represents a union with Christ's death and resurrection (2:12).

Once this has transpired, a new way of thinking and acting arise from this "new life," which is a life centered on eternal realities. *Christ is seated* (v1): The enthronement of Christ with the Father points to messianic fulfillment as foretold in Ps. 110:1. The earth-centered life now becomes part of the pre-baptismal past and is thus excluded (v2). The new life remains temporarily hidden, to be fully revealed only with Christ's return (vv3f; Rom 6:2 - 5). This interim period must be one of vigilance. The full nature of what has transpired in the Christian is not yet apparent. Glory is seminal only.

The list of vices to be avoided is more an accepted catalogue than anything of which the Colossians might be specifically guilty (v5; Rom 1:29; Gal 5:19ff). The purpose of the list is to draw attention to the ungodliness of their former way of life. In an image possibly drawn from the baptismal ritual, Christians are reminded of their new "investiture" in having removed the old clothes of paganism and assumed the new vesture of God (vv9f). This is the assumption of the new "self" in Christ. *Being renewed* (v10): Following on the first image (Gen 1:26f), this refers to the new image of God in the human person. It is continually being sharpened and refined through growth in virtue (Rom 8:29; 2 Cor 3:18). This insertion into the one body of Christ through baptism is all-encompassing in its unifying force, eliminating any social or ethnic barriers (v11; 1 Cor 12:13; Gal 3:27f).

Third Reading

Luke here begins a section of his gospel dealing with a proper attitude toward material goods (12:13 - 48). As is often the case, the discourse is initiated with a request. Jesus is asked to intervene in a family inheritance case which he firmly refuses to do (vv13f). Rather he directs his response to the petitioner's greed, a matter of greater importance (v15). It is not with possessions as such that Jesus argues but rather with the danger which they represent. The desire for further accumulation suffocates the spirit. Moreover, goods of this world are not related to the disciple's true destiny.

The parable's point is easily drawn. The man's wealth

increases (v16); this leads to new construction (v18). He then sees himself as well situated and settles in for an unconcerned life of luxury (v19; 12:45). His self-centered moral posture can be gleaned from the repeated use of the personal and possessive pronoun in the first person throughout. It is at this point that death intervenes; all his efforts are brought to nought and the destiny of his goods is questionable (v20). The question posed is ironic. The goods could have gone to the needy (12:33) if the man, wise in the things of this world, foolish in the things of God (v20), had achieved a true spiritual vision.

The disciples are encouraged to avoid such greed and acquire true riches, those things that matter to God (vv21, 34). Totally at odds with this man's conduct is that of the person truly dependent on the Lord (vv22 - 34).

Say what we will, the greater part of our waking hours goes into providing for ourselves and for others. In addition, we grow up with our attention riveted on succeeding. First of all, we want to make sure that we have enough for ourselves and our children. But then the strong consumerism of our society forces our standard of living to an ever higher level. It is all too easy to become entangled in the things that are "passing away." We also build bigger and better barns. We don't really avert to the possibility of its all ending suddenly and earlier rather than later. Today's scriptures are not a prediction of an early death. Nor does Qoheleth tell us to stop working. It is basically a reminder to keep perspective. We cannot risk to lose ourselves in the transient and forget or neglect that "which is above." It also tells us to use wealth generously while we are alive rather than have people fight over it after we are gone. Without calling for a rigorous poverty, there is no doubting the fact that a simplicity of life keeps our vision clear. It doesn't hurt to be rather spartan. It keeps us in shape for the marathon in life that really counts.

In addition, Paul reminds us that immersion in the things of this world can easily tempt us to greed and immorality. And that means we run the danger of losing everything. Why trade new clothes for old? With our Christian values in place, we have the wealth that really counts. Why become impoverished for the "fleshpots of Egypt"? Let's keep our gaze riveted on the "things that are above." We want to be good providers and take care of the concerns that God has entrusted to us. We have to work diligently. But let's keep the horizon before our eyes. And when the day comes to move on, we shall have done well but not have lost our freedom—or our real inheritance.

Homiletic and Catechetical Helps

1. The wise use of possessions.

2. The danger of greed: concrete examples.

3. The certainty of death as tempering human desires.

4. Graft, extortion, in-house trading in the light of Christian values.

5. Material prosperity: false values versus authentic values.

6. Seeking the things above: honesty, integrity, generosity, simplicity.

7. Being renewed in Christ: growing in virtue.

8. The body of Christ and divisions in society.

NINETEENTH SUNDAY OF THE YEAR
Year A

Readings

> 1 Kgs 19:9, 11 - 13
> Rom 9:1 - 5
> Mt 14:22 - 33

Theme: A Peaceful Presence

The first book of Kings relates the story of Elijah's finding God in the "sounds of silence." In today's gospel the apostles experience Christ's steadying hand on storm-tossed waters as a calm and reassuring presence. In the letter to the Romans, Paul grieves deeply over his separation from his Jewish brothers and sisters, the people through whom God first spoke to the world.

First Reading

Elijah, who was a principal instrument of Yahweh in covenant renewal, retraces the exodus journey. With his life threatened (v2), he begins a desert sojourn of forty days, echoing Moses' forty days on Sinai (Ex 34:28) and Israel's forty years in the desert (v8). He makes his way to Horeb, the name for Sinai in the Elohist and Deuteronomic traditions. Like Israel (Ex 16), he is miraculously sustained on his desert journey (vv6ff). This exodus motif prepares the reader for the encounter with Yahweh which takes place after the prophet takes shelter on Horeb (v9).

During Moses' forty day stay on Horeb, he was given a "glimpse of God," i.e. an insight into Yahweh's nature (Ex 34:5ff). Elijah's experience parallels this. In both experiences, the Lord "passes by" (v11; Ex 34:6). The Sinai covenant theophany had been characterized by heavy storms, earthquakes, and volcano-like phenomena (Ex 19:16 - 19). Such is not the present case. Although the elements all make their presence felt—wind, earthquake and fire—the Lord is not to be found in any of them. *A tiny whispering sound* (Heb: *qol demamah daqqah;* lit. "the sound of a fine silence" (v12). The expression is enigmatic, pointing to an imperceptible sound. The paradox of a sound in silence alludes to the transcendent, even inexplicable presence and activity of God. Elijah's God is not one of power and might but one of a quiet awesome presence. The prophet realizes that he stands in God's presence and, like Moses before him, covers his face (v13; Ex 3:6).

Responsorial Psalm   Ps 85

The nearness of salvation to those who fear God continues the theme of the day. For commentary, see the Second Sunday of Advent in Year B.

Second Reading

This passage begins Paul's treatise on the place of Jews and Gentiles in the plan of salvation (cc. 9 - 11). He expresses his profound regret that his former co-religionists, sharers in the Jewish faith, had not come to a recognition of Christ as Messiah and Lord. *In Christ* (v1): His veracity is linked with his life in Christ, by reason of the gift of the Spirit (2 Cor 11:31). His own conscience and the Holy Spirit converge in attesting to his truthfulness. Paul's anguish is such that he is willing to sacrifice his own spiritual life and inheritance for the sake of his former co-religionists, linked with him by physical descent (v3). Like Moses, he would be willing to have his own name stricken from God's list in the interests of his people (Ex 32:32).

Paul lists eight ways in which the Jews are linked with God. *Israelites* (v4): Paul uses the name of honor conferred upon his people in the patriarch Jacob (Gen 32:29), not the more common name "Jews." Their privileged state lies in their *adoption* (sonship) as a people made God's own (Ex 4:22; 19:5f; Deut 14:1); the *glory*, the visible manifestation of God's otherness experienced in the desert theophany and in temple worship (Ex 16:10; 40:34; 1 Kgs 8:10f); the *covenants*, the various bonding relationships with God embracing Noah (Gen 9:8), Abraham (Gen 15:18), Moses (Ex 24:7f), the *law*, given through Moses to the people at Sinai (Ex 20); the *worship*, the honor given Yahweh in temple cult with divinely established norms; the *promises*, the assurance of God's abiding presence and direction given to the *patriarchs* (Gen 12:2; 21:1f; Deut 18:18; 2 Sam 7:8 - 17); the patriarchs, especially Abraham, Isaac, and Jacob, immortalized in Jewish prayer and thought and the pledge of blessings for God's people (Rom 11:28).

Finally Paul sees Christ as the high point in Jewish distinctiveness and singularity. *From the Jews, according to the flesh, came the Messiah, Christ the Lord. God who is above all be blessed forever* (v5). On the basis of differing manuscript witnesses, the punctuation of this verse is controverted. If the period is removed from midverse, in the position taken here, a balance is struck between human descendency from the Jews and divine origins as God. This would maintain the seemingly intended parallelism juxtaposing human and divine origins. The other position retains the period. What follows then is a distinct idea treating of God (the Father) alone who is to be praised, i.e. "God who is above all be blessed forever."

Third Reading

This narrative is found in that section of Matthew which is often termed "the book of the church" (13:54 - 18:35), wherein the requisites of discipleship and leadership in the church come to the fore. Today's account must be read against that background of first century ecclesial life.

The apostles find themselves in the boat on a stormy sea (v24), while Jesus is at prayer (v23), one of two mentions of such prayerful activity in Matthew (26:36). The stormy sea is symbolic of chaotic evil over which Yahweh triumphs (Ps 77:17; Job 9:8; Is 43:16). The story combines a nature miracle (v32; 9:23 - 27) with a salvific "rescue" story, symbolic of Christ's mission (vv30f). The boat represents the church wherein the apostles conduct their mission, a church beset by persecution, opposition and apostasy, symbolized by storm and night ("the third watch": between 3 and 6 A.M.) (vv24f).

In the midst of turmoil, it is clearly the abiding presence of Christ that saves. His lordship is underscored in various ways. He walks on the water (v25; Ps 77:20); he identifies himself in revelatory terms: "it is I" ("I am"), reminiscent of Yahweh's self-identification in Exodus (3:14). Peter addresses him as "Lord" and pleads for salvation (vv28, 30). In contrast to the Marcan ending with the apostles' astonishment (Mk 6:51), Matthew ends with a full post-Easter faith affirmation (v33). The serene composure of Jesus throughout the narrative is intended as a message of encouragement in difficult ecclesial circumstances.

The disciples also represent the Christian people, with their strengths and weaknesses. They register fear and lack of recognition of the Savior (v26). The Petrine tradition provides Matthew with the insert on Peter's action (vv28 - 31) not found in the Marcan account. His initial reaction to Jesus' presence is spontaneous and faith-filled. But as was so often the case in the early Christian experience, faith wavered in the course of time (13:20ff). However, weakness that leads to awareness of God's saving power is beneficial (v30). Jesus simply extends his hand. *You of little faith* (v31): Peter is not faulted for his initiative or for stepping out into the unknown. Rather his deficiency lies in his lack of courage and wavering in the face of obstacles. Human factors frequently overrode the call for faith (Jn 20:24 - 29).

The calm returns. The triumph of Christ is recognized; his presence with the church is assured (v33). The picture of Jesus' serenity in the story contrasts sharply with the panic of the disciples.

The sounds of silence. We think all too little about solitude and God's presence therein. Yet it is all too true. Some of the greatest leaps forward in Christian history came from hearing God's speech in quiet tones–Benedict at Subiaco, Francis at LaVerna, Ignatius at Manresa, Teresa in her Spanish cloister. Christ was with his apostles even though their panic made them fail to realize it. So too with us. Christ does not abandon his church or any one of us. But we need time and space to let the truths of God penetrate our lives. The Christ of today's gospel is the picture of serenity and steadfastness. It is the Christ we all need in a very harried world. It also reminds us of our own presence to others in their moments of need: the loss of a dear one, the news that an illness is terminal, the tragic end of a marriage. It is often our presence, not our words, that speaks volumes. Words at times seem very empty. Elijah heard God in the sounds of silence. Jesus was silently present to his disciples in distress–but it was a strengthening presence.

The Jews are the people of the promise. We share such an inestimable patrimony. The tragedy of history is that so much hatred has been heaped upon them, often by Christians. Hatred is not the answer to any problem if we are truly Christian. We continue to regret that the fullness of the promises is not yet theirs. But the glass that is half empty is also half full. From them we have received God's word. Their beliefs have profoundly influenced our own. On the human side, they gave us Christ. We have to avoid stereotyping and adopting negative attitudes. We have to join hands when we can. And where we cannot be one, let's pray for a better day.

Homiletic and Catechetical Helps

1. Christ's presence with the church.

2. The importance of a trusting faith.

3. The value of silence in our lives.

4. The significance of retreats and days of recollection.

5. Peter: the importance of stepping out in faith.

6. Peter: doubt in the face of difficulty.

7. The Jews in God's saving plan.

8. Prayer for and with our Jewish neighbors.

9. Positive attitudes regarding other faiths.

10. Our shared heritage with the Jews.

NINETEENTH SUNDAY OF THE YEAR
Year B

Readings

> 1 Kgs 19:4 - 8
> Eph 4:30 - 5:2
> Jn 6:41 - 51

Theme: Food for the Journey

In today's first reading, Elijah is strengthened enough by the angel's food to make a forty day journey. The gospel continues Jesus' bread of life discourse as Christ present himself as the nourishment for our life's journey. Ephesians teaches that immoral conduct by those who are called to be imitators of God "saddens the holy Spirit."

First Reading

Elijah, a prophet of covenant renewal, is a new-Moses figure, echoing many features of the latter's life. His altar on Mount Carmel with its twelve stones "according to the number of tribes of the sons of Jacob" (18:31f) matches the altar of Moses at Sinai (Ex 24:4). In today's narrative, his journey of "forty days and forty nights" (v8) recalls the stay of Moses on Sinai (Ex

24:18); his later entering the cave at Horeb (v9) recalls the location of Moses when gaining his glimpse of Yahweh (Ex 33:22).

The event takes place after Elijah's life has been threatened by Jezebel (v2). The prophet flees for his life to Beer-sheba in southern Judah and then on to the desert (vv3f). His state of depression leads to a death wish (v4). He is twice miraculously fed by an angel, a visible manifestation of Yahweh himself (vv6ff). The twofold eating fortifies him sufficiently for the trip to Horeb, the name for Sinai in the Elohist and Deuteronomic tradition.

Together with the Moses motif, the experience of the prophet is intended to reproduce the experience of Israel in being provided food and drink in the desert (Ex 16 - 17).

Responsorial Psalm   Ps 34

"To taste and see" the Lord is to know him through a faith experience, not simply through credal acceptance. This idea is at the heart of the bread of life discourse. Commentary on this psalm is found on the Fourth Sunday of Lent, Year C.

Second Reading

One of the results of life in the Spirit is the imitation of God after the example of Christ, as today's passage illustrates (5:1f). By their baptism, members of the Christian community were *sealed* (or stamped) in the Spirit, as a pledge of their definitive redemption at the time of the parousia (v30; 1:13f). The Spirit expresses itself in unity and love; any conduct to the contrary within the community is said to "sorrow the Spirit." The list of vices, a type of general listing frequently used (Col 3:8), here centers on uncontrolled irascibility (v31), a type of conduct which is seriously disruptive.

Christians, on the contrary, must take God as their example, principally in forgiving (v32) and showing charity. The exhortation to forgiveness reflects the petition of the Lord's Prayer (Mt 6:12, 14) with a reversal, however, in the order of forgiveness. The example of God's charity is Jesus who offered himself in sacrifice for the world (5:2). This same person of Christ is the model of love, compassion, and kindness.

Third Reading

In this part of the bread of life discourse, the Johannine Jesus accents his divine origins with the Father and the destiny of all those who accept him in faith. Thus, the Father, faith, and eternal life serve as the triad of the discourse.

Desert resonances continue to be heard in this discourse, well after the loaves and fish narrative (vv1 - 15). The *murmuring* of the Jews (vv41, 43) is evocative of the Israelites' conduct prior to the provision of manna and quail (Ex 16:2, 8f). There is, moreover, an explicit reference to the manna (v49), which picks up on Jesus' earlier rebuttal of the Jews (vv31f).

To Jesus' "spirit" level declaration of origins (v41), the Jews remain on the "flesh" level, seeing no farther than his human parents (v42). Jesus sees their inability to accept him as overcome only by *faith*, which is ultimately a gift of the Father (v44). It is the Father alone who convinces and in eschatological language, by a free adaptation of Isaiah (54:13), is the only teacher (v45).

Each time Jesus speaks of accepting his teaching in faith, he notes the *eternal* quality of faith. Thus it leads to resurrection (v44), life forever (vv47, 51), a life without death (v50). Like the living water (4:14), this bread finds its proper terminus only in everlasting life.

Only the Father can be the author (v44) and instructor (v45) in faith. However, he has consigned the task to the Son as the one who has insight and access to the Father (v46; 1:18). To know Jesus, then, is to know the Father (14:8f).

The Johannine Jesus concludes this part of his discourse with the assurance that the one who accepts him unreservedly in faith is destined for eternal life (v51a). The discourse then takes a new turn (v51b) in preparation for the eucharistic bread of life section which follows (vv52 - 59). Here for the first time the bread (Gr: *artos*) is spoken of as flesh (Gr: *sarx*). This is a transposition to another key wherein eating and drinking flesh and blood will come to the fore. There is convergence however. The bread of Jesus' person and teaching receive sacramental expression in the eucharist.

There is no substitute for faith. That sounds very trite, but there is no other way to say it. Faith is certainly food for the journey. We have all known persons whose personal code of conduct is irreproachable. But they just can't believe, and they really don't see the need. Perhaps "agnostic" best describes them. They just don't know. They follow their conscience for humanitarian reasons. When it comes to eternal life, they are very skeptical. Sometimes we love them so much we agonize over their plight. And then there are people whose faith is utterly indomitable. They live a faith life of vigorous intensity. Dogged by a fatal illness, they face the future with the same optimism and resoluteness. "Why be distraught?" they ask. Isn't this what I have been living for?" That is a gift. That is being taught by God. The person's entire value system bears the imprint of faith. We have to pray to grow in faith, just as we remember those who do not have it.

Anger can be a very frightening thing. It finds expression in forms of passion that can scarcely be called human. At its worst, anger ends in violence, even death. In lesser forms, it means outrage and irrational conduct. It devastates people, destroys family relationships, and inflicts serious harm. Anger is often fomented by alcohol, with things said and done that should never occur. The author of Ephesians says that it even grieves God. It can have no place in a loving, compassionate community of believers. It is so much better to promote growth than to destroy it, to extend the warmth of forgiveness rather than the fire of insult, to speak the kind word rather than to deal the harsh sentence. God does not treat us with hostility. Be imitators of God.

Homiletic and Catechetical Helps

1. Faith in Jesus as an experience.

2. Understanding the truths of faith.

3. Faith in Christ as the food for our journey of life.

4. Jesus, bread of life, and the eucharist.

5. Faith as a gift of God.

6. The various forms of anger.

7. Forgiveness as a reflection of God.

8. Controlling our anger.

9. Examples of patience from daily life.

NINETEENTH SUNDAY OF THE YEAR
Year C

Readings

> Wis 18:6 - 9
> Heb 11:1 - 2, 8 - 19
> Lk 12:32 - 48

Theme: The Vigilant Servant

Wisdom reflects on the Israelites in Egypt awaiting their salvation. Their posture was one of alertness, courage, and prayer. Jesus in Luke's gospel advises an alert spirit, also, on the part of servants expecting their master's return, a spirit which expresses itself in fidelity to duty. Hebrews recalls the faith of Abraham and Sarah and sees it as an unwavering confidence in the Lord's promises.

First Reading

In recounting the events of the exodus, the author of Wisdom parallels punishment and liberation, the misfortunes which befell the enemy and the benefits shown God's people. In this passage, the night of the death of the Egyptian firstborn and the deliverance of the Israelites is seen as the night of Yahweh's justice. It appears clearly in the vindication of his own people (v7) but also in the punishment of Israel's tormentors (v8).

That night (v6): This was the time of the final plague, the killing of the Egyptian firstborn and Israel's celebration of the first passover. With the lamb's blood sprinkled on the lintels and doorposts, the Lord "passed over" the homes of the

Israelites (Ex 12:21 - 30). *Our fathers* (v6): A reference to the Genesis patriarchs who predicted the Egyptian bondage and eventual deliverance (Gen 15:3f; 46:3f). Confident in the Lord's power to fulfill his word as expressed in his oaths of fidelity, the patriarchs knew that eventual salvation was assured (12:21).

The people awaited God's intervention (v7) that night in a spirit of vigilance and alertness, with their loins girt and sandals on their feet, ready for flight (Ex 12:11). This manifestation of God's power was two-pronged in saving Israel and in punishing Egypt. The latter action, directed against a much greater political and military force, would redound to the glory of God's favored people (v8; 19:22). *Summoned* (v8): called to be God's people, his elect (Ex 19:5f).

At the very moment of the death of the firstborn, the Israelites were offering their first passover sacrifice behind closed doors, according to the divine prescription (v9: Ex 12).

Responsorial Psalm   Ps 33

The just are exhorted to praise the Lord for his goodness in creating the universe (vv1 - 9) and in fashioning a nation (vv12 - 19). The note of election and expectation connects the psalm with today's theme. For a commentary, see the Second Sunday of Lent, Year A.

Second Reading

In this chapter dealing with the example of patriarchal faith, the author cites three examples from the life of Abraham. The first was his willingness to set out for an unknown land at God's injunction (vv8ff). The second was the faith of Abraham and Sarah in the promise of a child in their advanced years (vv11f). Finally there was the obedient faith of the patriarch in his willingness to sacrifice his only son, Isaac (vv17ff).

In faith the unseen is made present and apprehended. The future reality becomes part of present existence. *Realization* (Gr: *upostasis*) (v1): Frequently translated "substance," the meaning here includes subjective apprehension of the objective reality. *Evidence* (Gr: *elenchos*) (v1): A word with both a subjective and an objective dimension, with the latter more to the fore. It looks to the external evidence upon which conviction is based.

The fact that Abraham lived in the promised land more as a transient than as a permanent citizen, longing for his lasting home above (vv9f), makes him a model for the Christian whose aspirations are the same (13:14). This is a form of midrash or free adaptation of a scriptural incident or passage to a new situation.

From the dead regenerative powers of the patriarch and his wife came the progeny of countless descendants (v12; Gen 15:5). All the ancestral figures, not only Abraham, are seen as yearning for an eternal homeland, even though it was perceived as a far distant reality. The proof of this is the fact that they lived a nomadic existence, never taking up "permanent residence" (v13). They were nomads not just because they were landless people; they could have returned home at any point (v15). The fact is that their hopes were in heaven, their ultimate destiny. In all of this, the author continues to review the past and make applications out of his Christian experience.

Even though Isaac was the son of promise, the carrier of future progeny, Abraham was willing to sacrifice him (vv17f). So strong was his faith that he was convinced that God could bring his son back from death to realize the promise (v19). *Symbol* (v19): Isaac's "return" from death was actually a deliverance from death. Here however the use of "death" is figurative, symbolic of Christ's true return from death in resurrection.

Third Reading

The "servant" theme joins a number of the Lucan Jesus' thoughts in today's gospel. There is the conclusion to the "lilies of the field" teaching on providence (vv22 - 32), which centers on the priority of the heavenly treasure over every other good (vv32ff). This is followed by a parable on the importance of vigilance (vv35 - 39) and finally a parable on responsible stewardship (vv41 - 48).

Little flock (v32): little in terms of numbers but also endowed with a humble spirit. The contrast is evident. The little ones are destined to receive the greatest gift, the kingdom of God. In the light of their heavenly spiritual destiny, they are to substitute the perishable for the imperishable (v33). In one of scripture's greatest verities, the disciples are told that their human forces will be totally absorbed by their priorities and goals, for good or ill (v34).

Addressing himself to members of the church, the Lucan Christ urges vigilance (vv35ff). The loins bound for the journey suggest the readiness for the exodus departure (Ex 12:11), and the lighted lamp is a New Testament figure for alertness (Mt 25:1 - 8). Christ, the master, already present at the eschatological wedding feast, will return at the parousia, for which the servants are to stand in readiness. At this point, there is an unusual reversal of roles (vv37f). At whatever watch the Lord comes, he will respond to vigilance not simply by inviting the faithful to the heavenly table but rather will himself become the servant. This reference to the servant role of Jesus, woven into his entire ministry and teaching, is now presented in an eschatological setting (22:24 - 27; Jn 13:1 - 11).

At this point (vv39ff), the "master of the house" passes from Christ to the vigilant servant. However, the same point of vigilance is made, an alertness that prevents the intrusion of a thief. This must be the posture of the Christian in expectation of the end.

Peter's question (v41) moves the discourse to an ecclesial setting. Jesus' words are intended not solely for his companions but for later Christians, especially those called to leadership. Leaders in the church were termed "servants" (Rom 1:1; Gal 1:10) as well as "stewards" (v42). What is allegedly an exposition of the preceding is actually a new parable (vv42 - 48). The emphasis moves from vigilance in light of the parousia to the manner of exercising ministry within the ecclesial community.

The parable addresses different categories of people charged with responsibility. The *food allowance* may be a reference to charitable activites connected with material needs, a prevalent part of the early church's *diakonia* (Acts 6:1 - 7). There are those who show unflagging dedication to their designated service; they will receive even greater responsibility (vv42f). When end-time expectations ran high, this was a commonly found posture; problems began to arise with the delay in the Lord's return. This even led to misconduct and mistreatment (v45). In such cases punishment is definitive and severe, with the return taking place unexpectedly (v46). Finally a theology of "mitigating circumstances" is introduced. Culpability is not the same for all. The measure of punishment will depend on the steward's awareness. Ignorance tempers divine judgment (vv47f). This ending reflects the parable's ecclesial setting where moral nuances are beginning to emerge.

Today we lament the absence of competent service. All too often in business it seems that customer satisfaction is not a high priority. The quality of merchandise is frequently less than what should be expected. Fixed appliances often return speedily to a state of disrepair. Today's scriptures remind us that the same thing can happen in church ministry. A lack of interest and enthusiasm results in perfunctory ministry at best. Or church can become a playing field where careerism takes precedence over people's concerns. Homilies poorly prepared or poorly delivered become a scourge. Hospital visits deferred, catechists not properly renewed and updated, careless eucharistic ministers–for those called to ministry in a sacred setting, all of this represents a lack of vigilance. On the other hand, a well-prepared liturgy with a thematic coordination of hymns of proven worth and ministries willingly and efficiently performed can make a genuine contribution to faith. In this age of multiple and diversified ministries, for which we can only be grateful, the decision to serve should be weighed and then approached with a true sense of dedication.

It is good to read Hebrews. Its faith is so dynamic, personal, and engaging. We recite a creed each Sunday. Does it touch our lives? Faith for Abraham involved testing, holding on in the face of the unbelievable. Faith is seen in our actions. It makes us do what we would otherwise not do. Therein lies the difference. Simply to accept truth costs very little. It will hardly distinguish believer from non-believer. When faith carries us to the brink, brings us to stand up for our convictions, even to suffer for them, then we are talking the language of Hebrews.

Homiletic and Catechetical Helps

1. Vigilance in church ministries.

2. Israel's vindication through punishment of enemies.

3. Faith as trust in God's providence.

4. Authority as a ministry in the church.

5. The liturgical and social ministries.

6. Faith as the present realization of future realities.

7. Faith as experience in Abraham's life.

8. Faith as experience in our lives.

TWENTIETH SUNDAY OF THE YEAR
Year A

Readings

Is 56:1, 6 - 7
Rom 11:13 - 15, 29 - 32.
Mt 15:21 - 28

Theme: An Open House

All three readings this Sunday evolve around the theme of universalism. Third Isaiah in a remarkable oracle sees people of all backgrounds making their way to the temple for sacrificial worship. Paul reminds the Gentile Christians that the Jews' rejection of Jesus, which is only temporary, has worked in their favor in producing a church that is open to all. The Matthean Jesus stands on the borders of Gentile territory as he commends a Canaanite woman's faith.

First Reading

Third Isaiah (cc. 55 - 66) completes the prophetic book, dating from a different period and setting than Second Isaiah. The temple has been rebuilt (therefore after 515 B.C.) and the setting is Palestine itself. The conditions of the exile have passed, with new concerns now to the fore, such as ritual regulations, sabbath observance, and fasting. In comparison with the broad sweep of Second Isaiah's vision, the view has somewhat narrowed. But in the area of universalism, Third Isaiah is in the forefront. He stands in the tradition of Jonah and Ruth. Today's passage marks a startling breakthrough in Israel's sense of inclusiveness.

The belief in the Lord's definitive intervention in history remains strong (v1). In preparation the prophet exhorts the people to covenant fidelity (Heb: *mishpat, sedeq*) in view of the fact that Yahweh's own fidelity to the alliance will soon be manifest for all to see. This matching faithfulness underscores the bilateral character of the covenant.

Foreigners living in Israel had been historically accorded limited rights and an overall protection (Ex 22:20; Deut 10:18f). There was less openness toward people living in surrounding countries due to the hostilities that had marked Israel's contact with many of them in the past. The Deuteronomic school shows a gradual and partial opening in the latter's regard with the passing of time (Deut 23:2 - 9). The present Isaian oracle is especially noteworthy since it comes at a time when contact with foreigners was again under attack by a "ghetto" mentality (Ezr 9 - 10).

Those aliens who accept Yahweh and the terms of the covenant—in short, converts to Judaism—will be accorded the full ritual rights of the Jews (vv6f). *Ministering to him* (v6): This customary reference to priestly duties is here used figuratively in the sense of a cultic faith response. The sabbath observance is underscored in view of its renewed emphasis in the post-exilic community (56:2). The traditional sacrificial offerings to be presented by foreigners will have equal value with those of the Jews. The temple, the revered locus of Yahweh's presence reserved to his own people (1 Kgs 8:29f), will be open to all the nations without exception.

There is no suggestion, here or elsewhere, of any active proselytizing on the part of the Jews to attain this universal faith accord. Israelite universalism is presented as a fact, not as a program of action.

Responsorial Psalm　　Ps 67

This hymn of praise may well have been written in thanks for a plentiful harvest (v7). It has a strong universalist strain. The prayer for God's continued kindness (v2) echoes the priestly blessing of the people (Num 6:22 - 27). God's visible goodness to Israel will have an apologetic value in bringing the nations to recognize his universal rule (vv3, 5). The entire earth, then, is seen as giving God praise (v8).

Second Reading

Paul in speaking to the Gentile Christians here explicitly calls himself their apostle (v13; Gal 2:7f). He expresses the hope that the success of his Gentile mission will move the Jews to jealousy resulting in the conversion of at least some of them (v14). *My race* (v14): In the human order, Paul still identifies closely with the Jews ("my flesh"; Gr: *ten sarka*). *Their rejection* (v15): a subjective genitive, i.e. the Jews' rejection of the Christian message. Here the apostle passes to an *a fortiori* argument. If the Jews' failure to respond has resulted in the message's widespread diffusion in a Gentile culture, their ultimate acceptance of Christ will be a remarkable summons from death to life for them (v15; 6:4). *Reconciliation of the world* (v15): Christ's redemption not only has embraced the Gentiles but has touched the universe as a whole (Col 1:20; Eph 1:9f).

The ultimate conversion of the Jews is certain since the divine call is irrevocable (v29). In the typical Pauline antithesis of negative producing positive (5:12 - 20), the Gentiles were saved from their original disobedience (the pagan rejection of God, 1:18 - 32) by another disobedience, i.e. the failure of the Jews to accept Christ. Now that God's forgiveness has touched the Gentiles, the Jews will also be delivered from their disobedience (vv30f). On the same negative-positive note, Paul sees the evil of this widespread sin as overcome by the greater, all-encompassing mercy of God (v32; 5:20).

Third Reading

Matthew shares this narrative with Mark (7:24 - 30). Although it deals with a cure, it does not have the customary miracle story form, resembling more a pronouncement story with its strong didactic note. It combines the exclusivist mentality of

Matthew's Jewish-Christian community with an openness toward the Gentile mission.

Jesus moves to northern Galilee, precisely to the border with Phoenicia. The actual site is left generic enough to support Matthew's position that the mission of Jesus' earthly life was limited to Palestine (v21; 10:5f). The woman evidently comes into Palestine from the Gentile territory to intercede on behalf of her "possessed" daughter. Identified specifically with her home territory by Mark (7:26), Matthew refers to her as a Canaanite, conjuring up all the hostile connotations which the term held for the Jews. Her ardent faith in Jesus and in his power to heal is deeply woven into the story. She twice calls him "Lord" (vv22, 25). Her petition for mercy is frequently used in human recourse to a forgiving God (v22); the posture of kneeling veneration (Gr: *proskuneo*) is often used cultically (v25). A Gentile, she explicitly recognizes Christ as the davidic messiah (v22).

Reserve marks Jesus' initial reaction. This serves to enhance the theme of an exclusively Jewish mission of Jesus as well as to highlight the woman's persistent faith (vv23f). In responding to the woman's plea, Jesus uses a rather startling metaphor (v26). The Gentiles were not infrequently referred to as dogs by the Jews. With this colorful semitic expression, Jesus points strongly to his Jewish mission, without the softening which Mark gives in upholding the priority given the Jews but not the exclusivism (Mk 7:27).

The woman spars with Jesus verbally and manages to emerge with the final word (v27). It is this persistence which merits Jesus' encomium ("a great faith" is singular in Matthew) (v28). The cure is immediate but has already receded into the background, with focus centering on the faith of a woman and a Gentile who has ventured courageously into a Jewish world.

The Canaanite woman is a fascinating personality. She is a woman in a male-dominated society. She is a foreigner who ventures alone into a Jewish milieu. Upon finding a seemingly detached and distant Jesus, she refuses to give up. She has daring and a sense of humor. And she ends up by being one of the most highly commended persons in the gospels.

Persistence can show a great deal of conviction and fortitude. Dogged determination says a great deal about a person. It can say even more when faith moves one to the limits in pursuit of a desired goal. Gandhi was so convinced of the value of non-violent opposition to colonial rule that he not only obtained his goal but made the means a way of life. Frances Xavier Cabrini was so determined to establish her missionary community for poor immigrants that Pope Leo XIII simply said: "Cabrini, you have the spirit of God." Yet persistence without humor can become very intense and unpleasant. Humor is a vital ingredient of accomplishment. It brings relief to intensity, joy to earnestness, happiness to vision. A sense of humor makes the most bitter medicine palatable.

Christ came for all. Paul uses language which is as frank as it is uncustomary if one compares it with that of a sanitized bureaucracy. If nothing else, he says, I will make my people jealous of my accomplishments. But he says it in the interests of emphasis. God really wants everyone at the table. The book of Isaiah said it in a startling way in the late sixth century: sacrifices offered by the unclean! The Canaanite woman was quite convinced that she had a place at that table, and nothing would stop her. We would probably all say that we believe today's scriptural message. But practice says so much to the contrary. There are many negative attitudes toward minorities today; there is all too much stereotyping. To maintain a universal love is at the heart of our faith. But that faith is tested every day as we turn the next corner. It is much more than theory. For each of us it has to become fact.

Homiletic and Catechetical Helps

1. Israel's major leap: foreigners in the temple.

2. Common prayer as an ecumenical imperative.

3. Faith and perseverance.

4. The gift of humor in life and faith.

5. The courage of the Canaanite woman.

6. Paul's antithesis: sin as a key to grace.

7. The eventual unity of Christians and Jews.

8. Universalism and attitudes toward minorities.

TWENTIETH SUNDAY OF THE YEAR
Year B

Readings

> Prov 9:1 - 6
> Eph 5:15 - 20
> Jn 6:51 - 58

Theme: Eucharist as Wisdom

Wisdom in the biblical sense looks to the proper ordering of life according to the norms of faith. In Proverbs, Wisdom presents herself as a hostess offering food and drink, a metaphor for the instruction which leads to life. In his conclusion to the bread of life discourse, the Johannine Jesus presents the eucharist as the food which is equated with life. On the practical level, Ephesians speaks of the way that wisdom-life is expressed in conduct that is circumspect and Spirit-filled.

First Reading

In this chapter of Proverbs two women are the central figures, Wisdom and Folly. The former leads her adherents to the fullness of life; the latter, to death. It is Lady Wisdom who appears in today's reading. True wisdom, which here points to the content of the entire book, is instruction in God's law. Observance leads to a full and satisfying terrestrial life. Wisdom is here presented as a woman who invites people to dine in her home. The food is wisdom's instruction, providing a sumptuous and satisfying banquet.

Wisdom's house is the created universe (v1). *Seven columns* (v1): The Hebrew universe was composed of three tiers: the heavens, the earth, and the subterranean world. The entire structure rested on pillars or columns for support. Wisdom takes up domicile, then, within the world. She was present at the world's creation (8:27 - 30) and found her recreation among humans (vv30f).

Within her earthly home, she has prepared her banquet and then through her maiden emissaries has summoned her guests (vv2f). Divine instruction described in terms of food and drink is a recurring biblical motif (v5; Sir 24:18ff; 51:23f). To enter wisdom's home is to turn away from the path of error and death by walking in the way of God's truth.

Responsorial Psalm   Ps 34

This is a thanksgiving song with a strong wisdom motif. It is an alphabetic psalm, each verse beginning with a successive line of the Hebrew alphabet. In praising the Lord for his deliverance (vv5, 7), the psalmist gives encouragement to the poor in their plight (vv2f). *Fear the Lord* (v10): This is a reverential fear of God rooted in the observance of the law. Fear of God is true wisdom (Prov 1:7) and leads to the fullness of life. *The powerful* (v11): literally "the lions," symbol of power and might.

The wisdom motif appears in the latter verses (vv11 - 15). The antithesis to the lot of the powerful is that of the lowly (children) (v12). The path to life and prosperity is built on proper speech and conduct, often requiring a conversion of life (vv14f).

Second Reading

Wisdom continues as a theme in this reading from Ephesians. It still leads to life (v15) but here in a fuller sense than in Proverbs. It is life in Christ that is co-terminous with Christian wisdom. Vigilance is called for in view of the elements of "flesh" still present in the Christian but even more so in the world at large (v16). Foolishness (v15) and ignorance (v17) are to be avoided, like Proverb's Lady Folly (Prov 9:13 - 18), as the antithesis of true wisdom. An example of foolishness is excess in eating and drinking (Prov 23:31f).

On the contrary, Christian wisdom lies in the liturgical praise of God in joy and unity (vv19f; Ps 33:2f; Col 3:16f). Gratitude is an integral part of praise to God, the author of all good. Characteristically praise is directed to the Father in and through Christ (v20).

Third Reading

The sixth chapter of John, read on the last three Sundays, reaches a high point today with Jesus' eucharistic discourse.

At this point in the chapter, there is a transition from Jesus as God's self revelation, presented as the bread of life (v51a), to Christ as the eucharistic bread, when he speaks of giving "my flesh for the life of the world" (v51b). From this point on, the discourse will center on "flesh and blood" and "eating and drinking," expressions quite different from those used in the bread of life part of the discourse. The Johannine Jesus here begins his eucharistic catechesis. The transition clause (51b), reminiscent of the synoptics' eucharistic formula ("my body given for you"—Lk 22:19), may well be drawn from the liturgy of the Johannine community.

The Jews' "flesh" or natural level question becomes a springboard for Jesus' further teaching (v52). They understand "flesh" only in a physical, even cannibalistic sense. Jesus continues to speak on the "spirit" level of sacramental language, understood well within John's faith community. To "eat flesh" and "drink blood" (vv53, 54, 56) is to partake of the transformed bread and wine of eucharist. This is *true* (Gr: *alethes*) food and drink (v55) as opposed not only to material food but also to the food providentially provided for the Jews in the desert (v58). Hence, the Christian community is blessed beyond not only the pagan nonbelievers but also the Jews, still glorying in their ancestral past.

Two different verbs are used for "eating" in the discourse, the more conventional verb "to eat" (Gr: *esthio, phagomai*) and the less common "to munch" or "to gnaw" (Gr: *trogein*). The latter stresses the concrete non-figurative meaning of an authentic eating and not solely a faith acceptance of Jesus.

In establishing the necessity of eucharistic reception, the effects are repeatedly expressed in terms of *life*. This is an important link with the former part of the discourse, with both faith in Jesus and the eucharist offering life (vv47f). Thus "eating" and "drinking" brings "life within you" (v53), resurrection life (v54), "life because of me" (v57), life forever (v58). This life is effected through the indwelling and abiding presence of Jesus within the believer (v57b). That same life which from the "living" Father (v57a) passes to Jesus is then shared with the believer. Just as Jesus and the Father dwell within one another (14:10), so too the believer and Jesus (v56; 15:4). Just as the living water issues in eternal life (4:14), so too the life-giving bread of the eucharist.

The eucharist is presented, then, as a true living in the Lord through a mutual indwelling which culminates in eternal life. It has been suggested that the eucharistic discourse was directed at the factionalized Johannine community in the interests of a unified spirit. What is certain is that it gives a solid base for Christian unity. In addition, while transposing the bread of life discourse to a new key, it is in continuity with it. The acceptance of Jesus in faith has its concrete and lived expression in the eucharist.

Today we would probably define wise people as those who "have their act together." They are people who have ordered their lives properly—for Christians, in accord with the teaching of Christ. That teaching comes from more than textbooks and classrooms. It comes from knowing the Lord, in the biblical sense of experiencing God. The eucharist stands at the very heart of that experience. It can be viewed from different angles. Paul is strong on its social dimension. John stresses the internal transformation which the eucharist effects—Christ in us and we in Christ, just as the Father in Christ and Christ in the Father. We live under God's roof and share the same household, as in any household that involves speaking the same language and sharing the same vision. That is the eucharist as wisdom. God, the source of all wisdom, is instructing and guiding us on the journey of life. Reflection and the eucharist go hand in hand. We need the time in silent prayer in conjunction with the mass to know the Lord. Christ, the way, the truth, and the life, leads us in all wisdom. The eucharist is our pledge of eternity. We really have nothing to fear from sin or death. We are walking in the best of company.

Christian wisdom avoids loose conduct or debauchery. Anything less than rational is less than Christian. Rather we cherish all that is truly human, honorable, and just. Realizing God as the source of all good, wisdom wants to praise him. Vatican II said that the liturgy stands at the apogee of the Christian life. It is our noblest task, bringing the whole of our being to the public expression of God's presence in our lives, the actual reenactment of the death of the Lord until he comes. It is also our source of strength for the journey. Frequent attendance at the eucharist is commendable as long as it never becomes matter of fact. It should bring us always deeper into the family circle of God.

Homiletic and Catechetical Helps

1. Biblical wisdom personified as a woman.

2. The meaning of Christian wisdom.

3. The eucharist as guiding and directing our lives.

4. Meditation and the eucharist.

5. The eucharist and eternal life.

6. Living in Christ.

7. The wisdom of sobriety and the foolishness of substance abuse.

8. Full participation in the liturgy.

TWENTIETH SUNDAY OF THE YEAR
Year C

Readings

>   Jer 38:4 - 6, 8 - 10
>   Heb 12:1 - 4
>   Lk 12:49 - 53

Theme: The Prophet's Pain

Of all biblical vocations, that of the prophet is the most difficult. For his truthful but ominous oracles, Jeremiah is viewed by Judah's leaders as a demoralizing force; he is thrown into a cistern and left to die. Jesus today speaks of the pain which his mission will entail, his own death and a later division even among family members which faith in him will cause. Hebrews looks to the outcome of it all in pointing to God's vindication of the prophet. Jesus was brought through trial to glory. So too will we if we remain faithful.

First Reading

The accusation against Jeremiah is treason. Repeatedly he had advised Judah's capitulation to the enemy and the transfer of its citizens to Babylonian custody (38:2f; 21:8ff). For this he had aroused the ire of the king's court which led to their request for his death (v4). *He demoralizes the soldiers* (v4): literally, "he weakens their hands," an expression with extra-biblical parallels indicating a breakdown in their ability to respond. Jeremiah had been confined to the quarters of the military guard (37:21). It is argued that his survival bodes nothing but ill for the welfare of the people. The story highlights the weak character of King Zedekiah, whose capitulation accurately summarizes his reign as king (v5). Ironically Jeremiah is saved from his fate by a foreign courtier, Ebed-melech (vv8f).

This is the second reported imprisonment of Jeremiah (37:15 - 21). The present account is strikingly similar to the fate of the patriarch Joseph who was thrown intro a cistern by his brothers (Israel) and saved by a caravan of Midianites (Gen 37:20 - 28).

Responsorial Psalm   Ps 40

It was really Yahweh who drew Jeremiah from the pit, as in the earlier case of Joseph. It is the same Yahweh who brought Jesus from the tomb to new life. Today's psalm celebrates the Lord as deliverer. The needier the suppliant, the greater the Lord's assistance (v18). The psalm is divided into two parts: thanksgiving (2 - 11) and personal lament (12 - 18). The psalmist describes his deliverance from an unspecified misfortune as being drawn from a muddy body of water (v3), a possible allusion to the Mesopotamian trial by ordeal with the submersion of the accused in a river and survival giving assurance of innocence. He is gifted by God with a hymn of praise to express his thanks (v4).

Second Reading

The author of Hebrews has cited ancestral figures within Israel whose faith and endurance offer examples to Christians (c. 11). He here concludes by proposing Christ as the principal model for all of his followers. The examples of the past are geared to motivate believers to leave behind all relics of "the flesh" in sinful inclinations and press on to the finish line, in the language of the games (v1; 2 Tim 4:7). Jesus was certain of his ultimate vindication by the Father, and this made his sufferings endurable. As the enthroned Messiah, Christ fulfills the prophecy of Davidic ascendency (v2; 10:12; Ps 110:1). Christians are to draw inspiration from the trials and hardships of Christ in his coming to glory. In similar trials, even to the point of martyrdom (v4), they will also share a similar destiny (v3).

Third Reading

The Lucan Jesus speaks of the hardship that his mission will entail for himself (vv49f) and his followers (vv51ff). The passage mirrors difficulties of a domestic nature which were arising in the early church. *Earth on fire* (v49): This is a purifying fire connected with the eschatological messenger (Mal 3:2f). The Baptist had spoken of the mission of Jesus as a purifying and separating fire (3:16ff), distinguishing good from bad, believer from non-believer. *Baptism* (v50): This is clearly a reference to Jesus' death spoken of in metaphorical terms. In Christian terms, baptism was a bath of transition, a passage from death to life. Jesus, as the "firstborn of many," experiences this passage in his death. It is Jesus' ardent desire that his salvific death, anticipated with anguish, be soon accomplished (v50; Mk 10:38).

The peace that Jesus brings (2:14; Mic 5:4) is the restoration of harmony between God and humankind and the universe through reconciliation. It is not necessarily equated with domestic or social peace. In fact, just the opposite was often the case. Jesus' message and the response that it evoked resulted in division, even within the family. In this sense he came to bring not peace but division (vv51ff). But as Jesus elsewhere indicates, new family relations are now established among his disciples which transcend those of blood bonds (8:19ff). The attention given to women's concerns in this passage points to the importance they have assumed among Gentile Christians of the Lucan church.

Suffering for belief is not something of the past. In various ways in modern times, in a variety of political settings, the prophetic stance has taken a staggering toll: Mindszenty, Stepinac, and Beran in communist Europe; Oscar Romero, the Jesuit university community, and the four American churchwomen in El Salvador. No less true today is the saying that the seed of faith is nourished by the blood of martyrs. Where faith is tested, it is strengthened. The prophet is the one who stands unhesitatingly on God's side because it is impossible for him or her to stand anywhere else. This may mean standing firm against atheism; it may mean standing with God's poor against totalitarian regimes, sometimes of a "Catholic" character. To die for others is to die for Christ, as did Maximilian Kolbe at Auschwitz. These are all forms of martyrdom. It still happens that families divide over a member's faith decision—and it can be very painful. But peace at any cost is no answer. Christian principle cannot settle for that. But this is the faith that counts. If we look at Jesus against the background of Jeremiah and the prophets, we cannot help but see that at given moments we have to stand tall.

But it is not a somber picture. Hebrews reminds us of our destiny once the trial is over. Irish lore speaks of it as the tavern at the end of the road where we shall together lift the cup—rather terrestrial imagery, and very Irish. But describe it any way you want because it is indescribable anyway. The point is that it makes all the prophet's pain worthwhile.

Homiletic and Catechetical Helps

1. Contemporary examples of a prophetic stance.

2. Human reaction and the pain of prophecy.

3. Zedekiah: weakness in authority.

4. Baptism as a synonym for suffering.

5. Explaining Christ as an agent of peace and division.

6. Relationships: the primacy of the spiritual over the natural.

7. The power of example: Christian role models.

8. Faith as a purifying fire, separating the good from the bad.

TWENTY-FIRST SUNDAY OF THE YEAR
Year A

Readings

> Is 22:15, 19 - 23
> Rom 11:33 - 36
> Mt 16:13 - 20

Theme: Keeper of the Keys

In telling of the substitution of one royal official for another, Isaiah describes him as the keeper of the keys, the one who admits or prohibits access to the king as he deems fit. After his profession of faith at Caesarea Philippi, Peter is also designated a key keeper, the one given an important and singular authority within the church. It is not surprising that it is Matthew, the church-conscious evangelist, who preserves this account. At the conclusion of his treatise on God's plan for Jew and Gentile, Paul hymns God's over-arching wisdom which is far beyond an poor mortal's ability to plummet.

First Reading

This replacement is reported as occurring during the reign of King Hezekiah at the height of Isaiah's prophetic career. As the text stands (v15), one Shebna, the king's principal administrator, something of a royal chief of staff in charge of day to day administration, is to be replaced for his misconduct. The charges, not given in their entirety, were evidently connected with the use of his office for personal gain (vv16 - 19). He is to be replaced by Eliakim whose forthcoming investiture is described (vv20 - 23).

Both Shebna and Eliakim are elsewhere identified as royal officials—the former as the scribe, the latter as master of the palace (36:3). There the role of Eliakim agrees with the provisions of today's text. Shebna as the scribe, however, evidently retains a high administrative post in government even after his predicted departure in disgrace. Furthermore, there is evidence that his name and rank ("master of the palace") was a later addition to the text of 22:15, the original being an unidentified "that official." In short, although the message is clear enough, lack of certainty continues to surround the actual personalities involved.

As master of the palace, Eliakim is to be solemnly invested with the robes of office (v21). *Father to the inhabitants* (v21): the chief provider of temporalities (Gen 45:8; Job 29:16). *Key of the house of David* (v22): This symbol of authority is explained in the verse itself. He has the right of admittance to and exclusion from the king's palace. More than a doorkeeper, he provided access to royal employment, benefits, and privileges. The master's position and rank will be firmly established within the government (v23).

Responsorial Psalm   Ps 138

God's responsiveness to the poor and lowly is in harmony with the position accorded the weak and erring Peter. For a commentary on the psalm, see the Fifth Sunday of Year C.

Second Reading

In reviewing God's intention to embrace both Jew and Gentile in his plan of salvation, with the unusual turn it took, Paul is prompted to conclude with a hymn to the wisdom and goodness of the Lord. The human mind cannot begin to plummet the infinite depths of God's knowledge and providential care in directing the path of human events and world order (v33). The hymn echoes the wisdom literature in extolling the unsearchable designs of God (Job 11:7; Ps 139:6; Wis 17:1).

In all that he accomplishes, God is in no need of counsel or assistance. Paul cites two scriptural texts in support of his argument. The first is taken from the Greek version of Isaiah 40:13; the other cannot be identified with certainty (vv34f). The latter is often identified with the Greek of Job 41:3, to which it bears a general resemblance; the Hebrew of that verse is corrupt and largely unintelligible. Conclusions, then, are tentative at best. However, the sense that Paul gives the passage is clear enough.

To God be given glory, he who is the origin ("from him"), the supporter ("through him") and the goal ("for him") of all creation (v36; 1 Cor 8:6). Everything depends on him who guides the human order according to a well-determined plan, as illustrated in the epistle's Jew-Gentile elaboration (cc. 9 - 11).

Third Reading

One of the most important ecclesial passages of the gospels, this profession of Christ on Peter's part (vv13 - 16) and the confirmation of Peter on Christ's part (vv17 - 20) reflect early church life, with a singular authority accorded the first of the apostles.

In comparing the Matthean account of the Caesarea Philippi incident with its synoptic counterparts (Mk 8:27 - 30; Lk 9:18 - 21), the reader is impressed with the Christological and ecclesial expansion found in the first gospel. In analyzing the narrative, its post-resurrection imprint cannot be disregarded. This is seen especially in Peter's full-blown profession of Christ as Son of God, possible only after the conferring of the Spirit, and the references to the "church" (Gr: *ekklesia*), found only here and in 18:17 in all of the gospels. Even in incipient form, the church is presented as an organized community with a basic structure of direction.

Located in the northern most part of Palestine, north of the sea of Galilee, close to the borders of the Gentile world, the incident still keeps Jesus within Jewish territory, following the Matthean design (10:5). *Caesarea Philippi* (v13): So called to distinguish it from the coastal Caesarea, the city was built by Herod's son Philip, the ruler of Galilee in the period of Jesus' ministry. *Son of Man* (v13): Matthew substitutes the synoptics' "I" with this title of Christ. Derived from Daniel (7:13), it is eschatological and stresses the note of humanity. It will be complemented by the further "sonship" of Peter's profession (v16). Matthew retains the synoptics' public conjecture on Jesus' identity: the Baptist *redivivus* (14:2) and the end-time-returning Elijah (Mal 3:23f), with the addition of Jeremiah, a prophetic type of the suffering Jesus (v14).

Peter's recognition of Jesus' identity goes beyond the synoptics' acknowledgement of his messiahship (v16). In seeing Jesus as both *Christ* and *Son of the living God,* Peter gives a full faith profession possible only by a special revelation of God (v17). The post-resurrection understanding of Jesus' Lordship and unique filial relationship to the Father, given to Peter and all the disciples by the risen Christ (Lk 24:34; 1 Cor 15:15), is here retrojected into an incident which was considered paramount in Peter's career. *Flesh and blood* (v17): humanity in its unaided weakness; natural forces. This recognition of Jesus was not possible by human insight alone; it is the result of divine enlightenment, i.e. the gift of God's Spirit (1 Cor 12:3).

Jesus' confirmation of Peter's faith in conferring broad ecclesial authority at Caesarea Philippi is exclusively Matthean. Peter is first identified as Rock (v18), then keeper of the keys (v19a) and the one who binds and looses (v19b). Substituting the name Rock (Gr: *Petros*) for Simon, son of Jonah, is symbolic in the play on words. In the original Aramaic, the name and the word for rock are identical (*kepa*). In Greek there is a slight change by reason of gender: *Petros: petra* (rock). Peter was known by the name Cephas or Petros within the Christian community (1 Cor 1:12; Gal 1:18; 2:7f). With this designation Peter is constituted the firm foundation of the church. So steadfast will the church be, rooted in the faith-filled Peter, that not even death itself (the gates of hell) will hold any sway over it. This is a church founded on the fullness of life where death has no part.

Keys of the kingdom (v19a): The imagery drawn from the Isaian expression found in today's first reading (Is 22:22) looks to admitting and excluding from the reign of God, the eschatological destination to which the church points. *Whatever you bind...whatever you loose* (v19b): In Jewish categories this connotes the power to excommunicate and reintegrate as well as to give authoritative instruction. It is conferred on all the disciples in a context which points strongly in the direction of excommunication (18:15 - 18). The present context, where there is indication of substituting for the Jewish religious authority (16:5 - 12), may lean more toward the teaching role. However, neither need be excluded from Peter's mission. Decisions made within the church are seen as having binding force even within the end-time reign of God. Matthew concludes with the injunction to silence about the Messiah (v20), here rejoining the other synoptics' level of recognition and preparing for the subsequent passage on the Messiah who suffers (vv21ff).

Some conclusions from this narrative are to be borne in mind. The authority conferred singularly upon Peter is in part conferred on the other disciples as well. In addition, traditional polemics as to whether the church is built upon Peter the man or upon the faith he expressed is overcome in realizing that both are present in the text. The church is built on the believing Peter. Finally, it is important to note that this text continued to have significance as a lived reality at the time of Matthew's writing, at least twenty years after the death of Peter.

The Catholic papacy has been something of the eye of almost every religious hurricane in the course of Christian controversy. Pope Paul VI spoke of it as the major obstacle to Christian unity. But in recent years there have been some positive, if halting, steps forward. It is wrong to say that the New Testament offers no support for the papal claim. It is equally wrong to say that the scriptures explicitly envision everything that the papacy has become. From a doctrinal viewpoint, there is no doubt that Peter is accorded a singular position of authority in the church. And the Matthean text comes from a church preserving that text long after the death of Peter. On the other hand, the ways in which the papacy developed were determined not solely by doctrinal considerations but also by historical circumstances. It is the theologian's task, in concert with the church's teaching office, to separate the two.

Today we recognize the wisdom in having an ultimate arbiter in questions that can easily become divisive. All of Christianity profits by a single voice who authoritatively expresses the belief of the church. This is seen by many, even outside the Catholic fold, as a positive good. At the same time, the role of chief shepherd must be seen as truly pastoral, at the total service of God's people. Moreover, the chief shepherd is called to hear the voice of the faithful in whom the Spirit is also at work. It is, in addition, a mission to be exercised in close concert with the college of the apostles, the bishops of the church. It is a collaborative exercise of ministry where governance and decision making are truly shared. Ecumenical progress around the role of the pope has been notable since the Second Vatican Council. Future steps will take wisdom and courage. With good will and integrity, matched by an ardent desire for unity. the will of Christ for a church that is one can become a reality.

Homiletic and Catechetical Helps

1. The pastoral role of the pope.

2. A threefold papal authority: to teach, rule, and sanctify.

3. The Matthean text: essential features of Peter's role.

4. Peter and the apostles: collaborative leadership in the church.

5. God's wisdom in the direction of the world.

6. Ways of teaching in the church: ecumenical councils, synods, encyclicals, decrees.

7. The holy see: the organism of papal teaching.

8. The conference of bishops and episcopal teaching.

TWENTY-FIRST SUNDAY OF THE YEAR
Year B

Readings

> Jos 24:1 - 2, 15 - 17, 18
> Eph 5:21 - 32
> Jn 6:60 - 69

Theme: Christian Freedom: The Right To Stay Or To Leave

Forced love is no love at all. Since God wants a free response from us, our liberty is never violated. Once settled in the land of promise, Joshua gathers the Israelites at Shechem to renew the covenant and express their intention of remaining with Yahweh or not. At the conclusion of his bread of life discourse, Jesus in John's gospel asks his disciples a similar question: Do they wish to stay with him or to leave? In our reading from Ephesians today, husbands and wives are a living reflection of the love between Christ and the church.

First Reading

The conclusion to the book of Joshua (c. 24) is considered by many authorities to be an appendage, a later composition containing some primitive material. The occupation of Canaan is presented as a *fait accompli,* brought to a conclusion during Joshua's lifetime. There is good evidence, some of it extra-biblical, to indicate that it was a longer process. Nonetheless, after the fashion of the deuteronomic Moses (Deut 11:26 - 29; 27:11ff), Joshua moves to determine whether or not his people desire to remain covenant-centered or not.

All the tribes of Israel (v1): The picture is idealized. The land was not simply overrun by the Israelites, who after defeating the native population decide to renew the covenant. Shechem, for example, an important Canaanite city, never destroyed during the occupation, is the locale of this covenant renewal. It later became an important center of Israelite cult (Gen 33:18ff).

What Joshua does not mention is the gradual assimilation of native peoples who had not been part of the exodus. With their acceptance of the Yahwistic faith, they became part of the Israelite family. Thus, a ceremony of covenant renewal was that for some; for others it was an act of official incorporation.

The language of the renewal can also be explained by this assimilation of new people. To offer the original Sinai covenanters the option of Yahweh or other gods (v15a) would seem to be an unlikely option. The incorporation of new members into the covenant community would make it much more likely. *The gods your fathers served* (v15a): the Mesopotamian gods worshiped by Abraham's ancestors in the land beyond the Euphrates. *Gods of the Amorites* (v15b): the deities worshiped by a sizable part of the pagan population displaced (and absorbed) by Israel at the time of the conquest (4:9). The gathered population is offered the choice of renewing the Sinai commitment (Ex 19 - 24) or not, with Joshua indicating the clear choice of himself and his household (v15c).

There is a brief recital of the saving acts of God during the exodus (vv17f), presented in a more expanded form by Joshua in the introductory ceremony (vv2 - 13). In neither account is there any mention of the covenant at Sinai, an absence which is noted in other sources as well (Ex 15:1 - 17). This may be due to a tradition from segments of the Israelite population which had not participated in the Sinai experience. A more likely explanation is that a ceremony of covenant renewal would not include an account of the original covenant. The covenant-making occurs with the renewal; the inclusion of its precedent would be cultically inappropriate.

The people in unison and without dissent make their option for the Lord as the covenant is renewed with verbal acceptance (v18b).

Responsorial Psalm   Ps 34

The lowly and the authentic poor of God do not reject him or walk in another direction. They are praised in today's thanksgiving psalm, a commentary on which is found on the Thirtieth Sunday of Year C.

Second Reading

This code of moral conduct, probably drawn from the household ethos of Greco-Roman culture, is structured hierarchically to reinforce the social patterns of the time (Col 3:18 - 4:1). Here its distinctly Christian bent is reinforced by the inclusion and interpretation of the Genesis quotation (v31; Gen 2:24)

A moral posture of respect measured by a willingness to be in second place characterizes Christian conduct (v21; 1 Pet 5:5). The marriage relationship calls for recognition of the husband's leadership (v23; 1 Cor 11:3). These forms of subordination are related to faith, not social norms or norms of Gentile domesticity; it is a case of respect for Christ who is present in all the faithful (v30). The husband, on the other hand, is bound as well by Christian principle, i.e. the willingness to sacrifice himself entirely for his wife as did Christ for the church (v25; 1 Cor 11:3; Col 1:18).

The marriage bond mirrors the union between Christ and his church (vv25 - 28). Christ loved the believers to the extent of surrendering his life for them. This offering of Christ results in a "bathing" of the bride, an obvious reference to baptism. *Bath of water with the word* (v26): the ritual of water baptism accompanied by a verbal formula. This effects the transition from sin to grace, from death to life (Rom 6:3f). The purified church is the cleansed and fair-skinned bride on behalf of whom Christ acted with a total love. This is the love which the husband is to manifest as well (v28).

The body of Christ theology reinforces the moral point (vv28ff; Rom 12:5; 1 Cor 6:15). By reason of the unity in Christ, with all being members of the one body, the husband in loving his wife actually exhibits love for himself, for his own body.

The argument is strengthened by the use of the Genesis (2:24) quotation. The deep mutual adherence experienced in the union of man and wife is symbolic of the parallel Christ-church bond. *Mystery* (Gr: *mysterion*) (v32): the recurring Pauline "secret" hidden in God in the past and revealed only in this final era. The mystery here is the fuller understanding of the Genesis text as pointing to the bond between Christ and the church.

Third Reading

These concluding verses of the Johannine Jesus' major discourse on himself as the bread of life, as well as the sacramental flesh and blood, throw into strong relief the reaction of his disciples to his teaching. The initial "murmuring" which accompanied the bread of life discourse (vv41, 43) continues here (v61). The passage continues also the distinction between "flesh" and "spirit," so important to Johannine theology. The former exhibits a purely natural understanding of Jesus' teaching, which fails to come to any authentic understanding. The latter is a God-given gift which leads in faith to the full acceptance of his words (3:6f).

Jesus has concluded his lengthy discourse in which he treats of his own teaching (bread) and the eucharist (flesh and blood). This proves to be a strong test of faith. *This saying* (Gr: *logos*, word) (v60): This refers to the entire content of the preceding teaching (c. 6). The continued *murmuring* of his disciples echoes the conduct of the Israelites in the desert (v61, Ex 16:2, 8f; 17:3). The question which Jesus raises in the face of their incredulity is unfinished in the Greek text, with the first part only (protasis) of the conditional sentence (v12). The meaning, however, is not lost. The shock (literally, scandal) caused by Jesus' words in the preceding discourse will be as nothing in comparison to their reaction in the face of his death by execution with his subsequent return to the Father. Here as elsewhere in John, death and ascension are one movement from the cross to glory (3:13f).

Jesus makes his final appeal for faith acceptance. Spirit and flesh are at odds; only the former confers life, with the latter, in the face of a failure to understand, bringing only death (v63). Only a new birth will bring spirit and life (3:6). Some of those who had heard his teaching and accompanied him remain unbelieving, a situation reflected as well in the apostasies of the early church. But Jesus returns to one of his recurring themes. Faith is attained not by human effort, even though cooperation is essential, but by the action of God drawing the believer (vv64f; 6:37; 8:46f).

At this point there is a major division in the ranks of the disciples. The twelve (the first Johannine use of the term) remain faithful; many others depart (v66). Peter then gives expression to the faith of the twelve in what might be termed John's Petrine profession, given in a different form and a different scenario in the synoptics (Mk 8:27 - 30). Peter fully affirms the teaching of Jesus as the key to life in words that almost repeat Jesus' own (vv68, 63). *God's Holy One* (v69): This act of faith recognizes Jesus as the consecrated one. In the Hebrew scriptures, the people were consecrated to God (Jgs 13:7; 16:17). Jesus is consecrated as the dwelling place of God (10:36; 1:51). It is another manner of expressing Jesus' divine filiation (Mt 16:16).

People choose to walk away from Christ today for various reasons. But most often it is not with Christ that people have difficulty. They would say that their problem is with the church more than with Christ, whose gospel message they find challenging and appealing. Others admit openly that it is the pull of the world or their attraction to sin that destroys their Christian allegiance. So while Christ is seen as the teacher, the "man for others," even the world's Savior, our "murmuring" today takes a different direction: the church's failure to respond, a disinterested clergy, an intransigent authoritarianism, a second or third marriage, questions of morality. And so the list goes on. We can only say that the church is not yet the spotless bride that Christ intends. The church has a human dimension and does not always measure up to our expectations. But it is still our key to God, the custodian of his teaching, the locus of our sacramental life. It is the church that accompanies us from the baptismal font to the cemetery. Yes, we are always free to walk away. But as Catholics we can hardly say that we walk away from the church but remain with Christ. The church is still the bride of Christ, even if all the wrinkles have not yet disappeared.

The Paul of Ephesians is often taken to task for his insensitivity to women's concerns. There is no doubt that he saw a certain headship in the husband's role, although he would certainly have championed decision making by mutual agreement. But it should be remembered that he sees this in religious, not sociological terms. The willingness to be subordinate is part of any Christian's posture because it was the "mind" of Jesus himself. But the fact is that Ephesians asks more of the husband than of the wife when it comes to self-denial and sacrificial dedication on behalf of the spouse. The husband is called to subordi-

nate his own interests to those of his wife just as Christ did. The basic question from either side is one of Christian mutual respect and love. It is this that keeps many a marriage on course today, just as its absence can lead to marital shipwreck.

Homiletic and Catechetical Helps

1. Adult education: growing in faith understanding.

2 The meaning of covenant renewal for the Israelites.

3. The eucharist and our covenant renewal.

4. Departures from Christ in our age.

5. Departures from the church.

6. The meaning of apostasy and heresy.

7. Peter's profession: staying with Christ.

8. Marriage as a sacrament.

9. Submission and mutual respect in marriage.

10. Living the Christ-church symbolism in marriage.

TWENTY-FIRST SUNDAY OF THE YEAR
Year C

Readings

> Is 66:18 - 21
> Heb 12:5 - 7, 11 - 13
> Lk 13:22 - 30

Theme: The Wide Road and Narrow Gate

There is a real paradox in today's gospel. The Lucan Jesus attests to the universal character of the church and at the same time warns about a complacent spirit of easy salvation. In today's first reading, once again we see Third Isaiah's remarkable sense of the universal call of Yahweh. Citizens of distant lands make their way to Jerusalem, with some of them even chosen to minister in temple worship. A measure of discipline makes us all better people. Hebrews today invites us to see the hand of God in our hardships and difficulties.

First Reading

With this stirring passage, the third and final part of the Isaian prophecy moves toward its conclusions. A call addressed to all nations invites them to the worship of Yahweh in Jerusalem. *My glory* (v18): the visible manifestation of God's presence seen in major historical events, as the return from exile (40:5), but especially in his temple (tent) presence (Ex 40:34). A sign (v19): the summons of the Gentiles together with Jews of the diaspora to temple worship. From among the Gentiles a certain number will be sent to "evangelize" even more distant lands (v19): *Tarshish* (Spain), *Put and Lud* (North Africa), *Mosoch* (?), *Tubal and Javan* (Ionia, Asia Minor). There the Gentile fugitives will announce the "glory" of Yahweh. Again, it is interesting to note that it is Gentiles and not Jews who are involved in what might be termed a proselytizing effort. Repeatedly in Hebrew universalism, conversion is due to the action of God more than to any active initiative on the part of the Jews.

The Gentiles, now accompanied by Jews of the diaspora ("your brothers," v20), approach Jerusalem in solemn caravan. As the native population makes its own ritual offerings, the Gentiles offer symbolically the Jews who have been separated from temple and land. *Priests and Levites* (v21): In light of the preceding verse, the "some" mentioned here could be Jews or Gentiles. However, the sense of the verse, in a context of a strong and unconventional universalism, leans toward an interpretation of Gentiles serving in temple ministry. This comes at a time when official Judaism was retrenching on Gentile contact (Ezr 9 - 10) and restricting temple ministries even among the Jews (Ez 40:46; 44:10 - 16).

Responsorial Psalm   Ps 117

The note of universalism is dominant in this shortest of psalms. Commentary is found on the Ninth Sunday of Year C.

Second Reading

In dealing with the problem of suffering under the direction of an all-just God, the Hebrew scriptures frequently explain it in terms of sanctions, i.e. punishment for sin. That such an explanation did not always fit the case is evident from Job and Qoheleth. The book of Proverbs sees testing as a reason for suffering (3:11f; 17:3), a notion with which Hebrews concurs in citing the Proverbs text (vv5f). In the present chapter, Christians are encouraged to persevere in the face of trial and suffering. In addition to finding in Christ their role model (v2), they are exhorted to realize that suffering can lead to a strengthening of faith. Sonship is the Spirit's gift (Gal 4:6), and every son receives a measure of discipline from his father, as a sign not of rejection but of love (vv5ff; Deut 8:5).

The pain of discipline will have a joyful outcome. It will produce an upright spirit, strengthened by adversity. As a person lame from a painful injury must continue to walk on level ground for healing purposes, so too the person once disciplined must avoid the uneven ground of sin in moving virtuously ahead.

Third Reading

This catechesis of Jesus on the rejection and acceptance of his message forms part of his teaching on the Christian journey as he himself makes his own way to Jerusalem (v22).

In illustrating the obstacles to salvation, in answer to a question on the number to be saved (v23), Jesus uses two separate images: the narrow gate (v24) and the locked door (v25). The former points to the necessity of qualifications for admittance, the latter to tardiness and indifference in making the response. In their original context, both metaphors were applicable to Jesus' Jewish contemporaries whose failure to enter was due to their rejection of Jesus and his claims (v24; 13:34f; 14:15 - 24).

The image is that of the larger city gate where throngs passed easily and the narrower, single-file entrance.

The second parable (vv25 - 27) deals with the unexpected time of the Lord's return at the parousia when dalliance and a false sense of inclusion will meet with a negative response. The fact that Jesus and the Jewish community shared much in common will serve as no warranty of salvation. Forceful exclusion will be the result once the time for decision making has passed.

The grief of the rejected Jews will be augmented with the entrance of the Gentile world into the kingdom (vv28f). Israel's authentic strain, represented by the patriarchs and prophets, will be joined by people from all parts of the world at the eschatological banquet. In the oft repeated refrain (v30), the inversion of rank appears. The "last," the discarded and demeaned Gentiles, take precedence over the people of election, who now remain outside.

While the Jew-Gentile ironic situation is clear in the parables, the Lucan use of the stories is not so restricted. The parables are a warning to Christians in the early church for whom vigilance and repentance is an ongoing theme (13:1 - 8; 12:35 - 40) and for whom detachment is essential (12:13 - 34). Laxity may well make it impossible to enter through the narrow gate or find entry at the unforeseen hour. Thus, even though foreigners now find themselves within the church, they may well find themselves in the same position as the unbelieving Jews if they are not vigilant.

"But by comparison..." Consciously or not, many of us may assess our moral posture with those words. Considering everything around me, I really don't look too bad. But comparisons don't always hold up. Today's scriptures draw us in two directions. One stretches our vision, When it comes to God's plan, both Isaiah and Luke envision an open door policy. In God's design exclusivism has no place. Yet it is surprising how much that principle is accepted in theory and bypassed in fact. There are fine practicing Christians who have severe blind spots when it comes to ethnics and minorities. In many neighborhoods today young people grow up and finish high school with little or no contact with people of a different race apart from some competitive sports.

Many churchgoers find no place for "those people" in their neighborhood, their schools, or their parish. This is hardly reconcilable with the Christian message.

But the other point of comparison has to be considered as well. We really can't say that because we are under the "church roof," we are home safe. Yes, Jesus said, there was room for everyone at the banquet, but one person not properly attired was shown the door. The Christian life does take effort. It means self-giving and detachment, going the extra mile, turning the other cheek. Just saying "Lord, Lord" is not sufficient. My Christian responsibility does not finish when I return from mass on Sunday morning. Every day presents its challenges. All of us stand on the brink of serious sin. All of us are called to new challenges in living our faith. That is the mix of life.

So that is the great paradox. There is room for everyone, but not everyone wants to stay. We can always lose our footing. Confirmation, it is noted, is a strengthening sacrament. And that means putting our shoulder to the wheel. Without living in fear and with much hope, it is still salutary for all of us to remember that the door which opens can also close.

Homiletic and Catechetical Helps

1. Christian universalism: practical implications in our neighborhood.

2. The parish: the home for all Christians.

3. The danger of religious indifference.

4. Vigilance versus false security.

5. The danger of a narrow religious vision.

6. Mission in the church.

7. Suffering as a discipline.

8. The growth of faith in hardship.

TWENTY-SECOND SUNDAY OF THE YEAR
Year A

Reading

> Jer 20:7 - 9
> Rom 12:1 - 2
> Mt 16:21 - 27

Theme: Adherence to the Will of God

There is a deep spirituality in the simple prayer of former Secretary General of the United Nations, Dag Hammarskjold: "For all that has been, 'thanks'; to all that will be 'yes.'" The message of today's scriptures centers around that unqualified "yes." Jeremiah accepted his God-given mission even though it was tortuous and he was strongly compelled to turn away. Jesus does not allow voices from any quarter to draw him from his appointed destiny. Even though it was to lead him through the valley of death, he was irrevocably set upon the path that his Father had determined. It is this type of "living sacrifice" that, Paul tells us, we should offer to God.

First Reading

The book of Jeremiah contains mainly the prophet's oracles on Jerusalem's final days before the exile. It is an important index to the political, social, and religious events of that period. At the same time it contains a series of the prophet's personal reflections on the demanding calling that he had received. Today's reading is taken from these "confessions of Jeremiah." It represents one of the strongest and, in a sense, audacious conversations with Yahweh in the Hebrew scriptures.

The book's editor has placed this present passage immediately after a threefold prediction of Jerusalem's destruction, made at great personal cost by the prophet. The first was made at the Potsherd Gate near the city dump (19:1 - 3); the second, in the temple area (19:14f); and the final one, before the priest

Pashhur (20:1 - 5). For such alleged profanation, Jeremiah was publicly punished by being placed in stocks (20:2).

In the present passage, well placed after the difficult ordeal, the prophet addresses Yahweh in the language of sexual seduction (v7). God has seduced (Hebrew: *pata*, Ex 22:15) and seized him (Hebrew: *hazaq*, Dt 22:25; 2 Sam 13:11). Admittedly such language was used in a figurative sense; however its strength and boldness would not have been lost on the prophet's audience. In its daring, the lament serves well to underscore the pain that his mission entailed; frustration has led to this strong confrontation. The brighter side of his original calling—"to build and to plant" (1:10b)—was in no way evident. God, he says, has not dealt with him honestly.

And what has been his lot for speaking of punishment and destruction (1:10a)? Derision, hostility and rejection (7b, 8b). To this physical abuse has been added.

The final verse (v9) offers an interesting insight into the psychology of prophetic inspiration. Yahweh's word is compared to a raging fire (15:14; 23:29). Attempts to restrain it or leave it unuttered become insufferable. As much as he might have desired to do so, Jeremiah is simply unable to remain silent. God has so taken hold of his life that the word, as terrifying as it may be, must be spoken.

Even though we are dealing here with the language of poetry, the idea of a strong divine direction in prophecy stands out in bold relief. There is an inexorability about God's word. Once embarked on his mission, the prophet finds that there is no turning back.

Responsorial Psalm   Ps 63

The psalmist's sentiments of trust echo those of a prophet or disciple. It is only confidence that makes their hardship supportable. Placed at a distance from the sanctuary with a resultant spiritual aridity (v2), the psalmist sees the temple as the focal point of faith and the source of renewal (v3). Through this prayerful experience, intimacy with Yahweh is intensified, with the psalmist led to proclaim God's love. The vivid imagery of clinging to the Lord, with the right hand of God never loosening its grip (v9; Dt 10:20) has a spiritual richness highlighting the importance of trust.

Second Reading

This short passage from Romans continues to build on the idea of identification with God's will. Paul uses his own distinctive imagery. The disciple is likened to the temple sacrifice, making his body (i.e. body person, Rom 6:12f), the offering (v1). The language draws on Jewish cult, but differences are quickly underscored. The temple offering is a dead animal; the disciple is living. The temple offering has only an efficacy "in the flesh" (Heb 9:9f) and is powerless over sin (Heb 10:3f) whereas the Christian offers a worship "in the spirit." It is an oblation endowed with internal personal sentiments, deriving its worth from the offering of Christ himself (Heb 9:13ff).

The use of sacrificial imagery underlines total self-surrender. The conversion or transformation of heart (v2), by which the Christian is being constantly configured to Christ, is the work of the Spirit (2 Cor 3:17 - 18); it involves an ongoing disengagement from a world/age which is passing away (1 Cor 7:31) with an accompanying ever fuller engagement in Christ. The human mind (Gr: *nous*) itself is renewed in a conversion wherein God's will becomes ever more central.

Third Reading

The passage is a turning point in Matthew's gospel (as well as in Mark's—8:31 - 36). It is preceded by Peter's profession of Jesus as Messiah and God's Son (16:13 - 20). Here the topic moves from glory to the cross. The temporal transition in Matthew—"From that time on" (v21)—separates the profession and passion prediction more logically than in Mark.

The key notion in this passage is engagement in God's will on the part of Jesus (vv21 - 23) and those who would follow him (vv24 - 28). Distancing himself somewhat from Peter's profession, Jesus speaks of his impending suffering. Originally such predictions, during the lifetime of Jesus, were undoubtedly a general indication of what he was to endure. The specifics given here (v21), which even include the third day resurrection, represent a sharpening "after the fact." Prophetic predictions are characteristically very general in nature. The gospels are written and "fine-tuned" after the resurrection in the light of Easter faith, as is seen in the case of Peter's recognition of Christ as Son of God (Mt 16:16).

Peter's attempt to dissuade Jesus and the latter's sharp rebuke (vv22f) do not fit well with the accolades accorded Peter only a few verses before (16:17 - 18). They are, however, integral to the author's combined glory–suffering theme. The "Satan" designation of Peter attaches itself to his attempt to deflect Jesus from his God-given mission (cf. 4:10). Peter's thinking is an obstacle blocking a determined path; it is human rather than God-related reasoning (v23).

The sayings on discipleship (vv24 - 28) are well suited to their Matthean context. Cross-bearing and self-denial are integral to any true following of Jesus. It need not be sought out; it flows from the Christian life itself. Cross bearing derives its *raison-d'être* from the following of Jesus.

It is important to note the inversion of values which discipleship entails. Human salvation is a Christian loss while human loss is Christian salvation. The Christian is prepared to sacrifice everything, even life itself, in the interests of eternal values. For those who adhere to God's designs, Christ's return in glory offers an imperishable recompense (Mt 25:31 - 40).

Today's liturgy of the word is an extended commentary on the Lord's Prayer: "Thy will be done." Jeremiah's very human and understandable lament points up the difficulty in accepting God's will without reservation. Once he accepted his mission, the prophet paid a dear price. Yet the call of the living God and the correctness of the cause convinced him that he could not do otherwise.

The New Testament in its entirety shows us that it was Jesus' "will" which saved us. As painful as it may have been, Jesus was not to be dissuaded from fulfilling his call. Before the "no" of Adam and his descendants, the New Adam utters an unequivocal "yes."

As followers of Jesus, bearing the name Christian, we are asked to make God's will our own in countless ways, large and small. This is what it means to grow in holiness. The demands made on us will be less vivid than those of Jeremiah or Jesus. But what is important is that every day in many ways we make God's will our own.

Homiletic and Catechetical Helps

1. The psychology of a prophet

2. Difference between a prophet and an inspired writer, e.g. evangelist.

3. Anger with God: a sign of faith

4. Christian soteriology: Jesus' will

5. Understanding gospel composition as reflection on the life of Jesus.

6. Self-denial in our daily life.

7. Doing God's will in our daily life.

8. Human possessions versus spiritual holdings.

9. Sacrifice: its cultic and figurative meaning.

10. Explain: "Thy will be done on earth as it is in heaven."

TWENTY-SECOND SUNDAY OF THE YEAR
Year B

Readings

> Dt 4:1 - 2, 6 - 8
> Jas 1:17 - 18, 21 - 22, 27
> Mk 7:1 - 8, 14 - 15, 21 - 23

Theme: Law and the Christian Life

Life without law is chaotic and unmanageable. Life with too much law is repressive and dehumanizing. Today's scripture points up the positive and negative features of religious law.

The positive values in the law, seen as a gift of God, are set forth clearly in Deuteronomy. Jesus had a sound respect for the Hebrew law in its basic formulation. But, as in today's gospel, he criticized the Jewish legalism of his time. James today speaks of care for the needy as authentic worship.

First Reading

Although the book of Deuteronomy is attributed to Moses, it comes to us in its present form some seven centuries later. It is composed of a corpus of laws drawn up to guide all phases of Hebrew life. Some of the laws may well date from Moses' time, but in the main they span many centuries, with the mantle of Mosaic authority covering the entire legislative code.

"Hear, Israel" (*Shema'*). The invocation is solemn in the Deuteronomic literature. In the early chapters of Deuteronomy, it serves as a prelude to the subsequent body of laws, a cultic summons to be attentive to God's word. Statutes and decrees (v1) are not synonymous. Statutes were broad legal precepts expressed in positive form; decrees were casuistic and more restricted in their application.

A frequently re-emerging leitmotiv of Deuteronomy is that faithful observance of the law leads to life, and life, in concrete terms, is identified with possession of the land of promise. Life here is natural, human, and terrestrial, not heavenly or eternal. Then there is the injunction, frequent in ancient law codes, not to make any later additions or deletions (v2). There is wisdom in the law (Sir 24), and through its observance Israel will give evidence of superior status (vv6ff). This occurs in two ways. As an immediate expression of Yahweh's will and a ready avenue of access to his favor, the law shows God's closeness to his people. This God is not known through lofty speculation and has no need of heavenly beings to convey his intentions. Secondly, comprehensive and rooted in justice, the law is unmatched among the nations. Its observance is certain to illustrate the wisdom of the people and the God who has espoused them.

The reading is typical of the Deuteronomic exhortations. The book is strong on motivation for Torah observance, a motivation ultimately based on Yahweh's love for his people.

Responsorial Psalm   *Ps 15*

The psalm's opening verse (not read today) poses the question as to the qualities required in one engaged in temple worship.

The psalm sees the genuine worshiper as a law observer who maintains proper relations with God and neighbor in thought, word and action. The dealings of such persons with others are marked by correctness, enabling them, in turn, to distinguish the bad and the good in the conduct of others (v4). In financial matters, the just will not be swayed or be bribed at the expense of innocent people nor will they take interest on a loan, a serious violation of another's personal integrity and a form of extortion in Hebrew law (Ex 22:24; Lev 25:36f).

Second Reading

This letter attributed to James, leader of the Jerusalem church and "brother of the Lord" (Mt 13:55; Mk 6:3), is more a general exhortation than a letter. Today's passage centers on God as the first gift-giver. He transcends all the heavenly bodies, which are themselves his gifts (Gen 1:14 - 18). Unlike the planets which increase and diminish in visible brightness, God's brilliance remains unaltered (v17).

In addition, there is the gift of his word. Just as God's word in Genesis was creative, so the word in the new dispensation brings about a new spiritual creation. The word brings believers to new life (vv17f; Jn 3:5f), like a seed producing fruit (Mk 4:1 - 20). Like Christ himself (1 Cor 15:20; Rom 8:23), Christians are the first fruits; they will bear abundant fruit if their roots are deep. The word has the power to save if acted upon. James has strong feelings about a merely nominal faith which does not express itself in deed (vv23ff).

The word is particularly effective in outreach to the needy in society (v27). Widows and orphans epitomize need since a fatherless family has no tangible means of support (Deut 27:19; Sir 4:10). This is coupled with remaining undefiled by the world (used here in its unredeemed sense, in opposition to God). These two examples (v27) constitute "pure and undefiled religion," not in an exhaustive sense but as integral to any authentic expression of Christian belief.

Third Reading

Jesus in today's gospel takes issue with the legalism of the Pharisees. In so doing he surfaces the ultimate source of sinful conduct, a personal internal spirit. This chapter in Mark (c. 7) deals with Christ's attitude toward a number of issues: purification ritual (vv1 - 8), human tradition and divine commandments (vv9 - 13), and Jewish food laws (vv18 - 23).

In failing to wash before eating, Jesus' disciples are in violation of Jewish law (vv1 - 8). Writing for an audience unschooled in Jewish tradition, Mark explains the precept to his readers. Purification rites had become an increasingly important part of the law. What was originally prescribed for Levites only (Num 8) was extended in legal tradition to all Israelites and in a broader form as well. These were detailed unwritten prescriptions stemming from early Jewish teachers and codified by the rabbis. These "traditions of the elders" were eventually given the same weight as the Torah itself. Among such laws were those on the ritual washing of body parts and culinary objects before eating. The failure of the disciples to observe these norms occasions the criticism of Jesus' opponents.

Christ's reply (vv6f) is a reworded quotation from the Septuagint touching on two aspects of Pharisaic hypocrisy (Gr: *hypokrites*, a masked actor). The first is the marked emphasis on external conformity (lip service) with no change of heart. The second is the penchant for ranking secondary precepts with the Torah itself. In some cases, divine law is even dismissed in favor of human precept, e.g. the qorban case (7:9 - 13).

Jesus states publicly that sin comes not from violations of external observances but rather from evil internal dispositions (vv14f). Later in private conversation with his disciples (v17), he elaborates on this teaching, showing the difference between legalistic ritual and true morality (vv21 - 23). Internal evil manifests itself in single or habitual acts of sinfulness. The evils cited are in large part related to the decalogue, therefore basic in character (Gal 5:19f). Not included in the reading today is the editorial comment that Jesus therewith abrogated the Jewish food laws (v19). It is unlikely that such was Jesus' initial intention; if he had so intended, the early church would have had a clear precedent in dealing with this thorny issue (Acts 10:1 - 16). However, the statement of Jesus would certainly have lent itself to support later church action in abolishing such laws.

Today's liturgy gives us a balanced approach to law. Deuteronomy sees it as positive and life-giving. Properly understood, law gives direction to life and certainty of God's will, and it establishes positive social patterns of conduct. Anti-nomianism is not a part of the true Judeo-Christian tradition.

However, law must be rooted in the love of God and be an expression of it. It is a means and not an end in itself. Laws should not be multiplied, and the danger of that happening is not insignificant. Laws give security, and security in religious conduct is paramount for some people. Law observance can convince us that God is well served, when actually the authentic spirit of religion, as a loving response to God, is woefully lacking.

Jesus, in today's gospel, inveighs against a legalistic spirit. His Jewish contemporaries were lost in detailed prescriptions and had forgotten the true meaning of religion. Their adherence to external observance often took precedence over faith, or even excluded the fundamental responsibilities of that faith.

As in most things in life, law requires a balanced outlook. Where and when it is necessary, it must be enforced and observed. But it must never suffocate the spirit which leads the Christian above and beyond anything the law might ask (Gal 2:22f). Every law must be evaluated in the light of the greatest law: the love of God and neighbor. Notice how succinctly James summarizes the spirit of religion: holiness of life and care for the needy.

Homiletic and Catechetical Helps

1. The value of law in the Christian life.

2. The danger of law in the Christian life.

3. Legalism—examples from daily life.

4. The code of canon law—role in the church.

5. The primacy of the law of love.

6. Conversion: internal versus external morality.

7. Nominal Catholicism and a new evangelization.

8. Usury and interest rates.

9. The "widows and orphans" of our day.

10. Faith: hearers and doers.

TWENTY-SECOND SUNDAY OF THE YEAR
Year C

Readings

> Sir 3:17 - 18, 20, 28 - 29
> Heb 12:18 - 19, 22 - 24
> Lk 14:1, 7 - 14

Theme: Humility

No one can boast before God, says Paul, and if there is any boasting to be done at all, it can center only on our weaknesses. Today's liturgy stresses the importance of humility in our lives, a virtue not greatly esteemed in our competitive society. Sirach offers some practical insights, and the gospel teaches the meaning of humility in parable form. The reading from Hebrews contrasts the two covenants, pointing out the blessedness and joy proper to the new dispensation.

First Reading

The work of one Ben Sira, a Jerusalem Jew of the early second century B.C. and translated into Greek by his grandson some fifty years later, appears in the final years of Israel's Wisdom literature. Sirach follows a traditional line of thought in expressing practical norms of life.

The humble person is more appreciated than a generous benefactor, and the higher one goes in life, the more essential humility is (vv17 - 18). Characteristic of the humble person is contentment with his/her lot. The pursuit of lofty objectives brings disappointment and disillusionment, especially when ability does not match aspirations (Ps 131:1).

Proud people are obsessed with their own thinking and their often unrealistic goals. The wise person is attracted to the wisdom of others and learns from the insights which only experience can give (v28). Practical charity, e.g. almsgiving (7:10; 16:14), atones for one's sinful past, just as water is an antidote for a spreading fire (v29).

Responsorial Psalm   Ps 68

The Hebrew text of Psalm 68 is obscure in a number of verses. It is a cultic hymn probably used for the solemn enthronement of the ark of the covenant. Today's liturgy selects only those parts of this long psalm related to the theme of God's concern for the powerless. The choir calls upon the just to proclaim God's goodness, especially his concern for orphans, widows, the homeless, and prisoners. Widows and orphans get prime consideration (Deut 10:18; 27:19) because, in the absence of male support, they are most vulnerable (vv6f). The land of promise is renewed at God's will for the benefit of his people, especially the poor. The land is always considered the greatest of God's blessings. The majesty of Psalm 68 is tempered by its emphasis on Yahweh's tender love for the least remembered.

Second Reading

The letter to the Hebrews contrasts in various ways the old and new covenants. In today's reading, the author stresses their differences from a cultic perspective. The covenant made on Mount Sinai with Moses as mediator was marked by a terrifying theophany (vv18f; Ex 19:12 - 13, 16 - 19; 20:18f). In their fear, the people asked that God not address them directly (Ex 20:19).

Much different is the experience of the new covenant, sealed in Christ's blood (vv22ff). A celestial liturgy is depicted (Mount Zion, Jerusalem) in which Christians, by reason of their baptism, are already participants. The first covenant was an earthly reality concerned with the history-bound future of God's people. The present covenant is other-worldly and eternal. It is marked by serenity, the presence of angels, the faithful of the former covenant ("just made perfect"), and the Christians who have died ("first born enrolled in heaven," Jas 1:18), as well as Jesus and the Father. This is a permanent and lasting bond between God and his people, characterized by peace and joy. In a verse not included, the author exhorts his readers to listen to God's voice (v25).

Third Reading

Luke returns to one of his most emphatic points in today's gospel. The parable of Jesus, with its treatment of banquet protocol, states that just as the poor are closest to Jesus and his mission, they should be close as well to his disciples (vv12 - 14). A second point is made as well: humility should be a part of every disciple's life (vv8 - 11).

The banquet or wedding feast as an eschatological symbol is frequent in the New Testament, appearing again in the present chapter of Luke (cf. vv15 - 24). Christ is the host (v24), and all people without exception are welcome, with the necessary internal disposition always presupposed (Mt 22:10 - 14). Emphasis falls on the presence of those who would ordinarily be kept at arm's length in Jewish society.

The first verse in today's gospel (v1) is connected with a following discussion (vv2 - 6). With the arrival of Jesus at the Pharisee's house, a sick person was presented to him. Jesus questions the Pharisees about the appropriateness of a sabbath healing, with silence being their only response to the dilemma he presents. Meanwhile Jesus has healed the man and dismissed him (v4).

Jesus then passes to the question of banquet protocol (vv7 - 11). The teaching in itself is basic etiquette, a practical wisdom of the type found in Proverbs or Sirach. In the absence of "place cards," do not move too far up the table lest you later be asked to move down. There is no embarrassment whatever in being asked to advance and occupy empty places. But Jesus' teaching is more profound, as his final remark indicates (v11). Self-promotion has no place in God's reign or at his table. On the other hand, the humble person, who in honesty recognizes what God has done in his or her life, is the one who is lifted up. The sentiments match those of Mary in the Magnificat (Lk 1:48f). There is a "double entendre" in the word "invited" (Gr: *keklemenoi*, also meaning "called, elect"). The parable has a broader scope in looking at position in the reign of God.

At this point (vv12 - 14), the theme reverts to the lot of the man with dropsy (vv2 - 6). Jesus teaches that in the interests of love and concern, he is willing to set aside legal prescriptions. In his personal comportment, he departed from religious and social convention in associating and eating with the "untouchables" of his time (7:36 - 44; 19:1 - 10). His teaching conveys the same idea. At the final banquet there is place for all, just as there is room for God's healing action at any time.

All of this flies in the face of a Greco-Roman ethic of reciprocity whereby one good turn deserved another. An act of kindness was expected to be returned. The charity of Jesus sees no possibility of favorable recompense. It is done solely for the good of the other (Mt 5:46f).

Love becomes more visible when it touches the neediest, the specially designated recipients of Jesus' message (Lk 4:16 - 19). Here Jesus speaks mainly of the handicapped, whose lack of physical wholeness made them misfits in society. Even the Qumran literature from late pre-Christian times finds no place for them at the eschatological banquet (1QS 2:5 - 22). The listing (v13) includes "the poor" as well. Their lot differs little from that of the handicapped, and they are equally incapable of repayment.

The reward for openness to the needy is eternal (v14). Once again in the gospels, it is the standard of love of neighbor that is the norm of final judgment (Mt 25:31 - 46).

Two ideas emerge in today's gospel: the importance of humility and of love for the humble of the earth. Are they related? The answer is in the affirmative when we understand that humility is the honest recognition of personal status in the presence of an all-good and beneficent God. All are marked by weakness and inadequacy. The realization of the fact convinces us that we have no claim to superiority or exclusivity. The humble person realizes that the poorest at the table are as worthy, perhaps worthier than he or she is.

The liturgy today calls us to humility and to attentiveness to the humble. It is a virtue about which we hear little today, perhaps because it is so much at odds with self-determination, human ambition, and aggressiveness. But it is too dominant a scriptural value to be bypassed. However vaguely or confusedly understood, the truth is clear. Humility calls us to turn our lives over to God and recognize that all we are and all we do derives ultimately from him.

Sin is always a misfortune. But it, too, has its positive side. If it makes us more aware of our inadequacy and our need of God's help, then sin has been productive of good.

Even a cursory reading of the gospels makes the point. The people most deaf to Jesus' word are the self-sufficient, the religious professionals, the spiritually skilled—Pharisees, scribes, priests. Those who hear most readily are the sinners, the social outcasts, those aware of their humanness and their need for God. These are the humble of the earth.

Homiletic and Catechetical Helps

1. Understanding humility.

2. Pride as a capital sin.

3. The spiritual life: loss means gain.

4. Meal sharing as a Christian experience.

5. Are all people welcome at our family table?

6. Meal sharing, eucharist, heavenly banquet: inter-relatedness

7. Consciousness of the handicapped.

8. Sharing with no hope of repayment.

9. God's concern for the poor, the outcast, the sinner.

10. Earthly and heavenly liturgy: Sunday mass—"a little bit of heaven."

TWENTY-THIRD SUNDAY OF THE YEAR
Year A

Readings

Ez 33:7 - 9
Rom 13:8 - 10
Mt 18:15 - 20

Theme: Admonition

God's word this week speaks of our Christian responsibility to be willing to correct our brothers and sisters when the need arises. Ezekiel speaks of admonition in terms of the prophetic ministry wherein it was not infrequently demanded. The gospel today speaks of the procedure to be followed in the Christian community in dealing with the unrepentant offender. The gospel also speaks of community prayer. The second reading from Romans highlights love as the summary and epitome of all the commandments. While not directly related to the other readings, it nonetheless offers the basis for understanding the why of Christian admonition.

First Reading

Ezekiel's prophetic career began among the first wave of deportees in Babylon (597 B.C.). He is the first prophet to receive his calling in a foreign land, one of the reasons why he emphasizes the universal interests of Yahweh, a very "mobile" God (1:15 - 20). A contemporary of Jeremiah, Ezekiel addresses the already departed exiles and, in his early years, informs them of the impending tragedy of Jerusalem's destruction (586

B.C.). It was a bitter task, in spite of Yahweh's efforts to make it more palatable (3:1 - 4).

The present passage appears twice in the book (3:17 - 19); the present chapter builds around the idea of the watchman (1 - 6, 7 - 9). The first section describes the watchman's duties in time of war. He is to sound the trumpet so that people may avert sudden death; his failure to do so will render him culpable for the deaths that ensue.

The second part (7 - 9), read today, is more general in character. The designated watchman has the duty of bringing culpability to the attention of the guilty. The "son of man" appellation is synonymous with "man." The watchman is like a sentinel standing guard to protect his people. He has a responsibility to Israel as a whole (v7) as well as to the individual (vv8f). This latter dimension is consonant with the strong personalism that comes to the fore in Israelite thought at the time of the exile. With Judah's dispersion and the destruction of Jerusalem, the spirit of nationalism recedes and the personal relationship with God emerges more strongly (33:10 - 20; Jer 31:27 - 33). Guilt is personal as well, and retribution is individual.

The watchman is to indicate the seriousness of a person's sin. First cited is the case of a person who does not turn from his sinfulness. If he has been warned, the watchman's task has been discharged. The wrongdoer pays the price of his waywardness, but the watchman is not responsible.

When the warning has not been given, for whatever reason, the watchman is held accountable.

Despite its strong note of severity, the passage illustrates Yahweh's concern, with the prophetic voice seen as the key to possible conversion up to the final moment. The stress falls on the responsibility to admonish rather than on the response of the offender.

Responsorial Psalm   Ps 95

Commentary on this psalm may be found on the Fourth Sunday of Year B.

Second Reading

This Romans passage is of great importance in understanding Paul's teaching on Christian freedom from the law. Such freedom is not to be identified with anti-nomianism or licentiousness. If the basic Christian commandment of love is observed, then the dictates of the decalogue (Ex 20:13 - 17) or of any other religious or civil precepts will be met. If the positive command to love one's neighbor is central, then negative prohibition against harming another, which are basic requirements, are observed *ipso facto*. Love respects the law but calls for much more.

Love is the only debt which Christians have to pay, in Paul's figurative language (v6). In responding to Christ's command of unlimited love (Mk 12:28 - 34), Paul states that the law is totally fulfilled (v10).

Third Reading

The Matthean context deals with the offender in the Christian community. The sinner who departs the community is to be sought out (18:10 - 14). In the gospel read today, a formal procedure is given for the unrepentant offender who remains within the community. The context indicates that this is more than a private offense. It is in the public forum and has communal consequences.

The formal procedure (vv15 - 17), reflected in both the Qumran literature and rabbinic sources, deals with the recalcitrant person who does not make amends. The first step is direct confrontation alone, and then, this failing, in the presence of witnesses. The presence of two or three witnesses was required for public denunciation (Deut 19:15); in the Christian community, the possibility of a single witness is recognized (v16). This moves the accusation into the public forum.

If this fails, there remains the right to convoke the local ecclesial community. If the accused still persists in his or her obstinacy, the final step is expulsion from the church, i.e. returning to the state of a non-believer (Gentiles or tax collectors).

The legal decision is upheld by the divine judge (v19). The use of the theological passive here avoids the use of the divine name. The power to bind and loose meant effective authority to convict or exonerate. It included the right to excommunicate. In this regard, church authorities are here given the power that is elsewhere given to Peter alone (16:19). The process upholds the church's desire to resolve its problems internally without recourse to civil magistrates (Lk 12:57 - 59; 1 Cor 6:1 - 6). The emphasis on procedure should not obscure the underlying rationale: "To win over your brother" (v15). Full restoration to the community is the desired result.

The concluding verses (vv19 - 20) speak of the efficacy that Christ's presence in the community brings to prayerful supplication. (The opinion that this refers to the preceding juridical decision being brought before God is doubtful.) The reference here is to prayer in general, uttered by even a small number of people. It is related to the preceding passage only thematically (community action, divine confirmation).

Christian prayer is efficacious because Christ prays with the believers. It is his Spirit that "comes to the aid of our weakness and intercedes with irrepressible groanings" (Rom 8:26f). The Father does not remain insensitive to the needs of the praying community.

The epistle is of paramount importance for today's theme. Love is the yardstick of all Christian conduct. Law, precepts, and procedures must reflect love. Canon law, for example, has validity to the extent that it regulates conduct in the church by respecting clearly the dignity and worth of each person.

Admonition is at times necessary in the interests of our neighbor's welfare. An early step in dealing with chemical dependency, for example, is intervention. The dependent person is kindly but firmly confronted by others regarding his or her illness. This is a painful experience for the sufferer as well as for the confronter. The results are often salutary and mark the beginning of conversion; sometimes it can lead to alienation and bitterness. It remains, however, a good example of admonition. The well-being of the person demands a painful encounter, but it springs from a desire to heal, not to hurt.

The same is true in dealing with other personal ills in church or society. The prophets admonished in their time; basic church struc-tures provided for it in New Testament times. Even today there are times when the church has to use judicial procedures to correct the errant.

On a personal level, all of us have a certain responsibility. Some problems are overlooked for years and never addressed. Heavy drink-ing, drug addiction, marital infidelity, laziness, negligence of family, lack of social responsibility–examples can be multiplied. All too often failure to address a person's weakness leads to moral and/or physical deterioration. Even people in authority often prefer to avoid difficult or uncomfortable situations.

The scriptures today remind us that there are times when we as church–diocese, parish, school–or as individuals must follow the diffi-cult path in addressing another's wrong doing. To be avoided is any spirit of vindictiveness, on the one hand, or a spirit of laissez-faire *and inaction, on the other.*

Homiletic and Catechetical Helps

1. Admonition: concrete examples—When? How? Why?

2. Love—the motive of all admonition.

3. Meaning of love as the "fulfillment of the law."

4. Jesus and the woman taken in adultery: example of admonition.

5. Dealing with addictions in the family.

6. The power "to bind and loose" in the church.

7. The meaning of collegiality.

8. Community prayer and private prayer.

9. Civil law, church law—their relationship to the "law of love."

10. Distinguishing admonition from "putting someone in his or her place" or "telling someone off."

TWENTY-THIRD SUNDAY OF THE YEAR
Year B

Readings

> Is 35:4 - 7
> Jas 2:1 - 5
> Mk 7:31 - 37

Theme: The Gift of Hearing

Human life is seriously impaired when deafness occurs. Because of deafness, Beethoven never heard some of his greatest masterpieces. The Israelites saw impaired hearing, like all other handicaps, as a lack of wholeness or integrity. Such a person was incapable of full participation in the life of a holy (i.e. whole) community.

In today's first reading, Isaiah, in one of his great lyric poems, sees Israel's future liberation as a healing of human illness, a restoration of wholeness. In the gospel, Jesus, the fulfillment of Isaiah's hope, heals a man's deafness as a sign of the end-time's arrival. In the epistle of James, a very practical lesson on equality and just treatment of others affords us some important considerations for our life today.

First Reading

The reading is couched in terms of a return from exile, similar in theme to Isaiah 40 - 55. As in the original exodus experience, Yahweh takes the lead. His deliverance of the people is, in a sense, an act of justice to himself (v4). If Yahweh were not powerful enough to vanquish Israel's foes, then he would be inferior to their gods, a thesis categorically excluded (Ex 15:11 - 16).

The deliverance of Yahweh vanquishes evil. In Hebrew thought evil is masked in various guises: physical illness, handicaps, burned and scorched land without vegetation, sinful conduct and death itself. With the deliverance spoken of here, a journey experience reminiscent of the exodus, the restoration of life (water) to the desert is important (vv6 - 7; Is 41:18ff). Aridity and drought give way to abundant irrigation.

Yahweh's strength brings new life to the physically impaired as well. This "era of grace" is more than a spiritual experience; it has physical results as well. The blind, the deaf, the lame and the dumb are major beneficiaries. Their restored health, coupled with the desert's irrigation and fertility, becomes an eschotological sign. God makes all things new.

Responsorial Psalm   Ps 146

Yahweh's providing for the unfortunate links this psalm with the theme of the day. The author calls for trust in Yahweh who has given ample evidence of his creative power and fidelity (vv5f). The liturgy uses only the latter part of the psalm (vv7 - 10) wherein the Lord's concern for the oppressed and hungry (an exodus allusion) is coupled with love for the sightless and the subdued. Widows and orphans, who epitomize the helpless Israelite (Deut 10:18), are highlighted, together with the just and the stranger. The way of the self-sufficient and the cunning will be laid waste (v96). The final inclusion invites the community to acknowledge God's beneficent reign. Again, it is the least of this world who are the chief beneficiaries.

Second Reading

In speaking of table protocol, Jesus in Luke's gospel stresses the importance of humility on the part of the guest in taking the lower place at the table (Lk 14:7 - 11). In today's reading, James, in the example he uses, stresses the proper attitude of the host, as the writer inveighs against discrimination within the Christian community. A higher place is not to be accorded a person on the basis of appearances, be it of wealth or status, while the poorly clad person is practically dismissed (vv2ff). The case is one of self-serving favoritism.

The determining factor is faith in the "glorious Lord Jesus Christ" whose singular status excludes all other considerations of rank or privilege (v1). Anyone who discriminates is judging by human and corrupt standards (v4), not by God's norms.

Privilege belongs only to the poor, the special recipients of God's favor, the elect of the reign (v5; Lk 7:22; 6:20).

Third Reading

This miracle story is clearly presented as the fulfillment of Israel's future hope, even including an oblique reference to the Isaian text (v37; Is 35:5f). In Jesus, the final era is present.

The historical event itself is captured vividly in the Marcan account, e.g. the imposition of one hand, the use of spittle, the touching, the Aramaic word, the groaning. The stylized miracle story form is present in the general description of the illness (deafness, speech defect) (v32), the action of Jesus (vv33f) and the completeness of the cure (v35).

The cure takes place at the sea of Galilee after a very circuitous, even puzzling journey from Tyre in coastal Phoenicia, north to the city of Sidon, then southeast to Caesarea Philippi, to a point on the east of the sea of Galilee (v31). This is hardly a direct route to Jesus' destination. It is, however, a journey through Gentile country and thus a likely Marcan allusion to Christ's universal mission.

To correct the man's handicap, Jesus becomes physically involved (vv33f). The use of such contact in healings would not have been considered unusual. The fingers were inserted in the ears and spittle was placed on the tongue (cf. Mk 8:23; Jn 9:6). Jesus groans out of compassion and his gaze goes upward in prayer. The word of cure is Aramaic, editorially translated.

The cure is immediate and complete. Jesus again tries to impose secrecy (v36). This is part of the "Messianic secret" in Mark, variously interpreted by commentators. The understanding of Jesus and his mission is complete only after the resurrection. It is not to be distorted by partial glimpses of Christ as a healer or wonder-worker. In addition, Jesus studiously avoids forms of human acclamation. In Mark's gospel, there is a gradual unfolding of Jesus' personality, made by him to his apostles.

The injunction to silence, however, is thwarted; the cure produces the opposite effect (vv36f). The people's "proclamation of Jesus" carries post-Easter overtones of kerygmatic preaching

(14:9; 16:15). The account closes by echoing the Isaian text of fulfillment (v37).

So often in the New Testament we note that there are many who hear but do not grasp. Christ exhorts us: "Whoever has ears to hear ought to hear" (Mk 4:9).

Today's readings remind us that Jesus came to restore integrity to the disabled. This was God's way of making crooked ways straight at the dawn of a new era. It was Jesus' way of casting out evil from the arena where it held sway–in sickness, disease, disability and death. Finally he put sin itself to death on the cross. In Jesus' cure of a deaf man, more than compassion is evident. The final battle between good and evil is taking place. But deafness is more than physical. It is moral as well and is no stranger to our times. There is a difference between hearing and listening. The latter requires attentiveness; the former does not. Music may serve to enhance a restful environment while desk work is being done. The music is heard, little more. Attendance at a symphony or a musical, however, evokes a posture of listening, concentration and attentiveness.

All too often we hear God's word but do not listen. Attention is lacking, and sometimes our will as well. The word takes no root within us. We are often addicted to sin in some form and remain obtuse to God's will. At times the cry of human needs is deafening and we go on our way oblivious of an evident call. Yet God has been generous. His voice is ever present in word, sacrament, church teaching, and Christian insight. He speaks to us also in the eyes of the poor. Our deafness can be overcome in many ways. James today gives us a very practical example. Discrimination is un-Christian. Yet how often Christians fall prey to its designs. Cultivating persons of rank, showing preferential treatment, eliminating people of inferior status from our company on the basis of color, creed or ethnic background–all of this flies in the face of Christian belief. When God's word is proclaimed, we so often hear but do not listen. Today's liturgy reminds us that our deafness can be cured.

Homiletic and Catechetical Helps

1. Hebrew thought: relationship of physical and spiritual integrity.

2. The miracles of Jesus as part of the final battle.

3. Healing: a sign of God's compassion.

4. Healing: our ministry to the sick—in family, parish, neighborhood.

5. Spiritual healing: our relationship to the non-religious, the alienated, the embittered; the sacrament of reconciliation.

6. Listening to God's word: in liturgy, catechetics, private scripture reading, church teaching.

7. Listening to God in daily life: events at home, school, office, parish.

8. Examples of favoritism from personal experience.

9. Examples of discrimination from personal experience.

10. Hearing: the value of "auricular" (ear) confession.

TWENTY-THIRD SUNDAY OF THE YEAR
Year C

Readings

> Wis 9:13 - 18
> Phlm 9 - 10, 12 - 17
> Lk 14:25 - 33

Theme: The Cost of Discipleship

True wisdom comes from God and enables a person to be guided by the interests of the soul rather than those of the body. This is the lesson from Wisdom in today's liturgy. In Luke's gospel, wisdom is translated in Christian terms as meaning total commitment to discipleship regardless of the cost. Half-measures will not do. We cannot carry water on two shoulders. We cannot serve God and mammon. From prison, Paul, in today's second reading, writes to his friend Philemon on behalf of the latter's slave Onesimus, asking him to receive this recently converted Christian as a brother.

First Reading

The book of Wisdom was authored in the first century B.C. by an Alexandrian Jew. It is written in Greek and therefore not a part of the officially accepted Hebrew Bible within the Jewish community. Wisdom is written in a sophisticated intellectual environment by a devout Jewish sage who finds true wisdom in a sacred revealed tradition rather than in philosophical pursuit. While no champion of Hellenistic philosophy, the author of Wisdom, pseudonymously presented as King Solomon, is nonetheless influenced by the thinking of his time.

Who can know the plan of God? No mere mortal, unless God chooses to share it. This is the principal idea of today's reading (9:13 - 18). *Counsel of God* (Gr: *boule;* vv3, 17): This refers to God's design for human conduct rather than wisdom in general. No human being can ever attain that unearthly knowledge—for a variety of reasons, weakness and uncertainty among them (v14). The principal reason, however, is that the soul with its intellectual power is burdened by the body and thus rendered incapable of transcending such limitations (v15). Here the author speaks the language of Greek anthropology, alien to most of the Hebrew scriptures, which speak of body person or a living body rather than a body-soul composite. The result was that through most of Hebrew history any form of life without the body was unthinkable. Wisdom obviously represents a new way of thinking. The soul is spiritual; the body is corruptible.

Humans have difficulty in deciphering earthly realities; they can hardly attain the heavenly (v16). The only way to know God is through attention to his revelation (vv17f). Wisdom can be ours, not because of philosophical inquiry, but because God has made it possible, especially in outlining the path that humans are to follow. Implicit in the author's presentation is a subtle polemic against the philosophical and humanistic emphasis in the Alexandria of his time. He draws constantly on Hebrew tradition to show where true wisdom lies.

Responsorial Psalm   Ps 90

The lament is blended with wisdom motifs in underscoring another facet of true wisdom: the recognition of human mortality. In the opening verses of the psalm (not found in today's liturgy), the eternity of Yahweh is highlighted. This is followed by a reflection on the fragility and shortness of human life (vv3 - 4). The "return to dust" motif echoes the Yahwist narrative of human creation (Gen 2:7, 3:19). There is a contrast between God in his agelessness and the human person as a passing shadow (v4). Like short-lived grass under the oriental sun, human life is brief and transient (vv5f). Such sober thoughts lead to a prayerful plea for the experience of God's presence whose absence has been felt (vv3ff). His presence is sufficient to make a limited life span a period of happiness and prosperity.

Second Reading

The short letter (one chapter) to Paul's friend Philemon is written from prison, possibly in Rome, and deals with Philemon's slave Onesimus from Colossae (Col 4:9), who has visited and assisted Paul in his captivity. He was converted to Christianity during his stay with Paul and is now being sent back to his master.

Paul describes himself as an elderly man (Gr: *presbytes*, not *presbeutes*, ambassador) who is now imprisoned (v9). He intercedes for one who has become his spiritual offspring, an expression elsewhere used by Paul to express his role in conversion (1 Cor 4:15, 17; Gal 4:19).

The apostle implies discreetly in the letter that he would like to retain Onesimus' service and company but does not want to be in violation of Philemon's rights (vv13f). Onesimus now returns to his master as a fellow Christian. Paul speaks of the temporary separation of slave and master as now superseded by a permanent homecoming. *"Forever"* (v15) should be understood as meaning more than lifelong; it refers to the lasting bond of Christian kinship. This makes Onesimus more than a slave. In Christian terms he is now Philemon's brother, with

God as their common father (Gal 4:5f). In Christ the slave-master relationship has been transposed to another key (Gal 3:27f).

While the apostle does not contest Philemon's rights over Onesimus, he asks him to receive the slave as a brother (vv15f). The latter is now known to Philemon in two ways: humanly, "in the flesh" as a man, and spiritually, "in the Lord" as a brother. In view of the spiritual ties that bind all three—Paul, Onesimus, and Philemon—the apostle sees them as equal and asks for equal treatment (v17).

It is interesting to note that while Paul makes a strong appeal for human and Christian treatment of the slave, he does not take issue with the institution of slavery as such. It had long been a part of his religious and social culture. In the course of time, slavery will be seen as incompatible with Christian values, a conclusion implicit in Paul's own teaching (Gal 3:28). Only after many centuries of developing ethical insight was such a conclusion possible. It is a good example of how moral understanding is conditioned by many factors and is subject to a process of development.

Third Reading

The wisdom of God as related to human conduct and revealed in Jesus comes to the fore in today's reading from Luke. The wisdom of Christian discipleship is summarized in one central idea: total dedication. Family relationships (v26) and possessions (v33) must be subordinated to the following of Jesus with whatever cross-bearing that may entail (v27).

The strong semitic emphasis, e.g. hating family members, should not be pressed (v26). The idea is that priority in the Christian life must go to the claims of Christ, and all other considerations are secondary, even those of family. Whenever any conflict arises, it is clear where the Christian's allegiance must go. The notion of cross-bearing brings the image of Christ's form of death into the disciple's life (v27). It is not suffering for itself that is extolled; it is the suffering entailed in coming after Jesus

The two Lucan parables (vv29 - 32) stress the importance of

weighing well the consequences of discipleship before setting forth. One should not embrace a life of such inevitable sacrifice without the will to see it through to completion. Once the hand is set to the plow there is no turning back. Like the person constructing a tower or advancing against enemy troops, the potential disciple must do a careful calculation beforehand in order that the objective be realized. Discipleship is costly and cannot be adopted casually.

Just as the embrace of the objective must be total and not half-hearted, so too the renunciation and sacrifice which it entails must be made without reservations (v33). Jesus is not calling for a sudden surrender of property for all of his followers, nor is he asking all Christians to leave family ties behind. Such could be chaotic and even destructive of authentic religious values. But the point being made is important. It is necessary to live with such a spirit of detachment that in the interests of Christ, one is ready at any time to leave all behind. Human priorities must be subordinate to those of God's reign.

The teaching of God's word today is not easy to accept at face value. It makes bold claims regarding discipleship. Many of us would find great difficulty in surrendering our positions or leaving our family behind in the interests of following Christ. We breathe a bit more easily because the ultimatum has never been set before us. Others have had a different experience. Some people have preserved the faith at great personal cost in the face of persecution over many years. Lay people, even married couples, have given up a prosperous livelihood to serve the poor in Latin America, Asia, or Africa. Others make room in their homes for unwanted or parentless children at considerable personal sacrifice. Yet many Christians feel the pinch very little. While they remain faithful church-goers, their personal lives remain largely undisturbed. Their attitudes toward worldly goods differ little from those people of no religious persuasion. Today's liturgy gives us the occasion to pause and to think. We are even advised to weigh well the cost of discipleship before embarking on the Christian venture. Ours is not a comfortable religion, tailor-made for Sunday morning consumption. To take it seriously is to walk a rocky road.

But we should take courage. We are not asked to begin with a quantum leap. When Jesus speaks about family ties and possessions, he is primarily asking for a change in mindset. All of us can begin to think differently. We can be less consumerist, more simple in our tastes. We can begin to find more room for others. We can find more time to serve the less fortunate. The doors of our home and of our heart begin to open more. Prayer becomes more real in our lives. It may mean less television and more conversation. It may mean less money for recreation and more for God's poor. Like Paul we begin to see slaves—other races, colors, nationalities—as our brothers and sisters. And with a certain measure of courage, we may ask others to do the same. Our psalm today reminds us that we have a relatively short span of life. Our most important task is bringing Christianity to life. To begin by taking measured steps is better than doing nothing at all.

Homiletic and Catechetical Helps

1. Examples of giving Christ priority over my family ties.

2. Examples of giving Christ priority over my possessions.

3. How much do I know about the cost of discipleship?

4. What forms can cross-bearing take practically in our daily life?

5. Do we tend to view our life as permanent rather than transient?

6. Living discipleship: the role of religious life in the church.

7. The single unmarried person: a way of discipleship.

8. The married couple: a way of discipleship.

9. Development of church teaching; the slavery question.

10. All baptized persons: my brothers and sisters.

TWENTY-FOURTH SUNDAY OF THE YEAR
Year A

Readings

> Sir 27:30 - 28:7
> Rom 14:7 - 9
> Mt 18:21 - 35

Theme: The Christian: Forgiven and Forgiving

Today's liturgy presents Christian forgiveness as the human counterpart of God's forgiveness. The reading from Sirach speaks of Yahweh's dealing with his creatures as being a reflection of the ways in which they treat one another. The Matthean parable is a clear self-explanatory presentation of the Christian teaching on forgiveness. Beginning with God's treatment of us, Jesus makes an appeal for a similar spirit of mercy among his followers. The passage from Romans speaks of Christ's Lordship over both the living and the dead. We are now intimately linked with Christ in both the present and the future life.

First Reading

Ben Sira writing in the second century before Christ reflects the traditional position on retribution. While not uncontested (e.g. the book of Job), it had prevailed in Hebrew circles for centuries. In the question of sanctions, each action had its own inherent effect. With what might be called a "boomerang" quality, sin rebounded upon its perpetrator with a certain inexorability. Cain was faced with murdered Abel's blood crying out for vengeance (Gen 4:10); the rebellion of Dathan and Abiram finds the earth opening to destroy them and their families (Num 16:25 - 31); David's sin with Bathsheba, the wife of Uriah, leads swiftly to the death of their child (2 Sam 12:13 - 18). While Yahweh executes judgment against the sinner, the evil itself, once unleashed, moves inevitably toward its goal of retribution. "The wicked man is overthrown by his wickedness" (Prov 15:32).

At the same time, retribution in human affairs was regulated. One could exact from another no more than one had received (Ex 21:23ff). Unlimited retribution was excluded. So, too, in Yahweh's dealings with human sinfulness, it is in the area that one falls short in dealing with others that one will be repaid in kind, e.g. vengeance for vengeance, animosity for animosity.

The reading from Sirach reflects these patterns of thought. If one harbors a vengeful spirit, he or she invites the same from God (v1). To nurture a spirit of hostility toward another is to find God equally unforgiving (vv3f). Wickedness is thus repaid in kind; sinful actions return to haunt their perpetrator.

On the other hand, virtue too has its ripple effect. A posture of godness finds its echo in God's comportment. If forgiveness toward neighbor stamps a person's character, God shows the same when pardon is sought (v2). It is in this way that Sirach urges a forgiving and merciful spirit. It is the surest way to assure the same treatment from the Lord.

The finality of death also helps to ensure virtue; it is a sobering thought that moves one to keep accounts in order (v6). For Sirach, death and decay were final and definitive; he harbors no glimmer of after-life hopes. An evil life may simply accelerate the time of death or at least make life addedly sorrowful. To live virtuously, according to the thesis espoused by Sirach, is to live serenely.

Added motivation will be found in remembering God's goodness in covenanting himself with his people and giving them his law (v7). All of this offers motivation for a spirit of forgiveness. It is interesting to note that shades of this thought on retribution remain in the New Testament as well.

Responsorial Psalm   Ps 103

God's forgiveness serves as the dominant theme of the psalm. It is a hymn of thanksgiving on the part of one who has evidently recovered from a serious illness (3b, 4a). Illness is closely related to sin in Hebrew thought (3a, 10, 12; Job; Ps 32:3 - 5). In being freed from sickness, the psalmist realizes that his sins are forgiven as well. This is due solely to God's covenant love (*hesed*), his concern for the people he has espoused (v11).

There is a consoling note in the lyric expressiveness of the final verses (vv11f). God's love is as expansive as the height of the over-arching sky, his forgiveness as broad as the distance from one end of the earth to the other. This is no God preoccupied with accounts or detailed tabulations of wrong-doing. A humble and contrite heart is what he seeks (Ps 51:19).

Second Reading

Paul emphasizes repeatedly that the new life of the Christian is lived exclusively for God (6:10f; Gal 2:19). A transformation takes place with the assumption of this new life in baptism. A new freedom has been acquired which leaves behind sin, law, and death. One's sole allegiance is to the Lord Jesus.

In today's short passage, Paul states that the sovereignty of Jesus extends to both living and deceased Christians. These who have already died belong to Christ no less than the living. By the power of the same Lord they will rise again (1 Thes 4:14). Jesus has acquired this total sovereignty because he himself experienced the reality of both life and death.

Third Reading

The Matthean text draws on a saying of Jesus (Lk 17:4) and with it constructs a Peter - Jesus discussion on the frequency of forgiveness. To Peter's question of how often forgiveness should be extended, Jesus responds that it should be without limit (vv21ff). Seven is a perfect number; its multiples express the incalculable, seventy times seven pointing to forgiveness that cannot be limited to a certain number of times. It may also be sounding a contrary note to Lamech's unlimited vengeance in the Genesis narrative (Gen 4:24).

The parable of the unforgiving servant (vv23 - 35) illustrates the pardon principle but does not entirely fit the present context which is dealing with multiple acts of forgiveness. The story, dealing with a single act only, may be an extended commentary on another injunction to forgiveness (e.g. 6:12 - 15) and attached here because of its general relevance.

The parable of the king who cancelled the large debt (ten

thousand talents) of one of his ministers ("servant" is thus frequently understood), with a similar spirit lacking in the minister himself, differs from the Sirach exhortation in one interesting respect. It is the superior who first forgives the servant; the latter is then the recipient of pardon before he turns on his own debtor. His spirit should have been more magnanimous because of his own experience. The Christian, already the recipient of God's forgiveness through baptism and countless other moments in life, is in a unique position to offer that same spirit to others.

There is a strong dramatic build-up in the story. The scenario shifts from the king and his minister to the minister and his own subordinate, then to the other ministers (employees of the king), back to the king, and finally the conclusive encounter between the king and minister once again. Retribution is meted out to the minister with the solemn reminder that God's justice will not overlook harbored hostility in the moment of final reckoning (v35).

The retribution follows a gradual and logical pattern; it does not return to the offender as reflexively as is often the case. But this element is not totally lacking. There is something inherent in the sin itself which evokes the punitive response. A forgiving act comes back in forgiveness; a spirit of unforgiveness produces a punishment without mercy. Thus it is contradictory for an unforgiving person to pray that he or she be repaid in terms of God's forgiveness. God responds in kind according to what might be said to be "in the nature of things."

With his death and resurrection, Jesus forged bonds of love among Christians in and through the Holy Spirit. That oneness in Christ must be consciously and constantly brought to life in the Christian community. This unity is a vital witness to the power of God.

At the same time, we recall that it was in our weakened and sinful state that God reached out to us. Despite humanity's repeated failures, forgiveness was not lacking. Christ's teachings give us remarkable insight into God's mercy: the lost coin, the lost sheep, the lost son.

He personally extends his hand to the tax collector, the prostitute, other sinners of his time. So many times in our own lives has that pardoning presence of the Lord touched us as well. After baptismal for-

giveness, God has reached us repeatedly through the sacraments of reconciliation and other avenues of his mercy.

Today's liturgy calls us to extend that same spirit to others–yes, even to the point of taking the initiative and not waiting for the other person. Continued hostility runs contrary to the unity of the Christian spirit and makes a mockery of God's goodness toward us. In the Lord's Prayer we ask for pardon in view of the fact that we are ourselves forgiving. And if we are not? We must deal with the consequences of our petition.

We are also reminded that a divided Christianity has often been marked by scandalous hostility. In both the division between east and west and the sixteenth century reformation, there was enought fault on both sides to exclude later recrimination. The fact is that today a lack of pardon and forgiveness is unconscionable. Pardon and forgiveness are the first steps toward a restoration of unity. The spirit and activity of ecumenism is not limited to the work of church officials. It begins in each neighborhood, in each parish.

Homiletic and Catechetical Helps

1. Explain the relationship between divine and human forgiveness.

2. Dealing with hostile feelings.

3. The eucharist and forgiveness: the penitential rite, the Lord's Prayer, and the sign of peace.

4. Communal celebration of penance as related to today's theme.

5. Forgiveness and restitution.

6. Forgiveness and capital punishment.

7. Forgiveness and local ecumenism.

8. Jesus, Lord of the living and the dead.

9. The communion of saints.

10. Praying for the deceased.

11. Saints in the church–canonization.

TWENTY-FOURTH SUNDAY OF THE YEAR
Year B

Readings

    Is 50:4 - 9
    Jas 2:14 - 18
    Mk 8:27 - 35

Theme: Jesus, the Suffering Messiah

The third song of the servant of the Lord serves as our opening reading today. It is taken from the second part of the book of Isaiah (cc. 40 - 55), called Deutero- or Second Isaiah, and dates from the end of the Babylonian exile. It describes the suffering which the servant is called to endure. The gospel reading is a turning point in Mark, with Peter's profession of faith and Jesus' speaking of his impending passion and death. The letter of James sheds light on one of Christianity's major questions: the relationship between faith and good works.

First Reading

There are four songs of the Lord's servant in Deutero-Isaiah (42:1 - 7; 49:1 - 7; 50:4 - 9; 52:13 - 53:12). They are woven into the book's context but can be detached and treated separately. The songs have an inner dramatic progression. The servant's identity, as originally intended, remains problematic. He has both collective (Israel) and individual features. He is perhaps best described as a prophetic figure who suffers on behalf of others; he is the faithful remnant of Israel concretized in some unknown individual, whether ideal or real.

In the third song (vv4 - 9), the servant is already launched upon his mission as teacher-disciple. At this point he is meeting severe opposition which has taken the form of both physical and verbal abuse. To fulfill his prophetic mission, the servant remains attentive to the Lord's voice and has not reneged on his vocation (vv4f). He has been physically assaulted and beaten, with the plucking of his beard a particularly strong insult. Yet he is resolute and determined (vv4f). The servant's unwavering stance in the face of such strong opposition is in the great prophetic tradition. The "face like flint" (v7), now covered with spittle, recalls Ezekiel (3:8f), yet is even stronger with its vivid note of hatred and rejection.

The literary genre shifts in the final verses (vv8f) to one of legal proceedings. The defense is the Lord himself who supports the servant's cause. The prosecution had best weigh things well since the servant, with his defense, is prepared to argue the case to its conclusion.

The strong sense of the correctness of the servant's cause, of being an authentic prophetic emissary, enables him to endure all manner of rejection. Both his suffering and his strong convictions will be enhanced in the final servant song.

Responsorial Psalm   Ps 116

The sentiments of this individual thanksgiving hymn, written after a recovery from a mortal illness, accompany those of both the servant of the Lord and Jesus himself in today's readings. A note of appreciation is struck initially (vv1f). The illness is likened to an entrapment in binding ropes as death attempts to take its toll (v3). Supplication is made to the Lord (v4) and deliverance is granted. God is praised for his goodness as the psalmist is freed from the risk of death to a new life among his own (vv5 - 9). This note of suffering and deliverance links the psalm with the first and third readings.

Second Reading

Faith finding expression in the works of love is at the heart of this reading from James' letter. By faith, James understands the full acceptance of God's revelation including his expressed will for human conduct. To say that one believes and to ignore faith's injunction to act in accord with that belief means nothing in the order of salvation (v14). The example of the needy poor person (vv15ff) illustrates the point clearly and succinctly.

Faith and good works are in no way incompatible; in fact, they are basically complementary.

Is this teaching of James at odds with that of Paul (e.g. Rom 4:5f), as was often suggested in the past? The response is in the negative when the perspective of both is kept in mind. Paul argues that observance of laws (works), even when coupled with faith, can never bring one to justification. Faith is entirely a gift made possible through the saving action of Christ; to introduce works is to destroy the gratuity of the gift. James does not argue this point. Once justification takes place, however, it is essential that the spirit of love (grace) find expression in works, which are prompted by faith itself. This is a point which Paul himself affirms (Gal 5:6).

Third Reading

In Mark's gospel, Peter's profession comes after various glimpses into Jesus' identity and mission (1:24, 27; 3:11; 4:41; 6:15), coupled with Christ's own attempts to divert public recognition (1:25, 34, 44; 3:12). The present moment serves as a high point of the gospel in terms of the disciples' growth in understanding and a turning point as Mark thematically moves the messianic mission of Jesus toward its final stage, the Jerusalem experience of death - resurrection. This joining of the fulfillment of centuries of hope (vv27 - 30) and the prediction of future suffering (vv31 - 33) serves as the hinge of the entire gospel.

Situated at Palestine's northernmost point, Caesarea Philipi stands at the base of Mount Hermon where the confluence of four streams marks the beginning of the Jordan river. It is in this vicinity, looking out over a world much broader than that within Palestinian Judaism's borders, that Jesus poses to his disciples the question of his identity (vv27f). The response to the initial question regarding public opinion was to be expected: he is a prophet—perhaps John the Baptist resurrected (6:14), Elijah, the expected messianic forerunner (9:9 - 13), or another prophet.

The question is repeated and addressed to the disciples as a group (v29). Speaking for the twelve, Peter answers that Jesus is the Messiah, the Christos, the Anointed One. This is the title that had attached itself to the hoped-for descendant of David who would be part of the final era. Anointing accompanied the designation of a king and in time became a specific designation for the future king like David, the anointed one (Heb: *mashiah;* Gr: *christos*). In Jesus' case, it eventually became the equivalent of a surname.

The title "Messiah" has no connotation of divinity in itself. Hence the profession of Peter here does not carry the weight of the recognition scene in Matthew (16:16). However, it does represent a watershed in the disciples' evolving understanding and more logically reflects the actual historical scene in Jesus' ministry. Peter sees Jesus as the promised one of Israel. Again Jesus enjoins secrecy (v29), in keeping with his intention not to deflect public attention from God's design for him. The term "Messiah" carried a broad, even political meaning which Jesus studiously desired to avoid, as his subsequent remarks make clear.

At this point Jesus shares with his disciples the meaning that will be given to messiahship and the consequences it will have for them as well (vv31 - 35). The "Son of Man" reference may stem from the narrative's editor or from Jesus himself. It had eschatological overtones (Dan 7:13), less nationalistic in character, and meant basically "human."

The precise prediction of the form that Jesus' death would take (v31) is not in keeping with prophecy in general. The future is spoken of in much broader terms. This account has no doubt been sharpened after the fact. However, it does not exclude Jesus' indication of his impending passion along broad lines. The "Satan" designation for Peter (v33) is connected with his attempt to dissuade Jesus from following his Father's plan. In playing the Satan role, Peter would place an obstacle to the realization of God's will. This also reflects the historical fact. It is hard to imagine the early church creating such a designation for the first of the apostles. Interesting to note is the openness with which Jesus now speaks of his death - resurrection (v32) in view of the circumspection which earlier surrounded comments on his identity.

Finally Jesus addresses both the disciples and a broader audience (v34) in pointing out the meaning of discipleship. After speaking of his own future, he asks the same spirit of his disciples. If the expression "cross-bearing" were used by Jesus himself, his hearers would have understood the figurative image from their own knowledge of this Roman form of execution. It would have connoted submission to authority, in this case God's. In a post-Easter setting, however, there is no doubt that the text would have been understood in the light of Christ's own form of death.

Discipleship, then, means accepting the suffering which the following of Christ entails and a willingness to sacrifice human values and interests for the sake of those which are lasting (vv34f). We should note the distinctive Marcan note in the quotation: losing one's life "for the gospel" (cf. Mt 16:25; Lk 9:24). It looks to total dedication to living and proclaiming the "good news" of Jesus the Christ, dead and risen.

Human suffering remains an enigma. But God has given it new meaning. The historical identity of the servant is not as significant as what he accomplishes. His prophetic role is exercised through suffering–rejection, abuse, eventual death. And yet in the end Yahweh vindicates his servant. The early church saw Jesus as the servant. The parallel between the lives of the two is striking. In both there is the acceptance of God's will, with personal sacrifice, in the interests of God's people.

Today's liturgy reminds us that the name "Christian" configures us to one person: Jesus the Christ. The pursuit of the Christian life is certain to entail hardship and sacrifice if it is taken seriously. There is no need to seek the cross or invent it. For example, James speaks of faith's call to action, especially in the service of others. We cannot look at the poor and simply wish them well. But to do more will often mean sacrifice, and that is not a popular word in our vocabulary.

Asceticism and penance in the service of God's reign; doing without in order that others may have; foregoing a ball game or the theater to be available to a sick person; giving a year of one's life to assist God's people in a developing part of the world–examples of cross-bearing can be easily multiplied. It may be difficult but certainly not outmoded. We cannot forget either that our home, or parish, or town–just like ourselves–can become very self-centered and uncaring. Yet if we look about us, the cross-bearers are always there. The prophets and lovers–their faith lives in action.

Homiletic and Catechetical Helps

1. The servant of the Lord in Deutero-Isaiah.

2. Compare Peter's profession of faith in Mark and Matthew.

3. Cite some examples of cross-bearing in your experience.

4. Cite some examples where cross-bearing could be present and is not.

5. Discuss the faith-works controversy in reformation and post-reformation thinking.

6. The meaning of the term "Messiah."

7. Understanding the secret of Jesus' identity in Mark.

TWENTY-FOURTH SUNDAY OF THE YEAR
Year C

Readings

> Ex 32:7 - 11, 13 - 14
> 1 Tim 1:12 - 17
> Lk 15:1 - 32

Theme: God's Love for the Sinner

God relents of his plan to destroy his people, following Moses' intercession on their behalf, in today's reading from Exodus. Persuasion tempers his anger and the people are spared. As generous as this may be on Yahweh's part, it is but a glimmer of the concern for the sinner that is reflected in today's gospel, chapter 15 of Luke. The joy over the single sinner who repents resounds throughout heaven, as illustrated in the three Lucan parables. In the first letter to Timothy, Paul presents himself as the classic repentant sinner. He had wandered far yet God's love reached him.

First Reading

The narrative which is read today was part of Israel's desert experience. In Exodus, it occurs after the covenant-making with Yahweh (cc. 19 - 24) and is a record of the first violation of the covenant norms. It centers around the calf of god incident (32:1 - 6) in which Aaron himself was an accomplice. The molten calf is intended as a representation of Yahweh, the people's deliverer from Egyptian bondage (v8), not as an image of a foreign deity. This is a clear violation of the basic commandment which forbade any form of image, whether of Yahweh or other gods (Ex 20:4). The calf or bull was a symbol of strength, representing either the god himself or his animal throne.

The narrative in Exodus is probably refracted through the prism of a later experience in Israel. The king Jeroboam (922 - 901 B.C.) apostatized in erecting gold calves in the north to divert the people from going to Jerusalem for worship (1 Kgs 12:26 - 32).

In Exodus, Yahweh, angered by the idolatry, decides to destroy the people (v10). Moses then makes his plea on behalf of the Israelites (vv11 - 14). It is two-pronged. Destruction of the Israelites would only evoke scorn from the Egyptians who, having experienced Yahweh's power in defense of his people, would now see the same power turned against them. In addition, Moses appeals for compassion on the basis of Yahweh's love for the past patriarchs whom the Lord had chosen and to whom he had committed himself in promise. Admittedly, this argumentation is circuitous. There is no attempt to excuse the people themselves whose conduct is thoroughly reprehensible. But Moses is a convincing defender. Yahweh repeals his judgment of punishment.

Responsorial Psalm   Ps 51

The celebrated Miserere, an individual lament, places in relief the dispositions which accompany turning to God from a path of sin. Echoing the sentiments of David after his sin, as the heading of the psalm indicates (vv1 - 2), the psalmist asks for forgiveness and the total remission of sin and guilt (vv3f). He bases his request on Yahweh's lasting love and willingness to pardon. What he requests is a new heart and spirit more responsive to Yahweh's will (v12; cf. Ez 11:19; Jer 31:33f).

Because of the favor received, the psalmist wants only to sing God's praises and to bring before him not animal sacrifices, but the authentic offering of a deeply internal and penitent spirit. The latter, as the true spirit of religion, is repeatedly contrasted with empty cultic formality (Ps 40:7; 1 Sam 15:22).

Second Reading

The first letter to Timothy is one of the three pastoral letters (two to Timothy, one to Titus). They are presented as personally authored by Paul, but authorities in increasing numbers in recent times have argued that the attribution is pseudonymous. While there is no unanimity on the question, doubts center around the notable differences in style, language, and theology between the letters that are certainly Pauline and the pastorals. Authorship, however, remains a secondary question; the inspired character of the letters, regardless of their author, is not questioned.

The reading is bracketed by words of praise and thanksgiving (vv13, 17). Framed within the two acclamations is their *raison d'être:* the mercy shown to Paul in God's bringing him from sinfulness to service in the church. His sinful past as a persecutor of Christians (Acts 9:1 - 9; 26:9 - 11; Gal 1:13) is stressed (v13a). His ignorance is a reason for the mercy he has been accorded (v13b).

The reasoning follows these lines. Paul was converted as the worst of sinners (v15), was given merciful treatment, and was even brought to ministry within the church (v12). His transition from a sinful state to a life of conversion can only be explained by grace; hence, his conversion testifies to the fact that Christ came for sinners (v15), as Jesus himself claimed (Lk 19:10; Jn 3:17). In Paul, Christ's patience and long-suffering are most evident, giving encouragement to all those coming to belief (v18). Christ's mercy reached Paul, the most distant, in order that hope might be given to all. For this Paul praises the invisible and eternal God (v17).

Third Reading

Christianity is wholly indebted to Luke for two of these parables: the lost coin and the lost son; the third, the lost sheep, is
shared with Matthew. All three make one major point: the
boundless, even humanly incomprehensible joy over the conversion of a single sinner. In the Lucan context, controversy initiates the discourse; there is question about Jesus' friendship and
food sharing with sinners (v2). At an early stage of church life,
Gentile Christians did not enjoy the status of Jewish Christians
and there was controversy about table fellowship with them
(Gal 2:11f). Thus Jesus justifies his own outreach to sinners
(and the early church justifies its inclusion of both sinners and
Gentiles) in the three ensuing parables.

The lost sheep (vv4 - 7) is found also in Matthew (18:12 - 14),
although in the Matthean context the emphasis falls on the disciples' responsibility to seek out the erring person. Here the
main point centers wholly around heaven's joy over the converted sinner. The evident exaggeration (ninety-nine sheep for the
sake of one) is intended. It underscores God's unlimited concern for the sinner. The shepherd's conduct is not normal or
rational and is not meant to be. The joy over conversion takes
place in heaven, implying an invitation to the Christian community to participate.

The woman who has ten coins (literally, drachmas) loses one
(vv8 - 10). The loss is insignificant; the effort to find it is extraordinary; the merrymaking upon recovery is rather unrealistic.
But again the parable wants to underscore unlimited love and
concern. Heavenly and earthly joy result from the sinner's
restoration

To speak of the "parable of the lost son" (vv11 - 32), so called
because of its relation to the two previous "losses," fails to highlight the father as the central figure of the narrative. The outcome of the story is the same: joy over the recovery of a great
loss. In this story, however, there are many secondary features
which color the narrative and contribute to its impact. It evokes
memories of earlier "brother stories," especially Jacob and Esau
(Gen 25:27 - 34; 27:1 - 36).

The younger son's selfishness leads him to demand his inheritance in advance of his elder brother in violation of prevailing custom (v12). The depth of his subsequent descent, financial and moral, is strikingly seen in his Gentile occupation, feeding pigs (v5). At the lowest point in his life, still guided by self-interest (v17), he decides to return home.

The son's prepared speech (vv18f) is abbreviated in its actual recitation (v21); no suggestion of a degraded status is allowed to be uttered. The reunion itself is poignantly dramatic. Even though running violates the norms of patriarchal propriety, the father does not hesitate to do so in his excitement at the son's return (v20). The embrace and kiss take place with no questions asked. The son's total restoration to his place in the family is seen in the ceremonial robe, the signet ring, and sandals. The festive banquet lifts the occasion to an even higher level of acceptance (vv22f).

The elder brother's failure to appreciate the reception is understandable from a certain point of view. His own obedience and loyalty (v29), commendable in itself and never equally applauded, have dulled his appreciation of what family ties mean. He views the whole scene from the perspective of duties and obligations (the attitude of the Pharisees, v2). He cannot bring himself to say "my brother" (v30), but his father puts the words in his mouth (v32).

In this story, the three men illustrate dramatically the forgiveness of God: the young son in his hardened attitude and superficial remorse; the elder son seeing the return in terms of a servant-employer relationship; the father who casts aside norms and convention in welcoming home a wayward son, who has passed from death to life (v32).

God's pardon in Exodus and the forgiveness presented in the Lucan parables are strikingly different. The God of Exodus reluctantly concedes pardon to a people with no registered sense of guilt. He does so largely on the basis of past promises and respect for the person of Moses. It is basically anger withdrawn. And there it rests

Luke offers us a remarkable insight into the God of Jesus. There is consolation for every Christian in Luke 15. The story of the forgiving father contains countless riches. The mean-spiritedness and selfishness of the younger son is the shadowy background for the bright hues of the father's love. The exactitude and sense of justice of the older son only serve to accent the absence of parameters in the unquestioning embrace of the father. In short, God's goodness cannot be measured. His ways are not ours. Sins red as scarlet become white as snow. In God's home, there is room for all.

Is it not regrettable that for many people their first impression of the church is of an organized, exacting and even harsh institution? Too much emphasis on law and conformity has often hurt the church. Its better side, its Christ side, with real concern for people, should leave the dominant impression. Today people are far from the church for various reasons: divorce and remarriage, alleged or real insensitivity on the part of church authorities, grappling with difficult sexual issues, a past abortion. These are people for whom Luke 15 is intended. It is important for them to hear it but, even more importantly, to see it lived by caring Christians.

The Paul of 1 Timothy can almost glory in the fact that he was the worst of sinners, the reason being that his conversion was visibly God's work and not his own. Sinners are so often deeply conscious of their need for God. And so they enter the kingdom while the self-righteous, even "religious" people remain aloof.

Three years will pass before the liturgy again takes up Luke 15. Most of us cannot wait that long. We should probably resolve to read it monthly. More importantly, we want to begin to live it now.

Homiletic and Catechetical Helps

1. The calf of gold: Where is it present today?

2. The first commandment of the decalogue.

3. Defining the importance of Luke 15 today.

4. With which of the three persons in the parable of the forgiving father can you most identify?

5. Spiritual alienation in church and world.

6. The act of contrition.

7. Distinguishing biblical authorship from inspiration.

8. How can being a sinner become a good?

TWENTY-FIFTH SUNDAY OF THE YEAR
Year A

Readings

> Is 55:6 - 9
> Phil 1:20 - 24, 27
> Mt 20:1 - 16

Theme: God's Generosity

Deutero-Isaiah in today's first reading warns against trying to make God fit into pre-determined categories. The gospel illustrates the points in parable form as it recounts the tale of the laborers hired at different times of the day and all of them receiving the same pay. In the reading from Philippians, Paul sees life in Christ as his primary good and thus would prefer death to the present life if apostolic demands were not weighing upon him.

First Reading

The ordinary way to "seek the Lord" (v6) was in temple cult. The injunction looked to public worship within a determined setting. Deutero-Isaiah, however, written after the experience of the exile, has been influenced by the personalism that has become so much a part of Israelite thought, reflected especially in Jeremiah and Ezekiel. The Lord is to be sought in the inner recesses of the heart, no longer dependent on a fixed time or place (Jer 33:3; 29:10 - 14). This was now a people dispersed, with no fixed place of worship, their temple in ruins, gradually coming to realize that their relationship to Yahweh remained intact. In fact, it could only become richer with a covenant written on the heart and an experience of God not requiring a human teacher (Jer 31:33f).

For the Lord to be found by the sinner, it was now sufficient to turn to him and to turn away from wrongdoing (v7). His mercy and generosity will not be found lacking.

The limitless mercy of God defies human boundaries (vv8f). Difficulties arise only when the yardstick used to measure normal human responses is applied to the Lord. Divine transcendence means many things, one of which is that God's nature moves on a distinctly different plane. It will never be fully understood.

Responsorial Psalm   Ps 145

The psalm is acrostic, the verses beginning with the successive letters of the Hebrew alphabet. It is an individual hymn of praise (vv1 - 10) for Yahweh's lasting kindness (vv14 - 21). It is this note of God's graciousness toward humankind that links the psalm with today's theme.

In the parallelism of the opening verses (vv1f), Yahweh is praised and pronounced blessed. The reason, often repeated in the psalter, is his covenant fidelity, characterized by a limitless patience and forgiveness which excludes no one (vv8f; Ps 86:5; Ex 34:6). Fault cannot be found with his mode of acting; he is close to his creation (vv17f).

Second Reading

Imprisoned, probably in Rome, Paul considers his future lot. By reason of his baptism, he now lives in Christ, a life that will intensify whether he lives or dies (v20). The "body" (*soma*) is more than the sum of one's physical parts; it means the body person. Life in Christ has become Paul's "all" (Gal 2:19f). In his actual circumstances, if Paul were to be sentenced to death, this would be a gain since he would be liberated from earthly trials for an even closer union with Christ. If he were to be acquitted, it would mean more missionary activity on behalf of Christ (vv21f). Either path is blessed; the apostle has difficulty choosing.

If Paul were to die, it would be the crowning point of his existence; it is what he longs for (v23). The idea expressed here has theological importance. Paul's customary emphasis on blessedness after death is connected with bodily resurrection (1 Thes 4:13 - 17; 1 Cor 15:53f). He says little about the interim state between death and resurrection. The present text points to a continued and uninterrupted union with Christ.

Paul is willing to set aside his personal desire in the interests of his apostolic mission for the benefit of the Philippians and others (v25). Finally he exhorts them to live in accord with their belief (v27).

Third Reading

This parable is bracketed by the saying of Jesus on the reversal of fortune in the reign of God (19:30; 20:16), for which the parable serves as an extended commentary. The parable is found only in Matthew and gives no hint as to its original context or application. In its present setting it is a clear statement on the equality which obtains in the reign of God. The inheritance is the same for all regardless of past history.

The vineyard (v1) frequently symbolizes Israel (Is 5:1 - 7) and flows into the New Testament reign of God (Mt 21:33 - 45). The landowner hires day laborers at five different intervals, agreeing to pay the earliest hired a denarius, the customary day's wage (vv2 - 7). The workers evidently waited at the usual place of employment and were anxious to obtain work.

In the parable's denouement the earliest hired are the last paid, simply to have them present while the others are remunerated (vv9f). All receive the same amount. From a human viewpoint, there is a certain lack of equity since not all have rendered the same service. Yet a real injustice cannot be claimed since all received the amount agreed upon (vv12f). Was the landowner at fault for deciding to remunerate the workers in the way he did? Here the discussion moves from one of equity to one of generosity and kindness. Those who serve God on the basis of strict legal observance will inevitably find this type of action incomprehensible (cf. Lk 15:25 - 30). But God's response is not so measured and is marked by divine largesse (Lk 15:31f). Without doing any injustice to those who serve long and well, he reaches out to those who are distant and emarginated. This embrace of God coupled with the person's change of heart results in equal entitlement.

Matthew writes for a Jewish-Gentile Christian community.

The parable may well be addressing certain tensions between the "first employed" Jewish segment and the Gentile "late-comers" within early Christianity. All enjoy equal status (cf. Mt 21:31 - 46; 22:1 - 10).

Experience demonstrates the fact that the only way we have of speaking of God is in human terms. Anthropomorphism is the word which describes our human speech about a God who is totally other. It is not surprising, then, that our way of looking at divine sanctions is conditioned by the way sanctions emerge in human affairs. There is a great deal behind the saying that we get what we ask for. Our courts are established to uphold justice. The innocent are protected and the guilty are punished in proportion to their wrong-doing. In business affairs, through efforts of management and labor, the just wage is axiomatic.

Our first reaction is to want to see God acting in the same way. Many of us were raised with a notion of strict retribution for sin on the day of reckoning. Even for sins forgiven, there is a "temporal punishment" due. Indulgences atone for sins on a somewhat mathematical basis.

God's way of acting does not follow human standards. The reward or compensation is not commensurate with the work done. The parable can be transposed in different keys. Sincere contrition can avert definitive separation from God at any moment in life. The faithful servant and the repentant sinner can stand on completely equal footing before God. It is the goodness of God that far outweighs any other characteristic. And all of us, tainted by sin, can only be grateful for that. It is a lesson that bears repeated emphasis. Many people are so burdened with guilt that they see no way out. For them there is no hope. And yet the word of God teaches just the opposite.

And we should go and do likewise. How often we want to exact our "pound of flesh." We are willing to put hostility aside only to the extent that it is matched by the other person. In the matter of debts, we are not too willing to take into consideration the differing economic circumstances of our debtors. In daily affairs our steps are too measured. We are willing to go only as far as the other person goes.

From Jesus' teaching we know that this is not the way God acts with us. In the face of a change of heart, God's response is boundless forgiveness. Those who enter God's reign at the last moment are as welcome as the first-comers. Yes, it is quite unusual. But it is God's norm, not ours.

It is also unusual for a person to prefer death to life. For Paul it was perfectly normal. The only reason that would make him opt for the present life was to serve others at greater length. Another Christian paradox–we hold on to life tenaciously even though we believe that a fuller destiny is ours. And our desire to live on is not usually marked by strong motives of service, as was Paul's.

In the Christian life, our deeds often fail to match our words. We want to condition our belief by other concerns. Yet God is constantly breaking the shell of our security. He calls us to go beyond the ordinary, the normal, the expected. His ways are not ours. The task is to make our ways more like his.

Homiletic and Catechetical Helps

1. The full-day employee: Was he fairly treated?

2. Reconcile God's justice and mercy.

3. The just wage: an economic and moral issue.

4. Equity: first and third world economics.

5. Where is lack of equality present in your experience?

6. Lifelong virtue and deathbed conversions.

7. Paul's meaning of life in Christ.

8. The understanding of life after death.

9. Examples of God's "irrational" goodness in your experience.

TWENTY-FIFTH SUNDAY OF THE YEAR
Year B

Readings

Wis 2:17 - 20
Jas 3:16 - 4:3
Mk 9:30 - 37

Theme: Service to the Lowly

In the reading from Wisdom today, the wicked are pitted against the just man. They are determined to rid themselves of his presence simply because his justice itself is a reproach to them. In today's gospel, Jesus concludes his Galilean ministry speaking once again of his approaching passion and instructing his disciples on the true meaning of rank or position among his followers. In the epistle of James, the author shows how God's wisdom imparts virtue while vice originates within the human heart.

First Reading

The book of Wisdom is important for its teaching on human immortality, a late concept in Hebrew thought. It developed to a great extent in a Hellenistic milieu. The wicked, who are the protagonists of today's reading, reject both immortality and justice. In fact, justice or correct living is seen as futile and senseless since everything ends with death (2:1 - 5). In words strikingly similar to those of Ecclesiastes (vv6ff; Eccl 2:24 - 26), the wicked uphold a life of sensuous satisfaction, while stifling the voice of the just at every turn.

The description of the just man is a collage of freely adapted texts from the Greek version (Septuagint) of the Hebrew scriptures, principally Isaiah, Jeremiah, and the psalms. The wicked are determined to silence him because of his accusations against them (v12). In addition, he has made claims which his opponents wish to test. The first claim is that in time of need, Yahweh will be the just person's deliverer (vv19f; Ps 22:23ff). *Son of God* (v18): The reference here has only generic significance, an observer of God's law. The second claim of the just is that in the face of death he will be saved (v20). This could be a reference to deliverance from death itself (Ps 22:9), or more likely, in terms of one of the book's major themes, it points to the immortality of the just (1:15; 3:1 - 5; 4:7f).

The views of the wicked in chapter 2 of Wisdom are completely world-centered and reflect a clear moral void. In support of their position they draw on other parts of the scriptures echoing views which in their own time were orthodox enough. The beauty of life and its fragility (vv1 - 5) and the enjoyment of this world's goods (vv7f) are themes that appear frequently in the wisdom literature on the lips of the just. In Wisdom, immortality with its after-life sanctions makes all the difference. Earlier views are now employed by evildoers to justify their sinful ways.

Responsorial Psalm   Ps 54

An individual lament, the psalmist prays for deliverance from enemies. God's "name" is God's person (v3). His opponents are not only ruthless; they are godless as well (v5). In the face of such evil, God's assistance is assured. Confident of victory, the psalmist pledges a sacrifice of thanks (vv8f).

The notion of conflict between the just person and his opponents in the first and third readings gives the psalm an appropriate setting.

Second Reading

James deals with disharmony within the Christian community. The causes listed are internal. Foul play springs from inordinate self love (v16). On the positive side, wisdom is a gift from God and a sure guide for human conduct; it produces the virtue necessary for the personal and communal good resulting in harmony and peace (vv17f). The fruits of Wisdom here are equivalent to those of the Spirit in Paul (Gal 5:22f).

There is a sharp contrast between the gift of Wisdom and the causes of conflict (4:1). Contention and hostility spring from passion (literally: pleasure). Prayer is either absent or improperly centered (vv2f), looking only to self-indulgences.

Third Reading

The Galilean ministry of Jesus is drawing to a close as the journey toward Jerusalem begins (v30; 11:1), with a continued concealed character to Jesus' movements. The note of privacy is here linked with his instruction of the disciples. In his second passion prediction (v31), Jesus is less specific about the circumstances of his death (cf. 8:31). The expression "handing over" (*paradididotai*) may be a theological reference to the Father's action in executing the divine plan; more probably, however, in view of the verb's repeated use with a determined subject (15:1, 10, 15), it simply refers to the human agents who will consign him to his executioners. The disciples' failure to understand (v32), even after the earlier disclosure (8:31ff), is part of the Marcan motif regarding the disciples' lack of acceptance of the Father's plan.

With the group's arrival in Capernaum en route to Jerusalem, they stop at a house, perhaps Peter's (cf. 1:29), where Jesus again questions them (v33). The issue of rank among the disciples (v34) is here linked with the previous statement on their lack of understanding. Jesus moves the discussion to the level of servanthood; it is only the least who have any status at all (vv35ff). A child has no legal rights or claims. To help a child is to expect nothing in return.

This moves the topic totally away from one of priority or pre-eminence to one of service and availability. There is no superior status in the reign of God; authority is totally identified with service (Mt 20:25ff). The child represents Christ himself, as Christ represents the Father. To receive one is to receive all three (v37, Mt 10:40).

In Matthew (18:1 - 5) the narrative takes a different direction. The disciple is first called to resemble the child and only secondarily is he called to receive the child.

When it comes to leadership, there should be a marked difference between the Christian community and secular governments and organizations. Ambition often leads people to take exceptional, even unethical steps to get ahead. It often leads to position which is undergirded by power. Worldly power is one of the most dangerous and potentially lethal forces in life. As Lord Acton said, it tends to corrupt, and when it is absolute, it corrupts absolutely. Human experience shows clearly the evils brought to humanity by people who craved power, even to the point of their own downfall.

Jesus here speaks with incredible insight. Status was to have no place in the reign of God; it was to be absent from the church. There was little that Christ had to say about eventual structures within the church; what he did say, however, is of primary importance. Those who exercise authority in the community are not to resemble the "rulers of this world, who lord it over them."

It is sad to note that in the history of Christianity this clear teaching of Jesus was frequently neglected. While it is true that many Christians who grasped the authentic spirit have left an inspiring legacy of service, it is also true that others have used the church to further their own personal aims. They have sought to be served rather than to serve.

The danger is always present. The reading from Wisdom speaks of the evildoers who simply want to eradicate the good person. The reason is that the person is a reproach to them. Jesus, soon to be crucified because he is a reproach, will see his death as undergone in total service to humankind. And yet his uncomprehending disciples are discussing rank. Jesus is quite forthright. Disciples are called to serve, even to death if necessary, and the service they render will bring with it no human acclaim or compensation–the Christian paradox! We have yet to grasp how different we are called to be.

James warns us to beware of our interior motives. Exteriorly we can seem to be Godlike. But within? James assures us that selfish ambition will only lead to "disorder and foul practice." It is said today that some people are willing to pay any price to get ahead. So it may be. But let us not compound the evil by labeling this as service to the reign of God. It is when we serve the neediest, the beloved of God, that we come closest to what Christian leadership means.

Homiletic and Catechetical Helps

1. Authority in the church: its gospel meaning.

2. The seven capital sins: the root of evil.

3. Connect Jesus' prediction of death and his words on service.

4. What it means to be childlike.

5. Is ambition always wrong?

6. Conflict in our own life: its roots.

7. The fifth commandment.

8. The eighth commandment.

TWENTY-FIFTH SUNDAY OF THE YEAR
Year C

Readings

> Am 8:4 - 7
> 1 Tim 2:1 - 8
> Lk 16:1 - 13

Theme: The Use of Material Goods

Often called the prophet of social justice, Amos inveighs against the unjust practices of his time in which the disadvantaged were clearly being exploited. The Lucan parable, combined with accompanying sayings of Jesus, speaks of the proper use of material goods within the context of the Christian community. The author of 1 Timothy stresses the importance of extending one's prayer to include all people, Christian and non-Christian, in the interests of peace and good order.

First Reading

Writing in the eighth century B.C., Amos, a livestock farmer, does not, by his own admission, come from prophetic stock (7:14). In fulfilling his mission, he strongly decries the injustice within Israel and accuses those who do violence to the poor. In today's reading he addresses merchants who exploit the people in buying and selling. *The new moon* (v5; Num 28:11 - 15): a monthly day of rest with no business transactions. Prescribed sacrifices were offered. Like the sabbath, it had become a formality for many merchants anxious to return to business.

"Tipping the scales" was customary. The *ephah* was a dry measure equal to a bushel; the *shekel* was a unit of stone weights. In buying or selling, the scales were adjusted to the advantage of the agent, while the poor paid more or received less. In addition, the poor could be bartered for a price. In the midst of all manner of social abuse, religious formalities were still observed. The "pride of Jacob" (v7) is decried as an exaltation of the country at the price of the neediest. It is used with a note of sarcasm (6:8). The Lord is determined to bring injustice to a court of accountability.

Responsorial Psalm   Ps 113

The hymn begins with the customary acclaim of the Lord's name (vv1f). The otherness of Yahweh finds expression in spatial terms; his enthronement in the heavens is to the fore. At the same time, this is matched by his closeness to the neediest whom he raises to a position rivaling that of royalty (vv7f). The idea of lifting up the anawim is an important scriptural theme (1 Sam 2:1 - 10) and is repeated in Mary's Magnificat (Lk 1:46 - 55).

While not intimately linked with today's theme, the idea of Yahweh's concern for the needy reflects the teaching of the Amos reading, as well as the gospel's implication that material goods should serve the needs of the poor.

Second Reading

The author urges that prayers be offered for all, regardless of their belief, especially for those holding civil authority. Commentators speculate on whether or not this reflects a lack of concern for non-Christians on the part of the Ephesian community. Early Christians were solicitous about their appearance as good citizens since they did not participate in the government's official religious cult. Paul asks for prayers for civil leaders on two scores: it will lead to the concession of an undisturbed and respected life for the Christians (v2); it may lead to their leader's conversion and salvation (v3).

What follows this exhortation is an early liturgical formula (vv5 - 6a), centering on the heavenly destiny of all people. Since God is one, there can be no question of other competitors. In addition, Christ's role of mediation is also singular. This mediation with the one God on behalf of all humans is attained through one who was human himself and therefore capable of bridging the gap between heaven and earth (Heb 5:1f). Christ's mediating role consists in his giving himself for humankind's redemption (v6a; Mk 10:45). In this way Christ attests to God's fidelity to his plan of salvation (v6b), a plan destined for all without exception (v6a). Paul himself bears witness to the plan's universality in working among the Gentiles (v7; cf. Rom 9:1).

The Ephesus community is encouraged by this exhortation to find a place in their prayers for all people, since in the plan of salvation, wrought by the only God who exists, all have a place.

Third Reading

The Lucan parable ends with v8a. It has attracted to it other sayings of Jesus dealing with fiscal responsibility (vv8b - 13). The story, misleading if not considered in its historical context, is of a piece in itself. Why is the steward praised at the parable's conclusion? It is because of his ability to use finances prudently in his own self-interest. It does not moralize on other aspects of the steward's conduct. The story looks to one thing alone: his ability to act decisively in the face of an imminent crisis.

In the Palestine of Jesus' time, the list of charges given to a buyer contained a sum beyond the product's cost. This was a "middle management" fee to cover the cost of the agent's work. In some instances it went entirely to the person handling the transaction; in other cases it did not. In the story it can be safely presumed that the manager would have given the agent the amount reduced as his payment.

As the story opens, the steward is accused of mismanagement (v1). Other references to his dishonesty in the story (v8) refer back to this initial accusation. At any rate, he is to be fired. Faced with a very uncertain future, he decides to take action which will be to his benefit (vv2ff). He summons his employer's debtors and reduces the charges owed by eliminating the "service charge," the sum that would ordinarily go to him. The fact that the story speaks of this sum as due to his master does not militate against its being the sum due to the agent after payment (v5). It is his hope that this financial consideration will help him in terms of future need (v4). He is then commended by his master (v8). The reason is simple. He had acted with decisiveness in a moment of crisis in his use of material goods.

He was enterprising and judicious, and this merits commendation. The parable has nothing to say about other aspects of his moral comportment.

The adjunct sayings (vv8b - 12) have been attracted to the story on the basis of the common theme: use of material goods. They are otherwise unrelated. The first (v8b) compares unbeliever and believer. Those unrelated to the faith (children of this world) use material goods, like the servant in the parable, for their own interests, and it surpasses that of the faithful (children of light) in using the same goods for eternal gain. *Dishonest wealth* (v9) (literally: mammon of iniquity): so called for the way it is generally used rather than as referring to money in itself. The point is that it should be used in such a way as to assure eternal happiness, i.e. for the good of others (12:33f).

Fidelity in stewardship is also commended (vv10 - 13). Finally, basic choices must be made. One is either pledged to worldly, passing concerns (mammon—the object of one's love) or to God (v13). A person is absorbed in one or the other. To opt for the Lord is to place trust and confidence solely in him (12:22 - 34). To center oneself on earthly possessions is to act counter to the gospel. Divided loyalties are impossible.

There is an increasing awareness among Catholics of the church's social agenda. This attention to the social needs of people dates from the 1891 encyclical on labor of Leo XIII. The social teaching of the church reached its highpoint in the document Gaudium et Spes *of the Second Vatican Council. Later in 1971 the international synod of bishops spoke of the promotion of justice in the world as being a "constitutive element of evangelization." Since then numerous papal statements have reinforced this position. The idea of human promotion, coupled with the eschatological or other-worldly dimension of salvation, stands at the heart of Latin America's liberation theology. On the more official level of church life today this is spoken of as integral salvation.*

This ecclesial social teaching can easily be inferred from today's readings. Amos' concern with the injustice done to the poor is dominant. Unjust business practices are clearly labeled as exploitative. The reduction of people to chattel by impoverishing them is a violation of human dignity. In the gospel, the steward is applauded by his master because of his enlightened use of material goods. Two other statements speak of honesty and fidelity in administering the wealth of others and the dangers inherent in becoming enslaved to material goods.

Material goods, not evil in themselves, are necessary for life and are meant to be shared. This is true on a personal as well as societal level. It is decidedly immoral for a portion of the world to become rich at the expense of the poorer segments of the earth. The broad chasm that today separates the first and third worlds calls for a major revision of our economic system so that the poorer nations may have a more equitable share of the goods of life.

When we show we are concerned for the disenfranchised in our towns, cities, and nations, even in a small way, we resemble the manager who disposed of his material goods in an enlightened way. He did it to get on in life. We are called to be more altruistic in acting just as decisively. We are the "children of light" who have much to learn from the "children of this world." In making the church's social agenda our own, we are making friends with wealth and using it in such ways as to assure our standing with God.

To promote an economy that provides jobs rather than adds to the proliferation of armaments; to be concerned about a just wage and living conditions for migrants and their families; to curb rampant development which devastates the environment; to protect the unborn; equal opportunity; minority job opportunities; combating a militaristic mindset—all of these are not simply secular or political concerns; they are moral issues as well.

Homiletic and Catechetical Helps

1. Personal and social sin.

2. The seventh commandment: its narrow and broad ramifications.

3. The conduct of the manager in the parable.

4. Consumerism: To serve God or mammon?

5. The meaning of sin?

6. Examples from your experience of using material goods in an enlightened way.

7. Respect for civil authorities.

8. Prayer of the faithful: its role in the liturgy.

9. Praying with and for the non-believer.

TWENTY-SIXTH SUNDAY OF THE YEAR
Year A

Readings

> Ez 18:25 - 28
> Phil 2:1 - 11
> Mt 21:28 - 32

Theme: Mindset

Have you ever journeyed with someone who prefers a well-traveled road, narrow and winding, to a number of newer highways now available? The old route is better, it is said—more scenic, less traffic, etc. The person is of a particular mindset. Today's reading from Ezekiel speaks of a change of mindset for the better, which we would call conversion. The parable taken from Matthew speaks of those who experience a change of mindset and those who do not in the face of new opportunities. The second reading, the famous passage from Philippians, encourages us to live in a spirit of humility or to have the mindset of Christ.

First Reading

The context of the Ezekiel reading is a chapter (18) dealing with individual responsibility. It marks a new development in Israelite thought that has to be viewed against a centuries-old tradition of collective responsibility. Culpability for parents' sins could be heaped upon their children due to the strong sense of family and clan solidarity that existed (Ex 20:5; 34:7; Dt 5:9). During the period of the exile, with the loss of land

and country, that strong sense of unity in guilt gave way to the emerging strain of personalism, a sense of individual responsibility (Jer 31:29f; 2 Kgs 14:6). In the future, each person was to have an individual relationship to God and would be held personally accountable for sinful or virtuous conduct.

The present chapter treats the question at length, commenting on the invalidity of the proverb cited in v2, which depicts the fathers eating green grapes and their children gritting their teeth. There is to be henceforth a neat distinction between a virtuous father (vv5 - 9) and a sinful son (vv10 - 13), a faithless father and a faithful son (vv14 - 20).

The final section, read in today's liturgy, carries the argument one step further. If a good person turns to evil in the course of his life, he will pay the price of his wickedness (v26). So, too, if an evildoer has a change of heart and lives virtuously, that person will be favored by God (v27).

The reference to the accusation of unfairness on Yahweh's part (v25) probably refers to prevailing sentiment on collective responsibility, i.e. children paying the price of their parents' sin. Ezekiel in setting forth his position rejects any notion of unfairness on God's part. Physical death (v26) represented a definitive separation from God, who had no access to the realm of the dead (Ps 88:6; 86:13). Its finality, especially when premature and untimely, was considered Yahweh's definitive punishment. Deliverance from death, on the other hand, meant restoration to life with its possibilities for joy and continued worship of the Lord (v27). This is the lot of the virtuous person (Prov 11:30). A long life was the sure sign of God's favor (Prov 11:27).

Not only is God's way just; it is generous. Not only will sins of progenitors not be visited on their children, but not even the sins of the individual will be remembered when there is conversion and remorse. By the same token, all the good of a person's life can be eradicated by a decision to turn away from God at any moment in life. Neither virtue nor vice is hereditary. It is a personal mindset that makes the difference, and even that is subject to change.

Responsorial Psalm   Ps 25

The psalm is a prayer for God's guidance (vv4f, 8f). The "way" of God (v9) is his teaching on righteousness. Interspersed in the psalm is the author's recognition of his own sins together with Yahweh's forgiveness.

The note of conversion, as the psalmist sees his own sins in the light of God's goodness, is suitable accompaniment for the change of mindset in the first and third readings.

Second Reading

In his appeal for a sense of unity and humility, Paul utilizes a Christological hymn (vv6 - 11). Whether the hymn was drawn from the liturgy of the early church or was composed by Paul himself is an unresolved question. It serves to encourage humility within the Christian community after the example of Christ himself.

The Christians' motivation for harmony and peace is their being rooted "in Christ" and enjoying fellowship in the Holy Spirit (v1). This ontological reality should produce a mindset of unity and common purpose (v3). Nowhere is this more evident than in humility which works to the good of others over one's personal concerns.

It is at this point that Paul introduces the celebrated hymn which unfolds the tale of Christ's profound sense of humility. There are two major movements in the hymn, one of descent and one of ascent, both of which center around the mission of Christ. It is the Christ "in the form of God" who stands at the beginning and end of the poem (vv6, 11).

Initially Christ is presented as pre-existent, with the Father eternally. This is not simply the divine nature or Christ as eternal Son but the God-man who is present to the Father from the beginning. He was divine by nature and possessed all the qualities that accompany his state (thus: "in the form of God"). But unlike Adam, who, created in God's image (Gen 1:26f), was akin to Christ, Jesus desires to exercise no hegemony. He did not want to "grasp" equality with God in the sense of selfish exploitation for his own ends (v6).

Rather Christ takes an opposite turn. His self-abasement is described in terms of a descent (vv7f). First of all, he "empties himself" (v7), an expression studied at great lengths by exegetes and theologians through the centuries. Its meaning is best derived from its complement (v7b). He emptied himself in becoming a slave, i.e. one without position, rank, or power of any sort. Paul elsewhere sees unredeemed humanity in this condition by nature (Gal 4:1 - 11; 4:21 - 31; Rom 8:1). Now Christ is seen and recognized simply as human. If his former "likeness" was godlike, his present appearance is totally that of man. He enters the enslaved state of humanity.

The descent continues (v8). Jesus, not content with the self-abnegation already realized, takes the added step, in profound humility, of submitting to the first major consequence of humanness: death. And this he does in accepting the ignominious form of crucifixion. Together with the humility of Christ, his obedience is stressed, a virtue to be emphasized in an exhortation, following the hymn (vv12ff).

At this point, the ascent of Christ begins (v9). God regards the humility and obedience of Jesus as the reversal of Adam's earlier disobedience (Rom 5:19) and finds it totally acceptable. Jesus is, therefore, exalted and reinstated to his former position (v2) but given a new name (v11). In this process, there is no mention made of resurrection or, in any explicit way, ascension. The hymn moves on a different Christological plane in expressing the entire redemptive act. By reason of this new name or title, the disclosure of which is saved for the final strophe, Jesus is placed above all the faithful just and the angelic beings. In short, he presides over the universe as a whole (Col 1:15f).

In continuing this theme of ascent, all tiers of creation—heaven, earth, and underworld—render homage in recognizing Jesus' new name (v10). The title he has won is that of Lord (*kyrios*). The word is used in the Hebrew and Greek scriptures to avoid the use of the sacred name, Yahweh. Hence, Jesus receives the same title given to God himself without belief in the unicity of God being sacrificed. In fact, God himself confers it and will give Christ the final glory (v11).

With lordship added to the godhead that is already his (v6), Christ is fully experienced and recognized as God. The ascent to his original place is now complete. The humility of Jesus is the centerpiece. By reason of their life in Christ, his followers are exhorted to have a similar mindset.

Third Reading

This parable is found only in Matthew. It is one of three consecutive stories (21:28 - 22:14) which form an extended commentary on the earlier cited obduracy and duplicity of the Jewish leaders (21:23 - 27). It is to them that Jesus' discourse is directed.

The vineyard as a metaphor for God's reign is frequent (20:1; 21:33; Is 5:1 - 7; Jer 2:10). The two sons, as the parable makes clear, represent two segments of Judaism. The first son (v28) stands for sinners within Israel (tax collectors, prostitutes) who, despite their initial negative response, ultimately answer favorably Jesus' message. The second son (v30) clearly represents Jesus' audience, the religious leaders of the Jews, the recipients of God's revelation to his people. It is a message to which they and their forefathers had initially given their assent. But when God's plan is brought to its fulfillment, first of all, in the preaching of John the Baptist, they refuse acceptance. In their response to Jesus' question (v31), they accuse themselves. The paradox was almost unthinkable by Jewish standards. The teachers of Israel are self-excluded while the outcasts enter God's reign. *The way of righteousness* (v32): This refers to his conformity and compliance with God's saving plan for the redemption of humankind (cf. 3:15).

The two categories referred to are clearly segments of Judaism, and this was undoubtedly the parable's earliest and dominant meaning. However, the frequent equation of the social outcast with the Gentiles makes it likely that the parable was also read, at least by Matthew's time, in terms of the Gentile movement toward the church while the Jews remained aloof.

The religious leaders represent a mindset of Jewish thought. Their "I will" was tailored to their pre-determined understanding of God's message and there they remained. The sinners, more open to God's healing action, respond with an openness of mind that enables them to move in a new direction.

Human conduct weighs in heavily before God. It is a thought that emerges clearly from today's readings. There are many factors that contribute to the way we act. There is a pattern of virtue, just as there is a pattern of vice. It is even argued that to inherit a parent's sins today means to be born into a life of deprivation and vice from which it is very difficult to emerge.

But freedom, as dulled as it may become, still offers the possibility of change. This may mean a move away from God or a move toward him. In the former case, people with strong moral principles find their ideals becoming more elastic with years. In the face of a critical decision, one can turn from God decisively, as today's first reading reminds us. Yet a mindset can also be changed for the better. Some people see the folly of their ways and experience genuine conversion. They begin anew. God's forgiveness is assured. It is never too late.

There is a certain relevance in today's gospel for our times. The one son promised to go to the vineyard and never went. His mindset proved too inflexible. Today there are sincere and well-intentioned Christians who are incapable of change. Since the Second Vatican Council, the church is clearly set on a new course. This requires a willingness to see things differently. Our non-Catholic neighbors, for example, are not an anonymous "they"; rather, they are believers also. The poor who inhabit our inner cities are not to be ignored. We share a common responsibility for our fellow human beings. In addition, our environment is sacred; ecology is a religious concern and a Christian duty. Yet all too often, mindsets do not change. Things remain the way they were. And yet conversions still take place. A new mindset takes over. We meet it often in life; we see it in the Matt Talbots and the Dorothy Days, not to speak of our own acquaintances. Some people begin by saying "no" to the master of the vineyard but end by giving their assent. They give themselves to the reign of God with limitless generosity. Life has countless paradoxes.

And for those whose life is largely undramatic, the Philippians' hymn is worth reading and rereading. We have no reason to boast or make claims of virtue. We simply bow humbly before the goodness of God. The humility of Christ in his suffering and death reminds us of our own unworthiness. If we fail to make our way to the vineyard, it is because we resist his grace. If we do go, it is because his love has touched us. There are many unknowns on the path which we walk. The only sure way is to make Christ's our own.

Homiletic and Catechetical Helps

1. Which of the two sons is closest to your own attitude?

2. Explain collective and personal retribution.

3. The importance of the Babylonian exile for Hebrew religious thought.

4. The understanding of repentance.

5. A mindset is a consistent way of thinking; show how it can be an obstacle or a grace.

6. The descent-ascent theme in the Philippians hymn.

7. The "name" given to Jesus.

8. Humility as a key Christian virtue.

9. The difference in Christ before and after the descent in Philippians.

10. The pre-existent Christ.

TWENTY-SIXTH SUNDAY OF THE YEAR
Year B

Readings

> Num 11:25 - 29
> Jas 5:1 - 6
> Mk 9:38 - 43, 45, 47 - 48

Theme: Tolerance

The readings today move in a number of different directions, any one of which merits development in itself. The notion of tolerance, however, emerges forcefully in the first and third readings. The reading from Numbers contains an incident from the time of the Israelites' desert sojourn. The gospel passage from Mark is a collage of sayings of Jesus drawn together on different bases, sometimes a word or a phrase. The reading from James is another example of this letter's straightforward and practical teaching, here related to social justice.

First Reading

The story of Eldad and Medad is concerned with the sharing of Moses' charismatic spirit among the people at the time of the desert experience. Earlier in the chapter, Moses had complained to Yahweh about his inability to provide for the people's needs by himself. The burden had become too great (11:1 - 13). The Lord decides in favor of shared responsibility, taking a portion of Moses' charismatic spirit and distributing it among seventy trustworthy and proven elders of the community (vv24f). The reference to their "prophesying" (v25) looks to a form of ecstatic language, rooted more in verbal enthusiasm than in intelligibility. It was not uncommon in Israel (1 Sam 10:10ff; 19:20ff) or the early church (1 Cor 13 - 14).

The account then centers on two men who were inexplicably absent when the outpouring of the spirit took place at the tent of meeting. Since they had been designated to be a part of the group, the spirit of Moses comes to rest on them within the camp itself (v26).

The stand-off between Joshua, the trusted aide, and Moses is unusual (vv28f). Moses' response is clear. Exception should not be taken to the two men's being gifted outside the ordinary procedure. Moses wishes that the distribution of the spirit were even more widespread (v29).

The question arises: Why was the event, rather insignificant in itself, preserved in Israelite tradition? Exodus events became part of tradition because of either their importance or their relevance to some later set of circumstances. The disagreement between Joshua and Moses may be a reason for its preservation.

It is quite likely, however, that the story took on particular significance at a later time when there were strong efforts to institutionalize the charism of prophecy. There were recognized groups of prophets in Israel whose membership was clearly determined (1 Sam 10:10 - 13). The prophet Amos clearly distinguishes himself from the class of "professional" prophets

(Am 7:14f). Since prophets were interpreters of God's will, their authenticity had to be tested. There were false prophets who were agents of deception (1 Kgs 22:19 - 23; Jer 28). The Torah gives clear admonition in this regard (Deut 13:1 - 6).

There was evidently some attempt to bring this prophetic spirit in rein through institutional control. As desirable as boundaries may have been, there were inherent obstacles to the limitation of a free gift of God. The narrative in Numbers does not favor placing limits to the action of the spirit; Moses encourages an attitude of tolerance. The narrative, then, can be said to have a distinctly polemic tone opposing efforts to limit charisms or exercise the type of control which institutionaliza- tion would inevitably entail.

Responsorial Psalm   Ps 19

This hymn has two distinct parts—one praising God for the work of creation (vv1 - 7), the second extolling God for the Torah, the guide for a correct moral life (vv8 - 11). It closes with a prayer for help to bring about faithful observance (vv12 - 15).

The Torah is spoken of with a variety of synonyms—decrees, ordinances—and its attributes amply extolled—perfect, trustwor- thy, true, just (vv8, 10). In view of the perfection of the law itself, the psalmist can only pray that his life approximate this perfection through upright conduct (vv12ff).

The psalm is related to the broad range of concerns expressed in God's word today, all of them related to faithful adherence to the teaching of Jesus.

Second Reading

The last chapter of James' letter registers a sharp contrast between the rich and the poor, with the injustice inflicted by the former on the latter brought to the fore.

The injunction to the rich (vv1 - 6) is probably literary and not addressed explicitly to Christians. *Impending miseries* (v1): This refers to the expected end time. Wealth is depicted as dis- integrating, even corroding the person (vv2 - 4). Ironically the treasures stored up for the "last days" point only to final tribulation (cf. Lk 12:16 - 21).

Wages as a tool of exploitation was long condemned in Israel (Lev 19:13; Deut 24:14f). Here such injustice is once again explicitly condemned (v4). Amassed wealth at the expense of the poor is but a preparation for final judgment (v5). The condemnation and murder of the innocent in their powerlessness is poetic for economic injustice (Sir 34:22).

Third Reading

In the gospel there is a linking of separate sayings of Jesus, with no single consistent theme. Some linkage is based on a similar thought, some on a word or a phrase. This commentary does not attempt to treat them as a block; each segment is treated separately.

The first statement (vv38 - 40) is linked with the reading from Numbers thematically. The note of tolerance is again present. In Mark, it is connected contextually with the story of receiving a child in Jesus' name; the sole connecting link is "in my name (vv37, 38, 39).

Jesus argues that anyone engaged in exorcism, in his name, even through not part of his company, is involved in a good work. He should not be impeded. At the very least, it is unlikely that an authentic adversary of the evil one would at the same time be opposed to Jesus. In the clear "black and white" lines of semitic thought, the one who is not my adversary is my ally (v40).

This tolerance of Jesus sheds light on the saying's origin. Although it is utilized by the early church, it was not created by it. This expansive vision is best explained as deriving from Jesus himself. Despite attempts by fraudulent exorcists to co-opt the apostolic Spirit (Acts 8:18f; 19:13f), there was the recognition that good was being accomplished beyond the boundaries of institutional direction. The present passage served to authenticate this exception. The story of Apollos (Acts 18:24 - 28) illustrates the point well. He was a Jew who had received only John's baptism but was instructed in Christianity. He is found in

Ephesus vigorously preaching the way of the Lord, even though unbaptized. Again, the Spirit breathes where it will.

The subsequent saying (v41) has "the name" of Christ in common with the preceding, thus in Greek: "because you have the name of Christ." Charity extended to one who is a disciple of Christ is rewarded, just as it was conversely stated earlier (v37) that the Christian who assists another person responds to God himself.

The following sayings of Jesus (vv42 - 48) treat of temptation to sin, linked together by the common word: "scandalize, cause to sin." To scandalize means to put an obstacle in a person's path; in the moral order, it is to block deliberately one's journey on the path of virtue. The seriousness of such obstruction is underscored by the gravity of the sanction: the desired loss of the tempter's life (v42).

The gravity of sin weighs in heavily in the final sayings (vv43 - 47). It is not self-mutilation that Jesus calls for. Rather, in strong semitic fashion, he exaggerates the measures to be taken to avoid sin only to heighten the notion of the seriousness of sin, which is in itself invisible and its effects not immediately evident. Gehenna would be referred to as hell today. Literally it meant the Valley of Hinnon, outside of Jerusalem, where child sacrifice was once practiced (2 Kgs 23:10) and which became known as a locale of the poorest repute. It is well described in the words taken from Isaiah (66:24) which conclude the passage.

This gospel is a scriptural collage of a variety of Jesus' sayings. The homilist or catechist is advised to deal with either the principal theme (connecting the first and third readings) or with one of the subsidiary themes. It is a thankless, even confusing task, for the homilist especially, to attempt to treat all the ideas comprehensively.

Tolerance is a more accepted virtue today than it was in years past. For example, to speak of religious tolerance at one time connoted a form of indifference. It implied that all religious bodies were of equal value. The word suffered from another ailment as well. Toleration often meant simply "to put up with, to endure." It was passive and lacked any positive thrust.

The idea of tolerance is best understood as opposed to bigotry, racism, sectarianism, or sexism. Its best synonym is inclusiveness, which connotes a breadth of vision. As today's scripture tells us, no restriction can be placed on God's action. Human restraints cannot be placed on the ways of the Lord.

Today, for example, we refer to other Christian bodies as churches. We recognize God's presence among them as well as within our own church. This is not to deny important differences; it is but to recognize a fact. We realize that we all have something to learn from each other. Tolerance is an active virtue when we seek to draw closer to others in inclusiveness. The days of bigotry may be passing but we do not want to replace it with "holy" indifference.

When we speak of other faiths, we want to include the Jewish people. Our attitudes toward them in the past have often been intolerant. To realize that God's word was first given to the Hebrew people, the "children of Abraham," gives us a common heritage. In addition, we believe that God is present in the other world religions. All of this was clearly stated at the Second Vatican Council.

Tolerance also means inclusiveness for people of other races. They have a proper and legitimate place as well in our social and economic structures. Tolerance means asking ourselves if we see men and women as truly equal in our church and society. The word means many things for many people. But basically it has to mean a broadening of vision and an opening of heart.

Today our scriptures also speak of sin and its serious consequences. Contemporary attitudes toward sin are sterilized and antiseptic. Without becoming guilt-ridden or neurotic, we have to recognize sin's seriousness as a sharp rupture between God and ourselves. This is not be to victimized by a "sin complex." It simply implies a realistic look at the world, our own weakness, and, above all, the need of God's grace.

James, in his usual straightforward manner, addresses the question of social injustice. His words have a clear contemporary resonance where the rich still exploit the poor, but perhaps in more complex forms. Societal corruption is not today an occasional, sometime sort of thing. It is widespread and worldwide. It even finds its way into religious bodies where it does great damage to the human spirit.

Corruption in the political field, on all levels, touches every country, especially the poorest. In industry, it infects both management and labor. This is not to deny the presence of good and qualified men and *women in public life today. But that very presence is too often offset by a negative picture that has led to a great deal of human cynicism. The words of James are sobering: "You condemn, even kill the just man." How often in our own day have those words had not a figurative but a literal meaning. The word of God still remains our two-edged sword, our stab of conscience.*

Homiletic and Catechetical Helps

1. Tolerance in church, society, and business.

2. Where is intolerance most present in our life?

3. The Vatican II documents on ecumenism and world religions.

4. The meaning and application of the word "scandal."

5. The definition of serious sin; the meaning of "fundamental option."

6. Applying today's epistle (James) to contemporary life.

7. Forms of exploitation: a Christian response.

TWENTY-SIXTH SUNDAY OF THE YEAR
Year C

Readings

> Am 6:1, 4 - 7
> 1 Tim 6:11 - 16
> Lk 16:19 - 23

Theme: True Riches

The Christian paradox of where lasting wealth really resides is at the heart of today's readings. The sheepherder prophet Amos in the eighth century B.C. speaks forcefully against his contemporaries in the northern kingdom who amass riches with little concern for the less fortunate. Luke's celebrated story of the rich man and Lazarus contrasts the final lot of the rich and the poor. The first letter to Timothy calls for unwavering perseverance until the Lord's return, with a firm grasp on eternal values.

First Reading

The words of Amos are directed to the complacent rulers of the southern (Zion) and northern (Samaria) kingdoms (v1). The "beds of ivory" (v4) are now known from archeological studies conducted in the Samaria region. They were actually beds with ivory inlays along the side for decorative purposes. The picture of undisturbed luxury and inexhaustible food supplies presents a picture of gross self-indulgence (vv4 - 6). By this date, David's musical ability has already been established (v5).

With all its wealth, the ruling class was oblivious to the moral decline of the kingdoms; Joseph (Israel) is in a state of disintegration (v6). The contrast is striking. A population in moral, economic, and political disarray is ruled over by unconcerned leaders who live only for the moment. The outcome is inevitable. Those who have enjoyed the most will be the first to suffer loss, to be led away in the impending deportation (v7).

Responsorial Psalm   Ps 146

This post-exilic hymn praises God as Creator (v6) and as redeemer of the poor and oppressed (vv7ff). Yahweh's fidelity to his covenant promises (v6) leads him to champion the cause of the needy. Some of these, as feeding the hungry and liberating captives, recall the exodus event. Granting sight to the blind and freeing captives are synonymous expressions (Is 42:7; 61:1). Orphans and widows (v9) were the most helpless in society since they had no male provider (Ex 22:20f; Deut 10:18). Just as Yahweh enables the just, he causes the wicked to stumble (v9; Ps 1:6). God's redemptive action is integral to the establishment of God's reign (v15).

This concern of God for the poor lies at the heart of Christian responsibility. In this way, it is connected with today's theme.

Second Reading

In this letter Timothy is presented as having a spiritual responsibility for the Christian community at Ephesus (1:3f). Paul (perhaps pseudonymously) holds him to the highest standards of behavior, just as he reproves the attitudes of those with base motives (6:3 - 10).

In the present passage, Paul bases his moral motivation on belief in eternal life (v12). Upright conduct (v11) springs from a belief in a life which will not end. Timothy professed belief in these values in his baptism, "the noble confession" (v12); Jesus himself bore witness to them in facing his passion and death (v13). In the name of God and Jesus, the apostle urges fidelity to the "commandment" (v14), i.e. Timothy's total commitment to the Christian life, which includes his actual duties.

All of this is held for the day of Christ's appearance, when promise will become reality and fidelity will be rewarded (Tit 2:11ff). The passage ends with a final doxology to God the Father in whose hands alone the future lies, including the time of Christ's return (vv15f).

Third Reading

The story of the rich man and Lazarus appears only in Luke. It is an extended commentary on the same gospel's version of the beatitudes (6:20, 24). It is basically a statement on after-life reversal of roles. While the rich man is faulted for his lack of concern for the poor, the story is not in itself a treatise on the general moral failure of the rich man nor of the virtue of the poor man.

To understand the story well, one must keep in mind that through most of the Hebrews' history good conduct was believed to be rewarded in this life just as sinful behavior was punished here. The after-life, if such it could be called, was sheol, the shadowy realm of the dead, which as a state of being was more negative than positive. God was not present there. It was not a place of sanctions. Since moral accounts had to be settled on this side of the grave, wealth and poverty become measures of virtue and sin. In practice, of course, this presented endless difficulties and contradictions, as seen in Job and Ecclesiastes, but these were the only parameters offered.

The message of Jesus brings after-life sanctions to the fore, as the Lazarus story indicates. No longer is the present lot of a rich man or that of a Lazarus to be seen as reward or punishment. A future accounting will take place after death occurs. It is only then that the truth will emerge. It is then that the true riches become evident.

The story has two distinct sections with their respective message. The first deals with the after-life lot of the two central players (vv19 - 26): the second concerns the lesson to be learned by the living on care for the poor (vv27 - 31). In the first parts, vivid contrasts are again to the fore. Lazarus is destitute, even dehumanized in full view of the rich man, whose life style is that of the wealthiest class (vv19f). While the reversal of fortunes after death is elsewhere present in oriental literature, the exchange between the rich man and Abraham is quite distinctive (vv23 - 26). The after-life itself is depicted in traditional Jewish terms. Elsewhere the Lucan Jesus speaks of the eschatological banquet in the company of Abraham, Isaac and Jacob (13:28f). Lazarus' privileged position at the table enables him to recline on the "bosom of Abraham" (v22; Jn 13:23).

The rich man's later lot carries him to the underworld, sheol, the realm of the dead. It is the lowest tier in the Hebrew cosmogony; there were heaven, earth, and the underworld, with a yawning chasm of separation between heaven and the underworld. The verbal exchange between Abraham and the rich man is clearly literary. The excruciating thirst of the rich man (v24) recalls the image of the hungry Lazarus lying at the man's door. Verse 25 capsulizes the importance of the story. The accounts are now settled.

The second section of the story is an exhortation to the Christian community (vv27 - 31). The repeated references to Abraham as "father" (vv24, 27) are of no avail since the rich man has not shown himself a son of Abraham in his moral standards (Jn 8:39). The point of the dialogue here is that the living must learn from the scriptures and the teaching of Jesus. The teaching of the Torah and the prophets (v29) is clear enough on respect for the poor. Further intervention, even if miraculous, will not change the hearts of the self-centered. The Lucan audience is reminded to seize the present opportunity to hear and obey God's word and not to put it off for some future day. This concluding exhortation has carried the original story a step beyond illustrating the reversal of fortunes.

True riches, then, will come to the rejected as part of God's reign. At the same time, the wealthy must realize that true riches for them lie in alleviating the needs of the less privileged, not in amassing greater wealth.

Latin American theology often speaks of seeing God in the eyes of the poor. St. Vincent de Paul said that to serve the poor is a true form of prayer. The poor, whatever may be said of the deprivation they experience, are a privileged people in God's plan.

Today's readings remind us to keep that vision before our eyes. Many people do. They always find time to assist the poor; they give generously of their time and resources; some serve directly in leaving home for other cultures. The history of the church is rich in its expressions of outreach.

But the poor still suffer. They are crushed not only by neglect but by exploitation. The causes of poverty today are more elusive, more difficult to label. It frequently involves complex economic systems. But it is as merciless and cruel as the conduct of the rich man eating sumptuously with a starving beggar at his gate. New forms of oppression do not excuse us from looking squarely at the basic reality. Certainly we need people who go directly to the slums, the barrios, and favelas to bring comfort, food, and assistance. But we also need those who lobby in Congress, track voting records, raise questions at stockholders' meetings, and use the media as a sensitizing strategy.

We have God's assurance that the lot of the poor will one day be altered. The unconcerned affluent will not have the final say. But we cannot wait for the final day. The rich man paid the price for not alleviating Lazarus' pain while he lived, while the chance was there. We cannot ease our conscience by saying that one day the record will be set straight, "Now is the acceptable time." "Carpe diem!" "Seize the day."

The first letter to Timothy is a source of meditation for those in authority. It reminds them of their awesome responsibility to live an upright life. Failure to do so causes untold damage within the community. Their vision must be, in the words of today's reading, "firmly fixed on eternal life." They will then be helped in viewing the events of daily life with a Christian perspective; it will prevent them from acting for purely human motives or, worse, for personal gain. It is frightening to think of God's church being used for personal advantage. Christian leaders, with their attention riveted on God's reign and Christ's return, are daily reminded that the outcasts of this world will be honored guests in the age to come.

Homiletic and Catechetical Helps

1. The story of Lazarus and the rich man as applicable today.

2. Where does our society today see the "true riches"?

3. The corporal and spiritual works of mercy.

4. Practical outreach to the poor.

5. The history of religious life and concern for the poor.

6. Church authority and integrity of life.

7. Authority: teaching by example.

8. Possible changes in church structure.

9. The sacrament of orders.

10. The teaching of Timothy: baptism and witness.

11. The relation of the after-life and sanctions.

TWENTY-SEVENTH SUNDAY OF THE YEAR
Year A

Readings

Is 5:1 - 7
Phil 4:6 - 9
Mt 21:33 - 43

Theme: The Rich Harvest: Fidelity to the Lord's Will

The biblical image of Israel as the Lord's vineyard finds one of its finest expressions in the Isaian song read in today's liturgy. It speaks poignantly of Yahweh's disappointment with the "wild grapes" produced at harvest time. The same imagery is present in Matthew's parable of the vineyard; in fact, the song and the parable conclude in much the same way—on a note of disillusionment. Fidelity to God's will produces the abundant harvest. The second reading from Paul's letter to the Philippians, exhorting the community to peaceful relationships, has its own sense of serenity and a striking appeal to love and respect whatever in life is wholesome and sound.

First Reading

A carefully constructed poetic piece, the song of the vineyard uses metaphor effectively in building dramatic tension around the issue of covenant infidelity. Only at the end of the song are the friend and his vineyard identified as Yahweh and Israel.

The prophet is presented as detached from his friend's lament (v1) as he recounts the story. Initially the poem deals with the constructing of the vineyard—spading, clearing, planting, conserving, and preparing for cultivation (v2). With everything done with care, there is a heightened expectation of a good harvest. But the outcome is one of bitter disappointment. With the vineyard still unidentified, Judah is ironically called to render judgment (v3). The defendant himself imposes the sentence, as in the case of Nathan's parable incriminating the guilty David (2 Sam 12:1 - 6).

The latter part of the poem corresponds to the earlier part on the construction of the vineyard in antithetical parallelism. The vineyard is dismantled: protective wall and hedge removed, no proper cultivation, and parched land (vv5f). The song becomes parable only at the end with the vineyard's identification as the unfaithful Judah. It ends with a play on words: judgment (*mishpat*) and violence (*mishpah*), justice (*sedeqah*) and outcry (*sehaqah*) (v7). The Lord looked for covenant fidelity and uprightness, especially as regards the rights of the poor (cf.

1:17) but found only selfish disregard and treachery. The point is clearly made. Because of the people's lack of regard of Yahweh and his providential care, their lot will be one of destruction and deportation.

Responsorial Psalm   Ps 80

The theme of the vineyard is continued in this psalm of lament and petition for Israel's deliverance, originally identified with the needs of the northern kingdom. Israel (the vine) was taken from Egyptian slavery and settled in Canaan, the land of promise. The vine grows in impressive heights, poetically presented as towering over the mighty Lebanon cedars; it is God's own handiwork (Num 24:6). Israel's geographical expanse is ideally presented as embracing what was then known of the civilized world, from the Mediterranean (the Sea) to the Euphrates (the River). But it has been brought to ruin by invasion; it is feeding ground for wild beasts. A communal petition for deliverance is uttered with a pledge of future fidelity in exchange for restoration.

Second Reading

In the final part of his letter to the Philippians, Paul instructs the community to put aside their preoccupations and turn to the Lord in prayer (v6). Then that gift of God which is his peace will be theirs. Biblical peace springs from harmonious relations between God and his people and then among the people themselves. It is found when one turns his or her life over to the crucified and risen Christ (Col 3:15). In its effectiveness it surpasses the human capacity to understand (v7).

The apostle does not hesitate to recommend a number of Stoic virtues to his Christian audience (v8), in celebrating those human values which elevate the human spirit and are thus related to the God of peace. The good in life is not solely connected with the world beyond but also includes natural beauty, the accomplishments of the human spirit and natural beauty in all its forms.

Third Reading

The parable of the vineyard is found in all of the synoptic gospels and is built upon the vineyard song of Isaiah 5. Israel, God's people, remains the vineyard and Yahweh, the absentee landlord. The Matthaean parable has taken on allegorical features as it developed in early church life, but its basic point of rejection and replacement is reflective of the ministry of Jesus himself.

The two sets of servants sent to the tenants are the Hebrew prophets. They are rejected, abused, even killed. The son, the final emissary, is Jesus himself, with an allusion to his death outside of Jerusalem (v29; Jn 19:17; Heb 13:12f). Once again sentence is passed by the hearers, here the Jewish religious leaders (v23). Ironically they pass sentence on themselves.

The quotation from Psalm 118 (v42) was used in the early church as a prophetic illustration of Jesus' rejection by his own people and his ultimate triumph. The messianic era with Christ as its foundation has passed from the Jews to the Christian community which in Matthew's historical context was made up of Jew and Gentile converts. Elsewhere Paul argues that at a future time the Jews will be fully integrated into this saving plan (Rom 9 - 11).

Privilege and status are meaningless in the reign of God. Israel's special election was not in itself assurance of lasting favor. Election was intended to elicit a grateful response leading to a faithful compliance with God's will. The readings from Isaiah and Matthew indicate what actually occurred. In religious belief there is always the danger of intractability, the inability to allow for growth and development. Fidelity to Yahweh is paramount, but on his terms, not ours. A true adherence to the Lord is certain to lead us down paths never envisioned.

Paul calls us to a spirit of peace and serenity in a world often beset by chaos and confusion. With a clear spiritual vision we are capable of dealing with the plethora of problems that are part of daily life. That spirit, coupled with the ability to see the hand of God in a multi-faceted world with its beauty and nobility as well as its failings, makes for a strong and steady hand at the helm during our earthly sojourn.

Homiletic and Catechetical Helps

1. God's call and our response.

2. The election of Israel (Vatican II's statement on the Jewish people).

3. Reconciling God's justice and forgiveness.

4. Relations between Christians and Jews; antisemitism.

5. Dealing with anxieties.

6. Meaning of biblical peace.

7. Christianity and the arts.

TWENTY-SEVENTH SUNDAY OF THE YEAR
Year B

Readings

> Gen 2:18 - 24
> Heb 2:9 - 11
> Mk 10:2 - 16

Theme: The Marriage Commitment

The reading from Genesis is part of our religious pre-history. Its significance lies in its doctrinal importance, not in questions of historical origins. Today's reading deals with the creation of woman, man's partner and mate. The gospel builds on the marriage theme in Jesus' clear enunciation of the permanence of the married state. The passage from Hebrews explains Jesus' historical and temporary inferiority to the angels in his human condition; such was necessary for him to bond with the sinful people whom he came to save.

First Reading

The passage comes from the J or Yahwish tradition of the Pentateuch and is characterized by a vivid and picturesque literary style in its manner of depicting "the beginnings." The basic framework of the passage is Yahweh's stated intention to create a partner for man (Adam). The creation of the animals, then, is a literary inclusion illustrating their inability to serve as a suitable companion as the author moves toward the creation of woman. The account of the animals being brought before man also serves another purpose. The person who attaches the name exercises a certain dominion over the one designated (Gen 17:5; 32:24); thus the narrative points to nature's subordination to the human person who stands at the apogee of creation.

The rib drawn from man's side expresses figuratively woman's equality with man and explains the physical attraction between the two. Woman's relation to the man is without parallel in the order of creation. In man's expression of his satisfaction at this turn of events (v23), there is a clear play on words. The Hebrew word for woman (*issha*) contains the root for man (*ish*), as is the case of the English *wo-man*. Adding the possessive pronoun "her" to "man" (Heb: *ishah*) makes for a euphonic closeness to "woman."

The biblical teaching here is one of complementarity and equality, with the note of a certain authority attached to the man, consonant with Hebrew culture, in his naming his partner. Permanence and exclusiveness seal the new union (v24), characterized by a closeness that is both effective and physical (one body).

Responsorial Psalm   Ps 128

The psalm is sapiential or didactic. The author extols upright conduct (v1), human industry (v2) and strong family life (v3). It is this last feature that links the psalm to today's theme. Fertility and numerous progeny were clear signs of divine favor, since the parents were seen as living on in their offspring. Childlessness was seen as a great misfortune. The comparison of wife and children with features of Palestinian horticulture presents an idyllic picture of peace and prosperity (v3). Such an experience of married life is a sure sign of God's blessing.

Second Reading

The author of the letter to the Hebrews is at pains to show Christ as the single and definitive intermediary between God and humanity, superior to all others including the angels. As God's Son "in the flesh," Jesus was only temporarily on a lower plain than the angels, and that for the sole purpose of sharing the human condition. In solidarity with this world's "many children," he brings them to glory through his death on their behalf.

God is spoken of as the origin and model of the whole created order (v10; 1 Cor 8:6). He is also the author of human salvation which he has effected through the suffering of his Son. Having led the way, Christ is now in a position to bring his human followers to glory as well. His role as "consecrator" (v11) is connected with his office as high priest and his entrance into the heavenly sanctuary (4:14ff). Jesus is consecrated in his secerdotal role and thus in a singular way is enabled to consecrate those who follow him. They, too, constitute "a royal priesthood, a holy nation" (1 Pet 2:9). Since Christ and his followers share the same humanity, he appropriately addresses them as brothers and sisters.

Jesus stands at the pinnacle of all creation, superior to all other mediating powers. His suffering in the world was a predestined detour in the interests of his return to glory with a newly acquired entourage, members of the human family.

Third Reading

Today's gospel contains two distinct narratives: the teaching on divorce (vv1 - 12) and on a child-like spirit (vv13 - 16).

The discussion on divorce is found in all the synoptics. The more primitive Mark is a forthright statement on the indissolubility of marriage admitting of no exception or qualification (Mt 5:32). To his opponents' subtle presentation of Moses' concession to divorce (v4; Deut 24:1 - 4), Jesus answers in rabbinic fashion, citing scripture for scripture. In quoting Genesis 1:27 and 2:24, he argues for and upholds the original divine plan for an indissoluble union, citing the Mosaic exception as a concession to human weakness (vv5 - 9).

In Marcan fashion, Jesus instructs his disciples privately on the question (vv10f). Remarriage after divorce is adulterous; the original bond remains intact. Interestingly Mark admits of circumstances wherein the woman also might sue for divorce (v12), a frequent practice in Roman law, while less frequent but not unknown in Jewish practice.

The narrative of Jesus and the children is expressive of a salient New Testament teaching (vv13 - 16). The reign of God is to be received with childlike simplicity. Children are capable of gaining or meriting nothing. By the same token, God's favor is totally gift, and the only possible human response is grateful acceptance. Since God's love is totally gratuitous, no "price tags" can be attached. The only acceptable posture of the beneficiary is a humble and open spirit.

Today's teaching on the permanent and indissoluble character of Christian marriage is as inspirational to some as it is painful for others. There are those in every Sunday assembly who have lived this ideal with generosity and intensity. Others have endured great suffering because that ideal could no longer be lived. Yet in the church there is room for everyone. It continues to proclaim this teaching on marriage because it has no choice. It not only comes from Christ but its wisdom lends itself to building up the human family, the church, and society. On the other hand, the church suffers with those who have found it impossible to live this commitment. Human weakness tells us that we all fall short in one way or another. Today the church's pastoral ministry seeks to alleviate where possible the pain connected with broken marriages, as we all strive to move, if only by inches, closer to that heavenly sanctuary where Christ has preceded us and to which he calls all of us without exception.

Homiletic and Catechetical Helps

1. The permanence of marriage: the teaching of Jesus.

2. The church's pastoral ministry to divorced Catholics.

3. Marriage as a sacrament.

4. Understanding the Christian childlike spirit.

5. The meaning of the reign of God.

6. The meaning of Christ the high priest.

7. The Catholic priesthood: its relation to the high priest.

8. The priesthood of all believers.

TWENTY-SEVENTH SUNDAY OF THE YEAR
Year C

Readings

> Hab 1:2 - 3, 2:2 - 4
> 2 Tim 1:6 - 8, 13 - 14
> Lk 17:5 - 10

Theme: The Power of Faith

Habakkuk reminds his contemporaries that Yahweh will render judgment and final deliverance in his own time. He calls for a steadfast faith. Today's gospel presents two consecutive pronouncements of Jesus, perhaps initially unconnected but joined in Luke to underscore the power of faith, a gift which remains always undeserved and unmerited. The second letter to Timothy reminds the young church official that belief must be manifest in courage and strength and preserved integrally as a precious patrimony.

First Reading

Writing shortly before the Babylonian invasion of Judah (597 B.C.), Habakkuk, in the short book which bears his name, questions Yahweh's governance of the world. The Lord answers with the assurance of an eventual emergence of order and salvation; the present moment of suffering and chastisement calls for a living and dynamic faith. In today's reading from the first chapter, the prophet's cry is one of desperation surrounded as he is by countless evils. "Violence" is a key word in Habakkuk (1:3, 9; 1:8, 17); here it refers to the serious violations of human rights within Judah. The wicked are rapacious in their greed and do violence to the poor and underprivileged. This has led to a spirit of lawlessness and anarchy.

The Lord promises a brighter future but only after chastisement has taken place, i.e. the destruction of Judah and Jerusalem. The hope-filled promise is written down to underscore its permanent and definitive quality (vv2:2ff). Deliverance will be delayed only to permit the period of trial to transpire. Once again the scriptures are at pains to reconcile the justice and mercy of Yahweh, as well as showing the importance of fidelity to his word.

The rash man is without principle. Verses 4b and 5 depict his conduct: a greed, which like a bottomless pit or Sheol itself, cannot be satisfied or filled. The future reality, or even the present signs of the times, say nothing to him. He is in sharp contrast with the just person whose life is rooted in faith. Habakkuk's statement on faith (v4b) is the book's most remembered verse used by Paul in his treatment of justification (Rom 1:17; Gal 3:11). It is faith in Yahweh's fidelity that enables the virtuous person to endure the pain of the present reality, confident that the Lord's design will ultimately triumph.

Responsorial Psalm   Ps 95

Commentary on this psalm may be found on the Fourth Sunday of Year B.

Second Reading

In the second letter to Timothy, the imprisoned Paul is presented as giving counsel and encouragement to his younger emissary, whose unspecified location may have been Ephesus. Most scholars see the letter as emanating from a Pauline school rather than from the apostle himself. The imposition of hands (v6), a sign of transmitting authority (Num 27:18 - 23; Deut 34:9), here guarantees the authenticity of Timothy's mission. It is one of a variety of ways in which the Spirit was communicated in the early church.

Paul's exhortation is twofold. The first calls for courage and strength in bearing witness to the Lord, as well as in upholding Paul himself, even though he is now detained and deprived of his freedom for the sake of Christ (v8). In what is evidently a difficult and trying ministry, Timothy will be provided with the strength needed. Secondly, the apostle calls for a clear and orthodox presentation of the faith which he summarizes in verses 9ff of the same chapter (not part of today's reading). Paul proposes himself as a model of fidelity to the original teaching received from the Lord (1 Cor 15:1f). There were forces at work within the church, probably Gnostic in character, which looked for a type of synthesis or adaptation within Christianity. The pastoral epistles are clearly at odds with such efforts. The faith received from the apostolic witness is to be retained in its purity and integrity.

Third Reading

To his disciples' request for greater faith, Jesus moves away from any quasi-quantitative response. Any person's basic faith is capable of producing remarkable results (vv5f). The mulberry tree was large and deeply rooted, not easily transplanted and certainly not likely to sink its roots in deep water. The point being made is clear: a true faith, even though incipient, defies human expectations and makes all things possible.

Moreover, even well-intentioned requests for an increase of virtue must be assessed and viewed with caution. The parable of the homecoming servants, found only in Luke, offers an interesting antidote to the story of the returning master, whose graciousness goes well beyond the ordinary limits (12:35 - 38). Those who render services for which they are employed deserve nothing more than the terms of the agreement provide (vv7ff). So, too, with the Lord's disciples. Jesus' final pronouncement (v10) is not a "put-down" of his disciples nor is it meant to show a lack of appreciation. The point is that the Christian vocation, a gift in itself, gives no one a claim on the Lord. In being the beneficiaries of God's saving work in Christ, his followers are already "gifted"; anything to which they are subsequently called as Christians is, as might be said, done "in the line of duty." God's added favor, while very frequently not lacking, is, by the same token, not due. Good things in the Christian life are received with gratitude—and surprise.

There are those whose faith is largely centered on the miraculous; the ordinary route of faith is never sufficient. There are others who discount miracles and are content to live with a faith largely undisturbed. True belief lies somewhere in between. Faith does make a difference in the way we view our life and the world reality. But it could make a greater difference than it does. Faith tells us that we don't have to accept things the way they are. That doesn't mean that everything requested is granted or that God is held to intervene at our behest. But faith can change more things than we are inclined, in our caution and even timidity, even to request. In daily life, moreover, it is our faith that makes it possible to sustain many a cross that appears to be otherwise unsupportable. And yet we can make no claims on God. Gifts remain gifts; they are not guarantees or warranties. God will not be outdone in generosity but he is not a contractual partner.

The letter to Timothy reminds us also that faith is best tested in adversity and is a pledge of an ultimate positive outcome. Retaining basic belief, while always open to a better understanding, is the task of every generation of disciples.

Homiletic and Catechetical Helps

1. Prayer of petition: For what do we pray?

2. Illustrate ways in which faith colors our view of life.

3. Faith as God's gift.

4. Faith as a theological virtue.

5. Transmission of the faith—personal and collective responsibility.

6. Courage in living the faith.

7. Retaining the apostolic faith: the role of theology.

TWENTY-EIGHTH SUNDAY OF THE YEAR
Year A

Readings

> Is 25:6 - 10
> Phil 4:12 - 14,19 - 20
> Mt 22:1 - 14

Theme: Banquet Guests

In today's liturgy food plays a part in all three readings. The salvation of the elect in Isaiah is depicted in terms of a mountaintop banquet celebrating Yahweh's victory over death, replete with choice meats and "vintage" wines. From prison, Paul speaks to the Philippians of good and bad times, times when food was plentiful and when it was scarce. It all mattered little since Christ was his sustenance. In the gospel Jesus describes the final era which he inaugurates as an elaborate dinner with many participants but also unfortunately many "regrets."

First Reading

This passage is taken from what is commonly termed the little apocalypse of Isaiah (cc. 24 - 27); it is generally recognized as coming from a later period than that of the eighth century prophet. It is eschatology at its most vivid. Yahweh inaugurates his kingship and is installed on Mount Zion, after subduing the cosmic powers, evil in the world, and finally death itself. The imagery used is effective, if somewhat jarring in its contrasts. From devastation and desolation (24:1 - 4), affecting even the sun and the moon (24:23), there is a transition to heightened festivities as the nation gathers on Mount Zion to celebrate Yahweh's triumph (v6). The imagery is wholly consonant with the Israelite belief that enjoyment of the good things of this world was a sign of divine favor. That belief is given an apocalytpic dimension in the deliverance of the elect. With the participation of all the nations (v7), the note of universalism is present.

The destruction of death assumes different symbols: the veil (v7a) and the web (v7b). The veil stands for the mortal shroud encompassing all people from which there is no escape, The web entangles and entraps, offering no avenue to freedom. Death is seen as the principal consequence of sin (Gen 3:22f), representing total alienation from God, a moral death for which physical death was the seal. For this reason the final triumph of Yahweh had to include victory over death. With the departure of death go grief and affliction as well (v8).

The passage closes with a chorus of the saved who proclaim Yahweh's fidelity in joyous acclamation, with Zion once again the focal point of God's presence (vv9f).

Responsorial Psalm   Ps 23

God's protective care of his servant is presented in this celebrated psalm in both pastoral (vv1 - 4) and banquet (vv5f) imagery. The king is often described as a shepherd in the literature of antiquity. Here the solicitude of the shepherd is marked, with the psalmist compared to a lamb or small calf which is well pastured and watered (v2). Moral guidance is intended as the shepherd selects only safe and tried routes, with accompanying dangers, leading to moral death, studiously avoided. The "staff and rod" (v4) were used to keep the sheep in proper order and to ward off threatening predators.

The banquet table is prepared by Yahweh, the host (v5), replete with the perfumed oil for the head (Mt 26:7). All favor is explained by Yahweh's covenant fidelity, with the psalmist seeing his greatest joy as rendering thankful praise in the Lord's temple sanctuary (v6).

Second Reading

The Philippians have sent a gift to Paul in prison to assist him in his temporal needs. Paul welcomes the spirit behind the gift more than the gift itself. He has always provided for his own needs (4:11) but applauds their renewed interest in his welfare (4:10, 14).

Paul states his willingness to accept either abundance or scarcity with equanimity, as long as he enjoys the living presence of Christ (vv12f). All else amounts to nothing in comparison with "knowing Christ Jesus" (3:8). Christ, living in the believer, imparts strength sufficient to deal with any obstacle (v13; Col 1:29).

His benefactors' generosity will be rewarded by God's goodness on their behalf (v19). The "riches" in Christ are found in the gift of the Spirit. The Spirit builds them up, and this ultimately redounds to the glory of God the Father (v20). The Christian is constantly being transformed into greater glory as he or she contemplates that glory of God manifest in Christ (2 Cor 3:18; 4:6). All of this gives praise and adoration to God.

Third Reading

The parable of the banquet, coming from the Q source, is common to both Matthew and Luke, yet nuanced differently by each. Matthew has allegorized many features of the original parable. Its primitive setting probably found Jesus justifying his presence in the midst of sinners and outcasts.

The "reign of God," so pivotal to Matthew's thinking, explains why the "man" of the original parable becomes here a "king" and "his son" (v2), a reference to the Father and Jesus. The end time as a banquet is frequent enough but nowhere more notably than in the Isaian passage of today's liturgy. In Matthew it is further specified as a wedding banquet, blending both the banquet theme and the eschatological nuptials between God and Israel. The twofold sending of servants (vv3f) is not as concerned with the two groups of servants as with the two different responses. The first is a simple refusal (v3). The second, characterized by indifference and maltreatment, aggravates the situation and is more serious than the first (vv5f). The two groups of servants would refer then to Christian missionaries sent to their Jewish contemporaries whose attitude worsens with time.

Allegory again enters the story, abruptly and unrealistically, in the king's interruption of banquet preparations in order to destroy the city of the invited guests (v7). The reference is clearly to the destruction of Jerusalem in 70 A.D., which Matthew sees as punishment for the Jews' harsh treatment of the early Christians.

The Gentile mission is justified in the third wave of emissaries. The crowds from the "main roads" (v9), unprepared for the banquet, were originally the outcasts of Judaism and later the Gentiles. It is both "the bad and the good" (v10) who enter the banquet hall, a specification necessary for the story's denouement.

The parable has both a realized (present banquet) and a future (the king's judgment) eschatology. The king's entry into the banquet hall is the moment of final judgment (v11). The wedding garment symbolizes the quality of an active Christian faith. Membership in the Christian community is not sufficient; one's life must be an expression of what faith means (7:21f). Thus, in the church's life, both the good and the bad will be found (13:47ff). Salvation will be finalized only with the Lord's return. Failure to be "properly attired" will result in ejection from the kingdom and consignment to a state of punishment (v13). The final *logion* (v14) is not a contrast of opposites but rather a relative comparison. The "called" (Gr: *kletoi*) are far more numerous than the "elect" (Gr: *elektoi*). And even then, among the latter, salvation should not be taken for granted.

In that banquet hall, which is God's church, all of us have a place. To be sure, it's an unusual mixture of people—a very egalitarian dinner, to say the least. There are guests of every color, nationality, and Christian denomination; backgrounds vary as well—white collar and blue collar people, as well as the unemployed, the poorest and the wealthiest. And there is to be no preferential treatment. Each eucharist reminds us concretely of what it means to be hosted by the Son of God. We all come around the Lord's table with no consideration of prestige or status. We are one in the same Lord.

But we need constant reminders. Fortunately each eucharist means hearing God's word. We are constantly reminded to grow in the Christian life and not to become complacent. Tattered, dirty clothes will not be acceptable when our final reckoning takes place. Each liturgy, then, calls us to alertness. We are hope-filled people, but we must keep our eyes riveted on our goal. As we reread the invitation which we accepted years ago, we should not forget to read the fine print: "Appropriate dress is required."

Homiletic and Catechetical Helps

1. The biblical meaning of meal-sharing.

2. The family and meal-sharing.

3. The eucharist as messianic banquet.

4. Responses to God's word: refusal, indifference, hostility.

5. The eucharist and the unity of all people.

6. The ministry to the imprisoned.

7. Growth in Christ and spiritual direction.

TWENTY-EIGHTH SUNDAY OF THE YEAR
Year B

Readings

> Wis 7:7 - 11
> Heb 4:12 - 13
> Mk 10:17 - 30

Theme: The Wisdom of Renunciation

Worldly wisdom and God's wisdom are often at odds. The book of Wisdom, written in a sophisticated intellectual milieu about 100 B.C., speaks of the inestimable value of that wisdom which comes from God; it is the path to a life with true meaning and far surpasses the riches of this world. In the gospel, the man who approaches Jesus seeks that wisdom which leads to life. The response of Jesus is clear, but the price is costly. He calls for a radical decision. The letter to the Hebrews sees the word of God as penetrating and incisive. That word is true wisdom, but it can also be deeply disturbing in its demands.

First Reading

Solomon, in whose name the author of Wisdom often speaks, asked early in his reign as king for the gift of wisdom in order that he might be an understanding and discerning judge for his people (1 Kgs 3:5 - 15). Today's reading recalls that event in the monarch's life (v7). It was a gift to be preferred over all others and is strongly contrasted with this world's wealth (v9). It surpasses physical well-being or attractiveness (v10a). Its light illumines the path of life (v10b; Prov 6:23). Wisdom offers riches of its own, which are far superior to those which pass away (v11; Prov 8:19).

Responsorial Psalm   Ps 90

This psalm defies strict categorization. It combines features of the lament with those of the wisdom literature. Its use in today's liturgy centers around the prayer for wisdom (v12), which occurs in what is actually the third part of the psalm. *Return* (v13): A period of distress and misery signaled God's absence from the sufferer's life. Restoration bespeaks God's return. The use of the plural throughout would seem to allude to some sort of collective, even national suffering, for the cessation of which the psalmist ardently prays.

Days filled with happiness begin with a dawn experience of God's covenant fidelity (v14). The request is for a future of happiness at least equal in length to the period of suffering (v15). This experience of God's saving action will go beyond the present generation and be recognized by their progeny as well (v16). The psalm ends with a prayer that their human undertakings will be blessed (v17). The bracketed repetition is a copyist's error.

Second Reading

The context of the fourth chapter of Hebrews speaks of the effect of God's word addressed to his people in the past and its meaning in the present (4:2, 7). This is followed by an analysis of the word, read in today's liturgy. The word is compared to a sword capable of deep and incisive penetration (v12; Is 49:2). As an extension of God himself, the word is seen as living and reflective.

The word distinguishes evil from good, as the process of human discernment takes place. It reads the innermost thoughts of the soul and determines motives. "The soul and the spirit" (v12) are two separate anthropological components but as intimately linked as "joints and marrow."

In summary, the word brings one to decisions of right and wrong in discerning human conduct, and it plummets the most interior chambers of the human heart. In the passage, there is an implicit interplay between the Word and the believer.

Third Reading

In this passage from Mark, there are three pronouncement stories, all of them related to worldly possessions: the story of the rich man (vv17 - 22), a teaching on wealth and the reign of God (vv23 - 27), and assurances to those who surrender possessions (vv28 - 30).

The account of the *man seeking the reign of God* (vv17 - 22) presents him initially as impetuous and enthusiastic (v17); only later will he be described as rich (v22). His one desire is to find and make his own the reign of God, the evident meaning of "eternal life" (cf. v23). *Good teacher* (v17): The man courteously addresses a respected rabbi. Jesus' response sounds rather harsh, making a clear distinction between himself and God. It is a response easily understood if coming from the time of Jesus' ministry. Even the early church had to struggle with Jesus' equality with and yet distinction from the Father (Yahweh). Here the reference is to Yahweh from whom Jesus makes himself clearly distinct. Matthew finds the statement difficult and rather awkwardly alters the meaning, thus blunting the unqualified distinction of Mark (Mt 19:17).

Jesus' initial injunction urges an observance of the decalogue, especially those precepts touching on social relationships (vv18f). The first plateau of Christian discipleship lies in obedience to the basic norms of the covenant relationship. With the man's indication that he is willing to go further, Jesus calls for the renunciation of his wealth (v21). This call to perfection should be understood as a call to the following of Christ as a disciple. There is no reference here to a special or select calling. Moreover, it is particularized, i.e. possessions are the obstacle for this man, impeding his self-donation. This is the only instance in the gospel where Jesus' invitation is rejected in what remains a very moving scene (v22).

Wealth and the reign of God (vv23 - 27) are frequently in conflict. The astonishment of the apostles (v24) arises from the fact that Hebrew belief saw wealth as a sign of divine favor. This is a position with which Jesus is completely at odds. Riches are an obstacle not only for the man of the previous narrative but for the wealthy in general. The unrealistic comparison of the camel and the needle's eye is meant to emphasize the problem, even while straining the imagination (v25). It is the perennial question of serving God or mammon, with no middle ground.

To the disciples' query as to whether or not salvation is even a possibility, Jesus roots his response in the power of God (vv26f). Under any circumstances, salvation is wholly the work of God, who is also able to overcome insuperable difficulties accompanying redemption (Lk 1:37).

The benefits of renunciation (vv28 - 30), as listed in Jesus' response to Peter, reflect the experience of the early church. Not only is a future life with God assured but blessings in this world as well (v30). Elsewhere Christ teaches that physical or "flesh" relationships are exchanged for those in the Spirit (Mk 3:31 - 35). The life of Christian community will substitute for the support and happiness of the families and properties left behind. The present, "this world" Christian life is meant to be joyous. With persecution (v30): a disjunctive insertion, not harmonizing with the list of benefits. It was, however, one of the main ingredients of the Christian life at the time of the gospel's composition, thus warranting its inclusion.

The teaching of the three pronouncement stories points up the grave difficulty that riches present in terms of discipleship as well as the blessings that redound to renunciation in both the present and the future life.

There is a great deal of wisdom in today's gospel. But we are frightened by it no less than the man who came to Jesus. The truth is that many of us in today's world and in today's church have an embarrassment of riches. We don't hear much about "creature comforts" anymore, perhaps because we have become so accustomed that they no longer appear to be comforts. Yesterday's comfort becomes today's necessity. While much of the world goes hungry, we are trapped by consumerism. But the word remains that two-edged sword. We stand under its judgment. There is no escape. It is not a question necessarily of people who live on estates and others who live in modest circumstances. Elizabeth of Hungary and Louis of France were royalty, lived in comfortable environments, and became saints. Their possessions counted for nothing; their treasure was in the reign of God.

Most Christians cannot walk away from everything tomorrow. But all of us are called to personal assessment. If God becomes our all, then we live more simply, ask more questions about accruing possessions, and are more conscious of the needy. It is not a question of surrendering things. That just creates a vacuum. It is because we have a spiritual treasure already in our heart that there just is not room for much more. So the question remains. What stands between us and God? What blocks our path? Like Solomon we pray for wisdom–the wisdom to know the answer.

Homiletic and Catechetical Helps

1. Wisdom in the Bible: Wisdom literature, Jesus as wisdom, wisdom in Paul.

2. The decalogue and the Christian life.

3. Christianity and consumerism.

4. Our attitudes toward possessions.

5. What are the joys of God's reign in this world?

6. The sacrament of God's word.

TWENTY-EIGHTH SUNDAY OF THE YEAR
Year C

Readings

2 Kgs 5:14 - 17
2 Tim 2:8 - 13
Lk 17:11 - 15

Theme: The Gratitude of Strangers

Gentiles had no real recognition within Israelite society. While they were to be accorded decent treatment, they were always in a subordinate, even marginal position. A leper was considered unclean and was barred from contact with the community. To be both a Gentile and a leper was to come as close to being a non-person as could be imagined. It is a pagan leper who comes to Elisha in today's first reading, and it is a Samaritan leper who returns gratefully to Jesus after his cure in today's gospel. In the hymn quoted in today's reading from Timothy, there is a forceful reminder that the destiny attained by Jesus will also be that of the believer if faith does not wane.

First Reading

Naaman was an officer in the Aramean army. He suffered from a type of serious skin disorder, commonly referred to as leprosy (Lev 13 - 14). While he has learned of Elisha's healing power through an Israelite servant girl (5:2f), he undertakes the journey to see the prophet only at the direction of his king, with a letter of introduction to the king of Israel (5:5f). He finally arrives at the simple, unimpressive locale of Elisha where with considerable reluctance he agrees to bathe in the Jordan (5:12f).

In today's reading, Naaman's efforts are rewarded; his cure is complete (v14). In gratitude he returns to the prophet, convinced of the authenticity of Israel's God as opposed to the ineffective and therefore non-existent gods of the Gentiles (v

15; 1 Kgs 18). Elisha's refusal to accept a gift shifts attention away from the human agent; the cure was the work of Yahweh to whom alone honor is due (v16). Naaman's personal conversion is complete. He asks for soil upon which to build a sanctuary to Yahweh in Aram where sacrifice can be offered. Ancient deities were closely tied with the land of their worshipers. They could not be worshiped on foreign soil (Ps 137:1 - 5). In relocating some Israelite earth, Naaman was able to fulfill his cultic desire.

Responsorial Psalm   Ps 98

In keeping with the day's liturgical theme, this psalm carries a note of universalism. Israel's deliverance is recognized and chanted. This is a manifestation of God's power (v1) as well as his covenant fidelity (v3). Although salvation is experienced by Israel, it is a sign to the nations as well (v2). In view of this evidence of the true God's presence to his people, the nations are exhorted to join Israel in giving praise (v4). The universalism of the Hebrew scriptures stresses the recognition of God in and through his action in favor of Israel, not involving any type of missionary thrust.

Second Reading

The reading from 2 Timothy contains part of an early Christian hymn, retained in its basic poetic form (vv11 - 13). In this letter, pseudonymously attributed to Paul according to most commentators, the apostle recalls his "gospel," centered on the two basic features of the kerygmatic preaching: the human descent of Jesus ("seed" of David) and his resurrection from the dead as Son of God (Rom 1:1 - 4) (v8). It is the faith acceptance of this *kerygma* that results in election, justification and eventual eternal glory (v10; Rom 8:30). Paul endures imprisonment and suffering because, in spite of his detention, God's word will continue to bear fruit.

The poetic symmetry of the hymn is striking, with a well-constructed parallelism in each verse. The Christians' spiritual death with Christ in baptism assures them of ongoing life with him (v11). Perseverance in the "now" of present redemption leads to participation in the "not yet" of the eternal reign (v12a). Yet judgment remains a constant. Rejection of Christ is reciprocal (v12b). However, human infidelity is not matched by the same in Christ. Even his denial of the unrepentant is an expression of his fidelity to his word (v13). *For he cannot deny himself* (v13c): There is a break here in the poetic flow of the hymn in what is evidently an addition. It explains further Christ's punitive action in the event of Christian apostasy. For the Lord to fail to act would be for him to compromise his own premises.

Third Reading

The parallels between the Elisha-Naaman narrative and the Jesus-Samaritan account are evident. With universalism one of his major themes, Luke wants to highlight both the cure and the response of a Samaritan leper. As Jesus began his journey to Jerusalem, the Samaritans were introduced at an early stage (9:51 - 55), and, as its title indicates, Luke's story of the good Samaritan places a foreigner in a very favorable light. This account of the Samaritan leper also appears only in Luke.

The fact that Jesus is traveling in the neighborhood of Samaria (v11) accounts for the leper's presence on the way. The group of lepers professes faith in Jesus and all are cured (vv13f). In showing themselves to the priests and being pronounced clean, the lepers could be reintegrated in the community (Lev 13:16f). The Samaritan who returns offers glory to God and prostrates himself before Jesus in adoration (vv15f). This is a strong expression of faith in both the God of Israel and Jesus his emissary offered by a person of non-Jewish origin. Jesus recognizes the prayerful gratitude of the healed man, not simply his belief (v18).

The narrative ends on an eschatological note. The man has been *saved*, not merely cured (v19). The gospel is looking at the cure on two distinct levels. Liberation from the illness points to the same saving power of God which liberates from sin and confers the gift of eternal life. And the personal ingredient for both is faith.

There are many "outcasts" in today's world. Yet Christians are expected to see a place for all people in God's plan. Since it is harder to deal with the individual, people are lumped together in one category or another. In that way they remain faceless and are easily consigned to mental oblivion. It is much easier to speak of real people as "they" or "those." Elisha was at ease with a pagan military officer. Jesus reached out to Samaritans as well as all the other social rejects. Lepers in Jesus' time were unapproachable. But Jesus drew near. There are lepers in today's society who are also stigmatized and kept at a distance. Would Jesus act any differently today than he did then? Jesus expects to be present today in us.

The Samaritan came back in gratitude. His faith was channeled through thanks. Perhaps the other nine were too elated with their cure to remember. It is strange to think of how often gratitude is overlooked. In fact, the people who do the most are often the most overlooked. How many children take their parents for granted. How easy it is to forget the gratitude due to an aging parent when he or she becomes difficult to care for. And when it comes to our forgetfulness, God may well top the list. He has brought us out of darkness to light, given us an incomparable vision, and the assurance of everlasting life. That is more than sufficient reason for gratitude. And let's remember that our own "thanks" for being loved when we were "unclean" is best expressed by embracing the lepers and Samaritans of today. Do we have the will—and the courage?

Homiletic and Catechetical Helps

1. Elisha and Jesus: being open to others.

2. Prejudice: Where is it in my life?

3. The prayer of thanksgiving; the meaning of the eucharist.

4. Understanding the mercy and justice of God.

5. Our ministry to the ill.

6. Concern for the homeless and the unemployed.

7. Heart of the *kerygma:* Jesus, God and man.

TWENTY-NINTH SUNDAY OF THE YEAR
Year A

Readings

Is 45:1,4 - 6
1 Thes 1:1 - 5
Mt 22:15 - 21

Theme: God and Caesar

The history of salvation, while divine in its origin, is played out on the stage of human history. The scriptures illustrate the relationship of both Israel and the early church to civil governments. Those relations were sometimes positive, sometimes negative. At the end of the exile in Babylon, the Persian king Cyrus ordered the return of the Jews to their homeland and the rebuilding of Jerusalem. In today's reading from Isaiah, Cyrus is held aloft as an agent of Yahweh's will. In today's gospel, Jesus is questioned about his attitude toward the Roman authorities. His answer is balanced and does not "tip the scale" in either direction. In the reading from 1 Thessalonians, Paul sees the Spirit's active presence within the community as a result of the apostolic preaching.

First Reading

Cyrus, a pagan ruler, is singled out and commended in Deutero-Isaiah. No other foreign monarch receives such honorable citation in the biblical literature. Cyrus overcame Babylon in 538 B.C., liberated the Jews, restored their homeland, and ordered the rebuilding of the temple. In today's passage , the literary depiction is that of a god installing a king, used biblically for Yahweh's designation of an Israelite king (Ps 2:7ff; 110:1ff). Here Yahweh commissions Cyrus. *Anointed* (v1):The Hebrew word for Messiah and the Greek *Christos* are derived from this word. The king was anointed when he came to power. Here it is a figurative title given to Cyrus as an emissary of Yahweh in describing the former's victory over his opponents.

It is ultimately for Israel that Cyrus has been chosen and personally designated (v4). That Israel's God should guide one of the major political and military powers of the ancient world reinforces one of Isaiah's major themes, an unqualified and absolute monotheism (v5; Is 43:10; 44:6; 46:9). Even though Cyrus had allegiance to his own god Bel-Marduk, this fact never enters the purview of the prophet. Although the king is unaware, it is Yahweh who orchestrates his career. The purpose behind this is clear. The existence of Israel's God, as the sole and exclusive deity, will be recognized by all people (v6). According to the thinking of the time, the God who *acts* equals the God who is.

Responsorial Psalm   Ps 96

This is a hymn praising God in what is perhaps a ritual celebration of his enthronement. It builds on today's reading from Isaiah in celebrating Yahweh as the sole deity, a fact to be recognized by all the nations. The psalm throughout is addressed to all peoples of the earth (vv1, 7, 9), who are called to acknowledge and express liturgically Yahweh's lordship and kingship (v10). This will follow upon Israel's public proclamation of what Yahweh has done for her (v3). This ingathering of the nations carries no missionary thrust; it is simply an expected response once Israel's story is chanted. As the liturgical scene is presented, the Gentiles participate in temple worship (vv7f).

His glory (v3): This is God's "otherness," his awesome majesty which finds external expression in his saving acts. Glory rendered to Yahweh (vv7f) is the recognition of his sacredness and is the human complement to God's personal glory; it is rooted strongly in cultic prayer. This psalm is striking for its strong universalism woven through the hymn as a whole.

Second Reading

The opening verses of 1 Thessalonians follow the classical epistolary form (v1). The sender is mentioned first. Here Paul links himself with his co-workers Silvanus (Silas, Acts 15:40f) and Timothy (Acts 16:1ff). The three are presented as joint senders of the letter. The addressee is explicitly cited, "the church of the Thessalonians." This is the use of the term "church" at an early stage and is applied to the local community of believers. They are the *qahal* of God, an elect cultic community brought into existence by God's call. A local church had the basic ingredients of faith, ministry, and worship found in the broader church as a whole. The final part of the epistolary form is the greeting. Here *grace* and *peace* are pregnant with theological meaning. The salutation points to the gift of the Spirit (grace) with its accompanying restoration of harmonious relations with God and neighbor (peace). Finally, the church lives in Jesus, acknowledged as the Messiah (Christ) and Lord, directly related to God as Father, who receives first mention.

Paul underscores the place that this community, located in what is now northern Greece, holds in his prayers (v2). It was through prayer that bonding among the early churches primarily occurred. He is reminded of their *faith, love* and *hope*, the earliest mention of the three theological virtues as a unit (v3). The "work of faith" and "labor of love" describe the virtues as operative, active, and effective. "Hope" is given final mention since it touches on one of the letter's major themes, the expected return of Christ in glory. The Thessalonians persevere in this hope through vigilance and alertness (5:4 - 8). They are here reminded of their election, which is adequate proof of God's love for them (v4).

Paul speaks of *our gospel* which has produced this fruit in Thessalonica (v5). This is not a reference to the content of the preached *kerygma* but rather the manner in which it reached them. The preached word was accompanied by the Spirit which made its acceptance possible (1 Cor 12:3); it is this accompanying power of God which accomplishes much more than human eloquence (1 Cor 2:1 - 5). The personal comportment of the apostle was an integral part of his mission. In speaking of his personal conviction, he brings to mind the single-mindedness and integrity which he brought to the task.

Third Reading

In today's gospel Jesus' opponents present him with a dilemma. Matthew emphasizes the role of the Pharisees; the

Herodians, a political rather than a religious party, play only a secondary role (vv15f). In the Matthean church the Pharisees are still formidable antagonists, whereas, by this time, the Herodians were insignificant and had largely vanished from sight.

The two groups recognize hypocritically but accurately Jesus' integrity (v16). The dilemma posed regarding the Roman tax (v17) would make an affirmative response to the question of payment offensive to religious Jews, in this case the Pharisees. It would represent no problem for the political Herodians. A negative answer would label Jesus an insurrectionist, like the Zealots of his time, and would create difficulties for the Herodians.

Jesus' answer is carefully nuanced and elusive, understandable in light of the malice and hypocrisy of his questioners (v18). At the same time it has its own logic. Asked to produce the coin in question, Jesus' opponents entrap themselves. They are evidently benefiting from Caesar's service and at least implicitly render him obeisance. The coin's image bears Caesar's likeness; the inscription reveals his formal title (v20).

Repay to Caesar (v21): For benefits received from Caesar, payment is due. Jesus does not set forth any political-religious theory. He deflects the question as having nothing to do with the reign of God, his sole interest. This is a matter of temporalities and therefore outside of his purview, having nothing to do with his mission. If one uses roads or public facilities, then one pays for them. The role of civil authority is not questioned in the New Testament (Rom 13:1 - 7; 1 Pet 2:13 - 17), nor is it accorded any importance in God's reign.

Repay to God (v21): The Pharisees have repeatedly tried to thwart Jesus as God's emissary, conduct which merited some of Jesus' harshest words (Mt 23:1 - 11). Here Jesus moves away from the Caesar question and calls for a basic respect for God's will. This is not a question of God's over-arching authority being shared with Caesar. The response to God must be total, not in any way divided. Questions of civil authority are secondary, even peripheral. In submitting totally to the sovereignty of God, the concerns of lesser authorities will be met. But allegiance to God must be seen as absolute.

Questions of church and state loom large on the American scene. There are those who argue against any official recognition of religion on the part of the state. Others argue that this "wall of separation" has gone far beyond anything envisioned by the nation's founders. Questions regularly arise which tax the legal acumen of a Supreme Court and the theological expertise of our best religious thinkers. Unfortunately, or perhaps fortunately, the New Testament sheds little light on these complex issues. Jesus' response to the Pharisees showed a basic respect for civil authority but not much more. Christian thinking is focused on God's reign, and any temporal reality, including civil government and political authority, is to be seen in that light.

As good citizens, we pay taxes, obey laws made for the common good, and play our part in the political process. This is all to the good. But there are dangers in canonizing the state or any form of government. When conflict arises between the state and God's law, there can be no doubt where our allegiance must lie. In the words of the apostles, we must serve God, not human beings. It is our commitment to God above all that moves us at times to fault the state for its sins of commission or omission. Health care, housing, protection of the defenseless, preservation of all human life–these are all state issues but with a strong moral component. Even the state must repay to God what is his.

There is no reason why a Christian cannot be a good citizen or a good elected official. Hopefully he or she brings to the task a conscience formed in faith. It is not always easy to know how to apply one's convictions to particular issues. But we are never excused from doing so. For conscience remains the litmus test of all our behavior. All of us live in the human city, but we are always mindful of our primary citizenship in the city of God.

Homiletic and Catechetical Helps

1. Respect for civil law.

2. Dissent from civil law.

3. The state's sins of omission.

4. Contemporary church-state theories in our society.

5. Jesus and the state; priority of the reign of God.

6. Definition of the three theological virtues.

7. The gospel and the Holy Spirit.

8. Cyrus: God's activity in the events of the world.

TWENTY-NINTH SUNDAY OF THE YEAR
Year B

Readings

> Is 53:10 - 11
> Heb 4:14 - 16
> Mk 10:35 - 45

Theme: A Question of Status

To the ambitious request of Zebedee's two sons in today's gospel for a position of status in God's reign, Jesus answers that only a reverse type of precedence is to characterize discipleship: service and suffering. The painful experience of Jesus, and his apostles after him, was foreshadowed by the Isaian servant of the Lord, who appears in today's first reading. His is a life of service even to the point of dying in atonement for the sins of others. The reading from Hebrews brings all of this together in stressing our good fortune in having Christ as our high priest. Because he shared our human lot, he knows what weakness means. In his spirit of service, lowliness, and willingness to die, he remains the model for his disciples.

First Reading

This passage comes near the end of the fourth and last song of the servant of the Lord in Deutero-Isaiah. The servant's sufferings, which have become more intense, eventually lead to his death (53:3, 5, 8). But the chorus of onlookers realizes that he was innocent, and his suffering was endured for the sins of his people (53:4f).

Today's verses speak of the servant's vindication. It should be noted that the Hebrew text of these verses is badly disturbed, making it very difficult to grasp the full sense. Verse 10 is usually bracketed because its authenticity is questioned by many scholars.

There are certainties, however, around which the text as a whole converges. First, the servant's suffering and death are seen by God in a very favorable light. *The Lord was pleased* (v10): God's satisfaction in view of the outcome, redemption, not the suffering and death itself. It is willingness to comply with Yahweh's pre-ordained plan that gives the Lord pleasure in Deutero-Isaiah (v10c; 44:28; 48:14). The servant's self surrender is described in sacrificial terms (v10b).

Second, the Lord's appreciation will be seen in the servant's vindication. He shall be gifted with many descendants whom he shall live to see (v10b), with multiple progeny a sure sign of divine favor (Ex 20:6). The era of light in a long life is synonymous with liberation, joy, and tranquillity (v11; 9:1ff). It will be, in short, a life totally opposite to the painful lot that he has experienced.

Finally, the servant will effect redemption through the vicarious atonement which he offers (v11).

Does this vindication of the servant take the form of a personal resurrection? The description that is given makes the suggestion feasible. However, at this point in Israel's still underdeveloped after-life thinking, an actual return to life would not be expected. The hypothesis is made more difficult by the fact that the servant is a collective individual, i.e. while he is depicted as a person presented in concrete terms, he remains throughout the songs a representative of the faithful Israel as a whole. Therefore, "after-life" features regarding the servant may well refer to the continuation of the faithful remnant, the reborn people.

There is the further question of the servant's identity. spoken of elsewhere in this commentary. There is no convergence of views on who this collective individual is. Looked at from a Christian perspective, there is no doubt that there are many similarities between the mission of the servant and that of Christ. For this reason, the early church often describes the salvific work of Jesus in servant terms.

Responsorial Psalm   Ps 33

The hymn extols the fidelity of Yahweh. Just as the servant's steadfast dedication led to his final vindication,, so too the psalmist sees deliverance from death as a sign of Yahweh's trustworthiness (v19). Yahweh is first presented in terms of his fidelity to the covenant relationship. Both his word and his work reflect his inherent goodness (vv4f). This leads to a spirit of confidence in the believer. For those who are correspondingly faithful, Yahweh is never far away. His "eyes" follow them; hardship and misfortune will never have the final word (vv18f). The psalm closes with the petitioners' prayer that their hope and confidence will be repaid by the experience of God's saving help (vv20ff).

Second Reading

The priesthood of Christ is a major theme in Hebrews. Jewish liturgical images come to the fore. The entrance of the high priest into the inner sanctuary once a year finds its final expression and fulfillment in the once-for-all sacrifice of Jesus (Heb 9:11 - 14). Today's passage examines certain aspects of Christ's sacerdotal role.

Great high priest (v14): The expression is found only here in the letter. It probably underscores Jesus' superiority to the Jewish high priest. The resurrection-exaltation of Jesus is here described in liturgical terms which allude to the high priest's entrance into the holy place. He does this as Son of God, a post-resurrection title (Rom 1:4). *Our confession* (v14): a reference to the baptismal profession of Jesus as Son of God, here spoken of in the image of the high priest entering the heavenly sanctuary (3:1; 10:19 - 22).

The high priest's efficacy hinges not only on his present state but also on the fact that, as one who came "in the flesh," as totally human, he is in a position to understand the debility and corresponding needs of humankind (v15). Christ was exempt from no form of temptation. His human experience was total. It is not stated that he could not sin, only that he did not. This clear statement is at odds with any effort to "divinize" Christ by diminishing his humanity and its accompanying experiences.

This human condition of the heavenly Christ is to inspire trust in prayer and recourse (v16). *Throne of grace* (v16): This is access to the Father, not to the throne of Christ (10:19 - 22). God's throne is now one of "grace" because of the access to his favor which Christ's sacrifice has made possible. Every believer may now approach God's sanctuary because Christ the high priest has penetrated the veil and provided a direct and immediate contact.

Third Reading

The Jesus of Mark's gospel responds to the request of the sons of Zebedee (vv35ff) with three distinct pronouncements: the assurance of their suffering (v39), the allotment of places in God's reign (v40), and the role of leadership in the church (vv42 - 45).

Matthew softens the Marcan request of the two ambitious apostles in having it made by their mother (Mt 20:20). They request positions of precedence flanking Jesus in the age to come (v37). This may refer to Jesus seated in final judgment or at the messianic banquet. In either case, their request is in no way consonant with the discipleship which they have embraced. *Drink the cup* (v38): a figurative expression for sharing in the sentiments of another, in this case those of God. Frequently it has a punitive sense, accepting a destiny related to God's anger (Ps 11:6; Is 51:17 - 22). Here it refers to a share in the sufferings which Jesus will undergo at the behest of the Father. *Baptized with the baptism* (v39): Tragedy is frequently described in terms of submersion in water (Ps 42:7f; Is 43:2). Jesus' baptism is his death by which he makes Christian baptism effective (Lk 12:50). In addition, the Christian reader would see baptism as a transition from death to life. Jesus death brought about that passage in his life. The response that the apostles receive is totally different than expected. It is not position they are promised but suffering. Moreover, the designation of places (v40) is not for Jesus to make; that this is the Father's task is implicit in Mark and made explicit in Matthew (20:23).

Mark links this story on status-seeking with Jesus' statement on authority within the Christian community. There is, first of all, a comparison with worldly, pagan authority (v42), followed by a statement on leadership as servanthood (vv43ff). The language describing Gentile rulers is particularly strong: "lording it over" and "using power over." It clearly connotes a domination which contrasts sharply with the ensuing description of Christian leadership.

Among his disciples, and within the Christian community, leaders are to resemble two figures well known in the Palestinian and Hellenistic world: the servant (*diakonos*) and the slave (*doulos*). Servants were those who waited on table (Acts 6:2) and performed domestic duties. Their subordinate role was one of support and facilitation. Any notion of domination was incompatible with the role. The role of slave was of an even lower rank. Paul unhesitatingly speaks of his service to the community in terms of slavery (1 Cor 9:19; 2 Cor 4:5). Within any household the slave held the lowest position, subservient to all.

Jesus is himself the model for the exercise of leadership. The Philippians hymn speaks of his coming "in the form of a slave" (Phil 2:7). Jesus' posture was that of service to humankind, a dedication which carried him to death (v45). It is symbolically reflected in his washing the apostles' feet (Jn 13:1, 11). There are distinct echoes of Isaiah 53:10 - 12 in this final verse. *Ransom* (Gr: *lytron*) (v35): This was the price paid to redeem or reacquire a person or an object. It is figuratively applied to Yahweh's acquisition of his people (Is 63:4). The death of Jesus is here presented as an act of reacquisition of an enslaved people.

Jesus here presents his life of service, which included death itself, as the model of authentic Christian authority. It is diametrically opposed to any form of "power" government. Its exponents take last place in the community in their willingness to serve.

Christ's teaching on Christian authority is clear and forthright. It often seems that we are quite capable in developing elaborate theses on issues about which Christ has little to say, and yet we pass so glibly over other teachings which are direct and unequivocal. There is a time-

less quality to Jesus' response to the ambitious disciples. It may be because the problem is always with us. Christ's followers have been woefully slow in learning the lesson. The history of Christianity has been badly scarred by power-seeking, careerism, and manipulation at the service of ambition.

A general chapter of one religious order met to renew its constitutions after the Second Vatican Council. Eight full days were spent in discussing precedence, with interminable discussion about seating arrangements in chapel and dining hall according to rank. And, of course, it was always priests before brothers. In the end this proved to be an exercise in futility. Precedence was found to be lacking sound biblical roots. Even our language of appointments betrays us. People are still "elevated " to high office. Christ spoke of going in the opposite direction.

But then there is always the positive side. The author visited a house of retired brothers in Ireland. It was a house that hosted many visitors. But it was not solely to visit the aging friars. The local minister was the magnet. He was a brother who cared for the elderly with remarkable love and solicitude. It gained him widespread respect. People of all ranks came to express their gratitude and to be in his presence. He knew what Christ said about authority–and he lived it. In him Christ the servant was present to his brothers.

Homiletic and Catechetical Helps

1. The dangers of ambition.

2 Christ as the model of service in his life and death.

3. Personal experiences of true Christian leadership.

4. The servant of the Lord and vicarious atonement.

5. Christ the priest and the Christian priesthood.

6. The sinlessness of Christ.

7. The total humanity of Christ.

8. The diaconate: its biblical roots, its meaning today.

TWENTY-NINTH SUNDAY OF THE YEAR
Year C

Readings

Ex 17:8 - 13
2 Tim 3:14 - 4:2
Lk 18:1 - 8

Theme: Perseverance in Prayer

To continue steadfastly in prayer is a test of faith. Moses' upraised hands assured Yahweh's protection but required uninterrupted supplication. The widow in today's gospel persisted in her request until the annoyed judge acceded. The second letter to Timothy sees the apostolic ministry in similar terms; it is a constant call to be carried out tirelessly at great personal cost.

First Reading

This is one of those scriptural stories that centers around the name of a particular place or site. Rephidim (v8) is connected with the word for "support." The memory of an altar built on the site named "Yahweh-nissi"(vv15f) or "The Lord is my banner" also tended to draw to this locale the story of Yahweh's support in battle through the instrumentality of Moses' extended staff (banner) (v9). In antiquity the deity's standard was often used in battle to assure divine protection.

From the top of the hill, Moses extends the "staff of God" during the battle, to be identified with the rod he used to defeat Pharaoh (9:15; 14:16). The Amalekites were a nomadic tribe located in southern Palestine. The mention of this encounter with them in Deuteronomy does not reflect as favorable an outcome for the Israelites as is here presented (Deut 25:17ff). Joshua leads Israel's forces (v9). He will become Moses' trusted collaborator and eventual successor. Hur (v10) is elsewhere mentioned in conjunction with Aaron (24:14), with a possible priestly association.

The outcome of the battle is determined not by military prowess but by the prolonged assistance of Yahweh (v11). This is the significance of Moses' extended hands, which could not be lowered until the battle's end without placing Israel in a position of defeat. Moses' weariness (v12) may be a prelude to his ensuing decision to share his authority (18:18).

Responsorial Psalm   Ps 121

The note of confidence is woven into the fabric of this psalm. Its appropriateness lies in the fact that trust in the Lord's fidelity is the central theme of today's liturgy. The speaker (vv1f) addresses another person in the body of the psalm (vv3 - 8). This may be a temple priest and a pilgrim. *The mountains* (v1): the hilly landscape where Zion and the temple were located. Here confidence is placed in Yahweh, the powerful Creator (v2).

The same Lord is seen as perpetually vigilant in his concern for Israel (v4) as well as for the individual (vv5 - 8). *Sun...moon* (v6): The harmful effects of too much sun were well known; the ancients saw bad omens connected with the moon as well. *Coming...going* (vb): Entrances and exits served to express the start and finish of any action, hence the meaning of "all the time" or "at every moment" (Deut 28:6).

Second Reading

Constancy also appears in today's reading from 2 Timothy. The passage deals with instruction in God's word (3:14ff) and with its proclamation (4:1f). *Remain faithful* (Gr: *mene*) (v14): standing firm in the faith contrasts with those teachers who have wandered from authentic belief (2:17f).

Timothy is exhorted to retain the faith which he received in his early years. He was schooled in the scriptures, which here would refer to the Hebrew Bible (v15). It is the scriptures that outline the path of salvation (wisdom) but which must be read in and with the faith of the church. As the basic guide, they point out human error just as they build up virtue. This prepares one intellectually and morally for the Christian life (vv16f). In short, the Christian stands under the judgment of

God's word. *Inspired* (Gr: *theopneystos*) (v16): literally, "breathed by God." Here God is seen as the origin of the scriptures, His breath or spirit is used to refer to activity outside of himself, as creation and prophecy. While the scriptures have human authors, they are ultimately the work of God who subtly guides the work of human authorship. Scripture is the word of God in the words of humans.

The solemn charge that opens chapter 4 marks another major break in the letter (2:14). The apostle issues the directive in light of the Lord's return as judge (v1). While the parousia is not spoken of as imminent, as in earlier New Testament writings, it remains an important datum in the pastorals (1 Tim 6:14: Tit 2:13). Timothy is to be steadfast and totally committed in his preaching of the word. Here the word (v2) is broader than the scriptures referred to previously. It includes the proclamation of the New Testament kerygma. Since time is running out, there must be a constant willingness, unmindful of personal convenience, to make the truth known in teaching, correcting and strengthening the faithful.

Third Reading

This parable, found only in Luke, teaches the necessity of constancy in prayer. The judge is described as dishonest (v6); he is neither God-fearing nor respectful of others (v2). The scriptural widow (v3) makes frequent appearances symbolizing the disadvantaged; without the support of a husband, she is dependent on God and others for her needs. The point of the parable is that her perseverance obtains the desired end, her vindication before her accuser. God will do the same for those who are steadfast in prayer. A second point lies in the contrast between the unjust judge and a just God. If a dishonest judge ultimately responds to a persistent widow, a faithful Lord will do no less for his suppliants. *Strike me* (v5): literally a blow to the face. It may be figurative for wearing down one's resolve.

Faith lies at the root of the parable as is evident from the final verse (v8). The return of the Son of Man, presented at length in the preceding chapter (17:22 - 37), has been delayed. The decisive question which Jesus poses points to the faith which undergirds prayer; he wonders if it will perdure until the parousia. It is, then, more a steadfast posture of faith which expresses itself in persevering prayer rather than a constantly repeated verbalization of prayer that Jesus seeks.

Prayer does not always result in a request granted. But perseverance in prayer strengthens rather than diminishes faith. That may seem strange, but it is so. Perseverance enables us to see beyond particular needs and to view ourselves as part of a larger plan, which, as baffling and disconcerting as it may be at times, ultimately brings us to God. St. Monica prayed many years for the conversion of her son Augustine. Her hopes were dashed when he decided to leave her and go to Italy. But it was there that he met Ambrose and his conversion took place. Those years of constancy in prayer made of Monica a stronger woman. What impresses the pilgrim most at Lourdes is not the number of cures but the faith of the sick who return year after year, their faith strengthened with every visit.

The prayer of petition is a very noble form of prayer. It is the prayer of the anawim, the poor of God who willingly acknowledge their dependence. Today's scripture is a strong reminder that God is mindful of our needs but, even more importantly, it points up the need for trust. Everything may not turn out the way we hope, but we have the greatest assurance that our prayer does not fall on deaf ears. Our experience bears that out.

The Bible is a primary source of strength in our ongoing life with God. The rebirth of scriptural scholarship in the church was effected by Pope Pius XII and carried forward by the Second Vatican Council's opening the word to all the faithful in liturgy and all avenues of the spiritual life.

The faithful come to love the scriptures and are always thirsty for more. Those who preach and teach within the church have a weighty responsibility. The Bible expresses God's will for our salvation. Indeed, we stand under its judgment.

Homiletic and Catechetical Helps

1. The meaning of prayer.

2. The types of prayer: praise, contrition, thanks, petition.

3. Prayer as an expression of faith.

4. The eucharist: the perfect prayer.

5 Perseverance in prayer.

6. Prayer in the home.

7. Prayer for others.

8. Understanding scriptural inspiration.

9. Studying and praying the scriptures.

THIRTIETH SUNDAY OF THE YEAR
Year A

Readings

>   Ex 22:20 - 26
>   1 Thes 1:5 - 10
>   Mt 22:34 - 40

Theme: Love: Summary of the Christian Life

The law of the covenant (Ex 19 - 24), Israel's oldest law code, shows a marked respect for disadvantaged Israelites and resident non-Israelites. It calls for equity in personal dealings. This is reflected in today's first reading. Jesus, who came to bring the covenant law to perfection, goes beyond fair treatment in joining two passages from the Hebrew scriptures and placing love at the summit of religious belief. In a move that will forever characterize Christianity, he links indissolubly love of God and love of neighbor. In the reading from 1 Thessalonians, Paul speaks of modeling the faith. He was a model to the Thessalonian community and they, in turn, to other believers.

First Reading

This reading from the covenant law code looks to three categories of dependent people, otherwise unprotected members of society: resident aliens, the fatherless family, and the needy borrower.

Aliens (Heb: *gerim*) were non-Israelites residing within the country. They retained their own identity as people apart and were not accorded equal status (Ex 20:10), but the law insisted on fair-handed treatment and a concern for their welfare (23:9; Lev 19:33; Deut 24:17). They are often spoken of together with widows and orphans. In the absence of the male providers, the latter were often dependent on the community for their needs. Yahweh assured them special protection. Therefore, they became, in a sense, wards of the state and their rights were guaranteed (Is 1:17). Because the alien was not landed and had no protection from clan or tribe, he enjoyed a position akin to that of widows and orphans (Jer 7:6).

The injunction is to avoid any form of mistreatment of the aforementioned classes of people (vv20ff). Motivation for fair treatment of aliens is rooted in the similar experience of the Hebrews as "displaced persons" in Egypt (v20). In the case of widows and orphans, with no male defender, Yahweh himself will be the vindicator. Retribution will be meted out with parity, as is characteristic of the covenant code (21:23ff). The guilty party will himself die, leaving his wife and children in the same condition as the people mistreated.

The second section deals with situations of disadvantage within the Israelite community (vv24ff). When a needy Israelite requests a loan, no interest is to be charged. Interest would prove to be to the lender's advantage and clearly put the borrower at a further disadvantage. There is no law against interest on a loan to a wealthy or landed person nor on a loan made to an alien, although this norm seems to have gone through some alteration in the course of time (Deut 23:20ff).

Pledges on a loan were a common form of security for the lender. But human considerations put limits on this as well. The large and ample cloak (v25) often served as a blanket at night, especially among the poor. Thus, if taken in pledge, it is to be returned before evening. Yahweh's own compassion is to be the measure of this response (v26). Primitive laws like these are noteworthy for their very clear humanitarian concern.

Responsorial Psalm   Ps 18

The psalm is found in another version on David's lips after his deliverance from his enemies (2 Sam 22). It is a hymn of thanks which begins with the psalmist responding to the Deuteronomic command of love (v1). The Lord is given various titles, appropriate to David's gratitude for victory, all of them underscoring Yahweh's firmness and stability. He is "strength," "rock," "fortress," "shield" and "stronghold" (vv2f). *Horn of my salvation* (v3): The horned bull was the symbol of invincibility, an idea here transferred to Yahweh's power to save. The king expresses appreciation for victory over enemies (vv48f). He concludes with a paean of praise to Yahweh for his covenant fidelity (Heb: *hesed*), here referring to the covenant made with the Davidic dynasty (v51).

Second Reading

Two important Pauline ideas emerge in today's reading from 1 Thessalonians. The first is that of "modeling." Paul sees the example of his life as an integral part of his mission. First of all, he himself is an imitator of Christ (1 Cor 11:1), especially as related to his sharing in his suffering (Col 1:24). Now, in their end-time suffering on behalf of the gospel (word), the Thessalonians have become imitators of Paul (v6; 2 Thes 3:9). This combination of "affliction" and "joy" is eschatological and unites the Christian with Christ through "fellowship in his suffering" as well as through the Spirit-filled "power of his resurrection" (Phil 3:10). Now the Thessalonians, in turn, become a model for other Christians (v7). This idea of "modeling" the gospel is teaching through the power of example. The Thessalonians profit as well by the example of suffering given by the churches in Judea (2:14). Thessalonica's conversion adequately witnesses to the power of God's word; there is no need for Paul to add anything to it (v8).

The second important theme in this passage is that of conversion (vv9f), Other churches have reported on Thessalonica's "turning to God." This is an early expression of Christian *metanoia*. The underlying Hebrew idea (*shub*) was a complete turn-around on the road, a heading in the opposite direction. With the preaching of God's word in Thessalonica, the people responded by turning from their own gods to the one God. *Idols* (v9): images of deities which were believed to capture or attach the gods themselves. The gods were present to and with the idols. For Paul they are empty "no gods" (1 Cor 8:4f). The empty idols play an important part in Paul's description of conversion as the sinful "extreme" from which the Gentiles turn to engage themselves in a God who is "living" and "true." He is living as opposed to "dead" pagan gods, true since he is faithful to his promises. In this Spirit-led, radical turnabout, they have become a model to other churches.

An end-time note concludes the passage. Conversion conveys the notion of a certain urgency in view of the Lord's return. Jesus is Son of God and returning Son of Man as a result of his resurrection (v10; Rom 1:4). He will return to deliver the just from the final tribulation.

Third Reading

Jesus' teaching on the greatest commandment is found in the three synoptic gospels (Mk 12:28 - 34; Lk 10:25 - 28). It lends perspective to the New Testament attitude toward the Jewish law and illustrates the way that Jesus' teaching transcended the extensive legislation and casuistry of the Pharisees. Introducing the Pharisees and Sadducees (v34) effects a transition from the preceding controversy between Jesus and the Sadducees (22:23 - 33). A lawyer approaches Jesus (v35). Matthew never uses the term "lawyer" for a "scribe" elsewhere, but the meaning is the same: a person skilled in the Hebrew Torah. The question (v36) is not meant to be an easy one; in fact, it is posed in a "testing" fashion. There were more than six hundred commandments of the law, making some sort of prioritization a necessity among the Jews.

Jesus' answer joins two unrelated verses of the Hebrew scriptures (vv37ff). In quoting from the great Shema' (Deut 6:4f) he is on safe ground. This was one of Judaism's most sacred ethical precepts, as well as an important affirmation of monotheism. The love of God involves a commitment of will (heart), life itself (soul), and mind. Here Matthew substitutes Deuteronomy's (and Mark's) "strength" with "mind," relating this quality more with the first mentioned "heart" which in Hebrew thought was connected with knowledge and volition rather than with affection. In short, the love of God must be a total response in covenant fidelity with no competing attachment.

Although Jewish teaching coupled love of God and neighbor, never heretofore were the two so inextricably linked. The two verses joined here had not been so paired before. The quotation from Leviticus (19:18), obscurely placed in the Torah, becomes paramount in Jesus' teaching (Mt 19:19) and is accorded prominence as a principle in the epistolary literature (Rom 13:8 - 10; Gal 5:14; Jas 2:8). In its original Leviticus context, neighbor meant another Israelite. For Jesus it extends beyond all ethnic or national boundaries in terms of both the one treated as a neighbor (Lk 17:11 - 19) and the one acting as such (Lk 10:29 - 37). The statement that love of neighbor is to match love of self indicates an acceptance of a legitimate self-love within Christianity.

Jesus' answer goes beyond the limited legal outlook of the questioner and sees love of God and neighbor as the over-arching precept which embraces all other laws and against which all others must be measured. Skillfully Jesus reinforces the basic principle of law but moves away from concentration on a multiplicity of precepts as stepping stones to holiness. To his questioner's request as to what is the greatest commandment of the law, Jesus responds on a much broader level. He does not say that among all the laws this is the greatest but rather that the whole of the scriptures (law and prophets) must be interpreted in the light of this commandment (v40). This gives the law of love a singular and paramount importance.

Today's first reading calls for basic respect for others' rights. But it is limited and circumscribed. Jesus' call is as all-embracing as it is frightening. The commandment of love is an inspiring and challenging summary of what it means to be a Christian. There is no aspect of human conduct which it does not embrace. Yet to live wholly for God is no mean feat. Compromise is with us daily, if not hourly, and compromise places God in second place to something else. It diminishes the force of our love. Paul holds up the example of his new Christians because they did an about-face from "no gods" to the only God. Frequently our turns are ninety degrees rather than one hundred and eighty. Today's gospel says it all: Give God everything. He deserves nothing less.

We are told that to ignore our neighbor in our embrace of God is self-defeating. The two are inseparable. John's epistle had it right. Sometimes it is much easier to love the God we don't see and ignore the brother or sister at our side. Some religions can do that. Ours cannot. We cannot step over the homeless to enter our churches. Nor can we attend mass with sincerity while determined not to speak to another person. Such makes a mockery of faith.

Gandhi felt that if all Christians took Christ seriously, their impact on the world would be immeasurable. We seem to have a credibility gap. Today's gospel, heard so often, is our constant reminder. Like water dripping on a rock, it can eventually make a difference. We pray that it will.

Homiletic and Catechetical Helps

1. Explain the great commandment as the summary of Christian ethics.

2. To love God totally: its practical expression.

3. Love of neighbor: its all inclusive character.

4. The morality of interest on loans.

5. Contemporary forms of molesting the disadvantaged.

6. Models of Christianity today.

7. The parish as a model of the great commandment.

8. The meaning of conversion.

THIRTIETH SUNDAY OF THE YEAR
Year B

Readings

Jer 31:7 - 9

Heb 5:1 - 6
Mk 10:46 - 52

Theme: The Overlooked People

When in today's liturgy Jeremiah heralds the return of the northern exiles, it is mothers, expectant mothers, and the handicapped who are in the forefront. In the gospel, a scarcely noticed blind man is heard in the crowd when he persists in his cry to Jesus. The response of Christ is at least partially explained by the second reading: he knew what human weakness meant. Now, in God's plan, the people who are left on the wayside of life will be overlooked no longer.

First Reading

In one of Jeremiah's most celebrated chapters, the prophet speaks of the return of the exiles of the northern kingdom who had been deported by the Assyrians after their victory in 721 B.C. Those who had lived through the devastation now make their return. They are the "remnant of Israel" (v7), a term often used to describe that limited and small part of the Israelite population spared in catastrophe to be the survivors through whom God's lasting fidelity will continue (Am 5:15). Gradually this remnant takes on the moral qualities appropriate for deliverance (3:13 - 21). In today's reading the remnant is identified with the more disadvantaged members of society. Mothers and pregnant women, mentioned without husbands accompanying them, would be dependent on society for provision. The blind and the lame, often viewed as carrying the weight of their personal or family sins, were looked upon in their impairment as being imperfect and less than "whole" for the life of cult and community. These are the segments of society to be the first repatriated, as the special subjects of Yahweh's love. Their departure in mourning now finds them returning in joy (v9a; Ps 126)

With the passage dealing entirely with the Assyrian deportation, it is evidently written before the fall of Judah. Yahweh is said to be the father to Israel and Ephraim (v9b). The journey home is facilitated by leveling the road (Is 40:3f) and providing an ample water supply (Is 35:6). Their return from the north is also described as from "the ends of the world," an equivalent expression (v8).

This motif of deliverance bringing special favor to the physically impaired is a recurring theme in the prophetic literature (Is 35:5f).

Responsorial Psalm   Ps 126

The psalm echoes the sentiments of the returning exiles in the first reading. A heartbreaking departure for exile now results in joyful restoration, described in the agricultural image of sowing and reaping (vv5f). The return to Jerusalem is a moment of great joy and is, as well, a sign to the nations of God's saving power (vv1f).

Now that the homecoming has taken place, the people pray for the completion of their good fortune in the rebuilding of their city and temple (vv4ff). *Torrents in the southern desert* (v4): Heavy rains in a very dry area have a "flash flood" effect. A deluge of blessings is the object of the prayer.

Second Reading

The priesthood of Jesus is seen by the author of Hebrews against the background of the Israelite priesthood, its scriptural type. In today's passage, there is emphasis on the humanness of Christ as well as on his present glorified state. On both grounds he is uniquely suited to be of help to his adherents. The high priest of the temple was consecrated for God but in the interests of humanity (v1). Since his task was to offer sacrifice for sins, with the author thinking mainly of the Day of Atonement ritual (Lev 16:30, 34; Heb 9), then it was appropriate that he be in a position to sympathize with human weakness. Prone to sin himself (v2), he could extend help to those who were also weak.

The high priest was designated by the Lord through the line of Aaron (v4). This assured him acceptability and authenticity in exercising his sacred office. In terms of divine appointment, Christ is well qualified to be high priest. Subsequently the author will develop the human dimensions of Christ's priestly role (5:7ff). Here he speaks of his divine call which is seen as initiated with his death-resurrection (8:1ff). His designation as priest by the Father is supported by the citation of two biblical quotes (vv5f). The first is from a royal psalm wherein the king is designated God's son (Ps 2:7). Jesus enters into his sonship fully with the resurrection (Rom 1:4). Here that same filiation is related to the office of high priest. A second divine designation of Jesus is seen in the adaptation of another royal psalm (Ps 110:4). The psalm itself is frequently applied to Jesus in the New Testament, but never the verse cited here.

The priesthood of Jesus, like that of the king in the psalm, is not of the levitical line. Rather it is seen as similar to that of the priest-king Melchizedek who makes a brief appearance in Genesis (14:17 - 20). The author of the epistle at this point, in citing the psalm verse, wants to substantiate his claim that Christ was divinely chosen. This legitimates his high priestly role. At a later point in the epistle, the author will explain the Christ-Mechizedek likeness. The king's name means "righteous king"; as king of Salem, he is "king of peace" (Heb: *shalom*) (7:2). Both titles are appropriate as applied to Christ. The king appears with no mention of his human lineage with Christ being comparable in his divine origin (7:3). Finally the levitical priesthood, already present in Abraham's loins, pays honor to Melchizedek and tithes to him, a type of the superiority of Christ' priestly state over that of the Levites (7:4 - 9). The fact that the Genesis Melchizedek offers bread and wine to his guest plays no role in Hebrews' typology.

Jesus, then, as both human and divinely designated, is well suited to be the high priest of the new covenant.

Third Reading

The account of Bartimaeus' recovery of his sight is Mark's final miracle before Jesus enters Jerusalem (c. 11). Mark has it take place on the way out of Jericho, located about fifteen miles from Jerusalem (v46); Luke places it on the way into Jericho (Lk 18:35). Jesus is recognized by the blind man as the Davidic Messiah (v47), a title accepted by Jesus at this point but to be carefully interpreted by him as he enters Jerusalem as the humble and lowly Messiah (11:1 - 10).

The account combines features of a miracle story and a vocation narrative. Bartimaeus is one of the few people cured who is identified in Mark; he was seemingly well known in the Marcan community. Beggars were given scant notice on the roadside. Bartimaeus calls to Jesus twice after first being silenced (vv47f). This underscores his persistence in faith. Even though he gives Jesus his royal messianic title, it is God's mercy that he requests. His hopes were well founded since, as the first reading makes clear, healings were believed to be an important part of the messianic era.

The vivid description of Bartimaeus' call by Jesus is typically Marcan, bringing the reader close to the event (v50). It is interesting to note that Jesus' question to the blind man as to what he would like (v51) is the same as that posed to the sons of Zebedee in the preceding narrative (10:36). The irony is evident. The request on the one hand is marked by ambition; the other is a simple request made in faith.

The sight that Bartimaeus receives is obviously physical. But for Mark's readers it is meant to be seen on a deeper level. Biblical blindness is frequently identified with lack of faith, and sight with faith itself. Jesus brings out the faith dimension in his final statement (v52). Faith not only "saves" from physical blindness; it saves from eternal death as well. The man now deepened in his convictions follows Jesus "on the way" to Jerusalem with his disciples (v52; 10:32). The "way" of Jesus and of his followers is one that inevitably leads to Jerusalem and suffering. Bartimaeus has passed from a suppliant to a disciple, from the danger of being overlooked to a life of faith and favor.

In our contemporary society there are any number of people who are overlooked. They may be homeless, unemployed, elderly, institutionalized, or disadvantaged in some way. In addition, there are people who are lackluster, dull and uninteresting. It is so easy for us to look past people. It is amazing to think of the number of people who enter and exit our life, and how many of them go largely unnoticed. But how we brighten up in the presence of people of means, stature, or influence.

In his triumphant cortege Jeremiah places pregnant and unescorted women and the people who today might have wheelchairs and canes in the front line. And how sensitive Jesus was to those left out. Whether it was an old and bent woman who touched his clothes, a mother on the way to her son's burial, a short and unimpressive Zacchaeus scurrying up a tree, or a rejected woman taken in sin, no one was overlooked. In reaching out to Bartimaeus, who could scarcely make himself heard, Jesus gave a man sight—and gained a disciple.

Our high priest stands before God on our behalf. We have a mighty intercessor but also a very human one—one who understands what it means to fail, to become disheartened, to be tested, even to be rejected in favor of the common criminal Barabbas. Jesus knows what it means to be overlooked. And in our dealings of every day, he asks us to remember.

Homiletic and Catechetical Helps

1. The overlooked people of our experience.

2. Society's responsibility for the handicapped.

3. Ministry to widows, unwed mothers, and the handicapped.

4. Sight as a symbol of faith.

5. Son of David as a messianic title.

6. The need for healing in our own life.

7. Understanding Christ as high priest.

8. Melchizedek and Christ.

THIRTIETH SUNDAY OF THE YEAR
Year C

Readings

> Sir 35:12 - 14, 16 - 18
> 2 Tim 4:6 - 8, 16 - 18
> Lk 18:9 - 14

Theme: The Cry of the Poor

The poor in Israel were a special group. Having no providers, they were totally dependent on Yahweh and therefore deserving of special care on the part of the community. Gradually this socio-economic condition was transformed into a spiritual posture. People of any social category were called to be the anawim, Yahweh's dependents. Those who were materially poor, of course, were ideally suited to develop these spiritual qualities. Their cry is certain to be heard. Sirach today speaks of Yahweh's inclination toward the weak and needy. The disreputable tax collector in the gospel has succeeded in making the moral dispositions of the anawim his own. His prayer, too, is efficacious and pleasing to God. In the second letter to Timothy, Paul's life has been given totally to the gospel but, like the poor of God, he has been sustained throughout by his one defender, the Lord himself.

First Reading

Jesus, the son of Sirach, wrote his book of Hebrew wisdom in Jerusalem in about 180 B.C. He is a traditionalist who extols the law, seeing it as an indispensable guide for human conduct. Honesty in human dealings is a reflection of God himself who never bends the norms of justice and equity (vv12f). Just as the Israelite was held to administer justice without partiality to the weak or the strong (Lev 19:15), Yahweh acts similarly in his dealings with humankind.

This having been said, the Lord is, however, particularly sensitive to the needs of the poor since they have no one to present their case or plead their cause. It is precisely because he wants to see justice done that Yahweh intervenes on their behalf (vv14f). It is the "widows" and "orphans" who repeatedly in the scriptures epitomize the needy of society (Ex 22:21). The reason for this evolves around the importance of the male provider in a patriarchal society wherein all rights, titles, and obligations were connected with the man. The absence of a husband or father often meant to suffer severe disadvantage.

Sirach stresses at the same time the dispositions which are to accompany the disadvantaged state (vv16f). Those who serve God and turn to him in prayer express that spirit of dependence characteristic of the anawim. Their plea goes unswervingly to God's throne. For them the Lord acts as defender and judge, administering justice on their behalf.

Hebrew law placed great emphasis on justice and the rights of society's members. Therefore, it was of considerable importance that those unable to provide their own defense receive equitable treatment. Yahweh becomes their principal spokesperson.

Responsorial Psalm   Ps 34

This song of thanksgiving highlights the Lord's presence to the poor in their affliction. In fact, the humble are to be encouraged by the psalmist's account of God's presence to the disadvantaged (v3). In the verses of the psalm which are ready today, two categories of people are introduced. The evildoers (v17) are struck down and their memory is obliterated, a definitive and bitter end in a culture where one lived on in one's descendants. It is the just, the broken-hearted, the crushed in spirit, God's servants, his suppliants who are rescued and redeemed (vv 18ff, 22). The psalm does not limit its understanding of the poor to the socially disadvantaged; it moves beyond that to a spirit of lowliness (v3), justice (v18), and dependence (v23).

Second Reading

In the second letter to Timothy, Paul is presented as writing in what is presumed to be his Roman imprisonment. His first trial has ended (vv16ff) but Paul feels that his death is imminent, a martyrdom described in sacrificial terms (v6). Athletics figure in his imagery as he describes the life he has given to the Lord (v7f). The work assigned to him (Acts 9:15) has been completed; the faith is intact; the victor's laurels are assured. *Crown of righteousness* (v8): This is the laurel wreath placed on the winner's head (2:5; 1 Cor 9:25). Righteousness is sanctification, the grace-filled transformation about which Paul writes extensively. All of this will occur with the Lord's coming. The parousia is regarded as the time when reward and punishment are meted out. Little is said about the interim period for those who die before the Lord's return.

Paul speaks about his trial. Little is known about Alexander the coppersmith mentioned in the present chapter (vv14f); he was evidently an opponent of Paul. In speaking of his defense, the apostle states that he was totally abandoned (v16). The Lord alone stood by him as part of the defense's case. But the trial had a satisfactory outcome to the advantage of those who waited for the gospel (v17). Now the end is in sight, and God's protection which has never failed will bring him safely to his heavenly homeland (v18).

Third Reading

This is the second of two successive parables on prayer in Luke's gospel. The first deals with perseverance in prayer (18:1 - 8). Today's parable sets forth the interior dispositions which must accompany prayer and which are captured in the spirit of the child as set forth in the subsequent narrative (18:15 - 17).

Self righteousness presents a grave obstacle to discipleship and participation in the reign of God (v9; 5:32; 15:7). Everything in the comportment of the Pharisee epitomizes that spirit. His prayer of "thanksgiving" is self-serving from beginning to end (vv11f). He compares himself with others in a demeaning fashion; others are "unrighteous" (Gr: *adikoi*), a statement implying his own righteousness; he proudly parades his works of supererogation, fasting and tithing. Noteworthy is that this is a member of a religious class, an authority on God-related matters.

The tax collector, on the other hand, belongs to a generally disliked class of people. They were Roman collaborators and commonly linked with extortion and graft (3:12f). As socially undesirable, they are a group touched by Jesus' outreach. In the parable the tax collector's direct access to God arises precisely from the recognition of his sinfulness. His words are few; his demeanor is humble. He asks only for forgiveness (v13). The contrast between the two men bears a striking resemblance to that between the sinful woman who anointed Jesus' feet and the critical Pharisee (7:36 - 50).

The conclusion emphasizes the tax collector's justification. This is a forensic type of justice, not the ontological justification of Paul. Here God acts as judge in pronouncing sentence on the man's conduct. The tax collector had the authentic spirit of the anawim with the realization of his utter dependence upon God and his need for forgiveness. In being master of his own fate and exhibiting little need for God, the Pharisee was found lacking in justice. The parable ends with Jesus' statement on the reversal of fortunes in God's sight (v14).

It is not easy to avoid self-righteousness. Even our conversation so easily takes a self-serving turn. Self-preservation means more than species survival. It also includes a constant struggle for recognition which probably never vanishes completely. But repeatedly Jesus puts us on guard. So much of Luke's gospel represents a plea for humility and lowliness. Those who emerge in a favorable light are sinners and outlaws for the simple reason that they know what the need for God means. They have nowhere to turn but to God—and they do so.

If we could learn to make as much out of our failures as we do our successes, our lives would be much more God-centered. Failure is sobering; it marks our vulnerability. Sin, as a part of failure, shows us how far we can distance ourselves from God. The key is bringing all of that before God as an expression of our helplessness. Then our whole life, even with its successes, will take on a new light. Our prayer becomes richer because it truly expresses our dependence.

The tax collector went home the winner. He gave nothing and received everything—and he realized it. Paul today speaks of his successes. Faith-filled and often tested in the furnace of adversity, he is fully convinced that it is God who has brought him through. His, too, is the cry of the poor.

Homiletic and Catechetical Helps

1. The relationship between prayer and humility.

2. The relationship between poverty and spiritual dependence.

3. The widows and orphans of today's society.

4. The significance of prayer before meals.

5. Examining our personal self-righteousness.

6. Sin and the spirit of the anawim.

7. Asking forgiveness of God and neighbor.

THIRTY-FIRST SUNDAY OF THE YEAR
Year A

Readings

Mal 1:14 - 2:2, 8 - 10
1 Thes 2:7 - 9, 13
Mt 23:1 - 12

Theme: The Responsibility of Religious Leadership

Malachi takes serious issue with the type of religious leaders present in his time. Personally unfaithful to the covenant, they were also guilty of misleading and misdirecting the people they were called to lead. Today's gospel contains some of Jesus' strongest words against the scribes and Pharisees. Seeking privilege and honors, they were far more interested in recognition than service. Against this background, Paul stands out as a model of Christian leadership. He worked tirelessly among the Thessalonians, even providing for his own needs, with the sole aim of letting his message take deep root among his hearers.

First Reading

The prophet Malachi, whose name means "My messenger," lived in the middle of the fifth century. Other than his name, which may be functional rather than personal, nothing else is known of him. His prophetic utterances gravitate toward the prevailing sins of priests and people alike. In speaking of the priests, he contrasts their conduct with the fidelity of Levi himself (2:4ff).

Yahweh is the presiding monarch whose reign is universal

(v14; 1:11). It is a type of religious universalism which may find its origins in the Persian claim to a religious hegemony going far beyond its own boundaries, with Yahweh here becoming the substituted deity. At any rate the respect presented as accorded Yahweh by foreigners contrasts sharply with the religious misconduct and disregard of the Jewish priests and people (2:2; 1:6 - 9). Their empty cult, devoid of genuine sentiment, has become meaningless (2:13).

The priestly line had been blessed in Phinehas, the son of Aaron, who had acted honorably in Yahweh's behalf (Num 25:6 - 13). Now this blessing is not simply revoked; it is converted into a curse (2:2). The sins of the priests lie in their infidelity and their failure to instruct the people properly (2:8). In their official decisions they have shown favoritism (2:9). Their base misconduct and ineffectiveness result in their rejection.

The closing reference to the single God and covenant and the forging of a single people (v10) is prelude to the subsequent section decrying marriage with foreigners (2:10 - 16).

Responsorial Psalm   Ps 131

This short psalm calls for trust and confidence in God. It has a spirit in sharp contrast with the attitudes of pride and haughtiness described in today's first and third readings. The psalmist is free of an ambitious spirit characterized by lofty and impressive plans (v1). The note of trust is poignantly described in the image of the nourished child nestled in its mother's lap without fear or concern (v2). It is this spirit of childlike confidence which the New Testament sees as the key to God's reign. The psalm ends on a collective note addressed to Israel as a whole (v3), which may have been addded with the psalm's incorporation into a liturgical setting. Once again the call is for total trust.

Second Reading

In a brief autobiographical sketch (2:1 - 12), Paul describes his early work in Thessalonica with his companion apostles, Silvanus and Timothy (1:1). He elaborates on a theme to which he will frequently return: the importance of modeling the gospel which is being proclaimed. In their mission the apostles were neither superior nor authoritarian, but rather gentle and caring (v7). They lived their message by sharing their life in dedication and service to a people dearly loved (v8). *Gospel of God* (v8): the gospel which has God as its source as well as its content in recounting his saving action. Finally, the apostles were self-supporting (v9). Rather than put the community at a disadvantage due to their presence, they worked to provide for themselves at the same time as they performed their apostolic service. For Paul this perhaps meant plying his trade as a tent maker (Acts 18:3).

Paul then gives thanks for the reception given to the apostolic preaching of the word, which came from "hearing" (v13; Rom 10:14). This was an acceptance in faith, not a mere human hearing. This word, once received, is now active within them, since it is always accompanied by the action of the Spirit. The word once sown in the heart is cultivated and nourished by the same Spirit.

Third Reading

This chapter in Matthew's gospel (c. 23) brings to a close Jesus' dealings with the scribes and Pharisees and their teaching, which was initiated at an earlier point (21:23). Several factors must be kept in mind in understanding the important teaching on authority presented in today's gospel. First, what seems at times to be an inconsistency is due to the Matthean blend of Jesus' teaching with adaptations required by conditions within the Matthean community. Second, the gospel teaching must be read against the background of problems within the church itself as well as prevailing tensions between Pharisaic Judaism and the early church.

Jesus addresses the "crowds" and "disciples" (v1), a likely reference to the broader Gentile Christian community and the Jewish Christians who constituted a major segment of the Matthean community. Major lines of opposition to Jewish leadership center on their failure to teach by example (v3), their imposition of insupportable burdens on the people (v4), and their ostentation (vv5ff). *Chair of Moses* (v2): a figurative expression for Mosaic authority.

The injunction to observe the Pharisaic teaching (v3) is contrary to much of the Matthean Jesus' teaching, even in the present chapter (vv13 - 20; 16:12). This is evidently a logion drawn directly from Jesus' own preaching, with his characteristic basic respect for the law and Jewish teaching (5:17 - 19). It is taken over here by Matthew as a palliative for his own community with its strong Jewish sensitivities. It must be remembered that respect for and even observance of the Jewish law did not vanish without a struggle within the Jewish Christian community.

The fact that the religious leaders imposed heavy duties and sanctions on the people without offering relief or solace stands in strong contrast with the type of "yoke" that Jesus offers (11:28f). Equally serious is their desire for recognition and honors. *Phylacteries* (v5): small boxes containing important scripture texts worn on the forearm and forehead at the time of prayer. *Tassels* ("fringes," v5): worn on the corners of the outer garment as a reminder of the importance of Torah observance (Num 15:37ff). Both phylacteries and tassels were enlarged to be more noticeable.

The mention of the desire to be called "rabbi" (v7) triggers a listing of titles forbidden within the Christian community (vv8ff). The implication is that these designations, in use in Jewish circles, were making inroads in the Christian community as well. "Rabbi" (literally, "my great one") was used by disciples in reference to their teacher or leader. It accorded respect and honor. "Father," used also of Jewish sages, is used repeatedly by the Matthean Jesus in speaking of God (6:1 - 15, passim) and is thus excluded on that basis as a human referent. "Teacher" (Gr: *kathegetes*) could refer to either an intellectual or a spiritual guide.

The reason for the exclusion of these titles is the common brotherhood of v8. All of the titles mentioned convey a note of a superior relationship and therefore have no place in a spiritually egalitarian society. It should be noted, however, that they are excluded as titles within the community of faith, not within the family or in society in general. All of this is to place in strong and clear relief God as Father and Christ as rabbi and teacher, both of whom preside over a community of equals where authority derives its meaning exclusively from service to the brothers and sisters (vv11f).

This teaching is not given by the Matthean Jesus in a detached fashion. It evidences the tension that existed in the late first century between church and synagogue as well as the inroads being made in the church by partisan, non-evangelical thinking. For subsequent generations to say that this simple and clear teaching was time-conditioned or that it deals with an underlying spirit rather than the titles themselves would have to be substantiated on grounds stronger than later historical custom.

In secular society positions of authority are generally accompanied by appurtenances of rank or status. These can serve as incentives and in some way compensate for the weight of the office itself. It is interesting to note that even in states which allege total equality, symbols of ranks are never completely eradicated. In the gospel read today, Jesus is emphatic in affirming the totally opposite character of authority within the church. This idea of leadership seen in terms of minority and service, avoiding pomp, ostentation, even titles, is strongly emphasized as a hallmark of the Christian communmity. To pass over it as something purely secondary fails to accord it the force that the inspired word of God itself gives it.

What can so easily happen is that the message that the distinctiveness of the church in its life style is called to give suffers from a reverse situation. We become imitators of worldly patterns rather than the world learning from us. Paul earnestly strove to model apostleship. There is no doubt that he exercised genuine authority, even to the point of some "wrist slapping." But he lorded it over no one nor did he ask for any form of privilege. He earned his daily bread working side by side with Christians and non-Christians alike. He was totally available to the community of faith.

All Christians are called to cultivate a humble spirit and way of life. Christian leadership has an even greater responsibility. It comes through in countless concrete ways, always rooted in the inspiration given by a servant messiah. The world is very unaccustomed to this way of acting, so the need for it will never diminish. Yes, the first are last—a statement hard to fully accept. But for some of us it has be the path of holiness.

Homiletic and Catechetical Helps

1. Church authority in teaching, ruling, and sanctifying.

2. Service as a characteristic of church leadership.

3. The levitical priesthood and its role.

4. Church leadership amd the alleviation of "heavy burdens."

5. Appropriate forms of address within the church.

6. The example of Paul's leadership.

7. The focus of all church attention: the Father and Jesus.

8. The teaching of Vatican II on bishops and priests.

THIRTY-FIRST SUNDAY OF THE YEAR
Year B

Readings

> Deut 6:2 - 6
> Heb 7:23 - 28
> Mk 12:28 - 34

Theme: The Great Commandment

"Hear, O Israel," or the "great Shema," as it was known, is a central expression of Israelite faith. The pious Jew recited it twice daily. It gives expression to the absolute claim of Yahweh's sovereignty as well as the total character of the human response. This major Deuteronomic act of faith becomes, in turn, a centerpiece of Jesus' teaching, as recounted in today's gospel. To the Shema, Jesus adds the Leviticus injunction on love of neighbor. Complementing this teaching on allegiance to the one God, the epistle to the Hebrews today speaks of the one new covenant sacrifice and its single priest.

First Reading

The opening verses (vv2f) bring to a conclusion a preceding discourse of Moses and serve as a closing exhortation. "Statutes" (Heb: *huqqim*) and "commandments" (Heb: *miswot*) are two forms of positive or apodictic law. They are general in character and are not based on case decisions. The former establish penalties; the latter state simply the positive or negative command. Law observance was the Israelite's response to the covenant. From his side, Yahweh pledges length of life, growth, prosperity, and abundance, the "land flowing with milk and honey" being a familiar Deuteronomic expression (11:9; 26:9, 15). This understanding of blessings in a material sense was rooted in experiencing God's favor in the present life. Any after-life belief at this period was nebulous at best.

The Shema ("Hear") opens solemnly, affirming Yahweh's exclusive claim to Israelite allegiance (v4). No other deity, much less a pantheon of gods, is tolerable. The Shema has long been viewed and even translated as a strong monotheistic statement. This is valid as long as the monotheism is seen as practical rather than theoretical. This is a call to exclusivity rather than a theological statement on God's unicity.

The love of God is expressed in terms of covenant fidelity and in evident Deuteronomic terms. Israel's relationship to Yahweh is rooted in historical experience, not abstract speculation. Undivided loyalty embraces the mind, the will, and all the forces of the human spirit. It is a love without measure.

Responsorial Psalm   Ps 18

This psalm gives liturgical expression to the injunction of love of the Lord, central to today's liturgy. A commentary may be found on the Thirtieth Sunday of Year A.

Second Reading

This passage from Hebrews highlights the singular character of the priesthood of Jesus and of the sacrifice which he offered. This the author does in situating the action of Jesus against the background of its counterparts in Israelite cult. In former times there were many priests because human mortality prevented any of them from continuing indefinitely (v23). It is not so with Christ who as priest has an eternal mission. Once having entered the heavenly sanctuary, he makes continual intercession on behalf of his people (vv24f). This intercessory power is related to the ongoing and permanent character of Christ's single sacrifice. The offering of Christ on Calvary has taken on transcendent significance with both priest and victim continuing in their sacrificial role (9:11 - 14; Rom 8:34). The result is that people of any generation have their intercessor already in place and have no need of further sacrifices.

Christ, the high priest, sinless and undefiled (4:15), is the heavenly mediator now distanced from sinners. Unlike the high priests of the past, who had to offer sacrifices repeatedly for themselves and for the people, Christ remains the permanent priest and offering (vv26f; 9:25f). *Day after day* (v27): exaggeration for the sake of contrast with the one sacrifice of Christ. The Day of Atonement ritual, here described, was actually offered only once a year (Lev 16:11 - 19)

Finally, the levitical priesthood was marked by moral inadequacy, as evidenced by sacrifices offered for their own sins (v27), whereas the priesthood of "Melchizedek's line" has come to rest in God's Son, perfect and eternal (v28; 5:9f). *Word of the oath* (v28): the promise of a new non-levitical priesthood in Psalm 110:4, pledged subsequent to the Torah (levitical law), now supersedes the priesthood of Levi.

Third Reading

The great commandment narrative is found in the three synoptics. For a more extensive treatment of the commandment itself, the reader is referred to the commentary on its Matthean presentation (Thirtieth Sunday of Year A). Consideration here will be largely limited to the distinctive Marcan features of the narrative.

In Mark the account evolves without confrontation on the part of the questioning scribe. Jesus is not being tested. The exchange remains amicable throughout. The question put to Jesus was one frequently directed to the rabbinic teacher, requiring some prioritization of Judaism's 613 precepts (v28). Departing from the other synoptics, the Marcan Jesus quotes the Shema from its beginning (v29). Its meaning in the Greek text falls more strongly on the note of God's unicity, a conceptual monotheism stronger than in the original Deuteronomy. Jesus' response joins Deuteronomy 6:5 and Leviticus 19:18 as a summary of the entire law (vv30f) The total human response to God in love must be accompanied by love of neighbor, a linking of the two precepts which is distinctly Christian. Jesus concludes by affirming this law's superiority to all others.

Only in Mark does the inquirer repeat Jesus' teaching and address him as "Teacher" (vv32f). He adds his own postscript in recognizing the teaching's superiority to forms of cultic and ritual expression (v33). The subtle contrast here is between cultic formalism and a truly internal religious spirit. Jesus acknowledges the man's good intentions which indicate his proximity to Christian discipleship (v34). At this important juncture all further questioning of Jesus ceases.

Confrontation immediately puts conversation on guard. We are ill at ease from the start. Friendly discussion, on the other hand, leads to mutual enrichment. The great commandment of love is reported in basically the same form in all the synoptics. But only Mark places it in a friendly framework. It almost seems as if the precept itself is already at work in the exchange between the participants. In carefully repeating Jesus' words, the scribe is making them his own. He is convinced of their truth and his respectful and kindly tone reflect it. So often our tone of voice or our body language convey an attitude which sets the stage for misunderstanding and hurt feelings. On the other hand, a gentle inflection marked by respect elicits a ready response. It is hard to escape the fact that the great commandment becomes flesh in daily conversation, in the considerate gesture, in the soft-spoken word.

When it comes to knowing much about high priests and their duties, many of us probably draw a blank. But it is not hard to grasp the point that Christ is our constant intercessor before the Father. Weak and frail though we are, we have a sinless but compassionate brother who speaks that word of offering and forgiveness constantly on our behalf. Calvary is not a past event. It has become a heavenly reality, to last until the end of the ages, with the mass its earthly reflection.

Christ brings us before the Father and compensates for our inadequacies. We have every reason to be confident.

Homiletic and Catechetical Helps

1. The Shema as a summary of Israelite faith.

2. The great commandment: a synthesis of Christian morality.

3. Israel's belief in earthly blessings.

4. Distinction between practical and theoretical monotheism.

5. Respectful speech.

6. Hurting with the tongue.

7. The Hebrew high priesthood and Jesus.

8. The one sacrifice of Christ and the mass.

9. Christ the single priest and the Catholic priesthood.

THIRTY-FIRST SUNDAY OF THE YEAR
Year C

Readings

> Wis 11:22 - 12:1
> 2 Thes 1:11 - 2:2
> Lk 19:1 - 10

Theme: To Seek and To Save

The reading from Wisdom today teaches that everything that comes from the hand of God is good. What is true of creation in general is especially true of God's human children. In forgiving sin God is aware of those positive qualities. In the amusing account of Zacchaeus' determined and enterprising spirit, Jesus sees in the disreputable tax collector an inherent goodness which is not to be lost. Once converted, the Christian grows in holiness by God's power as the image of God becomes increasingly visible. Paul reminds the Thessalonians of the need to pass from good intentions to accomplishment through God's grace.

First Reading

The biblical book most influenced by Greek thought is also one of its severest critics. Writing in the first century before Christ, the author here interrupts his treatise on Yahweh's superiority over pagan forces as evidenced in the events of the exodus from Egypt with a digression on God's mercy. Even though the universe itself is dwarfed in insignificance by God's omnipotence and grandeur (v22), God still considers the worth of every created thing. Grain *from a balance* (v22): a small particle used in weighing light objects. His mercy and forgiveness are rooted in his omnipotence (v23). The notion that eradicating sin, as well as sickness, is a work of God's power emerges in the New Testament as well (Mk 2:9ff). God's patience with humans allows time for repentance (v23; 12:10).

God's love is directed to all things created. In fact, the existence and preservation of the created order are explained by God's love (vv24f). This relationship between the whole of creation and a living God endows the former with a permanent and lasting stamp (12:1; 1:7).

Responsorial Psalm   Ps 145

This is an alphabetic psalm (each verse beginning with the subsequent letter of the Hebrew alphabet) which continues today's theme of Yahweh's providential care for his creation. There is strong emphasis on the kingship of Yahweh. The psalm begins with an exclamation of praise and blessing (vv1f). The Lord's anger and sense of retribution are far outweighed by his patient forbearance and covenant fidelity (v9). In line with the day's liturgy, God's concern goes beyond humanity to embrace all of creation, with that same creation invited to acknowledge his goodness (v10). Yahweh as king enjoys a sovereignty which is eternal, directed in a special way to the down-trodden and forgotten (v14; 1 Sam 2:8).

Second Reading

In today's reading from Paul's second letter to Thessalonica, Paul prays for the community's growth in faith and virtue in anticipation of the Lord's return (vv11f) and exhorts them not to be misled with reports about the imminence of the parousia (2:1f).

Election is not synonymous with salvation. Paul prays that the action of God in the lives of the Thessalonians, initiated with their call and its accompanying good intentions, may be fruitful and productive (v11; Is 66:5). At the time of the Lord's return (1:10), this will result in a reciprocal glorification (v12). Christ will be made manifest in his chosen ones, with their virtuous lives giving evidence of his grace at work in them. They, in turn, will receive final deliverance, brought to eternal life and glory by the action of God and his Son, here spoken of jointly as the authors of salvation (v12; 1 Thes 4:14 - 17).

As the first letter to Thessalonica indicates, there was a marked climate of concern about the parousia within the community. Avoiding any semblance of pinpointing the time, Paul simply encouraged the people to be vigilant and alert (1 Thes 5:1 - 11). In the present letter there is evidence of some agitation, even frenzy regarding the question (2:2). It was occasioned either by some alleged prophetic insight ("spirit"), an oracle, or a fraudulent letter attributed to Paul. Paul urges a sane and calm spirit in the face of such disturbances.

Third Reading

In the engaging story of Zacchaeus, the tax collector, which is found only in the third gospel, some important Lucan themes appear. As in the case of the blind beggar by the roadside in the narrative which precedes (18:35 - 43), salvation is not easily accessible, here due to the protagonist's low stature (v3). Like the beggar, he persists in his desire to reach Jesus. In a sense, he is a typical Lucan subject: a tax collector, engaged in an occupation synonymous with traitorous collaboration and extortion.

For salvation to reach Zacchaeus, his own compliance is necessary. He hosts the Savior in his home (v6); he is willing to surrender his wealth (18:24 - 27) and to correct any injustices of which he is guilty (v8). From Jesus' side salvation meant acceptance of the sinner and defiance of Jewish custom in engaging in fellowship and food sharing (vv5ff). Once outreach from both sides has taken place, salvation is confirmed. The twofold mention of salvation "today" (vv5, 10) is Luke's realized eschatology with redemption already present during the public ministry of Jesus. The *kairos* or definitive time of the salvific event is now present in Jesus' person (2:11; 23:43). *Descendant of Abraham* (v9): Even though rejected by his co-religionists, Zacchaeus through his acceptance of God's pardon in faith stands in the authentic line of Abraham. Once again Luke's leitmotiv of God's outreach to the emarginated and its positive acceptance is sounded (v10; 15:7, 10, 32).

Zacchaeus began with two strikes against him. He was not a believer in good standing and he was rich—not the best preparation for God's reign. A single meeting with Christ was sufficient to move him in the right direction. Christ recognized the problems but was not put off by them. On the contrary he saw sincerity and good intentions and built on that. We so often take a different tack in being judgmental, questioning motives, and impugning others' intentions. We forget that self-righteousness was the one sin that Jesus could not deal with effectively. People turn to God for a variety of reasons and at very unexpected times. Zacchaeus was "touched" while he was up a tree—not a very dramatic pose for a major conversion. Despite all the criticism, Jesus cut through hypocrisy and, undaunted, went to a sinner's home as a guest. Social mores manage to build all sorts of walls against outreach. Failure to move with courage can make us the prisoners of our own fears. The people who need us most may not be sitting beside us in church. The lesson of God's word today is clear. The most disreputable person means much to God.

Religious experience seems inexorably drawn to the exceptional.

Alleged visions, messages, and miracles never fail to attract adherents. Things were no different in Thessalonica, even though the circumstances were not exactly the same. Auxiliary supports of faith are helpful and are not to be ruled out. Miracles do happen. But the greatest and most exceptional reality is present to us each day. The reign of God is in our midst. The great wonder of Christ, Brother and Savior, is as close as our parish church and our own home; indeed, he is within our own heart.

Homiletic and Catechetical Helps

1. The bond between humanity and all of creation.

2. The sacredness of creation and environmental concerns.

3. Examples of ministry to the unchurched.

4. Creative ways to reach the unchurched.

5. Catholic schools for a non-Catholic population.

6. Welcoming minorities.

7. Essential and optional beliefs in Catholic life.

8. Christ in us and we in Christ: its meaning.

THIRTY-SECOND SUNDAY OF THE YEAR
Year A

Readings

> Wis 6:12 - 16
> 1 Thes 4:13 - 17
> Mt 25:1 - 13

Theme: Wise and Vigilant

Wisdom is different than knowledge. Wisdom orders what is known toward a determined end. In the Bible, that end is God alone. In today's first reading, personified wisdom comes to those who are morally attuned and prepared to receive her. Matthew's parable of the expectant virgins points to wisdom's lying in preparedness. On another issue, Paul today considers the fate of those who die before the Lord's return.

First Reading

In the heady atmosphere of Alexandria where Hellenistic philosophy made deep inroads, the author of Wisdom points to the true wisdom of those eternal verities which the true God imparts to his people. Here the author presents wisdom as a strikingly attractive woman (v12). Personified elsewhere as well in the Hebrew scriptures as one of Yahweh's attributes (Prov 8; Sir 24), wisdom was present with him in the creation of the universe and stands by his side in its preservation. Wisdom is also identified with God's own spirit immanent within the cosmos and as a directive force of physical and moral life.

In human affairs, then, wisdom participates in God's capacity to order all things properly. The wise person accomplishes in his or her own life what Yahweh does for the whole of creation. In the present passage, her attractiveness makes her alluring and captivating. So prone is she to self-manifestation (v13) that she seeks out devotees (v16). She is presented as moving through the city and being seated at the entrance of homes (vv14, 16; Prov 1:20f; 8:1ff). To possess her, she must be sought out and desired (vv12f) in a spirit of prudence and vigilance (v16). As in the book of Wisdom as a whole, the author sees Yahweh's revelation as the only true wisdom in life.

Responsorial Psalm   Ps 63

The theme of night which is suggested in Wisdom's moving through the city in the first reading and marks the time of the groom's return in the third occurs in this psalm as well. It is during the night that the psalmist ponders the Lord's goodness (v7). The psalm contains a strong note of both distress and trust. There is a strong yearning for the Lord (v2), linked with the temple, his dwelling place, from which the psalmist is locally distant (v3). To make Yahweh's covenant love (*hesed*) more precious than life itself is for the earthbound Israelite to give it the highest priority (v4). Liturgical prayer is central to the psalmist's thought; in addition to the temple, mention is made of the gestures and prayers proper to public worship (vv5f). The intimate longing to be with the Lord continues through the night with expressions of trust and confidence (vv7f).

Second Reading

In writing to the Thessalonians, Paul more than once addresses their "second coming" concerns. The question presented here is one that has come to the fore: What is to become of those Christians who die prior to the parousia? Initially the interim period between Christ's departure and return was thought to be very brief. At this point, the delay has resulted in deaths, a fact which in some way had to be reconciled with Christian hope. The problem had resulted in a certain disquiet and concern within the community (v13).

Paul bases his argument on doctrine. The resurrection of Christ is the cornerstone of all resurrection belief; he is the prototype of his followers, destined to rise as well (v14; 1 Cor 15:22f). Since Christ has risen, his followers will experience the same and will not be abandoned. *God through Jesus* (v15): As in the case of Jesus, so too with his followers, resurrection is principally the work of the Father (Acts 2:24).

Apocalyptic imagery of the end time (archangel, trumpet, descent) is employed as Paul outlines the sequence of eschatological events (v16). Those who have died before the parousia will take precedence in the final ingathering over those still living, among whom Paul continues to see himself (v15). *Word of the Lord* (v15): prelude to a prophetic utterance, not a reference to a particular teaching of Jesus.

The Lord's return on the clouds of heaven draws on the Son of Man imagery in Daniel, referred to also by Christ in his end-time discourse (vv16f; Dan 7:13; Mt 24:30). Both the dead and the living are swept up quickly to the Lord as if drawn hastily away from worldly woes and distress (v17; 2 Cor 12:2; Rev 12:5).

Thus all will attain salvation's end, union with the Lord (5:10; Phil 1:23).

Third Reading

Wisdom as preparedness for the Lord's return is the main point of this parable found only in Matthew. What may have been its earlier and more primitive form, an injunction dealing with a master's return from a wedding, is found in Luke (12:35ff). Regardless of what form the parable may have originally taken, its Matthean presentation evidences some redactional development.

The wedding (v1) as an eschatological symbol, pointing to the definitive marriage of God and his people, comes from the Hebrew scriptures (Hosea, Canticles) and appears elsewhere in the New Testament (9:14f; 22:1 - 14; Rev 21:9f). Here it gives the story a parousia setting without playing an integral part in its development. The "kingdom of heaven" is not likened to the ten virgins but rather to the main point of the whole story that follows. The virgins, who would have served as the groom's attendants in a Palestinian setting, are termed "wise" and "foolish" (v2) in view of the parable's outcome, not because of any antecedent considerations. Their role here is to symbolize the Christian disciple (2 Cor 11:2). Since all the virgins sleep, the point being made is preparedness rather than constant alertness. The oil need stand only for a state of readiness without giving it an added allegorical understanding as good works (v4), even though the latter are said to be illumined by "lighted lamps" elsewhere (5:15f).

The bridegroom's return late at night points to the uncertain and unexpected time of the Lord's coming (v6). There is no reason to read any moral point into the wise virgins' failure to share their oil (vv8f). A parable makes one moral point only; secondary literary aspects should not be pressed. Both the request of the excluded virgins and the groom's response (vv11f) center on the danger of disparity between belief and conduct (5:21f). Election of itself gives no assurance of final salvation. The parable highlights the importance of the interim period between faith's inception and its consummation. Faith must be nurtured and grow, accompanied always by a spirit of expectation (v13; 24:42, 44). Such is true Christian wisdom.

It is probably safe to say that the return of the Lord at the end of history does not weigh in as a priority for most people today. It remains a given but has no vital significance for most of us. But perhaps it is seen too much as a single event. There are repeated inbreakings of God in the world which speak to us of a Christ coming toward us. God's speech is not solely past or present. It is also new and unexpected. What does the second coming tell us? In our complacency and self-reliance, it reminds us that the world is God's and the final word will be his. He speaks to us not only out of past revelation but from the future as well. The returning Lord is the Lord of surprise. How often do we see the hand of God in unexpected events? World powers vanish from history. Prosperity suddenly becomes hardship. An unforeseen ecumenical council gives the church a new vision. Peace emerges where conflict had long been the order of the day. Do we see this as Christ coming toward us?

There is nothing wrong, of course, in reading the parable of the ten virgins and applying it to our personal encounter with the Lord. Like the Thessalonians, we too will probably see death before the second coming of the Lord. Preparedness should be the order of the day. This is not to argue for some sort of morose preoccupation with death. We are all commissioned for a full life of service. But we should be conditioned to expect the unexpected. Serious sin is always life for the moment, to the exclusion of all other considerations. Anxiety about the future and moral indifference reflect the lack of faith in our life. We may be guilty of too much "Lord, Lord" and too little oil in our lamps.

A good life always reckons with a Lord who is close at hand. And the fact is that we have everything to look forward to. Happiness is not a difficult subject for reflection. What we look forward to, we will prepare for as well. It's the wise thing to do.

Homiletic and Catechetical Helps

1. The difference between human wisdom and biblical wisdom.

2. Wisdom personified as a woman.

3. What is the biblical wisdom literature?

4. Wisdom and moral vigilance.

5. Explaining death to the young.

6. Christian remembrance of the dead.

7. Stages in the second coming of Christ.

8. Faith: "Lord, Lord" or lighted lamps?

THIRTY-SECOND SUNDAY OF THE YEAR
Year B

Readings

> 1 Kgs 17:10 - 16
> Heb 9:24 - 28
> Mk 12:38 - 44

Theme: Sacrificial Giving

Both widows in today's readings teach us something about the meaning of sacrifice. Elijah is fed with the last of the oil and flour left to the Zarephath widow. The impoverished woman, observed by Jesus in the temple, gave to God of what was necessary for her to live. In both instances charity cost a great deal. Sacrifice of a different order appears in today's reading from Hebrews. The one sacrifice of Christ perdures before God and will never be repeated.

First Reading

The story is one of the prophetic "wonder stories" connected with the figures of Elijah and Elisha. It occurs during a time of drought in Israel which, considering the locale of the incident in Zarephath, had afflicted neighboring Phoenicia as well. As a prophetic "miracle" story, its main point is to illustrate Yahweh's providential care of the prophet and his provider in a moment of great need, much as in the case of the raven-feeding in the preceding narrative (1 Kgs 17:1 - 6). The dire circumstances of the widow are intended to enhance the miraculous character of the provisions. Her charitable motivation in giving from the little she had is a secondary feature of the story.

The fact that Yahweh is directing the course of events appears in the repeated use of God's "word" (vv8, 16) or Elijah's "word" (v15), as they appear in the Hebrew text, and the clear promise of replenished flour and oil by God's decree (v14). The widow's willingness to offer water (v10) is dampened by the prophet's added request for food (v11). The widow's circumstances (v12) throw into relief the need of divine intervention to prevent her starvation and that of her son. The woman, a Gentile non-believer, carries out the directives of the prophet in blind faith as she provides a cake from the last of her flour and oil. Her observance of the Lord's word results in the fulfillment of the word of promise, a supply of food for the remainder of the drought (vv15ff).

This widow enters Jesus' teaching as an example of God's outreach to the Gentiles (Lk 4:26).

Responsorial Psalm   Ps 146

This hymn extols God as Creator (vv1 - 6) and liberator (vv7 - 10). Only the second part appears in today's liturgy with its appropriate note of God's faithfulness to the poor and needy. The Lord will champion the cause of those who are faithful. This is especially true for those who have no access to human resources: captives, the oppressed, aliens, and the two biblical categories repeatedly mentioned: widows and orphans (vv7ff). The widow appears three times in this Sunday's liturgy. Her condition was singular; in the absence of the male provider, she was especially deprived and thus dependent on society. "The wicked he thwarts" (v9) is an example of antithetical parallelism, contrasting poetically Yahweh's providence with punishment (Ps 1:6). Recognition of the eternal reign of Yahweh as king closes the psalm (v10).

Second Reading

The author of Hebrews consistently views the priesthood and sacrifice of Jesus against the background of its Jewish forerunners. In today's passage the superiority of the offering of Christ lies in its non-repetitive character. At a determined historical moment, Christ the priest entered the heavenly eternal sanctuary (v24). This was in no way a mere reproduction of the Jerusalem sanctuary; it belongs wholly to the realm of God. There Christ continues to offer on behalf of humanity the one sacrifice of Calvary, now transcendent in character (7:25; Rom 8:34).

The author then considers the way in which this sacrifice differs from the annual Day of Atonement ritual, also offered in expiation for sin. First, Christ's is not a sacrifice repeated on a regular basis. If such were the case, he would have had to perform this priestly service from the beginning, since it is offered for all people and all ages (vv25f). In fact he has appeared only once. That one sacrifice, now ever present to the Father, satisfies for all sin past and present. Second, the blood offered is not that of an animal but that of the high priest himself, Jesus, God's Son (v25). *End of the ages* (v26): the time of Jesus, the final era of redemption, to be closed with the parousia. Here the author clearly moves away from the tiered philosophical universe, with which he is conversant, to the traditional Jewish linear view of history.

Christ' sacrifice is as definitive as death itself (vv27f). Once experienced, death can never be repeated. Just as death is the door to judgment, never to be passed through twice, so Jesus' sacrifice, now complete, remains only to be applied in its' effects, in bringing final deliverance to its beneficiaries. *Christ takes away the sins of many* (v28): The allusion is to the servant of Yahweh in Isaiah 53:12. The "many" is the equivalent of "all" (Mk 14:24).

Third Reading

The gospel passage contrasts a false religious spirit (vv38ff) and a true one (vv41 - 44). At this point in Mark's gospel, Jesus' split with the scribes, the authorities in Jewish law, and the Jewish religious leaders in general is complete. At this juncture, Jesus no longer speaks of their teaching but limits his comments to their conduct. The immediately preceding verse (12:37) spoke of the "crowd's" enthusiastic response to Jesus, thus separating the Jewish people from their leaders.

The scribes are guilty of pride, privilege-seeking, and ostentation (vv38f). Worse still, they betray their trusteeship of widows' property with unreasonable demands of shares or money (v40). Their prayerful attitudes, for the sake of impression, are nothing more than hypocrisy. As in Matthew, this passage in Mark reflects not only Jesus' difficulties but also the growing impasse between Jewish leaders and the church at the time of the gospel's composition.

The mention of "widows" (v40) may have suggested the addition of the story of the poor woman's offering at this point. But even more important, it fits well as a contrast to the preceding in illustrating the true faith response so lacking among the Jewish authorities. Jesus himself observes the widow (v41) and later summons his disciples for the "teaching" moment (v43). The coins which she offers (Gr: *lepla*) were the smallest in circulation; their market value was minimal (v42). The offering of two insinuates that she could have kept one for herself.

Jesus' statement that hers was the major contribution requires explanation (vv43f). Others gave with little or no sense of sacrifice. Even after their donations, their needs would be amply met. But the widow deprived herself and felt the pain in giving from the little that she had. Hers was the true spirit of generosity and religious dedication.

The story of the "widow's mite" is not just an interesting insight into Jewish Palestinian life. It is really the type of generosity that we meet day after day. It is humbling to think of how people with limited resources and heavy financial responsibilities sacrifice themselves for others, whether at home or in foreign lands. And it is done with grace and a smile. Many times, writing a check is the easiest way to exercise charity. Certainly it is good in itself and not to be disdained. But so often a duty discharged through donation is forgotten ten minutes after it is done. There are people for whom it is much more important to give of their time than their money. Time is costly; we feel the pinch.

But there are always those little people who preach the best homilies by their lives. They give of the little they have. They may light a candle for a sick friend, request a mass card for a cause close to their heart, contribute to a food kitchen or a clothing drive. They seek those who are poorer than they at every turn. In northern India, among the Catholic tribals, people contribute to the church in kind. That means an egg or some rice in the Sunday collection. It comes from poverty but it comes with love. It is today's gospel come to life.

Christ is our priest. There was a time when the Catholic priest was termed "another Christ." It was never too felicitous a title and is not heard much anymore. There can never be another Christ, any more than there can ever be another sacrifice. The Catholic priest simply mirrors the eternal high priest making that one lasting sacrifice present to us in a tangible, sacramental way. The greatness of the mass is that it unites us with that one heavenly sacrifice which continues through the ages and throughout the world. Human beings and human signs make all of this possible. But we can't get lost in the human. The whole experiences of our faith ultimately leads to a single reality: the one eternal God and the Son whom he has sent.

Homiletic and Catechetical Helps

1. Sacrificial giving and its meaning in our life.

2. The prophet as God's mouthpiece.

3. Attitudes: difference between the scribes and the poor widow.

3. The meaning of trust in God.

4. Contributions to the church: significance.

5. Why is Christ's sacrifice not able to be repeated?

6. Relate the mass to Christ's one sacrifice.

7. Relate the priesthood to Christ the one priest.

THIRTY-SECOND SUNDAY OF THE YEAR
Year C

Readings

2 Mac 7:1 - 2, 9 - 14
2 Thes 2:16 - 3:5
Lk 20:27 - 38

Theme: Imaging Life After Death

A clear belief in the afterlife was a late development in Israel. Today's reading from the second book of Maccabees, written in the second century before Christ, finds this belief placed in strong relief. Jesus' words to the Sadducees in today's gospel points up the difficulty involved in imaging our future life on the basis of our present life experience. Paul today speaks of the word of God as active and dynamic, capable of producing a continued growth in virtue if cultivated and nurtured.

First Reading

The earliest clear afterlife belief appears in the second century book of Daniel (12:2) as a promise of resurrection. Both Daniel and Maccabees come from a period of intense persecution of the Jews by the Seleucid kings at this same moment of history with the attempted Hellenization of Palestine. The story of the mother and her seven martyred sons may be authentic historical recollection, even though lacking historical and geographical specificity, or it may have been one of the Jewish martyr legends which were prominent well into the Christian era. Historical or not, the story is meant to inspire and remains an important theological statement. It should be noted that this book of the Bible does not appear in the Palestinian canon and thus is not recognized as canonical by Protestants or Jews. Catholic tradition, however, has always upheld its inspired character.

The Seleucids waged incessant war on Jewish belief and practice. Accounts like this story of the faith-filled family offered examples of heroism to the people and served as a source of inspiration. Today's reading is an excerpt from the story, which is found in its entirety in chapter 7.

Neither the family nor the king are identified, with the latter depicted as the actual torturer without intermediaries (v1). The test of the sons' faith lies in their observance of the Jewish dietary laws, an area chosen by the Seleucids to undermine and destroy religious observance. All of the sons resist to the end, with each in turn professing his faith before death in a strong theological statement.

The first of the sons to speak argues that death is preferable to disregard of the Torah (v2). By this point in history, the Jews could be clearly identified as "the people of the book"; the law was sacrosanct and complete observance of its dictates, was a serious matter of conscience. The next brother clearly attests to future life sanctions in the resurrection of the dead (v9) The third emphasizes the same belief in a statement that suffers from literalism. The dismembered body, it is hoped, will be re-membered (v11) The fourth son affirms resurrection for the just but not for the evildoers (v14). A general resurrection does not appear at this early stage of after-life development. There is little speculation about the future of the wicked other than to exclude them from the full-life implications of resurrection. Future life in the true sense of the word is reserved for the just. It is important to note that the title to immortality is based on righteousness, not on the imperishable nature of the soul. The willingness of all the sons to endure torture and death hinges on their belief in subsequent resurrection.

Responsorial Psalm   Ps 17

In this lament the psalmist is sorely tried, probably as the result of unjust accusation (v1). He protests his innocence and calls upon Yahweh for vindication (vv5f). He is confident that his fidelity will eventually lead him to temple worship of Yahweh (v15). *On waking* (v15): probably an indication of a new meeting with God in temple worship after present difficulties are resolved. To see this as an after-life meeting exceeds the evidence in terms of the psalm's date before the emergence of this belief and the ambiguous character of the verse itself.

Second Reading

Disturbances within the Thessalonian community have evidently led to a certain measure of fear and instability (2:1f). Paul now prays for a strengthening of the people among whom he has labored (v17; 3:3). Christ's equality with the Father is unequivocally expressed in the prayer directed to both (v16). *Good hope* (v16): directed toward the parousia (1:10) and made possible by grace, i.e. the enlightening presence of the Spirit. This future hope serves as a solid platform for present conduct and strong confidence (v17).

Paul sees himself as a servant of God's word to be proclaimed unwaveringly even in the face of opposition (3:2; Eph 6:19; Col 4:3). He asks for prayer that this word may spread and take firm root in human hearts. The lived acceptance of the gospel redounds to the glory of the word itself as well as its author (3:1).

Although evil opposes the gospel and its adherents, something which Paul himself is experiencing, it is the Lord's fidelity that will see them through moments of weakness and preserve them safe from harm (3:2f; 2 Tim 2:13) For his part, Paul is convinced that his preaching and teaching among them continues to bear fruit (3:4). *Love of God...endurance of Christ* (3:5): The genitives could be subjective, i.e. God's love for them and Christ's endurance for them, or objective, i.e. their love for God and their endurance for Christ. The context's emphasis on God's action for the people (2:13, 16) seems to give the subjective genitive the edge; thus their attention is to be focused on the extent of God's love for them and Christ's endurance on their behalf.

Third Reading

Holding only to the Pentateuch, the priestly Sadducees adhered to the letter of the law and refused to give weight to oral tradition. This meant that a doctrine such as the resurrection was excluded (v27). The case presented to Jesus, border-ing, as it does, on the absurd, implies an attitude of ridicule and is meant to press Jesus on the after-life issue (vv28 - 33). The responsibility of a man to marry his deceased brother's widow and bear progeny to his name is Pentateuchal teaching (Deut 25:5 - 10) and therefore appropriately cited by the Sadducees.

The response of Jesus moves the discussion to a distinctly dif-ferent level (vv34ff). To translate marriage in the present life into resurrection terms is impossible; the same is true of any legislation regulating the married state. The transformation of the resurrected body from matter to spirit is so total that earth-ly considerations no longer have meaning (1 Cor 15:42ff). There is a point of comparison with the angels (v36a) whose non-corporeality excludes gender differences, pairing and prog-eny. Those who rise are no longer human children but children of God (v36b).

Jesus then directs the discussion to the question of resurrec-tion itself (vv37ff). In citing Yahweh's relationship to the three patriarchs (Ex 3:6), he centers his argument on that part of the scriptures which the Sadducees accept, in stating that only life would continue to bind the patriarchs to God after their death. He who is the source of all life remains the cause of resurrected life. As he upholds resurrection teaching, Jesus at the same time challenges a type of thinking that would model future life on the present and fail to appreciate the transformation involved in the passage to a new existence.

Belief in life after death is inextricably woven into the fabric of Christian faith. Christian practice, liturgy, private prayer–all center on the belief that those who have preceded us in death continue to live. A large measure of the sanction surrounding our conduct centers on the after-life belief. And yet when we begin to describe what lies before us we become more than a little tongue-tied. Years ago a prominent actor who was largely agnostic was asked if he believed in the afterlife. "I can't say," he answered, "but I'm intrigued by the idea." So is the believer. Trying to depict the future affords us little more than approxi-mating images. The scriptures use apocalytpic symbols and figures. Some will image heaven in terms of that breathtaking view of the Alps or an eternal hearing of Mahler's Second Symphony or Mozart's Coronation Mass. For others it is the beauty of a lasting friendship.

What we do know about our future life with God is that it is not only vastly superior to the present life, it is also vastly different. Discussion about that difference is not particularly fruitful. Paul himself found discussion of the resurrected body of little profit. It is as different from the present body, he said, as the full grown plant is from the seed that produces it.

The central joy of heaven is life in and with God with no fear of loss. There is the further belief, reflected in 2 Thessalonians, that we will be reunited with those who have gone before us. And while it may be said that there is considerable discussion about what it will be like, there is no discussion about the basic fact. Eternal life is a gospel given, a New Testament datum. Yes, there are moments when many of us have doubts. And there is nothing unusual about that. With Paul we simply pray to be strengthened, with the firm conviction that the God who is faithful will bring us home.

Homiletic and Catechetical Helps

1. Roots of the Christian belief in life after death.

2. Understanding death, judgment, heaven, and hell.

3. Speaking about eternal life.

4. Martyrdom for the faith: classical and contemporary examples.

5. The communion of saints.

6. Understanding the rite of Christian burial.

7. Burial and cremation.

8. The child's understanding of death and eternal life.

9. Heavy crosses in the light of immortality.

THIRTY-THIRD SUNDAY OF THE YEAR
Year A

Readings

Prov 31:10 - 13, 19 - 20, 30 - 31
1 Thes 5:1 - 6
Mt 25:14 - 30

Theme: An Industrious Spirit

Two interesting but contrasting figures appear in today's readings. Proverbs' wife and mother, with all of her domestic duties, finds time to develop her personal skills and to dedicate herself to the needs of others. In Matthew's parable of the talents, the rejected servant is totally devoid of an enterprising spirit. We are told today that the fruitful use of God's gifts enter into the final assessment of our lives. In the second reading, Paul urges vigilance in the light of the uncertainty of the time of the parousia.

First Reading

Taken from the final chapter of Proverbs, the reading sings the praises of the worthy wife. It is part of an alphabetic poem (each verse beginning with the successive letter of the Hebrew alphabet). Proverbs places considerable emphasis on the feminine in its personification of wisdom (Prov 1:20 - 32; c. 8); it is therefore appropriate that the book's final chapter should highlight the very practical wisdom of a wife and mother.

The value of the worthy wife is inestimable. The comparison with precious stones appears also when wisdom is spoken of (3:14; 8:11), with the woman's worth illustrated in a variety of ways. She brings her husband success and not misfortune (v12), success in Hebrew terms measured along the lines of material prosperity. Even though she has adequate domestic help (vv15, 21), she applies herself industriously to personal skills of spinning, weaving, and sewing (vv13, 19). She is marked by compassion and generosity for the poor. These are the lasting qualities of the true wife, far superior to a vanishing physical attractiveness (v30). *Fear of the Lord* (v30): A reverential respect for God and his sovereignty is the beginning of all wisdom (1:7). Finally the woman is extolled by her acquaintances at the city gates, the place of public assembly for commerce, transactions, and general communication. It is also the place where Wisdom makes her plea (1:21).

It is true that the woman of Proverbs comes out of a Hebrew culture, with her value largely defined in terms of function as wife and mother. Nonetheless the portrait remains an unusual one. When the chapter is read as a whole and not in excerpted form, the woman is seen as going beyond her expected role in enterprising business ventures and real estate investments (vv16, 18, 24). For its time it is a progressive view of the woman's role in home and society. She is a woman whose gifts are well employed for the good of the family and other members of her community.

Responsorial Psalm   Ps 128

This sapiential psalm again makes reference to the blessing of a worthy wife (v3) in extolling the virtues of family life in general. The fear of Yahweh is the psalm's centerpiece (v1). The person's work will be blessed in productivity (v2); his many children will surround him at table like young shoots at the base of the olive tree (v3; Ps 127:3). May Yahweh's blessing upon Jerusalem be extended to the family so that city and family alike may share comparable joy in perpetuity (vv5f).

Second Reading

The anticipation of the Lord's return is pivotal to an understanding of the letters to Thessalonica. In the present letter Paul has already considered the lot of those Christians who die before the parousia (4:13 - 18); in today's reading he speaks of the moral posture of those who are alive. He insists on the uncertainty of the time of Christ's return and the need for constant vigilance.

Speculation about the end time was not lacking in either Jewish or Christian circles. Paul insists that much of this is idle since it will come at a totally unexpected time (vv1f). *Day of the Lord* (v2): an expression for the final period of history, dating from early prophetic times (Am 5:18). The "Lord" originally referred to Yahweh; in the Pauline literature it refers to Christ (Phil 1:10; 2 Cor 1:14). Two similes are used to describe the suddenness of the end: the thief in the night (v2) and the woman in labor (v3). The former is used by Jesus in the gospels (Mt 24:43f; Lk 12:39f) and strikes the note of unexpectedness, not stealth. The woman in labor adds the note of inevitability or no escape. In fact, the end may be expected at a time of receding expectation and lack of vigilance (v3). This teaching of Paul echoes clearly that of Jesus (Mt 24:36 - 45; Lk 12:35 - 40).

The theme of light and darkness (vv4 - 6) appears in traditional Jewish apocalyptic as well as in the New Testament. In the Dead Sea Scrolls, the final battle is a war between the "sons of light" and the "sons of darkness" (1QS 3:13 - 14). Mention of the thief's arrival at night (vv2, 4) suggests the light-darkness image. The Christians are free of fear since, as children of the day (light), night plays no part in their life. Light, marked by openness and vision, aptly describes the Lord's reign. The works produced in light are visible to all. Darkness, on the other hand, symbolizes the reign of evil; its works are hidden and shameful; its conduct is clandestine. Before baptism Christians lived in darkness but now they have been brought to light, the reign of Christ (Eph 5:8 - 14; Col 1:13f). The light that is theirs gives their conduct a transparency suited to moral uprightness. On the day of the Lord they will have nothing to fear.

Third Reading

The context of the Matthean parable of the talents deals with the influence of the expected return of Christ on Christian conduct. Not only is improper conduct to be avoided (24:46 - 51) and vigilance to be observed (25:1 - 13), but, as today's parable indicates, a steady growth in virtue is also a hallmark of discipleship. The story comes from the Q source; the nucleus of its teaching is found in Mark (13:34), but Matthew and Luke are evidently drawing on a more expanded version. During the wealthy man's absence from home, he wants his capital to be productive. Three of his servants are allotted a determined amount to invest in his absence (vv14f). *Talents* (v15): This was the largest unit of currency known at the time. Its value varied according to the metal's value (gold, silver or copper). Luke has a more modest and realistic sum (Lk 19:13). The English word "talent," identified with giftedness, is derived from this parable where the two ideas are in juxtaposition in v15.

The master's return "after a long time" (v19) alludes to the delay in the expected parousia. He rewards the industrious and enterprising spirit of the two servants who had doubled the amount consigned to them (vv20 - 23). *In small matters* (vv21, 23): only in comparison to the fuller eschatological rank they are to enjoy in God's reign. The praise heaped on the two servants is in sharp contrast with the anger and scorn directed to the negligent servant, who according to the custom of his time saw valuables best protected by burying them (vv25ff). The servant's explanation exhibits little logic. Knowing full well that the master wanted a return with interest (v24), he decides to make no investment at all. The unproductive servant relinquishes his amount to the enterprising servant, is excluded from his position and consigned to oblivion. *Wailing and grinding of teeth* (v30): New Testament expression for the sorrow and distress of condemnation (8:12; 13:42).

The point is clear. Those who build on their baptismal commitment by a steady and active growth in virtue and apostolic zeal will be more than amply rewarded. Those who do nothing with this gift will lose whatever they have in final separation from God's reign (v29). It is the difference between industry and idleness in the Christian life.

At one point in the gospels Jesus reminds us that the children of this world often exhibit a more enterprising spirit than do the children of light. It is enough to note the extent to which manufacturers will go to find markets; athletes, to perfect physical prowess; musicians, to master a musical instrument. While there are many Christians who give of themselves with real dedication, it is also true that many see their faith in terms of Sunday mass attendance and keeping the commandments (more or less). The word of God today sees things quite differently. We are all called to mission, to grow in the grace of God, and to use our talents for good, not just for profit.

It is too easy to say "Let the church do it"–educate our children, prepare them for the sacraments, visit the hospitals, reach the unchurched. But we are all the church. Each of us has gifts of nature and grace which can touch the lives of others. We have to stop burying the talents and be up and doing. Remember the penitential rite at mass. We ask forgiveness for what we have done and–importantly–for what we have failed to do. We are called to be industrious and enterprising.

We are light people and have to be wary of our shadow side. There are aspects of our life about which we are not particularly proud. Let's put night behind us and make our life an "open book." Thefts, homicides, and rapes often occur at night. Darkness provides protection. Faceless people create terror in others. Yet, honesty, candor, and affability are as transparent as the coral on the floor of a limpid body of water. Such people bring us the serenity of a broad tree-lined lane at midday. Perhaps in a cynical age we need reminding that evil doesn't have to win.

Homiletic and Catechetical Helps

1. Examples of an enterprising Christian spirit.

2. The deficiencies in "Sunday morning" Catholicism.

3 Personal reflection: What gifts can I offer the church?

4. Woman's role in home, church, and society.

5. The man's role in home, church, and society.

6. Light and darkness as applied to my conduct.

7. Eliminating evil in my life.

THIRTY-THIRD SUNDAY OF THE YEAR
Year B

Readings

> Dan 12:1 - 3
> Heb 10:11 - 14, 18
> Mk 13:24 - 32

Theme: The Final Word

As the liturgical year draws to a close, the church traditionally has directed our attention to the end of history. The first reading from Daniel and Mark's account of Jesus' end-time discourse address this question from different perspectives. In both cases the scenario centers on God's final word. In the meantime, as the author of Hebrews reminds us, Christ, our high priest in the sanctuary above, continues to intercede for us.

First Reading

Today's reading from Daniel brings to a close the account of final warfare and the downfall of major foes (cc. 10 - 11). This passage is important because it is the first clear statement on final resurrection and eternal life found in the Hebrew scriptures. It is connected with a teaching on eternal sanctions for the just and the wicked. This breakthrough from the second century B.C. finally allows Hebrew thought to come to terms with the problem of retribution within parameters which go beyond the present life.

The picture is an impressive one. "Michael" (v1a) is the angel guardian of Israel, designated the protector of God's people (10:13f; Rev 12:7). Here he effectively delivers the faithful Israel from the tribulation of the final days. The saved are those predestined by Yahweh in virtue of their fidelity (v1b). *The Book* (v1b): the record in which the names of those to be saved are inscribed (Ex 32:32f; Ps 69:29).

The resurrection envisaged is limited to Israelites only. "Many" (v2) may therefore be used in this restrictive sense or be used as a not uncommon substitute for "all." There will be a separation of the faithful from their unfaithful co-religionists. The former shall go forth to "eternal life" (v2b), the literal translation of the Hebrew text; others, to rejection and condemnation. Little is said descriptively of the lot of the rejected at this time in comparison with that of the elect. The state of those who are saved as well as their sages and leaders has the brilliance of the star-filled heavens (v3; Wis 3:7). The passage has broken new ground in seeing a realm beyond, peopled by the holy ones of God.

Responsorial Psalm   Ps 16

The preparation for the Lord's return involves trust and confidence, the theme of this psalm. To express the idea of Yahweh as the sole good of his life, the psalmist uses various metaphors (vv5f). The "cup" is cultic for "destiny"; the "portion," the "measured places," and the "inheritance" are used especially for land or property rights (Jos 18:8, 10). All of this is applied to Yahweh as the psalmist's sole desire. All other goods are excluded.

The psalmist's trust remains unshaken even in the face of death (v10). Loss of life and consignment to Sheol, the shadowy realm of the dead, was a great tragedy for the devout Israelite. There Yahweh was absent and the person forgotten (Ps 88:6f). The speaker, perhaps himself recovering from illness, is confident that he will be saved from this misfortune and be given a new lease on life (v11). The fullness of life is to be found in the worship of Yahweh in the temple ("in your presence ").

Second Reading

Hebrews contrasts Christ's single offering with the daily sacrifices offered by the temple priests (vv11f). Since the author speaks of daily service, he is no longer referring to the annual Day of Atonement ritual, which figures prominently in the letter (c. 9). The sacrifices of the levitical priesthood are seen as ineffectual (vv11f); the single sacrifice of Christ, however, has limitless effectiveness and is non-repeatable (9:24ff).

The standing posture of the priests in their endless work contrasts with the seated posture of Jesus whose work has been realized (vv12f). The picture of Jesus enthroned and waiting for his foes to be finally vanquished directly echoes Psalm 110, a Davidic royal psalm. The sitting position, symbolizing work accomplished, is not at odds with the high priest image which depicts Christ as continually offering his one sacrifice in the eternal "now." The two are complementary, not exclusive. Christ's repose looks to the interim period prior to the parousia during which time the evil forces already doomed are being subdued. At the end his triumph will be complete. Meanwhile his one sacrifice continues to make holy those who appropriate its benefits (v14). With sin now forgiven and ready access to God assured, no further sacrifice is needed (v18).

Third Reading

The eschatological discourse, common to the three synoptics, finds its earliest expression in Mark's gospel, composed in the mid-60s prior to the destruction of the temple. Today's gospel presents only a part of Jesus' discourse. The first part deals with the parousia itself (vv24 - 27), the second with the time of its arrival (vv28 - 32).

Apocalyptic imagery from the prophetic literature is the backdrop for Jesus' presentation. The cosmos, as had been predicted, is profoundly affected by the termination of history (v24; Is 13:10; 34:4; Jl 2:10; 3;4). The ingathering of God's people draws on the oft expressed idea of the return of a dispersed population (Deut 30:4; Is 11:11, 16; Ez 39:27). In the former covenant these final events were presided over by Yahweh; here they are directly related to the dominion of Christ. In Jesus' discourse, the Son of Man is clearly himself (v26). This eschatological figure from the book of Daniel (7:13) is elsewhere applied by Jesus to himself (14:62). In its original setting it individualized the concept of a saved and restored humanity, a notion aptly applied to Jesus in summarizing his person and mission. In its Marcan setting, it complements Jesus' death-resurrection as he returns to conclude his salvific mission with the ingathering of the elect.

When will this occur? It is clear that the Marcan Jesus sees its arrival within the life-span of his first believers. The fig tree in bloom heralds the arrival of summer; so too the events about which Jesus has just spoken (13:1 - 23)—the period of persecution, the destruction of the temple, the time of suffering and tribulation—are prelude to his return in final triumph (vv29 - 31). Jesus has elsewhere spoken of the end time's occurrence within the life-span of his contemporaries (9:1). In conclusion Jesus solemnly attests to the veracity of his statement.

The end is near. On the other hand, its exact time cannot be specified as to month and day. Thus the type of speculation evidenced in some Christian quarters regarding end-time predictions is to be avoided (1 Thes 5:1ff). It is interesting to note that Jesus himself claims ignorance of the time of the parousia; it is knowledge had only by the Father (v32).

Mark's gospel was written shortly before the destruction of the temple. After it was destroyed and the church expanded its horizons, the expectation of an early parousia receded. The fact is that it did not take place as originally expected. The other synoptics attempt to soften the straightforward and clear words of the Marcan Jesus. But it did not occur in their lifetime; in fact, it still stands on the Christian horizon. Its symbolic force retains its significance. Christ's death and resurrection remain the centerpiece of his triumph over evil. That has occurred. It was logical at the time to expect God's final seal on that momentous event. The parousia stands for Jesus as Lord of history, a history which with its linear movement will one day have its end. And it is a history over which Christ himself presides. The final word will be his.

We have very little record of early Christian sentiment regarding Christ's failure to return as expected. Was there widespread dismay or relief? It's hard to say. There was certainly a period of adjustment when the importance of living the Christian life fully in the here and now came to the fore. The basic message still has an important ring. We are all destined to meet the Lord at some time, and preparedness is very much in order.

The important thing about the parousia is the fact that Jesus remains the Lord of history, regardless of when he returns. And the final word will be his. That is easy to forget when the seemingly overwhelming "tides of change" carry us along with an inexorable inner force. How will the abandon with which human life is taken from its inception even to its final stages be halted? When will the injustices inflicted by war and selfishness be unmasked? When will the little people have their day in court? Must things remain the way they are? The answer is in the negative if there be a God to whom we are accountable. The end-time discourse of today's gospel says precisely that. There is a new world order, and it is based on justice and equity. God will ultimately triumph. That is what the second coming means.

Some people may be uneasy with the fact that Christ himself could not pinpoint the end time. There are probably more ways that Christ overcame ignorance and grew in knowledge than we imagine. After all, he was like us in everything except sin. But the human factor only brings Christ closer to us and makes what he had to endure more deeply appreciated. The Jesus of Mark's gospel is closer to us than in the other gospels. It is a gospel that merits a careful reading. For Mark's presenting a Christ who suffers so much of the human, we can only be grateful.

Homiletic and Catechetical Helps

1. Explaining the meaning of the parousia.

2. The human knowledge of Jesus.

3. The eschatological discourse and scriptural inerrancy.

4. Distinguish eschatology, apocalyptic, and parousia.

5. The return of Christ and personal and social accountability.

6. Preparedness and our own meeting with Christ.

7. The single and non-repeated sacrifice of Christ.

THIRTY-THIRD SUNDAY OF THE YEAR
Year C

Readings

Mal 3:19 - 20
2 Thes 3:7 - 12
Lk 21:5 - 19

Theme: Hardship Before the End

Today's short reading from Malachi sees the day of the Lord as a time of reckoning for both the just and the unjust. The Lucan account of the end time deals at considerable length with the interim period before the end. It is to be a period of widespread distress and persecution. Perseverance, however, will be rewarded with ultimate deliverance. For Paul the time before the end is a period of tireless service. His enthusiasm for the gospel does not preclude his emphasizing the importance of certain amenities, such as working for a living.

First Reading

Fire as the end-time's purifying instrument appears earlier in Malachi (3:2f). Here it reduces the wicked to stubble. The "day" (v19) is clearly the "day of the Lord," the time of definitive sanctions with the reward of the good and punishment of the evil. Those faithful to the Lord will experience heat of a different type. The warmth of the sun with its restorative power is a metaphor for deliverance (v20). The sense is one of well-being and health, both signs of divine favor. Sun of justice (v20): the sun as an agent of Yahweh's redemption, probably related to the image of the pagan winged sun god. The day of the Lord, then, appears clearly as a day of sanctions, an expression of divine justice.

Responsorial Psalm   Ps 98

This psalm of Yahweh's enthronement betrays its liturgical setting with its musical instruments and vocalization (vv5f).

While it is enacted within the temple with Yahweh ceremoniously installed, its symbolism comes to the fore in a way appropriate for this Sunday's liturgy: Yahweh enters upon the human scene (his coming) to administer justice and equity (v9). The chant breaks out of the confines of the temple to embrace all of the earth. Poetic language has both the watery depths (sea, rivers) and the lofty peaks (world, mountains) join in liturgical celebration (vv7f).

Second Reading

Paul dissociates himself from a spirit of laziness or idleness, whether due to a misguided expectation of the imminent end (2:2) or simple inertia. Again Paul sees the importance of his not only preaching but modeling the gospel. For this reason he can ask for imitation of his conduct (v7; Phil 3:17). Paul was never a burden to the community in exercising his ministry among them. He provided for his needs (v8; 1 Thes 2:9). In recognizing the right that the missionary had to local support (v9; Mt 10;10f; 1 Cor 9), Paul had decided to forego such assistance to give an example of hard work, industry, and self support. The apostle reiterates a former admonition to shame the idle Christian (v10; 1 Thes 4:11). A "do nothing" spirit unfortunately has more than sufficient time to be involved in the affairs of others (v11). Paul earnestly exhorts the "spongers" to get to work (v12).

Third Reading

When Luke writes his gospel in the latter part of the first century, the temple has already been destroyed and Jerusalem sacked. As he includes Jesus' end-time discourse, largely dependent on Mark, Luke makes some important alterations. While he speaks of the cosmic upheaval that will mark the end, which is still proximate, even if less urgent, he separates that from preceding events, now situated much more in a distinctly historical setting. The period of persecution and the destruction of the temple presage the end, but they are presented as lived events with no eschatological overtones. Today's gospel, then, combines both the language of the actual experience and that of apocalyptic. In using the ambiguous expression "these things" (Gr: *tauta*), applicable to both periods, Luke moves back and forth between present and future events.

Initially Jesus gives an oracular statement to the people about the imminent destruction of the temple (vv5f). His respondents then ask when "all these things" will happen (v7). This marks a shift from the temple question to the broader area of eschatology. Jesus distinguishes between events which precede the end and the end itself. He cautions against heeding the voices of those who are too prone to read the "signs of the times" and announce the end (v8). He then de-eschatologizes events already experienced, such as wars and uprisings (v9). While no mention is made of the Roman sack of Jerusalem, it is by no means excluded (21:20 - 24). These things will preface the end but are distinct from it.

Jesus then returns to the traditional description of the end time in cosmic terms (vv10f). Universal warfare and grave disturbances of nature will mark the end. In the meantime, in keeping with Luke's general emphasis in his gospel, the day to day life of the church must be addressed. Again Luke historicizes. A major feature of the contemporary experience was the persecution to which Christians were being subjected (vv12 - 19). They were outlawed by the Jews (Jn 16:2) and tried before civil authorities. *Kings and governors* (v12): a probable reference to Paul's personal experience as told in Luke's Acts of the Apostles (cc. 24 - 26). At the appropriate time, Christians are assured of the ability to speak in their own defense (vv13ff; Acts 6:10). Severe opposition will stem from their own families because of their conversion (12:52f). Even though they are faced with persecution and even death (vv16f), their lives will ultimately be saved (v19). Physical death is not be equated with loss of life; indeed, it is the door to fuller life. In the present moment of trial, disciples are called to that endurance which characterized the comportment of Christ himself (2 Thes 3:5).

Luke is as much concerned with the Christian interim as he is with Christ's return. The church of his era was not having an easy time. A speedy deliverance was not at hand; a fair share of cross-bearing had to come first. Can we identify with those early times? Persecution today comes in different forms, from ridicule to total indifference. Convictions can stand in the way of promotion. Strong beliefs can be termed quaint or outmoded. Families are still divided over religious belief. And yes, we still have occasional millenarians who tell us the day and the hour when the end will come.

In one way or another we suffer for what we believe–perhaps in upholding honesty in business when "cutting corners" has become the fashion, or in maintaining the line in the children's formation in a permissive environment. It may be a march in opposition to abortion or the death penalty, or opposing discrimination or harassment because of sexual orientation. To take a stand on principle today is to invite opposition, even invective. The message of today's liturgy is to stand firm with an unshaken faith.

It was once said that it was far more important for Christians "to be" than "to do." This was directed against an excessive Christian activism and had a measure of truth. A wag's response would be: If everyone "is" and nobody "does," then who provides the bread? Paul believed in hard work. He plied his own trade and was a tireless missionary. We all have to be providers as well as witnesses. Or, better still, we can witness by providing. Let's not forget that there is something distinctly Christian about being tired at the end of the day. Christ could sleep in a boat on stormy waters. Sleep as the result of serving people and the reign of God is blessed repose.

Homiletic and Catechetical Helps

1. Suffering for Christian principle in today's world.

2. Some modern issues calling for a Christian stand.

3. The virtue of perseverance.

4. The justice of God: reward and punishment.

5. The Christian work ethic.

6. The dangers of laziness and idleness.

7. Family members working for the family good.

8. Volunteer work and Christian responsibility.

CHRIST THE KING
Year A

Readings

Ez 34:11 - 12, 15 - 17
1 Cor 15:20 - 26, 28
Mt 25:31 - 46

Theme: The Shepherd King

On the last Sunday of the liturgical year, the church celebrates the universal sovereignty of Christ. Equally emphasized is the fact that his is a kingship different from that of any other. Like Yahweh the shepherd in the Ezekiel reading, Christ is the shepherd and provider of his people. He will evaluate human conduct in the final judgment on the basis of our willingness to provide providential care for others. Today's gospel is one of the most celebrated passages in the New Testament. As Paul today explains to the Corinthians, Christ's is a reign which will one day come to an end.

First Reading

Yahweh viewed as a shepherd in the thought of a largely pastoral and agricultural society is not exceptional (Is 40:11; Jer 31:10; Jn 10:1 - 18). The context of today's reading from Ezekiel is one of reproach for the leaders of Israel (34:1 - 10), for they have lived off the sheep without responding to their needs. They provided no care for those who remained close and left those who strayed to their own resources. With their people in great danger, the religious leaders provided for themselves; even when many people were lost, there was no noticeable difference in their leaders' comportment.

Now Yahweh himself will assume the role of shepherd (v11). The restoration of the exiled Jews to their homeland is alluded to in the image of the shepherd's ingathering (vv12, 13f). Various categories of deprivation are listed: the lost, the wandering, the wounded, the ill, the needs of all of whom will be addressed (vv15f). *The sleek and the strong* (v16): The reference ill-fits the thrust of the verse with its emphasis on the needy and may well be a later addition. The point is that the evildoers will be the recipients of severe judgment just as the needy are the recipients of compassion. The final verse (v17) actually opens a new section on the shepherd as judge (34:17 - 24). The emphasis on Yahweh's compassion is balanced with this treatment of his justice. In separating the different species, the shepherd exercises an important function; here it becomes a metaphor for separating the good from the wicked. This passage has influenced the final judgment scene of today's gospel.

Responsorial Psalm   Ps 23

Today's liturgical theme of Christ the shepherd appropriately includes Psalm 23. For a commentary on the psalm, the reader is referred to the Twenty-Eighth Sunday of Year A.

Second Reading

Christ's reign will last until his mission is accomplished and all the forces contrary to God are subdued. In today's reading from 1 Corinthians, Paul speaks of the final resurrection of the just (vv20 - 23) and the subjection of all the forces of evil to the sovereignty of God (vv24ff, 28). The three Pauline personifications—Christ, Adam, and death—reappear here as the *dramatis personae* (vv20, 22, 26; Rom 5:12 - 20). Christians are bonded with each of these: with Adam in the order of nature, with Christ in grace, and with death in nature and grace.

In his resurrection, Christ rises as the prototype of all those united with him in the Spirit. *Firstfruits* (v20): the offering of the first harvest fruits to God symbolized the offering of the whole. Thus Christ stands for all of his followers. By reason of their union with Adam, all humans are affected by his sin and its consequences (Rom 5:12ff), so too those bound to Christ will share in his victory over death at the time of his coming (v22, Rom 5:18). This will follow the sequence which Paul has elsewhere described: Christ, then those who have died, and those alive at his coming (v23; 1 Thes 4:15ff).

Following this eschatological moment, both history itself and the story of salvation will come to an end. Paul, at this point, places God the Father in the ascendency (v24). First, Christ vanquishes all sinful opposition. *Sovereignty, authority, power* (v24): personifications derived from the current mythology and mystery cults signifying forces opposed to world and human order. Christ must reign until total subjection is complete, here expressed in the language of the psalms (vv25, 27; Ps 110:1; 8:7).

Secondly, death is the final enemy to perish (v26). Once resurrection is complete, death will be no more. Finally, the only one exempt from this universal subjection is God himself (v28). It is the Father who has placed everything in Christ's hands in giving him his salvific mission and therefore stands above the Son. Once Christ's redemptive mission is accomplished by his saving death and resurrection, his task will then be terminated. The kingdom will be turned back to the Father (v24), with Christ and his followers in a subordinate position as God alone permeates the whole of creation (v28). Mediation of any sort will no longer be needed.

Third Reading

In Matthew, this impressive picture of the final judgment brings Jesus' public ministry to a close. In the immediately preceding context much had been said about the need for preparedness and vigilance (cc. 24 - 25); here attention is centered on what alertness means in practice. The judgment is found only in Matthew and reflects important features of Matthean teaching: the Son of Man (24:30, 37, 39), separation of the good from the wicked (24:36 - 43, 47 - 50), the Christian life expressed in good works (cc. 5 - 7). The account is clearly universal in scope with Christ as king (v34), Son of Man (v31), and Lord (v37). Son of Man derives from the eschatological figure who ushers in the final age in Daniel (7:13). In its embrace of all peoples, the broad imagery of the judgment goes beyond the customary gospel categories, but the Matthean Jesus indicates that the end will come only after the gospel has been preached to the ends of the earth (28:19f).

The separation of the costlier sheep from the less valuable "kids" (v32) reflects the Palestinian sort which came at day's end after the mixed flock had grazed together during the day. It is also an echo of the Yahweh-judge imagery found in today's first reading from Ezekiel (34:17). The just are called to the "reign of God" (v34), a life of permanent unending joy. Although Christ presides as judge, he is simply executing the plan of the Father (v34). The basis of acceptance is responsiveness to the evangelical precept of love . The judgment (vv34ff) is not based on sinful versus non-sinful conduct or a decalogue morality but rather on the extent to which the authentic good of others has been pursued. The precept of love of God and neighbor (22:37ff) are blended in such wise that love of neighbor becomes love of God.

The six categories of deprived people have become enshrined in Christian tradition in the corporal works of mercy; it is a significant and timeless summary of human suffering. The climactic moment of the scene comes with the expression of the motive for outreach to the needy: Christ is identified with them (v40). The deprived are first called "brothers" (v40) and later "these least ones" (v45). To limit Christ's teaching on outreach to Christians only on the basis of "brothers" fails to take count of the broader use of the term in Matthew (5:22ff, 47; 7:3ff) and the universal setting of the final judgment itself. Christ here identifies with all the underprivileged of the earth.

In Christ's judgment of the unjust, the entire scene is repeated (vv41 - 46), an expression of the parity demanded by a covenantal theology. Both sides are evenly paired and contrasted, even at the cost of repetition. The lot of those who do not show concern is consignment to eternal condemnation. The severity of the judgment highlights the importance of the teaching. Preparedness for the Lord's return means an active pursuit of virtue in seeing the face of Jesus in the most forsaken members of society.

The powerful last judgment scene in today's liturgy elicits a great deal of thought. We wonder what this means for us personally. On what basis will we be judged? Many of the things that most worry us go unmentioned in Matthew 25. And yet we should not be surprised that love for the poor takes first place. The Hebrew scriptures depict Yahweh as shepherd repeatedly. The posture of Jesus in his earthly ministry is so eminently pastoral. He is always moving toward the outcasts of society. They appear often in his parables. So it is little wonder that this sense of outreach is what he will first look for in his followers. The church has a long history of concern for the neediest. Most religious congregations owe their existence to the poor and emarginated. Redemption hinges on an open heart. Salvation is as close as the nearest soup kitchen, shelter for the homeless, city jail, even the park bench, or that broken person on the block who needs my love–now and not tomorrow.

We all learned that Christ is the Father's equal. But how often do we think of Christ as a window to God? Even Christ, who is so pivotal to our lives and whose name we bear with honor, points beyond. Christ will ultimately hand us back to that Father whom he loved and obeyed with such trust during his earthly sojourn. Our final destiny is to live in a wholly new way which remains unspoken and undescribed. We try so hard to concretize our faith. But some things are better left unspoken. We do know that God wants us for himself. That is why he gave us his Son.

Homiletic and Catechetical Helps

1. The meaning of the final judgment: image and reality.

2. The great commandment and the final judgment.

3. The judgment in Matthew 25: its application today.

4. The corporal works of mercy.

5. The meaning of a shepherd-king.

6. The reign of Christ and its termination.

7. Explaining that God will be "all in all."

8. Our relationship to Christ, Adam, and death.

CHRIST THE KING
Year B

Readings

Dan 7:13 - 14
Rev 1:5 - 8
Jn 18:33 - 37

Theme: *Kingship of a Different Kind*

The Son of Man figure in Daniel, whose dominion is perpetual and whose leadership is indestructible, came to life anew in the New Testament presentation of Christ. The Johannine Jesus is questioned about his royal claims. While not denying his kingship, he indicates that it cannot be defined in Pilate's terms. In Revelation, Christ returns as sovereign at the end of history, a king who brings salvation to his people.

First Reading

This celebrated passage from Daniel gave rise to one of the titles most frequently applied to Jesus: the Son of Man. The figure appears in the prophet's apocalyptic vision in direct contrast to the four beasts that arise out of the sea, described earlier in the same chapter (7:1 - 9). Each of the beasts represents a well-known historical empire, presented as opponents of the reign of God. The "Son of Man" is also symbolic. He is in the forefront of the appearance of God's reign; he comes "on the clouds of heaven," figurative for the celestial realm of Yahweh (Ps 18:10f; 68:5). He is the symbolic representative of the new people of God, the saved or the elect, who are to receive dominion over the earth (7:18). *The Ancient One* (v13): Yahweh depicted as old, expressing his eternal nature (7:9). The Son of Man has a sovereign authority which is universal and perpetual. The collective understanding of the Son of Man becomes individuated in Christ, who may himself have appropriated the title.

Certainly, the New Testament authors use it extensively as a Christological title.

Responsorial Psalm   Ps 93

The psalm celebrates Yahweh as king and is possibly related to a feast ritualizing his enthronement after overcoming the powers of chaos. Yahweh is acclaimed as king and seen as adorned with beauty and power (v1). The stability of his reign is a dominant motif of the psalm. The poetic re-enactment of the king's subduing the watery depths leads to an outcome of firmness and security (vv2f). Stability reaches to the throne of God and is reflected in his lasting decrees (vv2, 5a). The temple where the king's power and wisdom are celebrated shares in his glory as well (v5b).

Second Reading

The imagery of Revelation, the Bible's final book, owes a great deal to the book of Daniel. Both God (Daniel's Ancient One) and the Son of Man, arriving on the clouds of heaven, from today's first reading, appear once again, with the latter now clearly identified as Christ. Today's passage is drawn from the author's salutation, in the name of the Father and his Son, to the seven churches, to which the book is addressed. Christ is described (v5) as a "faithful witness" (Gr: *martos*), one who testifies to God's truth even to the point of death, "firstborn of the dead," the first of many followers to triumph over death in a resurrected life (1 Cor 15:20 - 23), and "ruler of kings," the one who receives the "obedience of faith" as sovereign Lord (Rom 16:26; 1 Cor 15:25). Christ has come to his lordship through his love manifest in freeing humankind from sin (Is 40:2; Gal 2:20; Rom 5:6ff). *Kingdom, priests for God* (v6): The expression is a free adaptation of Exodus 19:6, "a kingdom of priests." In Revelation, the sense is that Christians by reason of their consecration and unique relationship to God serve as mediators between God and the world (5:10). A doxology closes the salutation (v6).

The majestic return of Christ, based on the apocalyptic scene in Daniel (7:13), presents Christ in glory visible to all, both his opponents who brought him to death as well as the world of the nations. As the lamb who was slain (5:6), his glory will not conceal the tragic event of his death (v7). *Alpha and Omega* (v8): the words of the Father. The first and last letters of the Greek alphabet express the eternity of God, the one who initiates history and brings it to a conclusion (v8; 1:17; 21:6).

Third Reading

The appearance of Jesus before Pilate, reported in the synoptics as well, becomes an important theological statement in John. This centers around the notion of kingship as applied to Jesus. Pilate's question (v33) picks up on the accusations of the Jewish authorities and the charges of political insurrection. Jesus' answer implies that he knows the source of the accusation (v34). Pilate's response carries a cynical note, an indication of his own bias against the people over whom he exercises political authority (v35). In answer to the accusation brought against him by the Jews, Jesus states that the kingship which is his is of a different order. It looks to an allegiance of the heart and a spiritual sovereignty which is in no way competitive with earthly power. He is totally devoid of militant adherents who could defend him in his hour of need (v36; 8:23).

The fact that Jesus insinuates some kind of kingship allows Pilate to reintroduce his question (v37). Jesus answers obliquely, giving at the same time an insight into the nature of the reign of God. Jesus has come to reveal the Father and his plan of salvation, the supreme truth (14:6). Those open to the truth hear the word of Jesus and accept it. In so doing they submit to the truth of God and become part of Jesus' dominion or kingdom. This interior adherence to Jesus in faith is unrelated to the political accusations made against him, to which Pilate seemingly acquiesces. Jesus' kingdom is of a different and higher order.

The Johannine Jesus when engaged in human conversation appears disengaged and somehow detached from what swirls about him. He is unlike the deeply involved, even thrust-upon, Jesus in Mark. The con-

versation with Pilate is more a serene doctrinal response than the answer of a pressured man on trial. Pilate's ideas and those of Jesus pass each other like ships in the night. Indeed, Jesus is a king, but his point is lost on the Roman procurator.

Most of us know little or nothing about a real monarchy–except from history, of course, and that is a very mixed picture. There were benign kings and there were despots. We have to struggle a bit to apply the title "king" to Jesus, and even at that there is a fair amount of adapting to do. There was a prayer years ago, certainly out of date today in language at least, which spoke of the "sweet empire of your love." All things considered, it said it fairly well. Christ does have a sway over our lives–a total sway–through the "obedience of faith." He shapes our thinking and colors our vision–or should. Yet his yoke is easy and his burden light. We are subjects in his reign wholly because we want to be. His love has grasped us. His royalty was gained, not just conferred. He "paid his dues" and ours as well. So if "king" doesn't seem to fit exactly, it is hard to suggest a substitute. Let's get beyond the title and understand the reality: Totus tuus–*"Totally yours." This is a king who was insulted by a Roman political appointee and rejected in favor of a common criminal, the king who presents himself as the lamb who was slain. It gives us much food for thought on this feast of Christ the king.*

Homiletic and Catechetical Helps

1. Son of Man: a biblical title applied to Jesus.

2. Understanding the kingship of Christ.

3 Christ as faithful witness.

4. The meaning of commitment.

5. The authority of church and state.

6. The Christian as a faithful witness.

7. Truthfulness in daily life.

CHRIST THE KING
Year C

Readings

> 2 Sam 5:1 - 3
> Col 1:12 - 20
> Lk 23:35 - 43

Theme: King from the Cross

The account of David's anointing, in today's first reading, speaks of his closeness to the people and his future role as a shepherd-king. In Luke's gospel, the inscription placed on the cross does, in fact, point to the reality, the reign of Jesus. But this descendant of David comes to the throne through the path of rejection and death. The criminal crucified with Christ is assured a place in the reign of God as death envelops both king and suppliant. The reading from Colossians speaks of the lordship of Jesus as embracing not only the church but all of creation.

First Reading

David's election as king in Hebron of Judah gives him full authority over all the tribes (v3), although this is his third recorded anointing. Even though these may derive from different traditions, they have been coherently brought together by the Deuteronomic editors. The first anointing occurred when Samuel was led by the Lord to discover the young son of Jesse who was shepherding his father's flock (1 Sam 16:13). His private anointing at that time makes his future steps toward the kingship divinely directed. Later he is anointed as the Judahite king and is thenceforth seen as their designated leader (2 Sam 2:4).

Here David stands before all the tribes. His blood ties (v1), military prowess (v2a), and divine designation (v2b) more than justify his selection as king. The idea of a shepherd-leader reappears in Nathan's oracle (2 Sam 7:8). David's "agreement" is literally a covenant (Heb: "cut a covenant") made with the leaders of the country; this is followed by his being anointed king over the united kingdom, a reign that was to last for more than three decades. An important theological note in this brief passage is David as deliverer and shepherd of his people.

Responsorial Psalm   Ps 122

In this hymn of pilgrimage, the pilgrim sees Jerusalem as the center of both worship (v1) and royal administration (v5). It was not only the seat of Yahweh but the seat of David and his descendants. The psalmist joins with others in their joyful entrance into the city (v1). Standing with awe within the city, he is impressed by its compact and well-fortified state (vv2f). The image of all of Israel making its way to Jerusalem in thanksgiving (v4), with the correct interpretation of Torah conveyed to the people by their authorities, echoes an idea found also in Isaiah (2:1 - 5).

Second Reading

The letter to the Colossians gives expression to the sovereignty of Christ in drawing upon an early liturgical hymn which places Christ at the center of the universe (vv15ff) and at the head of the church (vv18f). This relationship to creation and the church is effected through his activity in the fashioning of the created order (v16) and in the work of redemption (vv12ff, 20).

In the first part of today's reading, Paul exhorts his listeners to give thanks to the Father for the deliverance they have received (vv12ff). The descriptive language of transition has echoes of the exodus, in the transfer from Satan's realm to that of Christ's kingdom where there is the shared inheritance of all the redeemed (the holy ones). This is a transition made possible through the death of God's Son, which has resulted in the eradication of sin from their lives. Paul equates redemption with the forgiveness of sin (Eph 1:7; Rom 3:24f).

The letter then passes to the hymn of Christ's pre-eminence (vv15 - 20). It should first be noted that it is the pre-existent Christ, the God-Man, not solely the eternal Word, that is here extolled. It is the known and experienced Christ who is present in the entire hymn.

The hymn first relates Christ's primacy to the whole of creation. *Image of God* (v15a): Even more than humankind (Gen 1:27), Christ is the icon of God in being the personification of God's wisdom (Prov 8:22 - 31; Wis 7:22 - 8:1) and the one in whom the saving love of the Father has become transparent (2 Cor 4:4ff). *Firstborn of all creation* (v15b): As the incarnation of God's wisdom, he is an agent in the very act of creation (Prov 8:27 - 31; 1 Cor 8:6) and therefore is "born" before any other creature. As God's wisdom, Christ is the "blueprint" or plan for an ordered universe, with the result that all things come into being in him and through him (v16). This includes earthly and heavenly beings as well as the angelic mediators who played a dominant role in the mystery cults of the Hellenistic world—thrones, dominions (Eph 1:21), principalities (Rom 8:38), and powers (1 Cor 15:24). As the one who ultimately presides over all of creation, things are made not only in and through him but for him as well. This is one of the strongest Christological statements in the scriptures. In Christ all things find their meaning, cohesion, and finality (v17).

The hymn then passes to Christ's role in the order of redemption (vv18ff). *Head of the body* (v18): The "body of Christ" is a frequent Pauline image (1 Cor 6:15; Rom 12:4f) in spelling out the intimate union existing between Christ and the baptized. The notion of Christ as the head and all the members constituting the body appears late in the Pauline or post-Pauline literature (Eph 1:23; 4:15f; 5:23). *The church* (v18): Most commentators see this as an explanatory addition to the hymn, disrupting, as it does, the poetic structure. It gives a distinctly Pauline meaning to the body image. *The beginning* (v18): In the context this probably refers to Christ's priority in the order of redemption, not creation. *Firstborn from the dead* (v18): As the first of many to rise from the dead, Christ is accorded still another title of primacy (Acts 26:23; Rom 8:29). His pre-eminence (v18c) is complete in creation, redemption, and glorification. *Fullness* (v19): This may be a reference to the fullness of Godhead (2:9) or the gnostic fullness, referring to the whole body of heavenly beings (2:9f).

In a final soteriological note, the universe is again related to Christ; this time not in the order of creation but in that of redemption (v20). The world that had become alienated from humans and God through sin (Rom 8:20f; Gen 3:14 - 20; 9:2) has been reconciled through Christ's redemption (2 Cor 5:19; Eph 1:10). Like humanity itself, the world groans in expectation of its final deliverance (Rom 8:21f). The hymn has come full circle in placing at the center of creation and history the Christ who can truly be called cosmic.

Third Reading

This section of the crucifixion narrative in Luke centers theologically on the recognition of Jesus, especially in the titles accorded him. In today's gospel there is both the pain of opposition (vv35 - 38) and the consolation of conversion (vv39 - 42). The Lucan distinction between the "people," who act as spectators and later repent (v48), and the "rulers" (v35) is an important distinction in terms of responsibility for the death of Jesus. The cynical attitude of Jesus' opponents echoes that of the persecutors of the innocent persecuted psalmist (Ps 22:8f).

Ironically everything said of Jesus by his enemies is accurate. He is derided as "the chosen one," the "Messiah of God" (v35). He is the Savior of his people (v35), who becomes such not by "saving himself" but by surrendering his life in order to take it up again and leading others to life as well (9:22ff). The inscription above him on the cross (v38), strongly opposed by the Jewish leaders (Jn 19:21f), captures a central feature of Jesus' earthly mission; he is the promised Messiah, descendant of David. In all of these titles, though situated in a context of hatred and opposition, the early church saw encapsulated the salvific work of Jesus.

The picture changes dramatically with the sentiments expressed by the repentant criminal (vv39 - 43). The saving mission of Christ, brought to its fulfillment in his death-resurrection, is illustrated and, in a certain sense, begins in this teaching moment from the cross. The unrepentant man asks "to be saved" but only in a temporal "this-world" sense. True salvation can only be extended when the proper sentiments are present;

these are seen in the moral posture of the repentant criminal. Initially he recognizes the innocence of the Lord's servant, sentiments voiced by the chorus in the last song of the servant (vv40f; Is 53:4 - 7). He then acknowledges the kingship of Jesus who with his death is about to enter into his kingdom (v42). His request could not have been honored before the time of passage, the "exodus" of Jesus (9:31). As the "firstborn of the dead" (Col 1:18), Jesus must first enter into his glory before anyone else is admitted. The man's request is an implicit expression of repentance. Jesus, teaching from the cross (v43), assures him of salvation "today," indicating that with the Savior's death the moment of entry into the eternal reign will have arrived. It will be a life "with me," the reign being a lasting sharing with Christ, especially prepared for the rejected of this world, the blessed ones of his earthly ministry.

Many facets of Christ appear in today's liturgy. The Christ of the gospel today has a striking message for all those involved in church ministry. Entitled king, he teaches from the cross as the king who imparts forgiveness to a renegade criminal. There were allusions to this pastoral king in David's being a shepherd. But that is still a far cry from the king who rules from a cross. It is small wonder that Paul speaks of himself as being an ambassador of reconciliation. That is at the heart of ministry. Compassion was not secondary in Christ's life; it was the way he exercised his sovereignty. Today's world has so many examples of cruelty, harshness, the desire to exact an eye for an eye. How can one be a disciple of Christ and have any question about the inadmissibility of the death penalty? In a scene of execution, Jesus, dying himself, wants only to bring pardon and hope.

And then there is the cosmic Christ. We think all too little about the sacredness of the world and its redemption. There is a sacred stamp on every snow-capped peak, every majestic oak, the bluebonnets, the sea lions, and the whooping cranes. Created and reconciled by God in Christ, we can "see his blood upon the rose." Environmental concerns are far more than political issues. They should really spring from faith. Many would argue that we are already well on the way to the destruction of the planet. The tide has to be reversed if our sinfulness is not to deprive our children of their planetary inheritance. The cosmic Christ truly gives us pause. With Chardin, we offer our mass on the altar of the world.

Homiletic and Catechetical Helps

1. The meaning of David as a shepherd-king.

2. Christ as king in Luke's crucifixion narrative.

3. Criminal justice: incarceration and rehabilitation.

4. The morality of the death penalty.

5. Violence in society and the media.

6. The importance of compassion.

7. Worship and instruction in the Christian life (Ps 122).

8. Christ as head of the church.

9. Christ as the center of creation.

10. Cosmic and human redemption.

THE IMMACULATE CONCEPTION

Readings

> Gen 3:9 - 15, 20
> Eph 1:3 - 6, 11 - 12
> Lk 1:26 - 38

Theme: The Immortal "Yes" to God

The Immaculate Conception is the feast of Mary's sinlessness, the Catholic belief that at no time in her human existence was she ever subject to sin's domain. Both she and Eve figure prominently in today's readings. The first reading speaks of the results of the primeval sin: an ongoing struggle and entanglement between humans, the children of Eve, and evil, the seed of the snake. There is a note of hope, however, in Eve's name.

She will be the mother of the living as God's creative plan continues. In the gospel, the grace-filled spirit of Mary, the new Eve, is reflected in her generous "yes" to God, supplanting the "no" of the Genesis couple and beginning the process of redemption in the conception of a child. Ephesians reminds us that neither Mary's lot nor ours is unforeseen. It is an expression of an eternal design now made manifest in time.

First Reading

The sin of Adam and Eve has already transpired before Yahweh begins his late afternoon walk in the garden (v8). As is characteristic of the Yahwist tradition, God is presented in very human terms, walking and conversing with his human creatures. The first result of sin is the recognition of nakedness, here directly related to the eating of the forbidden fruit (vv10ff). The blame passes from the man to the woman to the snake. Punishment will be meted out in the order of culpability, the first being the snake, the most responsible (vv14 - 19).

Just as the man and woman are individual representatives of all humanity, so too the snake represents the over-all forces of evil. In all three cases, the punishment for the sin is drawn from the author's lived experience. The disorders in nature which were part of everyday life are presented as the consequences of sin, quite independent of any causal relationship. In short, the author begins with the experience and works back to the proposed cause. Today's reading presents only the retribution directed to the snake, and it is drawn from the natural appearance it makes. Its slithering form and alienation from other creatures suggest its wrongdoing (v14). It is cursed by God in its flat and groveling condition.

Between the serpent and humans, antipathy is to be perpetual (v15). The "offspring" of both refers to all future generations. The descendants of Eve (he: singular in Hebrew; they: sometimes plural in English translation) will be locked in unending conflict with the forces of evil. The struggle is depicted in the strike and counter-strike of the two opponents, That is as far as the Genesis text goes. Later tradition, including the biblical, saw the devil in the snake (Wis 2:24; Jn 8:44). The human's superior physical position in stepping on the snake's head has also been seen as the earliest indication of humanity's eventual triumph over evil in Christ. There is a lengthy Christian tradition which sees in this text the first announcement of the gospel.

The text itself, however, ends on a note of hope. The name is intimately identified with the person. To give a name is to fix a destiny. The woman (2:23) is now named Eve (Heb: *hawwa*). By a play on words she becomes the mother of the living (Heb: *hay*), thus continuing Yahweh's promise of progeny (1:28).

Responsorial Psalm   Ps 98

The psalm has a strong note of universalism. Israel's deliverance is recognized and chanted. This is a manifestation of God's power (v1) as well as his covenant fidelity (v3). Although salvation is experienced by Israel, it is a sign to the nations as well (v2). In view of this evidence of the true God's presence to his people, the nations are exhorted to join Israel in giving praise (v4). The universalism of the Hebrew scriptures stresses the recognition of God in and through his action in favor of Israel, not involving any type of missionary thrust.

Second Reading

Based on the Hebrew blessing of God or *berakah*, this hymn, here only partially reproduced, betrays its liturgical origins, similar in both style and content to the hymn of Colossians 1. God extends heavenly blessings in and through Christ in order that a reconciled and sanctified people may stand before him (vv3f; 5:27; Rom 8:29). It is the pre-existent Christ, present throughout the blessing, who is at the center of God's saving plan prior to the world's creation. This holy people becomes adopted sons and daughters, united with God's own Son in the bond of the Spirit (v5; Gal 4:4 - 7; Jn 1:12). The process of sanctification redounds to God's glory through the visible effectiveness of the grace that comes through Christ (v6; Col 1:13).

Predestined by God's choice as part of the mystery, the elect give praise to God (vv11f; Rom 8:29f). *His glory* (v12): This is the external and perceptible manifestation of God's wisdom and power, seen in the mighty deeds of the exodus and now seen preeminently in his plan of salvation.

Third Reading

The account of Jesus' conception in Luke, like that of Matthew, is a central Christological statement. As has been noted elsewhere, the two evangelists, as much as they converge around basic beliefs, show marked differences in their infancy narratives, which exclude any type of historical synthesis. On the other hand, there is no need to force convergence in light of the clear theological and literary perspectives pursued by both.

In Matthew's infancy narrative, Joseph plays a dominant role; in Luke it is Mary. Luke also contrasts, in a parallel fashion, the parentage, conception, and birth of John and Jesus, underscoring the superiority of the latter.

Three fundamental points are made in this passage from Luke read today. The narrative begins with the mention of Joseph's Davidic lineage (v27), and the initial intervention of the angel concludes on a Davidic note (v32). Since Mary was formally betrothed to Joseph, they were legally joined to each other, although cohabitation had not taken place. For Jesus to claim Davidic descent, it was required only that Joseph confer legal paternity. What Luke does here is to connect Jesus with the messianic hope of Israel, which had its beginning in the oracle of Nathan (2 Sam 7).

Luke's second major point is to present Jesus as Son of God (vv32, 35). This honorific title was especially used of the king (Ps 2:7) and pointed to a special relationship. As the angel uses it here, especially in view of the context, it clearly has a special transcendent meaning.

The conversation between Gabriel and Mary is a usual way of expressing divine communication in Hebrew thought, regardless of what form it might have taken. Akin to his role in the book of Daniel (c. 9), Gabriel is a herald of the messianic era.

Mary is greeted as a highly favored person (v28), a greeting which puzzles her and is explained in the angel's message (vv29ff). In God's plan there is to be the conception and birth of a son whose name Jesus is salvific ("Yahweh saves"). He will be the Messiah and Son of God. Mary's question (v34) simply sets the stage for the climactic response; its purpose is literary. The child will be Son of God through a conception effected in her virginal womb by the exclusive action of God. The child, fathered by God alone, is in that sense God's Son. Furthermore, Elizabeth's pregnancy at an advanced age will substantiate the angel's claim (v36).

The third point of the narrative is to highlight Mary's response. She is recognized as favored (vv28, 30), an appellation which at once points beyond her to the author of salvation. Her own spiritual posture reflects acknowledgement of this in her words of acceptance (v38). In this Mary is the prototype of the Christian. She accepts and activates God's word within her, for which she is and will be blessed (vv45, 48). What becomes increasingly evident in Luke's gospel is that relationship with Jesus is based on word-acceptance, not ties of blood (8:21).

Important to note is that the divine Sonship of Jesus, identified by Paul at one point with the resurrection (Rom 1:4), is here carried back to the time of human conception. His pre-existence prior to conception (Jn 1) will come to the fore as Christian understanding develops.

Mary has always played a prominent role in Catholic belief and practice. And despite the predictions of some post-conciliar doomsayers, there is no evidence that her place in the lives of the faithful has diminished. Certainly, better focus has been attained. Ecumenical dialogue has brought a sounder balance to our presentation. Stronger scriptural underpinnings for authentic Marian devotion have had a positive influence. Attempts to historicize excessively what we know about Mary from the scriptures are less frequent. But her place in faith is secure. She continues to be central to much of Christian prayer and devotion. In the words of the poet, she is "our tainted nature's solitary boast."

Today's feast focuses on one of the honors that God accorded Mary. There are others, to be sure–the divine maternity, the assumption, the mother of the church. But none of them says as much as the lesson taught in today's scripture. Mary is the model believer. She gave her unqualified "yes" to God and no prerogative can overshadow that.

One day a woman in the crowd wanted to honor Mary and singled out her physical motherhood for special mention. But Jesus gave her a gentle rebuff in what might be though to be a "put-down" of his mother: "More blessed are they who hear the word of God and keep it." The story is found only in Luke–the same Luke who gave us today's gospel. Mary was pre-eminently the hearer and keeper of God's word. Acceptance of God's word in total obedience is the heart of discipleship. Thus Mary is the first of the disciples.

Homiletic and Catechetical Helps

1. Eve and Mary: similarities and dissimilarities.

2. Explaining the immaculate conception.

3. The conception of Jesus: Luke's theological statement.

4. The struggle between sin and humanity.

5. Our personal struggle with sin.

6. The meaning of predestination.

7. The snake as a symbol of sin.

ASCENSION
Years A B C

Readings

> Acts 1:1 - 11
> Eph 1:17 - 23
> Mt 28:16 - 20 (A)
> Mk 16:15 - 20 (B)
> Lk 24:46 - 53 (C)

Theme: Leave Taking with a Promise.

In Luke-Acts, the exaltation of Jesus is expressed in temporally distinct stages: resurrection, ascension, and conferral of the

Spirit. This extends over a period of fifty days. Today's liturgy celebrates the second step in the Lucan presentation, the ascension of Christ. In the reading from Acts and in each of the gospel readings for the three year cycle, Jesus' departure is accompanied by words of assurance that his mission will be continued by the Holy Spirit, who will inaugurate a new era in salvation history. As for Jesus, as Ephesians states today, he passes to a life with the Father, exalted over heavenly and earthly powers, while also continuing, in Matthew's words, with the church until the end of time.

First Reading

The exaltation of Jesus, an event that transcends history, follows upon his death, even though it has distinguishable aspects which admit of literary separation. For their own purposes, the New Testament writers present this new and, in a sense, indescribable phase of Christ's existence in different ways. In Acts Luke separates the ascension from the resurrection by forty days, with Pentecost following ten days later. This enables him to set forth his own historical-theological framework, with its post-Easter instruction of the apostles over a forty day period (vv2f). The number is symbolic, reminiscent of the experience of Moses (Ex 24:12 - 18) and Elijah (1 Kgs 19:8), and, even more proximately, the period of preparation for Jesus' own Spirit-directed ministry (Lk 4:2, 14 - 15).

The introduction to Acts follows the classical form. It is addressed to a patron and is related to the former composition (vv1f). Where Luke departs from the traditional form is in bypassing an outline of his projected work and going directly to a narration of the post-Easter appearances (vv3 - 8). In the earlier volume, Luke presented what Jesus "began to do and to teach" (Gr: *erxato*, began). The period of Jesus' public ministry serves as the basis for the apostolic witness (1:22). This "beginning" launches the mission of Jesus which continues until his ascension. The "instruction" of the apostles (v2) embraces both the teaching of Jesus during his ministry and the insight into its meaning in the light of the resurrection.

One of the main purposes of the resurrection appearances

was to verify the fact that Jesus was truly alive, as well as to deepen the apostles' understanding of God's reign. "Through the holy Spirit" (v2) grammatically could go with "instructions" or "apostles. . .chosen." In view of the importance to be accorded the subsequent descent of the Spirit, Jesus' earlier experience in choosing the apostles seems preferable here.

The multiple appearances of Jesus to the apostles (v3) are not otherwise borne out by Luke, who mentions only two instances (Lk 24). Matthew's mention of appearances in Galilee (Mt 28:10) would play no part in Luke's Jerusalem-centered theme. The apostles are clearly instructed to remain in Jerusalem until the coming of the Spirit, who is "the promise of the Father" (v4; 2:33; Lk 24:49). For Luke, Jerusalem is the place of Jesus' destiny (Lk 9:51), where he was to die like the prophets before him (Lk 13:33 - 35), where he was to take his leave and send the Spirit to launch the universal mission of the church (v8). Jersualem in Luke serves as an important link between the old and the new Israel. The coming of the Spirit will empower the apostles to be ministers of the new baptism as opposed to the former water baptism, which distinguishes Jesus clearly from his forerunner (v5; Lk 3:16).

To the apostles' query about the restoration of Israel's autonomy with the establishment of God's reign (v6), Jesus deflects the question and moves their thinking in another direction. As to the parousia itself, only the Father sets the time (v7; Mk 13:32). In the interim period, another period will be introduced, that of the Spirit (v8), to be recorded in the ensuing chapters. The Spirit will empower the apostles to be the witnesses of the teaching and resurrection of Jesus for the forgiveness of sins (2:32 - 40). The geographical progression—Jewish Judea, "half-Jewish" Samaria, and the Gentile world, with its imperial outpost, Rome—will be that followed by the book of Acts itself.

The departure of Jesus in a literal ascension is a literary device not employed by the other New Testament authors. It serves to bring the era of Jesus to closure and sets the scene for the age of the Spirit (v9; 2:1 - 4; Lk 24:50ff). The observation of the heavenly figures (v11) indicates that the parousia, while deferred, is not removed. Christ's mode of departure, in fact, is patterned on the expected mode of return (7:56; Lk 21:27). In the meantime, there is no time for "sky-gazing"; after a period of prayer, the Spirit will send the apostles forth on their saving mission.

Responsorial Psalm   Ps 47

This is one of the enthronenment psalms, acclaiming the kingship of Yahweh and, according to some authors, finding its liturgical setting in a celebration of Yahweh as king. He is given the title of "Elyon," the Most High or chief god of the Canaanite pantheon (v2) Since his reign extends to all the earth, all peoples are to acclaim him (v2). The sense of drama is heightened as Yahweh ascends his throne (vv6, 9). The nations, especially those subdued during the Davidic and post-Davidic periods, are depicted as rendering homage. In today's liturgy, the hymn is applied to the exaltation of Christ and the inauguration of his universal reign.

Second Reading

This prayer asks for a deeper knowledge of God, enabling the Ephesians to appreciate the ultimate outcome of their election (v18). By reason of their baptism, they are destined to be part of the heavenly community. This is described as an inheritance "among the holy ones," i.e. an aggregation of the elect here with the members of the angelic assembly akin to the assimilation posited also in the Qumran community.

This immortal destiny is effected by God's "power" and "might" (v19; Col 2:12; 2 Cor 13:4). The fact that God's power has brought about Christ's resurrection gives assurance to those who have been promised the same (v20; 1 Cor 15:12 - 19). *Principality, authority, power, and dominion* (v21): These are heavenly or angelic powers placed in subordination to Christ. Their origins are to be sought in the pagan mystery cults where they are deified agents directing human affairs. Here they are stripped of any divine significance (Col 1:16).

All things are subjected to Christ's universal dominion (v22), with Christ himself subject only to the Father (1 Cor 15:27f).

Head of the church (v23): This relationship of Christ to his members is found only in the captivity epistles (Col 1:18); in the other epistles he is equated with the body itself (Rom 12:4 - 8). The head is related to the body both as source of life and direction. Christ's dominion extends to the entire universe as well as to the church; by reasons of its union with the head, the church shares in this universal rule (v22). The church has its own fullness of Spirit-life, received from Christ ("the one who fills"), who in turn receives from the Father (3:19; 5:18). It is this fullness of life from the head that is the source of unity and growth within the church (4:15f).

Third Reading (A)

These final verses of the first gospel are rich in Matthean theology. The scene has apocalyptic, end-time features as the risen Christ outlines the mission of the apostles. In Matthew the disciples are found in Galilee (v28), where Jesus had earlier instructed them to go (28:10), a geographical note peculiar to the first gospel. The "mountain" is unspecified; it is Matthew's literary focal point of Jesus' teaching during his ministry (5:1; 8:1; 15:29; 17:1).

The Matthean Christ is already glorified and Spirit-endowed. In the first gospel there is no ascension; it is subsumed in Christ's resurrection. Moreover, this is Matthew's first meeting of the risen Jesus with the apostles, at which time the recognition of his new status is seen in their act of veneration (v17). The mention of their initial doubt is understandable, if somewhat surprising; it is something of a relic of Peter's former hesitant faith (14:30f).

The mandate of Jesus to his disciples has three main features:

The power of Jesus (Gr: *exousia*) (v18). The language draws on Daniel's apocalyptic Son of Man, endowed by God with authority over all nations (Dan 7:13f). The "all" of Jesus' authority embraces the heavenly and earthly spheres (v8; Col 1:18ff).

The mission of the apostles (v19). In accord with the breadth of Christ's authority, his gospel mandate to the apostles is universal as well. The mission is to both the Jewish and the Gentile world. The exclusion of the Gentiles from the mission of the Matthean

Jesus during his earthly ministry (10:5f) is now lifted in an all-inclusive mandate. In the apostles' being missioned, there is no explicit mention of their receiving the Spirit.

Their mission is to "baptize," i.e. to "immerse" or "plunge" the believer into an incorporation with the triune God. This baptismal formula reflects the developed theology of the Matthean church where equality and distinction of persons is carefully articulated. Earlier baptism was administered "in the name of Jesus" (Acts 2:38; 10:48). Its importance here is cumulative and climactic, a summary of the whole gospel. The Son has submitted his will to the Father with the result that the Spirit, first conferred on the Son, is now shared with the believer. In this scene the resurrection, ascension, and Pentecost are collapsed into a single event.

The teaching of the apostles (v20).This embraces the content of the whole gospel but preeminently the sermon on the mount (cc. 5 - 7). The full mandate includes the gospel proclamation (kerygma), baptism, and the further teaching (didache) on the meaning of the Christian life. This last element constitutes the heart of the written gospels.

Finally, Jesus, the Emmanuel (God-with-us) present from the gospel's beginning (1:23), the one whose presence was assured to the believing community (18:20), gives final assurance of his continuation with the church ("I am with you") until the end of the age. The parousia, while not imminent, remains a significant data of belief.

Third Reading (B)

The Marcan account of the final mandate and ascension is found in an ending to the gospel which is missing from some of the earliest Greek manuscripts. It is not Marcan in either style or vocabulary. Hence it has problems of both canonicity and authorship. Roman Catholic tradition recognizes it as inspired, having expressed itself authoritatively on the question at the Council of Trent. It is best seen as a later addition to Mark, perhaps as late as the second century, bringing the gospel to an ordered conclusion by combining elements of Luke 24 and John 20.

The mandate is one of gospel proclamation to be accompanied by baptism (vv15f), with salvation hinging on acceptance or rejection of the latter. There is no explicit mention of the Spirit as the effective agent, although its presence in baptism is clearly presumed. The signs accompanying the apostles are those associated with the wonder workers of the time and are seen here as giving probative force to the apostolic message. Exorcism, healing, and speaking different languages are New Testament phenomena elsewhere attested (vv17f); there is also evidence for freedom from reptile harm (Lk 10:19; Acts 28:3 - 6). The "tongues" spoken of here is not the usual escstatic speech (1 Cor 14) but the gift of different languages found in the Lucan Pentecost (Acts 2:4, 8, 11).

The ascension has similarities with Lk (v19; Lk 24:50f) and echoes Psalm 110:1. The continued presence of Jesus with the apostles in their mission is in the form of signs which validate their work (v20).

The Marcan narrative, less developed and unified than the other synoptics, is at one with them in the mandate to preach and baptize and the assurance of Christ's continued presence through ratifying signs.

Third Reading (C)

The ascension account serves as the conclusion of Luke's gospel, containing a number of already familiar Lucan themes. Thus Jesus interprets his death-resurrection in the light of the scriptures as an event pre-ordained by God (v46; 9:22; 24:25ff). The preaching of the kerygma for the forgiveness of sins is the first fruit of the resurrection, with Jerusalem designated as the focal point of the message's emergence, proceeding from there to the nations of the world (v47; Acts 2:38; 1:8). *Promise of my Father* (vv47, 49): the Holy Spirit (Acts 1:4; 2:33). As in Acts, the ascension will be followed by the era of the Spirit.

For theologial reasons, Luke in Acts places the ascension forty days after Easter (Acts 1:3). Here its apparent connection with the day of the resurrection is due to a combining of all the post-Easter events in a single day in Luke's final chapter. This is the only account in the gospels which tells of Jesus blessing his disciples (v50); the blessing and the worshipful response of the apostles is reminiscent of the account of the priestly blessing in Sirach (50:20 - 24). With Jesus' departure, Jerusalem is again the point of reference as the disciples return to the city (Acts 1:4). A Lucan inclusion finishes the gospel with a joy, echoing that of Jesus birth (2:10) and a return to the temple, where the gospel began (v53; 1:5 - 24).

In this narrative Luke has joined the two covenants, prepared for the opening of Acts and the era of the Spirit, and clarified the role of the apostles.

As is his wont, Luke has a very distinctive approach to the Easter season. The ascension clearly separates the era of Christ from that of the Spirit whereas in the other gospels there is blending of the two. But there is merit in Luke's idea. It enables us to look at Jesus in a very distinct and detached way. His was a life that ran its course in thirty-odd years. He met a violent end but, as faith makes clear, he was vindicated and made the Lord of history by the God he called Father. It was the life of a Palestinian Jew which changed the course of history. Our calendar now sees all of history as either prior to or following his life. His teaching is admired by believer and non-believer alike. His life of limitless love and non-violence has influenced some of the world's most important figures. And with all the divisions his followers have experienced through the centuries, they are united in one thing. They bear the name Christian. Jesus was a man of history, living in a determined period and in a specific culture. There is a constant effort to capture as much as possible about the man Jesus, to get behind the faith expression that comes fron the gospels. Without the historical Jesus, the age of the Spirit would have no meaning. We would be rudderless and adrift in some sort of esoteric mystery religion. The Spirit's main role is to shed light on the meaning of Jesus the Christ.

The ascension brings that mission of Jesus to a close. It gives us a bit of respite, the chance to look back and reflect before moving ahead. How often, after the death of someone loved and admired, we are renewed in reviewing his or her life. So too the disciples in prayer had their moment of silent reflection. But Jesus, true to form, moves our attention forward as well. We are not to spend excessive time gazing heavenward. He will not leave us orphans. And so he reminds us, as we reflect on his life and teaching, to prepare ourselves for the next exciting phase of God's interaction with the world. Pentecost is on the horizon. Memory and hope are two vital features of the religious experience—a leave-taking with a promise.

Homiletic and Catechetical Helps

1. Resurrection-ascension-Pentecost: a single mystery.

2. Differences in the gospels' approach to the ascension.

3. The meaning of the ascension in the Christian life.

4. Relation of Christ to the Holy Spirit.

5. The universal mission of the apostles.

6. Gospel composition: projection back from Easter.

7. The virtue of hope.

8. Christ as head of the body.

9. The Trinity and baptism.

10. The three-deckered world: earth, heaven (up), hell (down)

THE ASSUMPTION

Theme: Pledge of Life to Come

The readings for the vigil and for the feast speak to the Christian of life after death as well as the path to be followed in order to reach it. In the assumption the church celebrates Mary's total victory over sin in her return to God after death, saved from both sin and its vestiges. In both readings from Corinthians, we are assured that such a destiny is ours as well, even though sin has taken a toll in our lives. The two gospel readings from Luke present the key to immortality: internalizing and living God's word. In the reading from 1 Chronicles, we can see the ark of the covenant, God's dwelling place, as a symbol of Mary. She is seen as well in the woman of the book of Revelation who symbolizes the chosen Israel parenting the Messiah.

VIGIL MASS

Readings

1 Chr 15:3 - 4, 15, 16; 16:1 - 2
1 Cor 15:54 - 57
Lk 11:27 - 28

First Reading

This account of the transfer of the ark from the hill country of Judah to Jerusalem parallels that found in 2 Samuel 6. The difference lies in the role accorded the Levites in the priestly-oriented narrative of 1 Chronicles. David summons the Levites to execute the transfer of the ark (vv3, 12). They carry it from its provisional location in Judah to the tent prepared for it in Jerusalem (v15). The musicians, who were part of the second temple liturgy at a much later date, were Levites and subject to levitical authority (v16). In Samuel, the non-levitical David is engaged in sacrificing and in blessing the people, a practice which reflects early tradition (2 Sam 6:17). In 1 Chronicles, to bring the narrative in line with priestly ascendency, the priests are included in offering sacrifice (16:1). By post-exilic times, cultic ministry was restricted to the Levites, including the conferral of blessings (Deut 10:8; 21:5; Num 6:22 - 26).

Responsorial Psalm   Ps 132

This psalm celebrates the ark, its resting place, and the priests and the king, who were the ark's attendants. The strong liturgical note may reflect an original setting as part of a procession bearing the ark into the temple in commemoration of its first relocation (2 Sam 6). *Ephratah* (Bethlehem) (v6a): the location in Judah associated with the line of David (Ru 4:11). *Fields of Jaar* (v6b): This is Kiriath-jearim, a town near Jerusalem where the ark was located for many years (2 Sam 7:1f; 2 Sam 6:2).

The procession makes its way to the tent (temple). *Footstool* (v7): With Yahweh enthroned on the cherubim above the ark, the ark itself served as a place for the Lord to rest his feet (Ps

99:5; 1 Chr 28:2). Both the priests and the king are remembered in prayer (vv9f), as Yahweh pledges his lasting commitment to Zion as the sacred locus of his presence (vv13f).

Second Reading

Commentary on this reading from 1 Corinthians is found on the Eighth Sunday of Year C.

Third Reading

In the Lucan context dealing with exorcisms (11:14 - 25), this brief exchange emphasizes the necessity of not only accepting the word of God but persevering in it as well (v28). Only in perseverance is there assurance that evil will not return to one's life. At the same time the exchange points up the superiority of the faith relationship over that which is solely human (v27). Far more important than ties with Jesus through human parenting or blood are those which derive from discipleship (8:19ff). Parenthetically it may be added that Mary is first in the order of discipleship, having internalized God's word and made it her own in a spirit of total acceptance (1:38).

MASS DURING THE DAY

Readings

Rev 11:19; 12:1 - 6, 10
1 Cor 15:20 - 26
Lk 1:39 - 56

First Reading

This end-time description of the birth and triumph of the Messiah and the vanquishing of evil is replete with biblical and extra-biblical images. Today's passage opens with the ark in the holy of holies visible to all, indicative of an exceptional revelation (v19). Three figures dominate this narrative: the woman, her child, and the dragon. The woman is the historical Israel, who brings forth the Messiah (v5) and in the new era becomes

the church (v6). Her initial appearance resembles that of god-
desses in antiquity with some possible biblical allusions in the
sun, moon, and stars (Gen 37:9f). The role of Zion in ushering
in the final era is depicted as a childbirth (Is 66:7ff), one not
without the anguish beforehand that was to precede the end
(v2). Following the birth of the Messiah, Israel, now become
church, goes to an idyllic desert place, reminiscent of the exodus, to be protected by God during the time of persecution.
The period of time (1,250 days or three and a half years) is one
half of the perfect number seven, symbolic of evil or a time of
duress (v6; 11:2).

The *child* is Christ the Messiah destined for universal sovereignty (Ps 2:9); he is presented here in a rapid passage from
birth to glorification (v5.).

The *dragon*, identified in the chapter as the devil and Satan
(v9), is the mythological sea monster, symbolic of the forces of
evil (Ps 74:13f; Job 26:12). The horns recall the beast of Daniel
(v3; Dan 7:7f) as does the sweeping action of the tail in dislodg-
ing the stars (Dan 8:10).

At the end of the eschatological battle (vv7ff), salvation is
acclaimed with the full inauguration of the sovereignty of God
and Christ, both spoken of equally in Revelation as sharers in
authority and recipients of worship (v10; 7:15ff; 22:3).

This drama is pure apocalyptic, the revelation of God in
veiled form. It announces the final deliverance of the church,
just as Christ himself was delivered from death, even though a
period of trial must precede the end. The old and new Israel
are linked in the person of the woman. A church tradition has
long seen the person of Mary in the woman. Although the
author gives no indication of seeing more than Israel here, the
fact that Mary was, in fact, the mother of the Messiah makes
her presence in the text at least plausible and certainly would
not exclude an adaptation of the text in that sense.

Responsorial Psalm   Ps 45

This is a royal wedding psalm containing a remarkably clear
outline of the solemn ritual. The verses read today describe the
bride queen splendidly attired for the occasion, as she takes her

place at her spouse's right (v10). She is advised to sever her ties with her family home and dedicate herself to her new duties and to the king (vv11f). Her attendants are present as the entire entourage makes its way solemnly toward the royal dwelling to the enthusiastic acclaim of the people (v16).

Second Reading

Commentary on this passage from 1 Corinthians is to be found on the Feast of Christ the King, Year A.

Third Reading

In this Lucan account of Mary's visit to Elizabeth, the two covenants meet. The central figures are the offspring to be born, Jesus and John. Up to this point in the infancy narrative, the two have been paired but separate. At this point they are joined.

The story has a dominant theological meaning. As John leaps in his mother's womb, the inferior recognizes the superior (v44). The one who has conceived at an advanced age is overshadowed by the one who has conceived without a human procreator.

A second point to be noted is the meeting of the two covenants, with Elizabeth, Zechariah, and John representing the former dispensation, and Mary, Joseph, and Jesus representing the new. The faithful Israel, as seen in the person of Elizabeth, gives a "Spirit-filled" (v41) recognition of the Messiah and acclaims him Lord (v43), a faith statement to be understood in the light of the church's post-Easter experience. Elizabeth further notes the favored state of both Mary and the child (v42), in words to be later included in the Hail Mary. Mary's blessedness rests primarily in her having believed what God had revealed to her (1:25 - 38).

Mary's Magnificat (vv46 - 55) is tied into the context only slightly; it is so loose that some manuscripts attribute it to Elizabeth rather than Mary. The first half is individualized (vv47 - 50), with v48 being the verse most clearly applicable to Mary. The second half (vv51 - 55) is general, treating of Yahweh's saving action in very broad strokes. There is nothing exclusively Christian in the hymn, much of it echoing Hannah's song (1 Sam 2:1 - 11). It is best seen as an early Jewish Christian hymn which Luke has adapted to give prominence to some of his main theological concerns.

The hymn makes use of opposites or contrasts throughout. God is acclaimed for his awesomeness and power to save (vv46f), and for the fact that he has concern for the lowly or anawim (v48). Mary, on the other hand, is humble (Gr: *tapeinosis*) and servant or handmaid (Gr: *doule*). Because she is lowly, she shall be seen as blessed (v48). This verse is more clearly Lucan than any in the hymn. Mary has already been identified as "servant" (1:38) and referred to as "blessed" by Elizabeth (1:42). The point of convergence between Mary and God is found in anything accomplished in her being attributed to God's holiness and power. Thus, what is affirmed from God's side is greatness, salvation, holiness and mercy; from Mary's (human) side, joy, lowliness, blessedness. and fear of God.

In the concluding section, opposites continue in the religious paradox often highlighted by Luke. The use of the past tense points to customary action, not to a single event. The newly disenfranchised are the arrogant (v51), earthly rulers (v52), and the rich (v53), The privileged are the lowly (v52) and the hungry (v53). Sharp contrasts are important in illustrating the reversal of fortune. Qualifications and distinctions regarding internal dispositions are irrelevant here. Nor is there any indication that specific groups within the early church are being addressed. The hymn simply sees the physically poor as the beloved of God and the rich as being rejected; it is a broad description of the new order. It is the theme developed at length in Luke's story of the rich man and Lazarus (16:19 - 31).

The beneficiaries of this blessing, the anawim of God, constitute the new Israel, heirs of the promise made to Abraham and continued through his lineage (vv54f). Luke consistently maintains continuity between the two testaments, with Christ seen as the fulfillment of messianic hope (1:72f; 13:28f; 19:9). With literary neatness, Luke has Mary exit the scene at the hymn's conclusion before proceeding with his juxtaposition of narratives of the two families, the next dealing with John, Zechariah, and Elizabeth (v56).

The lowliness of Mary appears even in liturgical choice. Of the six readings chosen for the feast of the Assumption, only one of them treats of Mary personally, and even there a fair portion of the visitation scene is dedicated to an early Christian hymn. It is interesting to note how seriously the evangelists take the sentiments which Mary expresses in not singling her out because of personal prerogatives. She always appears in some direct relationship to her Son and his mission. Thus, as today we direct our attention to Mary and our heavenly home, she gives us an important lesson for the journey. And the readings chosen do illuminate her role in salvation history. She is the new ark of the covenant, the bearer of God, and in the litany dedicated to her she is still invoked by that title. She is also the woman of Revelation—if not by the author's intent, then by free adaptation. She is the one who brought the Savior to the world and engaged herself in the final battle against the dragon of sin. And on this mid-August feast, she is the woman who, with Paul, points to the end of time, the resurrection and the final engagement in God. For her salvation has been finalized. We are still on the way.

As Christians look at Mary, it is her profound self-effacement, her authentic lowliness that comes to the fore. In a power-hungry and ambitious world where people are forever forgetful that within a century they will be a name on a tombstone, Mary is a constant reminder that the standards of the world do not last. But God's will does, and that goes well beyond the grave. The short Lucan gospel read at the vigil Mass speaks volumes about the real Mary, even though her name never appears. She heard the word of God and kept it.

Homiletic and Catechetical Helps

1. The meaning of the Assumption.

2. The final destiny of the Christian.

3. The meaning of resurrection of the body.

4. Mary and the ark of the covenant.

5. Spiritual and human kinship.

6. Mary's claim to fame: lowliness of spirit.

7. The end of Christ's reign.

8. Symbols in revelation.

9. The dragon: Adam, sin, and death.

10. The relationship of John and Jesus.

ALL SAINTS

Readings

Rev 7:2 - 4, 9 - 14
1 Jn 3:1 - 3
Mt 5:1 - 12

Theme: Heavenly Company

Today's feast which honors and celebrates all those who have entered heaven before us goes between the heavenly court of those who have been saved and the earthly locale of the baptized still involved in the fray. The reading from Revelation presents a spectacle of countless thousands from every nation on earth, standing before God and the Lamb, singing full throated "Amens" as the saved of God. The first letter of John reminds us that we are only a step away as God's children in the world. Even though the future remains elusive when it comes to description, we are reminded that it is well worth the preparation. The gospel recalls the great paradox. Those who are pushed to the edges in this life have priority of place in the reign of God.

First Reading

The elect stand before God (the throne) and Christ (the Lamb). Final salvation has been achieved. The large group is variously described. It is the reconstituted Israel of the new covenant, its completeness highlighted by the square of the twelve tribes multiplied by one thousand: 144,000 (v4). The wave of destruction which the four angels, who regulated terrestrial elements in the Judaic thinking of the time, hold in abeyance provides time for the signet ring to seal the elect of God, designating them as God's property.

The same crowd is viewed from another perspective (v9). They represent all peoples of the earth, the new Israel made up of Gentile and Jew alike. *White robes* (v9): symbolic of the baptismal purity, brought about by the redemptive work of Christ, of the elect who have suffered and endured much for the faith in the face of persecution (vv13f). Clothing was seen as intimately identified with the person and thus expressive of inner qualities. The palm branches symbolize the final triumph.

In their hymn (v10), the elect attribute their redemption (Gr: *soteria*) to both God and Christ, the Lamb. Early Christian doctrinal development is often best seen in liturgical practice, especially in early hymnody. The equality of the Father and Jesus is evident in the identical worship offered to both. Attendant at the throne besides the angels are the twenty-four *elders*, representing the twelve tribes and the twelve apostles (4:4) and the *four living creatures*, originally mythological figures that guarded pagan temples, which in Israel became part of the heavenly entourage (Ez 1:5 - 21).

The recognition of God concludes with the heavenly body singing a hymn of praise in recognition of what God has effected.

Responsorial Psalm   Ps 24

The psalm has strong liturgical features, probably in celebration of the ark's coming to Jerusalem and Yahweh's enthronement in the temple. Yahweh's universal dominion is extolled (v1). Hebrew cosmogony, reflected in Genesis 1, pictured the earth as a large disc resting upon water. The waters below the earth offer support, just as the waters above the dome of the sky gave rain and moisture. The waters below emerge in the form of oceans and rivers (v2).

The theme then turns to cultic worthiness. Only the upright of conscience before God and neighbor can participate in the procession to the temple (vv3f), as God, in turn, extends his blessing (vv5f). *Seeks the face of God* (v6): This is an expression for temple worship; the sanctuary of the temple housed the unique presence of God.

Second Reading

Children (v1): a term of affection in the Johannine community (2:1; 2:18; 2:28; Jn 21:5). It arises like the Pauline "sons of God" out of the new relationship with Christ that constitutes believers members of God's family. *We may be called...we are:* with the latter given special emphasis in the Greek text, it moves the designation beyond a mere figurative appellation.

This passage makes three affirmations. First, the failure of the world to acknowledge the Christians' new relationship to God should come as no surprise to the Christian community, since it failed to recognize Christ as well (v1; Jn 15:18f; 17:14ff). *World* is used here not as the object of God's love (Jn 3:16) but as the arena of evil. Second, the love of God, which is the Spirit life, is also a pledge of the glory yet to come (v2). This notion of the new life initiated here as issuing forth in the life to come is a strong Johannine theme (Jn 4:14; 6:40). Since Christ is the "firstborn of the dead" (Col 1:18), believers are destined to be transformed as he was; this is a transformation already begun in the recognition of God in the face of Jesus (2 Cor 3:18). Third, by reason of their hope and their conformity to Christ, Christians are held to duplicate in their lives the virtues of Jesus (v3; 2:29).

Third Reading

A comparison of the beatitudes of Matthew with those of Luke presents some interesting differences. The categories in Luke—the poor, the hungry, and the mourners—are mainly socio-economic in character, the people for whom the Messiah was to have a special concern (Is 61:1 - 4). In Matthew there is a spiritual adaptation given which deepens the meaning. The three above-mentioned categories, when addressed in Matthew, are all diverse expressions of the anawim.

The poor, the mourners, and the meek are bereft of human

consolation and support, looking to Yahweh for deliverance. In Matthew, the poor have become the "poor in spirit," which places emphasis on the spiritual notion of humility and lowliness accompanying poverty (v3). The mourners grieve because they see evil as having the upper hand (v4); the meek experience long-suffering and patience (v5; Ps 37:11).

Luke's hungry have become Matthew's "those who hunger for justice," i.e. those who long for the full establishment of God's reign (v6); the merciful are those who forgive (Mt 6:12 - 14) and are marked by love of neighbor (v7; 5:44 - 47). "Purity of heart" stands close to spiritual transparency, total sincerity in covenant fidelity (v8). Peacemakers, like the merciful, are involved in re-establishing harmonious relations among individuals and communities (v9).

The final beatitudes (vv10ff) reflect early church experience where persecution and hatred have been turned on Christ's followers. Here the distinct Matthean hand is more evident than is any direct echo of Christ himself. Their rejoicing in the face of adversity arises from the knowledge that they share the prophets' lot and that their present sufferings will lead ultimately to the joy of the reign

All of the beatitudes are addressed to the disadvantaged as they attempt to cope with the present world. They are assured a better lot. The first beatitude speaks explicitly of the anawim, but the underlying spirit of an authentic poverty and dependence on God is present in all the Matthean beatitudes. They are based on a confident trust that Yahweh will be their ultimate vindicator.

As much as our faith and hope are directed toward our heavenly homeland, we have to admit that we have little knowledge of what is in store for us. Human language, even biblical language, simply tries to give an idea. And that, of course, falls short. The idea of being part of a large chorus probably appeals to members of a Bach choral society. It is less likely to say a great deal to an NFL tight end. One of the certainties that we do have is that eternity will be characterized by love in a life that is totally different from anything we have experienced here. Since love of God and neighbor are inextricably interwoven here, we presume that the same will obtain there. Friendships, we sincerely hope, will not be lost. Today's feast encourages us to believe that ties will not be severed. The communion of saints reminds us that community continues in heaven. We also believe that the meaning of the triune God in our life will intensify. That is what the first letter of John states today. And the beatitudes are a great consolation. At some point the wrongs will be righted. The injustices of life are not cast in concrete. And those who have placed God's interests first in their life will not be forgotten.

The communion of saints points to the fact there is considerable interaction between heaven and our world. St. Thérèse of Lisieux prayed that she might spend her heaven in doing good upon earth. She evidently felt the ties strongly. In a feast like today we celebrate the church's hall of fame. Years ago it was possible to name many of the saints who had formal recognition. In recent years they have become so numerous that it is difficult to keep up. But it is consoling to know that the Spirit binds all of us together. Most of the saints we have known will never be canonized. But they are saints nonetheless, and they have modeled Christianity for us. Today we honor them as well. They may be family members, a dedicated priest or religious, an heroic sufferer, a modern martyr. Because of their closeness, they speak volumes to us. And today's feast reminds us that we always remain one.

Homiletic and Catechetical Helps

1. The meaning of sainthood.

2. The process of canonization.

3. The communion of saints.

4. The meaning of the "poor in spirit."

5. The peacemakers and the persecuted,

6. Understanding heaven, purgatory, and hell.

7. Prayer for the deceased.

PASSION (PALM) SUNDAY
Year A

Readings

Mt 21:1 - 11
Is 50:4 - 7
Phil 2:6 - 11
Mt 26:14 - 27:66.

Theme: In Fulfillment of the Scriptures

The liturgy of the word for Palm Sunday, with the reading of the passion, is considerably longer than on the ordinary Sunday. The account of Jesus' final two days is the longest continuous narrative to be found in the gospels. A more detailed commentary on these events is given in presenting Mark's passion account (Year B), since this is the oldest of the three. Here the distinctive Matthean themes will be treated: scriptural fulfillment, Jesus as the royal Messiah and Son of God, the responsibility of the Jewish leaders, and the response of other persons in the narrative.

Reading Before the Procession

Matthew draws on Mark for the account of Jesus' solemn entry into Jerusalem, which begins at the Mount of Olives, east of the city. Jesus sends for the donkey, an act which in Matthew is explicitly related to scriptural fulfillment. Two quotations are combined (v4). The first half of the verse is an eschatological exaltation of Zion (Is 62:11); the second half speaks of the humble and lowly character of the Messiah (Zech 9:9). Strangely Matthew has misinterpreted the Zechariah text which speaks of one animal but in repeated parallel form. Matthew sees it as two animals, an ass and a colt (v2, 5b), with Jesus straddling both of them for his solemn entry (v7). Matthew is simply taking the symbolism and applying it literally.

Whereas Mark gives the assurance that the colt will be sent

back at once after use, such a detail is of no interest to Matthew. He converts the meaning into an immediate response to Jesus' request (v3). This underscores the royal and authoritative character of Jesus' mission. Compliance with his request is immediate and unquestioning.

Jesus' entry is a procession with strong liturgical shading. The Hosanna ("Lord, grant salvation") was heard on Jewish feast days (Ps 118:25f); here it is an acclamation directed to the Davidic Messiah (v9). The crowd is presented, then, as recognizing Jesus as the Messiah and a prophet (v11). *The whole city was shaken* (v10): The "shaking" is cosmic in character; the language is eschatological and is evocative of the city's reaction to the magi's word (2:3). This solemn procession of acclamation will contrast sharply with the crowd's rejection of Jesus later in the week.

First Reading

The servant of the Lord appears four times in Deutero-Isaiah. In the first instance (42:1 - 4), his initial call is described; in the second (49:1 - 7), there are indications that his work has met opposition. Today's reading is the third song in which the servant is bitterly reviled. Only in the last song (52:13 - 53:12) will it be clear that the servant's mission consisted as much in what he endured as in what he preached.

The servant's is a prophetic role in which he provides a word of consolation to the needy (v4). It is to the faint-hearted and sorely tried that his message is particularly destined. The servant's statement that he has been tested but has not withdrawn (v5) prepares the reader for the startling description that follows.

The abuse which the servant has suffered is both physical and mental. His face has been struck and is covered with spittle. Plucking the beard (v6) was a demeaning and serious insult. Yet the servant remains undaunted in his determination (v7), thus following in the great prophetic tradition (Jer 1:8, 18; Ez 3:8f).

Nowhere in the Hebrew scriptures is the servant identified. He remained an enigmatic prophetic figure who suffers on behalf of others. New Testament writers see in the servant the profile of Jesus himself.

Responsorial Psalm Ps 22

An individual lament, the psalm has two main parts, which describe the suffering of the psalmist (vv1 - 22) and his deliverance (vv23 - 32). Appearing frequently in the passion narratives, the psalm has long been seen as being distinctly applicable to Christ's suffering and exaltation.

The cause of the psalmist's suffering is not indicated. Attention is directed to his mental duress caused by rejection and abuse. To part one's lips and to wag the head (v8) were cruel forms of derision. The conclusion that God had forsaken him (v9) is related to the Hebrew idea of retribution. Suffering results from sin, just as well-being accompanies a virtuous life (Ex 20:5ff). The notion of divine rejection made the bearing of pain and suffering even greater. This leads the psalmist to moments when he is close to despair (v20). His adversaries are depicted as fierce dogs in attack; they leave him broken and disconsolate. Taking him for dead, his enemies rob him and cast lots for his clothing (vv17ff). Finally, delivered from his trials, the psalmist is vindicated and sees the liturgical assembly as the appropriate place to acclaim the Lord's mercy (vv23f).

Second Reading

The Philippians hymn, like the first reading from Isaiah, appears on Palm Sunday in each of the three years (A, B, C). Because of its rhythmic character and distinct vocabulary, commentators today generally agree that it is an early Christian hymn which Paul has inserted here, with a possible single addition of his own. If such be the case, in analyzing its content it must be remembered that it is poetry and not a narrow theological treatise. The hymn raises many theological questions not all of which admit of an easy response because of the genre that is here employed.

The context of the hymn finds Paul underlining the importance of mutual concern and help in a spirit of humility within the Christian community. He continues here by indicating that the Philippians' mindset should be commensurate with their life in Christ, or, more briefly, they are to act as Christians should (v5). The mention of *Christ Jesus* is sufficient to serve as a bridge to the hymn, which will illustrate Christ's own spirit of humility.

The hymn has a majestic sweep. It can be divided into two major sections. The first (vv6 - 8) begins on the highest level of being in "God-like" form, followed by a dramatic descent to humanity and obedient death. With this "sweep" of descent complete, the second section (vv9 - 11) highlights the reascent of Christ. The move is from a humiliating death as a man to a recognized and proclaimed equality with God in lordship. It should be noted that the theological curve of descent/reascent is matched by the peerless structure of the hymn.

In the form of God (Gr: *morphe theou*) (v6): The "form" is the external appearance which serves as the key to what something truly is. Humans, animals, vegetables, all have their distinctive "form" which permits identification and classification. The "form" of the pre-existent Jesus was that of God-hood or divinity (Jn 1:1f). Holding such a formidable status, Christ does not see it as something to be jealously retained or guarded (v6b). *He emptied himself* (Gr: *ekenosen*) (v7a): This expresses the total self-surrender of personal interests and the claims accompanying Godhood which transpires in the incarnation. There is no mention of Christ's actual birth, only his emergence on the human scene.

The appearance of Jesus is that of a slave (v7). This is his new "form." Elsewhere in the Pauline literature, it refers to humanity in its weakened, unredeemed state (Gal 4:1 - 7), the condition of being "in the flesh." Thus he is now found "human in appearance" who began "in the form of God."

In this state of being weak and suffering, Christ manifests obedience, the centerpiece of Christian soteriology (Heb 10:5 - 10). It was an obedience which led him to death in a type of Roman execution which was hardly utterable (v8). At this point the hymn reaches its lowest point in speaking of complete abasement. *Even death on a cross* (8c): The expression disturbs the poetic structure of the strophe and is probably Paul's own addition. The entire verse may be a subtle allusion to the death of the Lord's servant (Is 53:12).

In the reascent, God places the man Christ in a position superior to all other created beings. There is a threefold repetition of the "name" (vv9f), which, as the final verse makes clear (v11), is the name "Lord." With the conferring of this title, there is poetic contrast between the acquired Lordship of Jesus as opposed to his previous state of slavehood. The description of universal acclamation reflects the recognition given Yahweh himself in Isaiah (45:23), with the addition of the various levels of the Hebrew cosmos: the earth, the heavenly sphere, and the underworld (v10).

In his exaltation, Jesus is re-established in his original position, with the added dimension of universal recognition of his lordship, which now embraces his humanity and obedient death. *Jesus Christ is Lord* (v11b): a common faith expression in the early church (1 Cor 12:3; Rom 10:9). With the curve of descent/reascent complete, all presented as accomplished by the Father, it is finally seen as done for him as well (v11). Christ is the manifestation of God's glory (Gr: doxa), the concrete revelation of his design for the reintegration of the created order.

Third Reading

As stated earlier, the commentary here will focus on the distinctly Matthean features of the passion narrative.

In Fulfillment of the Scriptures. In recounting the arrest, trial, and execution of Jesus, the evangelists are at pains to indicate that he was not simply a victim brought to his death by factors beyond his control. Moreover, those responsible, while not guiltless, are not seen as the principal agents. In short, it was not a human ploy that killed Jesus. Matthew places a strong imprint of the divine plan over the entire passion narrative. Much that occurs has already been foretold in the scriptures. This situates Christ in his appropriate setting as part of the plan of God and, at the same time, shows a continuity between the two covenants.

As the passion begins to unfold, the treachery of Judas in betraying Jesus draws on the prophet Zechariah (26:14ff). The thirty pieces of silver, the compensation for Judas' betrayal, is the price rendered to the rejected good shepherd in Zechariah (11:12). It is Matthew who also points out Judas' greed as he bargains with the Jewish authorities.

The account of the institution of the eucharist is a liturgical insert drawn from the life of the early church (26:26 - 29). Matthew's dependence on Mark for this is altered by his addition of the phrase *for the forgiveness of sins*, pronounced by Jesus over the cup. There is strong sacrificial language already present in the eucharistic formula, especially as related to the Sinai covenant (v28; Ex 24:6ff). Matthew at this point wishes to make more explicit the relationship between Jesus' death and atonement for sin. In view of the covenant context, there is a likely allusion here to Jeremiah's new covenant (31:31 - 34), which is also related to the forgiveness of sin.

In the arrest of Jesus (26:47 - 56), it is Matthew who has Jesus repeatedly prescind from the human machinations at work in pointing up the necessity for the scriptures to be fulfilled (vv54, 56).

The death of Judas (27:3 - 10) again sees Matthew drawing on the Zechariah prophecy in which the price given the rejected shepherd is returned to the temple treasury (11:12f). The hanging images Ahitophel's tragic end after turning against David, God's anointed (2 Sam 17:23). The reference to Jeremiah (v9) is puzzling here since nothing in the text directly relates to that book. It may have been suggested by the potter (Jer 19:1 - 13) and the buying of the field (32:6 - 9). That is conjecture, at best, but the note of fulfillment is dominant in the Matthean text. The difference in the two accounts of Judas' death (Acts 1:16 - 20) can be partially explained by Matthew's strong fulfillment motif.

When the assembled Jews accept responsibility for Jesus' death (27:24ff), the transition from the former era to that of the new covenant is seen. Pilate's handwashing proclaims his innocence (Deut 21:6 - 9). "All the people" (v25), an expression for the nation, assume responsibility. For Matthew's community, the point is made that the former Israel, by its own choice, has been superseded by the church, the new people of God.

The death of Jesus is replete with fulfillment imagery

(27:51ff). The earthquake often speaks the language of a divine inbreaking (Ps 68:9). The resurrection of the dead from the tombs draws on the foretold "resurrected" spirit of Israel repossessing the land after the exile (Ez 37:12). The tearing of the temple veil symbolizes the end of temple cult and an access to the (heavenly) sanctuary now open to all. In its language the account is symbolic and apocalyptic and should not be pressed in terms of literal fulfillment.

The Identity of Jesus. The recognition of Jesus' true identity plays an important part in Matthew's gospel, the passion narrative not excepted. This also avoids any notion of his being manipulated or victimized. Throughout he stands as the centerpiece of the narrative, not as one demeaned but as the true representative of God.

At the supper the disciples refer to him as "Lord" (26:22), with the unbelieving Judas addressing him simply as "Teacher" (Rabbi) (26:25, 49). In a very personal and singular way, Jesus speaks to "my Father" (26:36, 48, 53), implying that his Sonship is also unique.

Recognition of Jesus comes from his opponents as well. The irony should not be overlooked. The high priest questions him on being the Messiah and the Son of God, titles that clearly evoke Peter's faith expression at Caesarea Philippi (26:63; 16:16). Jesus responds in the language of Daniel's Son of Man returning in glory (26:64; Dan 7:13). In their scorn his mockers acknowledge him as the Christ (26:68), Pilate calls him "King of the Jews," as do the soldiers (27:11, 29). The same title appears as the inscription on the cross (27:37). His taunters will speak of "Son of God" (27:40, 43). This will become explicitly a faith expression on the lips of the pagan centurion at the time of death (27:54), matching and following upon Peter's profession at the gospel mid-point (16:16). Whether spoken wittingly or unwittingly, this is all part of the Matthean thematic presenting faith insights into the person of Jesus. Finally, Jesus' silence before the chief priests (27:12) and Pilate (27:14) reflects the conduct of the servant of the Lord (Is 53:7).

Jesus as the Presiding Agent. This Matthean characteristic accompanies the recognition of Jesus' identity. Jesus stands over and above the scheming and demeaning conduct of his opponents and the less than courageous response of his disciples. The Father orchestrates events and Jesus submits as Son. It is the Father's will that is at work throughout.

The events of Passover preparation are sparse in Matthew, but Jesus is clearly in command (26:17 - 20). The directives are given succinctly as Jesus speaks of God's pre-determined time (Gr: *kairos*) (v18). At the table, he readily specifies his betrayer (26:23, 25) and speaks of the future in clear terms. The disciples will be scandalized "because of me"(26:31, 33), i.e. the experience of his arrest, and they will do so "this night."

In his prayer to the Father in the garden, Jesus is composed and totally submissive (26:39, 42); his greeting to Judas is proper and restrained (26:50). Matthew alone reports the conversation between Jesus and the assailant of the high priest's servant (26:51 - 54). Jesus has no need of human protection; heavenly armies are at his disposal if so needed or so willed. Moreover, such retaliation only obstructs the ordained design of God. Repeatedly in the passion narrative, Jesus is said to be *handed over* (Gr: *paradidomi*). While human agents may be involved, in a deeper sense the Father's surrender of his Son is intended. Throughout the events of his trial and sentencing, the posture of Jesus is one of silent composure.

Participants in the Passion. The moral posture of Jesus casts light or shadow on other participants in the events of his final days. For example, the treachery and greed of Judas (26:14ff) are not only in sharp contrast with the teaching of Jesus, they are in marked opposition to the generosity of the woman who anointed Jesus in the immediately preceding incident (26:1 - 13).

In the garden (26:36 - 46), Jesus' persistence in prayer (only in Matthew, a threefold explicit mention) throws into relief the lack of moral vigilance by the sleeping disciples. While the event appears in all the synoptics, it is Matthew who heightens the separation between Jesus and the disciples.

Under arrest Jesus is accused of blasphemy, for which he is condemned (26:65f). Ironically the real blasphemy follows immediately in the action of his vilifiers (26:67). Jesus' truthful response regarding his role and destiny (26:64) is in contrast with Peter's denial that he even knows Jesus (26:70, 72, 74), a denial much more emphatic than in Mark, the Matthean source. Matthew underscores the choice made between Jesus and Barabbas, a common criminal, in having Pilate pose the question twice (27:17, 21), with the respondents moving from the religious leaders to the crowd (vv20, 21) and then to "the whole people" (v25). The intervention of Pilate's wife, a Gentile (27:19), bears a likeness to other divinely guided Gentiles who were also in contrast with the incredulous Jews (2:1 - 12).

The account of the Jews' initiative to guard Jesus' tomb (27:62 - 66) arises out of a post-Easter Jewish-Christian polemic regarding the veracity of the resurrection witnesses. To charges that Jesus' followers had stolen "the body" and reported a resurrection, the Christians respond that the guarded tomb precluded any such attempt. The background to all of this is not disclosed; it is certainly a part of the unequivocal affirmation that Christ had risen.

We cannot help but be impressed with the circumspection and respect that surround the gospel accounts of Jesus' passion. There is no dwelling on unseemly detail, no extended elaboration; the presentation is simple and direct. This is the part of the gospel that comes the closest to being an historical replay, even though each evangelist brings his own perspective to bear.

Matthew views the entire drama, frightening in many respects, as the culmination of a carefully devised plan to which the scriptures bear ample witness. His account should move us to an ever deeper sense of appreciation. This was a death that touches each one of us, a death long prepared for. From the time of Adam's rebellion and our subsequent alienation, God was at work to bring us back. When we open the scriptures and see ourselves included in this plan that took centuries to unfold, it can only lead to a deeper sense of gratitude for what occurred on a hillside outside of Jerusalem two millennia ago.

Homiletic and Catechetical Helps

1. The meaning of the death of Jesus in my life.

2. Salvation from Jesus' submission to God's plan.

3. Betrayal and denial: the difference between Judas and Peter.

4. Jesus and Barabbas: our acceptance of rejection.

5. Discussion of Matthew's approach to the passion and death.

6. Jesus' humanity in the face of death.

7. The biblical symbols of holy week: palm, light, water, the crucifix, foot-washing.

PALM SUNDAY
Year B

Readings

Mk 11:1 - 10
Is 50:4 - 7
Phil 2:6 - 11
Mk:14:1 - 15:47

Theme: Who Is This Man?

Reading Before the Procession

Jesus' entry into Jerusalem is simpler and less elaborate than in the other synoptics. Bethphage and Bethany (v1) were towns close to Jerusalem; the Mount of Olives ringed the city to the east. Although there is no direct quotation from Zechariah, Jesus' mounting the young donkey to make his entry is an allusion to the prophet's symbol of the humble, lowly Messiah (Zech 9:9). Jesus' specifying exactly where the colt will be found is to be credited to his foreknowledge. The Marcan note that it will be returned soon is probably actual historical recall and points up the almost casual character of the original event (vv2f).

The group surrounding Jesus as he enters does not appear to be that sizeable. A single mention is made of "many people" (v8), but no "crowds" (Mt 21:9) or "multitude" (Lk 19:37). If Mark is the more accurate reporter, such an entry at the time of a feast would not have occasioned great notice. The "Hosannas" (literally: "Save now") with the accompanying chant (Ps 118:26) and the leafy branches could well have been part of the overall liturgical scene, with the branches, however, being more appropriate for the feast of Tabernacles than for Passover. In the chanting of the psalm, Jesus is not directly addressed in messianic terms (vv8ff).

In context the narrative highlights the entry of Jesus as the final step in his salvific journey. The reign of God is about to be inaugurated. Mark sees the event against this end-time background and the other synoptics will build on it.

First Reading

(Same as Year A)

Responsorial Psalm

(Same as Year A)

Second Reading

(Same as Year A)

Third Reading

The Anointing and Betrayal (14:3 - 11). Mark gives few particulars surrounding the anointing other than the fact that it took place at Bethany close to Passover (15 Nisan). Neither the woman nor her critics are identified. The event takes on symbolic significance at this juncture in Jesus' life. His death is imminent, already foreshadowed in the plotting of his enemies (14:1f). The action of the woman is seen as a burial anointing (v8); its being performed on Jesus head (v3) gives it a royal, messianic note in contrast to the feet-anointing of Luke (7:38) and John (12:3). The symbolism points to Jesus' coming into his reign via death and burial.Faced with the accusation of inappropriate luxury, Jesus gives the event its symbolic meaning and indicates that the woman's action will be recounted wherever the "good news" is preached (vv8f).

Judas is in evident contrast with the dedicated and generous woman (vv10f). His cooperation with the priests enables them to move their death wish forward (v1).

Passover Preparations (14:12 - 21), Mark views the final supper as a Passover meal, celebrated on the evening of 15 Nisan; he is followed in this by the other synoptics. For John it is a farewell supper, celebrated on 14 Nisan, the day before the feast (Jn 18:28; 19:14). Both chronologies have strong theological concerns. In Mark and the synoptics there is the clear intention to unite the meal on the eve of Jesus' death with Passover, the great feast of deliverance and salvation. The feast, beginning in the evening, would then continue until dusk the following day, enveloping the whole of Christ's passion.

Jesus' knowledge of the place and the particulars (vv13ff) parallels his earlier prediction prior to the entry into Jerusalem (11:1 - 6). It casts a supernatural aura over the emerging events of this final week. This foreknowledge continues in his prediction of betrayal by one of the twelve (v18). Meal-sharing in antiquity had a sacred character. To share a meal was to wish another well in a way that carried the symbolism of a life-giving concern. Enemies did not share meals, and to do so with duplicity was particularly grievous (Ps 41:10). In addition, this meal was Passover, which added to its significance. Thus, the betrayal takes on the worst aspects of treachery (v20). For Mark, the death of Jesus is divinely willed, but such does not diminish human culpability (v21).

The Eucharist (14:22 - 31). The institution of the eucharist in a Passover setting underscores its sacrifical character. The formula (vv22ff), unrelated to the Passover ritual, is inserted into the narrative and is easily excised, reflecting its original liturgical setting in the life of the early church. The eucharistic formulas of Mark and Matthew (26:26 - 29) are largely the same; Luke (22:15 - 20) and Paul (1 Cor 11:23ff) reflect a slightly different tradition. The body to be eaten and the blood to be drunk anticipate the death of Jesus on the following day. This will inaugurate the new covenant (Jer 31:31-34), with a clear allusion made to the first covenant (v24; Ex 24:8). This presentation of the death of

Jesus is real, i.e. a living symbol. It is also placed in an end-time setting. The death of Jesus will inaugurate the reign of God at which time Jesus will participate in the eschatological banquet (v25).

As the group makes its way to the garden, Jesus sees his arrest and death as the occasion of the apostles' dispersion, drawing on Zechariah's prophecy (13:7). His resurrection, however, will bring about their reassembling (vv27ff), words reflective of actual post-Easter events. Despite Peter's protestations, Jesus predicts his denial, as Peter himself will have reason to remember (vv29ff, 62 - 72). It is the stark and even embarrassing truth about central figures in the narrative, such as Peter, that gives the entire picture an authentic ring. Such stories were not created.

Gethsemane (14:32 - 42). This incident vividly depicts the human dread of Jesus in the face of his impending death. Gethsemane was a garden on the Mount of Olives outside the city. The three disciples who witnessed Jesus' transfiguration glory (9:2) are now called to share the depths of his human anguish (v33). Jesus' request for watchfulness, the equivalent of moral alertness, is met with sleep, the symbol of spiritual torpor (v34). *Abba* (v30), the Aramaic familiar form for "father" was not customarily used of God without qualifiers. Here it points to Jesus' unique filial relationship. As Jesus struggles in the hope that the Father's decree might be altered, he nonetheless expresses complete acceptance (v36). Three times he returns to the disciples, who remain separated from him by sleep. It is the spirit that calls the Christian to the good, the ideal which beckons; the *flesh* is the residue of weakness and fragility drawing the believer away from the ideal (v35). Again Jesus foreknowledge (vv41f) puts him beyond human machinations in fulfilling a divine plan.

The Arrest of Jesus (14:43 - 15:2). The Marcan account of Jesus' arrest is summary and succinct. There is no mention of temple (Lk 22:52) or military (Jn 18:3) personnel accompanying the crowd that makes the arrest as directed by the religious authorities (v43). Judas gives the respectful disciple-master greeting in the form of a kiss. In Mark it carries the bitter note of duplicity, although no comment is made. The cutting off of the ear does not identify the wounded person nor the perpetrators (Jn 18:10f).

Jesus' comments again accent his control of events (vv48f). He is not surrendering as one besieged; he fulfills what the scriptures require. *Day after day* (v49): An indication of a longer Jerusalem ministry. Mark has no Jerusalem stay apart from the present one, which is quite brief. Attempts to identify Mark's naked young man (vv31f) render no adequate solution, although it was evidently a vivid memory at the time. The main point is that he fled like the rest.

Jesus and the Sanhedrin (14:53 - 65). While historically important in explaining the death of Jesus, this confrontation is theologically significant as well. The death of Jesus must take place within the day of Passover, in keeping with the gospel's design. This accounts for the highly improbable gathering of the sanhedrin at night, the eve of Passover at that (v53). Moreover a full complement is gathered (v53), part of the attempt to place the weight of the blame for Jesus' death on the Jews and thus lighten Roman guilt. It is also difficult to imagine such a large gathering taking place at the high priest's home (v54). It has long been recognized that Mark condenses a more protracted prosecution into a brief period of time in keeping with his literary and theological framework. Peter's presence is introduced early (v54) and will be woven into the trial account.

The testimony against Jesus is contradictory and therefore invalid (v56: Deut 19:15). His condemnation will have to depend on self-incrimination. How Jesus originally spoke of the temple's destruction and the substitution of himself for it is hard to determine. He certainly spoke of the passing of the old era, with its law and ritual, in view of the inbreaking of God's reign. The accusation has here been fashioned into a clear resurrection prediction (v58). Jesus' silence is that of the servant of the Lord (v61; Is 53:7).

The question of the high priest is ironically faith-filled (vv61f). The central theme of Mark's gospel is the identity of Jesus. "Who is this man?" (4:41) is woven into the gospel's fabric. The ultimate answer is foretold in the gospel's introduction: Jesus is the Christ and the Son of God (1:1). This is restated in the high priest's question. Jesus' answer is direct and affirmative, as he passes to his eschatological role as the Son of Man returning in glory (Dan 7:13; Ps 110:1). The Christological import of the exchange should be noted. Jesus is the Messiah, Son of God, the representative of the new humanity (Son of Man), and the end-time judge. It is more than sufficient for sentencing (v64).

Irony follows in the mockery that follows as well (v65). Prophecy is requested. The preceding exchange with the high priest was the highest form of prophecy. And in their very act of abuse, his mockers fulfill Isaian prophecy (Is 50:6).

Peter's Denial (14:66 - 72). Jesus responded affirmatively to the high priest's questioning. Mark brings out the contrast between the stance of Jesus and that of Peter in weaving the account of Peter's denial into the narrative at this point. Peter becomes increasingly more volatile before his questioners. He goes from simple denial (v68) to cursing (v71), as the number of interrogators mounts (vv67, 69, 70). Peter's denial brings to fulfillment Jesus' earlier prediction (14:30).

Jesus and Pilate (15:1 - 15). Marcan features continue in Jesus' appearance before Pilate. Jesus remains the silent servant of the Lord (v5); the primary responsibility for the sentence is placed on the Jews as the instigators, with Pilate simply an accomplice (vv8, 10f, 13, 15); the "king of the Jews," used repeatedly by Pilate (vv9, 12), has two levels of meaning, one religious-political opposing Roman authority, the other an affirmation of Jesus' sovereignty over the reign of God.

The choice of Barabbas over Jesus receives in Mark its simplest presentation, based on historical memory. To Pilate's seemingly well-intentioned questions about Jesus' guilt (vv12, 14), the cry of death is the only response (vv13f). That a common murderer was preferred to the Savior of the world left a deep impression on the early Christian conscience. The account appears in all of the gospels.

The Crucifixion (15:16 - 32). Once again certain concerns of Mark should be noted. As in the other evangelists, his account is restrained and limited to a simple statement of the facts. The crucifixion is treated with reverent circumspection. Before leaving the praetorium, the mockery of Jesus includes crowning him with thorns and vesting him in purple. This accompanies his recognition again as "king of the Jews" (vv16 - 20). All of this has to be seen against the faith background of the reality of Jesus' kingship, as it brought to mind the pain through which Jesus came to his sovereignty. This is borne out again in the inscription placed on the cross (v26). Finally, Mark again points up the suffering of Jesus as a pre-ordained part of God's plan. Psalm 22 plays an important part in illustrating the scriptural expressions of this plan. It appears on the lips of the dying Jesus (v34) and in the casting of lots for Jesus' garments (v24; Ps 22:1, 19).

The mention of Simon the Cyrenian who carried the cross-beam, as well as the names of his sons, would indicate that they were well known in the Marcan community (v21).

The time (v25) and circumstances (v27) of the crucifixion are noted without comment. The reviling jeers addressed to Jesus on the cross (vv29 - 32), like those at his trial, carry a clearly ironic note of truth. The titles belong to him by right. Moreover, the only way Jesus can save himself or others is by not descending from the cross.

The Death and Burial (15:33 - 47). As stark as Mark's presentation is, the death of Jesus is vividly painful (v37). The scriptural imagery highlights the note of fulfillment. This includes the psalm quote on Jesus' lips (v34), the darkness on the earth (v33; Am 8:9), and the cross inscription (v26). The rending of the temple veil (v38) symbolizes the end of the former era and the birth of a new covenant and cult, with the access to God open to all. *Eloi, Eloi* (v34): Jesus quotes the Aramaic version of the Hebrew psalm, leading to his hearers' misunderstanding that he is invoking Elijah (vv35f).

The words of the centurion are climactic in Mark (v39). The central theme of Mark's gospel is Jesus as the Christ and the Son of God (1:1). At mid-point, Peter acknowledges Jesus as Christ, the Messiah (8:29), and at the gospel's end the centurion sees him as Son of God. The fact that the latter is a Gentile portends the mission of the church to the world.

The circumstances of the burial serve two purposes. First, there is the clear affirmation that Jesus truly died. Pilate's doubts are allayed by the centurion's word (vv44f). Then the body is laid to rest in the presence of witnesses (v47) and the large sealing stone is rolled into place (v46). Possible misinterpretations of the resurrection make the establishment of death indispensable.

Second, the members of the Christian community who provided this service for Jesus are remembered with respect and affection. Joseph of Arimathea, a Jew and a member of the sanhedrin (v43), the two Marys and Salome are mentioned. Mark makes no mention of the presence of Jesus' mother. The presence of the women is important in witnessing to the three major moments: death (v40), burial (v47) and resurrection (16:1 - 6).

Death is inevitable, and one prays for a peaceful passing. When a death is tragic, it takes time for the healing process to give perspective and a broader understanding. It is Mark who brings us face to face with the stark reality of what Jesus endured. There is little adornment or alteration of the facts in his gospel. But as he presents all of this, he is answering the basic question: Who is this man? In one sense the great tragedy is that Jesus is no ordinary man, let alone a common criminal. Mark has answered the question in Peter's profession that this is the Christ and in the centurion's recognition of God's Son. In the midst of Calvary darkness, great light appears.

When a crazed psychopath rampaged through a Texas cafeteria at lunch hour, killing people on sight, the writer was living in the area. The initial reaction of the victims' families and friends was one of heart-rending, inarticulate grief. But gradually this gave way to the serenity of a rural people with a very simple faith. God was not held accountable; God was their solace. When asked as to their choice, these people did not want to have the cafeteria closed as a permanent memorial to a person gone berserk. They wanted it reopened, and it was–a testimonial to ongoing life and the hope of a better future. It was Calvary and the Son of God all over again. The lesson was a simple one. But it made a lot of sense.

Homiletic and Catechetical Helps

1. Mark's theme: Jesus as Messiah and Son of God.

2. Jesus and the disciples in the garden: the lesson.

3. Eucharist and Passover.

4. Gospel in liturgy and liturgy in gospel.

5. The meaning of Jesus as king in the passion narrative.

PALM SUNDAY
Year C

Readings

Lk 19:28 - 40
Is 50:4 - 7
Phil 2:6 - 11
Lk 22:14 - 23:56

Theme: The Passion: A Teaching Moment

For a more detailed comment on the events recounted in the passion narrative, the reader is referred to the discussion of Mark's gospel (Year B). Attention here will be focused on the distinctive Lucan features.

Reading Before the Procession

Luke's use of Mark's gospel in much of the passion narrative is evident. As is true of the other gospels, Luke's narrative must be read as part of his gospel as a whole. In the present passage, for example, Jesus' solemn entry into Jerusalem climaxes a journey begun much earlier in this gospel (9:51). It is both a geographical and spiritual ascent for Jesus, bringing him to the city where he will pass from death to glory. It is a "teaching" journey in which Jesus both instructs his disciples and presents himself as a model for their own way to the Father.

The identification of the young donkey (vv30 - 34), in underscoring Jesus' foreknowledge, places him in control of all features of his destiny. He is "the Lord" (vv31, 34). The allusion to Zechariah's mounted king (Zech 9:9) draws on Mark but is not "footnoted" in Luke; such would not have importance for

Luke's Gentile Christian audience. It does, however, point up the humble type of kingship which Jesus espoused.

In the procession, only the cloaks play a significant role (vv35f). Symbols of possession, they are cast before Jesus in a spirit of renunciation important to the third gospel (9:57 - 61). The procession praises God and Jesus the king (vv37ff). *Mighty deeds* (v37): the saving acts of Jesus' ministry, his teaching and healings (4:18f). The acclamation (v38) is an adaptation of Psalm 118:26, making it a reference to Christ and an echo of the angels' hymn at the time of Jesus' birth (2:14). Jesus is the king to come, the promised one, who will establish peace and harmony between God and humankind and who through his offering of self will give glory to God.

First Reading

    (Same as Year A)

Responsorial Psalm

    (Same as Year A)

Second Reading

    (Same as Year A)

Third Reading

The Image of Jesus. Written with the fuller understanding of Easter faith, the third gospel retrojects its grasp of the person of Jesus into the events of his passion. He speaks of himself as the *Son of Man* (22:22), the eschatological figure of Daniel (7:13), a title repeated before the sanhedrin (22:69), but eliminating Mark's emphasis on the *returning* Son of Man (Mk 14:62).

Asked before the council whether or not he is the *Christ* (22:67) or *Son of God* (22:70), and, before Pilate, if he is the *king of the Jews* (23:3), Jesus responds ambiguously. There was a sense in which such designations could be misconstrued; yet they were also true. There is irony in their being placed on the cross inscription (23:38) and on the lips of the sneering opponents (23:35ff). The Lucan Jesus avoids the use of such titles. The Son-Father relationship appears only in Jesus' personal address of the Father (22:42; 23:46) or in private sharing with the disciples (22:29).

In Luke Jesus appears clearly as *Savior* of his people. In the eucharistic formula, it is both "the body which will be given for you" and "the cup which will be shed for you." This additional clause over the bread may pre-date Luke or have been added by him. In either case, it fits the Lucan picture of Jesus' mission as strongly directed to his followers. In the garden scene when the disciple cuts off the slave's ear, the Lucan Jesus not only opposes any violent defense but performs a saving action in healing the man (22:51). Only in Luke does the crucified Jesus ask forgiveness for his opponents (23:34) and extend salvation to the criminal executed with him (23:39 - 43). There is a striking irony in the repeated calls for Jesus to save himself (23:35, 39). If Jesus is to save others, there is no way that he can save himself; indeed, he himself will be saved in his final exaltation only through his death. The first response to salvation after Jesus' death comes in the repentant attitude of the departing crowd (23:48).

The singular pre-eminence of Christ is emphasized in the passion narrative by his foreknowledge and control of events. He is not a mere player in this drama of human malfeasance. As God's Son his mission is pre-determined in every detail. As prophet he inaugurates the final era. In sharing the Passover with his disciples, he notes that it will be his last before the reign of God is inaugurated (22:15 - 18). He predicts the betrayal of Judas (22:21ff) and the denial of Peter (22:34). He foresees the future desolation of Jerusalem in his words to the women of the city. If this moment of the deliverance of Jerusalem (green wood) has met such a negative response, how will its citizens fare in the face of the anguish to come (dry wood) (23:27 - 32)?

The sense of Jesus' composure is more pronounced in Luke than the other synoptics. He uses the supper as a teaching moment, the final sharing before the end (22:24 - 30, 35 - 38). In the garden (22:39 - 46), Luke arranges the material to accent the prayer of Jesus rather than the sleep of the disciples. He withdraws from them only once and prays (vv41f). An angel appears to console him. He returns to the disciples and encourages them to pray in view of the imminent crisis or test. Jesus at prayer is a constant theme through Luke's gospel.

With the crowd's arrival in the garden, Jesus rises above them in his exercise of restraint. There is no direct physical contact with Judas, only a reproach (22:48). Jesus rejects defense and performs a healing (vv50f). He submits to arrest only because it is evil's final moment (v53). Throughout the trial and its accompanying abuse, he is largely silent. His opponents unwittingly give him messianic recognition. Unlike the anguished cry on the cross in Matthew and Mark (Ps 22:1), the Lucan Jesus is full of trust (Ps 31:5).

The exclamation of the centurion sees Jesus as a *righteous man* (Gr: *dikaios*) (23:47). The quality of righteousness points to a life lived in conformity with the covenant or, more generally, with God's will. The death of Jesus concludes a life of willing and unqualified acceptance of God's plan.

Jesus as Teacher. A rabbi is the instructor of his disciples. As Jesus makes his way to Jerusalem, beginning in Luke's ninth chapter (9:51), he constantly imparts teaching or didache to his followers. This same practice continues in the passion narrative. Luke places the teaching on humility and service in the context of the supper (22:24 - 30), in which Jesus presents himself as the model of servanthood (v27). The setting gives the dimension of Christian service to the eucharist. He also warns the disciples of ensuing crisis and persecution during the supper (22:35 - 38). The sword here is a symbol for opposition, not a call to bear arms (v36). The disciples are to expect persecution. If Jesus is counted among malefactors (Is 53:12), their lot will be similar.

The instruction continues on the way to Calvary. He stops to address the women along the way (23:28 - 31). On the cross he has words of forgiveness (23:34) and salvation (23:39 - 43).

Other Persons in the Drama. In Luke the *apostles* appear in a more positive light than in Matthew and Mark. In view of the important part they played in the life of the early church, as recorded in Acts, Luke's deference is understandable. At the supper Jesus lingers with the apostles in instructive conversation. He commends their fidelity for which they will be rewarded (22:28f). Before Peter's promise of continued fidelity, Jesus speaks of his future role of leadership in "strengthening your brothers" (22:31f).

In the garden, all the disciples are indicated as being with Jesus, not just the three (22:39). Jesus returns to them only once and does not dwell at length on their failure to stay awake (23:46). It is the disciples who try to defend him (23:49), and, in contrast to the other synoptics, there is no mention of their fleeing. Peter's denial of Jesus is softened in Luke (no oaths or curses) and his repentance is accentuated. He exits the scene before Jesus is humiliated (22:54 - 62). Jesus' "acquaintances" are present with the women at the crucifixion, who presumably include the disciples (23:49).

In treating of the Romans and the Jews, Luke does not exonerate either group in the death of Jesus. In Acts, guilt is equally distributed between Gentiles and Jews, between Pilate and Herod (Acts 4:27). In the passion, Luke lets the facts speak for themselves. That having been said, if there is any imbalance in the narrative it is in favor of Rome and against Jesus' Jewish opponents.

At the arrest in the garden, it is not a military cohort or even an unspecified crowd that comes to seize Jesus but rather the Jewish temple personnel (22:52). This group remains involved in the entire proceedings from arrest to trial (22:54; 23:1) to crucifixion (23:25f). The appearance of Jesus before Herod, the Jewish civil authority, is marked by contempt and abuse; before him Jesus says nothing (23:6 - 12). The repentant crowd at the crucifixion is clearly distinct from the religious leaders (23:48).

The Roman authority, on the other hand, declares Jesus' innocence three times (23:4, 14, 22). Pilate sins on the side of pacification for purposes of political expediency. He does not plot against Christ but rather makes earnest efforts to free him.

Among the Jews, however, Joseph of Arimathea receives a positive assessment (23:50 - 54). Luke indicates that he was an upright man who, though a member of the sanhedrin, was not party to the plot.

The position of Luke on this question must be seen against

the background of the times. In a Gentile Christian world, it was necessary to explain how it was that Jesus was rejected by his own people. Later antagonisms between church and synagogue undoubtedly exacerbated the situation and colored the gospel presentation. At the same time, it must be noted that Jesus' disciples and those who remained with him throughout his ordeal were themselves from the Jewish community.

In this gospel it almost seems as if Jesus does not want to terminate his last meal with the disciples. His words on service are significant in this context. Jesus has just given the eucharist to his closest companions and will soon die in total service to others. In considering the eucharist, Francis of Assisi stood in awe at the "humility of God." This same God gives himself to us in every eucharist. But it can't stop there. Jesus models what we are called to be: people of service to others—at home, at business, in the neighborhood, in the parish community.

Jesus remained at the table to teach. He even interrupts his painful walk to Calvary to instruct some women along the way. His words were never shared begrudgingly. It almost appears as if, in the shortness of time, there is so much to do. Even when pressures were the greatest, Christ had time for people. Our lives are so full and quality time is minimal. We have to admit that often we fail to be present to others because we lack time. We often reach our destination in stepping over many needy and lonely people. Jesus never did, not even under the duress of imminent death. The awareness of others is a valuable holy week lesson.

Homiletic and Catechetical Helps

1. Understanding Jesus as Savior, Son of God, and Son of Man.

2. Jesus as teacher in Luke's passion.

3. The apostles in Luke's passion.

4. Catholic teaching on the Jews and Jesus' death (Vatican II).

5. Jesus, the "upright man"—an example for Christians.

6. Women in the passion narrative.

SELECTED BIBLIOGRAPHY

Achtemeier, P., *Mark* (Proclamation Commentaries), Philadelphia, Fortress, 1986.

Achtemeier, P., *Romans* (Interpretation), Atlanta, Knox, 1985.

Barrett, C. K., *A Commentary on the Second Epistle to the Corinthians*, New York, Harper and Row, 1973.

Beasley-Murray, G. R., *The Book of Revelation* (New Century Commentary), Grand Rapids, Eerdmans, 1978.

Bright, J., *Jeremiah* (Anchor Bible), Garden City, Doubleday, 1965.

Brown, R., Fitzmeyer, J., Murphy R. (eds.), *The Jerome Biblical Commentary*, Englewood Cliffs, Prentice-Hall, 1968.

Brown, R., Fitzmeyer, J., Murphy, R. (eds.), *The New Jerome Biblical Commentary*, Englewood Cliffs, Prentice-Hall, 1990.

Brown, R., *The Gospel According to John* (Anchor Bible), Garden City, Doubleday, 1966-70.

Brown, R., *The Birth of the Messiah*, Garden City, Doubleday, 1977.

Brown, R., *The Epistles of John* (Anchor Bible), Garden City, Doubleday, 1982.

Bruce, F. F., *The Epistle to the Galatians* (New International Greek), Grand Rapids, Eerdmans, 1982.

Bruce, F. F., *The Epistle to the Hebrews*, Grand Rapids, Eerdmans, 1964.

Conzelmann, H., *The Theology of St. Luke*, New York, Harper and Row, 1960.

Conzelmann, H., *First Corinthians*, Philadelphia, Fortress, 1975.

801

Crowe, J., *The Acts* (New Testament Message), Delaware, Glazier, 1979.

Fitzmyer, J., *The Gospel According to Luke* (Anchor Bible), Garden City, Doubleday, 1981-85.

Harrington, W., *Mark* (New Testament Message), Delaware, Glazier, 1979.

Kaiser, O., *Isaiah 1-12, 13-39* (Old Testament Library), Philadelphia, Westminster, 1974-83.

Kingsbury, J. D., *Matthew*, Philadelphia, Fortress, 1975.

LaVerdiere, E., *Luke* (New Testament Message), Minnesota, Liturgical Press, 1980.

Lymon, C. (ed.), *The Interpreter's One Volume Commentary on the Bible*, Nashville, Abingdon, 1971.

Mays, J. (ed.), *Harper's Bible Commentary*, San Francisco, Harper and Row, 1988.

Meier, J., *Matthew* (New Testament Message), Minnesota, Liturgical Press, 1980.

Murphy, R., *Wisdom Liturature and Psalms*, Nashville, Abingdon, 1983.

Noth, M., *Exodus* (Old Testament Library), Philadelphia, Westminster, 1962.

Roetzel, C. J., *The Letters of Paul*, Atlanta, Knox, 1975.

Schnackenberg, R., *The Gospel According to St. John*, New York, Herder, 1968-82.

Senior, D. (ed.), *The Catholic Study Bible*, New York, Oxford Univ. Press, 1990.

Stuhlmueller, C., *Psalms* (Old Testament Message), Delaware, Glazier, 1983.

Taylor, V., *The Gospel According to St. Mark*, London, Macmillan, 1966.

Vawter, B., *On Genesis*, Garden City, Doubleday, 1977.

von Rad, G., *Deuteronomy* (Old Testament Library), Philadelphia, Westminster, 1966.

von Rad, G., *Wisdom in Israel*, Nashville, Abingdon, 1972.

Westermann, C., *Isaiah 40-66* (Old Testament Library), Philadelphia, Westminster, 1969.

INDEX OF BIBLICAL PASSAGES

Key:
A= Advent
L = Lent
E = Easter Time
O = Ordinary Time—i.e. Of the Year
A-2-C = Advent 2nd Sunday - Cycle C

804